Who's Who
IN TWENTIETH-CENTURY
WARFARE

THE ROUTLEDGE WHO'S WHO SERIES

Accessible, authoritative and enlightening, these are the definitive biographical guides to a diverse range of subjects drawn from literature and the arts, history and politics, religion and mythology.

Who's Who
IN TWENTIETH-
CENTURY
WARFARE

Spencer C. Tucker

ROUTLEDGE
Taylor & Francis Group

London and New York

First published 2001
by Routledge
11 New Fetter Lane, London EC4P 4EE

Simultaneously published in the USA and Canada
by Routledge
29 West 35th Street, New York, NY 10001

Routledge is an imprint of the Taylor & Francis Group

© 2001 Spencer C. Tucker

Typeset in Sabon by Taylor & Francis Books Ltd
Printed and bound in Great Britain by TJ International Ltd,
Padstow, Cornwall

British Library Cataloguing in Publication Data
A catalogue record for this book is available from the
British Library

Library of Congress Cataloging in Publication Data
A catalog record for this title has been requested

ISBN 0–415–23497–2

Contents

Preface

This book provides brief biographical sketches on more than 1,000 individuals who were important in twentieth-century military history. My criterion was that the person should have played a key role in twentieth-century warfare, even if only at the beginning of the century. I could not include everything about a particular individual, but I have tried to list schooling, major commands and battles, and selected promotions. Book size has necessitated that most of these be limited to 250 words or less. I hope that the entries provide sufficient information so that the book may serve as a useful reference source both for scholars and for those merely interested in twentieth-century warfare.

I have included those political leaders who, in my judgment, have had a major impact on military policy. Some choices were quite easy, such as Winston Churchill and Adolf Hitler. I have also endeavored to include principal army and air force generals and navy admirals, as well as those commanders or individuals who are worthy of note. For that reason I have included inventors such as J. W. Christie, John Garand, and Andrei Tupolev. I have also tried to include individuals who did not have a wide military impact but are identified by individual accomplishments, such as U.S. Army Sergeant Alvin York in World War I, or Russian pilot and leading woman ace Lilly Litvak and plastic surgeon Dr. Archibald McIndoe in World War II. I believe there are many entries here that are not found in other such reference works.

To save space I have incorporated some abbreviations, a listing of which is to be found at the end of the book. Chief among these are AEF (American Expeditionary Force), BEF (British Expeditionary Force), CofS (chief of staff), CinC (commander-in-chief), and CG (commanding General). I have tried to hold such abbreviations to a minimum.

I am grateful to the Virginia Military Institute for a discretionary fund that has allowed me to employ cadet assistants to help with vexing research questions, and I am appreciative of the work of Cadets Richard Donohue, Jr. and Alexander Haseley, and former Cadet, now U.S. Army 2nd Lieutenant, Colin Mahle – fine students and efficient workers all. I am also grateful to these colleagues who helped me with some aspect of the manuscript: Lt. Col. John R. Angolia, USA

Rtd.; Dr. Carl Boyd; Col. George M. Brooke, III, USMC Rtd.; Dr. Bruce Elleman; Dr. Paul G. Halpern; Dr. Jack McCallum; Dr. Malcolm Muir; Mr. Andrzej Suchcitz; Dt. Donald Thomas, Dr. Haruo Tohmatsu; Dr. Blair Turner; Dr. Bruce Vandervort; Dr. Mark Wilkinson; Dr. Laura M. Wood; and Col. Dr. David Zabecki. I am most grateful for the keen eye and many helpful suggestions of Morgen Witzel in copy-editing the manuscript. As always, I am especially appreciative of the assistance, support, and forbearance of my wife Beverly, which has made possible my long hours at the computer.

Spencer C. Tucker
Professor and Holder of the John Biggs Chair of Military History
The Virginia Military Institute

Abbreviations and terminology

AEF	American Expeditionary Force, U.S. troops sent to France in World War I
Annapolis	U.S. Naval Academy, Annapolis, Maryland
BEF	British Expeditionary Force, British forces sent overseas in World War I and II
Benelux	Belgium, The Netherlands, and Luxembourg
CNO	Chief of Naval Operations
CinC	Commander in chief
CG	Commanding general
CofS	Chief of staff
Dragoons	Mounted infantry, employing horses to get to a location where they then fought on foot
Frunze	Soviet military academy and most prestigious of its officer schools
GHQ	General Headquarters
IJA	Imperial Japanese Army
IJN	Imperial Japanese Navy
JG	*Jagdgeschwader* (Luftwaffe fighter wing)
Kriegsakademie	Prussian War Academy
Kuomintang (Guomindang)	Nationalist Party of China.
Luftwaffe	German air force
Medal of Honour	Highest U.S. military award for combat valor
NATO	North Atlantic Treaty Organization
NCO	Non-commissioned officer (corporal or sergeant)
Nürnberg	International War Crimes Tribunal
Oberst	German rank, equivalent to U.S. colonel
Oberstleutnant	German rank, equivalent to U.S. lieutenant colonel
RAF	Royal Air Force
Reichswehr	German army during the Weimar Republic (1919–33)
ROTC	Reserve Officer Training Corps, a U.S. program whereby

	college students can obtain a commission in the armed forces
Sandhurst	Royal Military College, Britain
SHAPE	Supreme Headquarters Allied Powers Europe (NATO military headquarters)
St. Cyr	French Military Academy
Stavka	Stavka Verkhovnogo Glavno Komandovaniy. Russian headquarters of the Supreme Army Command. Existing in Tsarist times, it was revived during World War II on 23 June 1941
USAAF	United States Army Air Force (World War II designation)
USAF	United States Air Force
Victoria Cross	Highest British military award for combat valor
Waffen SS (Armed SS)	Armed German SS formations during World War II
Wehrmacht	German Army during the Third Reich
West Point	U.S. Military Academy, West Point, New York
Whampoa	Chinese military academy, run by the Nationalists or Kuomintang (KMT, Guomindong)

A

Abd-el-Krim (1881–1963) Moroccan nationalist and leader of the Rif Rebellion. Known as "the Wolf of the Rif," Abd-el-Krim (Abdel Krim or Mohammed Abd-el-Karim el Khattabi) was a Berber nationalist from the Rif region of Morocco who organized resistance against the Spanish and French beginning in 1920. His greatest victory against the Spanish came in the battle of Anual (21 July 1921). He then proclaimed the Republic of the Rif and organized a modern military force that included artillery (1923). A French advance into the Wargla (Ouargla) Valley prompted him to attack them as well, and he advanced almost to Fez (April–July 1925), but was forced onto the defensive by French troops under General Louis Lyautey. Although he successfully gained the allegiance of many tribes, others opposed him, and the French and Spanish united their effort (September 1925–May 1926). The Rif Rebellion culminated with his surrender to the French (May 1926). Exiled to Réunion, he escaped while on his way to France (1947) and settled in Cairo.

Abe, Hiroaki (1890–1949) Japanese admiral. Abe graduated from the Japanese Naval Academy (1911) and Naval Staff College (1925). He rose through the ranks as a torpedo officer and during 1922–23 commanded a destroyer. He then commanded destroyer divisions, before commanding light cruiser *Jintsu* (1936) and battleship *Fuso* (1938). Promoted rear admiral (1938), he commanded 8th Cruiser Division in the attack on Pearl Harbor (7 December 1941). He led the bombardment groups in the attack on Wake Island (December 1941) and the Battle of Midway (June 1942). Instructed to bombard Henderson Airfield on Guadalcanal (November 1942) to cover the arrival of a task force of transports bearing 13,000 Japanese reinforcements, his force was intercepted by Rear Admiral Daniel Callaghan's U.S. Task Force 67.4. In the ensuing furious, short night action off Lunga Point (12–13 November), his two battleships, one cruiser, and eleven destroyers were ranged against a U.S. force of five cruisers and eight destroyers. Abe lost his flagship, the battleship *Hiei* (badly damaged, she was sunk the next day by carrier aircraft, the first Japanese battleship lost in the war) and two destroyers. The Americans lost two cruisers and four destroyers, and Callaghan was killed. Abe was unable to complete his mission and the Japanese transports turned back. Admiral Isoroku Yamamoto relieved Abe of duty (20 December) and he resigned from the navy (March 1943).

Abe, Koso (1892–1946) Japanese admiral. A career naval officer, Rear Admiral Abe commanded the troop-lift portion of the Port Moresby invasion force (May 1942).

The invasion was called off following the Battle of the Coral Sea (7 May) and his force returned to Rabaul. He subsequently commanded bases in the Marshall Islands.

After the war Vice Admiral Abe was tried on the charges of ordering the execution of nine Marines who had been captured in a raid on Makin Island (August 1942) and sent to Kwajalein for disposition. Convicted, he was hanged at Guam.

Abrams, Creighton Williams, Jr. (1914–74) U.S. general. A West Point graduate (1936), Abrams was posted to the 7th Cavalry Regiment, Fort Bliss, Texas. He took command of a tank battalion of the 4th Armored Division, which often spearheaded General George S. Patton's Third Army (March 1942) and led the relief of the surrounded 101st Airborne Division at Bastogne during the Battle of the Bulge (December 1944), earning battlefield promotion to colonel. Aggressive and hard-driving, he was described by Patton as the "best tank commander in the Army."

Following World War II Abrams was director of tactics at the Armor School (1946–48), graduated from the Command and General Staff College (1949) and the Army War College (1953) and was a corps CofS at the end of the Korean War (1953–54). Promoted to brigadier general (1956) and major general (1960), he held a variety of staff posts. He then commanded 3rd Armored Division (1960–62). Promoted to lieutenant general, he commanded V Corps in Germany (1963).

Promoted general, Abrams became the army's vice CofS (1964–67). He was deputy commander of the Military Assistance Command, Vietnam (MACV) (May 1967), and devoted himself to improving the South Vietnamese armed forces. He replaced General William Westmoreland as commander of MACV (July 1968) and shifted from his predecessor's large-unit search-and-destroy operations to small-unit operations emphasizing population security. He left Vietnam (June 1972) to become CofS of the army. Stricken with cancer, he died in office.

Abrial, Jean-Marie-Charles (1879–1962) French admiral. Abrial entered the French Naval Academy in 1896 and was a midshipman in 1898. During World War I he commanded a high seas patrol boat and by 1917 he was in the anti-submarine division of the Naval Ministry. Promoted commander in 1920, he commanded a torpedo boat, then a squadron of torpedo boats in the Mediterranean. After studies at the Naval War College, he was promoted captain (1925). He commanded a cruiser (1927) and was CofS of 1st Squadron at Toulon (1930). Promoted rear admiral in 1931, he held staff positions and in 1936, as a vice admiral, commanded the Mediterranean Squadron (1936–38) and then was maritime prefect at Toulon. Given charge of protecting the north coast of France and French overseas trade (December 1939). General Maxime Weygand named Abrial CinC, northern naval forces (May 1940).

Abrial was not informed by the British at the time of their decision that they would evacuate their forces through the port of Dunkerque, which was in his area of responsibility. Meanwhile he organized the beachhead there, convinced it could be held. Informed only when the British evacuation began (26 May), he used the Pas-de-Calais flotilla and requisitioned private boats to organize French maritime assistance, and began evacuating both French and British troops beginning on 29 May. Abrial was among the last to be lifted off.

As senior officer at Cherbourg, Abrial surrendered that port to the Germans (19 June). He was then governor general of Algeria (July 1940–July 1941) and Vichy secretary of the navy (November 1942–March 1943). Arrested after the liberation on charges of collaboration, he lost his pension (May 1945) and was sentenced (August 1946) to ten years of forced labor and national indignity. He was granted provisional release (December 1947) and amnestied (1954).

Abruzzi, Amedeo di Savoia-Aosta (1837–1933) Italian admiral and CinC of the fleet (1914–17). Better known by his title of Duke of the Abruzzi, he was the third son of the former king of Spain. He chose a naval career and became known for his geographical and scientific expeditions.

In World War I, Abruzzi commanded Italian battle squadrons at Taranto but conditions allowed only raids and counter-raids. He won praise for his role in the evacuation of the Serbian Army (early 1916) but he increasingly became the target for criticism as a consequence of the stalemate, and resigned (February 1917).

Adachi, Hatazō (1890–1947) Japanese general. Adachi graduated from the Military Academy (1910) and the Army War College (1922). Promoted colonel (1934) and lieutenant general (1940), he was CofS of the North China Area Army (army group) (1941–42). Following the death of Lieutenant General Tomitaro Horii (23 November 1942), Adachi took command of the Eighteenth Army at Rabaul and the north coast of New Guinea. General Douglas MacArthur's landings at Aitape and Hollandia (Jayapura) largely isolated his forces. A capable commander in adversity, he successfully evacuated by barge and forced marches some 14,000 men from the Huon Peninsula. Cut off at Wewak, he twice led breakout attempts, most notably at Aitape (July–August 1944). He surrendered at the end of the war (13 September 1945) with only 13,500 men of what had been nearly a 100,000-man force. Taking responsibility for the criminal mistreatment of Allied POWs at Rabaul, he was sentenced to life in prison (1947) and committed suicide (September).

Adam, Wilhelm (1877–1949) German general. Adam joined the army (1897), serving first in transportation and then in engineers. He attended the Bavarian Military Academy, and during World War I rose to be a staff officer in a reserve division.

Adam continued in the Reichswehr after the war and headed the Truppenamt (army secret general staff). After Adolf Hitler took power, he commanded the Bavarian Military District (late 1933). Promoted brigadier general (February 1930), major general (December 1931), lieutenant general (April 1935), and general (January 1939), he commanded the War Academy in Berlin, then and Army Group 2 at Kessel (March 1938), with responsibility for the defense of the western German borders. Vocal in his opposition to Hitler's Czechoslovakian policies, he was the seventh-highest ranking officer in the army when he was replaced by General Erwin von Witzleben (November 1938). He retired shortly thereafter. Although he maintained contact with some anti-Nazis, he was not involved in the plots against Hitler.

Aguinaldo, Emilio (1869–1964) Filipino revolutionary leader. Educated at Santo Tomas University, Aguinaldo became mayor of Cavite Viejo and local leader of the anti-Spanish Katipunan. He came to prominence in its armed revolt against Spanish rule and won a series of victories, including the Battle of Binakayan (November 1896). Elected president of the revolutionary government (March 1897), he reached agreement with the Spanish (December 1897) whereby he went into exile.

Aguinaldo returned to the Philippines during the 1898 Spanish–American War and became president of the new Philippine Republic (September 1898). Following transfer of the Philippines to the United States, he led Filipino nationalists against U.S. rule (February 1899) and in the 1900–02 Philippine–American War. He and he and his troops were soon forced into the mountains and took up guerrilla warfare. Betrayed, he was taken prisoner (23 March 1901) and took an oath of allegiance to the U.S.A. (April 1901).

Aguinaldo lost an election for president of the Philippines (1935) and sided with the Japanese during World War II in hopes of achieving independence. Briefly imprisoned after the war, he was released under presidential amnesty.

Ainsworth, Walden Lee (1886–1960) U.S. admiral. "Pug" Ainsworth graduated from Annapolis (1910) and was commissioned (1912). He participated in operations against Vera Cruz (1914) and had a number of ship assignments. During World War I he was a gunnery officer in transports. He then was on ordnance duty ashore. Following other ship assignments, he was on ordnance and navy yard duties (1923–25). He was then in the Asiatic Fleet, an instructor at Annapolis (1928–31), and served for a period at sea. He was stationed in the Panama Canal Zone (1934–35), graduated from the Naval War College, was an executive officer on a battleship, and then headed the Naval ROTC unit at Tulane University (1938–40). As a captain, he commanded Destroyer Squadron 2 in the Atlantic (July 1940–December 1941), and then commanded a battleship (1942). Promoted rear admiral (July 1942), he became commander Destroyers, Pacific Fleet.

Known as a strict disciplinarian, Ainsworth then commanded Task Force 67, carrying out the bombardment of Munda, New Georgia (5 January 1943), which was long considered a textbook operation. As commander of Cruiser Division 9 (January 1943–October 1944), he supported American landings in the Solomons and led U.S. light cruisers against ten Japanese destroyers in the Battle of Kula Gulf (5–6 July), in which a U.S. cruiser and two Japanese destroyers were destroyed. He then fought the Battle of Kolombangara (12–13 July) with three cruisers and ten destroyers against Rear

Admiral S. Izaka's one cruiser, five destroyers, and four destroyer transports. Japanese superior night-fighting techniques carried the day; Izaka lost his cruiser, while Ainsworth's three cruisers were damaged and he had one destroyer sunk.

Ainsworth subsequently commanded Cruisers and Destroyers, Pacific Fleet (October 1944–July 1945). After the war he commanded the 5th Naval District (1945–48) and retired as a vice admiral (December 1948).

Akiyama, Yoshifuru (1859–1930) Japanese general. Akiyama entered the Military Academy (cavalry) in 1877. He graduated from the War College (1885) and was attached to the Army General Staff. After study in France (1887–90), he commanded the 1st Cavalry Battalion (1892). He fought in the 1894–95 Sino-Japanese War, participating in the siege of Port Arthur (Lüshan) (1894). He then became director of the Army Cavalry School (1897). He fought in the 1900 Boxer Rebellion. CinC of the China Garrison (1901), he was promoted major general (1902). He was then CinC, 1st Cavalry Brigade (1903).

Known as the "Father of Japanese Cavalry," Akiyama effectively used his well-trained cavalry units against superior numbers of Russian cavalry during the 1904–05 Russo-Japanese War. He fought in the battles of Sha Ho (1904) and Sandepu (San Shih-Li-Pu) (1905).

As general inspector of cavalry (1906–13), Akiyama toured Europe (1907–08). He then commanded 13th Division (1913), the Imperial Guard Division (1915), and the Korea Garrison (1916). He was inspector general of Military Education (1920), then went on the reserve list (1923).

Albrecht Duke of Württemberg (1865–1939) German field marshal. Albrecht entered the army (1893). He became heir to the Württemberg throne (1903) and headed the Sixth Army Inspectorate at

Stuttgart and became colonel general (1913).

Upon mobilization for World War I, Albrecht commanded the German Fourth Army and led it into Champagne during the initial invasion of northeastern France. After the Battle of the Marne (September 1914), he was assigned to Flanders, where a new "Fourth Army" was formed. This ill-equipped and poorly trained force carried out the costly offensive of First Ypres (October–November). His army also participated in the Battle of Second Ypres (April–May 1915).

Promoted to field marshal (1916), Albrecht remained in charge of the crucial Flanders sector until February 1917. One of the more capable senior German commanders of the war, he then commanded an army group holding the southern portions of the Western Front and successfully defended his sectors in Alsace and Lorraine until the end of the war.

Alekseev, Mikhail Vasilevich (1857–1918) Russian general. Commissioned on graduation from the Moscow Infantry Cadet School (1876), Alekseev saw combat in the 1877–78 Russo-Turkish War. He graduated from the General Staff Academy (1890) and was a professor there (1898–1904). In the 1904–05 Russo-Japanese War he was a major general and chief operations officer of Third Army in Manchuria. He then commanded XIII Corps (1912).

On the outbreak of World War I, Alekseev became CofS of the Southwestern Front and planned the Galician offensive that nearly drove Austria-Hungary from the war. He then commanded Northwestern Front (March 1915). After the Germans launched their counter-offensive, he stabilized the Russian lines (August). When Tsar Nicholas II removed the Grand Duke Nicholas, and assumed personal command of the army (September), Alekseev became CofS and was allowed to plan and conduct military

operations. He did much to restore the fighting capacity of the Russian Army.

Ill health forced Alekseev to take medical leave (end of 1916). He returned to be confronted with the March 1917 Revolution. Appointed CinC of Russian forces, he relinquished this to General Aleksei Brusilov (May 1917). Following the November Bolshevik coup, he was helping to form an anti-Bolshevik army when he died of a heart attack.

Alexander, Harold Rupert Leofric George, First Earl Alexander of Tunis (1891–1969) British field marshal. Alexander attended Harrow and Sandhurst and was commissioned in the Irish Guards (1911). During World War I he was a line officer. Distinguishing himself for bravery, he ended the war a lieutenant colonel and battalion commander.

Following the war, he helped organize military forces in Latvia (1919). He graduated from the Staff College at Camberley and the Imperial Defence College, then commanded a brigade in India (1934–38). Promoted major general (1937), he took command of 1st Division on returning to Britain (1938).

On the outbreak of World War II, Alexander served in France and distinguished himself by commanding the rear guard in the retreat to Dunkerque and, briefly, the evacuation itself. He then took over Southern Command (November 1940). Commander in Burma (March–July 1942), he then took charge of British forces in the Middle East, where he got on well with Eighth Army commander General Bernard Montgomery and U.S. military leaders. Following attendance at the Cairo Conference (January 1943), he served as General Dwight Eisenhower's deputy for the remainder of the North African campaign (February–May).

Alexander commanded British and U.S. forces in the invasion of Sicily (July 1943) and then effectively directed the difficult and long Italian campaign (September 1943–May 1945). In reward, he was made field marshal (June 1944) and CinC of the Mediterranean Theater of Operations (December).

After the war Alexander became governor general of Canada (1946–52). He was then British minister of defence (1952–54).

Allenby, Edmund Henry Hynman, First Viscount (1861–1936) British field marshal. Allenby graduated from Sandhurst (1882) and was commissioned in the cavalry. He saw extensive service in Africa, especially in the 1899–1902 Boer War, when he was promoted brigadier general. Promoted major general (1909), he then became inspector general of cavalry.

On the outbreak of World War I, Allenby commanded the cavalry division (later cavalry corps) in France. He then commanded V Corps, and took over Third Army (October 1915), and had notable success in the Battle of Arras (April 1917). His disagreements with General Douglas Haig and the inability to use cavalry to advantage on the Western Front led to his transfer to the Middle East as replacement for Sir Archibald Murray commanding British forces in Egypt (June 1917).

Restoring morale after the earlier defeats at Gaza, Allenby made use of surprise and mobility to break the Turkish front with an attack at Beersheba (October). Known as "the bull" for his determination, Allenby took Jerusalem and then began a drive toward Damascus (September 1918). A cavalry charge following an elaborate deception broke the Turkish lines at Megiddo, and his forces then took Damascus.

After the war Allenby was promoted to field marshal and made Viscount of Megiddo. He was then high commissioner in Egypt (1919–25). He retired in 1936.

Almond, Edward Mallory (1892–1979) U.S. general. Almond graduated from the Virginia Military Institute (1915) and was commissioned (1916) and immediately promoted 2nd lieutenant. During World War I he commanded a machine gun battalion in France. He then served with occupation forces in Germany (1918–19). Following the war he had a variety of assignments and graduated from the Infantry School, the Command and General Staff School, and the Army War College. Promoted brigadier general (March 1942), Almond received command of the 92nd Infantry Division, the only division of black troops in the army (July). Promoted major general (September), he trained the 92nd and then led it in combat in Italy.

Assigned to Japan after the war, Almond became CofS to General Douglas MacArthur's Far East Command. He commanded X Corps for the Inchon invasion (September 1950) and continued in this dual role until July 1951. Promoted lieutenant general for his Korean service, he headed the Army War College until he retired (January 1953).

Ambrosio, Vittorio (1879–1959) Italian general. Ambrosio advanced in the army and served during the 1911–12 Tripolitanian War in the cavalry. During World War I he was a divisional CofS. After the war he commanded a corps, and by 1939 he commanded Second Army on the Yugoslav border.

During World War II Ambrosio's army participated in the invasion of Yugoslavia (April 1941). Recalled to be army CofS (1942), he was then chief of the general staff of the armed forces (February 1943). He sought to return Italian forces from Ukraine and the Balkans and, following the loss at Tunis (May 1943), saw nothing but disaster ahead. Following the Allied invasion of Sicily (July), he tried to convince Benito Mussolini to withdraw Italy from the war. With Mussolini unable to stand up to Adolf Hitler, Ambrosio helped remove him from power. He was then a member of Marshal Pietro Badoglio's military government and helped negotiate the armistice with the Allies (September 1943), which however, was sufficiently delayed to allow the Germans to occupy much of Italy. Shortly thereafter Badoglio dismissed him on the insistence of the Allies, who did not trust him.

Anami, Korechika (1887–1945) Japanese general. Commissioned in the infantry from the Japanese Military Academy, Anami was military aide to Emperor Hirohito (1926–32). He commanded the 2nd Imperial Guards Regiment (1933–34), then headed the Tokyo Military Preparatory School (1934–36).

Promoted major general (March 1935), Anami joined the War Ministry. Promoted lieutenant general (March 1938), he commanded the 109th Infantry Division in China (1938–39). He was then vice minister of war (October 1939–April 1941) before commanding first Eleventh Army in China (April 1941–July 1942) and Second Area Army in northern Manchuria. Promoted full general (May 1943), his army command was shifted first to Davao and then to Manado. Recalled to Japan (December 1944) after the loss of Leyte, he was inspector of army aviation before becoming minister of war (April 1945). The "fight to the death faction" sought his support for a coup against the group allied with Emperor Hirohito for peace. His refusal to go along led to the coup's collapse. He committed suicide (15 August) shortly before Hirohito's broadcast to the Japanese people.

Anaya, Jorge (1927–) Argentinian admiral. A career naval officer, Anaya was CinC of the navy (1982) and the most militant member of the three-man junta ruling the country. The chief architect of the 1982 invasion of the Falkland Islands, he was convinced that Britain would not fight to restore the status quo and that the United States would not rally to London's side. He turned down all peace proposals, confident that the navy could control the

South Atlantic. After the British torpedoed and sank the cruiser *General Belgrano*, he withdrew all his naval units to Argentinian waters, where they remained for the duration of the war.

Anders, Wladyslaw (1892–1970) Polish general. A former Tsarist cavalryman, Anders was a regimental commander during the 1920 Russo-Polish War. From 1926 he commanded a brigade. During the German invasion of Poland (September 1939) his cavalry brigade fought in the northern defenses of Warsaw. Eventually cut off, it was destroyed near Sambor (27 September) fighting against both the Germans and Russians. Wounded, he was captured by the Russians and imprisoned in Lubianka prison, Moscow.

Following the German invasion of the Soviet Union (22 June 1941) and consequent Polish-Soviet Agreement (30 July), Anders commanded the Polish Army in the Soviet Union. Stalin refused to arm the Poles but ultimately allowed Anders to move 70,000 men and 44,000 women and children to the Middle East, where he commanded Polish forces (1942–45) and the Polish II Corps (two infantry divisions and an armored brigade) intended for service in Europe. In the winter of 1943–44, II Corps joined Eighth Army in fighting in Italy. Among its accomplishments was the taking of Monte Cassino (May 1944), which opened the way to Rome. Transferred to the Adriatic coast, the corps took the port of Ancona (June), Pesaro (September), and then Bologna (April 1945).

Appointed acting supreme commander of Polish forces (February 1945), he held that post until the end of the war, ultimately commanding some 200,000 men. After the war he and all but seven officers and 14,000 men decided to remain in the West, where he became a leader of the Polish exile community in Britain.

Anderson, Frederick Lewis (1905–69) U.S. Army Air Forces general. Commissioned in the cavalry on graduation from West

Point (1928), Anderson earned his wings in the Army Air Corps (1929). A pioneer in strategic air warfare, he served in the office of CofS of the Army Air Forces (1941–43). He was CG 8th Bomber Command (July 1943), carrying out raids on U-boat bases in France, Messerschmitt plants at Regensburg, and ball-bearing plants at Schweinfurt. Despite disappointing results in these raids, he developed new techniques of shuttle-bombing, twilight raids, and bombing through cloud cover. Promoted major general (November 1943), he was then assistant CofS for operations and deputy commander of Strategic Air Forces, European Theater of Operations (February 1944–January 1945). He was assistant CofS for personnel at Headquarters, Army Air Forces until his retirement for reasons of disability (September 1947). He was later U.S. ambassador to NATO (1952–53).

Anderson, Sir Kenneth Arthur Noel (1891–1959) British general. Anderson graduated from Sandhurst (1911) and was commissioned in the Seaforth Highlanders. He saw combat on the Western Front during World War I. He commanded 11th Infantry Brigade (1930) and British troops in Palestine (1930–31).

At the beginning of World War II, Anderson commanded the 3rd Division in France and participated in the Dunkerque evacuation (May–June 1940). Promoted major general, he commanded the Eastern Task Force in Operation TORCH, the Allied invasion of North Africa (8 November 1942). He then assumed command of all Allied troops in Algeria, designated British First Army, for the advance to Tunisia. This force took the port of Bône (12 November).

Anderson commanded all forces on the Tunisian front (January 1943), including the U.S. II Corps. When General Sir Harold Alexander took command of overall Allied ground operations in North Africa (February), he was critical of Anderson and considered replacing him.

Although the Allies took Tunis (May 1943), Anderson never again held a major combat command. He did command Second Army in Britain, but was replaced before the Normandy invasion. After the war he served as governor of Gibraltar (1947–52).

Andrews, Frank Maxwell (1884–1943) U.S. Army Air Forces general. Andrews graduated from West Point (1906) and was commissioned in the cavalry. He completed flight training (1918) too late to see combat in World War I. He served in occupation forces in Germany after the war and was a leading advocate of air power in the interwar period.

Promoted temporary brigadier general (1935) and named to command the new GHQ Air Force, Andrews worked to organize the new command, the first time all U.S. air elements were under one commander. Promoted temporary major general, he angered the Army General Staff when, in Congressional testimony (1937), he argued for an independent air force. As a result, he was posted to Fort Sam Houston and reverted to the permanent rank of colonel (1939).

Shortly after his own appointment, Army CofS General George C. Marshall returned Andrews to Washington as assistant CofS of the Army for training and operations, the first aviator to hold that position. He then headed the Caribbean Defense Command as lieutenant general (1941), the first aviator to hold theater command. He commanded all U.S. forces in the Middle East (November 1942), then all U.S. forces in the European Theater of Operations (February 1943). At the time of his death in a plane crash three months later in Iceland, many thought him the leading candidate for supreme Allied command. Andrews Air Force Base is named for him.

Angelis, Maximilian de (1889–1974) German general. Born in Hungary, de Angelis was commissioned in the field artillery in the Austro-Hungarian Army (1910). He distinguished himself during World War I and continued in the Austrian Army after the war. He was a colonel and instructor at the Vienna War Academy at the time of the *Anschluss* with Germany (March 1938). Accepted into the Wehrmacht, he was promoted brigadier general (April 1938). First the chief of artillery in XV Motorized Corps, he then commanded the 76th Infantry Division. Promoted major general, he led his division in Poland, France, and south Russia. Appointed to head XIVL Corps and promoted lieutenant general (March 1942), he distinguished himself in fighting for the Kuban bridgehead. He briefly led the new Sixth Army, then took over Second Panzer Army (July 1944) and fought with it the remainder of the war in Yugoslavia, Hungary, and Austria. Captured by the Russians at the end of the war, he was held prisoner in the Soviet Union until 1955.

Antonescu, Ion (1882–1946) Romanian field marshal and dictator. Antonescu attended French military schools and held a variety of Romanian army positions until he became army commander (1937). Dismissed by King Carol II because of involvement in politics (29 November 1938), he was jailed but released shortly thereafter under pressure from the fascist Iron Guard. He became minister of defense, although Carol criticized the lack of preparations for war that forced Romania to make territorial concessions under German pressure to Hungary and the Soviet Union.

Carol was forced to appoint Antonescu premier with dictatorial powers (September 1940). As "conductor" (the Romanian equivalent of *Führer*), he initially shared power with the Iron Guard, joining Romania firmly to the Axis (November). When Iron Guard excesses threatened order, he had Adolf Hitler's support in crushing it in bloody fighting in Bucharest (January 1941). He then dissolved the Iron Guard and established a government

mostly of military officers. Assuming the rank of field marshal, he took nominal command of the Romanian field army of fourteen divisions that cooperated with the Germans in the invasion of the Soviet Union (22 June 1941), as a means of regaining lost territory.

When Soviet troops drove into Romania (20 August 1944), a coup brought King Michael to power and Romania switched sides. Michael then ordered Antonescu arrested. He was later executed for war crimes, including the murder of Jews and Gypsies.

Antonov, Alexi Innokentievich (1896–1962) Soviet general. Antonov attended the Pavlov Military School and was commissioned in the Russian Army (1916) during World War I. Following the November 1917 Bolshevik *coup d'état*, he joined the Red Army and was CofS of a brigade in the 1918–20 Civil War. He graduated from the Frunze Military Academy (1931). By 1937 he was CofS of a military district.

Antonov held numerous staff positions during World War II. Following the German invasion of the Soviet Union (June 1941), he was CofS of Southern Army Group and then of the North Caucasian and Transcaucasian Army Groups (1941–42), Appointed chief of operations of the General Staff (December 1942), after April 1943 he was also deputy chief of the General Staff. He helped plan the major Soviet offensives of the war, including Operation BAGRATION, the encirclement of the German salient in Byelorussia and East Prussia that brought the Red Army to the Elbe.

Antonov became chief of the Soviet General Staff (1945) and was then CofS of Warsaw Pact forces (1955) until his death.

Aosta, Amedeo Umberto di Savoia, Duke of (1898–1942) Italian general. A cousin of King Victor Emmanuel, Aosta entered the army and won distinction fighting the

Austrians on the Italian Front during World War I (1915–18). He left the army as a captain (1921) and traveled extensively in Africa (1922–25). He returned to Italy, reentered the army, and fought in the reconquest of Libya (1925–32). He then joined the air force (1932). Named viceroy of Ethiopia (end of 1937), he largely pacified the country after the turmoil of Marshal Rodolfo Graziani's rule. Named CinC of Italian East Africa (1940), he directed the Italian invasion of British Somaliland (August) and then defended against the British invasion (January–May 1941). Cut off from resupply and with two-thirds of his troops unreliable native levies, he was unable to halt the British invasion or capture of Addis Ababa (4 April). He surrendered to the British at Amba Alagi (18 May 1941) and died in a prisoner of war camp in Kenya.

Araki, Sadao (1877–1966) Japanese general. Araki graduated from the Military Academy (1897) and as a junior officer saw combat in 1904–05 Russo-Japanese War. After graduation from the Army Staff College (1908), he was in Russia as a language officer (1909) and then military attaché (1912). Later he was a staff officer in the Japanese expeditionary force to Siberia (1918).

As a major general, Araki commanded the 23rd Infantry Brigade (1923). Promoted lieutenant general (1927), he became superintendent of the Army Staff College (1928), then commanded 6th Infantry Division (1929), and directed the Department of Military Education (1931). As minister of the army (1931–36), he became a hero to young nationalist officers (KoJo faction) when he called for a military "spiritual reinvigoration." His sympathy for those participating in the abortive February 1936 rebellion forced his retirement. He rejoined the Hirota cabinet as minister of education for a short period (1938).

Tried and convicted on war crimes charges by the International Military Tribunal after the war, Araki was sentenced to life in prison in 1948. He was released on health grounds in 1955.

Arima, Masafumi (1895–1944) Japanese admiral. Arima graduated from the Japanese Naval Academy (1915) and had a number of ship assignments. He then graduated from the Naval Staff College (1928) and in the early 1930s switched to naval aviation. He commanded several naval air stations (1938–41), and aircraft carriers (1941–43), first a light carrier and then the fleet carrier *Shokaku* in the Battle of Santa Cruz (October 1942). Promoted rear admiral (1943), he commanded the 26th Naval Air Flotilla (1944) at Manila.

Just prior to the Battle of Leyte Gulf (October 1944), Arima led the air attack on Task Force 38 off Taiwan and may have crashed his plane into the carrier *Franklin*. He became a hero in the Japanese military for his sacrifice and is often falsely credited with having initiated the *kamikaze* campaign, which actually began during the Battle of Leyte Gulf.

Arnauld de la Perière, Lothar von (1886–1941) German admiral. Arnauld entered the navy (1903) and became a torpedo specialist. He attended the submarine commander's course (April 1915) and then commanded *U-35* in the Mediterranean. Operating out of Austrian bases, he completed fourteen cruises (November 1915–March 1918). During one cruise (26 July–20 August 1916) he sank no fewer than fifty-four steamers and sailing craft totalling more than 90,150 tons, and was awarded the *Pour le Mérite*.

The year 1917 was less spectacular for Arnauld, partially because his submarine was in dock for four months and was worn out. Moreover, the Allies had introduced and extended the convoy system in the Mediterranean and submarine successes were harder. His new command, *U-139*, a large so-called "U-cruiser" was also unhandy. In the one Atlantic cruise before the armistice he sank only five ships. Nevertheless his wartime total of 189 merchant ships (453,718 tons) and two small warships was a record for any navy of any war.

Arnauld left the German navy (1931) with the rank of captain and subsequently taught at the Turkish Naval Academy (1932–38). Recalled to service during World War II, he served successively as naval commander in Belgium and the Netherlands, Brittany and western France. Promoted vice admiral and named as Admiral Southeast, he was killed in a plane crash at Le Bourget airport, Paris while proceeding to take up his new command.

Arnim, Hans Jürgen Dieter von (1889–1971) German general. Arnim joined the German Army (1908) and was commissioned (1909). He served on both the Western and Eastern Fronts in World War I and ended the war as a captain. He continued in the Reichswehr after the war. He took command of 68th Infantry Regiment (1935) and was promoted brigadier general (1938). On the outbreak of World War II, he commanded the 52nd Infantry Division. Despite a lack of combat service early in the war, he was promoted major general (December 1939) and took command of the 17th Panzer Division (October 1940). He commanded this unit in the invasion of the Soviet Union (22 June 1941). Promoted lieutenant general (October), he ultimately commanded XXXIX Panzer Corps in Army Group North.

Following the Allied invasion of North Africa, Arnim received command of Fifth Panzer Army in Tunisia (December 1942). He assumed command of Army Group Africa on the departure of Field Marshal Erwin Rommel. Captured (12 May 1943), he remained a prisoner the rest of the war.

Arnold, Henry Harley (1886–1950) U.S. Army and Air Force general. "Hap" Arnold graduated from West Point (1907) and was commissioned in the infantry. He served in the Philippines (1907–09) and then was detailed to the aeronautical section of the Signal Corps and learned to fly (1911). He requested reassignment to the infantry and served a second tour in the Philippines (1913), then returned to the air service and was promoted captain. During World War I he had charge of all army pilot training.

After World War I Arnold filled a variety of assignments. He graduated from the Command and General Staff School (1929), was promoted to lieutenant colonel (1931) and commanded a bomb wing and a pursuit wing (1931–35). Promoted brigadier general (1933), he commanded 1st Wing, GHQ Air Force. He then became acting deputy CofS of the Army for air matters (October 1940) and chief of the renamed Army Air Forces (June 1941). Immediately after U.S. entry into World War II, he was promoted to lieutenant general. He then became commanding general of Army Air Forces and temporary general (March 1943).

As a wartime member of the Joint Chiefs of Staff, Arnold was an enthusiastic advocate of strategic bombing and daytime raids. He also pushed hard for a separate air force, which occurred in 1947. Promoted to general of the army (December 1944), he retired (June 1946) but was named first general of the air force (May 1949). He is the only individual to have been both general of the army and general of the air force.

Arz von Straussenburg, Baron Arthur (1857–1935) Austro-Hungarian general. Arz von Straussenburg entered the army (1878) and served on the general staff. He was a major general by 1908.

At the start of World War I, Arz commanded the 15th Infantry Division. Later that year he commanded VI Corps and led it with notable success in the Battle of Gorlice-Tarnow (May–June 1915). He then defended his native Transylvania against a Romanian invasion (August 1916) and bought sufficient time to allow Austro-German reinforcements to turn the tide. He then led the First Austro-Hungarian Army into Moldavia and fought Russian troops in northern Romania.

Arz succeeded Conrad von Hötzendorf as chief of the Imperial General Staff (February 1917). While a fine field commander, he did not understand the factors tearing apart the Dual Monarchy. He became supreme commander of the Imperial Armies (3 November), an hour before he issued an order to cease fighting. He retired that same month.

Asaka, Yasuhiko (1887–1981) Japanese general. Uncle of Emperor Hirohito, Asaka graduated from the Military Academy (1908) and from the Army Staff College (1914). Promoted lieutenant general, he took command of the Imperial Guards Division (1933).

On the outbreak of war with China (1937), Asaka commanded the Shanghai Expeditionary Army (August–December) and thus was at least partially responsible for the extensive atrocities committed at Nanjing (Nanking) after the fall of that city to the Japanese (13 December). He did not hold a prominent post after that date, although he held the nominal position of military advisor. Promoted full general (1939), he went on the reserve list (1945).

Despite his role in the Rape of Nanjing, Asaka was not brought to trial after the war, apparently because he was a member of the royal family.

Auboyneau, Philippe Marie Joseph Raymond (1899–1961) French admiral. Auboyneau entered the Naval Academy in 1917 and was an ensign in March 1918. He ended World War I aboard a torpedo boat. He held a variety of assignments and attended the Naval War College and then commanded a torpedo boat (1937–39). At the beginning of World War II, Auboyneau was with French forces in the Far East. Promoted commander (Decem-

ber 1939), he served as liaison officer to British naval commander in the Indian Ocean at Colombo, Ceylon. He then held the same post with British commander in the Mediterranean Admiral Andrew Cunningham (May 1940). After the defeat of France he rallied to Free French (FF) leader General Charles de Gaulle (August), and commanded 1st Destroyer Division, FF forces. Promoted captain (November 1941), he was appointed CinC, FF naval forces. Promoted rear admiral (June 1943), he commanded 3rd Cruiser Division (July 1944), participating in Operation DRAGOON, the invasion of southern France (August). Promoted vice admiral commanding French naval forces in the Far East (September 1945), he held that command during the Indo-China War and then was CinC of French naval forces in the Mediterranean at Algiers (August 1955). Promoted full admiral (December 1957), he directed French naval operations during the Algerian War until his retirement (1960).

Auchinleck, Sir Claude John Eyre (1884–1981) British field marshal. Following education at Wellington College and Sandhurst, Auchinleck was commissioned in the Indian Army (1904). In World War I he fought in Egypt and Mesopotamia and ended the conflict a lieutenant colonel. He then returned to India, attended the Imperial Defence College (1927), commanded a regiment (1929–30), taught at the Quetta Staff College (1930–33), and commanded the Peshawar Brigade (1933–36). Promoted brigadier general (1936), he became deputy CofS of the Indian Army (1936–38) and commanded the Meerut District (1938–40).

Promoted major general (January 1940), Auchinleck was recalled to Britain to command the expeditionary force at Narvik, Norway (May–June) and then Southern Command against an anticipated German invasion. He then returned to India as commander there (December). Prime Minister Winston Churchill then named "the Auk" to command British forces in the Middle East (June 1941), succeeding General Sir Archibald Wavell. Churchill applied intense pressure to launch immediate offensives against Axis forces under General Erwin Rommel, while Auckinleck insisted his command be properly trained and prepared. Although Tobruk fell (January 1942), he halted Rommel's advance in the first battle of El Alamein (July). Churchill, convinced Auchinleck lacked sufficient aggressive spirit, replaced him with General Harold Alexander (July 1943).

Auchinleck then returned to India as CinC and oversaw the reconquest of Burma (1945) and then division of his army into the forces of India and Pakistan. Promoted field marshal (1946), he retired in 1947.

Aung San, U (1916–47) Burmese general and nationalist leader. As a student leader at Rangoon University, he and U Nu led a students' strike (February 1936). Graduating from the university (1938), he became general secretary of the Thakin party (1939). He fled to Japan (1940–41) to avoid British arrest but returned to command the Burmese Independence Army, which he led during the Japanese invasion of Burma (February–May 1942). His force played only a minor role in the fighting but did assist the Japanese. Near the end of the war as the Japanese position deteriorated, Aung San began negotiations that led to his guerrillas joining the British (May 1945) and fighting the Japanese.

After the war he founded the Anti-Fascist Peoples' Freedom League (AFPFL) and then went to London and negotiated with Prime Minister Clement Atlee an agreement providing for Burmese independence (1946). His AFPFL won an overwhelming majority in the first general elections. He died at the hands of political assassins.

Auphan, Paul Gabriel (1894–1982) French admiral. Auphan entered the Naval Academy (1911), graduating as an ensign (1914). During World War I he participated in the Dardanelles campaign, organized an intelligence network in the Middle East, and served on a dispatch boat and in a submarine in the Adriatic. He commanded a submarine (1920–22) and studied at the Naval War College (1923–24). He held other commands afloat, including destroyers in the Mediterranean (1931–32). He then was deputy commander of the Naval Academy at Brest (1933) and on the staff of the minister of the navy (1234–35), before commanding a cruiser. Promoted commander, he took command of the naval school ship *Jeanne d'Arc*, in which he made an around-the-world cruise (1937–38). He was appointed deputy CofS of the French Navy (October 1939). Promoted rear admiral (June 1940), he was known as an administrator rather than a commander at sea. Following the armistice with Germany, he became director of the merchant marine (July 1940), then CofS of the navy (1941), and finally secretary of the navy in Pierre Laval's cabinet (April 1942).

Auphan was closely identified with Admiral Jean Darlan. He and Darlan both assured the English that France would never surrender its fleet to Germany (19 June 1940). Before and after the Allied invasion of North Africa (Operation TORCH) (8 November 1942), he and General Maxime Weygand urged General Henri Pétain to side openly with the Allies. He drafted the telegram whereby Pétain officially sanctioned the ceasefire signed by Darlan with the Allies (10 November). He then sent Admiral Jean Laborde instructions to destroy the French fleet at Toulon if the Germans moved against that port (11 November). He resigned (18 November) to protest the granting of full powers to Laval.

Pétain empowered Auphan to negotiate

a transfer of power to General Charles de Gaulle's provisional government (11 August 1944), but de Gaulle refused to reply and his government revoked Auphan's pension (September). After the war he was sentenced to forced labor in perpetuity and national indignity (August 1946); the charges including ordering the destruction of the fleet at Toulon. Freed (January 1955), he was rehabilitated in 1956 and wrote extensively on naval history.

Averescu, Alexandru (1859–1938) Romanian general. Averescu fought in the 1877–78 War of Independence against Turkey. He then studied military theory in Italy and returned to Romania as minister of war. He was army CofS during the Second Balkan War (1913).

When Romania joined World War I on the Entente side (August 1916), Averescu commanded Third Army. He took command of Army Unit South (September) against Bulgarian and Turkish forces. His attack across the Danube failed, and his troops were soon routed.

He restored his military reputation by directing defensive operations in the Carpathian Mountains and the defense of Marasesti (August 1917). King Ferdinand I appointed him prime minister to negotiate peace with Germany (February 1918). Dissatisfied with the treaty, the king then forced him from office, but he returned as prime minister in the fall.

After World War I Averescu founded the Peoples League (later the Peoples Party), which was victorious in the 1920 elections. He was prime minister (1920–1921 and 1926–28). He was made a field marshal (1930) and King Carol II appointed him a member of the permanent Crown Council in 1937.

B

Bachmann, Gustav (1860–1943) German admiral. Entering the navy (1877), Bachmann saw service in Africa and Australia. He was CofS of the East Asian Cruiser Squadron (1901–03), and as a rear admiral he headed the Central Division of the Navy Office (1907–10). Promoted vice admiral, he commanded scouting forces of the High Seas Fleet (1910–13), then was chief of the Baltic Sea naval station at Kiel (1913–15).

Appointed chief of the Admiralty Staff (February 1915), Bachmann was promoted admiral (March). He endeavored to secure greater operational freedom for the fleet, but this was rejected by Kaiser Wilhelm II. His major problem centered around unrestricted submarine warfare, and he soon came to be a strong advocate of this as the only means available to Germany to defeat Britain. He opposed concessions to the United States regarding submarine warfare, even after the sinking of the *Arabic* and *Lusitania*, and when the Kaiser ordered reversion to prize rules for submarine warfare, both he and Navy Minister Admiral Alfred von Tirpitz submitted their resignations (June). The Kaiser accepted only that of Bachmann (September). He then returned to his former post as commander of the Kiel naval station (September 1915–October 1918) and urged strong measures be taken against leftists following revolts in the fleet (1917 and 1918).

Bach-Zelewski, Erich von der (1898–1972) German SS general. Bach-Zalewski joined the German Army (1914) and fought in World War I. Commissioned in the Reichswehr after the war, he was forced out (1924) for reasons that are unclear. He rejoined the army (1934) as an enthusiastic Nazi and SS member, participating in the June 1934 Blood Purge. After commanding SS and Gestapo units, he was promoted SS general (1939).

During the invasion of Poland (September 1939), Bach-Zelewski personally participated in the massacre of Jewish civilians. Following the invasion of the Soviet Union (June 1941), he was SS Chief Heinrich Himmler's personal representative in charge of anti-partisan operations. As a general in the Waffen-SS, he frequently commanded these troops in battle.

Obergruppenführer Bach-Zelewski ruthlessly crushed the Warsaw uprising in Poland (August–October 1944) and was directly responsible for the excesses of German forces there. Following this he went to Budapest to help prevent Admiral Miklós Horthy from concluding a separate peace with the Russians.

After the war Bach-Zelewski surprisingly escaped both indictment by the War Crimes Tribunal and extradition to the Soviet Union. In 1951, however, he was sentenced to ten years in prison by a denazification court, but merely served house arrest. Indicted in 1961 for involvement in the Blood Purge, he received a prison term; a year later he was indicted again and sentenced to life in prison for murdering six Communists in 1933.

Bacon, Sir Reginald Hugh Spencer (1863–1947) British admiral and historian. Bacon entered the Royal Navy (1878) and specialized in submarines, mines, torpedoes, electricity, and ship design. Promoted rear-admiral (1909), he retired that same year to become managing director of the Coventry Ordnance Works.

On the outbreak of World War I, Bacon returned to active service and commanded the Dover Patrol (April 1915), which had the primary tasks of denying German U-Boats access to the Channel and ensuring passage to France of men and supplies. In 1917 government confidence in Bacon declined, because of the high number of German U-Boats transiting his area of responsibility. Although he was relieved of command (December 1917), Winston Churchill appointed him controller of the Inventions Department at the Ministry of Munitions.

Promoted admiral (September 1918), Bacon retired (March 1919) to become a naval historian. He defended Admiral John Jellicoe's handling of the Grand Fleet at the Battle of Jutland (31 May–1 June 1916), and then wrote, among other books, biographies of Lord John Fisher and Jellicoe, as well as studies of the Dover Patrol and his autobiography.

Baden-Powell, Robert Stephenson Smyth (1857–1941) British general and founder of the Boy Scout movement. Baden-Powell passed the army exams (1876) and was posted to India. He became a specialist in reconnaissance (often in disguise) and scouting, and wrote several manuals on the subject. He served in Zululand (1887) and in the Ashanti War (1895–96). Promoted colonel, he commanded the 5th Dragoon Guards in India (1897) and developed a training course for scouts.

Before the 1899–1902 Boer War, Baden-Powell was assigned to South Africa to raise two regiments of irregular mounted infantry. His 1,200 men successfully defended Mafeking against a 16,000-man Boer force. He became inspector general of cavalry (1903) and established the Cavalry School at Wiltshire (1904). Promoted lieutenant general (1907), he set up a trial Boy Scout camp in Dorset. In 1910 he retired from the army to devote more time to his passion for the Boy Scout movement.

Bader, Sir Douglas Robert Steuart (1910–82) British air force officer. Educated at Temple Grove School and St. Edwards, Oxford, Bader was a cadet at the Royal Air Force officer training school at Cranwell (1928–30) and was then posted to Number 23 Squadron. He lost both legs when his fighter crashed during a low-level stunt (1931). Fitted with artificial limbs, he taught himself to fly again but the RAF medical board steadfastly refused to certify his return to active duty. He then worked for the Shell Petroleum Company.

When World War II began, Bader volunteered for the RAF. After demonstrating his ability to fly, he was accepted as a pilot (November 1939). Within a few months he commanded 242 Squadron and became one of the leading British aces in the 1940 Battle of Britain. He then commanded a fighter squadron and was credited with 22.5 kills. He eventually commanded a fighter wing.

Bader was flying over France when he became separated from his group. He attacked a formation of six Bf-109s single-handed and shot down two of them, but another rammed his Spitfire from behind (9 August 1941). One of his artificial limbs was lost when he bailed out, but the Germans allowed the RAF to parachute in a replacement. After an unsuccessful effort to escape, he was confined at Colditz. Released (April 1945), he was promoted to group captain and took command of the

RAF Flight Leader School at Tangmere. Later he commanded North Weald Fighter Sector. He led the 300-plane victory fly-past over London (September), but re-signed his commission (February 1946) to return to Shell Oil. He was later knighted (1976).

Badoglio, Pietro (1871–1956) Italian general. Badoglio entered the Italian military as an artillery officer and participated in the campaigns in Abyssinia (1896) and Libya (1911–12). During World War I he commanded XXVII Army Corps in the 1917 Battle of Caporetto. His deployment and poor handling of his corps opened a gap in the Italian lines and facilitated the Austro-German advance. Despite this, he became deputy to CofS of the Italian Army General Armando Diaz.

In 1920 he commanded the Italian troops that forced Gabrielle D'Annunzio out of Fiume. He then became army CofS (1921), and chief of the general staff (1925). After a tour of duty as governor of North Africa (1928–33), where he oversaw the suppression of the Senussi rebellion, he commanded in Ethiopia, where he was named viceroy (May 1936). Promoted field marshal and awarded the title of Duke of Addis Ababa (July 1936), he was chief of staff for the Italian Armed Forces until he was forced to resign (December 1940) after the Italian failure in Greece. After Mussolini's arrest (July 1943), he became Italy's head of government and helped engineer the switch from the Axis to the Allied side as a co-belligerent. He was forced to resign in June 1944.

Baer, Heinrich (1913–57) German Air Force officer. Baer joined the Luftwaffe (1937) and became a pilot NCO, serving in JG-51 in Poland, France, and the Soviet Union. He then commanded JG-77 in Sicily, then JG-1 and JG-3. He then commanded the flying school near Augsburg, training pilots to fly the new Me-262 jet aircraft in Jagdverband (JV) 44

(January 1945). He succeeded General Adolf Galland as commander of JV-44 (April), ending the war as a lieutenant colonel.

One of the war's leading aces, Baer flew more than 1,000 missions and had 220 victories. He was shot down eighteen times. His 124 victories against western pilots was surpassed only by Hans-Joachim Marseille with 158. His sixteen victories in the Me-262 is still the record for jet aircraft.

Bagramyan, Ivan Khristoforovich (1897–1982) Soviet marshal. Bagramyan joined the Russian Army during World War I (1915) and graduated from officers' school (1917). Following the November 1917 Bolshevik *coup d'état*, he joined the Red Army and fought in the 1918–20 Civil War. He then held a variety of assignments and graduated from both the Frunze Military Academy and the General Staff Academy. Following the German invasion of the Soviet Union (22 June 1941), he was chief of operations and deputy CofS of the Southwestern Front (1941–42). He commanded the Sixteenth Guards Army (1942) and fought at Kiev and Kursk, then commanded the 1st Baltic Front (1943–45). Although blamed for the failure to take Königsberg, his successes on this front contributed to the later Russian capture of Berlin and German territory east of the Elbe.

After the war Bagramyan commanded the Baltic Military District. Promoted marshal (1955), he ended his career as deputy minister of defense and armed forces chief of rear services (1958).

Balbo, Italo (1896–1940) Italian air marshal. A lieutenant in the Alpini during World War I, Balbo joined the Fascist Party (1921). A brutal man, he became one of Benito Mussolini's top advisors. Following the 1922 March on Rome, he held various cabinet posts before becoming minister of aviation (1929), in which position he worked to make Italy a major air power. Despite numerous air records, the Italian Air Force was largely a paper tiger with few modern aircraft. Promoted Italy's first air marshal (1933), Balbo came to be seen as a political threat by Mussolini, who made him governor and commander-in-chief of Italian forces in Libya (January 1934). He was openly critical of Italy's alliance with Germany.

After Italy declared war (June 1940), Balbo accepted command of Italian forces in North Africa, but his plane was shot down over Tobruk and he was killed. The Italians blamed the incident on a British air raid, but the British said the plane was downed by Italian anti-aircraft fire. Mussolini, suspected of ordering his death, remarked later that Balbo was "the only one capable of killing me."

Balck, Hermann (1893–1984) German general. During World War I Balck served as an infantry officer on the Western, Eastern, Italian, and Balkan Fronts, ending the war as a captain. He continued in the Reichswehr with the cavalry. In 1938 he joined the Inspectorate of Mobile Troops within the army high command.

Balck assumed command of a motorized infantry regiment in his friend General Heinz Guderian's XIX Panzer Corps (October 1939). During the invasion of France (May 1940) he spearheaded Guderian's breakthrough at Sedan, securing a vital bridge. On Balck's suggestion, infantry and tank units were made into combined arms teams. He then commanded 3rd Panzer Regiment in the invasion of Greece (April 1941), breaking through the Metaxas Line and outflanking British forces near Mount Olympus. Appointed inspector of mobile troops (November 1941), he assumed command of 11th Panzer Division in the Soviet Union (May 1942). In one instance his division defeated an entire Soviet shock army. Promoted major general (January 1943), he commanded XIV Panzer Corps and in 1944 XLVIII Panzer Corps in the battles of Kiev, Radomyshl, and Tarnopol, de-

stroying in turn three Soviet armies. He assumed command of Fourth Panzer Army (August), halting a Soviet offensive on the Vistula.

Transferred to the Western Front, Balck took command of Army Group G (September 1944) with the mission of stopping the U.S. Third and Seventh Armies. Following clashes with Hitler, he was relieved (December) and ended the war in command of Sixth Army in Austria. One of the top German field commanders of the war, he received the Knight's Cross of the Iron Cross, with Oak Leaves, Swords, and Diamonds.

Barak, Ehud (1942–) Israeli general and political leader. Barak studied at Hebrew University in Jerusalem and at Stanford University in the U.S. He enlisted in the Israeli Defense Force (1959) and participated in a number of counter-terrorist operations. He commanded an armored regiment during the 1973 Yom Kippur War, then headed the Planning Department of General Headquarters and Central Command (1983–86), and was then assistant chief of staff of the army. CofS of the Israeli Defense Force (1991–95), he retired from the military as Israel's most decorated soldier (1995).

Barak joined the government as minister of interior (1995), and was then foreign minister. He then became head of the Labor Party (1997), prime minister (1999–2001), and defense minister (2001).

Barbey, Daniel Edward (1889–1969) U.S. admiral. Barbey graduated from Annapolis (1912) and served in various assignments afloat and ashore. As a captain, he headed the War Plans Section of the Bureau of Navigation (1938–41) and became interested in amphibious warfare. As CofS to the commander, Training Force, Atlantic Fleet (1941) he established the Amphibious Warfare Section of the Navy Department and developed U.S. Navy amphibious doctrine and practice. He personally designed the DUKW amphibious truck and supervised design of the LSD (landing ship dock), LCI (landing ship infantry), and other such craft.

Promoted rear admiral (December 1942), Barbey commanded VII Amphibious Force, Seventh Fleet (January 1943). As such he was responsible for all amphibious landings in the Southwest Pacific (56 landings in 30 months) through to the time of Luzon (January 1945). Promoted vice admiral (June 1944), he took the surrender in Seoul of Japanese forces there. He commanded Seventh Fleet (November 1945) and Atlantic Amphibious Forces (1946), then the Caribbean Sea Frontier and the 13th Naval District before retiring (May 1951).

Barkhorn, Gerhard (1919–83) German air force general. Barkhorn joined the Luftwaffe in 1937. He failed to shoot down a plane in the Battle of Britain (1940), but rose to prominence on the Eastern Front following the invasion of the Soviet Union (June 1941). Posted to JG-52, he ultimately scored 301 kills, most of them in a Bf-109F, making him the second-highest-scoring ace in history. Shot down nine times, he finished the war as a major. He joined the Federal Republic of Germany Air Force (1955) and retired a major general.

Barré, Georges (1886–1970) French general. Barré joined the army as a colonial officer in Morocco (1912). Promoted to brigadier general (December 1939), he commanded the 7th North African Infantry Division in France at the time of the German invasion (May 1940), when his division won official citation for its superior performance while sustaining losses of more than 30 percent from continuous combat.

Following the June armistice with Germany, Barré headed the delegation arranging demilitarization between Tunisia and Libya (the Mareth Line) and was then senior military commander in Tunisia (January 1942). Promoted to major general (January), he adopted a neutral posi-

tion regarding the Allied North African landings (Operation TORCH) (8 November) when 5,000 promised Allied troops failed to arrive in Tunisia. After German troops from Sicily came to Tunisia to establish an Axis beachhead there, he withdrew his forces into the hills while negotiating with the Germans, stalling to await Allied support. Despite a German ultimatum to withdraw from Medjez-el-Bab, he held that critical communications center under heavy German attack until British and American forces relieved him. His troops then joined the Free French XIX Corps for the remainder of the Tunisian campaign.

Bastico, Ettore (1876–1972) Italian marshal. Bastico fought in the 1911–12 war with Turkey and in World War I. A close friend of Benito Mussolini, he also fought in the Italian invasion of Ethiopia (1935), and the 1936–39 Spanish Civil War.

During World War II, Bastico became governor and commander in chief in Libya (July 1941–February 1943). Determined to assert his authority, he clashed with German General Erwin Rommel over the retaking of Tobruk. Rommel then secured Mussolini's authority to cut him out of the chain of command. Following the retaking of Tobruk, when Hitler made Rommel a field marshal, Mussolini promoted Bastico to marshal as well. He returned to Italy (1943) and retired from the army in 1947.

Batov, Pavel Ivanovich (1897–1985) Soviet general. Batov entered the army (1916) and fought in World War I. He joined the Red Army (1918) and fought in the 1918–20 Civil War. He then served as an advisor in Spain (1936–37) during its civil war, where he was wounded. He then commanded an infantry corps in the invasions of Poland (September 1939) and Finland (November 1939), and then was first deputy commander of the Transcaucasian Military District.

Promoted lieutenant general (June 1941),

Batov led IX Detached Rifle Corps in the Crimea, then was deputy commander of Fifty-first Special Army (October). He commanded Third Army on the Bryansk Front (January–February 1942), and was assistant front commander (February–October). He then commanded Fourth Tank Army, redesignated Sixty-fifth Army, in the Stalingrad area. After the Russian victory at Stalingrad (January 1943) he fought in the Battle of Kursk (July), the crossing of the Dneiper River, and the drive through Byelorussia into East Pomerania and across the Oder River.

Promoted colonel general (June 1944), Batov was in the Northern Group of Forces (1944–48), and was first deputy CG of Soviet forces in Germany. Promoted general of the army (1955), he commanded the Carpathian Military District (1955–58), the Baltic Military District (1958–59), and the Southern Group of Forces (1961–62). He was then CofS of Warsaw Pact forces (1962–65) and served in the Inspectorate until his death.

Battenburg, Prince Louis (1854–1921) British admiral. Born into the Hessian nobility, Battenberg was a career officer in the Royal Navy, who commanded several warships. He became assistant director of Naval Intelligence (1899), and then its director (1902). A naval reformer, he pushed for better conditions for seamen and a modern staff system for the navy. His marriage to Queen Victoria's granddaughter, Victoria of Hesse, gave him access to the royal houses of Europe and opportunity to gather information on the German naval build-up. Appointed first sea lord (December 1912), his major achievement during the next two years was to improve operational efficiency. He also supported an air arm for the navy.

While Battenberg was first sea lord during World War I, the army was transported across the Channel without loss, a blockade of Germany was implemented, and three German cruisers were sunk. He was undermined by setbacks, however.

The German battle cruiser *Goeben* reached Turkey, U-boats sank three British cruisers in one day, and Germany scored a clear victory off the Coronel Islands. The dreadnought *Audacious* also succumbed to a German mine.

Prime Minister Herbert Asquith asked for Battenberg's resignation (October 1914) and he spent the remainder of the war as a member of the King's Privy Council. He took the name Mountbatten (1917), and retired from the navy after the war (1919).

Bayerlein, Fritz (1899–1979) German general. Bayerlein fought as an officer candidate on the Western Front at the end of World War I. After a period in private business, he joined the Reichswehr as an infantry lieutenant (1921), but then transferred to the new armor (Panzer) force. Promoted major, he was staff officer to General Heinz Guderian in the invasions of Poland (September 1939), France and Benelux (May 1940), and the Soviet Union (June 1941).

Bayerlein was CofS to General Erwin Rommel's *Afrika Korps* (September 1941), and was promoted colonel (April 1942) and became CofS of the new *Panzerarmee Afrika* (February 1942). Briefly its commander (November 1942), he was promoted brigadier general (March 1943) and was wounded and then evacuated from Tunisia before its surrender (May 1943). Following recovery, he was chief of staff to the First Italian Army in Sicily. After the Allied conquest of Sicily, he fought in Italy, then on the Eastern Front as commander of 3d Panzer Division (October 1943–January 1944). He then commanded the elite Panzer Lehr Division (February 1944). Promoted major general (May 1944), he was transferred to the Western Front and participated with his division in the Normandy campaign and Ardennes Offensive (Battle of the Bulge, December 1944). He commanded LIII Corps (March 1945), but was taken prisoner shortly thereafter in the Ruhr

Pocket (April 1945). Following the war he helped write operational histories of the conflict.

Beatty, David, 1st Earl (1871–1936) British admiral. Beatty entered the Royal Navy as a cadet (1884) and became a midshipman at 15. He then had a variety of assignments, many abroad. He served in Egypt and the Sudan (1896–98), where he made commander (1898). He was promoted to captain (1900) and rear admiral (1910), and then became naval secretary to the First Lord of the Admiralty, Winston Churchill (1911).

Beatty commanded the battle cruiser squadron, the advanced guard of the Grand Fleet, in World War I (1914–16). He served in that capacity during the battles of Heligoland Bight (August 1914), Dogger Bank (January 1915), and Jutland (31 May–1 June 1916). All three battles were marred by problems of communication, confusion over targets, and poor staff coordination, for which contemporaries blamed Beatty. Nevertheless, when Admiral Sir John Jellicoe became first sea lord in December, Beatty was named commander-in-chief of the Grand Fleet. Promoted admiral (January 1919) and admiral of the fleet (April), he was then first sea lord (1919–1927), during which time the Royal Naval Air Service was shifted from the navy to the newly formed Royal Air Force, a serious blow to potential naval aviation capabilities.

Beaufre, André (1902–73) French general and military theorist. Attached to French Army commander General Maxime Weygand's headquarters, Beaufre accompanied Weygand as commander of Vichy French forces in North Africa (June 1940), remaining there following Weygand's dismissal (November 1941). He served on the staff of General Henri Giraud and rallied to the Allies following Operation TORCH, the invasion of North Africa (November 1942). Joining the Free French, he fought in Tunisia

(November 1942–May 1943) and Italy (September 1943–May 1945).

Following the war Beaufre was on the staff of French commander-in-chief in Indo-China, General Jean de Lattre de Tassigny (December 1950–September 1952), and also led troops in the field. Returning to France, he was promoted to lieutenant general and was deputy land force commander in the Franco-British assault on the Suez Canal (October–November 1956). He then commanded French forces in NATO and was deputy chief of staff for logistics at SHAPE (1956–60). Retired at his own request (1961), he published *Introduction to Strategy* (1963), which argued for the limited use of nuclear weapons. He was a leading proponent of the development of the French nuclear forces (*Force de Frappe*).

Beck, Ludwig (1880–1944) German general. Beck joined the army (1898) and as a lieutenant attended the Kriegsakademie in Berlin (1898–11). Promoted captain (1913), during World War I he served on the Western Front as a staff officer. He continued in the Reichswehr after the war and held a variety of posts, including command of the 1st Cavalry Division. Promoted brigadier general (February 1931) and major general (December 1932), he headed (October 1933) the Truppenamt (Troop Office), the staff organization prohibited by the Treaty of Versailles. The Truppenamt was later redesignated the general staff (1935).

Promoted lieutenant general (October 1935), Beck directed German rearmament and the creation of a modern, efficient military machine. He planned a defensive strategy and opposed Adolf Hitler's aggressive policy toward Czechoslovakia, believing it would bring a general European war and inevitable defeat. He was unsuccessful in an attempt to enlist other generals in a plot to overthrow Hitler. He sent an emissary to London urging the British government to act, also without success.

Promoted full general on his retirement (August 1938), Beck organized a resistance group of army officers and conservative civilians. Convinced of inevitable defeat, its members believed that only Hitler's death could save Germany from destruction. It organized several assassination attempts, the last being that of Colonel Klaus von Stauffenberg (20 July 1944). Convinced that Hitler had died in the bomb explosion, the group instituted their plan to seize power, Operation VALKYRIE, but with singular lack of resolution. On the failure of the coup attempt, troops loyal to Hitler stormed the conspirators's headquarters. Beck was then offered the opportunity to shoot himself. His self-inflicted head wound was not fatal, and one of his attackers administered the *coup de grace*.

Below, Fritz von (1853–1918) German general. The elder brother of Otto von Below, he joined the Prussian army and was commissioned (1873). Below attended the Kriegsakademie and thereafter had a variety of staff and command postings. He became commanding general of the newly formed XXI Corps (October 1912).

In World War I Below led XXI Corps on the Eastern Front, most notably in the Second Battle of the Masurian Lakes (February 1915). He then replaced the ailing Field Marshal Karl von Bülow as commander of Second Army in the Somme Region on the Western Front (April). Several weeks into the British offensive (July 1916), Below was made commander of First Army with responsibility for the northern Somme region. First Army was then moved to the Reims area (April 1917) where it helped to repel the Champagne (Nivelle) Offensive. In ill heath, Below went on leave (June 1918) and was placed on the standby list (August).

Below, Otto von (1857–1944) German general. The younger brother of Fritz von Below, he joined the Prussian army (1875) and attended the Kriegsakademie (1884–

87), rising to command 2d Reserve Division in East Prussia (April 1912).

During the World War I mobilization, Below took over the I Reserve Corps and led it with distinction in the early Battles of Tannenberg (August 1914) and Masurian Lakes (September). He succeeded General Hermann von François as commander of Eighth Army (November) and played a major role in the German victory in the Second Battle of the Masurian Lakes (February 1915). He then commanded the Niemen Army in defensive and offensive operations against the Russians (1915–16). Sent to Macedonia to take charge of the German and Bulgarian divisions (October 1916), he was then transferred to France as commander of the Sixth Army (Spring 1917). He was moved again (September), this time to the Italian Front. Appointed head of a newly formed German–Austro-Hungarian Fourteenth Army, he launched the highly successful offensive in the Isonzo region (the Battle of Caporetto) (October–November 1917).

Given command of the new Seventeenth Army in the Arras-Cambrai region of France (February 1918), Below participated in Ludendorff's Spring Offensive and, later, the defensive battles against the Allies. In the final weeks of the war, he and First Army commander General Bruno von Mudra exchanged commands. Following the armistice, Below went to eastern Germany as a corps commander. He was dismissed (June 1919) after vowing to lead an "uprising" against the Versailles Treaty if necessary.

Ben Gurion, David (1886–1973) First prime minister of the state of Israel. Ben Gurion first went to Palestine from Poland (1906) to work for the creation of a Jewish state. He joined a labor party and traveled extensively, then returned to Palestine, now under British control (1918), and became a leader of the Zionist movement there. Following Arab riots in Safed and Hebron, Ben Gurion formed the

Haganah (Defense) underground paramilitary terrorist group (1929). He became chairman of the Executive Committee of the World Zionist Organization (1935) and worked to secure arms and equipment for the Haganah. During World War II Haganah supported the British and Ben Gurion worked to form an all-Jewish brigade to fight Germany.

Following the war, when the British attempted to halt immigration into Palestine, Haganah and other Jewish terrorist groups such as the Irgun and Stern Gang increased their activities. Ben Gurion embraced the partition of Palestine, rejected by the Arabs. He then proclaimed the creation of the state of Israel (14 May 1948) and led it in war when it was invaded by its Arab neighbors. As commander-in-chief, he united the various terrorist groups to form a regular army and secretly worked with King Abdullah of Jordan. He retired (1953) but returned as prime minister (1956) and intrigued with France and Britain to initiate war with Egypt. He retired again in 1958.

Bennett, Donald Clifford Tyndall (1910–86) British air vice marshal. Born in Australia, Bennett pursued a career in aviation flying seaplanes for Imperial Airways. Commissioned in the Royal Air Force (1941), he commanded 10 Squadron (1942) and distinguished himself in a bombing raid against the German battleship *Tirpitz*, during which he and his copilot were shot down over Norway but made their way to Sweden and later returned to Britain.

Promoted to air vice-marshal (July 1942), the youngest in RAF history, he played a key role in the strategic bombing campaign against Germany. He was responsible for a number of night bombing innovations, including the Pathfinder Force of high-speed Mosquito aircraft that would locate and then illuminate German targets for attack, and the Light Night Strike Force of Mosquito bombers.

Bennett, Henry Gordon (1887–1962) Australian general. A reserve officer prior to World War I, he rose to the rank of brigadier general during that conflict. He left the army after the war, but on the start of World War II he returned to active duty as a major general. Initially in command of a training depot, he took command of Australian forces in Malaya (February 1941). With his 8th Division at Jahore, he tried to hold back the Japanese invasion and had some initial success before withdrawing to Singapore. With British surrender inevitable, he escaped without informing the British commander, General Arthur Percival. He made his way by junk to Batavia and then to Australia. Promoted lieutenant general (April 1942), he nonetheless came under severe criticism for abandoning his troops and never again held active command. After the war a court ruled he should have stayed at Singapore.

Benson, William Shepherd (1855–1932) U.S. admiral. An 1877 graduate of Annapolis, Benson held a variety of assignments afloat and ashore, including service at the Naval Academy and the post of commandant of midshipmen (1907–08). He commanded the Philadelphia Navy Yard in 1913. Promoted rear admiral, he was appointed the first chief of naval operations (1915), a position long advocated by naval reformers. Promoted admiral (1916) and the highest ranking U.S. naval officer, he reorganized and centralized administration in time to meet the demands of U.S. entry into World War I (April 1917). After the war in 1919 he was an advisor to the U.S. delegation at the Paris peace talks. He retired that September, and during 1920–28 was chairman of the U.S. Shipping Board.

Berenguer, Damaso (1873–1953) Spanish general. Born in Cuba, Berenguer joined the army (1889) and fought against the rebels in Cuba (1892–98). He then served in Spanish North Africa and fought against Moroccan rebels (1911–16). Promoted brigadier general (1913), he became military governor of Malaga (1916). He was then promoted major general, and made minister of war (1918). He chaired the high commission in Morocco (1919) and was made a count (1920). Held partly responsible for the disaster at Anual, where 12,000 men under General Fernandes Silvestre were killed by rebels led by Abd-el-Krim (21 July 1922), he was court-martialed and placed on the reserve list (1924). Soon amnestied, he became head of Alfonso XIII's military household (1926). Briefly premier (1930–31), he was again minister of war (1931). He spent most of the Republican era in prison (1931–39) but was released on the Nationalist victory.

Beresford, Charles, First Baron Beresford (1846–1919) British admiral. Entering the Royal Navy (1859), Beresford rose to prominence while commanding a gunboat in the bombardment of Alexandria, Egypt (1882). He then commanded the naval brigade in General Sir Garnet Wolseley's expedition to relieve General Charles Gordon at Khartoum (1884–85). During service at the Admiralty (1886–88), he helped establish the navy's intelligence arm.

Promoted rear admiral (1899), Beresford commanded the Mediterranean Fleet and was second in command overall to Admiral John Fisher. Although both men were reformers, they were markedly different in personality and clashed repeatedly. When Beresford was appointed commander of the Channel Fleet (1907), Fisher, then first sea lord, transferred many of his ships to a new Home Fleet. Following intensification of the feud, Beresford was ordered to resign from the navy (1909). Subsequent investigations of charges he made against Fisher, including the latter's failure to establish a naval war staff, cast discredit on both men and Fisher resigned (1910), although unlike

Beresford he later returned to the navy, serving again as first sea lord.

Bergeret, Jean Marie Joseph (1895–1956) French general. Bergeret volunteered for the army at the start of World War I (1914) and was selected for the special course at St. Cyr. On graduation he fought in the war, where he showed remarkable ability and enjoyed rapid advancement. On graduation from the École de Guerre, he transferred to the Armée de l'Air (1928). He was chief of operations on the air staff, and was promoted brigadier general just before the start of World War II (September 1939).

Following the defeat of France by the Germans (June 1940), Bergeret headed the commission negotiating armistice terms with Italy. He was air minister in the Vichy French government (September 1940–April 1942), and then inspector of air defenses. Shortly before the Allied landings in North Africa (8 November 1942), he rallied to General Henri Giraud and then became Admiral Jean Darlan's special assistant in Algiers. He was deputy high commissioner in North Africa until March 1943. Arrested in a Gaullist purge of the National Council of the Resistance (CNR) (October 1943), he was imprisoned until September 1945. All charges against him were later dropped (November 1948) and he was reinstated. He retired in 1950.

Berthelot, Henri Mathias (1861–1931) French general. Berthelot graduated from St. Cyr (1883) and served in Algeria, Tonkin, and Annam before becoming Secretary to the General Staff (1907–19), when he was promoted to command a brigade. On the outbreak of the war he became CofS to General Joseph Joffre. He took over command of reserves in the Soissons area (November), and then commanded 53rd division and later XXXIII Corps (1915). After taking part in the Battle of Verdun, he was sent to Romania (September 1916) to head the French military mission there. After the Romanian defeat he returned to the Western Front to command Fifth Army, which held the line west of Reims in the Second Battle of the Marne (1918). Fifth Army fared poorly in the German offensive (July); it was pushed back in disorder largely because Berthelot ignored General Henri Philippe Pétain's elastic defense scheme, which General Henri Gouraud had adopted for Fourth Army. The Germans were halted on the Marne only by determined American resistance and because French reserves were made available by Gouraud's success east of Reims. Berthelot then returned to the Balkans as commander in chief of the Danube Army. After the war he was governor of Metz and a member of the French Supreme War Council.

Beseler, Hans Hartwig von (1850–1921) German general. Beseler joined the army (1868) and fought in the 1870–71 Franco-Prussian War. He attended the Kriegsakademie and served in the War Ministry. Appointed deputy chief of the General Staff (1899), he was assumed to be the logical successor to Count Alfred von Schlieffen as chief of the General Staff, but the post went to Helmuth von Moltke. Promoted major general (1903) and lieutenant general (1907), he retired in 1910.

Recalled on the outbreak of World War I, Beseler commanded III Reserve Corps in First Army in the invasion of Belgium (August 1914). Entrusted with the reduction of Fortress Antwerp, he took the city in October. After fighting along the Yser River (November), III Corps was sent to the Eastern Front. Beseler became governor general of Poland (August 1915) and advocated a pro-Polish policy to recreate the Poland of the 1815 Congress of Vienna, but the proposal failed. Promoted full general (January 1918), he retired at the end of the war.

Besson, Antoine (1876–1969) French general. Commissioned on graduation from St. Cyr (1898), Besson joined the 4th Zouave Regiment and saw service in North Africa. During World War I he held staff and command positions on the Western Front, eventually commanding the 4th Zouaves.

Promoted full general and appointed a member of the Supreme War Council (July 1937), he commanded Third Army Group of three armies on the extreme right flank of the Allied line in the Colmar–Mulhouse Sector of the front during the German invasion of France and Benelux (May 1940). Following the German breakthrough, he began withdrawing on order to the Seine (8 June). Within a week, sensing the inevitable, he insisted that the government conclude an armistice. He spent the remainder of the war as a POW.

Béthouart, Marie Antoine Émile (1889–1982) French general. Commissioned on graduation from St. Cyr (1912), Béthouart began his military career with Alpine troops. Wounded three times during World War I, he held a succession of routine assignments after the war. A graduate of the École de Guerre (1923), he was military attaché to Yugoslavia (1934) and was with King Alexander when the king and French Foreign Minister Louis Barthou were assassinated at Marseille (9 October).

A colonel at the beginning of World War II (September 1939), he was soon promoted to general (April 1940). He commanded the Franco-Polish Expeditionary Corps sent to Norway and helped retake Narvik from the Germans (28 May). Following the defeat of France (June), he headed the Casablanca division in south Morocco. He cooperated with Allied plans to invade North Africa and ordered his troops to welcome the Americans as allies, but alerted his superior, Resident General Charles Noguès, who had pledged to oppose any landings. Noguès had him arrested for treason and he barely escaped execution.

Béthouart then headed a French military mission to the United States to arrange aid (December 1942), returning to Algiers as chief of the National Defense general staff. He joined the staff of Army Group B, which became First French Army, and then took command of its I Corps, which he led in the invasion of southern France (Operation DRAGOON) (August 1944), through the Vosges Mountains into Alsace, and eventually across the Rhine to the southern bank of the Danube. After the war he headed French occupation forces in Austria. Appointed commanding general of the army (1949), he then entered politics and became a senator (1955). He also published several volumes of memoirs.

Bigeard, Marcel Maurice (1916–) French general. Bigeard joined the army at the beginning of World War II. Wounded and captured by the Germans, he escaped (November 1941) and joined the Free French in Senegal. He parachuted into France to serve as liaison with the Resistance (July 1944).

Tough and resourceful, Bigeard became a legend in colonial warfare, first in Indo-China and then in Algeria. He fought in the 1946–54 Indo-China War as a captain and company commander, then a lieutenant colonel and commander of the 6th Parachute Battalion, which he led in the Battle of Dien Bien Phu, where he was captured when the French surrendered (May 1954). He returned to France (early 1955) and, as a colonel, commanded the 3rd Colonial Paratroop Regiment in fighting in Algeria (1956–58). He then commanded the 6th Combined Foreign Legion Regiment (1960–63). Promoted brigadier general (1967) and major general (1971), he served briefly as secretary of state for defense (1975–76).

Billotte, Gaston Herve Gustave (1875–1940) French general. Billotte graduated from St. Cyr and was commissioned in the naval infantry (1896). He served in the colonies until 1915 and commanded a division during World War I. Assigned to Indo-China, he became commander of troops there (1930). In 1937 he was military governor of Paris.

On the outbreak of World War II (September 1939), Billotte received command of First Army Group, consisting of four French armies and the BEF, which held the line facing Belgium from the English Channel to Montmédy. Billotte's forces moved into Belgium (10 May 1940) on the German invasion of the West, but German forces outflanked his southernmost army, the French Ninth, and he pulled his forces back. Badly injured in in an automobile accident at Ypres (21 May), he died two days later, creating more confusion in an already disorganized Allied command.

Birch, Sir James Frederick Noel (1865–1939) British general. Birch graduated from the Royal Military Academy and was commissioned in the artillery (1885). He spent his early career in the Royal Horse Artillery, commanding a battery in General John French's cavalry division during the Ashanti Expedition.

At the beginning of World War I, Birch commanded a brigade of the Royal Horse Artillery in France. He became artillery commander of I Corps (July 1915), and then was a major general commanding Fourth Army's artillery (March 1916). Following this he joined Field Marshal Douglas Haig's headquarters, becoming the top-ranking British artillery officer in France (May). He also supervised the gunnery of the Royal Tank Corps (May 1918) and assumed supervision of chemical warfare (June).

Birch's ideas on artillery employment were innovative, but he and other progressive British gunners, such as Major General Herbert Uniacke, often were overruled by their more conservative superiors, particularly Haig. Birch openly criticized infantry commanders who expected artillery preparation and the creeping barrage to get them to the objective unscathed.

After the war, Birch became director-general of the Territorial Army (1921). As master-general of ordnance (1923), he sponsored development of Britain's first self-propelled artillery gun, known as the Birch Gun. Promoted to full general (1926), he retired in 1927.

Birdwood, William Riddell, First Baron Birdwood of Anzac and Totnes (1865–1951) British field marshal and ANZAC commander. Birdwood served with distinction in the 1899–1902 Boer War and in India as military secretary to Lord Kitchener. Promoted brigadier general (1909) and major general (1911), during World War I he commanded Australian and New Zealand troops (ANZACs), leading them at Gallipoli (1915).

At Gallipoli, Birdwood launched a poorly prepared major assault (May). Forced onto the defensive, he maintained a policy of "cautious aggression." His attention to detail and regular tours of the trenches earned him the sobriquet "the soul of ANZAC." A stout opponent of withdrawal, he was appointed commander of the Mediterranean Expeditionary Force to oversee the final evacuations (November 1915).

Birdwood took the I ANZAC Corps to the Western Front and some of the most bitter fighting of the war (1916). His forces captured St. Quentin (September 1918). He replaced Sir Hubert Gough as commander of Fifth Army (May 1918). Promoted field marshal (1925), he was commander-in-chief in India (1925–1930). He was elevated to the peerage as First Baron Birdwood of Anzac and Totnes (1938).

Bittrich, Wilhelm (1894–1979) German SS general. "Willi" Bittrich was an army officer during World War I, served in the Freikorps after the war, and then returned to the army for secret pilot training in the Soviet Union. After Adolf Hitler came to power, he joined the SS (1934).

In World War II Bittrich commanded the Waffen SS Panzer Regiment *Deutschland* in the invasions of Poland (September 1939), France and Benelux (May 1940) and the Soviet Union (June 1941). Promoted *Oberführer*, he commanded first the *Das Reich* and then the *Hohenstaufen* divisions before being promoted *General der Waffen SS* and commanding 2nd SS Panzer Corps in Normandy. He also helped eliminate the British positions at Arnhem taken during Operation MARKET-GARDEN (September 1944). After the war he was held prisoner by the French until 1954.

Blamey, Sir Thomas Albert (1884–1951) Australian field marshal. Briefly a schoolteacher, Blamey won a commission through competitive examination (1906). He attended the staff college at Quetta (1911–13). During World War I he served in Egypt (1914–15) and at Gallipoli (October 1915–January 1916). He then served on the Western Front on the staff of Lieutenant General Sir John Monash. Following the war Blamey was Australian military representative in London (1919–23) and second chief of the Australian general staff (1923–25). He retired to become police commissioner for Victoria (1925), commanding 3rd Division of the Citizen Forces (Territorials) (1931–37). He was recalled to active duty on the start of World War II (September 1939).

Blamey went to Palestine as commander of the Australian corps formed for service in the Middle East (February 1940). He commanded the ANZAC Corps in its evacuation from Crete and Rhodes (May–June 1942). Recalled to Australia with two divisions (March 1942), he was both commander of the Australian Army and commander of Allied Land Forces, Southwest Pacific Area. He reorganized and trained the Australian Army, but suffered unfair criticism from General Douglas MacArthur for the performance of his troops. He took personal command in New Guinea (October 1942) and directed the successful Kokoda Trail Offensive that recaptured Buna (January 1943). He then directed additional offensives resulting in the capture of Lae (September). Late in the war he commanded Australian forces against the Japanese in Indonesia. Retiring (1946), he was briefly recalled (1950) to be promoted field marshal, the first Australian so honored.

Blanchard, Jean Georges Marie (1877–1954) French general. A graduate of the École Polytechnique (1899), Blanchard was commissioned in the artillery. He served in World War I in both line and staff assignments, ending the war as a major. Promoted to brigadier general (1932) and major general (1935), he directed French military education (1938).

At the beginning of World War II (September 1939), Blanchard commanded First Army at Cambrai in First Army Group. Following the German invasion of the West (May 1940), according to plan he moved his army to the Dyle River line to support the Belgians, meeting the German Sixth Army around Hannut. His army was cut off by the German left hook down the Somme River to the English Channel. Following General Gaston Billotte's fatal injury in an automobile accident (23 May), Blanchard took over his army group, where he proved totally out of his depth and seemed incapable of giving orders. After his evacuation from Dunkerque, he was placed on the reserve list (August).

Blandy, William Henry George (1890–1954) U.S. admiral. Graduating first in his class at Annapolis (1913), Blandy took part in the 1914 occupation of Veracruz, Mexico. After U.S. entry into World War I he was on convoy and blockade duties. Following the war he served with the Bureau of Ordnance (1919–20) and the Asiatic Fleet (1921–24). He returned to the Bureau of Ordnance (1924–27) and was naval attaché to Brazil (1930–34).

Chief of the Bureau of Ordnance (1934–43), Blandy then saw combat in World War II in command of Amphibious Group One in the Kwajalein invasion (January–February 1944). He commanded the floating reserve and coordinated operations for the invasions of Saipan (June–July) and Peleliu (September–November), and commanded the amphibious support group in the invasions of Iwo Jima (February–March 1945) and Okinawa (April–June).

Following the war, Blandy was deputy chief of Naval Operations (Special Operations). He commanded the task force in the Bikini atomic tests (July 1946) and then Eighth Fleet (1946) and the Atlantic Fleet (1947–50). He retired in 1950 but returned to service to head the Naval Reserve Evaluation Board (1953–54).

Blaskowitz, Johannes (1883–1948) German general. Blaskowitz fought on both the Western and Eastern Fronts in World War I. He remained in the Reichswehr after the war. Promoted lieutenant general (1936), he commanded Military District II (1936) and Third Army (1938), which he led during the German occupation of Czechoslovakia (March 1939). Promoted full general just prior to the outbreak of World War II, he commanded Eighth Army in the invasion of Poland (September 1939) and was then military governor there. A general of the old school, he protested against SS atrocities against Poles and Jews. His detailed complaints and demands for prosecution led to his dismissal. He briefly commanded Ninth Army in the invasion of France (May–June 1940) and was then military governor of northern France (1940) before commanding First Army along the French coast from Brittany to Spain (October 1940–May 1944). He commanded Army Group G along the Mediterranean and southeast coasts of France (May 1944) but was relieved of command following Operation DRAGOON, the Allied landings in south France (September 1944).

Commander of Army Group H defending Holland and northwestern Germany, Blaskowitz allowed food and medical supplies to reach trapped Dutch civilians. He surrendered to British forces in The Netherlands (March 1945). Arrested as a war criminal (1946), he committed suicide (February 1948) before he could be brought to trial.

Bliss, Tasker Howard (1853–1930) U.S. general. A graduate of West Point (1915), Bliss was commissioned in the artillery. He returned to West Point to teach modern languages and graduated from the Artillery School. He taught at the Naval War College (1885–88), and then was aide to the commanding general of the army, Major General John Schofield. Bliss next served as attaché in Spain, but was recalled on the outbreak of the 1898 Spanish-American War. He served with the 1st Division in Puerto Rico, then was collector of customs in Havana (1899–1902). Promoted brigadier general, he served as first president of the Army War College (1903). After a period of service in Asia, he was again president of the Army War College (1909).

Promoted major general (1915), Bliss became acting army CofS, then CofS (May 1917–May 1918), in which post he supervised the rapid U.S. military mobilization for World War I. He then was a member of the Allied Supreme War Council (May 1918). After the war he was one of the U.S. delegates to the Paris Peace Conference. An extraordinarily capable administrator, he had little opportunity to demonstrate ability as a field commander.

Bloch, Claude Charles (1878–1967) U.S. admiral. Bloch graduated from Annapolis (1899) and was commissioned (1901). He served aboard ship during the 1900–02 Philippine–American War and 1900–01 Boxer Rebellion. An aide and flag lieutenant to the commander of the Pacific Fleet (1907–09), he was assistant chief (1918–21), then chief (1923–27) of the Bureau of Ordnance. He commanded a battleship (1927–29), then graduated from the Naval War College (1929). Promoted rear admiral (July 1931), he was commander Cruisers, Battle Force (1932–33). He was judge advocate of the navy (1934–36), then commanded Battleship Division 2 (1936–37). Promoted admiral (January 1937), he commanded the Battle Force (1937–38), and then was CinC of the U.S. Fleet (1938–40). He took command of the 14th Naval District at Hawaii (January 1940). His refusal to allow installation of torpedo nets, even after the British torpedo attack on Taranto (11–12 November 1940), contributed to the success of the Japanese attack on Pearl Harbor (7 December 1941).

Whereas Pacific Fleet commander Admiral Husband Kimmel was retired after the disaster, Bloch continued in service until reaching mandatory retirement age (August 1942), when he retired as a full admiral. He was briefly recalled to serve on the General Board (1942 and 1946).

Blomberg, Werner von (1878–1946) German field marshal. Bomberg was an officer candidate in 1897. A staff officer in World War I, he headed the Truppenamt (secret general staff, outlawed under the Treaty of Versailles) (1927–29). He visited Russia to further secret military cooperation and was one of the first German generals to support Hitler. Recalled from the Geneva disarmament talks to serve as minister of war in Adolf Hitler's first cabinet (January 1933), he was an enthusiastic supporter of Hitler and was, as a result, made the first field marshal of the Third Reich (1936).

Blomberg issued the order congratulating Hitler and assuring him of army loyalty following the Blood Purge (June 1934), in which Hitler crushed supposed Storm Troop (SA) and other opposition. Among the dead were two army generals. After the death of President Paul von Hindenburg, he also ordered that the army swear an oath of loyalty to Hitler.

After Hitler revealed his plans for an expansionist foreign policy that would undoubtedly lead to war (1937), both Blomberg and Army commander General Werner von Fritsch voiced objections. Hitler was determined to get rid of them and purge the high command. His chance came when Blomberg remarried (January 1938). Hitler and Göring were the chief witnesses at the ceremony. Shortly thereafter, Heinrich Himmler, anxious to embarrass Göring, supplied evidence that Blomberg's new wife was a former prostitute known to the police. This shocked fellow officers, who called for and secured his resignation.

Blumentritt, Günther (1892–1967) German general. Blumentritt joined the army (1917) and saw service as a junior officer in World War I. He remained in the Reichswehr after the war, and was chief of operations planning for Colonel General Gerd von Rundstedt during the German invasion of Poland (September 1939) and France and Benelux (May 1940). He was then CofS for Field Marshal Hans Günther von Kluge's Fourth Army in the invasion of the Soviet Union (June 1941). Transferring back to Rundstedt's staff (1942), he carried out much of the planning to prepare for the Allied invasion of France. Although apparently not involved in the plot, following the 20 July 1944 assassination attempt on Adolf Hitler he was removed from his post in the general purge of the military (September). He ended the war as commander of Fifteenth Army (December 1944–April 1945) and participated in the December 1944 Ardennes Offensive (Battle of the Bulge).

Bock, Fedor von (1880–1945) German field marshal. Commissioned in the army (1908), during World War I Bock rose to command a battalion as a major. He remained in the Reichswehr after the war. Promoted to major general (1931), he received command of the 2nd Infantry Division. As commander of Eighth Army,

he directed German occupation forces first in Austria (March 1938) and then Czechoslovakia (September).

Promoted general, Bock commanded Army Group North in the invasion of Poland (September–October 1939) and Army Group B in the north during the invasion of France and Benelux (May–June 1940). Following victory in the Netherlands and in northern Belgium, in which his forces took both Brussels and Antwerp, he shifted his resources south to form the right wing of the German assault on France after the Dunkerque evacuation (June).

After the victory over France, Bock was one of twelve individuals raised to field marshal by Hitler (August). He commanded Army Group Center in the 22 June 1941 invasion of the Soviet Union, advancing as far as the suburbs of Moscow. Relieved of command by Hitler (December), he was replaced by Field Marshal Günther von Kluge. Recalled to head Army Group South (February 1942), he was again sacked following a dispute with Hitler (July). He died with his family in an Allied air raid (5 May 1945).

Boelcke, Oswald (1891–1916) German air force officer. Boelcke began his military career in a telegraph unit (1911), but became a pilot (1914). During World War I, in early 1915 Boelcke began flying the new Fokker Eindekker' monoplane fighter, and transferred (April) to a fighter unit. He became one of the first German air aces and, after Max Immelmann's death (June 1916), the High Command sought to protect him by removing him from combat. He returned to combat (July) at his own request to command a new air fighting unit on the Somme battlefront. He had forty kills to his credit when, trying to avoid a French aircraft during an aerial combat, he collided with another German aircraft and was killed. A leading air tactician, he is considered by some to be the father of air combat. The *"Dicta Boelcke"* include basics such as surprising the enemy from above and behind, using the sun, and planes working in formation.

Bohm-Ermolli, Eduard (1856–1941) Austro-Hungarian field marshal. Bohm-Ermolli entered military service (1870) and spent the next forty-four years as a cavalry commander and general staff officer. He began World War I as commander of Second Army, supporting the Austrian offensive against Serbia, but Russian pressure in Galicia forced the reassignment of his command to the Eastern Front (August). Poor planning scattered his army among various railheads and prevented it from operating as a whole until November, when it entered the fight in Silesia.

Bohm-Ermolli took part in the offensive to relieve Przemsyl (February 1915). Although most Austrian commanders doubted the Carpathian passes could be forced, he was confident. Weather, sickness, and Russian counterattacks stymied the attack. Another assault (April) brought the high point in his career, the capture of Lemberg (June). His forces continued eastward, and he assumed command of an Army Group south of the Pripet Marshes (October).

The Brusilov Offensive (July 1916) shattered Bohm-Ermolli's line. Temporarily relieved of command, he re-emerged in command of the three southernmost Austrian armies in Russia. His final campaign of consequence came when his troops turned back part of the last offensive by the rapidly disintegrating Russian armies (summer 1917).

Boisson, Pierre (1894–1948) French soldier and colonial administrator. Boisson entered the army (1914) and lost a leg in the Battle of Verdun (1916). He joined the colonial service (1919) and was commissioner of the republic to Cameroon (1936). At the start of World War II he was governor general of French Equatorial Africa (1936).

Loyal to the Vichy French government following Germany's defeat of France

(June 1940), Boisson was appointed governor general of French West Africa (26 June) and helped prevent the Anglo-Gaullist landing at Dakar (23 September). Arrested (December 1943), he was imprisoned for the duration of the war and then granted provisional freedom for health reasons. He died before he could be brought to trial.

Bonneau, Louis (1851–1938) French general. Bonneau fought in the 1870–71 Franco-German War, at St. Privat and in the Siege of Metz. At the beginning of World War I he led VII Corps in the French advance and victory at Mulhouse in Alsace (August 1914), but was forced to retreat following a German counterattack and was relieved of field command.

Bono, Emilio de (1866–1944) Italian general. Bono joined the army (1884) and saw action against Ethiopia (1887–88). He served in Libya during the 1911–12 Italo-Turkish War and, on Italy entering World War I (June 1915), was chief of staff of II Corps. As a colonel, he commanded a regiment with distinction in First through Fourth Battles of the Isonzo (June–December 1915). As a major general, he commanded the Savona Brigade and 38th Division during the Austrian Trentino Offensive (May–June 1916). Given command of II Corps (March 1918), he led it in the Battle of the Piave (June–July) and was promoted lieutenant general (1918).

Following the war, Bono was active in the formation of the paramilitary groups that were the basis of the Fascist party's Blackshirt militia. He played an important role in the 1922 Fascist March on Rome that brought Benito Mussolini to power and was rewarded by being made director of public safety, governor of Tripolitania, and minister for the colonies (1922–35).

Bono commanded Italian forces in the initial stage of the invasion of Ethiopia, but was replaced by Marshal Patrice Badoglio (December 1935). He voted to oust Mussolini from power (24 July 1943) and, when the Germans rescued Mussolini and restored him to power in northern Italy, Bono was arrested and executed.

Borghese, Prince Junio Valerio (1906–74) Italian navy commander. Known as the Black Prince, Borghese joined the navy and commanded a submarine. He achieved fame as a special operations officer, employing the submarine *Scirè* to launch two-man piloted torpedo teams to attach limpet mines. He had to abort his first attempts (September 1940) when he learned that Force H was away from Gibraltar. Several subsequent attempts were also unsuccessful. As commander of the underwater element of the 10th Light Flotilla (XMAS) (early 1941), he continued to develop techniques to sink Allied shipping. His teams sank a freighter and a tanker in the Bay of Gibraltar (September 1941), but his greatest success came against Alexandria when three teams from *Scirè* managed to enter Alexandria harbor and cripple the only two British battleships left in the Mediterranean, *Valiant* and *Queen Elizabeth*, and a tanker, as well as damaging a U.S. destroyer, all at a cost of only six frogmen captured (18–19 December 1941).

Borghese then commanded 10th Light Flotilla (May 1943), continuing operations against Gibraltar. He commanded a destroyer flotilla after Italy switched sides. A committed Fascist, as late as 1970 he attempted a *coup d'état* in Rome.

Bor-Komorowski, Taduesz (1895–1966) Polish general. A career army officer, Bor-Komorowski was from 1938 commander of the Cavalry Training Center. He was deputy commander of a cavalry brigade during the German invasion of Poland (September 1939). Following the defeat of Poland, he commanded the underground Krakow Home Army District. He was then (1941–43) simultaneously deputy commander of the Armia Krajowa (AK, Home Army) and the Western Home Army District. He took command of the entire AK (July 1943), with a strength of 250,000 men in summer 1944. He adopted "Bor" as a *nom de guerre*, and fought through the war as "General Bor."

Bor-Komorowski began Operation TEMPEST, in which Home Army forces openly assisted invading Soviet forces against the Germans (January 1944). He then led the Warsaw Uprising (1 August–3 October 1944). Betrayed by the Russians and largely abandoned by the West, his forces fought on alone. When the uprising was crushed, he was taken prisoner by the Germans. He survived the war and went into exile in the United Kingdom.

Borojević von Bojna, Svetozar (1856– 1920) Austro-Hungarian field marshal. Born in Croatia, Borojević was commissioned in the infantry from the Liebenau cadet school (1875). He became a General Staff officer and instructor at the Theresian Military Academy (1877). Promoted major general, he commanded VII Corps (1898). Promoted lieutenant general (1913), he commanded Third Army in Galicia at the beginning of World War I. One of the best field commanders of the empire during the war, he conducted a skillful withdrawal and tough stand in the Carpathians against a superior Russian force (September 1914).

Borojević opposed the abortive attempt to relieve the fortress of Przemysl (January 1915) and protested against renewing the attack. CofS General Franz Conrad von Hötzendorf then transferred command of most of his part of the front to the more pliable General Eduard Bohm-Ermolli. Borojević then took over Fifth Army, defending the approaches to Trieste following Italy's entrance in the war (May 1915) and displaying a mastery of defensive warfare during the First through Fourth Battles of the Isonzo (June– December 1915). His command had only a minor role in the Battle of Caporetto (October 1917). Favoring the defensive for 1918, he was overruled and his Piave Army Group participated in the offensive all along the Italian front (May). After few gains, he was able to pull his troops back in the face of heavy Italian pressure. The Vittorio Veneto Offensive (October–November) precipitated the collapse of his force, although he managed to conduct a fighting retreat from Italy, perhaps his most brilliant achievement of the war.

Botha, Louis (1862–1919) South African soldier and statesman. Although Botha opposed war with Britain, he joined the Transvaal commando during the 1899–1902 Boer War and helped defeat the British in a number of battles. He commanded Transvaal forces after the death of Petrus J. Joubert (March 1900) and proved adept at forging unity among the Boers. Following the loss of Johannesburg and Pretoria (late 1900), he skillfully directed a guerrilla war for two years.

Botha played a major role in peace negotiations and signed the treaty with Britain, something that angered many of his countrymen. He worked for reconciliation and was the first prime minister of the Union of South Africa (1910–1919). On the outbreak of World War I he supported Britain and suppressed an anti-British insurrection in South Africa. He then invaded and conquered German Southwest Africa (March–July 1915). After the war he attended the Paris Peace Conference.

Bothmer, Felix von (1852–1937) German general. Bothmer was commissioned from the Bavarian War Academy (1871) and rose to the rank of lieutenant general (1905). He was recuperating from an injury when World War I began, but received command of the 6th Bavarian Reserve Division (December 1914). He then commanded II Reserve Corps in Galicia (March 1915). He succeeded General Alexander von Linsingen as head of the *Südarmee* (South Army) (July), a force of German and Austro-Hungarian

(and later Turkish) units in the southern sector of the Eastern Front. Under his direction the *Südarmee* enjoyed success against numerically superior Russian forces, particularly during the 1916 Brusilov Offensive and the 1917 Kerensky Offensive.

Following the armistice with Russia, *Südarmee* was dissolved (January 1918) and Bothmer transferred to the Western Front. He then commanded the newly formed Nineteenth Army in Lorraine until the end of the war. Promoted full general (April 1918), he then retired in December 1918.

Bowhill, Frederick William (1880–1960) British air chief marshal. "Ginger" Bowhill was sixteen years in the merchant marine before undertaking flight training as a lieutenant in the naval reserve (1912). He was then appointed a flying officer in the Royal Flying Corps, Naval Wing. He was the first Englishman to fly an aircraft from a ship in an attack on an enemy ship. During World War I he led attacks on German submarine bases, commanded a squadron in Mesopotamia, and fought against Zeppelins raiding England. He ended the war a wing commander.

Promoted air marshal and knighted (1936), he helped develop the system of air–ground control that was a key factor in the 1940 Battle of Britain. Bowhill pushed for the use of barrage balloons against low-flying aircraft, and was also one of the creators of the Women's Auxiliary Air Force (WAAF). He then led Coastal Command (August 1937–June 1941) before going to Canada to head the new Ferrying command (1941–43), and then returned to Britain to head the new Transport Command (1943–45). He retired (1945) as an air chief marshal.

Boyington, Gregory (1912–1988) U.S. Marine Corps colonel. A graduate of the University of Washington (1934), "Pappy" Boyington briefly served in the Coastal Artillery Reserve, then enlisted in the

Marine Corps Reserve (1936) while working for Boeing Aircraft Co. He learned to fly and secured a commission as a lieutenant (1937). A flight instructor at the Pensacola Naval Air Station by 1941, he "resigned" to join General Claire Chennault's American Volunteer Group (AVG, the "Flying Tigers") in China. He shot down six Japanese planes and was the first Marine Corps ace of World War II. When the AVG was disbanded (July 1942), he became executive officer of Fighter Squadron VMF-122.

Major Boyington then was based on Guadalcanal and secured permission to form his own squadron, VMF-214. Inheriting a group of misfits and recruits, he was able thanks to his superb leadership and flying skills to form them into an excellent unit, the famous "Black Sheep Squadron." Flying the F4U Corsair and initially based at Espiritu Santo in the New Hebrides, the squadron attacked Japanese aircraft throughout the Solomans and conducted the first Allied fighter sweep against Rabaul (17 December 1943). The squadron had an excellent combat record and Boyington himself was credited with 28 kills before he was shot down over Rabaul (23 January 1944). He spent the remainder of the war as a Japanese POW. Released (September 1945), he received promotion to lieutenant colonel and the Medal of Honor. He retired a full colonel (1947).

Bradley, Omar Nelson (1893–1981) U.S. general. Commissioned in the infantry on graduation from West Point (1915), Bradley served in various posts in the U.S. and then taught at West Point. He attended both the Infantry School and the Command and General Staff School, and was an instructor at the Infantry School before graduating from the Army War College (1934). He served on the army General Staff (1938–41) and was promoted brigadier general (February 1941).

Bradley commanded the Infantry School before taking command of the

82nd Division as a major general (February 1942). He commanded II Corps at the end of the Tunisia campaign and during the fight for Sicily (July–August 1943), and First Army in the invasion of France (June 1944). He then commanded Twelfth Army Group (August), the largest force ever commanded by an American general and the southern wing of the Allied advance across northern France. Promoted general (March 1945), he was modest and unassuming, and regarded as a "soldier's general."

After the war Bradley headed the Veterans Administration (1945–47) and then became army chief of staff (February 1947). He was the first chairman of the Joint Chiefs of Staff (August 1949–August 1953). Advanced to general of the army (September 1950), he was President Truman's most trusted military advisor. He supported the use of U.S. forces to defend the Republic of Korea and military aid to the French in Indo-China. But he opposed expansion of the Korean War, believing Europe should remain the top U.S. military priority. He retired in August 1953.

Brandenburger, Erich (1894–1970) German general. Commissioned in the army, he was promoted colonel (August 1936), and was chief of staff for XXII Corps. He helped develop the tactics of close combined arms operations characterizing *Blitzkrieg*. Promoted brigadier general (July 1940), he commanded 8th Panzer Division in the invasion of the Soviet Union (June 1941). Advanced to major general (August 1942) and lieutenant general (August 1943), he commanded XXIX Corps in Army Group South Ukraine in the Balkans until, after the capture of General Heinz Eberbach, he was assigned to the Western Front to command the latter's Seventh Army (August 1944). He rebuilt Seventh Army and, by adroitly employing his inferior resources, successfully defended the Aachen–Hürtgen Forest–Roer Dam areas against the U.S. First Army. Seventh Army was one of the three

German armies in the Ardennes Offensive (Battle of the Bulge), but the objectives were beyond its means and it had not received the priority in equipment accorded the two panzer armies.

Brandenburger then fought delaying actions against the U.S. First and Third Armies in the Ardennes and into Germany proper. Facing overwhelming odds, he on occasion recommended withdrawing to more defensible terrain. He clashed with Field Marshal Walther Model, who relieved him (February 1945). He then received command of the greatly weakened Nineteenth Army of Army Group G in the Black Forest (March). Under relentless attack from the French First Army, he surrendered Nineteenth Army at Innsbruk, Austria (5 May 1945).

Brauchitsch, Walther von (1881–1948) German field marshal. Commissioned in the army in 1900, Brauchitsch was an artillery captain in World War I. He remained in the Reichswehr after the war, and by 1931 he commanded the training division and was then promoted to major general and made inspector of artillery (1932–33). He commanded the 1st Military District (1933–37) and Fourth Army Group (1937–38).

When General Werner von Fritsch resigned as commander-in-chief of the army in 1938, Brauchitsch replaced him. Adolf Hitler hoped to appease the officer corps by naming a respected military figure as Fritsch's replacement. While Brauchitsch opposed Hitler's plans for territorial expansion, he was not as vehement as his predecessor. He believed firmly in neutrality of the military in politics and felt honor bound by his soldier's oath to Hitler.

Brauchitsch coordinated the initial German victories in World War II, in Poland, France and Benelex, and the Balkans. Promoted field marshal (July 1940), he opposed Hitler's orders to stand fast in Russia, advocating withdrawal to more easily defended positions (early December 1941). Made a scapegoat for the failure of

the Russian campaign, he retired (19 December) and Hitler assumed personal command of the German armed forces.

Brereton, Lewis Hyde (1890–1967) U.S. Army Air Forces general. Brereton attended St. John's College (1906–07) before entering Annapolis. After graduation (1911), he exchanged his navy commission for one in the army. After a year in the artillery, he joined the Aviation Section of the Signal Corps (1912) and qualified as a pilot (1913). Following U.S. entry into World War I (1917), he commanded the 2nd Aero Squadron in France (March–October 1918).

Following occupation duty in Germany, Brereton was air attaché to France (1919–22), aviation instructor (1922–24), and commander of the 2d Bombardment Group. Closely associated with Colonel William Mitchell, he served as the latter's defense counsel at his court-martial (1925). He graduated from Command and General Staff School (1928). Promoted lieutenant colonel (1935), he was on the faculty of the Command and General Staff School (1935–40). As temporary brigadier general, he commanded 17th Bomb Wing (1940). As major general, he commanded Third Air Force (1941), and then was CG of Far Eastern Air Force in the Philippines (November 1941). Much of his force was caught on the ground and destroyed in a Japanese raid (8 December) on Clark Field, although he waged a determined struggle with his remaining planes (December 1941–March 1942).

Following the fall of the Philippines, Brereton was transferred to India as CG of the U.S. Middle East Air Force and then to North Africa to command Ninth Air Force, which raided the Ploesti oil fields. He then moved Ninth Air Force to Britain to prepare for the Normandy invasion. A meticulous planner and trainer, he helped minimize casualties. Following the Normandy invasion (6 June 1944), as a lieutenant general he took command of the Allied First Airborne Army – all U.S., British, and Canadian airborne units – and was responsible for Operation MARKET, the airborne portion of MARKET-GARDEN (September 1944). He also directed Operation VARSITY, the seizure of a bridgehead across the Rhine (March 1945).

Following the war, Brereton transferred to the U.S. Air Force (September 1947). He retired in 1948.

Brett, George Howard (1886–1963) U.S. Army Air Forces general. Brett graduated from the Virginia Military Institute (1909) and was commissioned in the Philippine Scouts (1910). He received a regular commission in the cavalry (1911), but then transferred to the Signal Corps (1915). After qualifying as a pilot (1916), he was assigned to the Signal Corps Office. Promoted captain, he went with the AEF to France in World War I and was in charge of purchasing for the air service. He did not see combat.

After the war Brett held a number of assignments related to logistics. He graduated from the Command and General Staff School (1930) and the Army War College (1936). Promoted brigadier general (January 1939), he was then chief of the Matériel Division at Wright Field, Ohio (1939–41). Promoted major general, he was appointed acting chief of the Army Air Corps (October 1940), and later chief of the Air Corps (May 1941–March 1942). After promotion to lieutenant general (January 1942), he commanded U.S. Forces in Australia, redesignated U.S. Army Forces in Australia (USAFA) (January 1942). He also commanded the new Fifth Air Force (February–August 1942). Continuing to command the USAAF, he also commanded the combined air forces in Australia and was head of all of General Douglas MacArthur's air forces in the Southwest Pacific Area (April–June 1942). He continued in Australia as CG Fifth Air Force until August 1942. He then took over Caribbean Defense Com-

mand (November 1942–1946). He retired in May 1946.

Bridgeford, Sir William (1894–1971) Australian general. Bridgeford graduated from the Royal Military College, Duntroon. He served in France during World War I, and afterward held a variety of staff and training positions in the Australian Army. He also attended the Staff College in Quetta and the Imperial Defence College in London.

During World War II, as a brigadier general, Bridgeford commanded the 25th Australian Infantry Brigade in Britain and then served in the Middle East and in the campaign in Greece (1941). He returned to Australia (1942) and served in New Guinea, commanding 3rd Armoured Division in the Bougainville Campaign.

After the war Bridgeford became quartermaster-general of the Australian military forces, then headed an Australian military mission to Malaya (summer 1950). Sent to Korea, he replaced General Sir Horace Robertson as Commonwealth commander-in-chief (November 1951–February 1953). His easy style smoothed over differences created by his acerbic predecessor. He retired from the army in 1953.

Brooke, Sir Alan Francis, Lord Alanbrooke (1883–1963) British field marshal. Commissioned in the artillery upon graduation from Woolwich (1902), Brooke served in Ireland and India. He fought on the Western Front in World War I, ending the conflict as a brevet lieutenant colonel and chief artillery officer of the British First Army. He was instructor at the Staff College, Camberley (1919, 1923–27) and at the Imperial Defense College (1927, 1932–34), and then was director of military training at the War Office (1936–37). He commanded Britain's first mobile division (1937) and the new Territorial Anti-Aircraft Corps, and was promoted lieutenant general in 1938. He then headed Southern Command (1939–40).

Brooke commanded II Corps in the

British Expeditionary Force (BEF) in France (September 1939), and had a major role in coordinating its retreat and evacuation (May–June 1940). He resumed his post as head of Southern Command (June) and then commanded Home Forces (July). Despite the fact that he had opposed Prime Minister Winston Churchill's decisions on several occasions, the latter named him chief of the Imperial General Staff (December 1941) and chairman of the chiefs of staff committee (March 1942). In this capacity, he was Churchill's closest military advisor during the war. He had some success with the Americans in pushing a Mediterranean strategy, although he was disappointed not to command Operation OVERLORD, the invasion of France (June 1944). Promoted field marshal (January 1944), he was made Baron Alanbrooke (September 1945), and finally Viscount Alanbrooke (January 1946), when he retired.

Brooke-Popham, Sir Henry Robert Moore (1878–1953) British air marshal. A graduate of Sandhurst (1898), Brooke-Popham joined the infantry. He completed pilot training (1911) and joined the Air Battalion of the Royal Engineers (1912). During World War I he was first a staff officer at the BEF headquarters in France. He then formed and directed an air wing in the 1915 Battle of Neuve Chapelle. The next year he was promoted brevet brigadier general. Just before the end of the war, he was assigned to the air ministry in London.

Following the war, Brooke-Popham was in the Air Ministry. He was commandant of the RAF Staff College at Cranwell (1921–26) and was the first Royal Air Force (RAF) officer to head the Imperial Defense College, Camberley (1931–33). He then commanded Britain's air defenses (1933–35). Promoted air marshal and made inspector general, he went to Cairo during the crisis over Italy's invasion of Abyssinia to command the Middle Eastern Air Force (1935–36). He retired and

became governor and CinC in Kenya (1937–39).

Brooke-Popham returned to service following the outbreak of World War II (September 1939) and set up the Commonwealth Air Training Scheme for aircrew. He was CinC of the Far East (October 1940) with headquarters at Singapore. Despite his pleas, most British resources went to the Middle East. London rejected his requests for a pre-emptive strike into south Thailand until after the Japanese had already landed. He returned to Britain (late December 1941), unjustly criticized for Japanese successes in Malaya, and held insignificant posts until his final retirement in 1945.

Brown, George Scratchley (1918–78) U.S. Air Force general. Brown attended the University of Missouri for a year before graduating from West Point (1941). He completed pilot training and was a bomber pilot during World War II with the 93rd Bombardment Group, Eighth Air Force. He distinguished himself in the Ploesti raids (August 1943) and was promoted to colonel (October). He ended the war as assistant operations officer of the 2nd Air Division.

After the war Brown held a succession of command positions, including that of chief of operations of Fifth Air Force during the Korean War (1952–53). After graduating from the National War College (1957), he served as executive officer to the CofS of the Air Force. Promoted to brigadier general (August 1959), he was then assistant to the secretary of defence until his promotion to major general (1963). He commanded Task Force 2, a weapons test unit, at Sandia Base, New Mexico (1964–66). Promoted lieutenant general (1966), he became assistant to Chairman of the Joint Chiefs of Staff General Earle Wheeler. Promoted general (August 1968), he commanded the Seventh Air Force in Vietnam, then the Air Force Systems Command, Andrews Air Force Base, Washington (1970–73). President

Richard Nixon appointed him chief of staff of the Air Force (July 1973), despite controversy over his falsification of reports regarding the bombing of Cambodia. He was chairman of the Joint Chiefs of Staff (1974–78) until his retirement.

Brown, Wilson (1882–1957) U.S. admiral. Brown graduated from Annapolis (1902). Following U.S. entry into World War I, Brown served on the staff of Admiral William Sims in London. Later he commanded a destroyer. He graduated from the Naval War College (1921) and then held a variety of positions. He was superintendent of the Naval Academy (1938–41) and was promoted to vice admiral (February 1941).

Following U.S. entry into World War II, Brown commanded the carrier *Lexington*, launching raids against Japanese positions. He took voluntary reduction in rank to rear admiral in order to serve as naval aide to President Franklin Roosevelt (April 1942). He retired as a vice admiral (1944), but continued as an aide to Roosevelt and then to President Harry Truman.

Browning, Frederick (1896–1965) British general and founder of British airborne forces. After Eton and Sandhurst, he joined the British Army in France (1915). Aged only twenty, he commanded a company. This earned him the nickname "Boy," which stuck with him throughout his life.

Browning took command of a brigade (1940), but later that year was given charge of organizing the 1st Airborne Division, which he did from scratch. He took easily to parachuting and set high standards for himself and his men. Elements of the division fought in Algeria and Sicily. Promoted lieutenant general (1944), he took command of I Airborne Corps, which he led at Normandy, Arnhem, and in the advance into Germany. Following the end of fighting in Europe, he transferred to the Pacific as Lord Louis

Mountbatten's chief of staff. He retired in 1948.

Bruchmüller, Georg (1863–1948) German Army colonel and artillerist. Bruchmüller was commissioned in the Foot Artillery (1885). He spent the next twenty-eight years in assignments with fortress guns and as an instructor. He received a medical discharge and was retired as a lieutenant colonel (1913).

On the outbreak of World War I, Bruchmüller was recalled to temporary active duty on the Eastern Front. His shorter duration, more effective artillery fire led to his steady rise in responsibility. Following the successful attack on Riga (September 1917) he transferred to the Western Front. He orchestrated artillery support for all of General Eric Ludendorff's 1918 offensives. Finally promoted colonel (March), he was also restored to the active list.

After the war Bruchmüller wrote several influential books about his methods. These were translated and widely studied abroad. The German Army belatedly promoted him to major general on the retired list (August 1939).

Brusilov, Aleksei Alekseevich (1853–1926) Russian general. Brusilov was commissioned in the cavalry (1872) and saw action in the 1877–78 Russo-Turkish War. He graduated from the Cavalry School, then was a teacher there and was appointed the School's commandant (1902–06). Promoted general (1906), he took command of a division, and then a corps. Deputy commander of the Warsaw Military District (1912), he was posted to the Kiev Military District.

The outbreak of World War I found Brusilov commanding Eighth Army on the Galician frontier. His troops performed well in the initial offensive into Galicia. Eighth Army took the brunt of the German counterattack (May 1915) and Brusilov carried out a masterly 200-mile strategic retreat, based on sharp, small attacks, often at night.

In spring 1916 Brusilov, almost alone, supported the idea of an offensive to relieve pressure on France at Verdun and aid Italy. Given command of the entire Southwest Front of four armies with fifty-five divisions, he was to launch a diversionary attack, with General Aleksei Evert's divisions to the north mounting the main offensive. Using innovative new tactics, his units broke the Austrian lines in four places in the most successful Russian offensive of the war (June). When Evert failed to move, the Germans were able to move units south and stop Brusilov. He later contended that if Evert had attacked as planned, Austria would have been driven from the war.

Brusilov was then appointed commander-in-chief of the army by Minister of War Aleksandr Kerensky (May 1917). Their July 1917 offensive achieved initial success, but discipline in the army broke down and within three weeks the Germans launched counterattacks. Totally exhausted, he was replaced by General Lavr Kornilov. He remained in Russia after the Bolshevik Revolution and, in 1920 during the war with Poland, offered his services to the Bolsheviks. He retired in 1924.

Bucher, Lloyd (Mark) (1927–) U.S. Navy commander. Adopted as an infant, "Pete" Bucher attended Boys Town near Omaha, Nebraska (1941–45) but left to serve two years in the navy. He then returned to Boys Town, graduating there and from the University of Nebraska.

Commissioned in the navy reserve (June 1953), he went on active duty and served as a submarine officer in Subfloat 7. In May 1967 he took command of the *Pueblo*, a small, 179-foot vessel transformed into a National Security Agency (NSA) intelligence-collecting ship.

Promoted commander (December 1967), Bucher took the *Pueblo* to sea. On 23 January 1968, the vessel was fifteen miles off the North Korean coast when she was attacked by North Korean torpedo boats and MiG aircraft. The Koreans towed the *Pueblo* into port, the first U.S. Navy ship taken at sea in over 150 years. Bucher and his crew were interrogated, tortured, and forced to read North Korean propaganda. Bucher was also forced to write letters in which he stated that the *Pueblo* was in North Korean waters and called on the U.S. government to apologize for the incident.

Bucher and his men were released in December 1969. Upon his return to the United States, Bucher was brought before a navy court of inquiry. He had been ordered to scuttle the *Pueblo* if threatened with capture but had failed to do so. His defense was that he was too busy destroying top-secret documents. The court's recommendation that he and one other officer be court-martialed was overruled by the secretary of the navy. Bucher never again received a ship command, and retired from the navy in 1973.

Buckner, Simon Bolivar, Jr. (1886–1945) U.S. general. Buckner attended the Virginia Military Institute (1902–04), then West Point, where he graduated (1908). He did not see combat in World War I. He taught at West Point (1919–24) and completed the Advanced Infantry Course. He was then instructor at first the Command and General Staff School and later the Army War College. He returned to West Point where, after a year as instructor, he was commandant of cadets (1933–36). Promoted colonel (1937), he commanded an infantry regiment and then Fort McClellan, Alabama. He became chief of staff of the 6th Division (1939).

Appointed to head the Alaskan Defense Command (1940), Buckner was promoted brigadier general. Promoted major general (1941), he directed the buildup of Alaska's defenses and construction of the Alcan Highway linking Alaska to the Continental U.S. Following the Japanese invasion of Kiska and Attu (June 1942), he helped direct their recapture, gaining promotion to lieutenant general.

In summer 1944 Buckner took command of the newly created Tenth Army, which provided the ground troops for the assault on Okinawa (April 1945). His slow frontal advance brought criticism, but he maintained a conservative, grinding offensive. Maintaining close contact with the front, he was killed at an observation post by a Japanese shell, the highest-ranking American officer lost to enemy fire during the war, only three days before the island was secured.

Budenny, Seymen Mikhailovich (1883–1973) Marshal of the Soviet Union. Budenny entered the army (1903) and saw service in the 1904–05 Russo-Japanese War. He attended the Imperial Cavalry School (1909) and during World War I fought as a sergeant major on the Caucasus front. He won four St. George Crosses, the highest Russian decoration for valor.

Budenny embraced communism (1917) and formed a cavalry unit that grew to 16,000 men during the 1918–20 Civil War. He fought at Tsaritsyn (later Stalingrad, now Volgograd) and in Ukraine, forming a close association with political commissar Josef Stalin. Transferred to the war against Poland (May 1920), he and Stalin refused to provide flank protection for General Mikhail Tukhachevsky's drive on Warsaw, bringing about Russia's defeat. He then defeated the remaining White forces in south Russia and secured the Crimea (1920–21).

Budenny played a key role in the development of Russia's extensive cavalry forces and was one of the first five Marshals of the Soviet Union (1935). As commander of the Moscow military district, he sat on the court that falsely convicted Tukhachevsky of treason and had him shot. As deputy commissar of defense (1939), he was the sole original marshal to survive Stalin's purges.

At the beginning of World War II Budenny commanded the Reserve Army.

He then commanded the Southwest Front in Ukraine (July 1941), but his armies were destroyed in great encirclement battles, such as Kiev (September). Budenny, who had urged withdrawal, only escaped by air. Relieved of his command, he received a training assignment. He commanded the North Caucasus Front (May–September 1942) and then (from May 1943) the cavalry in the Red Army, but held no further operational command.

Bull, Harold Roe (1893–1976) U.S. general. "Pinky" Bull was commissioned in the infantry on graduation from West Point (1914) and served with the AEF in France during World War I. After the war he was an instructor at West Point (1921–23), graduated from Command and General Staff School (1938), and was an instructor at the Infantry School (1928–32). He graduated from the Army War College (1934) and was secretary of the War Department General Staff (1938–39). Promoted brigadier general (July 1941), he was assistant division commander of the 47th Division, then assistant CofS for operations on the War Department General Staff (1942). Promoted major general (March 1942), he commanded Replacement and School Command (1942–43). He then commanded III Corps (June–September 1943). As deputy chief of operations to the chief of staff of the Allied Commander in Europe, he had a key role in planning the invasion of Normandy (Operation OVERLORD) (6 June 1944). Promoted major general, he was chief of operations for General Dwight Eisenhower at Supreme Headquarters Allied Powers Europe (SHAPE) (February 1944–45). He was then CofS of U.S. Forces European Theater of Operations (1945–46). Among other assignments after the war, he was commandant of the National War College (1949–52). He retired (July 1952) as a major general.

Bullard, Robert Lee (1861–1947) U.S. general. Commissioned in the infantry on graduation from West Point (1885), Bullard fought against the Apache Indians and in Cuba during the 1898 Spanish-American War. He then commanded a regiment in the Philippines. He graduated from the Army War College (1911) and saw duty along the Mexican border (1915–17), where he commanded all National Guard units (1916).

On U.S. entry into World War I, Bullard was promoted brigadier general (June 1917) and commanded a brigade of the 1st Division, and then the division itself. He established his reputation as a combat commander in the May 1918 Battle of Cantigny. He took command of III Corps (July) for the Aisne–Marne and Meuse–Argonne Offensives. Promoted temporary lieutenant general (October), he received command of Second Army.

Following the war, Bullard reverted to permanent major general and commanded II Corps. He retired in 1925. In 1930 he was promoted to lieutenant general on the retired list.

Buller, Sir Redvers Henry (1839–1908) British general. Following graduation from Eton, Buller joined the British Army. He served in India and then in China in the 1860 Third Opium War. In 1861 he was posted to Canada. He graduated from the Staff College and then fought in the Ashanti War, in the Transvaal, and against the Zulus. He won a Victoria Cross for action against the Zulus at Hlobane (28 March 1879). In 1882 he was in Egypt and took part in the expedition to relieve Khartoum. He was then sent to Natal (1899). With British Lieutenant General Sir George White trapped at Ladysmith on the outbreak of the 1899–1902 Boer War, Buller assumed command.

A series of defeats at the hands of the Boers earned Buller the sobriquet of "Reverse Buller" and led to a change in tactics. Buller then won the Battle of Tugela River (February 1900) and relieved Ladysmith. He also defeated the Boers at Biggarsberg and Lydenburg (August and September). Attacked in the British press, Buller retired in 1901.

Bülow, Karl von (1846–1921) German field marshal. Bülow participated in the 1866 Austro-Prussian War and 1870–71 Franco-German War. Although he never attended the Kriegsakademie, he was posted to the Prussian general staff (1876) and thereafter held staff and command positions. He was promoted colonel (1894) and commanded III Corps (1903–12). He was then head of Third Army Inspection and promoted full general (1912).

On mobilization for World War I, Bülow took command of Second Army. On the German right wing, it invaded Belgium and captured Namur, then defeated French General Charles Lanrezac's Fifth Army at Charleroi. But Bülow grew increasingly cautious, especially as a thinly veiled gap of over twenty miles had developed between Second Army and Colonel General Alexander von Kluck's adjacent First Army. Bülow agreed with emissary from German Army Headquarters Lieutenant Colonel Richard Hentsch that a withdrawal of the entire German right wing might become necessary (8 September). He then ordered his Army to retreat, forcing Kluck to follow suit (9 September). Second Army eventually moved to the St. Quentin region.

Bülow was promoted field marshal (January 1915). His health then deteriorated and he went on sick leave. Despite attempts to return to active duty, he was retired in June 1916.

Burke, Arleigh Albert (1901–96) U.S. admiral. A graduate of Annapolis (1923). Burke earned a master's degree in chemical engineering from the University of Michigan (1931). He held a number of assignments and was assigned to the Naval Gun Factory in Washington (1940).

During World War II Burke took command of a destroyer division (1943) and a destroyer squadron (August 1943). He won praise for his actions in the November 1943 Battles of Empress Augusta Bay and Cape St. George and earned the nickname "31-Knot Burke." He was then deputy chief of staff to Vice Admiral Marc Mitscher, commander of Carrier Division 3 (1944–45).

Burke was chief of staff to Mitscher when he commanded Eighth Fleet and then the Atlantic Fleet (1946–47). Burke then had charge of development of the navy's nuclear weapons program (1948–49). Promoted rear admiral (July 1950), he became deputy chief of staff to the commander of naval forces in the Far East and had charge of operational planning for the September Inchon landing. He commanded Cruiser Division 5 (1951) and then was temporarily detached to serve on the UN delegation to the armistice negotiations headed by Vice Admiral C. Turner Joy.

Burke served an unprecedented three terms as chief of naval operations (1955–61), when he pushed the Polaris missile program and helped bring the U.S. Navy into the nuclear age.

Burress, Withers Alexander (1894–1977) U.S. general. Burress graduated from the Virginia Military Institute (1914) and was commissioned in the infantry (1916). During World War I he served with the 23rd Regiment of the 2nd Infantry Division in the AEF. After the war he was an instructor at the Infantry School (1920–22). He graduated from the Command and General Staff School (1931), and then was an instructor there (1931–33). A graduate of the Army War College (1935), he was a professor and then commandant of cadets at West Point (1935–40), and then served on the War Department General Staff (1940–41).

During World War II, Burress was promoted brigadier general (March 1942) and major general (August). He was CG of 10th Infantry Division (1942–45), and then CG of VI Corps (1945–46). After the war he commanded the Infantry School

(1948–51), then VII Corps (1951–53) and First Army (1953–54). He retired as a lieutenant general in November 1954.

Busch, Ernst (1885–1945) German field marshal. Commissioned in the army (1904), Busch fought in World War I as a line officer, ending the war as a captain. He continued in the Reichswehr and steadily advanced in rank. A fervent Nazi, he owed his advancement after 1933 to loyalty rather than military ability.

Brigadier General Busch took command of 23d Division (1935). Promoted lieutenant general (1938), he commanded VIII Corps in the September 1939 invasion of Poland, figuring prominently in operations destroying the Cracow Army. As commander of Sixteenth Army, he had only a minor role in the May 1940 invasion of France and Benelux. Promoted full general (May 1940), he led Sixteenth Army in the invasion of the Soviet Union (June 1941) as part of Army Group North. Promoted field marshal (February 1943), he succeeded the injured Field Marshal Günther von Kluge as commander of Army Group Center (October 1943). Although he rigidly adhered to Hitler's orders, he was sacked in the wide-scale purge of commanders (June 1944). In the last weeks of the war he returned to active service as commander of Army Group Northwest, holding position from the North Sea to Magdeburg. He died in captivity in Britain.

Butler, Smedley Darlington (1881–1940) U.S. Marine Corps general. Butler obtained a commission in the Marine Corps (1899) by misstating his age. He did not see combat in the 1898 Spanish–American War but did fight in the 1899–1902 Philippine–American War and the 1900 Boxer Rebellion. His exploits won promotion to captain (1901). He saw service in the Caribbean and Philippines and was promoted major (1906). As commander of the Panama Battalion (1909–14) he led his troops into Nicaragua several times, most notably in 1912.

Butler won the Medal of Honor for his role in the capture of Vera Cruz (April 1914). He commanded a battalion in the intervention in Haiti (1915), winning a second Medal of Honor for capturing Fort Rivière (17 November). Promoted lieutenant colonel, he organized the Haitian Gendarmerie (1915–18). Promoted temporary brigadier general, he was sent to France to command a camp near Brest (1918–19).

Promoted colonel (1919), then brigadier general (1921), Butler commanded the Marine base at Quantico, Virginia, making it a permament installation (1920–24). He took leave to reorganize the police of Philadelphia (1924–25). He then commanded the Marine Barracks, San Diego (1925–26) and the Marine expeditionary force in China (1927–29). Promoted major general (1929) he incurred the dislike of the Hoover administration for speeches in which he criticized U.S. imperialism, especially interference in the Haitian elections. Passed over for the post of Marine Corps commandant, he retired in 1931.

Byng, Julian Hedworth George (1862–1935) British Army general. Educated at Eton, Byng joined the army (1883) and served in the Sudan and graduated from Staff College. He saw significant action in the 1899–1902 Boer War and was promoted to colonel. He then commanded the cavalry school (1907). Promoted major general (1909), he then commanded British forces in Egypt (1912).

During World War I Byng commanded 3rd Cavalry Division at Ypres (1914) and the Cavalry Corps (1915). He then commanded IX Corps at Suvla Bay (1915–16) on Gallipoli, after the landings had failed. He took command of the Canadian Corps in France (1916) and directed it in the capture of Vimy Ridge (April 1917). He

took command of Third Army that Spring and led it in the Battle of Cambrai, which proved the value of the tank in modern warfare. Third Army bore the brunt of the 1918 Ludendorff Offensive along the Somme, and then participated in the July–November counter-offensive.

Byng was made Viscount Byng of Vimy (1919). He was governor-general of Canada (1921–26) and was promoted to field marshal (1932).

Byrd, Richard Evelyn (1888–1957) U.S. admiral and explorer. Byrd attended the Virginia Military Institute for two years, then the University of Virginia, and graduated from Annapolis (1912). He qualified as a naval aviator and commanded the first American-Canadian naval air station at Halifax, Nova Scotia (1918). An inventor of navigational instruments, he also was involved in dirigible construction.

Byrd served in his first arctic expedition in 1924. Flying from and returning to Spitzbegen, Greenland, he and Brent Balchern made the first flight over the North Pole (9 May 1926) and were subsequently awarded the Medal of Honor. He then led an expedition to Antarctica (1928–30) and he, Balchern, and two others were the first to fly over the South Pole (29 November 1929). He commanded a second expedition to Antarctica (1933–35), during which he lived alone near the South Pole for five months (1935). He retired as a rear admiral (December 1939).

Recalled to active service during World War II, Byrd served on the staff of Chief of Naval Operations Admiral Ernest J. King. He commanded the U.S. Navy Antarctic Expedition (1946–47) with 4,000 men and thirteen vessels, during which he conducted experiments and training in cold-weather conditions and headed Operation DEEP FREEZE (1955).

C

Cadorna, Luigi (1850–1928) Italian general. Cadorna entered the army (1866) and became a major general (1898), divisional commander (1905), and corps commander (1910). Named chief of the General Staff (July 1914), during World War I he had a good grasp of strategic concepts but had difficulty cooperating with others. He also had a reputation as a stern disciplinarian with no empathy for the rank and file, which may have contributed indirectly to the disaster at Caporetto. Although made the primary scapegoat for the defeat at Caporetto, for which he was replaced, he did repulse the Austrians (1916), broke into the Bainsizza (1917), and held the Central Powers advance on the Piave after Caporetto (October 1917). He retired after the war (December 1918).

Callaghan, Daniel Judson (1890–1942) U.S. admiral. Callaghan graduated from Annapolis (1911), was commissioned, and took part in the U.S. intervention in Nicaragua (1912). During World War I he was on convoy duty. A variety of assignments followed, most of them on battleships.

Commander Callaghan was naval aide to President Franklin Roosevelt (1938–41), then commanded the cruiser *San Francisco* at Pearl Harbor and was there during the Japanese attack (7 December 1941). Shortly thereafter, he became chief of staff to Southwest Pacific commander Admiral Robert Ghormley. He helped plan the U.S. landings on Guadalcanal and commanded the task force providing fire support (August 1942). He fought with distinction in the Battle of Cape Esperance (October 1942) and was promoted rear admiral. As commander of Task Force 67.4 with five cruisers and eight destroyers, he intercepted a Japanese force of two battleships, a cruiser, and eleven destroyers under Admiral Hiroaki Abe off Lunga Point (Guadalcanal) on its way to shell Henderson Field. In a short, hard-fought night action (12–13 November), his force sank two Japanese destroyers and crippled a battleship (later sunk by carrier aircraft), at a cost of two cruisers and four destroyers of his own lost. Abe's task force and another carrying 13,000 reinforcements to Guadalcanal, which the first force was designed to mask, both turned back. Callaghan was killed by a shell that struck the bridge of the *San Francisco* during the action. Dubbed "the Fighting Admiral," he was subsequently awarded the Medal of Honor.

Calley, William Laws, Jr. (1946–) U.S. Army officer. Forced to leave junior college for poor grades, Calley worked at a succession of jobs until drafted into the army (1966) during the Vietnam War. Following basic training at Fort Bliss,

Texas, he was a clerk-typist at Fort Washington. He graduated from officer candidate school DCS at Fort Benning, Georgia and was commissioned a second lieutenant (September 1967).

In Vietnam, Calley commanded a platoon of C Company, 1st Battalion, 20th Regiment, 23rd Infantry Division. His company participated as a part of Task Force Barker, a scratch force of the 23rd, in an assault on My Lai 4 hamlet in Quang Ngai Province (16 March 1968), where his unit had previously taken casualties. Ordered by his company commander, Captain Ernest Medina, to burn and destroy the hamlet, believed to be the headquarters area of a Communist battalion, his platoon encountered only unresisting old men, women, and children. Nonetheless, over the next hour the platoon killed an estimated 500 Vietnamese civilians.

The massacre was later exposed despite an army attempt to cover it up. Calley was tried in a court-martial lasting more than four months, found guilty (March 1971), and sentenced to life in prison at hard labor, the only individual convicted in the massacre. In a highly unusual procedure, this sentence was later reduced to ten years, whereupon President Richard Nixon granted Calley parole (November 1974). He served three days behind bars.

Calthorpe, Sir Somerset Arthur Gough (1864–1937) British admiral. Calthorpe entered the navy (1878) and rose to command the 2nd Cruiser Squadron (1914). He then became second sea lord (1916). Named British commander in the Mediterranean (summer 1917), he coordinated scattered British naval commands with focus on enhancing anti-submarine efforts, including establishment of Mediterranean convoys. He was skeptical about convoys, especially as securing escorts was always a problem.

At the end of the war Calthorpe led the combined Allied fleet through the Dardanelles (12 November 1918). He was high commissioner at Constantinople (1918–19) and ended his active career as commander-in-chief, Portsmouth (1920–23).

Camm, Sir Sydney (1893–1966) British aircraft designer. After attending the Royal Free School, Windsor, Camm was apprenticed to a woodworker. He made gliders and model aircraft and then joined G. H. Martinsdyne Aeroplane Company as a designer throughout World War I. He then joined the Hawker Engineering Co., known for its Sopwith line of aircraft, as a draftsman (1924) and became an aircraft designer (1924), specializing in military aircraft (1925).

Camm designed the Hawker Hurricane, which was in full production when the war began. The first single-wing RAF fighter, it was fast, maneuverable, and rugged. Utilizing the new Rolls Royce Merlin engine and initially armed with eight machine guns, it was the principal British fighter in the 1940 Battle of Britain. Ultimately some 14,500 were built, many of them shipped to the Soviet Union. Its second-generation manifestation was the Typhoon fighter-bomber (1942), which gave way to the Tempest and the Sea Fury.

Camm also designed the jet aircraft Sea Hawk and its successor, the Hunter (1951), which set a world speed record, and he helped design the vertical takeoff and landing (VTOL) P-1127 Kestrel. He was knighted in 1953.

Campioni, Imigo (1878–1944) Italian admiral. Campioni fought in the 1911–12 Italo-Turkish War, World War I, and World War II. During World War II he commanded Italian naval units based at Taranto. In addition to escorting Italian ships for North Africa, his naval units participated in the Battles of Punta Stilo and Cape Teulada (1940).

Canaris, Wilhelm (1887–1945) German admiral. Canaris joined the navy (1905) and was promoted to full lieutenant (1911). He served on the *Dresden*, a commerce raider at the beginning of World War I, until she was scuttled. He escaped internment in Chile and bluffed his way back to Germany (1915). He then conducted espionage in Spain and Italy before entering the submarine service (1916) and commanding a U-boat in the Mediterranean.

After the war Canaris was active in covert operations to rebuild the German military. He worked in Japan with German designers to build submarines and then resumed his naval career, increasingly in intelligence activities. Promoted captain (1931), he commanded the battleship *Schliesen* (1932). Named head of military intelligence, the Abewehr (January 1935), he was promoted rear admiral (April). One of his first successes was to convince Hitler to intervene on the side of the Nationalists in the 1936–38 Spanish Civil War (July 1936).

An ardent nationalist and rightist, Canaris nonetheless came to oppose Hitler and worked to try to get Britain and France to stand up to Hitler during the 1938 crisis over Czechoslovakia. Although he supported and warned the putschists against Hitler, he did not himself take an active role. He was arrested after the bomb attempt on Hitler (July 1944), but initially there was no proof of his involvement. On the discovery of his secret diaries, he was tried and executed (9 April 1945).

Capelle, Eduard von (1855–1931) German admiral. Capelle joined the German Navy (1872) and held a number of shipboard commands before serving in the Naval Office (1905–14). An early associate of Admiral Alfred von Tirpitz, he helped prepare the naval budgets and dealt with the Reichstag. Ennobled (1912), he was promoted full admiral (1913). He served as under secretary of the Naval Office early in the war but broke with Tirpitz and retired (late 1915).

Upon Tirpitz's dismissal (March 1916), he became state secretary in his place.

Capelle believed that unrestricted submarine warfare would turn the tide of war. His lukewarm endorsement of additional battleship building programs and ill-fated efforts to purge the Reichstag of leftist deputies estranged him from fellow officers and civilian leaders alike. Despite growing unpopularity, Capelle continued in office until September 1918.

Capello, Luigi Attilo (1859–1941) Italian general. Capello was commissioned in the army (1878) and rose to major general (1910). He then took command of a brigade in the war against Turkey in Libya (1911). At the beginning of World War I, Capello commanded a division.

Promoted lieutenant general (September 1915), Capello led VI Corps to the first major triumph of Italian arms in the war at Gorizia (August 1916). However, he fell victim to politics and was exiled to the quiet Trentino sector (September). He returned to the Isonzo Front (spring 1917) in command of Second Army and played a key role in the Eleventh Battle of the Isonzo (August–September 1917) that led Vienna to seek reinforcements from the Germans, resulting in the Austro-German breakthrough at Caporetto (October 1917).

Capello and Italian army commander Luigi Cadorna bore responsibility for the debacle. Instead of following Cadorna's orders to withdraw his artillery to the west bank of the Isonzo, he prepared for a counteroffensive to hit the attackers' flanks, and he had his worst troops in the area of greatest danger. Ill and absent from his command before the battle, he returned to suffer a complete physical collapse. Cadorna rejected his advice to withdraw to the Tagliamento River, enabling the attackers to push to the Piave.

Capello did not return to command. After the war he was an early Mussolini supporter but parted company with him when the latter moved toward dictatorship.

Carden, Sir Sackville Hamilton (1857–1930) British admiral. Carden entered the navy in 1870. He participated in the 1882–84 Egyptian and Sudan campaigns, and was promoted captain (1887) and rear admiral (1908). He was then superintendent of the Malta dockyard (1912–14).

On the outbreak of World War I he became commander of the British Mediterranean Squadron (September 1914). He supported Winston Churchill's plan to attack the Dardanelles, and believed the Straits could be forced following methodical operations. His bombardment began on 19 February 1915, but it was difficult for the British and French warships to operate in the restricted waters of the Straits against the inner defenses. On 11 March the Admiralty ordered him to press forward, even at some loss.

Carden planned a daylight attack for 18 March, but two days before the attack ill health forced him to relinquish his command to Rear Admiral John de Robeck. He retired from the navy a full admiral (October 1917).

Carlson, Evans Fordyce (1896–1947) U.S. general. Carlson enlisted in the army (1912) and served in the Philippines and Hawaii (1912–15). Discharged (1915), he was recalled for service on the Mexican border (1916). After the United States entered World War I, he was a captain on General John J. Pershing's staff (1918–19).

Carlson left the service after the war but joined the Marines as a private (1922). Commissioned (1923), he served as an intelligence officer in Shanghai (1927–39) and in Nicaragua (1930). Returning to China (1933–35), he was promoted captain. He served with President Franklin Roosevelt's military guard (1935–37) before returning to China as an observer in the 1939–45 Sino-Japanese War. He went on two marches with the Communist Chinese Eighth Route Army. His praise

for the Communist army earned his superiors' censure, and this brought his resignation. He then traveled, lectured, and wrote two books on the Chinese army. Joining the Marine Corps Reserve as a major, he was called to active duty in May 1941. Promoted lieutenant colonel, he advocated the formation of commando units. He led 2nd Marine Raider Battalion (1942) and trained it with techniques learned from the Chinese and the motto "Gung-ho" (stick together). He then led "Carlson's Raiders" in a raid on Makin Island (17–18 August 1942) in which his 220 men wiped out the 83-man Japanese garrison. He also led his men on Guadalcanal in a 150-mile operation behind Japanese lines (November–December) that killed some 500 Japanese for only 17 Americans lost. An observer in the Tarawa (November 1943) and Saipan (June–July 1944) landings, he was severely wounded on Saipan. Promoted brigadier general, he was forced to retire as a consequence of his wounds (July 1946).

Carpenter, Alfred Nicholas Francis Blakeney (1881–1955) British admiral. Carpenter joined the navy and saw action on Crete (1898) and in the 1900–01 Boxer Rebellion in China. Promoted lieutenant commander (1911), he served on Admiral Sir John Jellicoe's staff (1914–15). Promoted commander (1915), he served on a battleship (1915–17) and then on the Admiralty Planning Staff (1917–18), where he and Admiral Roger J. B. Keyes planned raids against German bases at Ostend and Zeebrugge. As commander of the light cruiser *Vindictive*, he led the first attack on Zeebrugge (23 April 1918) and a second raid there in which he sank his ship in an effort to block access to the submarine pens (9 May).

After the war he taught a course at Cambridge for naval officers (1919–20), then held various posts including command of a battleship (1928–29). Promoted rear admiral (1929), he retired (1934). During World War II, he was commander of the Home Guard (1940–44).

Carranza, Venustiano (1859–1920) Mexican revolutionary leader and politician. Carranza was educated in Mexico City and entered politics in 1887, becoming governor of the state of Coahuila. He was a staunch opponent of President Francisco Madera and helped overthrow him, leading the Army of the Constitution. The latter consisted of scattered forces commanded by Alvaro Obregon, Pancho Villa, and Emilano Zapata, who were victorious and overthrew (August 1914) the forces of President Victoriano Huerta, who had seized power in a coup.

The revolutionary leaders then fought among themselves for the presidency. Thanks to the superior generalship of Obregon, Carranza won out. Obregon defeated Villa's forces (April 1915), but, after he was officially president, Carranza's order for the assassination of Zapata alienated Obregon and led to his own overthrow and death. Obregon replaced him.

Carton de Wiart, Sir Adrian (1880–1963) British general. Carton de Wiart left Bristol College, Oxford (1899) to join the army against the Boers and was wounded in the 1899–1902 Anglo-Boer War. He secured a commission in the 4th Dragoon Guards and then served in India and again in South Africa. He fought in Somaliland, where he was badly wounded and lost an eye, and in World War I on the Western Front, where he was wounded eight more times (for a total of 11 times by 1918) and lost his left hand. Awarded the Victoria Cross, he ended the war as a brigade commander.

After the war, as a lieutenant colonel, Carton De Wiart headed the British Military Mission in Poland (1919–24) and then resigned his commission to live on a Polish estate. On the eve of World War II he again headed the British military mission to Poland in Britain but disagreed with Polish military dispositions. Following the collapse of Poland, he escaped back to Britain, where he was promoted

major general and took command of the 61st Division. He then commanded the Central Norwegian Expeditionary Force (April–May 1940), before being sent to establish a mission in Yugoslavia. His plane crashed en route (21 April 1941) and he was taken prisoner by the Italians. After several attempts to escape, he was sent to Portugal (August 1943) to try to negotiate Italy's surrender. Less than a month later, Prime Minister Winston Churchill sent him, with the rank of lieutenant general, as his personal emissary to Chiang Kai-shek (Jiang Jieshi) (September 1943–46). He was knighted in 1946.

Cassels, Sir Archibald James H. (1907–96) British field marshal. Cassels was commissioned in the Seaforth Highlanders from Sandhurst (1926). He rose rapidly in rank and ended World War II as a major general commanding the 51st Highland Division.

After the war Cassels commanded the 6th Airborne Division in Palestine (1946). During the Korean War "Gentleman Jim" Cassels took command of the Commonwealth Division (July 1951) and proved adept at working with the different nationals and governments to form a division of infantry brigades representing Britain, Canada, and the other nations of the Commonwealth. Promoted lieutenant general (August 1952), he left Korea to hold a variety of other assignments including commander of I Corps in Germany, director of operations during the Malaya insurgency (1957–59), commander of Northern Army Group of NATO (1960–63), and chief of the British General Staff (1965–68). Promoted field marshal (1968), he retired from active duty the same year.

Castelnau, Noel Joseph Edouard de Curières de (1851–1944) French general. Castelnau graduated from St. Cyr (1870) and fought in the 1870–71 Franco-Prussian War. He later commanded various infantry units. As chief of staff to French army commander General Joseph Joffre (1912–14), he helped formulate War Plan XVII.

On the outbreak of World War I, Castelnau received command of Second Army in Lorraine. The Germans repulsed his Lorraine offensive and he then conducted defensive operations that saved Nancy and stabilized the front in Lorraine. He took command of Center Army Group (early 1915) and planned and conducted the costly September–November Champagne offensive, after which he became chief of staff to Joffre. During the Verdun crisis (February 1916), he recommended that General Henri Pétain command the defense.

When Joffre was replaced (December 1916), Castelnau was himself unemployed. He returned to active service to command Eastern Army Group in Lorraine (1918). After the war, he served in the Chamber of Deputies (1919–1924).

Cates, Clifton Bledsoe (1893–1970) U.S. Marine Corps general. Cates graduated from the University of Tennessee with a degree in law (1916). Commissioned in the Marines (June 1917), he went to France during World War I with the 6th Marine Regiment of the 2nd Infantry Division and distinguished himself in the Battles of Belleau Wood (June 1918) and Saint-Mihiel (September), and in the Meuse–Argonne Offensive (September–November), when he was gassed and wounded.

Following occupation duty in Germany (1919), Cates returned to the United States. He was an aide to President Woodrow Wilson, and served in Shanghai, China (1929–32, 1937–39). He graduated from the Army Industrial College (1932) and the Marine Corps School (1934), and the Army War College (1939).

Following U.S. entry into World War II (December 1941), Colonel Cates commanded the 21st Marine Regiment on Guadalcanal (August–December 1942). Promoted brigadier general, he com-

manded Marine Corps Schools at Quantico, Virginia (1943–44). As a major general, he commanded the 4th Marine Division in landings on Saipan (June–July 1944), Tinian (July–August), and Iwo Jima (February–March 1945).

After World War II Cates took command of the Marine Barracks at Quantico (1946). He was commandant of the Marine Corps (January 1948–January 1952) and promoted full general. He was then commandant of Marine Corps Schools until his retirement (1954).

Catroux, Georges Albert Julien (1877–1969) French general and political figure. Catroux graduated from St. Cyr (1898), entered the Foreign Legion and served in North Africa. In World War I he fought on the Western Front and was wounded and captured by the Germans (1916). Returning to colonial service after the war, he was promoted brigadier general (1931) and lieutenant general (1934). Promoted full general (1938), he commanded XXX Corps in Algeria and in 1939 vainly urged military reforms on General Maurice Gamelin. Placed on the reserve list, he was recalled by George Mandel (August 1939) as governor-general of Indo-China.

Catroux then was something of a colonial troubleshooter, known as an advocate of a liberal policy favoring accommodation with nationalism in the colonies. He came under intense pressure from the Japanese for bases in Indo-China. With France defeated by Germany and with the British and Americans unwilling to help, he had to give in. His independence of action and protest of the armistice with the Germans led to his replacement (July 1940). He then made his way to London and rallied to Charles de Gaulle, who named him Free French commander in the Near East, where he favored post-war independence for Syria and Lebanon.

Catroux played a key role in negotiations in Algiers after the 8 November 1942 Allied landings in North Africa.

Named CinC of all Free French Forces (25 November), he was then commissioner of state in the Committee of National Liberation (CNL). He then was governor general of Algeria (1943–44) and ambassador to Moscow (1944–48). He negotiated the return of Mohammed ben Youssef as sultan of Morocco (1955) and was appointed resident minister of Algeria (February 1956), but resigned four days later after pressure was put on Premier Guy Mollet by European settlers there.

Cavagnari, Domenico (1876–1966) Italian admiral. Cavagnari graduated from the Italian naval academy at Livorno (1895). He saw action in the 1911–12 Italo-Turkish War and in the Adriatic Sea during World War I, and was promoted captain (July 1918).

After World War I, Cavagnari held a series of posts, including chief of cabinet of the Naval Ministry (1922–25), commander of the naval arsenal at Le Spezia (1928–29), and director of the naval academy at Livorno (1929–32). He was then undersecretary of state for the Navy and chief of the naval staff (November 1933–December 1940). He was forced from office as a consequence of the successful British naval air raid on the port of Taranto, which crippled three of Italy's six battleships (11 November 1940). He then withdrew from active service.

Cavallero, Ugo (1880–1943) Italian field marshal. Cavallero first saw combat in the 1911–12 Italo-Turkish War. He distinguished himself during World War I in both the Trentino Offensive (May–June 1916) and Battle of Caporetto (October–November 1917). He ended the war as a brigadier general, but left the army to go into industry (1919). Benito Mussolini appointed him undersecretary of war (1925–28). Returning to active duty, he commanded Italian forces in East Africa (November 1937–May 1939).

Cavallero succeed Pietro Badoglio as chief of the supreme general staff (December 1940). He made it more efficient and transformed it from a mere advisory body into a true military high command. An admirer of Germany, he realized that Italy's fortunes in World War II were closely tied to those of that country, and he sent ten divisions and additional artillery to fight in the Soviet Union, even though these forces could have been put to better use in North Africa.

Mussolini began to view him with suspicion (late 1942) and dismissed Cavallero as too pro-German and as being responsible for the loss of Tripoli (January 1943). Accused of plotting against the government of his enemy, Badoglio, he was arrested (August). Released by the Germans, he nonetheless refused their demand that he lead Italian forces against the Allies. His death (14 September) was probably suicide.

Caviglia, Enrico (1862–1945) Italian general. As a junior officer, Caviglia served in Italian East Africa and fought in the 1895–96 Ethiopian War. Promoted major (1903), he was military attaché in Tokyo during 1905–11. He then fought in Libya during the 1911–12 Italo-Turkish War and was promoted colonel (1914).

During World War I Caviglia was promoted major general (summer 1915). He won distinction in the Third Battle of the Isonzo (October–November), in the Austrian offensive in the Trentino (May–June 1916), and in the retreat to the Piave River (November 1917) following Caporetto. As a corps commander, he led Eighth Army to victory in the battle of Vittorio Veneto (October–November 1918).

Appointed minister of war (1919), Caviglia the next year commanded the Italian troops that put down Gabriele d'Annunzio's short-lived state at Fiume. Later Caviglia was promoted field marshal. He returned to duty briefly (September 1943) to command the city of Rome and negotiate with the Germans.

Ch'ae Pyong-dok (1914–50) Republic of Korea (ROK) general. Ch'ae graduated from the Japanese Military Academy (1935) and was a Japanese officer during World War II, although he never commanded troops in the field. After the war he graduated from the U.S. Military English Language School for potential Korean officers, and was commissioned a captain in the Korean constabulary (January 1946). He rose rapidly in rank when the constabulary was transformed into the ROK Army (ROKA) (August 1948), a consequence of the patronage of President Syngman Rhee rather than his own military ability.

Ch'ae became chief of staff of the ROKA as a major general (May 1949). After early retirement (October 1949), he returned to the same post (April 1950). He bore heavy responsibility for the inadequate training and poor performance of the ROKA early in the 1950–53 Korean War. Following the North Korean invasion (25 June 1950), he ordered a series of piecemeal counterattacks that hastened the ROKA defeat, and he ordered the premature demolition of the Han River bridges, which forced the ROKA to abandon much of its equipment and supplies. Rhee relieved Ch'ae from his post (30 June) following U.S. General Douglas MacArthur's recommendation. Placed in charge of recruitment and training, Ch'ae was killed in the Battle of Hadong (July).

Chaffee, Adna Romanza (1842–1914) U.S. general. Chaffee received only a home education before enlisting (1861) to fight in the 1861–65 Civil War. He joined the 6th Cavalry, remaining with that regiment for more than a quarter of a century. As a consequence of his exemplary service record, he won promotion to sergeant and then was commissioned a 2nd lieutenant and promoted to 1st lieutenant (1865). Promoted captain (1867), he won a brevet promotion to major for service in an engagement with the Co-

manche Indians at Paint Creek, Texas (1868). He also participated in campaigns against the Cheyenne, Kiowa, and Apache Indians. He was promoted major (1888) and then lieutenant-colonel (1897).

Chaffee was promoted brigadier general of volunteers at the commencement of the 1898 Spanish-American War, then promoted major general of volunteers for his role in the Battle of El Caney (July). He then served as chief of staff to General Leonard Wood during the occupation of Cuba. He commanded U.S. forces in the Chinese relief expedition (July 1900), winning recognition for the successful relief of the foreign legations at Peking (Beijing) and the end to the Boxer Rebellion.

After receiving promotion to major general in the regular army (1901), Chaffee commanded U.S. forces in the later stages of the Philippine insurrection. Promoted lieutenant general (1904), he was army CofS until his retirement (1906).

Chaffee, Adna Romanza, Jr. (1884–1941) U.S. general. Chaffee graduated from West Point (1906) and was commissioned in the cavalry. He attended the Mounted Service School, Fort Riley, Kansas (1907–09) and the French cavalry school at Saumur (1911–12), served in the Philippines (1914–15) and taught at West Point (1916–17). During World War I he attended the General Staff College at Langres and was an instructor there (1918), and he participated as a staff officer in the St. Mihiel (September 1918) and Meuse–Argonne offensives (September–November 1918), finishing the war as a temporary colonel.

After the war Chaffee served in occupation forces in Germany and was an instructor at the Line and Staff School at Fort Leavenworth, Kansas (1919–20). Reverting to permanent captain, he was promoted major (1920) and lieutenant colonel (1929). A fine horseman who competed internationally, he nonetheless was an early advocate of the tank who sought to convince the army of the need for a separate armor force. During 1934 maneuvers at Fort Riley, Kansas, he demonstrated its potential, and as chief of the Budget and Legislative Planning Branch of the War Department General Staff (1934–38), he worked to secure funds. Vindicated by the German invasion of Poland (September 1939), he was promoted brigadier general (November 1938) and commanded the 7th Mechanized Brigade, which he led in the 1940 Louisiana maneuvers. Made commander of the Armored Force (July 1940), he was promoted major general (October) and organized I Armored Corps. Felled by cancer (August 1941), he was succeeded by Major General Jacob Devers.

Chang Fa-k'uei (Zhang Fakui) (1896–?) Nationalist Chinese general. A prominent member of the Kwangsi warlord faction, Chang joined the Nationalist Kuomintang (KMT, Guomindang) Army (1916) and rose to command a battalion, regiment (1923), and brigade. He then took command of 12th Division of Fourth Army (1925) and led it in the Northern Expedition against the government in Peking (Beijing) and warlords (1926–27). He was largely responsible for the defeat of Warlord Wu P'ei-fu (Wu Peifu) and the taking of Wuhan (September 1926). He then commanded Fourth Army (12th and 25th Divisions). He was then CG of Second Front Army (Fourth, Eleventh and Twentieth Armies). He suppressed the Communists in the August 1927 Nanchang Uprising, then moved his army to Canton (Guangzhou), where he attempted a rebellion himself (November 1927). On its failure, he escaped. He broke with Nationalist leader Chiang Kai-shek (Jiang Jieshi), and then attempted again to seize power at Canton (November 1929); he again escaped.

Restored to influence (1935), after the start of war with Japan (1937) Chang took command of Eighth Army Group at Shanghai and held the city against determined Japanese assault for four months

(August–November 1937), retreating only after taking 60 percent losses and being outflanked by Japanese amphibious landings. He commanded the Fourth War Area in Kwangtung (Guangdong) (1939–45), but when the Japanese began their ICHI-GO Offensive (1944) he was forced to retreat. He then tried unsuccessfully to set up a separate government. Confined to nominal duties, he was restored to favor after the start of the 1946–49 Civil War with the Communists. One of the more capable Nationalist generals, he was briefly CinC of Chinese Nationalist Land Forces. Realizing the Communists would win, he fled the mainland to Hong Kong (June 1949). He was identified in the 1950s as leader of the so-called Third Force Movement.

Chang Hsüeh-liang (Zhang Xueliang) (1898 or 1901–) Chinese field marshal. "The Young Marshal," Chang was the eldest son of Manchurian warlord Chang Tso-lin (Zhang Zuolin), "the Old Marshal." He studied at the National University in Peking (Beijing), but his father recalled him to attend the Fengtien Military Academy in Mukden (Shenyang). His father made him a colonel and gave him command of his personal bodyguard (1919). He then commanded a brigade and was promoted brigadier general (November 1920). Sent to Japan to observe military maneuvers, he returned with strong anti-Japanese attitudes, but he also instituted military reforms based on what he had seen. After fighting in the first Fengtien–Chihli War (1922), Chang commanded First Fengtien Army and also was commandant of the Fengtien Military Academy. He then won an important battle at the Great Wall in the second Fengtien–Chihli War (1924), then moved south, pacifying the lower Yangtse (Yangzi) Valley (1925).

Chang succeeded his father after the latter's assassination (1928). He then allied with Chiang Kai-shek (Jiang Jieshi) and the Nationalists, trying to modernize both the economy and army of Manchuria. On Chiang's request he moved against Warlords Wang Ching-wei (Wang Jingwei), Feng Yü-hsiang (Feng Yuxiang), and Yen Hsi-han (Yan Xishan)(1930).

Unprepared for the Japanese invasion (September 1931), he could not prevent the Japanese occupation of Manchuria (February 1932). He assumed command of the Northwest Army (1935), and Chiang ordered him to attack the Communist base at Yenan (Yan'an), but he had little success. Following a meeting with Communist leaders at Sian (Xi'an), he decided to make common cause with them against the Japanese. When Chiang upbraided him, he held Chiang hostage until the latter agreed to make common cause against the Japanese (December 1936). Subsequently court-martialed by Chiang, he was placed under house arrest, whereupon he became a noted scholar of Ming-period China. He was then transferred to Taiwan, where he remained under house arrest.

Chang Tso-lin (Zhang Zuolin) (1873–1928) Manchurian warlord. Chang had little education and first made his military mark as a bandit leader. He led Manchurian irregulars against the Japanese in the 1904–05 Russo-Japanese War. He then joined the Chinese Army and came to command its 27th Division, becoming governor of Manchuria's Fengtien Province (1916). Subsidized by the Japanese, he brought all Manchuria under his control (1916–18). Allying with Wu P'ei-fu (Wu Peifu), he defeated Tuan Ch'i-jui and gained control of several north China provinces (1921). In turn defeated by Wu and his allies (1922), he was driven back into Manchuria. Aided by the rebellion of Feng Yü-hsiang (Feng Yuxiang), he defeated Wu (1924) in north China and declared himself generalissimo of all Chinese forces (1926) and head of state (1927). Defeated in Chiang Kai-shek's (Jiang Jieshi) Northern Expedition (1928), he abandoned Peking (Beijing) and retired to Manchuria,

angering his Japanese backers. Radicals blew up his train as it approached Mukden (4 June 1928), hoping his death would bring a new political order. His son Chang Hsüeh-liang (Zhang Xueliang) succeeded him. His military skill earned him the title, "Tiger of the North." He was also known as the "Old Marshal," and his son as the "Young Marshal."

Chapman, Leonard Fielding, Jr. (1913–2000) U.S. Marine Corps general. Commissioned in the army on graduation from the University of Florida (1935), Chapman resigned his commission to join the Marine Corps. He was a captain when the United States entered World War II, and was artillery instructor at Quantico (1942). He saw combat in the Pacific in World War II and participated in the battles of the Coral Sea and Midway. Later he fought with the 1st Marine Division on Peleliu and Okinawa. After the war he was secretary of the General Staff, Fleet Marine Force, Pacific (1945–56). In 1956 he commanded the Marine Barracks in Washington.

Advanced to lieutenant general (1964), Chapman became Marine Corps chief of staff, where he promoted more effective management. He became Marine commandant with the rank of general in 1968. An expert on logistics and communications, he guided the Corps through the Vietnam War and subsequent social and racial upheavals. He retired at the end of his term (January 1972). He was then commissioner of the Immigration Naturalization Service (INS) until May 1977.

Charteris, John (1877–1946) British general. Charteris attended Woolwich and was commissioned in the Royal Engineers (1896). He formed a lasting association with General Douglas Haig before World War I, and served with him as both intelligence officer and personal confidant at I Corps, First Army, and General Headquarters. When Haig took command of the BEF in December 1915, Charteris became his head of intelligence as a brigadier general.

Charteris's overly optimistic assessments on German weaknesses and Allied chances of victory affected Haig's view of operations in the 1917 Battles of Third Ypres and Cambrai. Under pressure from Prime Minister David Lloyd George, Haig finally removed him in January 1918, although he remained at headquarters and Haig continued to consult him on intelligence matters. Charteris predicted the Germans would launch an offensive on the Western Front early in 1918. He retired (1922) and was a member of parliament from 1924–29.

Chauvel, Sir Henry George (1865–1945) Australian general. During World War I Chauvel commanded the 1st Australian Cavalry Brigade in the Battle of Ismalia (February 1915) and at Gallipoli (April–December 1915), where he was promoted major general and given command of the 1st Australian Division. In Egypt he commanded the Australia–New Zealand (AN-ZAC) Cavalry Division (January 1916), leading it in the unsuccessful First and Second Battles of Gaza (March, April 1917). He commanded with distinction the new Desert Mounted Corps under General Edmund Allenby during the Third Battle of Gaza (October–November 1917), capture of Jerusalem (December), Battle of Megiddo (September 1918), and capture of Damascus (October 1918).

Following the war, Chauvel became inspector general of Australian armed forces (1919) and chief of the general staff (1923). He retired in 1930.

Ch'en Ch'eng (Chen Cheng) (1897–1965) Nationalist Chinese general. Ch'en completed the Paoting (Baoding) Military Academy (1922) and served in several warlord armies before joining the Nationalist party or Kuomintang (Guomindang) of Chiang Kai-shek (Jiang Jieshi). He commanded a division in the Northern

Expedition (1927–28) and then commanded Eighteenth Army (1930). A close associate of Chiang, he was made governor of Hupeh (Hubei) Province and commanded the 6th War Area (1938–44). Directing the defense of Wuhan following the Japanese invasion, he was blamed for the fall of Yichang (Ichang) (1939).

Ch'en was named by General Joseph Stilwell to command the thirty Chinese divisions of Y Force in Yunnan for the invasion of Burma, but when the Japanese launched Operation ICHI-GO (1944) his divisions were shifted to defend Hupeh Province. In disfavor, he was replaced by Wei Li-huang (Wei Lihuang) April 1944). Although General Albert Wedemeyer recommended him to command Alpha Force defending Kunming, Chiang chose War Minister Ho Ying-Ching (He Yingqin). Ch'en then took Ho's place as war minister. Appointed chief of the general staff (1946), he commanded Nationalist forces in Manchuria, where his purge of former Manchukuo Japanese soldiers led them to join the Communists. This, coupled with his attacks on corruption, led to his appointment as governor of Taiwan (1948), where he played a key role in the retreat of Nationalist forces there. He was premier (1950–54, 1957–63) and then vice president of the Republic of China (1954–65).

Ch'en Chiung-ming (Chen Jiongming) (1878–1933) Chinese warlord. In the early 1900s Ch'en became a leading anti-Manchu leader and outlaw. After the Chinese Revolution (October 1911), he built up an army in Kwangtung (Guangdong). By 1918 he controlled most of the province, whereupon he invited Sun Yat-sen (Sun Zhongshan) to establish a civilian government, accepting Chiang Kai-shek (Jiang Jieshi) as his chief of staff (1918). Driven out of Canton (Guangzhou) by the Kwangsi (Guangxi) warlord clique (1918), he returned to defeat the clique (October 1920), recalling Sun. Disappointed in the latter's plans for the Northern Expedition to unify China, he revolted and brought down Sun's government (spring 1922), and then marched on the Nationalists when they established themselves at Canton (January 1924), but was defeated by Chiang's better trained Nationalist troops (1925). He then withdrew from public life.

Ch'en Yi (Chen Yi) (1901–72) People's Republic of China marshal. Born to a well-to-do family, Ch'en studied at both Shanghai University and Peking College of Law and Commerce and then in France (1919–21), where he met Communist leader Chou En-lai (Zhou Enlai). Expelled for political activities, he returned to China and joined the Kuomintang (Guomindang) Nationalist Party (1921) and the Communist party (1923). After study at the Sino-French University in Peking (Beijing) (1923–25), he joined the faculty at Whampoa Military Academy. He served on the staff of General Yeh T'ing's (Ye Ting) 24th Division at the beginning of the Northern Expedition (1926–27), then participated in the abortive Communist Nanchang uprising (August 1927). He then joined Chu Teh (Zhu De) in the Communist enclave at Kiangsi (January 1928) and commanded 12th Division of the Red IV Corps fighting the Nationalists during Chiang Kai-shek's (Jiang Jieshi) Bandit Suppression Campaign (1930–34). He did not participate in the Long March but stayed behind to maintain a Communist presence in the south and conduct guerrilla operations (1934–37).

On the establishment of the United Front against Japan (1937), Ch'en joined the New Fourth Army, becoming its commander (1941) and building it by 1948 into a force of 300,000 men. In the 1946–49 Civil War he encircled the Nationalist Second and Seventh Army Groups, destroying them in the Huai-Hai Campaign (November 1948–January 1949) and then advancing to take Nanking (Nanjing, April), Wuhan (May), and Shanghai (May). He was then mayor of

Shanghai and commander of the East China Military Region (1949–56), vice premier (1956), marshal of the People's Liberation Army (1955), and China's foreign minister (1956–68).

Chennault, Claire Lee (1890–1958) U.S. Army Air Forces general. Chennault graduated from Louisiana State University and was commissioned in the infantry (1917). He transferred to the Aviation Section of the Signal Corps and became a pilot (1919), then an instructor. As a pursuit squadron commander (1923–26), he developed an interest in fighter tactics. He graduated from the Air Corps Tactical School, Langley Field (1931) and published a book on fighter tactics (1935). He commanded an Air Corps exhibition group (1932–36) but retired on account of deafness with the rank of lieutenant colonel (1937).

Chennault was recruited to go to China to direct air operations against the Japanese (late 1937). He secured pilots and personnel in the U.S.A. and then began to train the American Volunteer Group (AVG) in China (August 1941). The AVG, known as "the Flying Tigers," began missions in December. During the next seven months the AVG shot down 299 Japanese aircraft and lost only 32. Recalled to active duty with the U.S. Army (April 1942), Chennault became chief of Army Air Forces in China. Promoted major general (March 1943), he commanded Fourteenth Air Force. He retired in October 1945.

Chernyakovsky, Ivan Danilovich (1906–45) Soviet general. A Jew, he was the youngest Soviet front commander of World War II. Chernyakovsky joined the Red Army (1924) and the Communist Party (1928) and was commissioned. He held a number of assignments before the war, graduating from Kiev Artillery School (1928) and the Mechanization and Motorization Academy (late 1930s).

By 1940 he was a colonel commanding the 28th Tank Division.

Following the German invasion (June 1941) his division fought on the Leningrad front (until July 1942) in XVIII Tank Corps. Promoted major general and then lieutenant general, he commanded Sixtieth Army, took part in the Kursk Offensive (1943), and was promoted colonel general (March 1944). Marshal Georgi Zhukov recommended him to command the Western Front, which he took over (April 1944) just before it was renamed the 3rd Belorussian Front. In the Belorussian Offensive his command participated in the taking of Minsk, moved through Latvia and took Vilna, and drove into East Prussia, eventually taking Königsberg (now Kaliningrad). Promoted general of the army (June 1944) just days before his thirty-eighth birthday and one of the finest Russian front commanders, he did not live to see the capture of Königsberg, being mortally wounded by artillery fire in February 1945.

Cheshire, Leonard, Lord (1917–1992) British air force officer. Cheshire learned to fly while a student at Oxford University and joined the Air Squadron there (1936). Commissioned in the RAF Volunteer Reserve (1937), when war appeared imminent he took a regular commission and was assigned to a bomber squadron. He first flew Whitleys in 102 Squadron and was the first junior British officer awarded the DSO in the war. He then moved on to fly Halifaxes in 35 Squadron. In early 1942 he became an instructor and wrote *Bomber Pilot*.

Cheshire then took over command of Guy Gibson's 617 Squadron (October 1943). He instituted new bombing techniques, including the use of pathfinder aircraft. Between 1940 and 1944 he flew and survived an incredible 100 bombing missions. His bravery in leading attacks earned him the Victoria Cross (October 1944). His status as a war hero led to his being withdrawn from combat duties,

although he was one of two British observers to the atomic bomb exploded over Nagasaki.

After the war Cheshire established the Cheshire Foundation Homes and Mission for the Relief of Suffering. This grew to a network of over 250 homes in fifty countries.

Chetwode, Sir Philip Walhouse (1869–1950) British field marshal. Educated at Eton, Chetwode was commissioned in 1889. He saw action in Burma during 1892–93 and in the 1899–1902 Anglo-Boer War. Promoted to colonel, he commanded a regiment (1908–12).

During World War I, Chetwode was in France, first as a brigadier general and commander of the 5th Cavalry Brigade (1914–15) and then as commander of the 2nd Cavalry Division (1915–16). Sent to Egypt, he led the Mounted Desert Column in the First and Second Battles of Gaza (March, April 1917). Given command of XX Corps, he successfully attacked Beersheba during the Third Battle of Gaza (October–November) and took Jerusalem (December). He also participated in the Battle of Megiddo (September 1918) and led the exploitation following that victory. Promoted lieutenant general (1919), he held a succession of important posts, including deputy chief of the Imperial General Staff (1920–23), chief of the general staff in India (1930–35), and commander-in-chief, India (1930–35). Promoted field marshal (1933), he was created a baron in 1945.

Chevallerie, Kurt von der (1891–1945) German general. Commissioned in the army (1911), Chevallerie served with distinction in World War I, rising to the rank of captain and commanding a company. He continued in the Reichswehr after the war and at the beginning of World War II was a brigadier general commanding the 83rd Infantry Division. Promoted major general, he commanded the 99th Light Division in the invasion of the Soviet

Union (June 1941). He then commanded LIX Corps as a lieutenant general (December). Sent to France, he commanded First Army in the area between the Loire and Pyrenees. Following the Normandy breakout, he was instructed to leave some troops to defend a pocket from La Rochelle to the Gironde, but to shift the bulk of his army to defensive positions on the Seine between Paris and Fontainebleau. When he failed to accomplish this impossible task, he was removed from command (August 1944). Still on the inactive list, he disappeared following the Red Army capture of Kolberg (now Kolobrzeg, Poland) (March 1945). He died either at this time or subsequently as a Soviet POW.

Chiang Kai-shek (Jiang Jieshi) (1887–1975) Nationalist Chinese general and president of the Republic of China (ROC). Chiang entered the Paoting (Baoding) Military Academy in 1906 and studied at the Preparatory Military Academy in Tokyo (1907–11). He returned to China to participate in the revolution at Wuhan (October 1911) and helped frustrate General Yüan Shih-k'ai's (Yuan Shikai) attempt to become emperor (1915–16). He then joined the Chinese Nationalist party or Kuomintang (Guomindang) and supported ROC President Sun Yat-sen (Sun Zhongshan). As a major general, he commanded the Whampoa Military Academy in Canton (Guangzhou).

Chiang succeeded Sun on the latter's death (1925) and began to purge the Communists, culminating in the 1927 "Shanghai Massacre." He also conducted military campaigns, known as the Northern Expedition, against the government in Peking (Beijing) and warlords (1926–27) that supposedly unified China, and made Nanking (Nanjing) the national capital (1928). He fought the Communists in five "Bandit Extermination" campaigns (1930–34).

When war with Japan began in 1937, Chiang put the struggle with the Commu-

nists on hold, although he seemed more interested in stockpiling arms to renew that struggle than in fighting the Japanese. Following the defeat of Japan, he received massive American military assistance, but when he sought to consolidate power in Manchuria, the 1946–49 Civil War began, which the Communists won (September 1949). He and the Nationalist remnants then fled to Taiwan. The outbreak of the Korean War (June 1950) helped him consolidate power and brought a U.S. military alliance. He remained ROC president until his death.

Choltitz, Dietrich von (1894–1966) German army general. Choltitz was an officer candidate (March 1914) and was commissioned in September 1914 at the beginning of World War I. After the war he continued in the Reichswehr and saw service in the cavalry until the early 1930s when he transferred to the infantry, eventually commanding 16th Regiment, which he led at the beginning of World War II.

Choltitz took command of the 260th Infantry Division (August 1942) and served briefly as an acting corps commander in Ukraine. He then commanded 11th Panzer Division and was interim commander of XLVIII Panzer Corps. Posted to Italy (1944), he was then assigned to France (June) and took command of LXXXIV Corps. As German defenses crumbled at Normandy, Adolf Hitler appointed him to command at Paris and ordered him to defend the city to the last. Despite his orders and greatly to his credit, Choltitz refused to use aircraft or heavy artillery and disregarded Hitler's express orders to destroy the city, surrendering it to Free French forces commanded by General Jacques Philippe Leclerc (August 25).

Chong Il-kwon (1917–94) Republic of Korea (ROK) general. Chong graduated from the Japanese Military Academy in Tokyo (1940), then served in the Japanese Kwantung Army in Manchuria. He returned to Korea after World War II, graduating from the U.S. military government's Military English Language School (January 1946). He then became the second chief of staff of the Korean Constabulary, predecessor of the Republic of Korea Army (ROKA).

When the Korean War began (25 June 1950), Chong was in the United States. He returned to Korea and was promoted major general and made ROKA chief of staff (1 July), replacing General Ch'ae Pyong-dok. Although ROKA commanding officer, he lost command authority when President Syngman Rhee approved a unified military command under United Nations commander General Douglas MacArthur. While Chong did not direct ROKA field operations, he had control over planning and security operations in rear areas, and he effectively coordinated activities between UN forces and the ROK government.

Relieved as chief of staff (July 1951), Chong attended the U.S. Command and General Staff College. On his return to Korea, Rhee arranged for him to command the ROKA 2nd Division (July–October 1952) so that he might gain battlefield experience. He was deputy commander of the U.S. IX Corps and then commanded ROKA II Corps. He returned as ROKA chief of staff (1954) and then became chairman of the ROKA Joint Chiefs of Staff (1956). He retired in 1957.

Christie, John Walter (1866?–1943) U.S. inventor. Christie first applied his genius to armaments design during World War I in a wheel-and-track carriage for an 8-inch gun. This experience led him to design the first American postwar tank, the three-man, 13.5-ton Medium Tank M1919 with removable track that could be stored around the tank hull during road operations. The M1928 was powered by a Liberty aircraft engine and had both great speed and a revolutionary suspension system of large weight-bearing wheels on torsion bars. The army ordered five of these. The M1928 was most studied overseas, first in the U.S.S.R. and then in Britain. The Soviets acquired two copies and used it as the basis for their BT series. Their T-34 tank, with a Christie suspension system, may have been the best tank of World War II.

The U.S. Army purchased three M1931 (U.S. designation, T-3) Christie tanks and the Soviets bought two. It was armed with a 37mm gun and a machine gun. His M1932 employed light-weight materials and had a forward-facing propeller so that it could be dropped from low-flying aircraft, fly, and hit the ground running. It could make road speeds of 36 mph on tracks or 65 mph on wheels, enabling it to leap a 20-foot gap from a 45-degree ramp. It was also sold to the Russians. His M1936, 6-ton, two-man tank was capable of cross-country speeds of up to 60 mph. In Britain it evolved into the first Cruiser tank.

Christie also designed for the U.S. the first standard turret track for battleships, as well as gun mounts and carriages. His amphibious platform for a 75mm gun, begun in 1921, led to the first amphibious tank.

Christie, Ralph Waldo (1923–87) U.S. admiral. A graduate of Annapolis (1915) with a MS degree from Massachusetts Institute of Technology (1923), Christie was a pioneer submarine officer and torpedo specialist. In his research at MIT he helped develop the magnetic exploder for torpedoes.

Christie commanded individual submarines (1918–20, 1923–24), Submarine Division 15 (January 1939–December 1940), and then Submarine Squadron 20 at Brisbane, Australia (1940–42). Promoted rear admiral (November 1942), he was at the Naval Torpedo Station, Newport, Rhode Island (January–March 1943). He then became commander of submarines, South Pacific operating out of Perth-Fremantle (1943–44).

Relying heavily on ULTRA intelligence, based on code-breaking and radio direction-finding operations, Christie's submarines mortally damaged Japan's ability to support its conquered territories and maintain its navy at sea. Although he appreciated Christie's abilities as a commander of submarines, Seventh Fleet commander Admiral Thomas Kinkaid clashed with him over management details, leading to his replacement (1944). He subsequently commanded the Puget Sound Navy Yard (February 1945–January 1948) and then naval forces in the Philippines. He retired as a vice admiral in August 1949.

Chu Teh (Zhu De, also Chu-Yü-chieh) (1886–1976) People's Republic of China marshal. Chu graduated from the Yunnan Military Preparatory School and fought in the Yunnan provincial army in support of Sun Yat-sen's (Sun Zhongshan) Chinese Revolution (October 1911). When General Yüan Shih-k'ai (Yuan Shikai) took power (1912), he commanded units along the border with Laos and Vietnam and became a warlord, amassing wealth and becoming an opium addict. He overcame his addiction and studied at Göttingen University, Germany (1922–24). In Europe he met Chou En-lai (Zhou Enlai) and joined the Communist party.

Arrested by the German police for his political activities, Chu was deported back to China (1926). He became a general in the Kuomintang (Guomindang) forces of Chiang Kai-shek (Jiang Jieshi). As commander of Ninth Army at Nanchang, he was one of the leaders of Chou's rebellion there (August 1927) but was forced to retreat on arrival of Nationalist forces. On the failure of the Nanchang Uprising, he joined Mao Tse-tung (Mao Zedong) in southwest Kiangsi (Jiangxi) (1928), where he formed the Red Army with Mao as political commissar and defended against Chiang's Bandit Suppression Campaigns (1930–33). He commanded the breakout leading to the Long March and was a major factor in the survival of the Communist forces. He then rebuilt the Red Army at Yenan (Yan'an) in Shensi (Shanxi) province (December 1936).

Chu commanded Eighth Route Army (1937) and directed the disastrous Hundred Regiments campaign in north China (August–November 1940) against the Japanese, thereafter abandoning large-unit actions. By 1945 he had built up the People's Liberation Army (PLA) to 800,000 men. He directed Communist military strategy during the 1946–49 Civil War, then served as defense minister (1949–54) and was the first of ten marshals created (1955) before he retired. He suffered persecution in the 1966–69 Cultural Revolution but was rehabilitated shortly thereafter.

Chuikov, Vasily Ivanovich (1900–82) Marshal of the Soviet Union. Chuikov joined the Red Army (1918) and fought in the 1918–20 Civil War and the 1920 Russo-Polish War. He later attended the Frunze Military Academy, and was Soviet military attaché in China (1926–1937).

Chuikov participated in the Soviet invasion of Poland (September 1939) and the 1939–40 war with Finland. A protégé of Georgy Zhukov, he was deputy commander, then commander, of First Reserve Army (later Sixty-Fourth Army). He then took command of Sixty-Second Army on the west bank of the Volga at Stalingrad (September 1942). His determined leadership was vital in holding the Germans until the Russians could mount a counteroffensive.

Chuikov then commanded Red Army forces in the drive through the Donets Basin, the Crimea, and into Belorussia. His troops reached Berlin (1 May 1945) where he accepted the German surrender. Following the war, he commanded Russian forces in Germany (1945–1953). He then headed the Kiev Military District until 1960.

Churchill, Winston Spencer Leonard
(1874–1965) British politician and prime
minister. Educated at Harrow and later
Sandhurst, Churchill was commissioned
in the cavalry (1895) and served in Cuba,
India, and the Sudan (1895–1899). Resigning his commission, he covered the
1899–1902 Boer War as a journalist,
where he was taken prisoner but escaped.

Returning to Britain, he won a seat in
the House of Commons as a Conservative
(1900). Crossing over to the Liberal Party
(1904), he held a number of increasingly
important posts: under-secretary of state
for the colonies (1905–08), president of
the Board of Trade (1908–10), and home
secretary (1910–11). As First Lord of the
Admiralty (1911–15), he reorganized the
navy and worked to assure readiness in
the case of war.

During World War I, Churchill was
involved in the defense of Antwerp
(1914). He promoted development of the
tank and was chief advocate of the
Dardanelles campaign to secure the
Straits, provide an easier means to reach
Russia, and drive Turkey from the war.
Poorly planned, the effort failed largely
because he insisted (despite his disclaimers
at the time and later) that the Straits
could be forced by ships alone and that
naval gunfire could silence the shore
batteries. When troops were brought in
(the Gallipoli Campaign), they were too
few and too late. Forced from office, he
became a lieutenant colonel and commanded a battalion of the 6th Royal Scots
Fusiliers, 9th Division on the Western
Front (November 1915). Returning to
England, he re-entered politics (June
1916) and became minister of munitions
(July 1917). Highly effective in this post,
he created a shell surplus.

During the inter-war years Churchill
was a staunch opponent of Communism
and supported Benito Mussolini in Italy.
A Cassandra regarding Adolf Hitler's
Germany, he sought to wake his countrymen from appeasement and turn them to
preparedness. He was out of parliament

twice in the 1920s and wrote his six-
volume memoir of World War I (*The
World Crisis*) and other books. Switching
to the Conservative party, he did not hold
a cabinet post again until he became First
Lord of the Admiralty for a second time
(September 1939).

Churchill replaced Neville Chamberlain
as prime minister (10 May 1940). Invigor-
ating the British war effort, he held that
post during most of the war. His policies
were influenced by a desire to preserve the
British empire, maintain Britain as a
major world power, and influence the
post-war settlement. To Churchill, the
great sin was inaction. He committed
British forces to the defense of Greece,
turned out commanders in North Africa,
forged an alliance with U.S. President
Franklin D. Roosevelt, fought hard and
unsuccessfully for an Allied offensive in
the eastern Mediterranean, opposed a
cross-channel invasion of France, and
sought to awaken the West to the threat
posed by the Soviet Union. In the latter
connection he wanted to "shake hands
with the Russians as far east as possible."

Turned out of office in an election (July
1945) after the end of the war in Europe but
during the Potsdam Conference, Churchill
then helped define the Cold War, wrote his
six-volume history of the war (*The Second
World War*), and served a second term as
prime minister (1951–55).

Chynoweth, Bradford Grethen (1890–
1985) U.S. general. Commissioned in the
engineers on graduation from West Point
(1912), Chynoweth held a variety of
assignments. He served with the 66th
Infantry Regiment (1939–1940) and with
the 53rd Infantry Regiment (1940–41).
Promoted brigadier general (1941), during
World War II he commanded U.S. forces
on Cebu Island, the Philippines.

Before his departure from the Philippines, General Douglas MacArthur left
Chynoweth in control of U.S. forces in
the Visayan Islands, including Cebu, Panay, Negros, Leyte, and Samar and in-

structed him to prepare for guerrilla operations. Contesting the Japanese landings, he fell back to the interior to conduct guerrilla warfare (April 1942). His forces were still largely intact when he was ordered to surrender against his wishes (18 May) by Brigadier General William Sharp.

Chynoweth survived the Bataan Death March and Japanese captivity and was released in 1945. He retired from the army in 1947.

Clark, Joseph James (1893–1971) U.S. admiral. "Jocko" Clark graduated from Annapolis (1917). Following sea duty in destroyers, he earned his pilot's wings (1925) and thereafter was identified with naval aviation. During World War II he led carrier formations as a rear admiral off Saipan, Iwo Jima, and Okinawa.

During the 1950–53 Korean War, Clark commanded Task Force 77 (September–November 1951). Promoted vice admiral (March 1952), he briefly commanded First Fleet and then received the Navy's premier combat command, Seventh Fleet (May 1952–December 1953). He worked well with Fifth Air Force commander Lieutenant General Glenn O. Barcus in carrying out raids against North Korea, named "Cherokee strikes" in his honor (Clark was one-eighth Cherokee Indian), against Communist supply dumps just beyond UN artillery range. Clark retired with the rank of admiral (December 1953).

Clark, Mark Wayne (1896–1984) U.S. general. Commissioned in the army on graduation from West Point (1917), Clark served as an infantry officer in World War I. He graduated from the Infantry School (1925) and the Command and General Staff School (1935), and the Army War College (1937). Promoted brigadier general (August 1941) and major general (April 1942), he became chief of staff of Army Ground Forces (May 1942). A month later he took command of II

Corps. He then led a secret mission to Vichy-held North Africa and met with French leaders (October). Promoted to lieutenant general (November 1942), he commanded land forces in North Africa. Beginning in September 1943, he led Fifth Army in its long drive up the Italian peninsula. Fifth Army took Rome (June 1944) and moved north. Clark then commanded Fifteenth Army Group with all Allied forces in the Mediterranean Theater (December 1944). His role in Italy was controversial, chiefly because of his determination to liberate Rome instead of trapping retreating German forces.

After the war Clark commanded occupation forces in Austria (1945–47), Sixth Army (1947–49), and then U.S. Army Field Forces (1949–52). He succeeded General Matthew Ridgway as commander of U.S. forces in the Far East and United Nations forces in Korea (May 1952). As with General Douglas MacArthur, he chafed at restrictions placed on his command. He returned to the U.S. (October 1953) and retired in 1954. He published two volumes of memoirs and served as president of The Citadel (1954–60)

Clay, Lucius DeBignnon (1897–1978) U.S. general. Commissioned in the engineers on graduation from West Point (1918), Clay was an instructor at West Point (1924–28) and then served in a variety of harbor and river assignments (1930–37). He served on General Douglas MacArthur's staff in the Philippines (1937–38) and then oversaw construction of the Denison Dam in Texas. A superb administrator, he headed the Civil Aeronautics Authority and directed construction and enlargement of 277 airports for military use (1940–42).

Following U.S. entry into World War II, Clay became deputy chief of matériel (March 1942). Promoted major general (December 1942), he oversaw military procurement and production. Following the Normandy invasion (6 June 1944), Clay sorted out problems at Cherbourg and helped substantially increase the flow of supplies to the front. He then became deputy chief of the Office of War Mobilization and Reconversion in Washington. He returned to Europe as General Dwight Eisenhower's civilian affairs deputy (April 1945), with responsibility for feeding and housing the population in the U.S. zone of Germany. He was then military governor in the U.S. zone (March 1947–May 1949) and a lieutenant general. He is best remembered for urging that President Harry S Truman take a tough stand following the Russian blockade of Berlin and for his oversight of the Berlin Airlift. He retired as a full general (May 1949).

Climo, Skipton Hill (1868–1937) British general. Climo joined the army and was commissioned in 1888. He saw considerable service in India and served in the 1897–98 Tirah Expedition and the 1900–01 Boxer Rebellion. He also participated in an expedition to Tibet (1903–04).

During World War I, Climo fought against the Turks in the Suez Canal area (1914–15). He then served in Mesopotamia, where he was wounded four times and promoted major general (1916). Following the war, in 1919 Climo fought in the Third Afghan War and commanded the force in the Waziristan Expedition (1919–20). He commanded a division in India (1930–22) and retired in 1923.

Cobbe, Sir Alexander Stanhope (1870–1931) British general. Educated at Wellington and Sandhurst, Cobbe became an ensign in the South Wales Borderers (1889). Promoted lieutenant, he transferred to the Indian Staff Corps (1892). He saw service in the Chitral Expedition (1895) and Nyasaland (1898–99), the Fourth Ashanti War (1900), and in Somaliland (1902). Promoted captain (1902) and major (1907), he served in staff positions in India and at the War Office (1902–14).

Cobbe served in France at the beginning of World War I but was then ordered to India. As a major general, he succeeded General Sir Stanley Maude (summer 1916) in command of III Indian Corps in Mesopotamia, leading it in the victory at Kut-al-Amara (February 1917) and the advance toward Baghdad. He captured Samarra (April) and had a major role in the victory at Ramadi (September). Defeating the Turks at Sharqat (October 1917), he captured Mosul (November).

After the war Cobbe was military secretary at the India Office (1919–22). Promoted general (1924), he had charge of Northern Command in India (1926–30) before returning to his post at the India Office until his death (1931).

Cochran, Jacqueline (1906?–80) U.S. pilot. Born into poverty, Cochran first worked in mill towns and then was a beautician. A chance meeting with an industrialist in New York City led to her taking flying lessons and becoming a licensed pilot (1932). Soon one of the world's premier fliers, she won the transcontinental Bendix Air Race (1938). After approval of the Lend Lease Act (March 1941) and encouraged by Air Army Corps commander General Henry "Hap" Arnold, she flew a bomber across the Atlantic to Scotland, then met with British officials to discuss a plan to train women fliers for service with the U.S. Army Air Forces. She was then appointed director of the Women's Air Service Pilots (WASPs) (July 1943). The Air Transport command used the WASPs to ferry aircraft, but principally for operational duties with Training Command, such as towing targets.

Despite Cochrane's best efforts, the WASP program was abandoned (December 1944), in part because the women had not been militarized. At the end of the war she became a foreign correspondent. She was the first woman to fly faster than the speed of sound (1953) and continued to set air records through the 1960s.

Collins, Joseph Lawton (1896–1987) U.S. general. Collins graduated from West

Point in 1917 as a lieutenant of infantry. He missed combat in World War I but served with U.S. occupation forces in Germany (1919–21). An instructor at West Point (1921–25) and Fort Benning (1925–31), he also served in the Philippines. He taught at the Army War College (1938–41). Promoted major general (May 1942), he took command of the 25th Infantry Division and deployed with it to Guadalcanal, where his aggressive tactics earned him the nickname of "Lightning Joe."

Collins commanded VII Corps (March 1944) for the invasion of Normandy (6 June) and then directed the attack on Cherbourg. VII Corps spearheaded the Normandy breakout and then pushed eastward across northern France, Belgium, and into Germany. Promoted lieutenant general (April 1945), he was vice chief of staff of the army (1947–48) and was promoted to general (January 1948). After a term as chief of staff of the army (1949–53), he was special envoy to the Republic of Vietnam (1954–55). He retired in 1956.

Collins, Michael (1890–1922) Irish revolutionary. Born in Ireland, Collins worked in England as a bank clerk (1906). He joined the Irish Republican Brotherhood (1909) and returned to Ireland (1916), joining the Irish Volunteers. He led attacks on the British during the April 1916 Easter Rebellion, but was forced to surrender. Simple luck spared him execution. Imprisoned, he led a hunger strike and was released (December). He then handled finances for the Nationalists and helped organize the Volunteers, Irish Republican Brotherhood, and Sinn Fein party. He also arranged the smuggling of arms, set up an effective espionage organization, and engineered the escape of Sinn Fein leader Eamon de Valera from Lincoln Prison. He created an elite unit, the "Squad," which assassinated nineteen British secret agents in Ireland in retribution for assassination of Irish nationalists

by the British "Cairo Gang." The British offered a £10,000 reward for his capture.

In 1921 Collins represented Irish nationalists in negotiations with London leading to a treaty (December 1921) that established the Irish Free State in southern Ireland. He split with De Valera, who rejected compromise regarding northern Ireland. Under Collins's urging, a majority of the Irish national assembly ratified the treaty, but De Valera and the "Irregulars" refused and civil war ensued. Chief of state, Collins also became commander-in-chief of the Free State Army and crushed the hardliners. He was killed in an ambush near Cork following a meeting with De Valera.

Collishaw, Raymond (1893–1976) Canadian air vice marshal. A native of British Columbia, Collishaw was with the merchant marine before he joined the Royal Naval Air Service (RNAS) during World War I. He took command of the "Black Flight" Squadron (1917) and was personally credited with sixty victories with both the RNAS and the Royal Air Force. He commanded a fighter squadron during the British intervention in Russia to aid the White forces (1919), shooting down two Red Army aircraft. With the rank of vice air marshal, early in World War II he commanded 202 and 204 Groups of the Royal Air Force in the Western Desert (1940–41), defeating the Italian Air Force there.

Coningham, Sir Arthur (1895–1948) British air marshal. Born in Australia, "Mary" (from Maori) Coningham was educated at Wellington College, New Zealand. He joined that dominion's army at the start of World War I and saw action at Gallipoli (April 1915–January 1916). Discharged for illness, he then joined the Royal Flying Corps (1916) and saw combat in France as a fighter pilot.

After the war Coningham served in Egypt and Iraq and was also an instructor at the RAF college and the Central Flying

School. Promoted air commodore on the outbreak of World War II, he commanded 4 Group (night bombers) in Yorkshire (1939–41). Promoted air vice marshal, he received command of the Desert Air Force in North Africa (July 1941). The Desert Air Force provided support first to the British Eighth Army, notably during the Battle of El Alamein (October–November 1942), and then to the Allies in the fighting in Tunisia. He commanded Allied First Tactical Air Force during the invasions of Sicily (July 1943) and south Italy (September). Returning to Britain (January 1944), he commanded the Allied Second Tactical Air Force during the Normandy invasion. His command then relocated to France for the remainder of the war. By the end of the war it had grown to 100,000 men and 1,800 aircraft.

After the war Coningham commanded the Flying Training Center and was promoted air marshal and knighted (1946). He was asked to retire the next year, a consequence of his lack of service on the air staff; he had spent his entire career as an active pilot.

Conolly, Richard Lansing (1892–1962) U.S. admiral. Commissioned on graduation from Annapolis (1914), Conolly served in destroyers in the Atlantic. He won the Navy Cross for actions during World War I in helping to save a transport damaged in a German submarine attack. He earned an MS degree from Columbia University (1922) and was an instructor at Annapolis (1925–1927). He then held destroyer commands and was again instructor at Annapolis (1936–39).

Conolly commanded Destroyer Squadron 7, and then Destroyer Squadron 6, in the Pacific (1939–42) and the destroyer screen for the Doolittle raid on Tokyo (April 1942). He was on the staff of Chief of Naval Operations (CNO) and Commander-in-Chief of U.S. Fleet Admiral Ernest King (1942–43), and was promoted rear admiral (July 1942).

During March–October 1943 Conolly

was with the Amphibious Force Atlantic Fleet and took part in the invasions of Sicily (July 1943) and Italy (September). Transferred to the Pacific, he was with amphibious forces in the Pacific and participated in landings at Kwajalein, Wake, and Marcus Islands. He commanded Group 3, Amphibious Force, Pacific Fleet during 1944–45 and led the landing on Guam (July 1944) and the Lingayen Gulf (January 1945).

After the war Conolly was naval representative to the 1946 Paris Peace Conference. He commanded Twelfth Fleet (September 1946–January 1947), then U.S. Naval Forces Eastern Atlantic and Mediterranean (1947–50). His last assignment was as the president of the U.S. Naval War College at Newport, Rhode Island (1950–53). He retired as a full admiral (November 1953) and was then president of Long Island University (1953–62). He and his wife were killed in a plane crash.

Conrad von Hötzendorf, Count Franz (1852–1925) Austro-Hungarian field marshal. Conrad graduated from the Maria Theresa Akademie and was selected for general staff training (1876). He distinguished himself during the 1878 Bosnia-Herzegovina occupation and thereafter served in a variety of other staff posts, including instructor at the Imperial General Staff College (1888–1892). The heir to the throne, Archduke Franz Ferdinand, facilitated his rapid advancement, and he became chief of staff of the army (1906).

Conflict with Foreign Minister Count Aehrenthal led Conrad to resign (1911), but he was reinstated with the 1912 Balkan War. In the crisis following the 28 June 1914 assassination of Archduke Franz Ferdinand, he urged a preventive war against Serbia, but his delay in mobilizing the final echelon of troops contributed to his army's poor initial performance. He cooperated only reluctantly with his German ally, to the detriment of the overall war effort. His fixation on the Trentino offensive against Italy prevented the dispatch of troops to stop the summer 1916 Russian drive into Galicia, which ended any hopes for Austro-Hungarian victory in the east. When Emperor Francis Joseph died (December 1916), new Emperor Charles dismissed him.

Given command of the Austrian Army in Tyrol (March 1917), Conrad proved an undistinguished commander. He had only a small role in the successful November Austro-German Caporetto offensive and had little success in the failed Piave offensive (June 1918). He retired in July.

Corap, André Georges (1878–1953) French general. Commissioned in the army on graduation from St. Cyr (1898), Corap fought with distinction in the 1920–26 Rif Rebellion, serving under Colonel Henri Giraud and capturing rebel leader Abd-el-Krim (1926). He commanded troops in Morocco (1935), and then a regiment (1936).

On the mobilization of French forces in World War II, Corap commanded Ninth Army. With the German invasion of France and Benelux (10 May 1940), on plan he wheeled his army north to the Meuse just west of Sedan. The Germans arrived there first, and in the ensuing battle, Ninth Army was all but destroyed by the German armored thrust. French CinC Northeast General Alphonse Georges blamed Corap for the German breakthrough and replaced him with General Henri Giraud (15 May). Corap was no more to blame, however, than General Charles Huntziger, commanding II Army to Corap's south, who later became Vichy minister of war.

Corap then commanded Giraud's Seventh Army (16–19 May) until he was dismissed. He accompanied the French government to Bordeaux in an unsuccessful attempt to clear his name, and then retired.

Cota, Norman Daniel (1893–1971) U.S. general. A graduate of West Point (1917),

"Dutch" Cota was commissioned in the infantry. He taught at West Point (1918–20) and was on duty in Hawaii (1924–28). He graduated from the Command and General Staff School (1931) and Army War College (1936). He was an instructor at the Infantry School (1932–33) and the Command and General Staff School (1938–40). He was on the staff of the 1st Infantry Division (1941–42), then its CofS (1942–43). Promoted brigadier general (February 1943), he was U.S. advisor to the combined operations branch of the European Theater of Operations (1942–43). He then became assistant division commander of the 29th Infantry Division (1943–44).

Cota had the distinction of being the first U.S. general officer ashore in the Normandy Invasion (6 June 1944). Later he commanded 28th Infantry Division, which he led in the liberation parade through Paris (29 August) as a show of support for General Charles de Gaulle. Promoted major general (September), he led his division in assaulting the Siegfried Line and in heavy fighting in the Hürtgen Forest and in helping to defeat the Ardennes Offensive (December 1944). He retired after the war (1946).

Crace, Sir John Gregory (1887–1968) British admiral. Crace joined the Royal Navy (1902) and saw action during World War I. As a rear admiral during World War II he commanded a squadron covering the sea approaches from the Japanese base of Rabaul. At first he escorted U.S. tankers supporting Admiral Wilson Brown's raid on Rabaul (21 February 1942) and then a strike against shipping off Lae and Salamaua. His Task Force 14, consisted of three Australian cruisers and several destroyers, joined U.S. Rear Admiral Jack Fletcher's TF 17 (6 May) in the Coral Sea. Heading westward the next day ("Crace's Chase") to protect Port Moresby, Crace's force successfully evaded a heavy Japanese air attack during the Battle of the Coral Sea

(7–8 May) and was thus a threat to the Japanese amphibious force bound for Port Moresby. The presence of his force and Japanese losses in the Coral Sea fight led Japanese Vice Admiral Shigeyoshi Inoyue to call off the invasion.

Shortly thereafter Crace retired from active service to become superintendent of the royal dockyard at Chatham until 1946. He was promoted (1945) to admiral on the retired list.

Cradock, Sir Christopher George Francis Maurice (1862–1914) British admiral. Cradock joined the navy (1875). During the 1900–01 Boxer Rebellion in China, he directed the storming of the forts at Tientsin. Promoted to rear admiral (1910), he took command of the North American and West Indies Station (February 1913), with responsibility for protecting the North Atlantic trading routes.

At the start of World War I Cradock's squadron failed to intercept two German cruisers, and the Admiralty then ordered him south to the Falklands to intercept German trade and attempt to destroy Admiral Maximilian von Spee's East Asian Squadron. Off Coronel near the Chilean coast, his two old heavy cruisers, one light cruiser, and one armed merchant cruiser encountered Spee's larger, faster, and more heavily armed squadron (1 November 1914). He forced the engagement anyway, perhaps hoping to inflict damage on the Germans far from their repair bases, even though it meant possibly sacrificing his own force. In the battle the Germans sank both heavy cruisers with the loss of all hands, including Cradock. An inquiry exonerated him of recklessness and blamed his defeat on late-arriving reinforcements and ambiguous Admiralty orders.

Crerar, Henry Duncan Graham (1888–1965) Canadian general. Crerar graduated from the Royal Military College (1909) and joined a militia unit in Hamilton, Ontario. An artillery officer in World War I, he transferred to the regular army after the war and served in the War Office. Returning to Canada (1927), he was assigned to the Department of National Defense, becoming director of intelligence (1935).

After the start of World War II, Crerar went to Britain (October 1940) and established a forward Canadian military echelon. He was then appointed chief of the General Staff (1940) and directed the expansion of the Canadian military. He resigned his post (November 1941) to assume the lower, combat command of the Canadian I Corps (1942), and led it in the invasion of Sicily (July 1943). Recalled to Britain, he then commanded First Canadian Army, which was in fact a multinational force. It landed in France near the mouth of the Orne River (July 1944), and had major responsibility for closing the Falaise Gap and securing the Channel ports, which he took one at a time. Criticized for his cautious approach, he in fact had little logistical support. Invalided to Britain (September 1944), he returned to duty in November.

Crerar's army broke through the Siegfried Line (February 1945) and participated in heavy fighting in the Rhineland. Cold and aloof, he was an exacting commander. He retired from the army after the war, little recognized for his achievements.

Cronjé, Pieter Arnoldus (*c.*1835–1911) Boer general. A leader in the Transvaal against British rule, Piet Cronjé commanded troops in the 1880–81 First Anglo-Boer War, forcing the surrender of the British at Potchefstroom, for which he became known as the "Lion of Potchefstroom". He also commanded the Boer force that halted the Jameson Raid (January 1896).

The chief Boer general on the outbreak of the Second 1899–1902 Boer War, Cronjé commanded forces in the west against Cape Colony and besieged the British garrison at Mafeking commanded by Colonel Robert Baden-Powell (October 1899). He was then called south to assist in the advance toward Kimberley and held against a British attack on the Modder River (November) before withdrawing. He held again at Magersfontein (December), inflicting heavy losses on the British. Forced to retreat by Field Marshal Lord Roberts's flanking advance (February 1900), he was trapped at Paardeberg (February) and forced to surrender. He was then held prisoner until the end of the war.

Crutchley, Victor Alexander Charles (1893–1986) British admiral. Crutchley won distinction, and a Victoria Cross, for his role during a World War I Royal Navy attempt to block Ostend, Belgium from German submarine access (April 1918). At the start of World War II he was captain of the battleship *Warspite* (1937–40). During the Norwegian Campaign (April–May 1940), his ship and nine British destroyers entered Narvik Fjord and sank all ten German destroyers supporting General Eduard Dietl's land force. He then commanded the Royal Navy Barracks at Devonport (1940–41).

Promoted rear admiral, Crutchley was named (Spring 1942) to succeed Admiral Sir John Crace in command of the Australian cruiser squadron at Brisbane, serving with the U.S. Navy Pacific Fleet in the Southwest Pacific and protecting transports landing Marines on Guadalcanal. Crutchley's dispositions off Savo Island were approved by U.S. Admiral R. Kelly Turner, who then called him away to a conference. Taking advantage of foul weather, Japanese Admiral Gun'ichi Mikawa launched a surprise night attack (8–9 August) during Crutchley's absence, leading to the loss of five Allied warships without a single Japanese ship sunk, in what became known as the Battle of Savo Island (or Battle of the Five Sitting Ducks). Attempts to make Crutchley a scapegoat were unsuccessful. As commander of the squadron until 1944, he participated in the remainder of the Southwest Pacific operations. He was then flag officer at Gibraltar (1945–47), before retiring (1947).

Cunningham, Sir Alan Gordon (1887–1983) British general. Younger brother of Admiral Andrew Browne Cunningham, a graduate of Sandhurst, he served in the artillery on the Western Front during World War I and in 1918 was promoted major general. In World War II, as a lieutenant general, he commanded British forces in Kenya (November 1940). In command of African and South Africa troops, he invaded Italian Somaliland (January 1941), rapidly securing Mogadishu (February) and Kismayu. Pursuing Italian forces into Ethiopia, he took Addis Ababa (April) and, in cooperation with General William Platt's British forces from the Sudan, converged on Gondar and received the surrender of 50,000 Italians, including the Duke of Aosta, at a cost of only 500 casualties (May), for which he was knighted.

Cunningham then was sent to Egypt (August) to succeed General Richard O'Connor in command of Eighth Army (replacing the old Western Desert Force). He directed Operation CRUSADER, General Claude Auchinleck's offensive for the relief of Tobruk (November–December 1941). But with scant time to prepare and being a stranger to armored warfare, he was outmaneuvered by German General Erwin Rommel. Only eight days into the offensive Auchinleck replaced him with General Neil M. Ritchie (26 November). He then commanded the Staff College, Camberley (1942–43) and the Eastern Command (1944–45).

Following the war he was promoted full general. He was the last British high commissioner to Palestine and Transjordan (Jordan) in the difficult period of the Jewish revolt (1945–1948). He was knighted on his return to Britain.

Cunningham, Sir Andrew Browne, 1st Viscount Cunningham of Hyndhope (1883–1963) British admiral. Cunningham joined the Royal Navy (1898) and served in the Naval Brigade in the 1899–1902 Boer War. He had a variety of postings before World War I, when he commanded a destroyer at the Dardanelles (1915) and distinguished himself in the raid on the German base at Zeebrugge (April 1918).

Cunningham was naval aide to King George V (1932–33). Promoted rear admiral (1934), he commanded a destroyer flotilla in the Mediterranean (1934–36), then the battle cruiser squadron. He was second in command of the Mediterranean Fleet (1938–39), and then its commander (June 1939).

Following the German victory over France, Cunningham's deft diplomacy secured neutralization of French naval assets at Alexandria (June 1940). Off Calabria (9 July 1940), he defeated Italian Admiral Angelo Campioni's slightly larger Italian force, damaging a battleship and cruiser. With aircraft carrier *Illustrious* he carried out the daring air attack on Taranto (11 November) that sank or badly damaged three Italian battleships and two cruisers and sank two auxiliaries, decisively altering the naval balance in the Mediterranean. In a night gunnery action off Cape Matapan (28 March 1941), he intercepted Admiral Angelo Iachino's main battle Italian fleet, sinking three cruisers and two destroyers. He carried out a costly evacuation of the British Expeditionary Force from Greece (April) and Crete (May–June), and his naval units kept Malta supplied despite heavy Axis air attacks (June 1941–June 1942).

Cunningham was then representative to the Combined Chiefs of Staff in Washington (June–October 1942). Promoted admiral of the fleet, he returned to the Mediterranean (October 1942) as Allied naval commander, overseeing the invasions of North Africa (November) and Sicily (July 1943) and receiving the surrender of the Italian fleet (8 September). He returned to London to replace Admiral Sir Dudley Pound as first sea lord (September 1943–1946). He then was created viscount and retired from the navy.

Cunningham, Sir John Henry Dacres (1885–1962) British admiral. Cunningham joined the navy as a cadet (1900) and then was a midshipman. He went on to specialize in navigation and was a junior officer in World War I.

Promoted vice admiral (June 1939), he commanded 1st Cruiser Squadron in the Mediterranean, which was transferred to the Home Squadron at the start of World War II (September). He supported operations in Norway (1940) and then was co-commander, with Major General N. M. S. Irwin, of the ill-fated attempt to take Dakar (September 1940). He then became Fourth Sea Lord (logistics and transport) (1941–43) and was knighted (1941). Appointed Commander-in-Chief in the Levant (late 1942), he was later promoted to full admiral. He was also deputy to Admiral Andrew Cunningham (no relation), before succeeding him as Allied commander-in-chief Mediterranean (October 1943).

After the war Cunningham again succeeded Andrew Cunningham, this time as first sea lord and chief of the naval staff (1946–48). Promoted to fleet admiral (January 1948), he retired in September 1949.

Cushman, Robert Everton, Jr. (1914–85) U.S. Marine Corps general. Commissioned in the Marine Corps after graduation from Annapolis (1935), Cushman held a variety of assignments. During World War II, as a lieutenant colonel (1943) he commanded a battalion of the 9th Marine Regiment on Bougainville, Guam, and Iwo Jima.

After the war Cushman was a student, then instructor at Marine Corps Schools, Quantico (1945–48). He then headed the

Amphibious Warfare Branch of the Office of Naval Research. He was detailed to the Central Intelligence Agency (1949–51) and promoted colonel (1950). He served with the Eastern Atlantic and Mediterranean Fleet (1951–53) and was on the faculty at the Armed Forces Staff College (1953–56). Promoted brigadier general (1957), he was then assistant for National Securities Affairs to Vice-President Richard Nixon. Promoted major general (1958), he commanded the 3rd Marine Division on Okinawa (1961–62) and was assistant chief of staff of the Marine Corps (1962–64). He then commanded Camp Pendleton (1964–67). He took command of the 3rd Marine Amphibious Force in Vietnam (April 1967). Its 160,000 men was the largest combined combat force ever commanded by a Marine. He then became deputy director of the CIA (April 1969). Promoted full general (January 1972), he was commandant of the Marine Corps until his retirement in June 1975.

D

Danilov, Yury Nikiforovich (1866–1937) Russian general. Danilov graduated from the Mikhailovsky Artillery School, served briefly as a line officer, and then graduated from the General Staff Academy (1892). He made his military reputation as a staff officer, teaching at the General Staff Academy and writing on military subjects. As a colonel, he returned to the General Staff (1908). In 1914 he was the army's quartermaster general, responsible for military planning.

On the outbreak of World War I, Danilov became deputy to Chief of Staff General Nikolai Yanushkevish. He urged that the army concentrate on defeating Germany, rather than Austria-Hungary, as its primary goal. He strongly supported an offensive into East Prussia, a proposal that was accepted. He did much of the planning for the campaign that led to the Russian disaster at Tannenberg, but his original plan was reshaped to provide for a second offensive against Austrian Galicia, dispersing Russian strength, something he opposed.

When Tsar Nicholas II took personal command of the Army (September 1915), Danilov received command of a corps. In early 1917 became chief of staff to commander of the Northern Front General Nikolai Ruzsky and for a time commanded Fifth Army. Following the March 1917 Revolution, he emigrated to France.

Dankl von Krasnik, Viktor (1854–1941) Austro-Hungarian general. Dankl graduated from the Maria Theresa Military Academy (1874) and the War Academy (1879). He joined the General Staff (1880) and was promoted captain (1884). He then served in a variety of assignments and was promoted major general (1903) and general of cavalry (1912), when he commanded XIV Army Corps at Innsbruck.

At the beginning of World War I, Dankl commanded First Army. A competent if unimaginative leader, he attacked north into Poland (August 1914). He defeated the Russian Fourth Army near Krasnik (August) and reached Lublin. Outflanked by the Russians (September), his army became part of the rout that followed. He played only a minor role in the see-saw fighting that raged across Galicia and Poland during the remainder of 1914.

Dankl transferred to the Italian frontier with an understrength corps to defend the Tyrol area (April 1915). He then took command of Eleventh Army (March 1916) and spearheaded the drive against Padua (May), but mountainous terrain, Italian heroics, and the meddling of headquarters thwarted his plans. The offensive only reached the Arsiero, and Austro-Hungarian Army commander General Franz Conrad von Hötzendorf blamed

Dankl. Infuriated, he asked to be relieved which was granted. It was his last troop command.

D'Annunzio, Gabriele (1863–1938) Italian writer and political activist. D'Annunzio demonstrated his literary ability early, publishing his first book of poetry at age sixteen. Elected to parliament (1897), he became an exponent of Italian nationalism and irredentism, championing the cause of regaining Italy's lost territory on the Adriatic. He enthusiastically welcomed World War I and advocated Italian intervention.

Following Italy's decision for war (May 1915), D'Annunzio joined a cavalry division and then became a torpedo boat commander and later a pilot. He lost an eye in an air operation but retained his enthusiasm. His most memorable exploit was to lead a flight of aircraft to Vienna, "bombing" it with leaflets he himself had written (August 1918).

After the war D'Annunzio became chief spokesperson for disgruntled nationalists and ex-soldiers who believed Italy had not been sufficiently compensated for its wartime sacrifices. In January 1919 he called on Italians to seize the disputed port of Fiume and all of Dalmatia. He then led a march on Fiume and for over a year held it with his devoted followers and army deserters (September 1919–January 1921). The rise of Mussolini eclipsed him; by the end of 1922 he had given up hope of coming to power himself and retired to private life.

Darby, William Orlando (1911–45) U.S. general. Commissioned in the field artillery on graduation from West Point (1933), Darby served with the 80th Field Artillery Regiment (1939–40) and then commanded a battery in the 99th Field Artillery Regiment (1941–42). Following a brief tour as aide-de-camp to the commander of the 34th Division in Europe, he was selected (June 1942) to organize the Ranger training program in Achnacarry,

Scotland, with assistance from British commandos. Charismatic and an excellent trainer, he led by example.

Officially Darby commanded only the 1st Ranger Battalion, but he trained and actually led the 3rd and 4th Battalions as well. These were known throughout the war as "Darby's Rangers." Promoted colonel (December 1943), he officially took command of the three battalions. The Rangers saw action in the Dieppe Raid (19 August 1942) and in the U.S. campaigns beginning with Operation TORCH, the invasion of North Africa (8 November 1942). After the 1st and 3rd Battalions were destroyed at Anzio, Darby took command of the 179th Infantry Regiment. He returned to the U.S. to serve in the Operations Division of the War Department's general staff (April 1944). He then commanded the 10th Mountain Division in Italy, where he was killed by artillery fire in the last days of the war. He was posthumously promoted brigadier general.

D'Argenlieu, Georges Thierry (1889–1964) French admiral and colonial administrator. D'Argenlieu joined the navy as a cadet (1905), served in Morocco, and during World War I served in patrol craft in the Mediterranean. After the war he became a Carmelite friar. Recalled to service at the start of World War II, he was stationed at Cherbourg. He escaped from German capture, and made his way to London, where he was one of the first to rally to General Charles de Gaulle. Named chaplain to the Free French Navy, he was wounded in the abortive attempt to capture Dakar but played a key role in other actions along the West African coast (1940). In 1941 de Gaulle named him high commissioner for French territories of the Pacific and Far East. Later he was promoted rear admiral. He returned to London to command French naval forces in Britain (1943) and was French naval advisor to the Normandy invasion (6 June 1944).

In 1945 de Gaulle named d'Argenlieu

first the vice president of the Supreme Naval Council and inspector general of French naval forces, then high commissioner to Indo-China with instructions to restore "French sovereignty." His Indo-China policies, especially the proclamation of a "Republic of Cochin-China" (June 1946), undercut the work of French diplomat Jean Sainteny and helped create war. His order of military action to "teach the Vietnamese nationalists a lesson" resulted in the shelling of Haiphong by the cruiser *Suffren* (23 November) and the outbreak of the 1946–54 Indo-China War (19 December). Recalled to France (February 1947), he resigned and re-entered the Carmelite Order.

Darlan, Jean Louis Xavier François (1881–1942) French admiral and political leader. Darlan was commissioned in the navy on graduation from the Naval Academy (1901). A specialist in gunnery, he was an instructor on the school ship *Jeanne d'Arc* (1912). During World War I he commanded a land battery of naval gunners on various fronts. After the war he was promoted captain (1926) and commanded the school ships *Jeanne d'Arc* and *Edgar Quinet* (1928). Promoted rear admiral (1929), he commanded 1st Cruiser Division in the Mediterranean, and was promoted vice admiral (1932). He then commanded the Atlantic Squadron (1934–36). Appointed chief of the naval staff (1936), he was advanced to admiral of the fleet and made CinC of the navy (1937).

On the defeat of France by Germany in World War II (June 1940), Darlan became minister of the navy in Marshal Henri Philippe Pétain's Vichy government. He assured Britain that France would not allow Germany to acquire its fleet and issued secret orders calling on ships to be scuttled should the Germans try to take them. Fearful that this promise would not be honored, British Prime Minister Winston Churchill ordered an effort to acquire the French fleet, which resulted in fighting and considerable loss of French

life at Mers-el-Kebir in Algeria (3 July 1940). Already anti-British, Darlan believed Germany would win the war and now sought closer cooperation with Berlin.

Darlan succeeded Pierre Laval as vice premier and foreign minister (February 1941–April 1942). He also took over the ministries of interior and defense and was designated Pétain's successor. Laval's subsequent return to power (April 1942) greatly diminished his influence, although he continued to command the French armed forces. He was in Algiers at the time of Operation TORCH, the Allied landings in North Africa, and agreed to cooperate with the Allies in return for their recognition of his authority. This drew much criticism in the United States, but the problem was solved when Darlan was assassinated by a French monarchist, supposedly acting alone, on 24 December 1942.

Davis, Benjamin O., Jr. (1912–) U.S. Air Force general. The son of Benjamin O. Davis, Sr., Davis graduated from West Point in 1936, even though he had been shunned during his entire cadetship. The first black graduate from West Point in the twentieth Century, he was only the fourth overall. He joined the 24th Infantry Regiment, an all-black unit, at Fort Benning. Among his subsequent assignments was that of Reserve Officer Training Corps Instructor at the Tuskegee Institute.

Although he had been turned down earlier because of his race, in 1941 Davis was allowed into the Army Air Corps. He graduated from flight school (1942) and was promoted major. As a lieutenant colonel, he commanded the 99th Pursuit Squadron, the first U.S. combat squadron entirely of African-Americans. He led it and then the 332nd Fighter Group, which absorbed the 99th (June 1944), over North Africa, Italy, and the Balkans. Promoted colonel (March 1944), he returned to the United States after the war to command the racially troubled 477th

Composite Group at Goodman Field, Kentucky.

Many of Davis' subsequent assignments were related to improving race relations. Promoted brigadier general (1954), he was the first black U.S. Air Force general officer and commanded Twelfth Air Force in Germany (1957–59). Promoted major general (1959), he became director of manpower and organization at Air Force headquarters. Promoted lieutenant general (1965), he was deputy commander of the U.S. Strike Command, McDill Air Force Base, Florida. He retired from the military in 1970.

Davis, Benjamin O., Sr. (1880–1970) U.S. general. Davis entered Howard University (1897) but left school after only a year to fight in the 1898 Spanish-American War as a lieutenant in the 8th Volunteer Infantry Regiment. Discharged after the war, he joined the 9th Cavalry Regiment as a private. He rose through the ranks to sergeant major and then passed a test for a commission (1901) and became a lieutenant in the 10th Cavalry. He was an ROTC instructor at Wilberforce University and the Tuskegee Institute, a National Guard instructor, military attaché in Liberia (1912–15), and served along the Mexican border.

Davis became the first black colonel in the army (1930) and its first black general officer (October 1940). He then commanded a brigade of the 2nd Cavalry Division at Fort Riley, Kansas. He retired when he reached mandatory retirement age (July 1941), but a day later General George C. Marshall returned him to active duty.

Davis then headed a special section in the army's inspector general's office to deal with problems of racial segregation within a rapidly expanding army. One device was a film, "The Negro Soldier." Despite his best efforts, he failed to achieve major change in army racial policies during his own career. He did,

however, lay the basis for the changes to follow. He retired finally in June 1948.

Dayan, Moshe (1919–81) Israeli general and politician. Born in a kibbutz in Palestine, he joined the Haganah (1929) paramilitary terrorist group and served in ambush and patrol units during the 1936–39 Arab revolt. Imprisoned by the British at the start of World War II as a member of an outlawed terrorist group, he was released (February 1941) when Haganah joined the fight against the Axis powers. He served as a scout during the British invasion of Syria and Lebanon, and lost an eye in fighting there (June 1941).

After the war, David Ben Gurion elevated Dayan to the general staff and he fought in the 1948–49 Israeli War of Independence, raising and then leading the 89th Commando Battalion, before commanding the Jerusalem sector. He attended Camberley Staff College in Britain (1953) and on his return became chief of staff of the Israeli Defense Forces (IDF). He had a lead role in planning Israel's 1956 invasion of the Sinai Peninsula. He retired in 1958 and then represented the Mupai party in the Knesset. He was minister of agriculture (1959–64) and then defense minister (June 1967), when he planned the incredible Israeli victory in the 1967 Six-Day War, but he departed under criticism (1974) after Israel was surprised by Egypt in the 1973 Yom Kippur War. As foreign minister, he helped negotiate the Camp David Peace Accords with Egypt, resigning in 1979 following differences with Prime Minister Menachem Begin over policy toward the Palestinian Arabs.

de Castries, Christian Marie Ferdinand de la Croix (1902–91) French general. De Castries enlisted in the army as a private (1921) and was commissioned in the cavalry (1926). Bored by garrison life, he resigned, and during the 1930s represented France in international equestrian events and obtained a commercial pilot's license. After the start of World War II (September 1939), de Castries rejoined the army as a lieutenant. During fighting in Lorraine he and his sixty men held out for three days against a German battalion supported by artillery and aircraft. Wounded, he was then captured. His fourth escape attempt was successful (1941), and he joined the Free French. He was wounded in Italy but recovered to take part in the invasion of southern France, Operation DRAGOON (August 1944), serving in Colonel Henri Navarre's regiment of the 3rd Moroccan Spahis in First Army. Promoted major, he led his forces in a maneuver that secured Karslruhe.

De Castries served in Indo-China (1946–49) and gained a reputation as an excellent commander of raiding forces. After study at the Army Staff College, he returned to Indo-China as a lieutenant colonel and took command of the critical Red River Delta sector (1951).

Named by General Navarre, now French commander in Indo-China, to command at Dien Bien Phu (November 1953), Colonel de Castries showed reckless bravery under fire but was also at times detached and withdrawn. His defensive dispositions have been criticized, particularly the separation of Gabrielle from the remainder of the French strongpoints. Promoted brigadier general during the siege, he was taken prisoner on the surrender of the fortress (7 May 1954) but was released after four months to return to France as a national hero. He commanded 4th Armored Division in Germany, retiring (1959) after an automobile accident.

de Gaulle, Charles André Marie Joseph (1890–1970) French general and politician. De Gaulle joined the 33rd Infantry Regiment in 1909 and graduated from St. Cyr (1912). He then returned to the 33rd, now commanded by Colonel Henri Philippe Pétain. Severely wounded at the beginning of World War I, it was seven

months before he rejoined his regiment as adjutant. Wounded again, he spent five months recovering. Promoted captain (September 1915), he returned to the 33rd and fought at Verdun, where he was again wounded and taken prisoner.

De Gaulle returned to France after the war and taught at St. Cyr and later at the École de Guerre. He was also aide to French Army commander General Pétain. He became an important theorist on armored warfare and published *Vers l'Armée de Métier* (published in English as *The Army of the Future*) (1934). Had his ideas been followed, the 1940 French defeat might not have occurred.

Promoted colonel (1937), de Gaulle took command of the 507th Tank Regiment. The day after the Battle for France (May–June 1940) began, he took command of the 4th Tank Division, which had one of the few successes of the campaign, near Laon. Promoted brigadier general, he became under-secretary of state for national defense. When the French government rejected his call to fight on, he went to London and established the Free French, becoming the leader of the Resistance. He was then provisional president of the Fourth Republic (August 1944–January 1946), until he abruptly resigned. He returned to power as president of the Fifth Republic (1958–69). Although he did have his negatives, he also created the strong presidential regime that survives today, developed the *Force de Frappe* (nuclear strike force), worked out an entente with the Federal Republic of Germany, gave independence to Algeria, and began the process of détente with the Soviet Union and Eastern Europe. He was France's greatest statesman of the twentieth century.

de Guingand, Sir Francis Wilfred (1900–79) British general. "Freddie" de Guingand graduated from Sandhurst (1919) and joined the West Yorkshire Regiment, beginning a long friendship with then Captain Bernard Montgomery. He was aide to

Secretary of War Leslie Hore-Belisha (1939–41). As a lieutenant colonel, he was instructor at the new Middle East Staff College, Haifa. Assigned to the joint planning staff, Cairo (1941), he became director of military intelligence in Middle East Command (February 1942) and, as a brigadier general, CofS to Eighth Army Commanders General Claude Auchinleck and Mont-gomery. He remained CofS to Montgomery for the remainder of the war, in North Africa, Sicily, Italy, and northern Europe.

Knighted in 1944, de Guingand fell out with Montgomery over the latter's attempt to take sole credit for military success and reconciling differences with Eisenhower, after which Montgomery inflicted a number of slights. De Guingand was promoted major general when he retired from the army in 1946.

de Haviland, Sir Geoffrey (1882–1965) British aircraft designer and manufacturer. Graduating from the Crystal Palace Engineering School, de Haviland designed one of the first successful British airplanes and engines (1908–10). This brought him to the attention of the British military and a position at HM Balloon Factory. Here he designed such aircraft as the FE-2, SE-1, BE-1, and BS-2. In 1914 he joined the Aircraft Manufacturing Company as chief designer and test pilot, producing, among other aircraft, the DH-4, DH-9, and DH-10. When the company went out of business (1920), he founded the De Haviland Aircraft Company (1920) and was its technical director until 1955. Most of his designs were of commercial aircraft, including the classic DH-60 Moth, which became the primary Royal Air Force (RAF) trainer.

With war looming, he produced the DH-91 Albatross (1937). During the war, to conserve metal, he designed the largely wooden Mosquito fighter, one of the best all-around aircraft of the war. He also produced some of the early British jet aircraft, including the Comet (1949) and Trident (1962). He was knighted in 1944.

Two of his three sons were killed in test flight crashes, and his company was forced to merge into the Hawker Siddeley Group in 1966.

De la Rey, Jacobus Hercules (1847–1914) Boer general. De la Rey had little education and no formal military training save experience gained in fighting the Bantus. He opposed President Kruger's policy of a preventive strike against the British. Appointed general at the beginning of the 1899–1902 Boer War, he was given command of Transvaal forces against Cape Colony in the west. He fought in the battles of the Modder River, Magersfontein, Doornkop, Zilikat's Neck, Nooitgedacht, and Tweebosch.

De la Rey excelled at guerrilla warfare and had great success against British columns, supply trains, and storage depots. At Tweebosch (7 March 1902), he captured British General Lord Methuen and destroyed his force of 1,200 men. He reluctantly agreed to a settlement with the British and then served in parliament. A staunch Afrikaner nationalist, he saw the outbreak of World War I as an opportunity to break free of British rule entirely. While on his way to start a rebellion in the Transvaal, he was accidently killed at a British roadblock.

de Lattre de Tassigny, Jean Marie Gabriel (1889–1952) French general. De Lattre graduated from St. Cyr (1910), and fought in World War I, where he was wounded six times and rose to command a battalion. After the war he fought in the Rif campaign in Morocco. After graduation from the École Supérieur de Guerre, he served as General Maxime Weygand's chief of cabinet and then CofS of Fifth Army. On the eve of World War II he commanded an infantry regiment.

During the Battle for France (May–June 1940), de Lattre commanded the 14th Infantry Division. Following the armistice he retrained what remained of the army and then commanded in Tunisia and an infantry division in France (January 1942). After the Allied landings in North Africa (8 November 1942), he deployed his troops to prevent German units from quickly reaching the Mediterranean coast, for which he was tried by Vichy and sentenced to prison. He escaped (September 1943) and made his way to Britain. Later he joined the Free French government in Algiers and commanded French troops in the invasion of Elba (June 1944) and then the Free French First Army in the invasion of southern France (August 1944). His forces liberated Belfort, and by the end of the war had fought to the Austrian border.

After the war de Lattre served on the Allied Control Commission for Germany. He was then inspector general of the army, overseeing its retraining and modernization, and then commanded Western European land forces (1948–1950). Following French defeats in Indo-China, he was sent there as both commander of French forces and high commissioner (December 1950). He restored morale, worked to turn over more of the burden of fighting the war to the Vietnamese, and won a series of pitched battles against General Vo Nguyen Giap's People's Army of Vietnam. He initiated the meat-grinder battle of Hoa Binh (December 1951–February 1952), which France won after he had already departed for France (December 1951), consumed by cancer.

de Robeck, Sir John Michael (1862–1928) British admiral. De Robeck entered the Royal Navy (1875) and served in two dozen warships before promotion to commander (1897). Promoted rear admiral (1911), he was on half-pay when World War I began. Recalled to active duty, he commanded 9th Cruiser Squadron. He was then appointed second-in-command of the Eastern Mediterranean Squadron for the Dardanelles expedition (1915).

When ill health forced the commander, Vice Admiral Sackville Carden, to relinquish his post, de Robeck led the unsuc-

cessful naval attempt to force the Dardanelles, which failed when the battleships ran into a recently laid, undetected and uncleared Turkish minefield (18 March). He then recommended that the navy wait until troops could be landed and seize terrain dominating the Narrows. From then on he steadfastly resisted pressure, including that from First Lord of the Admiralty Winston Churchill, for a renewed naval attack.

De Robeck's critics charged he doomed the Dardanelles campaign to failure. His supporters claim he simply said no to probable disaster. He commanded 2nd Battle Squadron of the Grand Fleet (1916–19), then was commander-in-chief, Mediterranean (1919–22); he was also high commissioner for Constantinople (1919–20), and ended his career as commander of the Atlantic Fleet (1922–24).

de Wet, Christiaan Rudolph (1854–1922) Boer general. Born in the Orange Free State, de Wet first saw combat in the 1867–68 Third Basuto War. In the 1880–81 First Boer War, he participated in the Battle of Majuba Hill. During the 1899–1902 Second Boer War he led an attack near Ladysmith and was then promoted general.

The outstanding guerrilla leader of the war, de Wet attacked British supply convoys and conducted hit-and-run raids. Early in 1900 he was appointed commandant general of Orange Free State forces. He launched an invasion of Cape Colony (November 1900) but was forced to withdraw (February 1901). Although he wanted to fight to the end he was persuaded to lay down his arms with the signing of a peace treaty (1902).

De Wet opposed reconciliation with the British and led a Boer revolt during World War I (November 1914–February 1915) that was crushed. Sentenced to prison, he was released after only a year.

Dean, William Frishe (1899–1981) U.S. general. Dean graduated from the University of California at Berkeley (1922) and secured a regular army infantry commission (1923). He had a variety of assignments and graduated from the Army Command and General Staff School, Fort Leavenworth (1936), the Army Industrial College (1939), and the Army War College (1940).

On U.S. entry into World II (December 1941), Dean was assistant to the secretary of the General Staff. Assigned to Headquarters, Army Ground Forces, he was promoted brigadier general (December 1942) and made assistant commander of the 44th Infantry Division, accompanying it to southern France (August 1944) and in fighting there and in Germany. As commander of the 44th (December), he was promoted major general (March 1945).

After the war Dean was on the faculty of the Army Command and General Staff School (September 1945) and assistant commandant (June 1946). He was then military governor of South Korea (September 1947), supervising elections and the inauguration of the Republic of Korea (August 1948). He then commanded 7th Infantry Division, taking it to Japan (January 1949). He commanded 24th Infantry Division (October 1949), the first U.S. ground combat unit to respond to the North Korean invasion of South Korea (25 June 1950). He assumed command of all U.S. forces in Korea and led in person the bitter defense of Taejon (July). Separated from his command, he was captured (August), the highest ranking UN Command officer taken prisoner during the war. He was awarded the Medal of Honor (February 1951) for his bravery at Taejon. Freed at the end of the war (September 1953), he became deputy commander of Sixth Army (December 1953), then retired in October 1955.

Del Valle, Pedro Augusto (1893–1978) U.S. Marine Corps general. Born in Puerto Rico, Del Valle graduated from Annapolis (1915) and was commissioned in the Marine Corps. He commanded the Mar-

ine detachment aboard battleship *Texas* during World War I. He then served in various posts, including that of naval attaché in Italy. He was the only U.S. military observer during the Italian invasion of Ethiopia (1935–36). He graduated from the Army War College (1937) and was promoted to colonel and commanded the 11th Regiment (1941).

Promoted brigadier general (August 1942), Del Valle commanded the 1st Marine Division artillery in the 1942 Guadalcanal campaign and then briefly commanded all ground units at the end of the Solomon Islands campaign (1943). He commanded III Corps artillery in the invasion of Guam and Tinian (July–August 1944). Promoted major general, he commanded the 1st Marine Division on Okinawa (April–June 1945).

After the war, Del Valle was Marine Corps inspector general (1945–48). He retired in 1948.

Delestraint, Charles Antoine (1879–1945) French general. A graduate of St. Cyr, Delestraint was captured early in World War I (1914) and spent most of the war as a POW of the Germans. After the war he joined the French armored forces but retired from the military in 1939.

Recalled to duty on the start of World War II (September 1939), at the time of the May 1940 German invasion Delestraint commanded an armor group that included Colonel Charles de Gaulle's division. He directed the counterattack at Abbeville (3–4 June). He retired again after the armistice (July), but formed a clandestine military headquarters with the intention of establishing a national redoubt on the Vercors plateau. On the recommendation of Resistance leader Henri Frenay, seconded by Jean Moulin, General de Gaulle in London appointed him head of the Secret Army in France (March 1943).

Betrayed in a trap set by the Gestapo chief in Lyon, Klaus Barbie, Delestraint was arrested in Paris (June 1943). He was executed at Dachau (19 April 1945) just before the arrival there of U.S. forces.

Dempsey, Sir Miles Christopher (1896–1969) British general. Dempsey graduated from Sandhurst (1915) and by the end of World War I was a captain. Promoted lieutenant colonel (1939), at the beginning of World War II he commanded the BEF's 13th Infantry Brigade in France, leading it with distinction in a delaying action to Dunkerque (May 1940). He then helped to train new British forces. Promoted major general (June 1941), he received command of an armored division.

Following the Battle of El Alamein, General Bernard Montgomery requested that Dempsey be transferred to command XIII Corps of Eighth Army. Subsequently promoted lieutenant general, he headed British planning for the invasion of Sicily (July) and fought there with his corps and in the invasion of Italy (September). When Montgomery moved to Britain to command Twenty-First Army Group, Dempsey took command of Second Army in the Normandy invasion (6 June 1944). Following the Allied breakout, his army raced to Belgium, liberating Brussels and Antwerp. He opposed Montgomery's cherished Operation MARKET-GARDEN, favoring an assault near Wesel. Later his army cleared the area west of the Maas, then crossed the Rhine and drove to the Baltic. He personally took the surrender of Hamburg (3 May 1945).

Already knighted, after the war Dempsey was advanced to KBE. He first commanded the reoccupation of Singapore and Malaya, then Allied land forces in Southeast Asia. Promoted full general (1946) he then became CinC in the Middle East. He retired at his own request in July 1947.

Denfeld, Lewis Emil (1891–1972) U.S. admiral. Denfeld graduated from Annapolis (1912) and during World War I served aboard destroyers on convoy duty in the North Atlantic. Following the war,

he received his first ship command, and served on a submarine and then ashore. Promoted commander (1933), he commanded Destroyer Division 11 (1935–37) and was aide to CNO Admiral William Leahy (1937–39). Promoted captain (1939), he commanded Destroyer Division 18 and then Destroyer Squadron 1 (1939–41). Assistant chief of the Bureau of Navigation (January 1942), he was promoted rear admiral (May). During 1945 he led Battleship Division 9.

After World War II, Denfeld was chief of the Bureau of Personnel (1945–46). Promoted vice admiral (January 1947), he commanded the Pacific Fleet (February) before succeeding Admiral Chester Nimitz as chief of naval operations (CNO) (December). He vigorously defended the independence and prerogatives of the navy in the so-called Revolt of the Admirals (1949), which however led to his dismissal (November) barely a month after his appointment to a second term as CNO (November). He retired in March 1950.

Denikin, Anton Ivanovich (1872–1947) Russian general. Of humble birth, Denikin distinguished himself as an officer in the Imperial Russian Army. He attended the Kiev Junker School and Academy of the General Staff, and he fought in the 1904–05 Russo-Japanese War. Promoted major general (June 1914), he was acting CofS of the Kiev District on the outbreak of World War I.

Denikin then became deputy CofS to General Aleksei Brusilov's Eighth Army. He then took command of the 4th Rifle "Iron" Brigade (September 1914) and fought with it in the Carpathians and Galicia. He took command of VIII Corps (1916) and fought alongside the Romanians during Brusilov's offensive. He was then CofS, Southwest Front.

Denikin welcomed the March 1917 Russian Revolution. That summer he became chief of staff to the supreme commander in the Aleksandr Kerensky regime, serving successively Generals Mikhail Alekseev, Brusilov, and Lavr Kornilov. He supported Kornilov's attempted coup (September) and was imprisoned with him.

Following the November 1917 Bolshevik Revolution, Denikin and Kornilov escaped (December) to join Alekseev in Don Cossack territory in south Russia. Here they formed the "White" Volunteer Army, a small force loyal to the Allies and dedicated to driving the Central Powers and the "Reds" from Russian soil. When Kornilov was killed (spring 1918), Denikin assumed control of the army. He led a series of brilliant campaigns in the north Caucasus area and along the Don, emerging at the end of the year as commander of the Armed Forces of South Russia. Having received limited Allied assistance, he launched a drive to capture Bolshevik-controlled Moscow (June 1919). His force reached Orel but was defeated (October), and by March 1920 it had been evacuated to the Crimea. Denikin then resigned his post and passed the remainder of his life in exile.

Devereux, James Patrick Sinnott (1903–88) U.S. Marine Corps general. A graduate of Loyola College, Maryland, Devereux enlisted in the Marine Corps (1923) and was commissioned two years later. When the United States entered World War II (December 1941), he was a major in charge of the 1st Battalion on Wake Island. Devereux led the 8–23 December defense of Wake Island that sank two Japanese destroyers and killed 900 men before surrendering. A POW until the end of the war, he retired from the Marine Corps as a brigadier general in 1948. He then served in Congress (1951–59).

Devers, Jacob Loucks (1887–1979) U.S. general. Devers graduated from West Point (1909) and was commissioned in the artillery. He returned there as an instructor (1912–16) and then served in Hawaii and at the Field Artillery School, Fort Sill. He did not see combat in World War I, although he served in the occupation forces in Germany (1919). Devers graduated from the Command and General Staff School (1925) and the Army War College (1939). He also served at West Point, on the War Department staff, and in the Panama Canal Zone, where he was promoted brigadier general (1939). He assumed command of 9th Infantry Division (October 1940) and was promoted major general. He commanded the Armored Force at Fort Knox (July 1941–May 1943), then the European Theater of Operations (May–December 1943) and the North African Theater of Operations, when he was also deputy supreme Allied commander in the Mediterranean (January–October 1944). Following Operation DRAGOON, the Allied landing in south France (August 1944), Devers received his long-awaited field command in Sixth Army Group (September), leading it north through the Vosges mountains to the Rhine (autumn) and then east into Baden and Bavaria (February–May 1945), linking up with Lieutenant General Mark Clark's Fifteenth Army Group in Austria.

Devers served as chief of Army Ground Forces (later renamed Army Field Forces) (June 1945) until his retirement (September 1949). He later served as chief military advisor to the UN mission attempting to resolve the Pakistan–India border dispute in Kashmir (1951–52).

Dewey, George (1837–1917) U.S. admiral. Dewey graduated from Annapolis (1858). His service in the 1861–65 Civil War included participation in the capture of New Orleans and the Battles of Port Hudson and Fort Fisher. Here he developed a reputation for coolness under pressure.

After the war Dewey returned as an instructor at Annapolis and then held a variety of commands. Promoted captain (1884) and commodore (1897), he assumed command of the Asiatic Squadron (January 1898). Immediately on receiving word of the beginning of hostilities with

Spain, he steamed from Hong Kong to the Philippines, then attacked and destroyed the Spanish squadron of seven ships at Manila (30 April 1898), at a cost to his own side of only seven wounded. Promoted rear admiral, he supported the army in its capture of Manila. Promoted admiral of the navy (March 1899), he made a brief run for the presidency of the United States but dropped out (1900) to become president of the newly formed Navy General Board. He served in that post until his death, helping to create a stronger U.S. Navy. He also chaired the Joint Army–Navy Board, beginning in 1903.

Diaz, Armando (1861–1928) Italian field marshal. Diaz joined the Italian army and served in the 1911–12 Italo-Turkish war. Promoted major general (1914) and lieutenant general (1916), he commanded XXIII Corps on the Isonzo front. Following the Caporetto debacle, he succeeded General Luigi Cadorna as chief of staff (November 1917), halting Austrian-German forces on the Piave.

Diaz did much to improve morale and conditions for his men. Although he was accused of being too slow to take the offensive, his subsequent attack at Vittorio Veneto (October 1918) routed the Austro-Hungarian army and earned him the title Duke of Vittorio Veneto (1920). Replaced as CofS by General Pietro Badoglio (November 1919), Diaz subsequently served as minister of war under Mussolini (1922–24) and reorganized the army. He was made a marshal in 1924.

Dickman, Joseph Theodore (1857–1927) U.S. general. Dickman graduated from West Point (1881). He fought against the Apache Indians and in Cuba during the 1898 Spanish–American War and the Philippines during the 1900–02 Philippine-American War. He also served with the Relief Expedition during the 1900–01 Boxer Rebellion. He graduated from the

Army War College (1905) and was promoted colonel (1914).

After the United States entered World War I (April 1917), Dickman was promoted brigadier general and then temporary major general in command of the 85th Division. He commanded 3rd Division in France, where he won renown for the defense of Château-Thierry (May 1918) and his role in stopping the German Marne Offensive. One of the best U.S. combat commanders of the war, he led IV Corps in the St. Mihiel and Meuse–Argonne Offensives. Later he commanded I Corps. Following the armistice, Dickman commanded Third Army in the German occupation. He returned to the U.S. (April 1919) and commanded the Southern Department (later VIII) Corps until his retirement in 1921.

Dietl, Eduard (1890–1944) German general. Dietl joined the army as a cadet candidate (1909) and was commissioned (1911) and assigned to the Bavarian 11th Regiment. He saw combat in World War I, being wounded several times. He continued in the Reichswehr after the war and joined the Nazi party. As a company commander he provided military instruction to Adolf Hitler's Brown Shirts and was active in the Munich Beer Hall Putsch (November 1923).

Promoted lieutenant colonel (February 1934), he commanded several infantry regiments. Promoted colonel (January 1935), he commanded the 99th Alpine Regiment during the Austrian *Anschluss* (March 1938). Promoted brigadier general (April 1938), he commanded 3rd Mountain Division (1938–40). He earned renown during the invasion of Norway (April 1940) at Narvik. Although outnumbered, his forces held out and he became known as "The Hero of Narvik." Promoted major general for this action (May 1940), Dietl commanded Mountain Corps Norway (June 1940). He was then promoted lieutenant general (July 1940).

Dietl commanded Twentieth Mountain

Army (January 1942), known as Lapp-land Army and was promoted full general. He died in a plane crash (23 June 1944) while returning to Norway following a meeting with Hitler.

Dietrich, Josef (1892–1966) German SS general. With little education, "Sepp" Dietrich joined the army (1911) and fought in World War I in an artillery unit, rising to the rank of sergeant. Discharged at the end of the war, he fought in the Freikorps against the Communists and then joined the Nazi party (1923). For many years, he commanded Adolf Hitler's personal bodyguard, which became the *Leibstandarte Adolf Hitler* (LAH). He took the lead in turning the LAH into a motorized infantry regiment. One of the leading figures in the Waffen SS (Armed SS), he led the LAH in the invasions of Poland and France. Raised to division status, the LAH then fought in Greece, Yugoslavia, and the Soviet Union.

Dietrich took the division to Italy (July 1943). He then commanded I Panzer Corps. Back on the Russian front (October), he was then posted to France in time for the Normandy invasion (6 June 1944). Promoted SS *Obergruppenführer* and full general in the Waffen SS, he took command of Sixth Panzer Army (October 1944) to spearhead the Ardennes offensive (Battle of the Bulge, December 1944), during which he was implicated in the massacre of U.S. soldiers (at Malmédy) and Belgian civilians. In early 1945 Sixth Panzer Army transferred to Hungary. After the war he was tried and convicted for his involvement in the Malmédy massacre but was released from prison in 1955.

Dill, Sir John Greer (1881–1944) British field marshal. Commissioned from Sandhurst (1901), Dill joined his regiment in South Africa and saw action in the 1899–1902 Boer War. When World War I began, he was studying at the Staff College at Camberley. He then became brigade major in the 8th Division (October). Appointed to the staff of the Canadian Corps and promoted major (1916), he saw action at Ypres (1917). At the end of the war he was on the operations branch of General Headquarters and temporary brigadier general.

After the war, Dill held a variety of posts. Promoted major general (1930), he commanded the Staff College (1931). Later he was director of military operations and intelligence at the War Office (1934). Promoted lieutenant general (1936), he served in Palestine. He was then promoted full general and knighted (1937). When World War II began (September 1939) he commanded I Corps in the BEF in France. He was first vice chief of the Imperial General Staff (April 1940), then its chief (May).

Dill's caution following the defeat of France (July) put him at loggerheads with Prime Minister Winston Churchill, who saw him as an obstructionist and had him retired with the rank of field marshal and posted as governor-designate of Bombay (November 1941). When Churchill visited the United States for a planning conference (December 1941), Dill went along as acting head of the British Staff Mission. His tact and good sense led to his being named its permanent head. He became close with President Franklin Roosevelt and U.S. military leaders, especially General George Marshall. Widely praised, he died in Washington and is buried in Arlington National Cemetery, the first foreign soldier so honored.

Djemal Pasha (1872–1922) Turkish general and government minister. Djemal graduated from the War College (1895) and was assigned to Salonika where he joined the reformist Young Turk movement (1906) that overthrew Sultan Abdul Hamid (1908). Political power came to be concentrated in the hands of Enver Pasha, Talât Pasha, and Djemal Pasha.

Djemal commanded a division in the 1912–13 Balkan Wars. He also played a prominent role in the reign of terror unleashed by the government to crush political opposition. He entered the cabinet (1913) and became minister of the navy (1914). In the July 1914 European crisis, he attempted to arrange an alliance with the Entente powers, which failed. He then supported friendly relations with the Central Powers but was a reluctant convert to joining their side in the war.

After Turkey entered the war (November 1914), Djemal continued as navy minister. He played a key role in fighting in the Arab lands and became governor of Syria (1915) where he treated the inhabitants with extreme ruthlessness, which in turn led to revolts against Turkish rule. His inept 1915 raid on the Suez Canal was easily defeated. After the fall of Jerusalem (December 1917), he left Syria for Constantinople. Forced from office along with other Young Turks (early October 1918), he fled the country the following month.

Dobell, Sir Charles McPherson (1869–1954) British general. Dobell entered the British army and saw action in the 1899–1902 Boer War and the relief of Peking in the 1900–01 Boxer Rebellion. During World War I he directed the conquest of German Kamerun (Cameroon) (1914–16). Sent to Egypt, he served under General Sir Archibald Murray and commanded British troops in attempts to take Gaza (March, April 1917). Relieved of command, he subsequently commanded a division in India (1917–19).

Doihara, Kenji (1883–1948) Japanese general. Doihara graduated from the Military Academy (1904) and the General Staff College (1912). During World War I he held staff and intelligence assignments in China (1913–18). He then was military advisor to Chinese warlords, including "Tiger of Manchuria" Chang Tso-lin (1918–29). Promoted colonel (1927), he was chief of the Special Service Agency at Mukden (1931–32) and is widely re-

garded as having set up the 1931 Mukden Incident that provided the excuse for the Japanese takeover of all Manchuria. Excelling at special operations, he became known as "Lawrence of Manchuria." He was responsible for the abduction of Henry Pu-yi, later installed as emperor of the Japanese puppet state of Manchukuo.

Promoted major general (1933), Doihara played a major role in Japanese expansion into north China (1933–35). He negotiated the Chin-Doihara Agreement (June 1935) that allowed the Japanese Kwantung Army into Inner Mongolia. Promoted lieutenant general (1936), he commanded 14th Infantry Division in combat in north China (1937–38). Despite suffering a serious reverse, he was promoted to command Fifth Army. He then took command of the Japanese Military Academy (1940) and was inspector general of military aviation (1941). Promoted full general (October 1941) after Hideki Tōjō became premier, his commands during World War II were limited to a succession of reserve armies. After the war he was tried, convicted, and executed (1948) on war crimes charges resulting from his activities in pre-war Manchuria.

Dollmann, Friedrich (1876–1944) German general. Dollmann fought in World War I and continued in the Reichswehr afterward. As colonel general, he led Seventh Army at the beginning of World War II and in the invasion of France (May–June 1940), when his forces penetrated the Maginot Line as French resistance collapsed. His army then remained in France in occupation duty. Responsible for the defense of Brittany and Normandy against invasion, he anticipated Operation OVERLORD and wanted a strengthening of forces in Normandy, but reinforcements went to Fifteenth Army in the Pas de Calais area instead. When the weather worsened, Dollmann ordered readiness relaxed. He was away from his headquarters when the invasion actually occurred (6 June 1944). He died of a heart attack the same month after ordering a counter-attack.

Dönitz, Karl (1891–1980) German admiral. Dönitz joined the navy as a cadet (1910). He began World I on the light cruiser *Breslau* but transferred to submarines (1916). While he was in command of *U-68*, the submarine was sunk and he was taken prisoner (October 1918).

Dönitz remained in the Reichsmarine after the war and was appointed head of the new submarine service (1935). Promoted rear admiral (October 1939) just after the beginning of World War II, he was also made flag officer of submarines. Although he deplored the small size of his force and Adolf Hitler's shift in allocation of resources away from U-boats, he inflicted significant damage against Allied shipping early in the war, especially in the North Atlantic. He clashed with Grand Admiral Erich Raeder, who wanted a balanced fleet and more conventional naval warfare.

Promoted to vice admiral (1940) and to admiral (1942), Dönitz succeeded Raeder as commander of the navy (January 1943). Despite his best efforts (including new tactics of wolf packs, night surface attacks, submarine tankers, and air reconnaissance), the Germans had lost the Battle of the Atlantic by mid-year. Innovations late in the war could not reverse this.

Named as his successor by Hitler in his will (30 April 1945), Dönitz presided over the last days of the Third Reich and surrendered unconditionally to the Allies (7 May). Tried and convicted of war crimes at Nuremberg, he was sentenced to ten years in prison and was released in October 1956.

Donovan, William Joseph (1883–1959) U.S. army officer and director of intelligence operations. "Wild Bill" Donovan graduated from Columbia University (1905), where he also earned his law degree (1907). He practiced law in New York City and also joined the New York National Guard (1912), seeing service along the Mexican border as a major (1916). During World War I he served with the 27th Division in France and rose to colonel. Wounded three times, he won the Medal of Honor. He then served briefly as a U.S. military observer in Asia.

After the war Donovan became active in Republican politics. He was a U.S. attorney and served in the office of the attorney general. Beginning in the late 1930s he made a number of trips abroad for the U.S. government and studied the British intelligence system (1940–41). President Franklin Roosevelt asked him to set up a U.S. intelligence agency, and he became Coordinator of Information (July 1941). This became the Office of Strategic Services (OSS), with Donovan as director (June 1942).

The OSS gathered intelligence and conducted covert and special operations in the European Theater and in India and Burma (General Douglas MacArthur would not permit it in his area of command). President Harry S Truman dissolved the OSS after the war (October 1945). Donovan was made a brigadier general (1943) and then promoted major general (November 1944).

Following the war Donovan served as aide to Justice Robert H. Jackson at the Nuremberg International War Crimes Tribunal. He was ambassador to Thailand (1953–54).

Doolittle, James Harold (1896–1993) U.S. Army Air Forces general. A student at the University of California, Doolittle left school (October 1917) to enlist in the Aviation Section of the Signal Corps. Commissioned (March 1918), he underwent pilot training and became a flight instructor. During the 1920s he gained fame through a series of pioneering flights. He resigned his commission (1930) to work for Shell Oil but continued to fly and set aviation records. He returned to active duty as a major (July 1940).

Following U.S. entry into World War II (December 1941), Doolittle was promoted lieutenant colonel and assigned to Washington, where he planned a bombing raid against Japan. The resulting strike, involving sixteen B-25 bombers and two aircraft carriers (18 April 1942) earned him advancement to brigadier general, the Medal of Honor, and assignment to the European theater of operations.

Doolittle took command of Twelfth Air Force in North Africa (September 1942), heading it through the early part of the Italian campaign. He then assumed command of Fifteenth Air Force (November 1943) and Eighth Air Force (January 1944), whereupon he ordered fighters to switch from escorting bombers to pursuing German aircraft. He was promoted temporary major general and then temporary lieutenant general (March 1944).

Following the end of the war in Europe, Eighth Air Force was sent to the Pacific but the war ended before any missions were flown. Doolittle then resigned his commission (January 1946) to return to Shell Oil.

Doorman, Karel W.F.M. (1889–1942) Netherlands admiral. Rear Admiral Doorman commanded the Royal Netherlands naval force in the East Indies at the beginning of World War II. He was appointed to command (2 February 1942) the ABDA (American, British, Dutch, Australian) Command strike force of five cruisers and ten destroyers that had been operating off Sumatra and Java against Japanese convoys for some months.

Northeast of Soerabaja in the Makassar Straits, Doorman prepared to engage a Japanese invasion force headed for Java. It was escorted by two heavy and two light cruisers and thirteen destroyers, commanded by Rear Admiral Takeo Takagi. In the ensuing seven-hour Battle of the Java Sea (27 February 1942), the Allied force was crushed. Although his

ships generally outshot the Japanese, Doorman was without air power for reconnaissance, scouting, or spotting. He also suffered from poor communications. The Japanese enjoyed superiority in torpedoes and tactics.

No Japanese ships were sunk and only one destroyer was badly damaged. On the Allied side only three cruisers and five destroyers survived. Doorman's flagship, cruiser *De Ruyter*, was among those sunk, the admiral going down with his ship.

Dorman-Smith, Sir Eric (1895–1969) British general. Dorman-Smith was one of the first British officers to understand the revolution in armored warfare. Serving in the 1930s as part of the SD-2 Section of the War Department, he helped develop British doctrine for the Royal Tank Corps. After a period in India, he was commandant of the Middle East Staff College, Haifa (1940).

On the invasion of Egypt by the Italian Tenth Army, Dorman-Smith was assigned to the staff of General Richard O'Connor, commander of the Western Desert Force, and played a major role in the subsequent British victory at Beda Fomm (February 1941). Then, as General Sir Claude Auchinleck's CofS, he planned the British victory at Alam el Halfa (July). Throughout, he stressed the importance of mobile warfare.

When Prime Minister Winston Churchill relieved Auchinleck (July 1943), Major General Dorman-Smith went with him, ostensibly because he had abandoned the strategically worthless position of Tobruk. After the war he successfully sued Churchill for libel over the latter's history of the Second World War and statement that British troops had lost confidence in Auchinleck and Dorman-Smith, forcing Churchill to revise his account of the North African campaign.

Dornberger, Walter (1895–1980) German general and rocket scientist. Dornberger served in the artillery in World War I, ending the war as a lieutenant. He remained in the Reichswehr and, still on active duty, graduated from the Berlin Technical Institute in mechanical engineering (1929). He became director of the army's ballistics weapons department (1930) and then began work on a prototype rocket, the A-1 (1932), bringing Wernher von Braun into the project. The two men were the leaders of the team that developed the World War II V-2 rocket. Colonel Dornberger established the research facility at Peenemünde (1937), where the Luftwaffe also worked to develop the V-1 buzz bomb. Although Hitler was opposed, the experiments continued.

Test firings on Dornberger's A-4 began in 1942, and in 1943 it received Hitler's enthusiastic support. Dornberger was promoted to brigadier general (May 1943). Although the British struck Peenemünde with a massive air attack (August), this set back the program by only six months, and Dornberger relocated manufacturing to the Harz mountains.

Surrendering to the Allies at the end of the war, Dornberger was charged as a war criminal for V-2 rocket attacks on Antwerp and London, but he was never brought to trial. He moved to the United States (1947) to become a missile consultant to the U.S. Air Force.

Douglas, William Sholto, 1st Baron of Kirtleside (1893–1969) British air marshal. Douglas left Oxford to fight in World War I in the field artillery. He transferred to the Royal Flying Corps (1916), and by the end of the war was a squadron commander.

After the war Douglas left the service to become chief pilot for Handley Page, but rejoined the RAF as a squadron leader (1920). He graduated from the Imperial Defense College and was director of staff studies at the Air Ministry (1936). Advanced to air vice marshal, he was assistant chief of air staff (1938).

Douglas was a leading critic of Air Chief Marshal Sir Hugh Dowding, whom

he succeeded (25 November 1940) as head of Fighter Command, when he was also promoted air marshal. He immediately instituted offensive operations and worked to improve night fighting techniques. Promoted air chief marshal (end of 1942), he was deputy to Air Marshal Arthur Tedder in the Middle East, then commanded Allied air forces under General Dwight Eisenhower in North Africa (April 1943) before succeeding Tedder. Preceding the invasion of France (June 1944), he headed Coastal Command and commanded British Expeditionary Air Forces, with responsibility for securing air space over the English Channel.

After the war Douglas commanded the British Air Forces of Occupation in Germany and was knighted (January 1946). Promoted marshal of the RAF, he succeeded Field Marshal Bernard Montgomery (June) as commander of British forces in Europe and military governor of the British zone in Germany. On his retirement (1948), he was raised to the peerage as a baron.

Douhet, Giulio (1869–1930) Italian general and leading air power theorist. Douhet joined the Italian Army as an artillery officer (1882). By 1909 he commanded Italy's first military aviation unit and soon was advocating a separate air branch.

Outspoken in advocacy of aviation during World War I, Douhet also criticized the Italian High Command. Convicted by a military court for publicly denouncing Italy's military leaders in a memorandum to the cabinet (1916), he was sentenced to prison. The Italian defeat at Caporetto proved his claims, and the government recalled him to service (December 1917) as head of Italian Army aviation. Promoted general (1924), he was briefly head of aviation under Mussolini (1922).

In 1921 Douhet published *The Command of the Air*. In this most influential book, he argued that aircraft were instruments of great offensive potential that could alone win a war because there was no effective defense against them, and that civilian morale would be shattered by bombardment of population centers. An enemy air force should be dealt with by destroying its ground installations and factories. He also argued that in the interest of economy for only one basic aircraft type: a self-defending bomber "battle-plane." His writings were widely translated and impacted air doctrine worldwide.

Dowding, Sir Hugh Caswall Tremenheere, 1st Baron (1882–1970) British air marshal. Commissioned in the artillery out of Sandhurst (1900), Dowding served in India and the Far East and attended the Staff College at Camberley (1910–12). He learned to fly (1912) and then transferred to the Royal Flying Corps (1914). During World War I, he held a variety of staff posts in England and France. Promoted brigadier general (1917), he remained in the Royal Air Force after the war as a group captain. He commanded No. 1 Group (1922–25) and then air units in the Middle East during the remainder of the 1920s. He was next a member of the Air Council for Research and Development (1930–36), pushing development of radar and the Hurricane and Spitfire fighters.

Named commander-in-chief of RAF Fighter Command (1936), Dowding prepared it for the Second World War. He clashed with Prime Minister Winston Churchill and succeded in getting the dispatch of additional air units to France canceled. Nicknamed "Stuffy" for his lack of humor, he masterfully directed Fighter Command in the pivotal Battle of Britain (July–October 1940). Succeeded by Air Marshal William Sholto Douglas (25 November), he served on an aircraft production mission to the United States (1940–1942). He then retired (1942) and was made a baron (1943).

Doyle, James Henry (1897–1981) U.S. admiral. Commissioned in the navy on graduation from Annapolis (1920), Doyle earned a law degree from George Washington University (1929) and was in the office of the Navy's Judge Advocate General (1932–35). During World War II he was an operations officer and staff commander of Amphibious Forces South Pacific, serving in the Guadalcanal and Solomons Islands campaigns. He then commanded a cruiser and was promoted rear admiral (1947).

In charge of submarine demolition at Coronado, California when the 1950–53 Korean War began, Doyle went to Japan at the behest of Far East Command commander General Douglas MacArthur, who valued his experience in amphibious tactics. In command of Amphibious Forces Far East (Task Force 90), he played a key role in the rapid buildup of men and supplies from Japan to Korea. He participated in planning for, and had charge of, landing X Corps at Inchon (15 September 1950). This occurred without incident and led to the recapture of Seoul and disintegration of the North Korean Army.

Doyle then oversaw the landing of X Corps at Wonsan (25 October), and, following entry of the Peoples Republic of China into the war, had charge of the evacuation of troops, civilians, and supplies from Hŭngnam and other North Korean east coast ports (December 1950). After the war he was president of the Navy Board of Inspection and Survey in Washington, DC, then chaired the Joint Amphibious Board. He retired in 1953.

Drum, Hugh Aloysius (1879–1951) U.S. general. Drum left Boston College and was commissioned from the ranks, and served in the Philippines (1898). He graduated from the Army Staff College (1912), saw service on the Mexican border, and went to France with the AEF after U.S. entry into World War I (April 1917). He rose to be deputy CofS, then

CofS, First U.S. Army and was promoted temporary brigadier general (October 1918).

After the war Drum held various assignments and was again promoted brigadier general (December 1922). He was assistant CofS of the army (1923–26), then commanded 1st Infantry Brigade (1936–37) and 1st Infantry Division (1927–30). He was inspector general of the army (1930–31). Promoted major general (December 1931), he was CG First Army (1931–33). Deputy CofS of the Army (1933–35), he then commanded the Hawaiian Department (1935–37), then Second Army (1937–38). Promoted lieutenant general (August 1939), in the 1939–40 army maneuvers in New York State he had troops carry wooden weapons and drive trucks with signs "tank" and "cannon" on them. While this helped gain national support for army preparedness, it led to criticism from within the service that he was attacking his superiors, including CofS General George Marshall.

Drum assumed that, as senior officer in permanent rank, on U.S. entry into World War II he would receive command of the army to invade Europe. He thus declined the command in China that went to Lieutenant General Joseph Stilwell. He then tried to secure the command, thus ending his career. He continued as First Army commander until he retired (October 1943).

Dubail, Auguste (1851–1934) French general. Dubail entered St. Cyr (1868), served in the 1870–71 Franco-German War, and graduated from the War College (1878). In 1911 he became French Army CofS. A member of the Supreme War Council, he negotiated with Britain regarding the size and disposition of forces in a possible war with Germany.

At the beginning of World War I, Dubail commanded First Army and carried out the planned offensive into Lorraine. Although this met with rebuff, he withdrew the army in good order and anchored the French line. In early September the French and British won the Battle of the Marne. This critical victory would not have been possible had his army given way or not been able to send reinforcements. He continued to carry out vigorous attacks and counterattacks and, at the end of the year, his sector was the largest on the Western Front.

Dubail then formally assumed command of the Eastern Group (January 1914), a role he had in fact held since September 1914. The Battle of Verdun was his undoing. In early 1915 he had officially stated that defenses there were adequate; but he worried when French Army commander General Joseph Joffre stripped the fortress complex of its artillery, and he warned Joffre of a possible attack. Nonetheless Joffre made him the principal scapegoat for the Verdun debacle and removed him from command (March), the highest-ranking officer ousted. He finished the war as military governor of Paris.

Duchêne, Denis Auguste (1862–1950) French general. Duchêne graduated from St. Cyr and served in Indo-China; by 1912 he was a colonel in the 69th Infantry Regiment. At the beginning of World War I, he was promoted to general of brigade. He became interim commander of the 42nd Division (October 1914), then was promoted to major general and took command of XXXII Corps (March 1915). He then commanded Tenth Army and led it in support of the Fifth and Sixth Armies during the disastrous Nivelle Offensive (April 1917).

Duchêne took command of Sixth Army (December 1917) with the task of defending along the Aisne River. The Allies expected a German attack, but he intended to retain the high ground of Chemin des Dames and ignored General Henri-Philippe Pétain's call for an elastic defense, instead placing the bulk of his twelve divisions forward in trenches along a twenty-five-mile front. Attacked by seventeen German divisions (May 1918),

Sixth Army collapsed. Duchêne was then sacked in June 1918.

Durand-Viel, Georges Edmond Just (1875–1959) French admiral. Durand-Viel entered the École Navale (1892) and became a torpedo specialist. He served in submarines and became known for his scientific inventions, including a telescopic sight that bore his name. During World War I he commanded a torpedo boat in the Adriatic, and then served in the military section of the cabinet, helping to coordinate anti-submarine operations. He then commanded a torpedo boat squadron in the Levant. After the war he attended the Naval War College and held increasingly important assignments at sea and at the ministry in Paris. He was promoted rear admiral (1924). He was then director of the École de Guerre and Centre des Hautes Études Navales (1927).

Promoted vice admiral (1928), he commanded the 1st Squadron (1929).

Durand-Viel became chief of the Naval Staff (May 1931) and continued the task of rebuilding the fleet begun in the 1920s by his predecessors and by Minister of Marine George Leygues. Under his leadership, France began construction of the *Dunkerque* class battle cruisers to counter the German *Deutschlands*, the powerful *Richelieu* class battleships, six-inch-gun *La Galissonnière* class cruisers, *Mogador* class and smaller *Hardi* and *Fier* class destroyers. By the time of his retirement on reaching the age limit (March 1937), France had built or was in the process of building a fast modern fleet. Durand-Viel was then vice president of the Suez Canal Company. His successor Admiral Jean Darlan refused to recall him to active service on the start of World War II (September 1939) and he played no part in the war.

E

Eaker, Ira Clarence (1896–1987) U.S. Air Force general. Eaker graduated from Southwestern State Teachers College in Oklahoma (1917) and was commissioned in the infantry when the U.S. entered World War I (April 1917). He transferred to the Aviation Section of the Signal Corps and became a pilot (1918). Following a tour in the Philippines (1919–22), he served in the office of the chief of the Air Service (1924–26). He earned a degree in journalism from the University of Southern California (1933) and was promoted major (1935). Among his accomplishments as a pilot was the first transcontinental instrument flight. He graduated from the Air Corps Tactical School (1936) and the Command and General Staff School (1937). In 1937 he co-wrote with Henry Arnold *This Flying Game*, a popular book on aviation. He followed this book with two more books, *Winged Warfare* (1941) and *Army Flier* (1942). He also traveled to Britain and observed the Royal Air Force in combat. Promoted temporary colonel, Eaker commanded the 20th Pursuit Group (1941).

Promoted temporary brigadier general (January 1942), Eaker was sent to England to head 8th Bomber Command (July), and he led the first U.S. heavy bomber (B-17) raid on German-occupied Europe (August). Promoted temporary major general (September), he commanded Eighth Air Force (December) and

helped direct the strategic bombing campaign of Germany. Promoted temporary lieutenant general (September 1943), he commanded Allied Air Forces in the Mediterranean (January 1944). He completed his military career as deputy commander Army Air Forces and then chief of the Air Staff (1945–47). He retired in August 1947 prior to the official formation of the U.S. Air Force but was then promoted to full general in retirement.

Eberhardt, Andrei Augustovich (1856–1919) Russian admiral. Eberhardt rose to become chief of the Russian Naval General Staff (1908). Appointed CinC of the Black Sea Fleet (1911), his command consisted mostly of old vessels. His appeals for an active defense plan were rejected. Capable and vigorous, during World War I he organized mining operations in defense of Russia's Black Sea ports and bombarded the coast of Turkish Anatolia, concentrating on mining areas and Bosphorus fortifications. His failure to counter the German submarine threat and prevent bombardment of the Russian coastline by Turkish cruisers led to his replacement (July 1916). He then became a member of the State Council.

Eichelberger, Robert Lawrence (1886–1961) U.S. general. Eichelberger attended Ohio State University, graduated from West Point (1909), and was commissioned in the infantry. He was involved in training during World War I. He served in the Siberian Expeditionary Force (1918–19) and then saw service in the Philippines and at Tientsin (Tianjin). He served in the intelligence division of the General Staff (1921–24) and graduated from the Command and General Staff School (1926), remaining at Fort Leavenworth as a staff officer (1926–29). He graduated from the Army War College (1930) and was at West Point (1931–35) and secretary to the General Staff (1935–38). Promoted colonel (1938), he commanded the 30th Infantry Regiment at San Francisco. Promoted brigadier general, he was superintendent at West Point (1940–42).

Promoted major general, Eichelberger commanded the 77th infantry Division (March 1942), then XI Corps (June). He then commanded X Corps in the Pacific Theater, leading it in combat in New Guinea (September). Promoted lieutenant general (October), he won a series of victories over the Japanese in New Guinea and New Britain (November 1942–July 1944). As commander of Eighth Army (September 1944), he landed on Leyte Island (December) and then directed operations on Luzon (January–April 1945), including the liberation of Manila (March). He then took much of the rest of the Philippines. Eighth Army then assumed responsibility for the occupation of Japan (January 1946). Returning to the U.S. (September 1948), he retired as a full general (1954).

Eichhorn, Hermann von (1848–1918) German field marshal. Eichhorn joined the Prussian army (1866), participated in the 1866 Austro-Prussian and 1870–71 Franco-German Wars, attended the Kriegsakademie, and rose rapidly through various staff and command positions. He was promoted major general (1897) and lieutenant general (1901). He then commanded Seventh Army Inspection (1912) and was promoted full general (1913).

Badly injured in a riding accident, Eich-horn did not receive command in World War I until January 1915, when he took the newly formed Tenth Army in East Prussia and led it to victory in the Second Battle of the Masurian Lakes (February 1915) and in subsequent fighting. He then took command of Army Group Eichhorn (Eighth and Tenth Armies) (July 1916) and operated with success against the Russians in the northern sectors of the Eastern Front until March 1918. He was promoted field marshal (December 1917).

Following the signing of the Peace of Brest-Litovsk, Eichhorn went to Kiev as commander of a new army group to occupy Ukraine and the Crimea. Although assisted by his capable chief of staff Lieutenant General Wilhelm Groener, he had only limited success in stabilizing the political situation there and in harnessing resources for the Central Powers. He was assassinated in Kiev by a young revolutionary. He was the only German of his rank to suffer violent death during the war.

Eicke, Theodore (1892–1943) German SS general. Eicke was a paymaster in the army during World War I and a policeman afterward, but had difficulty holding jobs because of his extreme right-wing political views. He joined the Nazi party (1928) and then the SS (1930). He fled to Italy (1932) following a political bombing but returned to Germany when the Nazis came to power. Heinrich Himmler appointed him commandant of Dachau concentration camp (1933). He was then promoted *SS-Gruppenführer* and made inspector of concentration camps and commander of the SS guard formations (1934). He took command of the Waffen SS (Armed SS) *Totenkopf* Division (1939) and fought with it in Poland, France, and the Soviet Union. Considered by many in the regular army as a brutal butcher, he was idolized by his men. He died on the Eastern Front when his plane was shot down.

Einem, Karl von (1853–1934) German general. Commissioned in the cavalry during the Franco-Prussian War, Einem was admitted to the General Staff (1880) without having attended the Kriegsakademie. He was minister of war (1906–09), then took command of VII Corps.

During World War I Einem led VII Corps into France as part of General Karl von Bülow's Second Army. He replaced the ailing commander of Third Army, General Max Baron von Hausen (September 1914). Promoted full general (January 1915), Einem headed Third Army until the end of the war. He held his sector of the Western Front in Champagne against a succession of Allied attacks until the Meuse–Argonne Offensive (September 1918) forced his retreat. He retired in January 1919.

Eisenhower, Dwight David (1890–1960) U.S. general and president. Commissioned in the infantry on graduation from West Point (1915), Eisenhower served in training assignments and did not see combat in World War I. He was then in the Panama Canal Zone and graduated from the Command and General Staff School (1926) and the Army War College (1928). He served in the War Department (1933–35) and in the Philippines (1935–39).

In 1941 Eisenhower was chief of staff of Third Army and was promoted temporary brigadier general (September). After U.S. entry into World War II, he was assistant chief of the Army War Plans Division (1941–42) and helped formulate the "Europe First" strategy. Promoted major general (April 1942), he went to London as commander both of the European Theater of Operations and U.S. forces in Europe (June). He directed the Allied invasion of North Africa (8 November 1942) and the invasions of Sicily (July 1943) and Italy (September). He was then commander of the Allied Expeditionary Force to invade Western Europe (December 1943). Promoted general of the army (December 1944), he oversaw the Normandy invasion (6 June 1944) and directed the defeat of Germany from the west. As supreme commander, Eisen-

hower showed a tendency to compromise and followed a broad-front strategy, but he was nonetheless a superb coalition leader.

Eisenhower commanded the occupation forces in Germany (May–November 1945), then returned to the United States as CofS of the Army until his retirement (February 1948). He was president of Columbia University (1948–50), when he took leave to become the first Supreme Allied Commander Europe and organize the North Atlantic Treaty Organization (NATO) headquarters in Paris. In November 1952 he was elected president of the United States. As president (1953–61) he emphasized nuclear forces at the expense of conventional arms ("More bang for a buck"), and he strengthened U.S. commitments around the globe during the Cold War.

Enver Pasha (1881–1922) Turkish general. Enver graduated from the military academy and entered the Ottoman Army and was one of the organizers of the 1908 Young Turk Revolution. Military attaché in Berlin (1909–11), he served with distinction during the 1911–12 Italo-Turkish War, then led the *coup d'etat* that gave the Young Turks full power (23 January 1913). He then became army chief of staff.

Promoted brigadier general, Enver became minister of war (February 1914). Although he always put Turkey's interests first, he played a key role in bringing his country into the war on the side of the Central Powers. As chief architect of Turkey's wartime military policy, he sought to expand his country's power into the Caucasus region and Central Asia.

When Turkey entered World War I (October 1914), Enver assumed personal command of Third Army facing Russia. His plans there were unrealistic, and his offensives met defeat at the hands of capable Russian commander, General Nikolai Yudenich. Enver's interest in the Caucasus intensified with the March 1917 Russian Revolution, depriving the

Germans of forces to meet General Edmund Allenby's Palestine offensive.

Enver's reputation was further damaged by Turkish massacres of civilians in Armenia. When the Young Turks fell from power (October 1918), he fled the country. He died in Uzbekistan while leading anti-Soviet Turkic rebels.

Essen, Nikolai von (1860–1915) Russian admiral. A graduate of the Naval College (1880) and Nikolaevsky Naval Academy (1886), Essen served in the Pacific and the Mediterranean. During the 1904–05 Russo-Japanese War he briefly commanded a battleship. At Port Arthur, he then moved to shore duty and was taken prisoner during his defence of the Tiger Peninsula guarding the entrance to the base (January 1905). Promoted rear admiral (1908), he then was CinC of the Baltic Fleet (1909). His principal task was to prevent a German attack against Petrograd through the Gulf of Finland. On his own initiative he ordered a protective minefield laid across the entrance of the gulf. Promoted admiral (1913), his hope of conducting offensive actions during war against Germany was blocked by his superiors.

During World War I, acting under authority of the army general commanding Petrograd, Essen managed to secure a free hand for his light forces to begin limited offensive operations (autumn 1914). These included extensive mining of the south and west Baltic Sea aimed at disrupting German trade and communications. There were also naval skirmishes with the Germans, but the overall defensive policy of his superiors cost an opportunity to catch a large part of the German Baltic Fleet's light forces at Libau (May 1915). His untimely death deprived the Russian Baltic Fleet of a capable and energetic leader.

Esteva, Jean Pierre (1880–1951) French admiral. Esteva entered the Naval Academy (1898) and held a variety of assignments on graduation, including in the Far East. During World War I he distinguished himself in the Dardanelles campaign (1915), when he was wounded. After the war he attended the École Supérieure de Marine (1920). A specialist in naval aviation, he was promoted rear admiral (1929) and vice admiral (1935). Inspector general of naval forces, he was then promoted full admiral (September 1937). He took command of French Naval Forces South at Toulon (August 1939) just before the beginning of World War II.

Under threat of Italian entry into the war, Esteva moved his headquarters to Bizerte in North Africa (17 May 1940), and his units saw action in the eastern Mediterranean in cooperation with British naval forces. Following the French capitulation, he became resident general of Tunisia (July 1940–May 1943). After the Allied invasion of North Africa (8 November 1942), he protested against the landing of Luftwaffe aircraft in French North Africa. But, loyal to the Vichy government, he went along with Pierre Laval's order placing French military bases in North Africa at the disposition of the Germans and invited French troops to cooperate with the German forces (11 November).

The Germans flew Esteva back to France (7 May 1943) and he retired. Arrested after the liberation of Paris and charged with failure to resist the German buildup in Tunisia (September 1944), he was sentenced (March 1945) to "military degradation" and life imprisonment, but was released because of failing health (August 1950) shortly before his death.

Estienne, Jean Baptiste (1860–1936) French general. A graduate of the École Polytechnique, Estienne was commissioned in the artillery. As a proponent of military innovation, from 1909 he pushed the development of French military aviation, which for a time led the world. At the beginning of World War I, he fought in Belgium (August 1914) and in the Battle of the Marne (September). In 1915 he commanded the artillery in the Vaux sector and then at Douaumont.

Estienne is best known as the father of French armor forces. During World War I, after the British had already started their own tank program, he wrote to French Army Commander General Joseph Joffre (December 1915), suggesting that France build caterpillar-type vehicles similar to the Holt tractors used by the British to move their artillery. After investigation, Joffre ordered 400 light tanks from the Schneider works.

In 1916 Estienne organized and commanded the French tank unit, the *Artillerie d'Assault*. His first general order (January 1917) called for tank attacks to be mounted in early morning and in fog, if possible. Attacks would be continuous with the tanks followed by carriers with fuel and supplies. He also stressed the need for thorough coordination beforehand with infantry, artillery, and air forces. He and his superiors saw the new weapon as "portable artillery" supporting infantry.

After the war the French Army rejected Estienne's call for an independent armored force of 4,000 tanks and 8,000 trucks. Light tank units were permanently allocated to infantry formations in the army (1920). Despite this failure, his ideas were taken up in the 1930s by reformers such as Colonel Charles de Gaulle. The formation of French armor divisions came too late, however, to deal effectively with the World War II German *Blitzkrieg*.

Eugene, Archduke (1863–1954) Austro-Hungarian field marshal. Eugene's early military career reflected his imperial connections. He was promoted a general of cavalry (1900) and then was inspector of the army (1908).

Eugene replaced General Oskar Potiorek as commander of the Serbian front following the failed 1914 Austro-Hungarian offensive there. He assumed command of the Italian Front (May 1915) and held this post until the end of the war. He was promoted field marshal (November 1916). Throughout he was hampered by constant interference by the Austrian Chief of Staff, Field Marshal Franz Conrad von Hötzendorf, and frustrated by the Germans' refusal to subordinate themselves to Austrian command.

Eugene also advocated offensive action in a theater that should have been strictly defensive. At the same time his reluctance to take risks dispersed the Austrian effort, dooming several offensives. He also allowed dynastic politics to interfere with his military judgement. After the war he fled to Switzerland, but returned to Austria in 1934.

F

Faisal, Prince (1885–1933) Arab military commander and king of Iraq. Son of the Sharif of Mecca, Faisal advocated Arab home rule. During World War I he assisted his father in the Arab Revolt against Turkey (June 1916), leading the Northern Hijazi Army with Colonel T. E. Lawrence as his liaison and staging guerrilla attacks on Turkish towns and railways. His forces captured Aqaba (1917), then moved north to Syria to protect General Edmund Allenby's right flank. His troops performed well in the Transjordan and helped rout the Turks in the Battle of Megiddo (September 1918). His forces liberated Damascus (October 1918), but he was dismayed to learn that France would have a mandate over Syria. The Syrian National Congress proclaimed him king (March 1920), but French authorities expelled him. He then became king of Iraq under the British mandate (August 1921).

Falkenhausen, Baron Ludwig von (1840–1936) German general. Falkenhausen joined the army and fought in the 1866 Austro-Prussian and 1870–71 Franco-German Wars. Called out of retirement at the beginning of World War I, he commanded Sixth Army on the Western Front. It bore the brunt of the British attacks in the Battle of Arras (April 1917) and, following the loss of Vimy Ridge, he was replaced by General Otto von Below and appointed German governor of Belgium (April 1917–November 1918).

Falkenhayn, Erich Georg Anton Sebastian von (1861–1922) German general. Falkenhayn attended cadet school before joining the infantry. As a military instructor in China (1899–1903), he participated in the relief expedition to Peking (Beijing) during the 1900–01 Boxer Rebellion. Appointed chief of staff of XVI Army Corps (1906), he then became Minister of War (June 1913).

Following the German defeat in the Battle of the Marne, Falkenhayn replaced General Moltke as chief of the General Staff (14 September 1914). He refused to gamble on weakening his armies on one front to achieve superiority on another and preferred marginal strength on all fronts; but he maintained that peace could be achieved only by a victory on the Western Front, and as the point of attack he selected Verdun. He planned a battle of attrition. The bloody stalemate of Verdun and Rumania's entry into the war (29 August), which he had not considered, cost Falkenhayn his command (August).

Replaced by General Paul von Hindenburg, Falkenhayn took command of Ninth Army against the Rumanians. Following his victory there, he commanded forces in Palestine (1917), which were defeated by General Allenby at Gaza (October), largely as a result of insufficient resources.

Removed from command by General Liman von Sanders (February 1918), for the remainder of the war he commanded the remote Tenth Army in Lithuania.

Falkenhorst, Nikolaus von (1885–1968) German general. Falkenhorst joined the army in 1903 and at the end of World War I was a staff officer in the German expedition to Finland. He served in the Freikorps before joining the Reichswehr. He then served in the War Ministry (1925–27). Promoted colonel (1932), he was then military attaché in Prague, Budapest, and Bucharest (1933–35).

As a major general commanding XXI Army Corps in East Prussia, Falkenhorst participated in the invasion of Poland (September 1939). His role in that campaign brought promotion to lieutenant general (October). Adolf Hitler then picked him (February) to plan and command Operation WESER, the German invasion of Norway (April 1940). Following the successful execution of these tasks, he was promoted full general (July 1940). Officially designated commander of the German Army of Norway (October), he planned joint German–Finnish operations as part of Operation BARBAROSSA, the invasion of the Soviet Union (June 1941), directing an offensive against Murmansk and Landalaksga. When the German drive faltered, Hitler created the Army of Lapland under General Eduard Dietl and Falkenhorst returned to Oslo. He was recalled to Germany (December 1944), after disputes with the Nazi proconsul in Norway, Joseph Terboven.

After the war, Falkenhorst was tried by a British military court for allowing the execution of British POWs under the commando order. The death sentence (1946) was commuted to life in prison. He was released in 1953 for health reasons.

Fayolle, Marie-Emile (1852–1928) Marshal of France. Fayolle was educated at the École Polytechnique and commissioned in the artillery (1877). He entered the École de Guerre (1889), where he later served as a professor of artillery (1897–1907). He was promoted general in 1910.

Fayolle commanded 70th Infantry Division at the start of World War I. Much of his subsequent wartime service was as a subordinate to General Henri-Philippe Pétain. Both men agreed on the futility of massive infantry assaults unsupported by adequate artillery fire. Fayolle succeeded Pétain as commander of XXXIII Corps (June 1915). He then commanded Sixth Army (February 1916) in support of the British Somme Offensive (July–November 1916).

When Pétain took command of the French Army, Fayolle replaced him as head of the Central Army Group (May 1917). Following a brief period in Italy commanding Tenth Army along the Piave Line, he returned to the Western Front. He then commanded the Reserve Army Group (GAR) on the front line south of the Somme (March 1918), the critical hinge where the French and British armies met. At the peak of action during the last phase of the war he commanded fifty-two divisions. Torn by conflicting directives from Pétain stressing the defensive and Foch ordering attack, Fayolle accepted Foch's aggressive approach. His troops drove steadily forward until the armistice.

Until October 1919 Fayolle served as commander of French forces in occupation of the Rhineland. He retired in 1920 but was promoted marshal of France the next year.

Fechteler, William Morrow (1896–1967) U.S. admiral. Fechteler graduated from Annapolis (1916) and during World War I was an aide to the Atlantic Fleet commander. Following the war he held sea assignments, served in Washington, and was an instructor at Annapolis.

During World War II, Fechteler was operations officer for Destroyer Command, assistant director of the Navy's

Personnel Bureau (1941–43), and captain of a battleship in the Pacific. Promoted rear admiral (January 1944), he commanded Amphibious Group 8 in Seventh Fleet Amphibious Force. He then directed amphibious operations in New Guinea and commanded VII Force in the assault on Biak (May) and Sansapar, New Guinea (July). During the Philippines campaign, he directed landings on Luzon and Palawan.

Promoted vice admiral (1946), he commanded cruisers and destroyers in the Atlantic Fleet, then served as deputy chief for personnel (1947–50). Promoted full admiral (February 1950), he assumed command of the Atlantic Fleet. He succeeded Admiral Forrest P. Sherman as chief of naval operations (August 1951–August 1953), and then commanded North Atlantic Treaty forces in southern Europe before retiring in 1956.

Fedorenko, Yakov Nikolayevich (1896–1947) Soviet marshal. Drafted into the navy during World War I (1915), Fedorenko took part in the revolt at Odessa (October 1917) and joined the Red Guard and the Communist party. During the 1918–20 Civil War he commanded Red armored trains. He graduated from the Kharkov Higher Artillery School and the Frunze Military Academy, and commanded a tank regiment (1934) before taking over the 15th Mechanized Brigade. He commanded armor formations in the Kiev Military District (1937–1940) before becoming chief of the Main Armored Directorate in Moscow (June 1940), where he increased production of the new T-34 medium and KV heavy tanks.

Following the German invasion of the Soviet Union (June 1941), Fedorenko became commander of Soviet armored and mechanized troops and deputy commissar of defense. In this position he showed great understanding of armored warfare, creating the first Soviet tank armies for deep penetration operations (1942). He and Pavel Rotmistrov became the only Soviet marshals of armored troops (1944). He held his posts until his death.

Fedyuninsky, Ivan Ivanovich (1900–77) Soviet general. Fedyuninsky joined the Red Army (1919) and the Communist party (1930). He distinguished himself in fighting while commander of the 14th Motorized Regiment in the Battle of Khalkhin Gol (Nomonhan) (20–30 August 1939) during the undeclared war with Japan. As a colonel he commanded xv Rifle Corps at Kovel (April 1941). Promoted major general soon after the German invasion of the Soviet Union (22 June), he commanded Thirty-Second Army. He then became General Georgi Zhukov's deputy in the defense of Leningrad (September), where he took command of Forty-Second Army. Briefly head of the Leningrad Front (October) until succeeded by General Mikhail Khozin, he took over Khozin's Fifty-Fourth Army. He went to the Moscow sector (April 1942) to command Fifth Army and was promoted lieutenant general (June).

One of the best Russian field commanders of the war, Fedyuninsky was then senior deputy commander of the Volkhov Front (October 1942–May 1943), then held the same position in the Bryansk Front (May–July 1943). He commanded Eleventh Army, then Second Shock Army (December 1943), helping to break the siege of Leningrad (January 1944) and then driving into East Prussia. Promoted colonel general (October 1944), his army joined General Konstantin Rokossovsky's Second Belorussian Front and attacked north into Pomerania. After the war he was deputy commander of Russian occupation forces in Germany (1945–52), then commander of the Trasnscaucasian and Turkestan military districts and was promoted colonel general in October 1955.

Fegen, Edward S.F. (*c.*1892–1940) British navy officer. Born in Ireland, Fegen joined the Royal Navy and served at sea in

World War I, eventually commanding a destroyer. Subsequent assignments included cruiser commands. At the beginning of World War II, Acting Captain Fegen commanded the 14,000-ton armed merchant cruiser and former passenger liner *Jervis Bay*.

Fegen was escorting eastward-bound North Atlantic Convoy HX 64 of thirty-seven merchant ships when the German pocket battleship *Admiral Scheer* attacked (5 November 1940). Despite hopeless odds – the *Jervis Bay* had only six-inch guns against the eleven-inch guns of the *Admiral Scheer* – Fegen attacked, his ship firing fast and accurately. The convoy immediately scattered.

Although torn apart by German shells, the *Jervis Bay* nonetheless diverted the *Admiral Scheer* until almost nightfall, allowing most of the convoy to escape in the darkness. Only five of its ships were lost. Fegen, who went down with his ship, was posthumously awarded the Victoria Cross for his action.

Feng, Yü-hsiang (Feng Yuxiang) (1882–1948) Chinese marshal. Feng joined the army as a private (1894). He won appointment to the Paoting (Baoding) Military Academy and rose to colonel commanding a regiment (1913). He commanded 16th Mixed Brigade and was a member of the Peiyang warlord faction (1918). He distinguished himself in Chihli faction operations against Manchurian warlord Chang Tso-lin (Yang Tsolin), then helped depose President Li Yuan-hung (Li Yuanhong) (1923).

Promoted field marshal and made commander of Third Army in Wu P'ei-fu's (Wu Peifu) Chihli faction (early 1924), Feng saw to it that his troops were well disciplined and indoctrinated in his brand of Christianity (he was known as "the Christian Marshal"). Ordered to invade Manchuria, he rebelled against Wu and occupied Peking (Beijing), bringing the collapse of the Chihli faction (October–November). He invited Sun Yat-sen (Sun

Zhongshan) to Peking (Beijing) (December), then reorganized his forces as the Kuominchün (People's Army). Defeated by the combined forces of Chang Tso-lin and Wu P'ei-fu (1926), he visited Russia and garnered some support there, reequipping his army (1926–27) and joining forces with Chiang Kai-shek (Jiang Jieshi) (1928). He rebelled against Chiang (1929) and was twice defeated by his Kuomintang forces (1929 and 1930). He then raised a volunteer force against the Japanese (1933) but remained an opposition figure within the Kuomintang. He visited the United States (1947–48) but died in an accident while returning to China aboard a Russian ship.

Fisher, John Arbuthnot, Lord Fisher of Kilverstone (1841–1920) British admiral. Fisher became a naval cadet (1854) and saw action in the 1854–56 Crimean War and in China. He commanded a battleship in the 1882 shelling of Alexandria. A specialist in naval gunnery, Fisher was director of naval ordnance (1885–1890). Promoted rear admiral (1900), he held a variety of important commands, including that of the Mediterranean fleet (1899–1902). Fisher became first sea lord (October 1904) and immediately launched a series of reforms. He stressed efficiency, economy, and the German threat. He introduced significant new ship types in the *Dreadnought* and the battle cruiser. Fisher preferred the battle cruiser, which he saw as a powerful and fast but less expensive capital ship. He also sought to concentrate British ships in the North Sea to enable the Royal Navy to deal with the German threat. He also improved conditions for sailors.

Controversy and schism swirled around the flamboyant Fisher, and he resigned as First Sea Lord (January 1910). Early in World War I, on the forced retirement of Prince Louis of Battenberg, First Lord of the Admiralty Winston Churchill, an admirer of Fisher, recalled him (October 1914), but their relationship deteriorated.

Fisher resigned (May 1915) over Churchill's Dardanelles Campaign, certain it would bring further reductions in the Home Fleet in the North Sea.

Fiske, Bradley Allen (1854–1942) U.S. admiral. A graduate of Annapolis (1874), Fiske was granted a year's leave to study electricity and oversaw its installation in new ships in the 1880s. Later he introduced new range finders, telescopes, and other devices. The greatest inventor of naval electro-mechanical shipboard appliances of his generation, he registered more than sixty patents.

During the 1898 Spanish-American War Fiske was navigator on a gunboat and participated in the Battle of Manila Bay. He then commanded a monitor and a cruiser squadron. He was second in command of the Atlantic Fleet and then aide for operations to the secretary of the navy (1910). Promoted rear admiral (1911), he was the first admiral to leave and return to a ship by aircraft. He also patented a torpedo plane (1912).

A staunch advocate of naval reform, Fiske urged changes in education and officer training. He also advocated creation of a naval general staff and national security council that would centralize national defense policy making. Partly as a result of his efforts, the office of chief of naval operations came into being (1915). A prolific author, he used his position as president of the U.S. Naval Institute (1911–23) to publish five books and many articles. He also originated the strategic war game. Following retirement from the navy (1916), he continued to write and advocate reform.

Fitch, Audrey Wray (1883–1948) U.S. admiral. Fitch graduated from Annapolis (1906) and was commissioned (1908). During World War I he served aboard the battleship *Wyoming*. He qualified as a naval aviator (1930). A graduate of the Naval War College (1938), he then commanded the Pensacola Naval Air Station

(1938–40). Promoted rear admiral (July 1940), he commanded Patrol Wing 2, then Carrier Division 1 (1940–41). He participated in the aborted relief expedition to Wake Island (December 1941), then commanded the aircraft carriers in the Battle of the Coral Sea (May 1942) that stopped the Japanese advance in the south Pacific and caused their Port Moresby invasion force to turn back. His own flagship, the carrier *Lexington*, was sunk in the battle.

As commander of all land-based U.S. naval and Marine aircraft in the South Pacific (September 1942–August 1944), Fitch played a key role in the offensive against Japanese-held south Pacific islands and naval forces. His aircraft destroyed more than 3,000 Japanese planes. Promoted vice admiral (1943), he was deputy chief of naval operations for air (August 1944–August 1945). He was then superintendent of the Naval Academy (August 1945–January 1947), the first qualified naval aviator to hold that post and the first as vice admiral. He was then special assistant to the secretary of the navy before retiring as a full admiral in July 1947.

Fleischer, Carl (1883–1942) Norwegian general. In 1940 during World War II, Fleischer commanded the Norwegian 6th Infantry Division. He was able to contain German forces under General Eduard Dietl at Narvik following their invasion there (April). As commander of forces in northern Norway, he counterattacked and dealt the Germans a major setback. Distrustful of the British and French after their withdrawal from Norway, he accompanied his government into exile in London (June). He then commanded the Norwegian army-in-exile. Following continued disagreements with the British, he was sent to Canada as military attaché (1942) and commander of Norwegian troops there, but he committed suicide shortly after his arrival at Ottawa.

Fletcher, Frank Friday (1855–1928) U.S. admiral. Fletcher joined the navy (1870) and served on the *Ticonderoga* (1878–81) during her circumnavigation of the globe. A scientist and naval reformer at a time when the U.S. Navy was undergoing rejuvenation, he participated in an expedition (1883–84) to determine longitudes. Assigned to the Bureau of Ordnance (1887–92), he helped design mechanisms for new rapid-fire guns and campaigned for range lights, which the navy subsequently adopted (1890). He was responsible for the developing U.S. torpedo warfare doctrine (1893).

Fletcher commanded the battleship *Vermont* in the Great White Fleet that circumnavigated the globe (November 1908–February 1910). Promoted rear admiral (1911), he held a succession of ship commands. He commanded forces off the east coast of Mexico (April 1914) during the crisis between that nation and the United States. Ordered by President Woodrow Wilson to seize the customs house at Vera Cruz, he was subsequently awarded the Medal of Honor for carrying this out. Promoted admiral (1915), he served during World War I on both the Army–Navy Joint Board and War Industries Board. He retired in November 1919.

Fletcher, Frank Jack (1885–1973) U.S. admiral. Fletcher graduated from Annapolis (1906) and was commissioned (1908). He received the Medal of Honor for evacuating refugees under fire at Vera Cruz, Mexico (1911). During World War I he commanded a submarine. On the eve of U.S. entry into World War II, he commanded Cruiser Division 3 at Pearl Harbor as a rear admiral. His mission to relieve Wake Island was aborted on its fall to the Japanese.

Fletcher formed Task Force 17 around the aircraft carrier *Yorktown* and conducted raids in the Marshall and Gilbert Islands (February 1942). He commanded U.S. forces during the Battle of the Coral Sea (May) and the three U.S. carriers in the Battle of Midway (June); he helped orchestrate the U.S. victory, but was criticized for abandoning the carrier *Yorktown*. As commander of Task Force 6 with his flag in the *Saratoga*, he oversaw U.S. landings on Guadalcanal but made a controversial decision to withdraw his carriers after the U.S. defeat at Savo Island (August). He then assumed command of forces in the North Pacific (December 1943), conducting raids and air strikes against the Kurile Islands. After the war he oversaw the occupation of the northern Japanese islands of Hokkaido and northern Honshu. Promoted full admiral (May 1947), he then retired.

Foch, Ferdinand (1851–1929) Marshal of France. Foch enlisted in the army during the 1870–71 Franco-German War but did not see action. He entered the École Polytechnique (1871) and was commissioned in the artillery (1874). He then attended the War College (1885–87) and was assigned to the General Staff. In 1894 he taught at the War College, where he stressed the importance of the commander's will and the offensive. Promoted brigadier general (1907), he then headed the War College (1908). Promoted to major general (1912), he commanded a division. He then took command of XX Corps (1913).

During World War I Foch distinguished himself in the Battle of the Frontiers (August 1914), and French Army commander General Joseph Joffre gave him command of the new Ninth Army during the Battle of the Marne (September). Joffre then appointed him deputy commander-in-chief to coordinate operations in the northern wing of armies (October). He next commanded Northern Army Group (January 1915).

When Joffre was dismissed in favor of General Robert Nivelle (December 1916), Foch was transferred to an unimportant advisory post. But when General Henri-Philippe Pétain became commander of the army (May 1917), he returned to prominence as chief of the General Staff, although command authority rested with Pétain. Premier Georges Clemenceau then appointed Foch to the military committee of the new Supreme Allied War Council (November 1917).

Foch's opportunity came in the spring of 1918 when the Allies, close to defeat during the Ludendorff Offensive, adopted unity of command. Clemenceau selected Foch as supreme commander, largely for his fighting spirit. Originally, he had power only to "coordinate" Allied operations, but soon he gained full control; and on 14 April he was named CinC of the Allied Armies, first on the Western Front, then over all other operations.

As generalissimo of the Allied armies, Foch directed the defeat of the German offensive. When the German drive had spent itself (July), he launched his own succession of offensives over the whole of the front to give the Germans no time to regroup. This continued until victory. In gratitude for that achievement, Foch was promoted to the rank of marshal of France (August).

Foch headed the Allied team in armistice negotiations with the Germans (November), insisting on terms that would make it impossible for Germany to renew the war. During the 1919 Paris Peace Conference, he advocated a tough stance toward Germany. He later denounced the Treaty of Versailles, predicting that the Germans would invade France again within a generation.

Foch was the only French general also to be named a British field marshal. He was also made a field marshal of Poland.

Fonck, Paul René (1894–1953) French army officer and pilot. Fonck joined the army (1914) and enrolled in flying school (February 1915). He first flew reconnaissance aircraft, but then transferred to fighter aircraft on the Western Front (April 1917). Known for his conservative use of ammunition, he often fought against great odds. On two occasions he shot down six planes in a single day. He had seventy-five confirmed kills, but claimed to have shot down 127 aircraft. At the end of the war he was the leading ace on the Allied side.

After the war, Fonck was a racing and demonstration pilot, and was inspector of fighter aviation in the French Air Force (1937–39). After Germany defeated France (June 1940), Fonck worked with the Vichy government.

Forbes, Sir Charles Morton (1881–1960) British admiral. Forbes was on the staff of Admiral Sir John Jellicoe when he commanded the Grand Fleet during World War I. After the war, he commanded battleships and held important staff positions, including deputy commander of the Mediterranean Fleet.

Promoted admiral (1936), Forbes was appointed CinC, Home Fleet (1938). Although the fleet as a whole was ready for combat on the outbreak of World War II, its bases, which lacked submarine and anti-aircraft defenses, were not, and the impact of air power on naval surface assets was not yet understood. He earned the enmity of First Lord of the Admiralty (later prime minister) Winston Churchill during the Norwegian Campaign (April–May 1940), although this did not prevent his promotion to admiral of the fleet (May). Replaced as commander of the Home Fleet (December) by Admiral Sir John Tovey, he then commanded Portsmouth Navy Base and helped plan the St. Nazaire raid (March 1942). He retired in August 1943.

Foulkes, Charles C.C. (1903–69) Canadian general. Foulkes came to Canada from Britain while very young and joined the Royal Canadian Regiment (1926). He was a general staff officer in the Permanent Force and graduated from the Staff College at Camberley (1939). He shipped overseas with the Canadian 1st Division as a brigade major (November 1939) and was rapidly promoted. CofS of General Henry Crerar's First Canadian Army, he assumed command of the Canadian 2nd Division as a major general (January 1944). Unsuccessful in his first battle following the Normandy invasion (June 1944), he was censored for high losses by Canadian II Corps commander General Guy Simonds but continued to command the division in costly battles in Normandy and in clearing the Scheldt estuary. He temporarily commanded Canadian II Corps when Simonds became acting army commander (August). Promoted lieutenant general (November), he commanded Canadian I Corps in Italy, returning to Holland when his corps was transferred to the Canadian First Army (Spring 1945).

After the war Foulkes served as the Canadian Army's first chief of General Staff (1945–1951), then was chairman of the Chiefs of Staff Committee (1951–60) until his retirement.

Foulois, Benjamin Delahauf (1879–1967) U.S. Army Air Corps general. Foulois enlisted in the army (1898) and served in Puerto Rico during the 1898 Spanish-American War, and was then in the Philippines. He passed an officer candidate test and was commissioned (1901). He returned to the U.S. (1905) and, following service in Cuba, attended the Infantry and Cavalry School at Fort Leavenworth and the Army Signal School. He transferred to the Signal Corps and embraced military aviation (1907). A skilled pilot, he pushed through numerous aircraft modifications, including wheels and radio. As a captain, he commanded (1916) the 1st Aero Squadron during the Punitive Expedition into Mexico. Promoted brigadier general soon after the United States entered World War I (April 1917), he went to France to bring order to the U.S. air arm but was soon replaced by General Mason Patrick.

After the war Foulois reverted to the permanent rank of major. Following service as an attaché in Berlin (1920–24), he attended the Command and General Staff School at Fort Leavenworth (1925). Promoted to brigadier general, in 1927 he was assistant chief of the Army Air Corps. In 1931 he became chief of the Air Corps as a major general. Despite budget limitations, he did much to modernize the Air Corps and created the General Headquarters (GHQ) Air Force (1934). He was forced to retire (1935) following problems handling civilian mail and because of his advocacy of a separate air force. He remained a forceful public advocate of air power.

Franchet d'Esperey, Louis Felix François (1856–1942) Marshal of France. Franchet d'Esperey entered the army from St. Cyr (1876). He served in North Africa and Asia but also travelled extensively in southeastern Europe. When World War I began, he commanded I Corps in Fifth Army. Its victory at Guise (29 August) won him command of Fifth Army. In late 1914 he argued unsuccessfully for a major military effort in southeastern Europe. He was promoted to head Army Group East (1916), then Army Group North (1917).

The failure of General Maurice Sarrail's 1917 Balkan offensive and Franchet d'Esperey's familiarity with the region led to his taking command of Allied forces in Salonika (June 1918). He launched an offensive (September) that forced Bulgaria to request an armistice, and by the end of the war his armies were on the Danube. Named marshal of France (1922), Franchet d'Esperey remained on active duty into his seventies.

Franco Bahamonde, Francisco Paulino Hermenegildo Teódulo (1892–1975) Spanish general and dictator. Franco was commissioned in the army from the Toledo Infantry Academy (1910). Rapidly promoted as a consequence of his service in North Africa, he rose to deputy commander of the Spanish Foreign Legion in Morocco (1920) and fought in the 1921–26

Rif Rebellion led by Abd-el-Krim. By the end of the war he was a brigadier general commanding the Legion. He then commanded the military academy at Zaragoza.

Following the overthrow of the monarchy (April 1931), the new Republican government sent Franco to command in the Balearic Islands (1931–34). After the conservatives came to power (1933), he played a major role in suppressing a left-wing revolt in Asturias and became army chief of staff (1935). When the leftist Popular Front won the next elections (February 1936), the new government sent him to the Canary Islands.

Franco joined forces with other right-wing enemies of the republic to revolt against the government (July 1936) and came to lead the Nationalist military effort. Thanks to German aid, he was able to airlift a large part of the Foreign Legion from North Africa, although his forces were repulsed at Madrid (September–October). He became leader of the Falange party (February 1937) and *de facto* chief of state of Spain following the fall of Madrid (March 1939).

Franco angered Adolf Hitler by maintaining a non-belligerent stance during World War II, although he did send the volunteer Blue Division to fight in the Soviet Union and secretly supported German submarines. The most durable of twentieth-century dictators, he moved to strict neutrality at the end of the war and gradually relaxed his rule in the 1960s, making arrangements for the restoration of the monarchy on his death.

François, Hermann von (1856–1933) German general. François joined the army and graduated from the Kriegsakademie (1887). He served in a variety of staff and command positions. Although a major general, he was entrusted with command of I Corps in East Prussia (October 1913).

Headstrong and offensive-minded, François played a major role in the first encounters with the Russian army in World War I, especially in the Battle of Gumbinnen (August 1914), but his penchant for ignoring orders caused difficulty. Promoted lieutenant general, he was briefly acting commander of Eighth Army (October–November 1914), but thereafter took over the newly formed XLI Reserve Corps. He served initially on the Western Front but returned to the East (April 1915). He then commanded VII Corps (June 1915), a position he retained until summer 1918. From July 1916 he was also responsible for "Meuse Group West," coordinating German operations in the left bank section of the Verdun region. He gave up command (July 1918) but remained on the standby list (until October), when he retired.

Fraser, Sir Bruce Austin, 1st Baron Fraser of North Cape (1888–1981) British admiral. Fraser entered the navy (1902). A specialist in naval gunnery, in World War I he was at the Dardanelles. He spent the years after the war at sea and in ordnance assignments and was promoted rear admiral (1938). During the first three years of World War II he was third sea lord with oversight over ship production and repair, and a vice admiral. He then commanded the Home Fleet with the principal task of escorting Allied convoys to Murmansk (May 1943). Highlights of this service were the crippling of the *Tirpitz* and destruction of the *Scharnhorst* in the Battle of North Cape (23 December).

Promoted admiral (August 1944), Fraser commanded the Eastern Fleet, the small British naval presence in the Pacific, and he represented the Royal Navy at Japanese surrender ceremonies. After the war he was rewarded with the title of Baron Fraser of North Cape and promoted admiral of the fleet. He served as first sea lord (1948–51), retiring in 1952.

Frederick, Robert T. (1907–70) U.S. general. Frederick graduated from West Point (1928) and was commissioned in the coast artillery. His service assignments included Hawaii and the Panama Canal Zone. A staff officer in the War Plans Division early in World War II, he recommended against a British proposal to create a special U.S.–Canadian special fighting force. It was approved anyway and he was selected to command the elite U.S.–Canadian 1st Special Services Force, known as the "Force" (1942) and the forerunner of today's U.S. Special Forces.

Frederick led by example, stressing physical fitness and preparedness. The Force trained for combat in all conditions and as paratroopers and amphibious soldiers. Assigned to Aleutian operations, it arrived there after the Japanese had evacuated. The Force was then sent to Italy (late 1943), where it served with distinction. It was also employed at Anzio and in other assignments in a straight infantry role. Frederick then commanded the 1st Airborne Task Force in Operation DRAGOON, the invasion of Southern France (August 1944). He ended the war commanding 45th Infantry Division. He had been wounded in action eight times, more than any other U.S. general officer of the war.

After the war Frederick commanded the 4th and then the 6th Infantry Divisions. He was then chief of the Military Assistance Advisory Group (MAAG) in Greece (1951) and retired in 1952.

Frenay, Henri (1905–88) French army officer and resistance leader. Commissioned in the army from St. Cyr, Frenay also graduated from the École de Guerre and the Centre d'Études Germaniques at Strasbourg. A captain during the Battle for France, he fought in the Vosges area and was taken prisoner but escaped (27 June 1940). He made his way to unoccupied France and joined the post-armistice army forming at Vichy as an intelligence officer. Disenchanted with Vichy policies, he went underground (February 1941) and began publishing resistance newspapers and then formed the resistance group "Combat." Initially de-

voted to propaganda, it expanded into intelligence gathering and, finally, into a fighting branch with a secret army organization. It grew to be the largest of French Resistance movements.

One of the key figures of the Resistance, and one who originated most of its techniques, Frenay was high on the Gestapo's list of wanted men but managed to avoid capture. He made several trips to London and also traveled to Algiers. Resenting the manipulation of the Resistance from London, he joined General Charles de Gaulle's provisional government only with great reluctance, serving as minister for prisoners, deportees, and refugees (1943). Almost legendary in France, he did not publish his memoirs, *The Night Will End*, until 1976. The major point in this best-selling book was that he and his colleagues handed over an already formed Resistance to de Gaulle. He also expressed frustration that the idealistic hopes of the Resistance for post-war France were not realized.

French, John Denton Pinkstone, Earl of Ypres (1852–1925) British field marshal. French served in the navy as a cadet and midshipman (1866–1870). He transferred to the army and then saw periods of colonial service in Egypt and India. Promoted brigadier general, he commanded a cavalry brigade. Promoted major general, he performed well as a cavalry commander in the Boer War and was promoted lieutenant general. He then commanded at Aldershot and implemented army reforms (1902–07). Promoted to full general (1907), he was inspector general of the army (1907–12). He then became chief of the Imperial General Staff (1912) and was advanced to field marshal (1913). He resigned (April 1914) in the aftermath of the Curragh Mutiny (March).

Recalled to duty at the start of World War I, French was a logical choice to command the BEF. His mercurial temperament, mood swings, and lack of understanding of modern war all hampered his effectiveness, however. His actions in the earliest battles of the war called into question his judgement and resolution. Secretary for War Lord Kitchener had to intervene to prevent him from pulling out of the line on the eve of the critical Battle of the Marne (September 1914). French's attacks on Neuve Chapelle and Auber Ridge (March and May 1915) were costly failures. He blamed the shortage of shells and Kitchener, charges that raised further questions about his judgement. His habit of seeking to avoid responsibility for failure and controversy over his handling of the Battle of Loos (September 1915) proved his undoing. Following his forced resignation, he took command of the Home Forces (1916–18). He was then Lord Lieutenant of Ireland (1918–21).

Freyberg, Bernard Cyril, 1st Baron of Wellington and Munstead (1889–1963) New Zealand general. Freyberg joined the New Zealand Army (1909) but took leave to fight with Pancho Villa in Mexico (1914). In World War I he fought in the defense of Antwerp (August–September 1914), and then in the Gallipoli campaign (April 1915–January 1916). He then fought on the Western Front. On the Somme he suffered four wounds in a twenty-four-hour period (November 1916) but refused to leave his battalion until the objective was secured, for which he was awarded the Victoria Cross. He became the youngest general in the British Army and took command first of a brigade (1917) and then the 29th Division (1917–18). He was wounded nine times.

After World War I Freyberg served in various command and staff positions. During World War II he commanded New Zealand forces in the Mediterranean Theater. He fought in the defense of Greece (April 1941) and, following defeat there, commanded British/Greek forces on Crete, where his forces inflicted heavy casualties on attacking German airborne forces (May 1941). Able to extract most of his force from the island, he then

fought in the Western Desert in North Africa as a corps commander in Eighth Army in the Second Battle of Sidi Rezegh and at Minqar Qaim, where he was wounded a tenth time. He led the breakout in the Second Battle of El Alamein (November 1942) and commanded the flanking force in the drive to Tunisia. He then commanded the New Zealand Corps in the Italian campaign, most notably in fighting for Cassino and breaching the German Gothic Line. His troops entered Trieste (2 May 1945). After the war he was governor-general of New Zealand (1946) and made a baron in 1951.

Friedeburg, Hang Georg von (1895–1945) German admiral. A career naval officer up until he became head of the organizational section of submarine forces (1938), Friedeburg was involved only with surface vessels. His hard work in training and deploying submarines from bases in France, and his ability to get along with head of the submarine service, Admiral Karl Dönitz, resulted in his promotion to admiral (1942) and, when his chief was advanced to head the German Navy (1943), to command of the submarine service.

Friedeburg is also remembered as the German officer sent to Lüneburg (3 May) to negotiate the preliminary surrender of German forces in northwestern Europe to British General Bernard L. Montgomery. He then signed the unconditional surrender document with U.S. General Dwight D. Eisenhower at Reims (7 May 1945) and a day later with Soviet Marshal Georgi Zhukov in Berlin. A few days later he committed suicide.

Friedrich, Archduke (1856–1936) Austro-Hungarian general. A member of the Habsburg royal family, Friedrich emerged from semi-retirement to serve as CinC of the High Command and titular head of the Imperial Armed Forces during the first two years of World War I (1914–16). His assessment of Austria's prospects proved grimly realistic. Friedrich believed the entry of Italy and Romania doomed the Austro-Hungarian war effort to failure. His pessimism led to his removal (December 1916) and he retired in 1917.

Friessner, Johnannes (1892–1971) German general. Friessner entered the army in 1911 and saw duty in World War I. He remained in the Reichswehr after the war. Inspector general of the army educational system, he was promoted brigadier general and fought on the Eastern Front in command of 102nd Infantry Division (May 1942). Promoted major general (October), he commanded XXIII Corps (January–December 1944). Promoted lieutenant general (April 1944), he commanded Friessner Group (later Army Group Narva) on the northern front (February). Promoted full general (July 1944) and briefly commander of Army Group North (July), he then commanded the new South Ukraine Army Group (later Southeast Army Group) of two German and two Romanian divisions in Moldavia. A major Russian offensive (August) virtually wiped out his command: the two Romanian divisions defected, and the German divisions were trapped and mostly destroyed. Hitler dismissed him from command in December 1944.

Fritsch, Werner Freiherr von (1880–1939) German general. Fritsch joined the army (1898) and during World War I he was on the General Staff, rising to the rank of major. He remained in the army after the war. A protégé of General (later president) Paul von Hindenburg, he was promoted brigadier general (November 1930), major general (October 1932), then lieutenant general and CinC of the army (February 1934), and full general (April 1936).

Fritsch oversaw, along with Minister of War General Werner von Blomberg, Adolf Hitler's rearmament of Germany. In 1937 both Fritsch and Blomberg expressed opposition to Hitler's plans for war, and

Hitler became determined to remove them. Blomberg was forced out (January 1938) and the next month Fritsch was falsely accused of homosexuality. Resigning his posts (February) he demanded a court-martial to clear his name. He was found innocent, but was not restored to high command. He returned to duty as an honorary colonel and died in action leading a reconnaissance during the Polish campaign. Reportedly, he deliberately sought his own death.

Fromm, Friedrich (1888–1945) German general. Fromm served in World War I and was commissioned a lieutenant (1918). He remained in the Reichswehr after the war and served in a variety of staff posts. Promoted colonel (February 1933), he became chief of the Army Department in the War Ministry. He enjoyed rapid promotion, being advanced to brigadier general (November 1935), major general (January 1938), and lieutenant general (April 1939). He was then appointed commander of the Replacement Army as well as chief of army equipment (September 1939). He was promoted full general (July 1940).

By fall 1941 Fromm believed the war was lost. Approached by his CofS, Colonel Count Klaus von Stauffenberg, to join the resistance against Hitler, he refused to join unless the plot was successful. Following the 20 July 1944 bomb attempt, he learned that Hitler was alive and refused his support. Arrested by the conspirators, he escaped and ordered their immediate execution to cover his own involvement. This failed to save him. Arrested himself the next day, he was imprisoned. Ultimately tried on a charge of cowardice, he was executed by firing squad in March 1945.

Frost, John Dutton (1912–93) British general. One of Britain's first airborne soldiers, Major Frost led Company C of the 2nd Battalion of the 1st Parachute Regiment on a successful raid against a

German radar site at Bruneval, northern France. As a lieutenant colonel, he commanded the 2nd Battalion the remainder of the war. He is best remembered for his role in his regiment's stand at Arnhem (September 1944). Wounded in action, he was taken prisoner. After the war he continued in the army and retired as a major general (1968). In 1977 the city of Arnhem renamed the bridge there after him.

Frunze, Mikhail Vasilyevich (1889–1925) Soviet general and political leader. Frunze studied at the St. Petersburg Technical Institute and joined the Bolshevik party (1905). Arrested several times for political activity, he was sentenced to internal exile (1905–09) and also to death, the latter commuted to permanent internal exile (1914). He continued revolutionary agitation (1914–17) and was elected to the First Congress of the Soviet of Peasant Deputies in Petrograd. He participated in the November 1917 Bolshevik *coup d'etat*, then helped put down an anti-Bolshevik uprising in Yaroslavl (August 1918). He played a key role in the 1918–20 Civil War, commanding Fourth Army of the Eastern Front (December 1918), then Southern Group (March 1919). He led successful operations against Admiral Aleksandr V. Kolchak's White forces. In command of Eastern Front (July), he won control of the Northern and Central Ural Mountain regions. He then commanded the Turkestan Front (August 1919–September 1920), destroying White forces in the Southern Urals and in Central Asia. He commanded the Southern Front in the Perekop–Chongar campaign, defeating General P. N. Wrangel's White Army (November 1920).

Frunze held political posts in Ukraine (1920–24) and was elected to the Central Committee (1921). Appointed deputy director of military affairs (1924), he succeeded Leon Trotsky as commissar for war (1925). Considered a father of the Red Army, he wrote several books and developed the "unitary military doctrine" combining offensive action, indoctrination, and world revolution. The Soviet general staff college is named for him.

Fuchida, Mitsuo (1902–76) Japanese naval air officer. Fuchida graduated from the Imperial Naval Academy (1924). He then completed flight school and joined the Yokosuka Air Corps, where he developed a new dive-bombing tactic. He attended the Naval Staff College (1938) and was transferred to an air group aboard the carrier *Akagi* as a squadron leader (1939). Appointed to lead the attack on Hawaii, he took over training for the Pearl Harbor attack and led it in person (7 December 1941).

In spring 1942 Fuchida participated in the extended Japanese raid into the Indian Ocean. Illness sidelined him during the Battle of the Coral Sea (May 1942) and the decisive engagement at Midway (June); he was stricken by appendicitis and could not fly. He was on board the carrier *Akagi* (4 June) when American dive bombers surprised the Japanese and sank all four of their carriers. Fuchida, severely wounded, managed to escape.

Fuchida subsequently served as a staff officer at Yokosuka and was involved in military planning. After extended tours of the Marianas and the Philippines, he returned to Japan to begin to prepare for defense of the homeland. He retired at the end of the war as a captain.

Fuller, John Frederick Charles (1878–1964) British general. Fuller was educated at Sandhurst and commissioned (1898). He served in the 1899–1902 Boer War, was promoted to captain (1911) and attended the Staff College at Camberley (1913).

A staff officer at the beginning of World War I, Fuller soon realized the potential of the tank to overcome the stalemate of trench warfare. Appointed CofS of the new Tank Corps (December 1916), he introduced new tactics and planned the attack at Cambrai (November 1917). He planned tank tactics for the 1918 offensives. His "Plan 1919" called for a coordinated attack of tanks and airplanes to win the war.

Following the war, Fuller taught at the Staff College (1922) and was assistant to the chief of the Imperial General Staff (1926). He continued to urge reform and called for a totally mechanized army coordinated with aircraft. Given command of the new Experimental Force (Tank) brigade at Aldershot (1926), his imperious manner, intolerance, and advocacy of reform and tanks brought an end to his military career. Promoted major general (1930), he was placed on half pay and then retired (December 1933), whereupon he became the military correspondent for the *Daily Mail* and a historian. He also embraced fascism. One of the premier military theorists, his influence on Sir Basil Liddell Hart and others helped revolutionize warfare in the late 1930s and during World War II.

Funston, Frederick (1865–1917) U.S. general. Funston attended the University of Kansas and then worked for the Department of Agriculture. He joined guerrillas fighting in Cuba against Spanish rule (1896) and rose to be an artillery com-

mander with the rank of lieutenant colonel. He returned to the U.S. a hero (1897). In 1898 during the Spanish–American War, he commanded the 20th Kansas Volunteer Infantry Regiment and took it to the Philippines, where it fought in the Insurrection. He distinguished himself there and was awarded the Medal of Honor and promoted to brigadier general of volunteers. He helped capture Filipino nationalist leader Emilio Aguinaldo (March 1901), which act brought promotion to brigadier general in the regular army.

Funston commanded the Pacific Division during the 1906 California earthquake and that same year took part in the U.S. intervention in Cuba. He then commanded the Army schools at Fort Leavenworth (1908–10), the Department of Luzon in the Philippines, and the Hawaiian Department (1913). In 1914 he commanded army troops at Vera Cruz and was briefly governor during the occupation there. Promoted major general (1914), he took command of the Southern Department the next year. He then commanded troops mobilized along the border with Mexico (1916). Had death not intervened, he might have commanded U.S. forces in France during World War I.

G

Galland, Adolf (1912–96) German air force general. Galland learned to fly gliders (1929), then joined the Luftwaffe (1934) and was commissioned. He flew with the Condor Legion in Spain (1937–38). During the invasion of Poland (September 1939) he commanded an air transport squadron. He transferred to fighters just before the invasion of France and Benelux (May 1940), during which he achieved his first air-to-air kills. He took part in the 1940 Battle of Britain, was promoted lieutenant colonel, and commanded a fighter group. He championed tactics that would free his fighters from the bombers and allow them to win command of the air.

Following Ernst Udet's suicide, Galland received command of Luftwaffe fighters (November 1941). Promoted brigadier general (1942), during 1943–44 he commanded German fighter defenses against the U.S. Army Air Forces and Royal Air Force bombing campaign. He argued with Adolf Hitler for additional aircraft, but received little of what he wanted. He also clashed with Hermann Göring over the latter's insistence on a perimeter defense. His failure to halt the Allied bombing campaign and his outspoken nature caused him to be relieved of his command (January 1945). His reputation was such that Hitler appointed him to command Jagdverband-44, flying the new Me-262 jet aircraft. Shot down and seriously wounded, he was later taken prisoner (May 1945). Officially he was credited with 104 kills. After his release in 1947, he served as an advisor for the Argentine Air Force, returning to Germany in 1955.

Gallery, Daniel Vincent (1901–77) U.S. admiral. Gallery graduated from Annapolis (1921). Following routine ship assignments, he became a naval aviator (1927) and a flight instructor (until 1932). He then commanded a scouting squadron and was chief of the aviation section of the Bureau of Ordnance (1938–41) until posted as naval attaché for air at London (1941).

Gallery next participated in antisubmarine patrols in the north Atlantic, commanding the naval air base at Reykjavik, Iceland (1941–43). He then commanded a submarine hunter-killer task group centered on the aircraft carrier *Guadalcanal* and five destroyer escorts (1943–45). He had the distinction of being the first U.S. Navy officer to capture an enemy vessel on the high seas since 1815, when his group took *U-505* after it had been forced to the surface and its crew abandoned ship (4 June 1944). The submarine yielded information on both German codes and torpedoes. Transferred to the Pacific theater (1945), Gallery was promoted rear admiral. After the war he was assistant chief of naval operations (CNO), and commanded first a carrier division in the Mediterranean and then an anti-submarine force in the Atlantic. He was then chief of naval reserve air training and commanded first the 9th Naval District and then the Puerto Rico Naval District. He retired in November 1960.

Galliéni, Joseph Simon (1849–1916) French marshal. Galliéni graduated from St. Cyr (1870) and was commissioned in the Marines. He fought with distinction in the Franco-German War and then served in Africa and Indo-China. He returned to France to command a corps (1905), then joined the general staff (1908) and served there until his retirement (1914).

On the outbreak of World War I, Galliéni was recalled to active service and became military governor of Paris and designated successor to French Army commander General Joseph Joffre (late August 1914). When he learned that the German First Army had turned southeast of Paris, making it vulnerable to a thrust by his Sixth Army and Paris garrison, he pressed upon Joffre the need for an immediate counterattack. On the afternoon of 5 September, Sixth Army opened the Battle of the Marne. Galliéni's efforts helped prevent a German victory in 1914.

Galliéni was minister of war (1915–16), until poor health and disputes with Joffre over the defense of Verdun forced his retirement. He was posthumously promoted marshal of France in May 1921.

Gallwitz, Max Von (1852–1932) German general. Gallwitz joined the army (1871) and was commissioned in the field artillery (1873). After attending the Kriegsakademie, he held staff positions and commanded a division. He then became inspector of field artillery (1911).

At the start of World War I, Gallwitz commanded the Guards Reserve Corps, which participated in the invasion of Belgium and then was sent to East Prussia. He next took command of a mixed German-Austro-Hungarian corps in Poland (November 1914). He then had

charge of the defense of East and West Prussia as head of "Army Detachment Gallwitz" (February 1915), renamed Twelfth Army (August). Later that same year he commanded Eleventh Army in the conquest of Serbia. He fought at Verdun as commander of "Meuse Group West" (March 1916). Sent to the Somme, he took charge of Second Army and temporarily supervised First Army. At the end of 1916 he was back at Verdun as commander of Fifth Army, later "Army Group Gallwitz" (Fifth and C Armies). His divisions fought well in the 1918 defense of the Meuse–Moselle region. He retired after the end of the war.

Gamelin, Maurice Gustave (1872–1958) French general. Gamelin was commissioned in the army on graduation from St. Cyr (1893). During most of World War I he was on the staff of French Army commander-in-chief General Joseph Joffre; late in the war he commanded a division. After the war he headed a mission to Brazil (1919–24). He was on the staff of commander of French forces in the Levant General Maurice Sarrail and later succeeded him in command (1926–29). He returned to France to command 20th Military Region at Nancy (1929). He was then deputy CofS of the army (1930) and CofS (1931). He was vice president of the Supreme War Council and army inspector general (1935). Not interested in technological advances, about which he knew little, he failed to prepare the army for the next war. In 1938 he became CofS for national defense, commander of all French land forces.

In August 1939 Gamelin declared that the army was ready for war. At the start of World War II (September 1939), he believed strongly in superiority of the defense. His nine-division offensive into the Rhineland (September–October) to assist the Poles, delayed by the need to get artillery out of storage, was at best timid. More resolute action could have carried his forces to the Rhine. Caught off guard by the German armored thrust through the Ardennes (12 May 1940), he acted indecisively. His dismissal by Premier Paul Reynaud and replacement by General Maurice Weygand (19 May) delayed French military plans for several critical days. Arrested by the Vichy government (September) and brought to trial at Riom on charges of responsibility for the French defeat (February 1942), he refused to testify. When the proceedings were suspended, he was returned to prison (April). Deported by the Germans, he was held in Germany (March 1943–May 1945). Released by U.S. troops, he returned to France and wrote his memoirs.

Garand, John Cantius (1888–1974) American ordnance designer. Born in Canada, Garand moved to the U.S. (1898) and followed his father as a machinist working with precision tools. At age thirteen he received his first patent. During World War I, he worked in armaments production and designed a lightweight, air-cooled, machine gun, which was rejected by the military. He was, however, recommended for a position as a designer, which he accepted (1918). He then became a senior designer in the government's Springfield Arsenal (1919).

Garand worked to develop a semiautomatic version of the bolt-operated, 5-round, M1903 Springfield rifle. Electing to keep the same caliber to utilize stocks of World War I ammunition, he produced (1921) the prototype eight-round, gas-operated M-1 Garand rifle. Accepted by the army (1936), it became the standard U.S. rifle of World War II, increasing the firepower of an infantry company five-fold. The "Garand" saw service during the Korean and Vietnam wars. Later he helped develop the M-14 rifle. He retired in 1953.

Garros, Roland (1888–1918) French fighter pilot. Garros went to Paris to study to become a concert pianist but,

following the Rheims air show (1909), he embarked on a full-time profession as an aviator. Learning to fly, he became an exhibition pilot and flew a plane from France to Tunisia across the Mediterranean (1913). Garros was in Germany lecturing on the military uses of aviation when World War I began, but managed to escape in his plane in a daring night flight to Switzerland. Back in France, he joined Escadrille M.S. 23 as a scout pilot.

Garros then came up with a system of metal cuffs on the propeller of his plane, allowing him to mount a machine gun on the fuselage. The cuffs deflected those rounds that did not pass through the propeller. He promptly shot down five German planes in little more than two weeks (March 1915), and an American journalist called him an "Ace," a term used ever since for pilots with five aerial victories. The next month, however, Garros' engine failed from enemy ground fire and he was forced to land behind German lines. He might have escaped had he not tried to burn his plane to protect his secret. He was captured before he could carry out his design, and the Germans then came up with a vast improvement, an interrupter gear developed by Dutch aircraft designer Anthony Fokker.

Garros was a POW until he escaped (early 1918). Retrained as a combat pilot, he returned to action. He was shot down and killed a month before the end of the war.

Gatacre, Sir William Forbes (1843–1905) British general. Gatacre joined the army as an ensign (1861) and was stationed in India. Promoted brigadier general (1890), he commanded an infantry brigade in the relief of Chitral (March–April 1895). He also commanded a brigade in General Horatio Kitchener's 1896–98 Sudan campaign and was knighted.

Promoted lieutenant general, Gatacre commanded 3rd Infantry Division under General Sir Redvers Buller in northwest Cape Colony (December 1899). Despite orders not to take risks, he decided on a costly night assault. His men became lost and stumbled into the midst of the Boer defenses at Stormberg (10 December), where they suffered a costly defeat. In his retreat, he left 600 men to be captured by the Boers. Despite this fiasco, he continued in command of 3rd Division in the advance on Bloemfontein (January–March 1900), but, when he failed to relieve a besieged British garrison, the commander-in-chief, Lord Roberts, relieved him. It was his last military command.

Gavin, James Maurice (1907–90) U.S. general. Gavin enlisted in the army (1924), then secured a special appointment to, and graduated from, West Point (1929). Following U.S. entry into World War II he took command of the 505th Parachute Infantry Regiment (July 1942), which joined Major General Matthew Ridgway's 82nd Airborne Division (March 1943). The 505th spearheaded the invasion of Sicily (July), then jumped into the Salerno beachhead (September). Promoted brigadier general and made assistant division commander (October), he helped plan Operation OVERLORD (November 1943–February 1944). He then jumped into Normandy (night of 5–6 June 1944) and in August took command of the 82nd. During Operation MARKET-GARDEN the 82nd captured the Nijmegen bridge (September) and he was promoted major general (October). He then fought with the 82nd in the Battle of the Bulge (December 1944–January 1945) and crossed the Elbe (April 1945).

Gavin commanded the 82nd until 1948. He then served as CofS, Fifth Army; CofS, Allied forces South; commanding general of VII Corps; and deputy CofS of the U.S. army. Promoted lieutenant general (March 1955), he was slated for promotion to general when he retired (1958), the result of disagreements with the Eisenhower administration's defense policy, particularly its reliance on nuclear forces. Later (1961–62) he was ambassador to France. He strongly opposed U.S. involvement in Vietnam.

Gehlen, Reinhard (1902–79) German general. A university graduate, Gehlen joined the Reichswehr (1920) and was subsequently commissioned in the artillery. He completed general staff schooling and then joined the General Staff (1936) in the operations section specializing in eastern Europe affairs. During World War II he came to head the intelligence section Foreign Armies East (April 1942), in the process rising from lieutenant colonel to brigadier general (December 1944).

Removed from his post by Adolf Hitler for his accurate reports of impending German defeat (April 1945), Gehlen surrendered to U.S. authorities (22 May) with his extensive files. He convinced U.S. officials that he could be of value to the West in dealing with the Soviet Union. Returning to Germany from the United States, he eventually created an intelligence organization in the Federal Republic of Germany to track developments in Eastern Europe and the Soviet Union. This organization became the Bundesnachrichtendienst (BND, 1956), the equivalent of the U.S. Central Intelligence Agency (CIA). Gehlen headed the BND until his retirement in April 1968.

Geiger, Roy Stanley (1885–1947) U.S. Marine Corps general. Geiger graduated from John B. Stetson University (1907) and enlisted in the Marine Corps (1907). Commissioned (1909), he served in Nicaragua, the Philippines (1912–13), and China (1913–16). He then completed pilot training (June 1917).

Following U.S. entry into World War I (April 1917), Geiger deployed to France as a major, where he commanded Squadron A in the 1st Marine Aviation Force and flew bombing missions. After the war he was stationed in Haiti (1914–21). He commanded the 1st Aviation Group, 3rd

Marine Brigade at Quantico (1920). He graduated from the Army Command and General Staff School (1925) and the Army War College (1929). After further service in Haiti (1925–27), he was director of Marine Corps Aviation in Washington (1931–35). Promoted colonel (1936), he graduated from the Naval War College (1941), and was promoted brigadier general (October) and was assistant naval attaché for air, London (1941–42).

Geiger then led the air wing at Henderson Field on Guadalcanal (1942). Promoted major general (August), he was then director, Division of Aviation in Washington. He returned to the Pacific to command I (later redesignated III) Amphibious Corps (1943–45) in the invasions of Guam and Peleliu (1944). He led III Corps on Okinawa (April–June 1945). Promoted lieutenant general (June 1945), he briefly commanded Tenth Army on the death of General Simon B. Buckner (June). He was the first (and only) Marine to lead an army. He represented the Marine Corps at the formal Japanese surrender ceremony on board the battleship *Missouri* (2 September). After the war Geiger commanded the Fleet Marine Force at Pearl Harbor (1945–46). He was posthumously promoted general in 1947.

Genda, Minoru (1904–89) Japanese navy officer and air force general. Genda graduated from the Naval Academy (1924). He became a carrier pilot (1931) and was then a flight instructor at Yokosuka Naval Air Station (1932), where he organized an aerobatic team (Genda's Circus). Promoted lieutenant commander (1935) and known for his unbending advocacy of the primacy of naval aviation, he graduated from the Naval War College (1937). He was then again flight instructor at Yokosuka (1938) before becoming air attaché in London (1938–40).

Promoted commander (1940), Genda was operations officer, First Air Fleet (1940–42). In this capacity, he developed the tactical plans for the strike on Pearl

Harbor and helped perfect the shallow-water torpedo attacks used there, based on the 1940 British success at Taranto. He then participated in the attack itself (7 December 1941); operations in the Indian Ocean (March–May 1942); the air attacks at Midway (June 1942), which he led; and the battles for the eastern Solomon Islands (August) and Santa Cruz Islands (October). He was then a staff officer for the Eleventh Air Fleet on Rabaul (November) and for the Naval General Staff (1943). Promoted captain (1945), he was assigned to home island defense.

After the war Genda became deputy chief of staff of the Japanese Air Self-Defense Force (1954), chief of the Air Defense Command (1957), and chief of staff of the Self-Defense Force (1959). He retired in 1962, and then served in the upper house of the Japanese Parliament during 1962–86.

Georges, Alphonse Joseph (1875–1951) French general. Commissioned in the army on graduation from St. Cyr (1897), he served in Algeria and graduated from the École de Guerre. Badly wounded in World War I (1914), on his recovery he served in staff positions, ending the war as Marshal Ferdinand Foch's chief of operations (1918). After the war he commanded a regiment in the Rhineland (1923) and was CofS to Marshal Henri-Philippe Pétain (1925–26) during the Rif Wars. He then commanded a division and an army corps in Algeria (1928–32). Appointed to the Supreme War Council (November 1932), he was badly wounded in the attack in Marseilles (9 October 1934) that killed Foreign Minister Louis Barthou and Yugoslav King Alexander.

Georges was a leading candidate to head the French Army, a post that unfortunately went to General Maurice Gamelin. He was then deputy to Gamelin (1935–40). On the start of World War II (September 1939), in accordance with war plans, he became CinC Northeast, commanding French field forces and the

BEF. He opposed the Allied movement into Belgium, and Gamelin restricted his freedom of action. Following the German breakthrough in the West when Gamelin was replaced by General Maxime Weygand (19 May), his separate command was abolished, but Georges remained on duty to assist his new chief. Following the armistice (22 June 1940), he was army inspector general until he reached mandatory retirement age (August 1940). The British got him to Algiers (May 1943), but General Charles de Gaulle refused to give him any significant role and he retired.

Gerow, Leonard Townsend (1888–1972) U.S. general. Gerow graduated from the Virginia Military Institute and was commissioned in the infantry (1911). He participated in the occupation of Vera Cruz (1914), and during World War I he went to France as a captain in the Signal Corps and fought in the Second Battle of the Marne (July–August 1918), and the St. Mihiel (September) and Meuse–Argonne (September–November) Offensives, rising to temporary lieutenant colonel.

Following World War I, Gerow commanded the Signal Corps School (1919–21) and was promoted major (1920). He graduated from the Infantry School (1925), and the Command and General Staff School (1926) and the Army War College (1931). He saw service in China and the Philippines (1931–33) and in the War Plans Division of War Department (1935). Promoted colonel (September 1940) and brigadier general (October), he headed the War Plans Division (December) and was later concurrently assistant army CofS (December 1941).

Promoted major general, Gerow took command of the 29th Infantry Division (February 1942), then V Corps (July 1943) in First Army. He led his corps in the Normandy invasion and subsequent fighting, in the liberation of Paris, and in northeastern France and Belgium, the Hürtgen Forest, and the Ardennes Offen-

sive. Promoted lieutenant general, he commanded Fifteenth Army (January 1945) in the reduction of German-held ports in western France. After the war he was commandant of the Command and General Staff School (1945–48) and then commanded Second Army, Fort Meade, Maryland, until his retirement in 1950.

Ghormly, Robert Lee (1883–1958) U.S. admiral. Ghormly graduated from Annapolis (1906), then held a variety of assignments and gained a reputation as an excellent staff officer. He graduated from the Naval War College (1938), was promoted to rear admiral, and became director of the Navy War Plans Office. He was assistant chief of naval operations (CNO) (1939–40) and then in Britain as a special naval observer (1940–42).

Promoted vice admiral (1941), Ghormly briefly commanded U.S. naval forces in European waters (April 1942). He then took command of the South Pacific Force and area (June). He had charge of operations in the Solomon Islands, and in particular the invasion of Guadalcanal. He commanded during the first four of seven principal naval engagements with the Japanese. This included the Battle of Savo Island (9 August), perhaps the worst defeat suffered by the U.S. Navy, and the hard-fought Battle of Cape Esperance (11–13 October). Pacific commander Admiral Chester Nimitz then replaced him with Admiral William Halsey (18 October).

Ghormly commanded the 14th Naval District and Hawaiian Sea Frontier (1943–44). He then had responsibility for demobilizing the German Navy. He retired as a vice admiral in August 1946.

Gibbs, William Francis (1886–1967) U.S. naval architect. After the United States entered World War I, Gibbs was naval architect to the Shipping Control Commission. After the war he and his brother Frederick organized Gibbs Brothers Inc. (1922), which became the nation's largest ship design firm. Among his innovations was the improvement of ship survivability by increasing the number of hold watertight compartments.

As a principal designer of U.S. Navy ships, Gibbs was approached in 1940 by the U.S. Maritime Commission to design a cargo vessel for mass production. His response was the "Liberty ship." Its simplified design and assembly-line techniques enabled each ship to be produced in only three weeks. Liberty ships were of critical importance in World War II.

After U.S. entry into the war (December 1941), Gibbs became controller of shipbuilding and introduced the same labor-saving techniques into warship construction. He also designed the passenger liner *United States*.

Gibson, Guy (1918–44) British air force officer. Gibson became an RAF officer (1937) and was assigned to 83 Squadron. He flew Hampdens, Beaufighters, and then Lancasters.

Gibson was selected to train a new squadron for "special duties" (1943). This became 617 Squadron, popularized as the "Dam Busters." With planes carrying special "skip" bombs developed by Barnes Wallis, 617 Squadron attacked the Möhne, Eder, Schwelme and Sorpe dams in Germany (night of 16–17 May 1943). Only the first two dams were destroyed. Gibson was awarded the Victoria Cross. He was killed on a bombing raid on Rheydt and München-Gladbach.

Giffen, Robert Carlisle (1886–1962) U.S. admiral. Giffen graduated from Annapolis (1907) and during World War I commanded a destroyer on anti-submarine patrol in the North Atlantic. He held a variety of assignments after the war. On U.S. entry into World War II (December 1941) he was commanding Destroyer Division 7. He commanded convoys bound for Britain and the Soviet Union, then a task force in Operation TORCH, the Allied invasion of North Africa (8

November 1942). Transferred to the Pacific Theater, he commanded fire support in the invasion of Makin Atoll (November 1943) and Kwajalein (January–February 1944). He commanded Cruiser Division 6 in bombardment of Truk (February 1944), Saipan (June–July), Guam (July–August), and Tinian (July–August). Promoted vice admiral, he commanded the Caribbean Sea Frontier (autumn 1944). At the end of the war he commanded the Atlantic Fleet Service Force (1945), before retiring in 1946.

Giraud, Henri Honoré (1879–1949) French general. Commissioned on graduation from St. Cyr (1900), Giraud graduated from the École de Guerre and held a variety of colonial assignments until World War I, when he fought on the Western Front as a captain. Captured by the Germans (29 August 1914), he escaped (October) and made his way back to France (February 1915). He distinguished himself in later fighting, rising to command a battalion (1917). After the war he was in Turkey (1918–22), then Morocco (1922–34). Promoted colonel (1925), he played a key role in the 1920–26 Rif Wars and his forces captured rebel leader Abd-el-Krim (1926).

Giraud joined the French Superior War Council (1938). On the eve of World War II he was military governor of Metz but had little comprehension of the changes in warfare; he believed in the superiority of the defense and opposed the use of armor en masse. On mobilization for war (2 September 1939), he took command of Seventh Army. Following the German invasion of the West (10 May 1940), he led French forces into Belgium and held up the German advance on Antwerp. After the German breakthrough to the south, he replaced General André Georges Corap in command of Ninth Army (15 May). Captured by the Germans, he was sent to Saxony but escaped (April 1942) and was spirited to North Africa (November 1942). British and U.S. leaders wanted to replace General Charles de Gaulle with him. Made commander of French forces in North Africa (December), he became co-president with de Gaulle of the Committee of National Liberation (May 1943). Politically inept, he was soon elbowed to the sidelines by de Gaulle and resigned (November 1943). Later he helped liberate Corsica in April 1944.

Glubb, Sir John Bagot (1897–1986) British army officer and Jordanian general. Glubb graduated from the Royal Military Academy at Woolwich (1915) and served in France during World War I in the engineers (1915–18). He volunteered for service in Iraq and served there during the Arab Revolt (July–December 1920). He resigned from the service (1926) to become a civilian official for the Iraqi government, but left that post (1930) to become "officer commanding, Desert Area, Transjordan," in effect second-in-command of the Arab Legion. He raised, trained, and led what became an effective constabulary force in the Transjordan region.

Glubb took command of the 1,350-man Arab Legion (August 1939) just before World War II. An effective commander who was fluent in Arabic, he led the Legion into French-held Syria as part of General Archibald Wavell's invasion (June–July 1941).

By 1947 "Glubb Pasha" (General Glubb) had built the Legion into a 6,000-man motorized division. The most effective military force on the Arab side in the 1948–49 Israeli War of Independence, the Legion secured for Jordan the West Bank area and the Arab portion of Jerusalem. Anti-British sentiment, however, led King Hussein to demand his resignation (February 1956). Glubb returned to Britain and was knighted (1957). In retirement he produced a number of books on the Legion and his experiences.

Goddard, Robert Hutchings (1882–1945) U.S. rocket scientist. Fascinated as a boy by Jules Verne's adventure books, Goddard was convinced space flight would one day become reality. He studied physics at the Worcester, Massachusetts Polytechnic Institute, then obtained his doctorate at Clark University, Worcester (1911). He pioneered modern rocket development and saw the clear advantages of liquid fuel. An ordnance expert during World War I, he returned to rocket development after the war and proposed building a rocket large enough to reach the moon. Using a grant from the Smithsonian Institution, he launched a rocket using liquid oxygen as a propellent (28 March 1926), the first to fly on liquid fuel. The Guggenheim Foundation, on the advice of Charles Lindbergh, advanced research money and he developed gyroscopic control, gimbal and jet vane steering, and pressurized fuel tanks. By 1935 his rockets reached 8,000 feet and attained supersonic speeds. Others used his research to develop the World War II V-1 rocket and the anti-tank bazooka, as well as post-war space rockets.

Godfrey, John H. (1888–1971) British admiral. Godfrey joined the navy (1903). Appointed to head the Admiralty's intelligence division (February 1939), he quickly reorganized it to make it more effective. He also established the Joint Intelligence Committee to provide for the sharing of information. He early recognized the value of ULTRA (intelligence gained through the ability to read German encoded radio messages) and deception (at which the British excelled in the war). Nonetheless, his abrasive manner of leadership led to his removal (1942). He then commanded the Indian Navy and retired in 1946.

Godfroy, René Émile (1885–1981) French admiral. During World War II Godfroy took command of 2nd Cruiser Squadron (April 1940) and was promoted vice admiral. After the armistice between France and Germany (22 June), British Prime

Minister Winston Churchill expressed fear that units of the French fleet might fall into German hands and insisted that those portions of it that the Royal Navy could reach be offered the chance to continue the fight against Germany, be neutralized in a foreign port, or be sunk (Operation CATAPAULT) (3 July). Admiral Andrew Cunningham, whose ships at Alexanderia were intermingled with those of the French, had no intention of opening fire if he could avoid it and exercised as much tact as possible in presenting the ultimatum to Godfroy, who commanded Force X there. Godfroy agreed to see his ships demilitarized in the harbor with reduced crews, thus avoiding the bloodshed and loss that occurred the same day at Mersel-Kebir.

Godfroy joined the Allied cause following the liberation of North Africa (1943) but was later removed from command. He was rehabilitated in 1955.

Goethals, George Washington (1858–1928) U.S. army engineer. Commissioned in the engineers on graduation from West Point (1880), Goethals assisted in work on the Ohio and Cumberland rivers and construction of the Mussel Shoals Canal on the Tennessee. He was an instructor at West Point (1894–98), and served in Puerto Rico during the 1898 Spanish-American War and then on the General Staff. He graduated from the Army War College (1907).

President Theodore Roosevelt appointed Goethals chief engineer and chairman of the Isthmian Canal Commission for completion of the Panama Canal (February 1907). He proved to be a hard-working, adroit, and effective administrator. Following completion of the canal ahead of schedule (August 1914), he was promoted major general, and during 1914–16 he was administrator of the Canal Zone. He then retired from the army.

Recalled to active duty when the United States entered World War I, Goethals

became quartermaster general of the army and had charge of acquisition and supply, a herculean task. He retired again in April 1919.

Golikov, Filip Ivanovich (1900–80) Marshal of the Soviet Union. Golikov joined the Red Army (1918) and graduated by correspondence from the Frunze Military Academy with a specialty in armor (1933). Following commands in the invasion of Poland (September 1939) and perhaps in Finland, he was promoted major general (May 1940) and assigned as deputy chief of the general staff and chief of military intelligence (GRU). Reporting only to Stalin, he passed along information from Russian spy Richard Sorge that Japan would strike south in 1941. Shortly after the German invasion of the Soviet Union (22 June 1941), he led missions to London and Washington to negotiate aid.

Golikov took command of Tenth Army (October 1941) before Moscow and led it in desperate fighting (December). He commanded Fourth Assault Army in the winter counteroffensive (February–March 1942) and then the Bryansk Front opposing German Army Group South's summer offensive (June 1942). During the Battle of Stalingrad (August–December 1942) he commanded first the Voronezh Front, then First Guards Army; he was also deputy commander of the Southeast and Stalingrad Fronts. He then headed the Voronezh Front (October 1942–March 1943) and took part in the Soviet push through Kursk and Kharkov.

Promoted colonel general (January 1943), Golikov was deputy commissar of defense for cadres and chief of the personnel directorate of the Red Army (1943–50). He was subsequently promoted general of the army (1945) and marshal in 1961.

Gorchkov, Sergei Georgievich (1910–88) Soviet admiral. Gorchkov entered the Russian navy (1927), graduating from the Frunze Naval Academy (1931). His early service was with the Black Sea Fleet, and during World War II he came to command a destroyer squadron. He was a close associate of Soviet leader Nikita Khrushchev, who appointed him CinC of the Soviet Navy (1956), a post he held until his death (1988).

Khrushchev initially charged Gorchkov with carrying out reductions in defense expenditures, but this ended in the intensification of the Cold War following the 1962 Cuba Missile Crisis. One of the great lessons of that event for the Soviet leadership was the inadequacy of Soviet naval power. Khrushchev and his successor Leonid Brezhnev embarked on a considerable increase in defense expenditures, especially in the naval sphere. Gorchkov transformed the Soviet Navy from essentially a coast defense force into one capable of projecting naval power around the globe in support of Soviet foreign policy objectives. He oversaw construction of the Soviet Navy's first aircraft carriers, as well as new nuclear submarines and warships comparable to Western designs. His theories of naval tactics and strategy were embodied in his major book, *The Sea Power of the State* (1976).

Goltz, Colmar Freiherr von der (1843–1916) German and Ottoman field marshal. Goltz joined the Prussian army in 1861 and fought in the Wars of German Unification. He spent much of his career in staff or teaching posts and was a military advisor in the Ottoman Empire (1883–95). He became a corps commander (1902) and army inspector general (1908). Promoted field marshal (1911), he was placed on the standby list in 1913.

When World War I began, Goltz sought a major field command but became governor-general of occupied Belgium. Dissatisfied with this post, he welcomed transfer to Constantinople as a senior advisor to the Ottoman high command (December). He did not get on well with head of the German military mission

in Turkey, General Otto Liman von Sanders, and he eagerly accepted transfer to the Persian–Mesopotamian theater of war (fall 1915). Commanding the Ottoman Sixth Army, he halted the British advance towards Baghdad (December), but died of spotted fever only days before the surrender of General Charles Townshend's Anglo-Indian division at Kut-el-Amara (29 April 1916).

Göring, Hermann Wilhelm (1893–1946) German marshal, commander of the air force and number two in the Nazi hierarchy. Göring graduated from the military academy at Gross Lichterfelde (1912) and was commissioned in the infantry. During World War I he transferred to the flying arm as a combat pilot (1915). Shot down and severely wounded, he returned to combat (1916). He became commander of the Richthofen Squadron (July 1918) and was credited with twenty-two kills in the war.

After the war Göring moved to Scandinavia, where he became a show flier and married a Swedish baroness. On his return to Germany (1922), he became a prize recruit for the National Socialist party. Seriously wounded in the 1923 Beer Hall Putsch, he fled Germany. He returned (1927), rejoined the Nazis, and was elected to the Reichstag (1928). His social contacts that produced financial backing were his biggest contribution to the rise of Nazism. He became president of the Reichstag (1932). After Adolf Hitler became chancellor, he garnered numerous titles and positions, including Minister for Air, in which post he began secretly building the German Air Force (1935). Hitler then gave him charge of the entire German economy (1936), and he was promoted *Reichsmarschall* in 1940. He soon had amassed a vast fortune.

During the war Göring intervened in policy in fits and starts, often with disastrous result, as in the 1940 Battle of Britain, after which he began to lose Hitler's favor. Initially popular with the

German people, he grew satiated and lethargic, and his popularity plummeted. Stripped of his posts when he sought to take control of Germany before Hitler's death, he was captured by the Americans at the end of the war. Tried at Nuremberg, he was found guilty but escaped the hangman by committing suicide.

Gort, Lord John Standish Surtees Pendergast Verker, Viscount Gort (1886–1946) British field marshal. Commissioned into the army in the Grenadier Guards (1905), Gort served in France during World War I, first as an operations officer and then as battalion commander in the Grenadier Guards (1917–18), winning the Victoria Cross. After the war he commanded the Staff College, Camberley, then a brigade. Advanced ahead of other officers, he became chief of the Imperial General Staff (1937) and a full general (1937). Knighted (1938), he turned over his post to General John Dill in order to command the BEF in France at the start of World War II (September 1939). Initially he commanded four divisions, the number later rising to thirteen.

Although preoccupied by details and hardly imaginative, Gort nonetheless saved the BEF following the German invasion of France and Benelux (10 May 1940). Outflanked by the advancing Germans, he recognized the inevitable and conducted an effective delaying action toward the coast. In the process, he rejected orders by both Prime Minister Winston Churchill and French commander General Maxime Weygand that he send divisions south in a last throw of the dice against the southern German armor thrust (27 May).

Ordered to turn over command to General Harold Alexander and return to Britain (31 May), Gort was appointed inspector general of training forces (1940–41). He was CinC of Gibraltar (1941–42), and then of Malta (1943–44). Raised to field marshal (1943), he ended his military career as CinC Palestine and

high commissioner for Transjordan (1944–45). On retirement, he was created First Viscount Gort (1945).

Gott, William H. (1897–1942) British general. Educated at Harrow and Sandhurst, he was commissioned in the army (1915) and fought on the Western Front during World War I. Badly wounded (July 1917), he had to be left behind during a retreat and was taken prisoner. He made three unsuccessful attempts to escape and received the nickname "Strafer" from the German phrase "Gott Strafe England."

Following the war, Gott served twice in India. Promoted lieutenant colonel (1938), he commanded a battalion of the King's Royal Rifle Corps. During World War II he served continuously in Egypt and Libya. He commanded 7th Armored Division's Support Group (1940–41), then 7th Armored Division (September 1941), and XIII Corps (February 1942). Much respected as an officer and commander, he was promoted lieutenant general (August) and named to command Eighth Army, replacing General Claude Auchinleck. He was killed on his way to assume his command in Cairo when his plane was strafed by a German aircraft (7 August 1942). General Bernard Montgomery succeeded him.

Gough, Sir Hubert (1870–1963) British general. Educated at Eton and Sandhurst, Gough was commissioned in the army (1889). He fought in the 1897–98 Tirah campaign and, in the 1899–1902 Boer War, was a successful commander of anti-guerilla operations before being severely wounded and returned to Britain. After the war he was a professor at the Staff College, Camberley. He played a prominent role in the "Curragh Incident" (1914) when a number of officers threatened to resign if ordered to use force to impose Home Rule on the Ulster Protestants. This forced the government to back down.

Gough commanded 3rd Cavalry Brigade in the early fighting of World War I.

He then commanded a cavalry division, an infantry division, and I Corps. In the Battle of the Somme (July–November 1916) he commanded Fifth Army. In July 1917 he led the opening phase of the Passchendaele campaign, but casualties caused Field Marshal Sir Douglas Haig to shift command to General Herbert Plumer. Haig then ordered Gough to take over forty miles of French lines. The defenses were in poor state, divisions were too thinly spread, and there were few reserves. As a result the Germans, with a threefold manpower advantage, achieved a breakthrough there (21 March 1918). Gough was held responsible and removed from command. His last job before retirement with the rank of general (1922) was chief of the military mission to the Baltic. He was belatedly recognized with a GCB (1937), and during World War II he was recalled to serve as zone commander of the Home Guard in 1942.

Gouraud, Henri Joseph Eugène (1867–1946) French general. Gouraud entered St. Cyr (1888) and was commissioned in the infantry two years later. Prior to World War I, he spent virtually his entire service overseas and made his military reputation in Morocco. Promoted brigadier general just before the start of World War I, he made major general (1915). In May 1915 he commanded French forces at Gallipoli, where he performed credibly and lost an arm.

Gouraud returned to duty as commander of Fourth Army in Champagne (December 1915). He became resident general in Morocco (December 1916), but returned to France to command Fourth Army (July 1917), which held fifty miles of critical front in Champagne. In these circumstances he issued his famous "stand or die" order to French and U.S. troops under his command. He played a key role in stopping the German offensive in the Second Battle of the Marne, which earned him the nickname of "the Lion of Champagne." Fourth Army then went on the offensive (September 1918).

After the war Gouraud became High Commissioner of Syria and commander in the Levant (1919–23). He then served as governor of Paris and member of the Supreme Allied War Council (1923–37).

Govorov, Leonid Aleksandrovich (1897–1955) Marshal of the Soviet Union. Drafted into the Russian Army (1916), Govorov was commissioned from the Konstanin Artillery School (1917). Drafted into anti-Bolshevik forces commanded by Admiral Alexsander Kolchak, he deserted and joined the Red Army (1920). During the 1918–20 Civil War he commanded an artillery battalion, but because he had served in Kolchak's forces, he was denied membership in the Communist Party until 1942. He attended staff schools, the Frunze Military Academy, and the General Staff Academy. He commanded an artillery corps (1936) and, during the 1939–40 Russo-Finnish War, was chief of Seventh Army artillery. Here he utilized heavy guns for direct fire against fortifications.

Govorov then commanded the Dzerzhinsky Artillery Academy. Following the German invasion of the Soviet Union (22 June 1941), he commanded Fifth Army (October 1941) in the defense of Moscow and was promoted lieutenant general of artillery (November), and played an important role in the counterattack around Moscow (December 1941). He then commanded the Leningrad Front (June 1942–July 1945). Promoted general of the army (November 1943) and then marshal of the Soviet Union (June 1944), Govorov broke the German siege of Leningrad, pursuing the Germans through the Baltic states. He took command of 2nd Baltic Front (February 1945). After the war he headed the Leningrad Military District, then was chief inspector, Soviet Army (1946–47), and commanded the air defense forces and became deputy minister of defense (1954).

Grandmaison, Louis Loyzeau de (1861–1915) French general and military theorist. Grandmaison joined the army (1881), was commissioned (1883) and saw extensive service in France and overseas. While serving on the French Army general staff as director of military operations (1908–14), he articulated the doctrine of the resolute offensive. This rested on "élan" and an emotional, determined response to any invader. This concept of the *offensive à outrance* was incorporated into French War Plan XVII (1913), implemented at the start of World War I. Promoted to major general (January 1915), he died of wounds received in combat at Soissons the following month while commanding the Fifth Army Group of reserve divisions.

Graves, William Sydney (1865–1940) U.S. general. Commissioned in the army on graduation from West Point (1889), Graves held a variety of postings, including tours in the Philippines. In 1909 he was secretary to the General Staff. Promoted brigadier general (1917), he became assistant to the chief of staff. Promoted major general (June 1918), he commanded 8th Division.

Graves then took command of the American Expeditionary Force sent to Siberia (August 1918). He served another tour in the Philippines and commanded in succession the 1st Infantry Brigade and the 1st Infantry Division. He then commanded VI Corps (1925) and was in Panama (1926–28). He retired in 1928.

Graziani, Rodolfo (1882–1955) Italian marshal. During World War I he served first in Libya, and then went to the Italian front where he was wounded twice and became Italy's youngest colonel. He commanded forces in Tripolitania (1928) and rose to be a corps commander (1932) and governor of Cyrenaica. Considered Italy's most effective desert commander, he used brutal pacification methods. Appointed military governor of Italian Somaliland (early 1935), he commanded troops that invaded Abyssinia (Ethiopia) (October). Made Marchese de Neghelli and marshal of Italy, he replaced Marshal Pietro Badoglio as viceroy of Ethiopia (May 1936), but opposition to his repressive rule brought revolt and his replacement by the Duke de Aosta (January 1938). He was then in virtual retirement as honorary governor of East Africa (1937–39) until named army chief of staff (October 1939). Although Italy joined the war (10 June 1940), its army performed abysmally against France.

Following the accidental death of Governor General of Libya Marshal Italo Balbo (June), Graziani succeeded him. After repeated delays he reluctantly invaded Egypt (September), but the offensive was a disaster. Recalled (March 1941), he resigned from the army. Following the overthrow of Mussolini and his subsequent rescue by the Germans, Graziani became minister of defense in Mussolini's puppet government in the north (September 1943). He surrendered to the Allies (April 1945), who turned him over to Italian authorities (1946). Tried in 1950, he was sentenced to nineteen years in prison but was released after a few months.

Grechko, Andrey Antonovich (1903–76) Soviet marshal. Grechko joined the Red Army (1919), fought in the civil war, and joined the Communist party (1928). He graduated from the Frunze (1936), commanded a cavalry regiment, and was CofS of 36th Cavalry Division. He participated in the invasion of Poland (September 1939) and, as a colonel, was assigned to the General Staff in Moscow just before the (22 June 1941) German invasion. He then commanded 34th Cavalry Division at Kharkov. Promoted major general, he headed V Cavalry Corps (January 1942), then Eighteenth Army (October 1943–January 1943), both on the southern front. Promoted lieutenant general, he commanded Fifty-Sixth Army in Ukraine (until October 1943), then was second in command of 2nd Ukrainian Front, where he developed friendships with Nikita Khrushchev and Leonid Brezhnev. He then took command of First Guards Army (December 1943). Promoted colonel general, he led this army the rest of the war, helping to liberate Kiev, the remainder of Ukraine, and Prague.

After the war Grechko commanded the Kiev Military District (1945–53). Promoted general of the army (March 1953), he was CinC of Soviet troops in East Germany (1953–55), crushing the June 1953 Berlin Uprising. Promoted marshal of the Soviet Union (1955), he was CinC, Soviet Ground Forces (1957–60). He was then first deputy minister of defense and CinC, Warsaw Pact Armed Forces (1960–67), when he became minister of defense (1967). He orchestrated the 1968 Warsaw Pact invasion of Czechoslovakia, and died in office in 1976.

Greim, Robert von (1892–1945) German air force general. Originally a gunnery officer in World War I, Greim became a fighter pilot, ending the war with twenty-eight victories and the *Pour le Mérite*. After studying law at the Univeristy of Munich, he organized the Nationalist Chinese Air Force (1924–27). After pursuing commercial aviation ventures he entered the Wehrmacht as a major (1934). Appointed inspector of fighters and dive bombers (April 1935), he headed the Air Ministry personnel section (1937).

During the German invasion of Poland (September 1939), Greim was a major general commanding V Air Corps. He participated in the invasion of France and Benelux (May 1940) and in the 1940 Battle of Britain. His corps was then sent to the Eastern Front for the invasion of the Soviet Union (22 June 1941). As colonel general, he headed Sixth Air Fleet (from February 1943).

Called to Berlin by Adolf Hitler (24 April 1945), Greim flew into the beleaguered city with Hanna Reitsch (26 April). His right foot was shattered by ground fire in the approach, and Reitsch landed the plane. Hitler then promoted him new commander of the Luftwaffe with the rank of field marshal, replacing Hermann Göring, who had proposed seizing power from Hitler. Greim and Reitsch, both fervent Nazis, asked permission to remain with Hitler in Berlin but were ordered to fly out of the city, which they managed to accomplish in a training plane (28 April). Greim eventually reached Admiral Karl Dönitz's headquarters. Captured by the Americans, he committed suicide in prison (24 May).

Griswold, Oscar Woolverton (1886–1959) U.S. general. Griswold attended the University of Nevada (1905–06) and was commissioned in the infantry from West Point (1910). He served in China (1914–17) and fought in World War I as a major with the 84th Division in the Meuse–Argonne Offensive (September–November 1918). After the war he was on occupation duty in Germany (1918–19). He graduated from the Command and General Staff School (1925) and the Army War College (1929). He served on the General Staff of the War Department (1929–31).

He was then a member of the infantry board (1932–36) and served in the office of the chief of infantry (1936–39). He commanded the 29th Infantry (September 1939–October 1940). Promoted brigadier general (October 1940), he commanded the 4th Infantry Division (1940–41). Promoted major general (August 1941), he commanded the Infantry Replacement Training Center, Camp Croft (1941), then 4th Mechanized Division, IV Corps, and XIV Corps (August 1941–August 1945). Griswold commanded XIV Corps in the Pacific Theater during the later stages of the New Georgian Campaign (July–August 1944) and in the Luzon campaign in the liberation of the Philippines (January–August 1945). He then returned to command 4th Infantry Division (1945–47) before retiring (October 1947).

Groener, Wilhelm (1867–1939) German general. Groener joined the army (1884) and was commissioned (1886). He graduated from the Kriegsakademie (1896) and held various staff and command positions. In 1912 he headed the Railroad Branch of the General Staff and played a key role in the rapid mobilization and deployment of the German Army in August 1914.

Promoted colonel (September 1914) and major general (June 1915), Groener continued in charge of German railway operations until October 1916. Promoted lieutenant general, he oversaw implementation of the "Hindenburg Program" to mobilize Germany's manpower for war production. He then commanded a division on the Western Front (August 1917), then a corps (December). He commanded I Corps in Ukraine, then became chief of staff to Field Marshal Hermann von Eichhorn, German commander in Ukraine (March 1918).

After General Erich Ludendorff resigned (26 October 1918), Groener took his place as first quartermaster general. He supervised the withdrawal of Germany's western armies, called for immediate armistice talks, and informed the Kaiser that the army no longer supported him. He also worked out an arrangement with the new socialist government in Berlin whereby the army would support the government as long as it suppressed radical elements (10 November). He retired in September 1919. He was minister of transport (1920–23), and then minister of defense (1928–32).

Groves, Leslie Richard (1896–1970) U.S. general. Groves attended the University of Washington and Massachusetts Institute of Technology before graduating from West Point (1918). He served in the Corps of Engineers and was a colonel in charge of completing the Pentagon building when he was promoted brigadier general and given charge of the top-secret MANHATTAN (Engineer District) Project to develop an atomic bomb (August 1942).

Groves was promoted major general (February 1944), and eventually controlled a $2 billion budget and had 125,000 people working for him. A gifted organizer and gruff no-nonsense leader, he was instrumental in the project's success. Later he helped develop the list of Japanese targets. After the war he advised President Harry S. Truman on atomic policy. Promoted lieutenant general (January 1948), he then retired in February.

Gruenther, Alfred Maximilian (1899–1983) U.S. general. Commissioned in the field artillery on graduation from West Point (1919), Gruenther was promoted captain (1935). He taught at West Point (1935–37), then graduated from the Command and General Staff School (1937) and the Army War College (1939).

Gruenther became deputy to CofS of Third Army General Dwight Eisenhower (October 1941). He was then CofS of Third Army. Promoted temporary brigadier general (August 1942), he became deputy CofS of Allied Force headquarters in London, helping plan the invasion of North Africa. Promoted temporary major general (February 1943), he became CofS to General Mark Clark's Fifth Army and helped plan the invasions of Sicily and Italy. He was then promoted CofS of Fifteenth Army Group. After the war he was deputy commander of U.S. forces in Austria (1945–46).

Gruenther returned to the U.S. to be deputy commandant of the new National War College and first director of the joint staff on the establishment of the Joint Chiefs of Staff (1947). Promoted lieutenant general, he became army deputy CofS for plans (1949). In December 1950 he became CofS, Supreme Headquarters Allied Powers Europe (SHAPE). Promoted general (1951), he then became Supreme Allied Commander Europe (July 1956), which post he held until his retirement (November 1956).

Guderian, Heinz (1888–1954) German general. Commissioned in the army (1908), Guderian concentrated on signal communication. He attended the War Academy, and during World War I served with the 5th Cavalry Division. By the end of the war he had fully grasped the importance of radio and the tank.

Following the war, Guderian continued in the Reichswehr and became inspector of motorized troops. Building on the work of British and French armor theorists, he experimented with tank warfare and by 1928 had developed plans to employ tanks en masse in combined arms attacks and was the father of *Blitzkrieg* (Lightning War). Hitler's enthusiastic support overrode General Staff opposition.

Commander of 2nd Panzer Division (1935), Guderian was promoted brigadier general (August 1936). In 1937 he published *Achtung! Panzer* (Attention! Armor), presenting his theories of armored warfare. Promoted major general (February 1938) and lieutenant general (November), he commanded XIX Corps in Fourth Army during the invasion of Poland (September 1939). During the Battle for France (May–June 1940) he led this corps through the Ardennes and pushed to the Channel. After the defeat of France, he was promoted full general (July 1940).

In the invasion of the Soviet Union (22 June 1941), Guderian commanded Second Panzer Group in Army Group Center, but Hitler ignored his appeals to press on to Moscow and subsequently refused to allow him to withdraw his forces from an exposed forward position. He then removed Guderian from command (December 1941).

Guderian returned to duty as inspector general of all panzer forces (February 1943) and CofS of the army (July 1944), but clashes with Hitler again led to his removal from command in March 1945. He then wrote his memoirs.

Guevara, Ernesto (Che) (1928–67) Cuban revolutionary and guerrilla warfare theorist. Guevara studied literature in college in Argentina and became a dedicated Marxist. While pursuing medicine at Buenos Aires University he became interested in advancing political change in Latin America, especially after extensive travels during a break in his studies revealed how many people lived in poverty. After securing his medical degree (1953), and to escape military service in the army of Argentine dictator Juan Perón, he moved to Bolivia and then to Guatemala, where he attempted to establish an armed group to oppose the government. In Mexico City he met Cuban exiles Fidel and Raoul Castro, and joined their effort to overthrow the government of Cuban dictator Fulgencio Batista. Taking the nickname "Che" (Argentine slang for "buddy"), he became proficient in guerrilla tactics.

Guevara accompanied the revolutionaries to Cuba (1956) and was a doctor in Fidel Castro's guerrilla army. Highly influential in the military overthrow of Batista, he helped push Castro to communism, serving as minister of industry (1961–65). He is credited with inventing the so-called *foco* theory, later expanded upon and popularized by French theorists Gérard Challiand and Régis Debray. It holds that, simply by surviving, insurgent groups may become centers of attraction (*focos*) for latent peasant disattisfaction. It survived as the mythical explanation behind Castro's stunning success in Cuba.

Guevara traveled widely in Latin America and in the Congo in Africa, endeavoring to incite other revolutions. While trying to create a *foco* in Bolivia, he was captured and killed by its army.

Guillaumat, Marie Louis Adolphe (1863–1940) French general. Guillaumat graduated from St. Cyr (1884) and served three years as an officer in the Foreign Legion. He was in China during the 1900–01 Boxer Rebellion, and in 1903 returned to St. Cyr as an instructor. In 1914 he was an aide to the minister of war, having already taken part in twelve colonial campaigns.

During World War I, Guillaumat commanded an infantry division in the battles of the Marne (September 1914) and Argonne (1915). Promoted to command I Corps, he then fought in the Battles of Verdun and the Somme (1916). He then commanded Second Army in battles to recapture areas around Verdun (December 1916–December 1917). He replaced General Maurice Sarrail as commander of the Armies of The East at Salonika (December 1917), then was recalled to France to command troops defending Paris (July 1918). He then took command of Fifth Army (October 1918).

After the war, Guillaumat helped reorganize the Greek Army, commanded the French Army of Occupation in the Rhineland (1924–26) and served briefly as minister of war in 1926.

Guillaume, Augustin (1895–1983) French general. A graduate of St. Cyr (1914), Guillaume fought in World War I and was promoted captain at its end. After the war he served in Morocco, then was assistant military attaché at Belgrade (1922–24). He attended the École de Guerre (1926–28), then returned to Morocco for eight years. He joined the Higher War Council in Paris but, on the declaration of war (3 September 1939), returned to Morocco. After the armistice with Germany (22 June 1940), he was director of political affairs in Morocco and established a clandestine military organization with native troops known as *goumiers*. After the Allied invasion and occupation, Guillaume was promoted brigadier general

(1943) and led *goumiers* under General Henri Giraud in liberating Corsica, in the Italian campaign, and in southern France, where he helped take Marseille. He commanded the 3rd Algerian Infantry Division in General Jean de Lattre de Tassigny's First French Army, fighting in Alsace and into Germany.

After the war Guillaume was military attaché to the Soviet Union (1945–47). He became an authority on the Red Army and published several books on the subject. Commander of French occupation forces in Germany (1948–51), he also briefly (1951) commanded Allied Land Forces, Central Europe. He was then resident general in Morocco (1951–54). As a full general he was chief of the general staff and president of the Chiefs of Staff Committee in Paris (1954–56).

Guisan, Henri (1874–1960) Swiss general. A militia captain (1904), during World War I Guisan was an observer on both the Eastern and Western Fronts. As a colonel (1926), he devoted himself entirely to military affairs. Just before World War II began he was chosen general, only the fourth to hold that rank, and CinC of the Swiss army. By summer 1940 he headed a force that would number 800,000 men and women.

Guisan strengthened the national redoubt system of Alpine fortifications. His secret agreement for military cooperation with the French (the Guisan–Gamelin military convention) against the Germans was discovered by the Germans after their defeat of France and remained a threat as the excuse for a possible German invasion of Switzerland. He retired in 1947.

H

Hackett, John Winthrop (1910–) British army general. Educated at Oxford University, Hackett was commissioned in the army (1931) and spent much of his early military career in the Middle East. During World War II he was an operations officer in North Africa (1942), then commanded 4th Parachute Brigade (1943) which he led in Italy and in the Battle of Arnhem (September 1944).

After the war Hackett commanded in succession an armored brigade, an armored division, and troops in Transjordan and Northern Ireland. He also served on the General and Imperial General staffs. He ended his career as commander of the British Army of the Rhine. After his retirement, he wrote several books, among them *The Third World War.*

Haig, Alexander Meigs, Jr. (1924–) U.S. general. Haig was commissioned following graduation from West Point (1947). An aide to General Douglas MacArthur during the 1950–53 Korean War, he studied at the Naval War College (1955–56). After service in the Pentagon, he was special assistant to the secretary of defense (1964–65). He was with the 1st Infantry Division in Vietnam (1965–67), initially as G-3, then as a battalion commander. He was then stationed at West Point.

Haig was a military assistant to National Security Advisor Henry Kissinger in the Nixon administration (1969–73). Promoted brigadier general (1969) and major general (1972), Haig was advanced by President Richard Nixon past 240 more senior generals to full general and army vice chief of staff (September 1972).

Haig retired from the army and became President Nixon's chief of staff (1973). President Gerald Ford recalled him to active duty and appointed him supreme commander of NATO forces (SACEUR) (1974). Haig retired again to support Ronald Reagan's bid for the presidency (1979) and was President Reagan's secretary of state during 1981–82.

Haig, Sir Douglas, Earl Haig (1861–1928) British field marshal. Haig graduated from Brasenose College, Oxford, and first in his class from the Royal Military College, Sandhurst (1885). Commissioned in the 7th Hussars, he served in India. He attended the Army Staff College at Camberley (1896) and fought in the Battle of Omdurman (September 1898). During the 1899–1902 Boer War he was chief of staff to General John French. Promoted colonel, he commanded the 17th Lancers in operations against Boer guerrillas (1901). He was inspector general of cavalry in India (1903–06) and was promoted major general (1905). He was then director of military training at the War Office (1906–09), where he worked to prepare for possible British participation in a

European war and published a book, *Cavalry Studies* (1907).

Knighted (1909), Haig was then CofS of the Indian Army (1909–12) and promoted lieutenant general (1910). At the outset of World War I he commanded I Corps in the BEF in France and fought at Mons (August) and the Battle of the Marne (September). Promoted full general with command of First Army (February 1915), he led offensives at Neuve Chapelle (March), Artois (May), and Loos (September–October). French was blamed for these failures, and Haig succeeded him as commander of British forces in France (December).

Haig's name is forever linked with the Battle of the Somme (July–November 1916). His defenders stress his determination to fight against all odds; critics said his plan was unrealistic and that he was inflexible and stubborn. Haig, now a field marshal (late 1916), sent the BEF on the offensive again in another bloodletting for little gain in the Battle of Passchendaele (Third Ypres) (July–November 1917).

Haig helped to repulse the Spring 1918 Ludendorff Offensives and carried out the successful counterattack, most notably the action around Amiens (August). He then directed the final offensive in Flanders (September–November). After the war he was created Earl Haig, Viscount Dawick and Baron Haig (1919).

Haislip, Wade Hampton (1889–1971) U.S. general. Haislip was commissioned in the infantry on graduation from West Point (1912). He served with the 19th Infantry Regiment on the Mexican border (1915–16) and with V Corps and 3rd Division in France during World War I. He participated in the St. Mihiel (September 1918) and Meuse–Argonne Offensives (October–November) and rose to temporary lieutenant colonel. After the war Haislip was with occupation forces at Coblenz (until 1921). An instructor at West Point (1921–23), he graduated from the Command and General Staff School

(1925) and Army War College (1932) and attended the French École de Guerre. An instructor at the Command and General Staff School (1932–36), he was in the planning division of the War Department General Staff (1938–41).

Promoted brigadier general (January 1941) and major general (March 1942), Haislip organized the 85th Infantry Division (May 1942). As commander of XV Corps (February 1943), he joined General George Patton's Third Army (December). Because Haislip had studied in France, General Philippe Leclerc's 2nd French Armored Division was assigned to his corps. He led XV Corps from Normandy, in the liberation of Paris, in fighting around Falaise, across France to Strasbourg, and in the Rhineland campaign. Promoted lieutenant general (April 1945), he commanded Seventh Army in occupation in Germany. He was then president of Personnel Board (1945–46) and deputy chief of staff for administration (1948–49). Promoted general when he became vice CofS (1949–51), he retired in July 1951.

Haldane, Richard Burdon, Viscount (1856–1928) British military reformer and statesman. Haldane served as a Liberal member of parliament (1885–1911) and as secretary of state for war (1905–12). Acting on recommendations from the 1903–04 Esher Committee Report and 1906 Anglo-French Staff talks, Haldane secured legislation modernizing the British Army along European lines by creating the Imperial General Staff, the British Expeditionary Force (BEF), the Territorial Army, and the Officer Training Corps. These reforms made possible the rapid deployment of the BEF to France (August 1914). In 1912 Haldane undertook an unsuccessful mission to Germany to persuade Kaiser Wilhelm II to slow warship construction. He was later lord chancellor.

Halder, Franz (1884–1972) German general. Halder joined the Bavarian army (1902), graduated from the Bavarian Staff

College, and served on the staff of Field Marshal Crown Prince Rupprecht during World War I. He continued in the Reichswehr after the war. Promoted colonel (1931), he was then promoted brigadier general (July 1934) and commanded 7th Infantry Division (1935). Promoted lieutenant general (August 1936), he was deputy CofS for training (October). Promoted lieutenant general (February 1938), he became deputy CofS for operations (March). He succeeded General Ludwig Beck as chief of the General Staff (August 1938) and developed plans to remove Adolf Hitler from power, but the collapse of the Western powers before Hitler in the 1938 Czech crisis brought an end to these.

Halder helped plan many of the German campaigns during the war, including the invasion of Poland (September 1939). He dissuaded Hitler from attacking the West that same year. Promoted full general (July 1940), he planned Operation BARBAROSSA, the invasion of the Soviet Union (22 June 1941). Dismissed by Hitler (September 1942) over his opposition to the 1942 campaign plans and made a scapegoat for Hitler's own failures, he retired. Although not involved, he was arrested after the failure of the bomb plot (20 July 1944). Imprisoned at Dachau, he was freed at the end of the war. He then wrote extensively on the war and his own role in it.

Hall, Charles Philip (1886–1953) U.S. general. Commissioned on graduation from West Point (1911), Hall returned there as an instructor (1914–17). After the U.S. entered World War I (April 1917), he went with the AEF to France and fought with 2nd Division at Belleau Wood (June 1918), in the Aisne–Marne Counteroffensive (July–August), Saint-Mihiel Offensive (September), and the Meuse–Argonne Offensive (September–November). After the war he graduated from the Command and General Staff School (1926) and Army War College (1930). He then served in the Philippines (1930–32).

Promoted brigadier general (January 1941), Hall was with the 3rd Infantry Division (1941–42). Promoted major general (March 1942), he commanded the 93rd Infantry Division (March–October). He commanded XI Corps in the Southwest Pacific and led it on New Guinea (January 1943–July 1944), Morotai (September 1944), and in the liberation of the Philippines (1945). Promoted lieutenant general, he was acting commander of Eighth Army in the occupation of Japan (1945–46).

Hall, William Reginald (1870–1943) British admiral and naval intelligence officer. Hall joined the Navy (1884) and became a captain (1905). For reasons of health, he took up naval intelligence duties in London (November 1914). Hall then became director of naval intelligence (DNI). As such he expanded the cryptologic operations known as Room 40 that achieved significant breakthroughs during the war, especially in the Battle of Jutland (May–June 1916) and the 1917 Zimmermann Telegram episode. He was promoted rear admiral and knighted for his handling of the latter event (1917). He retired as a vice admiral and later became a member of parliament.

Haller, Józef (1873–1960) Polish general. Haller first became a professional soldier in the Austro-Hungarian Army, retiring as a captain (1911). Active in the Polish independence movement, he organized the Field Sokól Troops, based on the patriotic sports organization (1912).

From 1914 he commanded first a regiment and then a brigade in the Austrian-backed Polish Legions during World War I. Haller switched sides in protest at the signing of the Treaty of Brest-Litovsk with Russia. He defeated Austrian forces and then commanded the Polish II Corps in the Ukraine. When it was defeated by German forces (May 1918), he made his way to France where he commanded Polish forces.

In the 1920 Russo-Polish War Haller commanded the Polish northern front during the crucial Battle of Warsaw. He was a cabinet minister in General Wladyslaw Sikorski's government (1940–43).

Halsey, William Frederick, Jr. (1882–1959) U.S. admiral. Halsey graduated from Annapolis (1904) and was commissioned (1906). He served in the Great White Fleet during its circumnavigation of the globe (1907–09). He was then in torpedo boats, and was commanding a destroyer as a lieutenant commander when the United States entered World War I (April 1917). During the war he commanded destroyers operating from Queenstown (now Cobb, County Cork), Ireland in anti-submarine patrol.

After the war Halsey held destroyer commands. He also served in Naval Intelligence and was naval attaché in Berlin (1922–24). Promoted captain (1927), he commanded the *Reina Mercedes*, the Naval Academy's training ship. This began his love of naval aviation. He completed both the Navy (1933) and Army (1934) War Colleges. Then, despite poor eyesight and advanced age (52), he completed flight training (1935) and was assigned to command the aircraft carrier *Saratoga*. Promoted rear admiral (1937), he commanded Carrier Division 2 (*Enterprise* and *Yorktown*) (1938). Promoted vice-admiral (1940), he escaped the Japanese attack on Pearl Harbor because he was returning from delivering planes to Wake Island. He then led carrier strikes against the Japanese, including command of Task Force 16 in the "Doolittle Raid" on Tokyo (April 1942).

Hospitalized because of a skin ailment, Halsey missed the Battle of Midway (June 1942) but was assigned command of the South Pacific Area (October). Promoted admiral (November), he played a key role in the Guadalcanal campaign. He then commanded the newly created Third Fleet (March 1943) but continued to command the South Pacific Area (until June 1944).

He was known as "Bull" by the press for his pugnacious nature.

Halsey's most controversial action came during the Battle of Leyte Gulf (23–26 October 1944) when he was decoyed into chasing after a Japanese carrier force in the Battle of Cape Engaño, leaving the Leyte landing site vulnerable to Japanese attack. Fortunately Vice Admiral Takeo Kurita broke off his assault prematurely. Another major controversy centered on Halsey's decision to lead the fleet into a typhoon, leading to the loss of three destroyers (December 1944).

Halsey supported the invasions of Luzon and Okinawa, and his carrier aircraft attacked the Japanese home islands. His flagship *Missouri* was the site of the formal Japanese surrender (2 September 1945). Halsey returned home with part of the Third Fleet (October) and was promoted admiral of the fleet (December). He was on special duty with the secretary of the navy until his retirement (April 1947).

Hamilton, Sir Ian Standish Monteith (1853–1947) British general. Hamilton joined the army in 1872 and served in the Boer War. He held a variety of posts before World War I, including commander-in-chief of Mediterranean forces and inspector general of overseas forces.

At the outset of the war, Hamilton took command of Britain's home defense forces. In March 1915, after naval operations failed to open the Dardanelles, he was appointed to command an amphibious assault on the Gallipoli Peninsula. A lack of intelligence information and Hamilton's indecisiveness doomed the operation. Hamilton spent forty days assembling the invasion force, a delay that allowed the Turks to repair and strengthen the defenses, and his invasion plan was also faulty. He also failed to exercise adequate control over his subordinates and was overly optimistic. Relieved in October 1915, Hamilton never again held active command.

Hanaya, Tadashi (1894–1957) Japanese general. Hanaya graduated from both the Military Academy (1914) and Army Staff College (1922). Promoted major, he commanded an infantry battalion (1929). He then headed the Special Services Agency at Mukden (Shenyang) in the Kwantung (Guongdong) Army in Manchuria and thus was involved in the manufacture of the "Mukden Incident" (18 September 1931) that became the excuse for the Japanese takeover of the remainder of Manchuria (1931–32). Promoted colonel, he commanded an infantry regiment (1937) and advised the army of the puppet state of Manchukuo (1939). Promoted major general, he commanded a brigade (1940). He then was CofS of First Army in South China (1941). Promoted lieutenant general, he commanded 55th Infantry Division in Burma (1943).

Known as a ruthless commander who was hard on his subordinates, Hanaya had considerable success in the Second Arakan campaign until halted by superior British air logistical supply (February–April 1944). His subsequent attacks along the lower Sittang River in south Burma allowed Twenty-Eighth Army to escape (May–June 1945). Appointed chief of staff for Eighteenth Army on Rabaul (July), he ended the war there.

Hansell, Haywood Shepherd, Jr. (1909–88) U.S. Air Force general. Hansell graduated from Georgia Tech (1924) and was commissioned in the Air Reserve (1928). An instructor at the Army Air Corps Tactical School (1935–38), he then graduated from the Command and General Staff School (1939). He held a series of staff assignments, culminating in the war plans division of the chief of the Air Corps. He then served with the War Department General Staff (1942). Promoted brigadier general (August 1942), he commanded the 3rd, then 1st Bomb Wing (1942–43). He was then assigned to headquarters Army Air Forces (1943–44). As CG of 25th Bomber Command, he

was involved in the air bombardment of Japan (August 1944–January 1945). He then commanded 38th Flying Training Wing (1945) and retired in December 1946.

Recalled to active duty during the 1950–53 Korean War (July 1951), Hansell was chief of the mobilization division, office of the deputy CofS for operations, Air Force (1951–53) and was promoted major general (September 1952).

Harbord, James Guthrie (1866–1947) U.S. general. Harbord joined the 4th Infantry Regiment (1889) after he failed to gain appointment to West Point. Commissioned in the 5th Cavalry Regiment (1891), he graduated from the Infantry and Cavalry School at Fort Leavenworth (1895). In the 10th Cavalry (1899) he became close friends with John J. Pershing. Sent to the Philippines as a captain (1902), he worked with the Philippine Constabulary. Returning to the U.S., he was promoted major (1914) and was attending the Army War College when the U.S. entered World War I (April 1917). Commander of the AEF General Pershing selected him as its CofS.

Instrumental in preparing the AEF for combat, Harbord was rapidly promoted to brigadier general. During the spring 1918 Ludendorff Offensive, Pershing assigned him to the Marine Brigade of the 2nd Infantry Division (May 1918) and helped stop the Germans at Belleau Wood (June). Promoted major general (June), he commanded 2nd Infantry Division in its successful counterattack at Soissons (18 July). He then took charge of the troubled AEF Services of Supply, which he reorganized effectively.

Promoted brigadier general in the regular army (November 1918), Harbord was then reappointed AEF chief of staff. Promoted major general (September 1919), he commanded 2nd Infantry Division in the United States. He became army deputy CofS when Pershing became Army CofS (1921), but he retired the next year.

He was promoted lieutenant general on the retired list in July 1942.

Harmon, Ernest Nason (1894–1979) U.S. general. Harmon attended Norwich University and graduated from West Point (1917). Commissioned in the cavalry, during World War I he fought in the Saint Mihiel (September 1918) and Meuse–Argonne (September–November) Offensives. Advanced to permanent captain (1920), he graduated from the Cavalry School (1921), the Command and General Staff School (1933) and Army War College (1934). He was an instructor at West Point (1921–25) and at Norwich (1925–31) and served on the General Staff (1935–39). Promoted lieutenant colonel, he was assistant chief of staff in I Armored Corps (1940). Promoted temporary brigadier general, he was then chief of staff of Armored Force headquarters (November 1941).

Harmon took command of 2nd Armored Division (July 1942) and was promoted major general (August). He led part of the division in North African fighting (November 1942–May 1943), including the Battle of the Kasserine Pass (February). He commanded 1st Armored Division (April) and fought at Salerno (September). Sent to Anzio, his division led the breakout there (May–June 1944). He commanded XIII Corps in Texas (July), but resumed command of 2nd Armored Division (September 1944) and led it in the fighting through the Siegfried Line and the latter stage of the Battle of the Bulge (December 1944–January 1945). He then commanded XXII Corps (January 1945–January 1946).

Following the war, Harmon established the U.S. military government in Germany (1945–47), including the U.S. Constabulary (May 1946). He was then deputy commander of Army Ground Forces until his retirement in March 1948.

Harpe, Josef (1887–1968) German general. Harpe joined the army in the infan-try, but after World War I became involved in mechanized warfare, taking charge (1931) of the Reichswehr secret tank training center in the Soviet Union. As a brigadier general (April 1940), he formed 12th Panzer Division (October) and led it in the invasion of the Soviet Union (22 June 1941) and the great encirclements of Minsk and Smolensk (July–August). Promoted major general, he commanded XLI Corps (January 1942) and then Ninth Army near Minsk (November 1943) in the central part of the Eastern Front. Promoted full general (April 1944), he headed Fourth Panzer Army in Ukraine, then redesignated Army Group North Ukraine (later Army Group A). Adolf Hitler refused strategic withdrawals and Soviet forces broke through his lines, whereupon Hitler removed him from command (January 1945). Recalled (March 1945), he commanded the remnants of Fifth Panzer Army on the Western Front. Trapped in the Ruhr pocket, his command was destroyed and he was taken prisoner on 17 April.

Harris, Sir Arthur Travers, 1st Baronet (1892–1984) British air chief marshal. Harris joined a Rhodesian regiment at the beginning of World War I. He then transferred to the Royal Flying Corps and became a pilot (1915). He was a squadron leader in the newly formed Royal Air Force (1918), commanded a training school, and served in both India and Iraq. He completed the Army Staff College (1927), returned to the Middle East, and held posts in the Air Ministry (1933–37).

On the outbreak of World War II (September 1939), Harris commanded No. 5 Bomber Group. He was then deputy chief of the Air Staff and led a mission to Washington. Dissatisfaction with the course of British strategic bombing led to his appointment as CinC Bomber Command and promotion to air chief marshal (1942).

An effective leader who inspired confidence in his subordinates, "Bomber"

Harris believed that strategic bombing would break the German will to resist and force an end to the war. He advocated incendiary rather than high-explosive bombs to destroy German cities and used new tactics in the first "thousand bomber raid" on Köln (Cologne) (May 1942). The development of Pathfinder force and electronic navigation systems brought successes in 1943, but raids on Berlin (beginning November 1943) shifted emphasis from industrial targeting and brought heavy bomber losses.

Harris remained convinced of the value of strategic bombing through the end of the war. On his retirement (1946) he was made marshal of the Royal Air Force. Offered a peerage (1951), he refused but accepted a baronetcy (1953).

Hart, Thomas Charles (1877–1971) U.S. admiral. Hart graduated from Annapolis (1897). He served aboard a battleship during the 1898 Spanish-American War. Among subsequent assignments, he was an instructor at the Naval Academy and co-authored *Ordnance and Gunnery* (1903). When the U.S. entered World War I, he commanded seven submarines based in Ireland (1917–18). Promoted captain (1918), he advised the chief of naval operations (CNO) on submarine matters. He commanded the Asiatic Submarine Flotilla (1921–22), attended the Naval War College (1923), and commanded a battleship (1925–27). He then commanded the Torpedo Station at Newport, Rhode Island. Promoted rear admiral (1929), he commanded submarines of the Atlantic and Pacific fleets (1929–31), and then was superintendent of the Naval Academy (1931–34), where he introduced more humanities into the curriculum.

Hart commanded Cruiser Division 6 (1934–36), and then served on the General Board of the Navy that considered new tactics and weapons (1936–39). As admiral and commander of the Asiatic Fleet (1939), he sought to remedy problems in that small, scattered, and poorly trained force. Following U.S. entry into the war, he clashed with General Douglas MacArthur over the disposition of the fleet. In January 1942 he took command of all Allied naval forces in the Far East. The next month he returned to the U.S. and retired, but was recalled to serve on the General Board until he again retired in February 1945.

Hartman, Erich (1922–93) German air force officer. Hartman became interested in gliding in the 1930s and, on completion of gymnasium, joined the Luftwaffe. He graduated from Fighter School No. 2 in Zerbst (March 1942) and was commissioned an officer. Posted to the Eastern Front in JG-52 (August 1942), "the Blond Knight" as he was known, logged more than 1,400 sorties and achieved an astounding 352 air victories, the highest total in the history of aerial warfare. Forced down seven times, he was once captured (August 1943) but escaped and returned to German lines. Most of his tally was achieved against the Russians, but he was also for a short time posted to Rumania, where he shot down five P-51 Mustangs. Turned over to the Russians at the end of the war, he was imprisoned until 1955, when he joined the air force of the Federal Republic of Germany. He retired in 1973 as a colonel.

Harwood, Sir Henry (1888–1950) British admiral. Harwood joined the training ship *Britannia* (1903) and became a specialist in torpedoes. During World War I he served in the Grand Fleet. After the war most of his service was ashore in staff positions and at the Imperial Defense College. Promoted commodore, he commanded the South American division of the America and West Indies Squadron (1936). A Roman Catholic, he got on well with his Latin American counterparts.

On the outbreak of World War II (September 1939), Harwood was alerted to search for the German pocket battleship and commerce raider *Graf Spee*, commanded by Captain Hans Langsdorff. Locating her (13 December) in the estuary of the River Plate, Uruguay, despite adverse odds he engaged with cruisers *Ajax* (flag), *Achilles*, and *Exeter*. His unorthodox attack from different directions quickly damaged the *Graf Spee* and Langsdorff took her into Montevideo for repairs. Bluffed into believing the British had been reinforced, Langsdorff scuttled his ship (17 December) and then committed suicide.

Promoted immediately to rear admiral, Harwood was also knighted. He then became assistant chief of the Naval Staff (1940) and so impressed Prime Minister Winston Churchill that he succeeded Admiral Andrew Cunningham as CinC Mediterranean. Promoted full admiral, he pursued aggressive actions until poor health forced him from his post (early 1943). He then commanded the Orkneys and Shetland Islands before being invalided out of the navy as a full admiral (1945).

Hasbrouck, Robert Wilson (1896–1985) U.S. general. Hasbrouck graduated from West Point (1917) and served with the 62nd Coast Artillery in the AEF in France (1918) during World War I. After the war he was an instructor at the Field Artillery School (1921–24) and ROTC professor at Princeton University (1927–32). He graduated from the Command and General Staff School (1934) and Army War College (1937). He then was on the War Department General Staff (1937–41). He was a battery commander, then executive officer of the artillery division in the 4th Armored Division (April 1941–March 1942).

Hasbrouck was then CofS of the 1st Armored Division (March–August 1942). Promoted brigadier general (September), he commanded a combat unit in the 8th Armored Division (August 1942–August 43). He was deputy CofS, Twelfth Army Group in Britain (1943–1944). Assigned command of the 7th Armored Division

(November 1944), he led it during the Battle of the Bulge (December 1944–January 1945). Promoted major general (January 1945), he led his division in the breakout from the Remagen bridgehead and in the reduction of the Ruhr pocket (March–April). After the war, Hasbrouck served as deputy CofS for Army Ground Forces (1945–46) before his retirement in September 1947.

Hasegawa, Yoshimichi (1850–1924) Japanese general. Hasegawa fought in the 1868 Meiji Restoration War. He joined the new Japanese army as a captain (1871) and commanded a regiment in the 1877 Satsuma Rebellion. After travel in France (1885–86), he was promoted major general (1886). He commanded a brigade in the 1894–95 Sino-Japanese War and distinguished himself in fighting at Pyongyang, Korea (September 1894). He commanded the Guards Division in First Army early in the 1904–05 Russo-Japanese War, and fought with distinction in the Battle of the Yalu (April–May 1904). Promoted full general (June), he commanded the Korea Garrison Army (September 1904–December 1908). He was then army CofS (1912–15) and was promoted field marshal (1915).

Hashimoto, Kingorō (1890–1957) Japanese army officer. Hashimoto graduated from the Military Academy (1911) and the Army Staff College (1920), then served with the Kwantung Army and the army staff in Manchuria (1922–25). Promoted lieutenant colonel, he headed the Russian Section of Intelligence Section of the General Staff (1930–31). An ultranationalist, he founded, along with Captain Isamu Chō, the Cherry Blossom Society (1930) of militant junior officers. Cashiered after his involvement in an attempted putsch (October 1931), he was recalled after the start of war with China (July 1937). Promoted colonel, he received command of the 13th Heavy Field Artillery Regiment. In this capacity, he instigated the shelling of the British gunboat *Ladybird* and U.S. gunboat *Panay* on the Yangtse River (December 1937). Despite the international crisis this caused, he retained command of his regiment. Hashimoto was a key figure in the *Jūgutsu Jiken* (October Plot) and probably participated in the atrocities at Nanking (Nanjing).

Hashimoto retired (1939) but then became executive director of the Imperial Rule Association (1940). He was later charged and convicted of war crimes. Sentenced to life in prison, he was freed two months before his death.

Hashimoto, Mochitsura (1909–) Japanese naval officer and submarine commander. In 1944 he took command of *I-58*. His submarine torpedoed and sank the U.S. heavy cruiser *Indianapolis* (28 July 1945), the last major warship lost during the war by the U.S. Navy. Her sinking cost 803 lives and resulted in a controversial court-martial conviction for her captain, Charles B. McVay III.

Haus, Anton (1851–1917) Austro-Hungarian admiral. Haus entered the navy in 1869. He rose to become fleet inspector (1912) and then its commander (1913). He rejected proposals from the German and Austrian High Commands that he deploy the fleet to Constantinople for operations against the Russians in the Black Sea, a move he thought impracticable. He insisted that the big ships be maintained as a fleet-in-being. Even after Italy entered the war on the Allied side, he refused to risk his capital ships, although he made use of light forces, submarines, and aircraft. He subsequently became a champion of unrestricted submarine warfare. He was promoted admiral of the fleet in 1916.

Hausen, Max Klemens von (1846–1922) German general. Hausen entered the Saxon army (1866) and fought against Prussia in the 1866 Austro-Prussian War.

He was an instructor at the military academy in Berlin (1871–74) and served on the General Staff (1875–87). On the eve of World War I he commanded XII Corps at Dresden.

In the invasion of France and Belgium (August 1914), Hausen commanded Third Army. In the advance he ordered the shelling of Reims (4 September 1914), doing widespread damage to its cathedral and creating a source of controversy afterward. He was relieved of his command following the Battle of the Marne (September 1914).

Hausser, Paul (1880–1972) German SS general. "Papa" Hausser was commissioned in the infantry (1899). A staff officer on both the Western and Eastern Fronts in World War I, he continued in the Reichswehr after the war, retiring as a major general (1932). He joined the SS (1934) and took charge of setting up its officer training schools. He in effect created the Waffen (Armed) SS and was its commander.

At Hausser's instigation, Waffen SS units served with the regular army in the campaign for France. He took command of new SS 2nd Division (*Das Reich*) (October 1939) and fought with it in the invasion of the Soviet Union (22 June 1941), where he was wounded and lost an eye (October). After exhorting Hitler to provide tanks to the SS, he took command of I SS Panzer Corps (later II SS Panzer Corps), attached to Army Group B in Ukraine (June 1942). Encircled at Kharkov, he managed to break free (February 1943) and then took part in the city's recapture (March–April). He also fought in the Battle of Kursk (July), where his corps performed well. Following refitting in France, his corps returned to Russia. Sent to France, he commanded Seventh Army (June 1944). Again wounded (August), he managed to escape the Falaise Pocket with a third of his force. Promoted *SS-Oberstgruppenführer* (January 1945), he commanded Army Group G on the Rhine. Dismissed (April), he spent the remainder of the war on the staff of Field Marshal Albert Kesselring in Italy.

Heinrichs, Axel Erik (1890–1965) Finnish general. Heinrichs commanded III Corps during the 1939–40 Russo-Finnish War, successfully blunting Russian attacks on the Taipale area. He then commanded the Kannas Army (February–March 1940) and held Russian gains to a minimum.

When Finland entered the war against the Soviet Union following the German invasion in order to secure the territory taken from it by that nation in 1940 (the so-called Continuation War), he commanded the Karelian Army and retook the Karelia–Ladoga region. Later he was chief of the general staff and then CinC of the Finnish armed forces.

Heinrici, Gotthard (1886–1961) German general. Commissioned in the army (1911), Heinrici served on both the Western and Eastern Fronts in World War I. Continuing in the Reichswehr after the war, he was promoted brigadier general (January 1936), major general (March 1938), and lieutenant general (Spring 1940). He commanded the 16th Infantry Division in the invasion of Poland (September 1939), then XIII Corps in First Army in the invasion of France and Benelux (10 May 1940).

Heinrici commanded XLIII Corps in the invasion of the Soviet Union (22 June 1941). Promoted full general (January 1942), he commanded Fourth Army in Army Group Center. One of the premier defensive commanders in the war, he developed tactics that featured aggressive patrolling to discover impending attacks, withdrawing front-line troops to escape preliminary bombardments, and then counterattacking to destroy the attackers.

Heinrici took command of First Panzer Army in the Carpathians (August 1944) and also temporarily commanded First Hungarian Army. He took command of Army Group Vistula (March 1945) and

held the Oder River line for almost a month. Although Adolf Hitler rejected his pleas to save lives by abandoning Berlin, Heinrici cooperated with Albert Speer to circumvent his scorched earth directive. Relieved of command (28 April) when he announced he would not obey Hitler's order to hold at any cost, he was taken prisoner by U.S. forces at the end of the war.

Henry, Prince of Prussia (1862–1929) German admiral. The younger brother of Kaiser Wilhelm II, Henry commanded the cruiser squadron based at Kiaochow and led German naval units during the 1900–01 Chinese Boxer Rebellion. Promoted grand admiral, he commanded the German Navy in the Baltic Sea during World War I, where he mounted aggressive operations and argued for greater resources.

Hewitt, Henry Kent (1887–1972) U.S. admiral. Hewitt graduated from Annapolis (1906) and was commissioned (1908). After ship assignments, he returned to Annapolis as an instructor (1913–16). Following U.S. entry into World War I (April 1917), he commanded destroyers in convoy and anti-submarine duty. Again an instructor at Annapolis (1918–21), he was on staff duty with the Navy Department (1923–26) and graduated from the Naval War College (1929). Promoted captain (1933), he commanded a cruiser and then Cruiser Division 8. Promoted rear admiral (December 1940), he commanded U.S. Atlantic Fleet task groups in neutrality patrols and then convoy escort.

When the U.S. entered World War II (December 1941), Hewitt commanded the Amphibious Force, Atlantic Fleet and had responsibility for the Western Task Force landings at Casablanca, Morocco in Operation TORCH (November 1942). Promoted vice admiral (November), he commanded U.S. naval forces in northwest African waters and then assumed command of Eighth Fleet when it became operational (March 1943) and assisted in planning and carrying out Operation HUSKY, the Allied landings in Sicily (July 1943) and Operation AVALANCHE, the landing at Salerno (September). He commanded the Allied force of nearly 1,000 vessels in Operation DRAGOON that landed the 400,000 men of Seventh Army on the French Mediterranean coast (August 1944). Promoted admiral (April 1945), Hewitt commanded Twelfth Fleet in European waters (1945–46), then served as U.S. naval representative on the United Nations Military Staff Committee until his retirement in March 1949.

Higashikuni, Naruhiko (1887–1990) Japanese general. Related to the emperor and a prince, he graduated from the military academy as an infantry officer (1908), then held a succession of command and staff assignments, primarily in military intelligence. This included seven years in Europe as a lieutenant colonel. As a major general, he was appointed to the General Staff (1929). He commanded 5th Infantry Brigade and, as a lieutenant general (1934), the 4th Infantry Division. He then headed the army aeronautical department before commanding Second Army in China (1938). Promoted full general (August 1939), he was then CinC, Home Defense Headquarters. He resigned (December 1941), but was recalled to head the "surrender cabinet" (17 August–5 October 1945), ending Japanese involvement in World War II. He resigned to protest General Douglas MacArthur's edict that U.S. occupation authorities would dictate changes in Japan's internal affairs.

Higgins, Andrew Jackson (1886–1952) American industrialist. Higgins attended Creighton University (1903–06) but did not graduate. Fascinated by boats, he eventually acquired a fleet and organized a shipbuilding company in New Orleans.

Higgins Industries produced a great many products during World War II, but by far the most important was the "Higgins boat" or Landing Craft, Vehicle Personnel (LCVP). Shallow and flat-bottomed with a protected propeller and shaft, it was sold before the war for use in Louisiana swamps and marshes. The military version could land thirty-six men, or twelve men and a jeep, then extract itself from the beach for another shuttle run. It was widely used in the Pacific and Atlantic theaters, including the Normandy Invasion (June 1944). General Dwight Eisenhower said that without Higgins "the whole strategy of the war would have been different."

Himmler, Heinrich (1900–45) German political figure and leader of the SS. In World War I Himmler went from clerk to officer cadet in the 11th Bavarian Regiment. After the war he served in the *Freikorps*, secured an agricultural diploma from a technical high school, joined the Nazi party, and played a minor role in the 1923 Munich Beer Hall Putsch. Remaining active in politics, he bought a farm and raised poultry. Appointed by Adolf Hitler head of the *Shutz Staffel* (SS), his personal bodyguard (January 1929), he built it from 200 men into a carefully selected formation 50,000 strong, with a distinctive black uniform and its own ethos.

Himmler gained control of all the secret police of Germany (1934). As *Reichsführer* of the SS and head of the secret police, he was a powerful figure. For his key role in the Blood Purge (June 1934), Hitler made the SS an independent organization subject only to his own immediate authority. Himmler then gained control of all the police forces of Germany (June 1936). He was also allowed to establish armed SS formations, known as the SS *Verfügungstruppen* (emergency troops), from which the divisions of the Waffen SS (Armed SS) emerged during World War II. A dreaded figure in the Third Reich, he remained one of Hitler's closest advisers.

During the war, with oversight over racial policies, Himmler carried out the Final Solution, the plan to exterminate the Jews. After the bomb attempt on Hitler's life (July 1944), he commanded the reserve army. Hitler then appointed him to command Army Group Rhine (November) for the Ardennes Counteroffensive and Army Group Vistula (January–March 1945), positions for which he was totally unqualified. Furious on learning that Himmler had been making peace overtures to the Western Allies, Hitler ordered his arrest. Captured by the British at the end of the war, when recognized he committed suicide by means of a concealed cyanide capsule.

Hindenburg, Paul Ludwig Hans von Beneckendorff und von (1847–1934) German field marshal. Hindenburg became a cadet (1860) and was commissioned in the Foot Guards (1866). He fought in the 1866 Austro-Prussian War and distinguished himself in the Battle of Königgratz (July). He also fought in the 1870–71 Franco-German War, distinguishing himself at Saint-Privat. He attended the Kriegsakademie (1872–75) and then held a variety of staff and command positions. He commanded a division (1900–03) and then was commander of IV Corps. Hindenburg was placed on the inactive list as a lieutenant general (1911).

Shortly after the start of World War I when there was a command crisis in East Prussia, Hindenburg was called from retirement and given command of Eighth Army with Major General Erich Ludendorff as his chief of staff (22 August 1914). The two men quickly adopted the plan developed by Lieutenant Colonel Max Hoffmann to crush Russian General A. V. Samsonov's Second Army in the Battle of Tannenberg (August) and then force General Pavel Rennenkampf's First Army out of East Prussia after the First Battle of the Masurian Lakes (September). Promoted full general, he assumed command of the new Ninth Army (September). He then took charge of all German forces on the Eastern Front and was promoted field marshal (November).

Hindenburg replaced Erich von Falkenhayn as chief of the General Staff (29 August 1916). Ludendorff continued with him as first quartermaster-general. The two presided over a successful campaign against Romania and stabilization of the Eastern Front. They then implemented Operation ALBRICHT, a phased withdrawal of several German armies in the West to the shorter Siegfried (Hindenburg) Line (March 1917). These successes were, however, counter-balanced by their support for the resumption of unrestricted submarine warfare (February 1917), which brought the United States into the war and by disruptive economic and manpower mobilizations within Germany.

Hindenburg and Ludendorff's increasing interference in German internal affairs was highlighted by the dismissal of Chancellor Theobald von Bethmann Hollweg (July 1917). Hindenburg also agreed with Ludendorff that Germany should launch major offensives on the Western Front in spring 1918. Following the defeat of these attacks, Ludendorff resigned (26 October) but Hindenburg remained at his post (until 25 June) just before Germany signed the Treaty of Versailles. After the war Hindenburg promoted the "stab-in-the-back" myth.

Hindenburg was elected president of Germany (1925) and re-elected (1932). He was persuaded to appoint Adolf Hitler as chancellor on 30 January 1933.

Hines, John Leonard (1868–1968) U.S. general. Commissioned in the infantry on graduation from West Point (1891), Hines fought in Cuba during the 1898 Spanish-American War and then served the first of three tours in the Philippines. He participated in the 1916 Punitive Expedition into Mexico. During World War I he served in the GHQ of the American Expeditionary Force (May 1917). Promoted temporary brigadier general, Hines commanded 1st Brigade of 1st Division. Promoted temporary major general (August 1918), he commanded 4th Division, then III Corps (October 1918). He was promoted permanent brigadier general (November 1918) and permanent major general (March 1921).

As army CofS (1924–30), Hines was faced with serious shortages and worked to improve training and army schools. He then succeeded General Douglas MacArthur as commander of the Department of the Philippines (1930) and held that post until his retirement (1932). In 1940 he was promoted to general on the retired list.

Hipper, Franz Ritter von (1863–1932) German admiral. Hipper joined the navy (1881) and rose to flag rank (1912) and took over the Scouting Forces of the High Seas Fleet, a post he held until 1918. World War I coastal operations against England (1914) and the Battle of the Dogger Bank engagement (24 January 1915) identified him as a bold tactician. His most conspicuous performance came in the Battle of Jutland (31 May–1 June 1916) when his scouting force of battle cruisers led Admiral Reinhard Scheer's main body of battleships. In the shake-up of naval command structure (August 1918), he was promoted to full admiral and succeeded Scheer as Chief of the High Seas Fleet. He planned the last-minute sortie of the battle fleet against England (30 October) that led to mutinies aboard his ships and presaged the end of hostilities. Hipper retired in December.

Hitler, Adolf (1889–1945) Dictator of Germany. After a troubled childhood and early adulthood in Austria, Hitler moved to Germany. He found identity and purpose in World War I. He joined the army and saw action in the First Battle of Ypres (1914), Neuve Chapelle (1915) and the Somme (1916). Wounded (October 1916), on recuperation he returned to the front (March 1917) and was promoted lance

corporal, taking part in the battles of Arras and Passchendaele (1917) and the Ludendorff Offensives (Spring 1918). Gassed in a British attack and temporarily blinded (October 1918), he ended the war in a hospital. In the war he was a *Meldegänger* (runner) carrying messages, and won the Iron Cross Second Class (December 1914) and Iron Cross First Class (August 1918), the latter quite uncommon for someone of his rank.

After the war Hitler worked in Munich for the army and reported on developing political parties. He then embraced politics full time and joined the German Workers' Party. Soon he was the driving force in the renamed National Socialist German Workers' Party (Nazis). In the Munich "Beer Hall Putsch" (9 November 1923), he attempted to seize power as a prelude to taking power in all Germany, but the movement was put down and he was arrested, tried, and imprisoned (1923–24). His trial made him a national, even international, figure.

Hitler ran against Paul von Hindenburg for the presidency of Germany (April 1932) but was defeated. Thanks to disillusionment with the 1919 Versailles Treaty, the 1923 catastrophic inflation, the early 1930s economic depression, and the political instability of the Weimar Republic, the Nazis registered steady gains and became the largest party in the Reichstag in national elections (July 1932).

Named chancellor (January 1933), Hitler set about consolidating power. On the death of Hindenburg (August 1934), he amalgamated the office of president and took control of the armed forces. In "The Night of the Long Knives" (July 1934) he purged the party. As *Führer* (leader) of what he styled the "Third Reich," he reorganized Germany administratively, making it a one-party state and arresting opponents. In foreign policy he tore up the 1919 Versailles Treaty and 1925 Locarno Pacts and rearmed Germany (1935). His most daring gamble was to remilitarize the Rhineland (March 1936).

He announced plans to his top advisors and generals for an aggressive foreign policy and war (November 1937), took over Austria (*Anschluss*, March 1938), seized the Sudetenland (October 1938), and took the rest of Czechoslovakia (March 1939). He then concluded a non-aggression pact with the Soviet Union (August 1939) and invaded Poland (1 September 1939), touching off World War II.

Success crowned his early military efforts. Poland was absorbed in a month; Norway and Denmark were invaded (April 1940), and France and Benelux taken (May–June). His first rebuff came in the Battle of Britain (July–October 1940), for which he was unprepared. He then invaded the Soviet Union (22 June 1941) and declared war on the United States (December 1941).

Germany suffered the consequences of strategic overreach, particularly as Hitler came to the rescue of Italy and sent resources to North Africa. His constant meddling in military matters and his divide-and-rule concept of administration both worked to the detriment of Germany's cause. On his command, millions of people, especially Jews, were rounded up and systematically murdered. He refused negotiation to the end, preferring to see Germany destroyed as unworthy of him. Rather than be taken by the Russians, he committed suicide in his Berlin bunker on 30 April 1945.

Hobart, Sir Percy Cleghorn Stanley (1885–1957) British general. Commissioned in the engineers from the Royal Military Academy at Woolwich (1904), Hobart was posted to India (1906), where he distinguished himself. Sent to France with the Indian Expeditionary Force (January 1915), he fought on the Western Front and in Mesopotomia, ending World War I as a major.

Hobart graduated from the Staff College, Camberley and then returned to India (1921). Convinced that the future

of ground warfare lay with the tank, he joined the Royal Tank Corps (1923). An instructor at the Staff College, Quetta (1923–27), he was breveted lieutenant colonel (1922) and colonel (1928). He was then second in command of 4th Battalion (1927–30) and commanded 2nd Battalion of the Tank Corps (1931–22). As inspector, then commander of the corps (1933–34), he raised and commanded 1st Tank Brigade (1934–37). Promoted major general and appointed to head military training (1938), he went to Egypt to raise what became the 7th Armored Division, championing its use apart from infantry formations. He retired from the army (1939).

During World War II Hobart was a colonel in the Home Guard when Prime Minister Winston Churchill recalled him to active duty to command first 11th Armored Division in England (1941–42) then 79th Armored Division with its unique engineering equipment. This gave Hobart opportunity for his innovative talents. The division's equipment included vehicles for mine laying and clearing, an amphibious tank, and a flame-thrower tank (the Crocodile). Such special tanks were known as "Hobby's Funnies." Hobart commanded his division in Twenty-First Army Group through the campaign in northern Europe to the end of the war. He then retired for a second time in 1946.

Ho Chi Minh (1890–1969) Vietnamese nationalist and leader of the Democratic Republic of Vietnam. Ho Chi Minh's real name was Nguyen Tat Thanh; later he changed it to Nguyen ai Quoc ("Nguyen the Patriot"), and finally to Ho Chi Minh ("He who Enlightens"). He attended high school at Hue, but left Vietnam (1911) and lived in London and then in Paris during World War I, where he became a leader of the Vietnamese community in France.

Ho joined the Socialist Party, and then was one of the founders of the French Communist party when it split off from the Socialists (1920). He became active in the Comintern and traveled in China and the Soviet Union, and was one of the founders of the Indochinese Communist Party (1930). During World War II he formed the Viêt Minh to fight first the Japanese and French, cooperating with the U.S. Office of Strategic Services (OSS). He took the lead in establishing the Democratic Republic of Vietnam with himself as president (December 1945). Entrusting the direction of military operations to Vo Nguyen Giap, he led the struggle for independence in the 1946–54 Indo-China War against France and then the long battle against the southern Republic of Vietnam and the Americans in the 1960s and 1970s. Implacable and determined, he measured the conflicts not in Vietnamese lives lost but in French and American casualties. Although he did not live to see final victory (April 1975), "Uncle Ho" is regarded by Vietnamese as the most important figure in their modern history.

Ho Long (He Long) (1896–1967) Communist Chinese general. Although of peasant origins and barely literate, Ho became an outstanding general. Active as a guerrilla leader (1912), he joined the Nationalist Koumintang (KMT, Guomindang) Army (1920). He then joined the Communist party (1926). During the 1926–28 Northern Expedition, he commanded Twentieth Army (1926).

When Kuomintang leader Chiang Kai-shek (Jiang Jieshi) began his purge of Communists, Ho led a revolt of Twentieth Army, the August 1927 Nanchang Uprising. When it failed he returned to Hunan–Hupeh (Hubei) border area to organize guerrillas. He commanded Second Red Army (1929), reorganized into Second Army Corps (1930). Named commander of Third Red Army (1932), he led Second Red Army against the Nationalists but was defeated in Hunan (1933). His Second Front Red Army and Fourth Front

Red Army served as the rear guard for the legendary 1934–35 "Long March."

Ho commanded 120th Division of the new Eighth Route Army (1937), engaging the invading Japanese (September). He directed a growing guerrilla operation against the Japanese and expanded his division to army group size. During the 1946–49 Civil War, his forces controlled much of northwestern China, trained replacement troops, and defended the Communist base areas. Following the Communist victory, he held a succession of military and government posts and was advanced as one of ten marshals of the People's Liberation Army (1955). He was severely attacked during the 1966–69 Cultural Revolution.

Ho Ying-ch'in (He Yingqin) (1889–1987) Nationalist Chinese general. Ho was educated at the Japanese Military Academy (Shimbu Gakko) and joined the Nationalist Kuomintang (KMT, Guomindang) at Canton (1924). Soon he commanded one of two training regiments of the Whampoa Military Academy. He led both regiments to take Kwangtung (Guangdong) Province and also secured northern Fukien province (1925–26). During the 1926–28 Northern Expedition he served on the staff of Chiang Kai-shek (Jiang Jieshi). Appointed inspector general of military training (1928), he was then minister of war and chief of the Supreme Staff (1930–34). He participated in the "bandit suppression" campaigns against the Communists but with little success.

With the beginning of war with Japan (1937), Ho commanded the Fourth War Area. In 1945 he became CofS of the army and directed its losing effort against the Communists. Recalled as minister of defense (1948), at the end of the war, he fled to Taiwan in 1949.

Hobby, Oveta Culp (1906–96) U.S. Army officer. A Texas lawyer, Hobby was appointed by President Franklin Roosevelt to head the Women's Division of the War

Department Bureau of Public Relations. She then commanded the new Women's Auxiliary Army Corps (WAAC) (May 1942). Commissioned colonel (September 1943), she was one of only two women colonels in the U.S. Army during the war. She resigned (July 1945) but joined the Eisenhower administration as secretary of the new Department of Health, Education, and Welfare (1953–55).

Hodge, John Reed (1893–1963) U.S. general. Hodge graduated from the University of Illinois and was commissioned in the infantry (1917). During World War I he served in France and was promoted captain. He fought in the St. Mihiel (September 1918) and Meuse–Argonne Offensives (September–November). After the war he was an ROTC instructor at Mississippi Agricultural and Mechanical College (1921–25). He graduated from the Infantry School at Fort Benning (1926), the Chemical Warfare School (1933), the Army Command and Staff School (1934), the Army War College (1935), and the Air Corps Tactical School (1936). He served on the War Department General Staff (1936–41) and was promoted lieutenant colonel (1940).

Hodge served on the staff of VII Corps (1941). Promoted brigadier general, he was assistant commander of the 25th Infantry Division on Guadalcanal (June 1942). Promoted major general (April 1943), he took command of the Americal Division and fought with it on Bougainville. He then commanded XXIV Corps, landing with it on Leyte in the Philippines (October 1944). He then took part in the fight for Okinawa (April–June 1945) and was promoted to lieutenant general.

After the war Hodge commanded U.S. forces occupying Korea south of the 38th parallel. After establishment of the Republic of Korea, he commanded V Corps at Fort Bragg, North Carolina (November 1948). He then commanded Third Army at Fort McPherson, Georgia (June 1950). Named chief of army field forces (May

1952), he was promoted to general (July) and retired in June 1953.

Hodges, Courtney Hicks (1887–1966) U.S. general. Hodges entered West Point (1904) but dropped out for academic reasons (1905) and enlisted in the army. He won a commission (1909) and served in the Philippines and in the 1916 Mexican expedition. In 1918 he went to France and fought in the St. Mihiel (September) and Meuse–Argonne offensives (September–November). He finished World War I a temporary lieutenant colonel.

Hodges attended the Field Artillery School (1920) and was then a tactical officer at West Point. He graduated from the Command and General Staff School (1925) and taught at the Infantry School and graduated from the Army War College. He returned to the Infantry School as assistant commandant (1938). Promoted brigadier general (1940), he became the school's commandant. Promoted major general, he was assigned as chief of infantry (May 1941).

Hodges then took command of X Corps (May 1942). Promoted lieutenant general, he took over Southern Defense Command (February 1943). Deputy commander of First Army, he took over the command when General Omar Bradley took command of Twelfth Army Group. First Army liberated Paris (August 1944), crossed the Siegfried Line (September), and bore the brunt of the German Ardennes offensive. First Army then linked up with the Russians along the Elbe (April 1945). Promoted full general (April), Hodges retired in March 1949.

Hoepner, Erich (1886–1944) German general. Hoepner joined the army in 1905 and served in the dragoons in World War I. He took part in the 1920 Kapp Putsch. A staunch opponent of Nazism, he joined the plotting against Adolf Hitler in opposition to the planned invasion of Czechoslovakia (1938).

An armored warfare specialist and

protégé of General Heinz Guderian, as a major general he succeeded Guderian as commander of XVI Corps and led it into Czechoslovakia (March 1939). Promoted lieutenant general (April), he led his corps in the invasion of Poland (September 1939) as a part of Tenth Army and then spearheaded Sixth Army's advance through Belgium (May 1940).

Promoted full general (July 1940), Hoepner commanded Fourth Panzer Group in Army Group North in the invasion of the Soviet Union (22 June 1941) but was moved to Army Group Center (September) and attacked toward Moscow (October–December), reaching the outskirts of that city until halted by the Soviet counteroffensive (8 December). His command was then redesignated Fourth Panzer Army (January 1942).

Hoepner withdrew his forces on his own responsibility to save them from certain annihilation. Adolf Hitler then dismissed him without trial and singled him out for special punishment, including cancelling his pension. Hoepner refused to recognize this illegal action and was allowed to retire (June 1942). He later joined the anti-Hitler conspiracy, but was among those failing to take decisive action in the aftermath of the bomb attempt (20 July 1944). Refusing to commit suicide, he was tried in People's Court, condemned, and hanged on 8 August.

Hoffmann, Carl Adolf Maximilian (1869–1927) German general. Hoffmann joined the army as an officer cadet (1887). He graduated from the Kriegsakademie (1898), and during the 1904–05 Russo-Japanese War served as a German military observer with Japanese forces. This experience increased his knowledge of the Russian military and helped him become operations chief of Eighth Army, charged with defending East Prussia.

On the outbreak of World War I, he relied on Russian radio intercepts and anticipated that General Pavel Rennenkampf's First Army would not rush to assist General Aleksandr Samsonov's Second Army. Hoffmann's Tannenberg battle plan was adopted by Generals Paul von Hindenburg and Erich Ludendorff who now took charge in the East (22 August 1914).

When Hindenburg and Ludendorff were posted to command in the West (August 1916), Hoffmann became chief of staff to new commander in the East, Field Marshal Prince Leopold of Bavaria, and was largely responsible for his 1916 and 1917 successes. In recognition of his role, Hoffmann was promoted major general.

Hoffmann concluded an armistice at Brest-Litovsk with the Bolsheviks who had seized power in Russia (December 1917). He insisted on major Russian territorial concessions, although less than those demanded by Ludendorff. He retired from the army in 1920. A supporter of Franco-German cooperation, his postwar writing was critical of Hindenburg and Ludendorff.

Hoge, William M. (1894–1979) U.S. general. Commissioned in the engineers on graduation from West Point (1916), Hoge's first assignment was to the Mexican border. He then commanded a company of the 7th Engineers at Fort Leavenworth Kansas (1917), accompanied his regiment to France (1918), was promoted major, and participated in the St. Mihiel (September) and Meuse–Argonne (September–November) offensives.

After World War I Hoge graduated from the Massachusetts Institute of Technology with a civil engineering degree and from the Command and General Staff College (1928). He commanded an engineer battalion of the Philippine Scouts and later was chief of engineers for the Philippine Army. He then oversaw construction of the 1,030-mile ALCAN highway across northwest Canada to Alaska (1942). He served briefly with the 9th Armored Division before going to Britain to command the Provisional Engineer

Special Brigade in the Normandy Invasion (June 1944). After his return to the 9th Armored Division, his troops seized the railroad bridge across the Rhine at Remagen (March 1945), providing the first Allied bridgehead east of that river. By the end of the war he was a major general commanding the 4th Armored Division in Third Army.

After World War II Hoge commanded the Engineer Center at Fort Belvoir, and then U.S. troops in Trieste. He commanded IX Corps in the 1950–53 Korean War (February–November 1951) during critical battles in central Korea. Hodge then commanded Fourth Army in San Antonio, Texas and Seventh Army in Germany, then U.S. Army forces in Europe. He retired as a full general in 1955.

Holcomb, Thomas (1879–1965) U.S. Marine Corps general and commandant. Appointed a Marine officer (1900), Holcomb served in a variety of posts. He fought in World War I as a battalion commander. He graduated from the Command and General Staff School (1925), the Naval War College (1931), and the Army War College (1932). Promoted brigadier general (1935), he commanded the Marine Corps School at Quantico. Promoted major general (1936), he became commandant of the Marine Corps and presided over its vast expansion in World War II, from 16,000 to over 300,000 men. He promoted doctrinal and technological changes in amphibious warfare and worked to define command relationships with the navy. He also instituted yearly fleet exercises and brought women into the Corps. He was promoted lieutenant general (1942), and on his retirement (1943) was promoted general. He was U.S. minister to South Africa during 1944–48.

Holland, Lancelot (1887–1941) British admiral. Assistant chief of the Naval Staff (1937–38), Vice Admiral Holland commanded 2nd Battleship Squadron in the Mediterranean at the beginning of World War II. He then commanded 3rd Battle Cruiser Squadron consisting of battle cruiser *Hood*, new battleship *Prince of Wales*, and six destroyers against the German battleship *Bismarck* in the northeast Atlantic (24 May 1941). He and all but three men of the *Hood* were killed when a fifteen-inch shell from the *Bismarck* pierced the ship's armour and ignited a magazine.

Holloway, Bruce K. (1912–99) U.S. Air Force general. Holloway studied engineering at the University of Tennessee before graduating from West Point (1937). He completed pilot training (1938) and served with a fighter unit in Hawaii. Following U.S. entry into World War II, he went to China and flew with General Claire Chennault's Flying Tigers (1942). He took command of the 23rd Fighter Group (January 1943), the successor to the Flying Tigers, and was credited with shooting down thirteen Japanese aircraft. Shot down himself, he made his way to friendly lines and then returned to the U.S. (1944).

Following the war, Holloway commanded the 412th Fighter Group at March Field, California, the first USAF jet-fighter unit. Promoted brigadier general (1953), he became deputy commander of the U.S. Strike Command, MacDill AFB, Florida (1961). He assumed command of U.S. Air Forces in Europe (1965), was vice chief of staff of the Air Force (1966), and, as full general, headed the Strategic Air Command (1967–72). He then retired.

Holtzendorff, Henning von (1853–1919) German admiral. Holtzendorff joined the navy (1869) and fought in the 1870–71 Franco-German War. He commanded Germany's 1st Battle Squadron (1906). He took command of the High Seas Fleet (1909) and was promoted to full admiral (1910).

Holtzendorff disagreed with Admiral Tirpitz over naval matters and retired

(April 1913). Reactivated as chief of the Admiralty Staff (September 1915), he cultivated close relations with the Kaiser and government officials. Although he supported fleet operations, he was convinced that only all-out submarine warfare would assure German victory over Britain. He was primarily responsible for persuading the Kaiser to resume unrestricted submarine warfare (1 February 1917), promising England's collapse before the end of the summer. He was promoted grand admiral just before his retirement (August 1918).

Homma, Masaharu (1887–1946) Japanese general. Commissioned in the infantry out of the Military Academy (1907), Homma graduated from the Army Staff College (1915) and served on the general staff before going to France as a BEF observer (1918). Promoted major (1922), he was a resident officer in India (1922–25), instructor at the Army Staff College (1925–27), and aide-de-camp to Prince Chichibu (1927–30). Promoted colonel (1930), he was military attaché in London (1930–32). He then commanded a regiment (1932). Promoted major general, he commanded an infantry brigade (1933–37). Raised to lieutenant general (1938), he commanded 27th Division in China, then the Formosa Army (December 1940).

Despite not having held a previous combat command, Homma commanded the invasion of the Philippines (December 1941). His forces easily took Manila (2 January 1942) but encountered difficulties in securing Bataan (he initially had only 43,000 men and was given just fifty days to complete the conquest). Reinforced, he then took Bataan (9 April) and U.S. General Jonathan Wainwright surrendered all the Philippines (6 May). Despite his considerable achievement, the operation had taken longer than expected. Recalled to Japan (August 1942), Homma was transferred to the First Reserve List.

Arrested after the war as a war criminal, Homma was charged with responsibility for the Bataan Death March (about which he claimed ignorance) and other actions in the Philippines. Tried in Manila (January–February 1946), he was found guilty and shot on 3 April.

Honda, Masaki (1889–1964) Japanese general. Honda graduated from the Military Academy (1910) and the Army Staff College (1917). Promoted major (1925), he lectured at the Infantry School (1930–32). Promoted colonel, he commanded an infantry regiment (1933–36); as a major general, he commanded an infantry brigade (1937–38). Promoted lieutenant general, he commanded the Infantry School (1939). He was then CofS of the China Expeditionary Army (1939) and later chief of the Armored Warfare Department (1941–43).

Honda then took command of Twentieth Army in Manchukuo (1943–44). Appointed commander of Thirty-Third Army in northern Burma (April 1944), he opposed operations mounted by British General Orde Wingate's Chindits and General Joseph Stilwell's Chinese troops (May–October). Forced to withdraw, his army was all but destroyed in fighting along the Irrawaddy River (January–April 1945).

Honjō, Shigeru (1876–1945) Japanese general. Honjō graduated from the Military Academy (1897) and served in Manchuria in the 1904–05 Russo-Japanese War. He graduated from the Army Staff College and was then on detached duty with the Gerneral Staff in China (1906–13). Promoted major (1909), he served in the China Section, Intelligence Division of the Army General Staff (1913–15).

Promoted colonel (1918), Honjō commanded a regiment in the Siberian Expeditionary Force (1919–20). Advanced to major general (1922), he was military adviser to China warlord Chang Tso-lin (1921–24). He then commanded an infantry brigade (1924) and was military attaché to China (1925). Promoted lieutenant general (1927), he commanded a division (1928).

As commander of the Kwantung (Guangdung) Army in Manchuria, Honjō directed the Japanese takeover of that entire province (1931–32). Promoted general and made a baron, he was named aide to Emperor Hirohito (1933). Placed on the reserve list (1936), he committed suicide (September 1945) after Japan's surrender in World War II.

Hore-Belisha, Leslie (1893–1957) British war minister. Hore-Belisha studied at Oxford and then enlisted in the British Army during World War I, rising to the rank of major in the Army Service Corps. Following the war he won his degree in law and was elected to parliament. He became minister of transport (1935), and Neville Chamberlain appointed him minister of war (1937).

Hore-Belisha's major contribution lay in modernizing the British Army. He alienated many by turning to Basil Liddell Hart for advice, but he improved conditions of service for soldiers, overhauled the career system for officers, doubled the size of the territorial army, and persuaded a reluctant Chamberlain to introduce conscription (April 1939). His criticism of Lord Gort for the slow rate of construction of field fortifications in France during an inspection trip there (1939) finally led Chamberlain to remove him from his post. Offered another position in the government, he chose instead to resign (January 1940). He remained in parliament, where he was a strong critic of Prime Minister Winston Churchill. He was later raised to the peerage (1954).

Horii, Tomitaro (1890–1942) Japanese general. Horii graduated from the Japanese Military Academy (1911) as an infantry officer. He was attached to the headquarters of the Shanghai Expeditionary Army during the Battle of Shanghai (January–March 1932). Promoted colonel (1937), he became a regimental commander (1939). Sent to Guam as commander of the South Seas Detachment centered around the elite 144th Infantry Regiment (1940), his troops took Rabaul from Australian troops (January 1942). Sent to New Guinea, he landed at Buna (Garara) and attempted to take Port Morseby overland (July 1942) by means of the Kokoda Trail over the rugged Owen Stanley Mountain Range. He got to within 30 miles of Port Morseby (September) before digging in to wait for an amphibious landing that was to occur a month later. This plan was upset by the American landing on Guadalcanal. After his attempt to attack alone was unsuccessful, he was ordered to withdraw while harassed by Australian forces (September 1942–January 1943), proof that Japanese troops could be beaten. He drowned when his improvised raft broke apart while crossing the turbulent Kumusi River (night of 12–13 November 1942). He was posthumously promoted lieutenant general.

Horne, Henry Sinclair, Baron (1861–1929) British general. Horne was commissioned in the artillery from the Royal Military Academy, Woolwich (1880). He saw service in the Boer War and began World War I as a brigadier general, commanding I Corps artillery. He commanded 2nd Division (1915) and then served briefly on Lord Kitchener's staff. He then commanded XV Corps on the Somme (1916) before being promoted again to command First Army the same year.

Horne was a competent commander who worked well with his subordinates. First Army's successes included the battles of Vimy Ridge (1917) and those on the left flank of the BEF during summer 1918.

Horrocks, Sir Brian Gwynen (1895–1980) British general. Commissioned in the Middlesex Regiment (1914), during World War I he was wounded at Ypres (October 1914), captured by the Germans, and held prisoner for the rest of the war. His career in World War II was closely linked to that of General Bernard Montgomery. He took command of a machine gun battalion in Montgomery's 3rd Division of the British Expeditionary Force (BEF) in France (May 1940). Following evacuation of the BEF at Dunkerque (May June 1940), he was promoted brigade commander and then (1941) division commander in Montgomery's corps in Britain.

Shortly after taking command of Eighth Army in Egypt (August 1942), Montgomery sent for Horrocks to command XIII Corps as a lieutenant general. His corps was the main force in the victory at Alam Halfa (August–September) and fought well in the Battle of El Alamein (October–November). He then commanded X Corps in the drive westward. Seriously wounded in an air raid before the invasion of Sicily, he was still recuperating in England when Montgomery sent for him to take over XXX Corps in Normandy (August 1944). He commanded it the rest of the war. XXX Corps performed well in the drive eastward through France and Belgium.

Montgomery entrusted Horrocks with responsibility for the ground portion of Operation MARKET-GARDEN, the attempt to secure a crossing over the Rhine at Arnhem (September), but his corps was not able to reach Arnhem in time to relieve the British 1st Airborne Division. It had more success in Operation VENERABLE, the approach to the Rhine. Horrocks retired in 1949.

Horthy de Nagybána, Miklós (1868–1957) Austro-Hungarian admiral. Horthy, a Hungarian, entered the Naval Academy at Fiume (1882) and subsequently became naval aide to Emperor Franz Josef. At the beginning of World War I he commanded a battleship. Horthy planned the raid on the drifter line maintaining the Otranto barrage (May 1917). This led to the largest naval action of the war in the Adriatic, in which he was wounded. Kaiser Karl selected Horthy over many

more senior officers to lead the Austrian fleet (February 1918).

Horthy planned another raid on the Otranto Straits but, when a dreadnought was sunk, he aborted the operation (June). He managed to keep the fleet intact until the end of the war, maintaining sea communications with Austro-Hungarian forces in Albania and supporting German submarine operations in the Mediterranean. After the war he led the counter-revolution in Hungary that overthrew the Communist regime of Belá Kun. Horthy was Regent of Hungary (1919–44). He brought Hungary into the war on the German side, but was overthrown when he tried to extract his country from the war.

Horton, Sir Max Kennedy (1883–1951) British admiral. Horton was commissioned in the navy (1904). Most of his early assignments were with submarines, his first command coming with the experiment A.1 (1905). During World War I he saw extensive service in submarines.

Promoted captain (1920), Horton then took command of a flotilla of the new K-class steam-driven submarines. He then held a mix of command and staff assignments. Promoted rear admiral (1932) and lieutenant admiral (1936), he then commanded the Northern Patrol (1938).

During World War II, Horton became flag officer of submarines (January 1940). His force savaged German ships involved in the invasion of Norway (April) and Italian supply ships bound for North Africa. He succeeded Admiral Sir Percy Noble as commander of Western Approaches (November 1942) and thus played a key role in the Battle of the Atlantic. Here he aggressively promoted the use of convoys and long-range aircraft to locate and attack German submarines. He retired at the end of the war.

Hosogaya, Boshiro (1886–1964) Japanese admiral. Hosogaya graduated from the Naval Academy (1908) and the Naval

Staff College (1920). He had various positions afloat and ashore, including battleship command.

Promoted rear admiral (1935), he commanded the Communications School, then the Torpedo School (1936–37). Promoted vice admiral, he commanded Port Arthur (Lüshan) naval base (1939), Central China Fleet (1940–41), and then Northern Area Force (July 1942).

In the process of escorting two transports to Attu Island in the Aleutians, Hosogaya's two heavy and two light cruisers ran into U.S. Rear Admiral Charles McMorris's task force of one heavy cruiser, one light cruiser, and four destroyers. In the long-range Battle of the Komandorski Islands (26 March 1943), he sought to defend his transports. Unable to defeat the smaller American force, he drew off. One cruiser on each side was damaged. For his timidity, he was dismissed from command and placed on the reserve list. He was then governor of the South Seas Agency on the mandated islands (1943–45).

Hossbach, Fredrich (1894–1980) German general. Hossbach joined the army (1913) and served on the Eastern Front during World War I. He remained in the Reichswehr after the war and was assigned to the General Staff as a captain (1927). As a major, he became adjutant to Adolf Hitler (August 1934) while continuing his position as chief of the Central Section of the General Staff. Soon promoted to colonel, he is chiefly remembered for his notes (the "Hossbach Memorandum") during a key meeting between Hitler and his military chiefs in Berlin (5 November 1937), in which the *Führer* spelled out his plans for an aggressive foreign policy leading to war. This became important evidence at the post-war Nuremberg Trials. Immune to intimidation, he also warned General Werner von Fritsch of charges impending against him. He was consequently dismissed from his adjutant post, although retaining his staff position.

Hossbach commanded the 82nd Regiment of 31st Infantry Division in the invasion of France and Benelux (May 1940). Promoted brigadier general (March 1942), he then commanded the 82nd Division (April) and briefly the 31st Division (May 1943) on the Eastern Front. He then took over LVI Panzer Corps (August) as a major general. Promoted lieutenant general (November 1943), he then commanded XVI Fourth Army (July 1944). Hitler relieved him from command (January 1945) when in East Prussia, under Russian pressure, he withdrew his forces without authority.

Hoth, Hermann (1885–1971) German general. Hoth joined the army (1904), graduated from the Prussian War Academy (1913), and became an intelligence officer. A staff officer during and after World War I, he became a specialist in armored warfare.

Hoth commanded 18th Division (1935) and was promoted major general. Promoted lieutenant general, he took command of XV Motorized Corps (November 1938) and distinguished himself in the invasion of Poland (September 1939), and of France and Benelux (May 1940), when he drove through the Ardennes Forest to the English Channel, and then into Normandy and Brittany. Promoted general (July), his formation was redesignated Third Panzer Group (November), which Hoth then led in the invasion of the Soviet Union (22 June 1941). He then commanded Seventeenth Army in Ukraine (October 1941–June 1944). He led Fourth Panzer Army (June 1942) across the Don River toward the Caucasus Mountains, then toward the lower Volga in an unsuccessful effort to relieve Sixth Army at Stalingrad.

Hoth's Fourth Army helped restore the German lines and participated in the Battle of Kursk (July 1943). Adolf Hitler dismissed the capable Hoth for his "defeatist attitude" (November). Tried by a U.S. military court after the war for "crimes against humanity" committed by subordinates, Hoth was found guilty and sentenced (October 1948) to fifteen years in prison. He was released in 1954. He then wrote on armored warfare.

Hsü Hsiang-ch'ien (Xu Xianqian) (1902–) People's Republic of China marshal. A member of the first class at Whompoa Military Academy, Hsü joined the Nationalist or Kuomintang (KMT, Guomindang) Army (1924). He fought in the Northern Expedition (1926) and joined the Communist party (CCP) (1927). After the split between the KMT and CCP (1927), he went to Canton and helped lead the uprising there (December). After its failure, he led his men to Hailufeng and merged them into the 4th Red Division, which he later commanded against the KMT, with mixed success (1928–31). Given command of Fourth Red Front Army (December 1931), he was besieged by KMT forces (December 1932) but broke free and fought in Szechuan (1933–35), where he met Mao Tse-tung (Mao Zedong). Following a crushing military defeat (December 1936), he escaped to Yenan (Yan'an) in disguise (1937).

At the start of the 1937–45 Sino-Japanese War, Hsü was vice commander of Eighth Route Army, and helped establish the Shantung Red Base (1939). During the 1946–49 Civil War he was vice-commander of the Shansi–Hopei–Shantung–HonanMilitary Region (1947), then commanded I Army Corps, North China Field Army, then the Taiyuan Front (1948) and Eighteenth Army Group (November). He was vice-commander North China Military Region (September 1949–December 1954). He then held a variety of political and military posts including member of the People's Revolutionary Military Council (1949–54). Appointed vice-chairman of the National Defense Council (1954), he was promoted marshal (September 1955) and then held a succession of important political posts.

Hu Tsung-nan (Hu Zongnan) (1895–1962) Chinese Nationalist general. Hu joined the Nationalist Kuomintang (KMT, Guomindang) party and graduated in the first class from Whampoa Military Academy (1925). He advanced rapidly in rank during the 1926–28 Northern Expedition. As commander of the 1st Division he helped suppress rebellions by Feng Yü-hsiang (Feng Yuxiang) and Yen Hsi-shan (Yan Xishan) (1929–30). His units in north China failed to prevent Communist forces from reaching Yenan (Yan'an) in the Long March (1935), but he then attacked the Communist base area (November–December 1936). He had little success stopping the Japanese invasion (1937). He then commanded KMT forces blockading the Communist base area at Yenan after the United Front collapsed (1941) until the end of World War II. Ordered to attack Yenan on the outbreak of the 1946–49 Civil War (March 1946), he launched an offensive (January 1947) and took Yenan (March), but was subsequently cut off and fell back on Sian (Xi'an), losing 100,000 men in the process (October–November). He was then constantly on the defensive, finally retreating to Hainan Island (December 1949). He launched an independent invasion of the mainland, but was soon driven back to Hainan (March 1950). He joined the KMT government on Taiwan and held several important military posts until his retirement in 1959.

Hunter, Charles Newton (1906–79) U.S. colonel. Hunter graduated from West Point (1929). In 1943, after promotion to colonel, he helped organize and train the 5307th Composite Unit, codenamed GALAHAD, a force of 3,000 volunteers trained for deep penetration operations in Burma.

Hunter was executive officer to GALAHAD commander Brigadier General Frank D. Merrill. Because his chief was ill, he actually led "Merrill's Marauders" much of the time. He led GALAHAD's operations in the Hukwang Valley in conjunction with Chinese General Li Jen's New First Army (January–August 1944). He took actual command (April) when Merrill suffered heart problems, leading GALAHAD in a deep penetration operation over difficult terrain to take Myitkyina (May–August), in which his own force was nearly destroyed. He then trained replacements.

Hunter served on the Staff of Army Ground Force Headquarters (1945–47). He held various command positions in Korea and Japan (1947–49), graduated from the National War College, and served with NATO (1954–58). He retired in 1959 as a colonel and deputy chief of staff, Fourth Army.

Huntziger, Charles Léon Clément (1880–1941) French general. A graduate of St. Cyr (1901), Huntziger chose the colonial infantry and spent most of his early career outside of France, in Madagascar (1902–04), Senegal (1905–07), and in Tonkin (1912–14). He spent most of World War I fighting in northeast France. In early 1918 he went to the Balkan Front and ended the war as commander of a battalion in Bulgaria. He then served in the Orient (1918–20), and in China (1924–28). He was in Brazil (1930–34) as chief of the French military mission there and then commanded French troops in the Levant (1934–38). He attended the École de Guerre (1909–11) and the Centre des Hautes Études Militaires (1921). Promoted colonel (1922), major general (1926), and lieutenant general (1933), he commanded a corps (1935). Assigned to the Levant, he was then recalled to France as a member of the Conseil Supérieur de la Guerre (Higher War Council) (1938), designated to command an army in time of war. By the time of World War II he was regarded as one of France's most promising general officers.

At the time of the German invasion of France and Benelux (May 1940), Huntziger commanded Second Army, which was destroyed by German armor at Sedan. He then received command of Fourth Army Group, which was defeated around Châlons-sur-Marne. He headed the French commission that signed the armistice with the Germans at Compiègne (22 June 1940).

Vichy Chief of State Marshal Henri Philippe Pétain then appointed Huntziger war minister and his close adviser (September 1940). Huntziger, however, cooperated with the secret army resistance. The Germans apparently learned of this and may have been responsible for the plane crash that claimed his life on 12 November 1941.

Hussein Ibn Ali (1852–1931) Sharif, Emir of Mecca, and King of the Hejaz. Hussein was born at Constantinople into the family of Hashem, traditionally held as descendants of Mohammed and therefore holders of the title *sharif*. Sultan Abdul Hamid II brought him to Istanbul (1892) and, although placing him on the Council of State, held him a virtual captive until he was appointed Emir of Mecca (1903). Hussein resented the Hejaz railroad as an encroachment on Arab autonomy, and feared the Young Turks who controlled the Ottoman government.

In 1915 Hussein discovered written proof that the Young Turks planned to depose him after the war. Through his son Abdullah, he had initiated talks with the British government in Cairo (1913 and 1914). The threat from Istanbul caused him to pursue that relationship, and he initiated the Arab revolt (1916).

Hussein wanted personal power, autonomy within the existing empire, and the hereditary right to the title of Emir of Mecca. Lord Kitchener wanted military support from an Arab guerilla force, the support of a descendant of the Prophet, and transfer of the caliphate from Istanbul to Mecca as the cornerstone of a British Arab Empire similar to that in India. The military value of the Arab forces has been subject to debate, but it diverted 20–30,000 Turkish troops. The propaganda and political value of the caliphate were never as great as Kitchener believed.

After the war, Cairo reluctantly continued to support Hussein over the wishes of the Foreign Office and the India Office, which favored his son Faisal and his enemies the Sauds. Faisal was given Syria but was deposed, and became king of Iraq under British protection. Abdullah became king of the newly created Transjordan. Hussein declared himself King of the Hejaz, but, lacking committed British support, was deposed by his Saudi enemies in 1924. He spent most of the rest of his life in Cyprus.

Hutier, Oskar von (1857–1934) German general. Commissioned in the army (1874), Hutier attended the Kriegsakademie (1885) and then became a general staff officer (1890). He held a variety of command and general staff assignments and then was chief quartermaster on the General Staff (1911). He then assumed command of the 1st Guards Division in Berlin (1912).

When World War I began Hutier commanded his division on the Western Front, and then took command of XXI Corps on the Eastern Front (1915). Promoted lieutenant general (1917), he received command of Eighth Army, which captured the Baltic port of Riga (September), knocking Russia out of the war. Transferred back to the Western Front to command Eighteenth Army (December 1917), Hutier led it in the Spring 1918 Ludendorff Offensives, most notably at St. Quentin.

Hutier is remembered for the large-scale introduction of new infantry tactics consisting of a brief intensive artillery bombardment, followed by the infiltration advance of small groups of troops armed with machine weapons that bypassed enemy strongpoints. These were mistakenly named for him; "Hutier Tactics" were rather the product of careful and methodical staff work that characterized the German Army, and Hutier simply commanded the first large-scale operation in which the new doctrine was applied. Hutier retired from the army after the war in January 1919.

Hyakutake, Haruyoshi (1888–1947) Japanese general. Commissioned in the infantry (1909), Hyakutake became a signals officer. He was in Poland in the mid-1920s and, as a colonel, headed the Hiroshima Military Prep School (1936–37). Promoted major general (March 1937), he became superintendent of the Army Signal School (April). He commanded the 4th Independent Mixed Brigade (March 1939) and was promoted lieutenant general (August). He was then inspector general of signal training (1940–42).

Following the beginning of hostilities between Japan and the United States (December 1941), Hyakutake commanded Seventeenth Army Headquarters on Rabaul (May 1942). His attempt to take Port Moresby was thwarted by U.S. Navy intervention (May 1942); another planned attempt was called off following the U.S. Marine landings on Guadalcanal (August). He grossly underestimated U.S. fighting strength and abilities, launching piecemeal attacks against the Americans, who had taken Henderson Field. Building up his force on Guadalcanal to 30,000 men, he then led them in person (October). Following Japanese naval reversals, however, Tokyo ordered an evacuation (31 December), which was completed the next month.

Hyakutake then commanded on Bougainville. Following U.S. landings there (November 1943), he established effective defensive positions, chiefly at Buin. He made an unsuccessful effort to break out (March 1944). He surrendered at the end of the war and returned to Japan in February 1946.

I

Iachino, Angelo (1889–1976) Italian admiral. A specialist in naval gunnery, Iachino held a variety of assignments during World War I. He was naval attaché to Britain (1931–34). When Italy entered World War II (June 1940), he commanded 2nd Cruiser Squadron.

Following the British raid on Taranto (11 November 1940), Iachino succeded Admiral Inigo Campioni as commander of the main battle fleet (December 1940). Although a capable and resourceful commander, he was handicapped by fuel shortages and restrictions imposed by the naval staff. Under German pressure, he sortied with the fleet and engaged British naval units commanded by Admiral A. B. C. Cunningham in the Battle of Cape Matapan (28–29 March 1941), in which he lost three cruisers and two destroyers. He later exacted a price from British naval units in the evacuation of Greece (April) and Crete (May–June). An advocate of naval aviation, he pushed for development of an aircrat carrier, but Italy left the war before one could be completed.

Ammiraglio D'Armata (admiral of the fleet) Iachino continued to lead forays against the British in the Mediterranean until January 1942. He escaped following the Italian surrender and did not return to Italy until 1945. He later wrote several books on his wartime experiences.

Ibn Sa'ud, Abd al-Aziz (1880–1953) King of Nejd and Saudi Arabia and founder of the Kingdom of Saudi Arabia. Sa'ud was descended from the founder of the Wahhabi sect. Forced to flee from invading Rashidis (1891), he lived a short time in exile in Kuwait. In 1902 Sa'ud captured Riyadh and reestablished rule by his family in the Nejd. Early in World War I, Britain recognized him as ruler of the Nejd and Hassa. London paid him a subsidy, for which he maintained a position of benevolent neutrality.

Sa'ud then defeated the Rashids (1920–21) and became Sultan of the Nejd. In 1924 he defeated the Hashemites led by Sharif Hussein of Mecca and soon became "King of the Hijaz and the Nejd." In 1932 Sa'ud proclaimed himself king of Saudi Arabia and worked to promote nationalism in the kingdom. He granted oil concessions that made his country immensely wealthy.

Ichiki, Kiyonao (1892–1942) Japanese army officer. Ichiki graduated from the Military Academy (1916). Promoted major (1934), he commanded a battalion in 1st Infantry Regiment, China Garrison Army (1936) and helped provoke the war with China that followed skirmishing at Marco Polo Bridge near Peking (Beijing) (7–8 July 1937). He was then an instructor in infantry training schools (1938–40).

Promoted colonel (1941), Ichiki commanded the 2,000-man ground element assigned to take Midway Island. After the Japanese were defeated in the naval battle off Midway (3–6 June 1942), his unit was diverted to assault American positions on Guadalcanal, where the headstrong and overconfident colonel, contemptuous of his enemy and largely ignoring Marine dispositions, died along with most of his men in the Battle of the Tenaru River (21 August).

Ichinohe, Hyōe (1855–1931) Japanese general. Commissioned in the army (1876), he served with distinction in the 1877 Satsuma Rebellion and was promoted lieutenant. During the 1894–5 Sino-Japanese War, he won recognition while commanding the advance guard in the Battle of Songhwa (July 1894). He commanded a battalion in the Battle of Pyongyang (September). In the 1904–05 Russo-Japanese War, he commanded a brigade and fought in the siege of Port Arthur (June 1904–January 1905). His brigade played the crucial role in securing Hill 203; its capture sealed the fate of the Russian fortress. He also fought in the Battle of Mukden (February–March 1905). A methodical planner, he achieved objectives with few casualties. After the war he commanded 17th Division (1907), 4th Division (1911), and 1st Division (1912). He was then appointed military counselor and promoted full general (1915). He was then inspector general of Military Education (1915–19) and president of Gakushūin, the school for members of the imperial family and their peers, during 1920–22.

Iida, Shōjirō (1888–1980) Japanese general. A graduate of the Military Academy (1908) and Army Staff College (1915), Iida was on the Special Research Commission studying the lessons of World War I (1916–18). Promoted major (1924), he taught at the Infantry School (1922–26; 1927–20; 1930–34). Promoted colonel

(1932), he commanded a regiment (1934), then was chief of staff of 4th Division (1935). Promoted major general (1937), he was CofS of First Army (1938). Promoted lieutenant general, he commanded the Imperial Guards Division (1939–41).

As commander of Fifteenth Army (1941), Iida had charge of the Japanese occupation of Thailand (December) and invasion of Burma (January–April 1942). Placed on the reserve list (1944), he was recalled to command Thirtieth Army in Manchuria (July 1945). Captured by the Soviet Army (August), he was released in 1950.

Ijūin, Matsuji (1893–1944) Japanese admiral. A graduate of the Naval Academy (1915), Ijūin early specialized in torpedoes and submarines. He then commanded destroyers (1925–33) and was aide to Japanese puppet Emperor of Manchukuo, Henry Pu-yi (1932). Promoted captain (1938), he commanded destroyer flotillas (1938–39).

During World War II Ijūin took command of battleship *Kongō* (December 1942). Then, in command of 3rd Destroyer Squadron, he fought in the battles of Vella Lavella (6–7 October 1943) and Empress Augusta Bay (2 November). He died in an accident in Singapore.

Ilyushin, Sergey Vladimirovich (1894–1977) Soviet general and aircraft designer. Ilyushin began work as an aircraft mechanic (1916) and also learned to fly. He joined the Red Army (1919) and commanded an aircraft maintenance unit during the 1918–20 Civil War. He graduated from the Zhukovsky Air Force Engineering Academy (1926) and became an aircraft designer. He rose to become chief of the Central Design Office (1931) and a colonel general.

Ilyushin is credited with development during World War II of the Il-2 Stormovik, a highly effective well-armored ground-attack aircraft known to the

Germans as the "Black Death" that appeared in spring 1941. More than 36,000 were produced during the war, a greater number than any other warplane in history. It evolved into the Il-10 variant (1942). After World War II Ilyushin developed the jet ground-attack IL-40; the twin-engine IL-28 attack bomber, the Soviet Union's first jet bomber; and the Il-62 transcontinental passenger plane.

Imamura, Hitoshi (1888–1968) Japanese general. Commissioned in the infantry (1907), he was long associated with the British Army, first in England, then in France during World War I with the BEF, and finally in India (1926–30). Promoted major general (March 1935), he was vice chief of staff of the Kwantung Army in Manchuria (1936–37). He then headed the Army Administration Bureau (1938). Promoted lieutenant general (March 1938), he commanded 5th Division in China (1938–1940), and then became deputy inspector general of military training (1940–41). He returned to China to command Twenty-Third Army (July 1941).

During World War II Imamura commanded Sixteenth Army in the landing on Java (March 1942). His ship was among the Japanese transports sunk off Java by U.S.S *Houston* and H.M.S. *Perth* (28–29 February 1942), but he survived. Following surrender of the Netherlands East Indies, he established a liberal occupation policy there. He then took command of the new Eighth Area Army, headquartered at Rabaul (November 1942) to control Japanese forces on Guadalcanal and New Guinea. Promoted full general (May 1943), he continued to command 70,000 well-trained and equipped troops around Rabaul. He surrendered when instructed to do so by the emperor. Tried and convicted after the war of war crimes, he was released in 1954.

Immelman, Max (1890–1916) German fighter pilot. Immelmann joined the army

but resigned his commission (1912) to become an engineer. Recalled to active service at the start of World War I, he requested reassignment to the Flying Corps and passed the examination (March 1915). His first assignment was as a reconaissance pilot near Lille. Bored by this, he soon established his reputation as a fighter pilot and developed a flying maneuver that bears his name. Promoted lieutenant (April 1915) and then first lieutenant (September), Immelman, known as the "Eagle of Lille," had fifteen kills when he was shot down and killed on 18 June 1916.

Ingenohl, Friedrich von (1857–1935) German admiral. Ingenohl was an early supporter of Admiral Alfred von Tirpitz and distinguished himself in various ship and shore commands. He attained flag rank (1908) and was enobled (1909). Tirpitz promoted him chief of the High Seas Fleet (April 1913) with the rank of full admiral.

Ingenohl kept the fleet trained and at a high level of combat readiness and reluctantly respected orders that limited his offensive operations to surprise raids, mining operations, and U-boat warfare. German defeats in the Battles of the Falklands (December 1914) and Dogger Bank (January 1915) led to his replacement by Admiral Hugo von Pohl in February 1915. Ingenohl subsequently commanded the Baltic Naval Station until he retired in August 1915.

Ingersoll, Royal Eason (1863–1976) U.S. admiral. Ingersoll graduated from Annapolis (1905). During World War I he was attached to the office of the chief of naval operations, where he developed the navy's communication office (1916–18). He was communications officer for the U.S. delegation at the Paris Peace Conference (1919), then headed the branch of Naval Intelligence responsible for working to break the Japanese codes (1921–23).

Promoted captain (1927), Ingersoll held

a variety of staff assignments and twice commanded heavy cruisers. He also headed the Navy Department war plans division that helped develop "Plan Orange," for a war against Japan. Promoted rear admiral, he took command of Cruiser Division 76 (1938). He then was assistant to Chief of Naval Operations (CNO) Admiral Harold Stark (1940).

Following U.S. entry into World War II (December 1941), Ingersoll commanded the Atlantic Fleet (1942) with responsibility for protection of the Atlantic convoys and Atlantic U.S. coast and (until creation of the Tenth Fleet) anti-submarine warfare. He was promoted vice admiral and then admiral. The invasion of North Africa (Operation TORCH) (8 November 1942) was under his overall command and he was involved in the invasion of France (Operation OVERLORD) (6 June 1944). He then commanded the Western Sea Frontier in San Francisco (1944) with responsibility over all aspects of the projected invasion of Japan. He then became deputy CNO and deputy commander, U.S. Fleet before his retirement in August 1946.

Ingram, James Howard (1886–1952) U.S. admiral. A graduate of Annapolis (1907), Ingram was an outstanding football player and later coached football at the academy (1915–17). For his actions in the U.S. occupation of Vera Cruz (1914), he was awarded the Medal of Honor. He later directed athletics at the academy (1926–30).

Ingram commanded the Atlantic Cruiser Division (1941) and then Allied Naval Forces in the South Atlantic, in which capacity he helped secure naval cooperation with Brazil. His cruisers and destroyers sank or captured a half dozen German blockade runners and sank a number of German submarines. He succeeded Admiral Royal Ingersoll as CinC, Atlantic Fleet (November 1944) and was promoted full admiral. He warned of a German missile attack from submarines on New York City. Although this did not materialize, his hunter-killer groups did break up the last German U-boat operations off the Eastern United States. He retired in April 1947.

Inouye, Shigeyoshi (1899–1975) Japanese admiral. A graduate of the Naval Academy (1909), Inoye was trained in navigation. Resident officer in Switzerland and France (1918–21), he was promoted lieutenant commander (1922). He graduated from the Naval Staff College (1924) and held staff posts in the Navy Ministry (1924–32). Promoted captain, he commanded the battleship *Hiei* (1933). Promoted rear admiral, he headed the Naval Affairs Bureau (1937). Then promoted vice admiral, he was CofS of the China Area Fleet (1939). Known as a brilliant strategic thinker, he became convinced of the importance of naval aviation and secured appointment as chief of the Naval Aeronautics Bureau (1940). In this post he drafted a paper attacking the emphasis on battleships in naval procurement and urged an emphasis on shore-based aircraft and fortification of the mandated islands. For such "incorrect thinking" he was transferred to command Fourth Fleet (August 1941).

At the start of World War II, Inoue directed the capture of Guam and Wake Islands (December 1941). He then assumed overall command of Operation MO, the Japanese plan to take Port Moresby and secure the northern Solomon Islands. This led to the Battle of the Coral Sea (7–8 May 1942), after which, reluctant to risk his transports, he called off the invasion. He was then commandant of the Naval Academy (October 1942–44) and vice minister of the navy (1944–45). Promoted full admiral (May 1945), he joined the Supreme War Council, where he advocated a Japanese surrender.

Ironside, Sir Edmund, Baron of Archangel and Ironside (1880–1959) British field marshal. Nicknamed "Tiny" for his 6'4" height, Ironside was commissioned in the artillery from Woolwich (1899) and served in the 1899–1902 Anglo-Boer War. Fluent in seven languages, he served as a gunnery officer in the Royal Horse Artillery and was promoted captain (1908). He graduated from the Staff College, Camberley (1913), and served in France during World War I as a staff officer, ultimately with the 4th Canadian Division, seeing action in 1917 at Vimy Ridge and Paschendaele. As a temporary colonel, he led a machine gun school until he returned to the front in the Ludendorff Offensive (spring 1918) and took command of 99th Brigade of 2nd Division.

Immediately after the war, Ironside was promoted temporary major general and commanded the Allied force sent to Archangelsk to assist the Whites in the 1918–20 Russian Civil War. Knighted (1919), he became permanent major general. He then held posts in the Middle East and commanded the Staff College at Camberley (1922–26). Promoted full general (1936) he then headed Eastern Command (1936–38).

Ironside became CinC at Gibraltar (1938–39). He then should have retired, but became inspector general of Overseas Forces. Appointed chief of the Imperial General Staff (September 1939), he was thought too old for a field command and he clashed with War Minister Leslie Hore-Belisha. Replaced by General John Dill (May 1940), he was CinC, Home Forces (May–June) when he was replaced by General Alan Brooke. Promoted field marshal (1940), he retired and was elevated to the peerage as 1st Baron of Archangel and of Ironside (1941).

Ishihara, Kanji (1886–1949) Japanese general. A graduate of the Military Academy (1909) and Army Staff College (1918), he was commissioned in the infantry. He studied in Berlin and was an instructor at the Army War College (1925–28). In a series of lectures, he

propounded the theory of "The Final War," a great global conflict between Japan and the United States. This was inspired by the Nichiren Sect, a mystical and militant Buddhist group. Ishihara's theories were published in his book *Thoughts on the Final Global War*.

As operations officer for the Manchurian Kwantung Army (1928–32), he helped plan the swift takeover of all Manchuria (September 1931–February 1932). Promoted colonel (1932), he headed the Operations Section of the Army General Staff and helped crush the expansionist Young Officers' Rebellion (February 1936). Promoted major general, he headed the Operations Division of the General Staff (1937). His position of urging military restraint on the Asian mainland became increasingly unpopular in the army after the outbreak of war with China (July 1937). He was then CofS of the Kwantung Army (1937–38), but his personality and unorthodox views brought his assignment to unimportant posts (1938–41). Promoted lieutenant general, he was forced into retirement (1941).

Ishihara then led the *Tōa Remmei* (East Asian League) movement, which eventually became one of the rallying points for anti-Tōjō elements in World War II Japan. He returned briefly as an advisor to the "Surrender Cabinet," urging that Japan conclude peace in 1945.

Ismay, Hastings Lionel, 1st Baron Wormington (1887–1965) British general. Born in India and a graduate from Sandhurst (1905), he was commissioned into the Indian Army and saw action on the northwest frontier and then in Somaliland in World War I. After graduating from the Indian Staff College, he held a variety of staff posts in India and Britain. He then served on the Imperial Defense Committee and, as a major general, became CofS to Winston Churchil when the latter became prime minister (May 1940). Promoted lieutenant general (November 1942), he acted as a conduit between the service chiefs and Churchill, and later the Americans, trying to brake the prime minister's impetuous nature and his often impossible demands, and working to reduce friction and build consensus. Without personal ambition, he was a loyal subordinate who would also speak his mind, and he enjoyed Churchill's complete trust. Promoted full general (1944), he retired from the army and was made a peer as 1st Baron Wormington.

Ismay returned to government service as CofS in India to Lord Louis Mountbatten during the 1947 partition crisis. He was secretary of state for Commonwealth Relations (1951–52) and then first secretary general of NATO during 1952–57.

Isogai, Rensuke (1886–1967) Japanese general. A graduate of the Military Academy (1904) and Staff College (1915), he served on the General Staff (1916–28). In 1944 he headed a division of the General Staff. He was then military attaché in China (1935), then headed the Department of Military Affairs of the Ministry of War (1936).

Promoted lieutenant general (March 1937), Isogai commanded 10th Division sent to China and paired with Seishiro Itagaki's 5th Division for an offensive along the Tientsin (Tianjin)–Shanghai railroad. The 10th Division was ambushed at Tai'erzhuang (Taierchwang) (April). Although Itagaki's division broke through and relieved Isogai, it was at heavy cost in lives and prestige. Isogai took blame for the debacle and never again held active combat command. During World War II he was governor of Hong Kong.

Itagaki, Seishirō (1885–1948) Japanese general. Commissioned in the army (1904), Itagaki became a specialist in China and had lengthy staff, command, and attaché assignments there (from 1919). As a colonel in the Manchurian Kwantung Army (1928), he and his subordinate Kanji Ishihara implemented the

Kwantung Army's plan to take over Manchuria (1931).

Itagaki then had a series of important staff assignments in China, including negotiating with the Nationalist Chinese government over Japanese claims in north China. Appointed CofS of the Kwantung Army (March 1936), he was promoted lieutenant general (April). He then commanded the 5th Infantry Division at Hiroshima (March 1937) and took it to China, where it was paired with General Rensuke Isogai's 10th Division, which he saved from destruction in the Battle of Tai'erzhuang (Taierchwang) (April). Itagaki was himself defeated in battle with Chinese Communist guerrillas under Chu Teh (Zhu De) (September 1937) at Pingsinkuan, near the Great Wall.

Itagaki then held staff appointments and was minister of war (January–August 1939), before becoming CofS of the Japanese army in China (1940). Promoted full general (1941), he commanded the army in Korea. In the last months of World War II, he was appointed to head 7th Area Forces at Singapore and surrendered that place (12 June). After the war he was convicted of war crimes and hanged.

Itō, Sei'ichi (1890–1945) Japanese admiral. Itō graduated from the Naval Academy (1911) and the Naval Staff College (1923). He held cruiser commands and then commanded a battleship (1936). He was then promoted rear admiral and became CofS of Second Fleet (1937). He served in the Naval Ministry (1938–40) and then commanded Cruiser Division 8 (November 1940). Appointed CofS of the Combined Fleet (April 1941), he then became vice chief of the Navy General Staff (September). As such, he was a central figure in planning the Pearl Harbor strike (7 December 1941) and in Japanese naval strategy during the Pacific War. He was promoted vice admiral (October 1941).

Toward the end of the war Itō supported the use of *kamikaze* pilots. As commander of Second Fleet (from December 1944), he commanded the giant battleship *Yamato* and its support ships on a suicide run to Okinawa in order to try to destroy the U.S. invasion fleet. He died when his ship, a cruiser, and four destroyers were sunk by U.S. carrier aircraft well short of their destination in the Battle of the East China Sea (7 April 1945).

Ivanov, General Nikolai Yudovich (1851–1919) Russian general. Ivanov graduated from Mikhailovsky Artillery College and fought in the 1877–78 Russo-Turkish War. By the end of the 1904–05 Russo-Japanese War he had command of a corps. In 1906, as governor general of Kronstadt, Ivanov put down a military mutiny. Promoted general of artillery two years later, he then commanded the Kiev Miliary District.

When World War I began Ivanov took command of Southwestern Front of four armies facing Austria-Hungary. Although popular with his staff and troops, he was a poor field commander. Unduly cautious, Ivanov proved utterly unable to react to changing battlefield conditions. He was "kicked upstairs" as military advisor to Tsar Nicholas II (March 1916).

Ivanov remained loyal to the Tsar during the March Revolution, and he took command of the White Southern Army on the Don (October 1918), but died in south Russia of typhus.

Iwabuchi, Sanji (1893–1945) Japanese admiral. Vice Admiral Iwabuchi commanded battleship *Kirishima* and participated in the Battle of Midway (3–6 June 1942) and campaign for the Solomon Islands (1942–43). He is best known for his role late in the war, when he took command of Naval Defense Forces to defend Manila in the Philippines. Ordered to withdraw by General Tomoyuki Yamashita, he embarked instead on a suicidal defense. The month-long battle (February–March 1945) resulted in widespread destruction and great loss of life. He made his last stand at Intramuros, where he was killed. His efforts cost the lives of over 100,000 Filipinos, 16,600 Japanese, and 1,000 Americans.

Iwakuro, Hideo (1897–1970) Japanese army general. As a colonel, Iwakuro was a section head in the Military Affairs Division of the Ministry of War. He was involved in negotiations between the United States and Japan in the spring and winter of 1941.

When the war began between Japan and United States, Iwakuro fought in the Malaya campaign as a regimental commander in the 5th Division. Later promoted major general, he organized the anti-British Indian Nationalist Army in Burma. As CofS of Twenty-Eighth Army, he planned defensive operations after the 1944 Imphal debacle.

Izzet Pasha, Ahmed (1864–1937) Turkish general and politician. Izzet studied in Germany and saw service in Greece and Yemen. During the first two years of the First World War, he was in semi-retirement. He took command of Second Army in Anatolia as part of the effort to recapture Erzurum (April 1916). He attacked late and failed to concentrate his forces, which were driven back.

Izzet then served in a variety of diplomatic and administrative roles that culminated with his elevation as Grand Vizier (October 1918). This ended in November. He later held ministerial positions until 1922.

J

Jackson, Sir Henry Bradwardine (1855–1929) British admiral. Jackson joined the navy (1868) and helped introduce radio into the fleet (1900). He was third sea lord and comptroller of the navy (1905–08) and later headed the new Naval War College at Portsmouth. He then became chief of the War Staff of the Admiralty (1913).

On the outbreak of World War I, Jackson coordinated attacks on Germany's colonial possessions. He then replaced Admiral John Fisher as first sea lord. His forte was in scientific innovation, and he ordered extensive mine-laying operations in the North Sea. He opposed a naval operation in the Dardanelles without a land occupation of the Gallipoli peninsula.

Disappointment over the course of the war at sea led to Jackson's replacement by Admiral John Jellicoe (November 1916). Jackson ended the war as president of the Royal Naval College at Greenwich and aide-de-camp to King George V. Promoted admiral of the fleet (1919), he retired from the navy in 1924.

Jány, Gusztáv (1883–1947) Hungarian army general. As a colonel general, Jány commanded Second Hungarian Army in the German invasion of the Soviet Union, participating in offensive operations in Ukraine toward the Don River, where it established defensive positions south of Voronezh and north of Stalingrad. It was stretched thin over some 120 miles of front with few supplies and little ammunition. When the Red Army launched its counter-offensive at Stalingrad, the whole line began to crumble. The Italian Alpine Division on Second Army's right gave way and Jány sought permission to retire, which the Germans denied. His request to be reinforced by the Hungarian armor division in reserve was also denied. Russian troops got across the river and, although Jány flew from unit to unit trying to shore up defenses, Second Army's lines were breached (January 1943). As many as 80,000 men in Second Army were casualties, the bulk of these killed or taken prisoner, in Hungary's worst military defeat since 1526.

Although he did not deserve it, at the end of the war Jány was tried and found guilty by a people's court and executed as a scapegoat for the Don Bend disaster. He was rehabilitated in 1993.

Jellicoe, John Rushworth, first Earl (1859–1935) British admiral. Jellicoe joined the Royal Navy (1872) and specialized in naval ordnance. He served in the 1900 Peking Relief Expedition during the 1900–01 Boxer Rebellion and was seriously wounded. Appointed Third Lord of the Admiralty under Sir John Fisher (1908), he supervised the introduction of improved gunnery methods in the fleet.

On the outbreak of World War I, Jellicoe assumed command of the Grand Fleet. He made it clear in memoranda that he would act prudently if and when the German and British battle fleets met. Later he was faulted as being overcautious and lacking initiative.

Although Jellicoe deployed the Grand Fleet in precisely the correct formation, the results of the Battle of Jutland (31 May–1 June 1916) were indecisive. On two occasions he turned the entire battle fleet away from the Germans on receiving reports of torpedo attacks. The net effect of the battle, however, was to leave Britain in control of the North Sea.

Jellicoe then became first sea lord (December 1916). Within a year, he fell victim to the crisis of the German U-boat campaign and Prime Minister David Lloyd George dismissed him. In 1919 he was made Viscount Jellicoe of Scapa and admiral of the fleet. After the war, Jellicoe was recalled to serve as a diplomat and was governor general of New Zealand (1922–24).

Jeschonnek, Hans (1899–1943) German air force general. Jeschonnek was originally in the infantry during World War I but learned to fly in 1917. He had scored two aerial victories by the end of the war. He was then involved in the secret building of the Luftwaffe and became adjutant to Aviation Minister Erhard Milch (1933). As Luftwaffe chief of operations (1937), he was promoted colonel (1938).

Jeschonnek was chief of the General Staff of the Luftwaffe (February 1939–August 1943) and was promoted brigadier general (August 1939) and full general (1942). Convinced that the war would be short, he sacrificed long-term planning and built a tactical air force designed for support of the army, to include dive bombing. Germany had no production strategic bomber. Made scapegoat by Hermann Göring for air force failures, especially the Allied bombing of Germany and inability of the Luftwaffe to

supply Sixth Army at Stalingrad, he committed suicide.

Jodl, Alfred (1890–1946) German general. Jodl joined the army in 1910. An artillery officer, Jodl was both a line and a staff officer during World War I. He was promoted captain (1919). When Adolf Hitler came to power (January 1933), he worked to advance the Führer's complete control over the military. A protégé of General Wilhelm Keitel and a brilliant organizer, Jodl headed the war plans division of the General Staff (1935) and then the Land Operations Department when the Oberkommando der Wehrmacht (OKW) was set up. Promoted brigadier general (April 1938), he briefly commanded an artillery unit and then became chief of the Wehrmacht Operations staff, a post he held throughout the war (1939–45).

Jodl strongly supported the new theory of *Blitzkrieg* (lightning war) and directed most of Germany's World War II campaigns. Keitel, nominal OKW head, was actually Hitler's spokesman. Jodl enjoyed Hitler's confidence. He often argued with him over decisions, but remained completely loyal to the *Führer*. He considered himself merely an apolitical soldier. Promoted major general (1940) and lieutenant general (1944), his judgement declined as the war went on. He was injured during the July 1944 attempt on Hilter's life. Jodl signed for head of state Grand Admiral Karl Dönitz the instrument of German surrender (7 May 1945). Condemned as a war criminal at the International Military Tribunal at Nuremberg (October 1946), he was hanged. In 1953 a German court posthumously exonerated him of having broken international law.

Joffre, Joseph Jacques Césaire (1852–1931) Marshal of France. Joffre graduated from the École Polytechnique and fought in the 1870–71 Franco-German War. He was then stationed in the Far

East and Madagascar. He joined the Supreme War Council (1910) and became chief of the general staff and commander-in-chief designate (1911). His War Plan XVII, intended to secure Alsace-Lorraine, failed to anticipate the main German deployment through Belgium because he was convinced the Germans would not use their reserves on the front lines. Following defeat of the French offensive and development of the German threat to the north, he skillfully redeployed his assets and conducted a fighting retreat to the Marne.

Joffre orchestrated the Battle of the Marne (5–11 September 1914). This critical battle ended in a German withdrawal and was the high point of his career. His major offensives of 1915 and 1916, including Champagne, the Somme, and Artois, were failures. He justified them as convincing Italy to join the Entente and taking pressure off Russia.

By the end of 1916 Joffre was under severe criticism, especially when the German offensive at Verdun (February) caught him by surprise and with French defenses unready. He was also blamed for the Romanian disaster (late 1916). Removed as commander of French forces on the Western Front (December 1916), he was made marshal of France and named technical advisor to the government. He then headed the French military mission to the United States (1917), retiring after the war.

Johnson, Harold Keith (1912–83) U.S. general. Johnson graduated from West Point (1933) and was commissioned in the infantry. He graduated from the Infantry School, Fort Benning (1938) and was promoted captain (1940). On U.S. entry into World War II (December 1941), he was assigned to a regiment of Philippine scouts and advanced to lieutenant colonel. Following the Japanese conquest, he spent the remainder of the war in a succession of POW camps (1942–45). After the war Johnson graduated from

the General Staff college, Fort Leavenworth (1947) and the Armed Forces Staff College, Norfolk (1960). He commanded a regiment in the 1950–53 Korean War, then was assistant CofS of I Corps (February 1951) and promoted colonel. He graduated from the Army War College (1953) and was promoted brigadier general (January 1956). He was then CofS of Seventh Army (September 1957) and assistant CofS of the U.S. Army in Europe (April 1959). In late 1959 he was CofS of Central Army Group of NATO as a major general. He then headed the Command and General Staff College (August 1960). Selected from far down on the list of lieutenant generals, he was promoted general and assigned as CofS of the army (1964–68).

Admired for his high standards and dedication, Johnson headed the army at a critical time, during the rapid expansion of the U.S. effort in Vietnam. His work was made more difficult by the Johnson's administration's refusal to call up reserves. Although publicly supporting U.S. commander in Vietnam General William Westmoreland's tactics, privately he had misgivings and favored a program emphasizing pacification, which was ultimately instituted by General Creighton Abrams, Westmoreland's successor, (1968). Johnson retired from the army in 1968.

Jones, David C. (1921–) U.S. Air Force general. Jones attended the University of North Dakota and then Minot State College until the U.S. entered World War II, when he enlisted in the army (December 1941). He underwent flight training and was commissioned (February 1943). He was an aviation instructor in the U.S. until the end of the war.

After the war Jones was posted to Japan (1945–48). He then attended various air force schools, and saw his first combat during the 1950–53 Korean War with the 19th Bombardment Squadron (1950–53). Promoted lieutenant colonel, Jones commanded 22nd Air Refueling Squadron, then 33rd Bombardment Squadron (1953–54). He was then aide to Strategic Air Command commander General Curtis Le-May (1955–57). Promoted colonel, he commanded the 93rd Bombardment Wing in California (1957–59). He graduated from the National War College (1960) and was assigned to Air Force Headquarters in Washington. While serving as inspector general of U.S. Air Forces in Europe (USAFE), he was promoted brigadier general (December 1965) and was deputy CofS, USAFE (1967–69).

Promoted major general, Jones was deputy CofS and vice commander of Seventh Air Force in Vietnam (1969). Promoted lieutenant general, he then commanded Second Air Force in Louisiana (1969–71). He returned to the USAFE as vice commander (1971). Promoted general, he was commander of USAFE (1971–74), then CofS of the Air Force (1974–78) and chairman of the Joint Chiefs of Staff (1978–82).

Josef Augustin, Archduke (1872–1962) Austro-Hungarian general. Born into the House of Habsburg, Archduke Josef devoted his life to the Austro-Hungarian Army and commanded IV Corps in Hungary prior to the outbreak of World War I. During the war he commanded first a corps, then an army, and finally an army group on the Russian, Romanian, and Italian Fronts. By the end of the war he had charge of the Tyrolean Army Group.

At the beginning of 1918, Josef began to shift his loyalty from the empire to his native Hungary. He favored the creation of a separate Hungarian army, hoping thereby to reinvigorate the Magyar enthusiasm for the war. By October he was openly advocating an immediate armistice. He was deeply involved in post-war Hungarian politics, and was briefly regent there.

Josef Ferdinand, Archduke (1872–1942) Austro-Hungarian general. Josef Ferdinand was one of the less competent commanders of the Austro-Hungarian army during World War I. After the outbreak of hostilities, he had charge of a number of units on the Eastern Front, culminating with his appointment as commander of Austrian Fourth Army in Galicia. Believing his defenses impregnable, he organized hunting parties while the Russians prepared to attack. Receiving the initial assault of the Russian Brusilov offensive, Fourth Army was destroyed as an effective fighting force in a matter of hours. Only massive German reinforcements saved the whole Austro-Hungarian army from disintegration. Josef Ferdinand was relieved of his command three days after the start of the attack.

Joy, Charles Turner (1895–1956) U.S. admiral. Joy graduated from Annapolis (1916) and served on a battleship during World War I. He earned a master of science degree from the University of Michigan (1923) and served on the Yangtze Patrol, before commanding a destroyer (1933). He also held ordnance assignments ashore and was stationed at Annapolis.

During the first two years of World War II, Joy served aboard a cruiser and then a carrier. He then helped plan operations against the Solomon and Aleutian Islands and commanded a cruiser, before heading the Pacific Plans Division in Washington (August 1943–May 1944). Promoted rear admiral, he rejoined the Pacific Fleet and held commands during the Marianas, Philippines, Iwo Jima, and Okianawa campaigns.

After the war, Joy helped transport Nationalist Chinese troops from south to north China and Manchuria. He then commanded the Naval Proving Ground, Dahlgren, Virginia (1946–49). Promoted vice admiral (August 1949), he commanded U.S. Naval Forces Far East. From Tokyo he directed U.S. and United Nations Command (UNC) naval forces fighting to halt the North Korean invasion of South Korea (June 1950). His surface and air units shelled North Korean troops and lines of communication and established control of the Yellow Sea and the East Sea (Sea of Japan). They also carried out amphibious landings at Inchon (September) and Wonsan (October) and evacuated UN forces at Hungnam (December). He was then senior UNC delegate to the armistice negotiations (June 1951–May 1952) until, frustrated by the lack of progress, he asked to be relieved. He was superintendent at Annapolis (1952–54) before cancer forced his retirement.

Juin, Alphonse Pierre (1888–1967) Marshal of France. Born in Algeria, Juin graduated first in his class from St. Cyr (1912) and joined the 1st Regiment of Algerian Tirailleurs in the *Armée de l'Afrique* in Morocco. He fought in the Battle of the Marne (September 1914) as a lieutenant commanding a platoon in the Moroccan Brigade. He was awarded the cross of the Legion of Honor, but was badly wounded. Promoted captain, he returned to action to command a company.

Juin graduated from the War College (1921) and fought in the Rif War against Abd-el-Krim (1925). He served on the Higher War Council in Paris (1925–27), was promoted major, and commanded a battalion in Algeria. As a lieutenant colonel, he joined the War College as an instructor (1933). After additional service in Algeria and Morocco, he was promoted brigadier general (1938). On the outbreak of World War II, he commanded the 15th Motorized Infantry Division. Following the German invasion of the West (10 May 1940), his unit advanced into Belgium and was cut off. Taken prisoner by the Germans (30 May), he was promoted to major general (effective February 1941). Marshal Henri-Philippe Pétain arranged his release (1941) as an "African specialist."

Juin then commanded Vichy French land forces in North Africa. Furious at not having been informed of the Allied landings of Operation TORCH (8 November 1942) beforehand, he nonethless convinced Admiral Jean Darlan to order a ceasefire. Promoted lieutenant general, he commanded XIX Corps. Promoted full general, he formed the French Expeditionary Corps (CEF) and led it in Italy (November 1943–August 44). An able commander, his troops distinguished themselves in hard fighting. Juin then became CofS of National Defense under Charles de Gaulle (August 1944–1947).

Juin was resident general in Morocco (1947–51), then CinC, Land Forces, Central Europe in NATO. Promoted to marshal of France (1952), he retired (1956). In 1961 he opposed Algerian independence and de Gaulle removed him from the Supreme Defense Council and forbade him to visit Algeria.

K

Kamio, Mitsuomi (1856–1927) Japanese general. First a sergeant, Kamio was promoted to officer rank (1879). He was military attaché in China (1892–94) and then a staff officer in Second Army during the 1894–95 Sino-Japanese War. He was CinC, 3rd Imperial Guard Regiment (1897). He was then CofS, first of 1st Division (1900), and then of 10th Division (1901). He was CinC of 22nd Brigade (1902) and CofS of Lyadong Garrison. He then was CinC of 9th Division (1908) and 18th Division (1912).

During World War I, Kamio led the assault on Germany's base at Tsingtao (Qingdao), China. Skillfully employing vastly superior artillery assets, he forced Tsingtao's surrender (7 November 1914).

Kamio was then governor of the captured territory and later commanded the Tokyo garrison. He was promoted full general (1916) and retired in 1925.

Kamimura, Hikonojō (1849–1916) Japanese admiral. Kamimura was a *samurai* foot soldier in the 1868 Boshin (Restoration) War. He graduated from the Naval Academy and was commissioned an ensign (1879), then had various assignments afloat as a junior officer. His first command was a gunboat (1891–93). During the 1894–95 Sino-Japanese War, he commanded a cruiser in the Battle of the Yalu (17 September 1894). He then held a succession of staff and command assign-ments. Promoted vice admiral (1903), he commanded Second Fleet during the 1904–05 Russo-Japanese War, with instructions to blockade the Russian fleet at Vladivostok. He was blamed when Russian cruisers sank Japanese transports in the Sea of Japan (April–June 1904) but redeemed himself in the Battle of Ulsan (14 August). He led Second Fleet in the Battle of Tsushima (27 May 1905).

After the war Kamimura commanded Yokosuka naval base (1905–09), then First Fleet (1909–11). Created a baron (1907), he was promoted admiral (1910) and named a naval advisor (1911). He went on the reserve list in 1914.

Kammhuber, Josef (1908–86) German air force general. Enlisting in the army in 1914, Kammhuber served in the engineers during World War I and continued in the army afterward. Although he qualified as a pilot (1919), he remained in the engineers until he took command of the Reichswehr's secret pilot training school at Lipetsk in the Soviet Union (1930). He joined the Luftwaffe in 1933 and then held various developmental and command positions, including night fighter and bomber groups.

Given command of all German night fighter units (September 1943) during the height of the British night bombing campaign, Kammhuber developed the network of radar and fighter control stations that inflicted heavy losses on the British bombers. Effectiveness of the so-called "Kammhuber Line" declined following the institution of Allied countermeasures, however. At the end of the war, Lieutenant General Kammhuber had charge of a task force devoted to developing new tactics and equipment to defeat Allied bombing.

After the war Kammhuber joined the Federal Republic of Germany Air Force (1956) and advanced to inspector general with the rank of full general. He retired in 1962.

Kang Kon (1918–50) Korean People's Army general. Together with fellow Korean Kim Il Sung, Kang joined the anti-Japanese struggle in Manchuria (1932). He fled with Kim into Soviet territory (1940) and at the end of World War II was an officer in the 88th Independent Brigade of Koreans and Chinese in the Red Army on the Far Eastern Front.

Kang returned to North Korea (summer 1946) to help establish the Korean People's Army (KPA) and became its chief of staff (September 1949), playing a key role in planning the North Korean invasion of South Korea (25 June 1950). While serving as KPA chief of the General Staff, he was killed in action by a land mine (8 September 1950). Lieutenant General Nam Il succeeded him. The Kang Kon Military Officers Academy of the Democratic People's Republic of Korea is named for him.

Karl I, Emperor of Austria (1887–1922) Last Austrian emperor and Hungarian king (as Charles IV). Karl Franz Josef was the grandnephew of Emperor Franz Josef and became heir presumptive to the Austro-Hungarian throne upon the assassination of his uncle Franz Ferdinand (28 June 1914). As a colonel at the start of World War I, he was liaison to the Austro-Hungarian army in Galicia. In summer 1915 he was promoted major general, and he then commanded XX

(Edelweiss) Corps on the Italian front (May 1916). Soon afterward he was sent to Eastern Galicia as commander of a new army corps.

On the death of Emperor Franz Josef, Karl succeeded to the throne as Emperor of Austria (21 November 1916). He forced Field Marshal Franz Conrad von Hotzendorf to resign and appointed General Arthur Arz von Straussenburg as CofS. Karl, however, lacked the experience and willpower to make decisions. His desire to command the armed forces personally undermined confidence, as did his decisions to abolish dueling, end physical punishments, and grant amnesty for political crimes. He objected to German military dominance of the alliance and Berlin's decision to resume unrestricted submarine warfare. He also attempted to negotiate a separate peace for Austria-Hungary. Karl stepped aside as head of government (11 November 1918). He twice attempted to regain his Hungarian throne, but was blocked by Allied opposition.

Kataoka, Shichirō (1854–1920) Japanese admiral. A graduate of the Navy Academy (1871), he trained aboard German warships (1877–78). He served with the navy at sea (1881–86), then was an instructor at the Navy Academy (1886–88), before returning to Germany for advanced study (1880–90) and service as naval attaché in Berlin (1890–94). During the 1894–95 Sino-Japanese War, he was on the Navy General Staff (1894) before receiving ship commands (1895). He then had a series of assignments ashore and afloat (1895–1903). He was promoted rear admiral (1899) and vice admiral (1903). Early in the 1904–05 Russo-Japanese War, he commanded Third Fleet and participated in the Battles of the Yellow Sea (10 August 1904) and Tsushima (27 May 1905). After the war he became chief of the Department of Ships in the Navy Ministry (1906). Created a baron (1907), he was promoted admiral (1910) and then went on the reserve list in 1911.

Kawabe, Masakazu (1886–1965) Japanese general. The older brother of Torashirō Kawabe, he graduated from the Military Academy (1907) and the Army Staff College (1917). Promoted major general (1923), he taught at the Staff College (1927). He fought in the 1937–45 Sino-Japanese War, and was the commander on the spot during the Marco Polo Bridge incident. He authorized the attacks on the Chinese garrison that began the war. Promoted lieutenant general (1939), he twice served as CofS of the China Expeditionary Force (1938–39 and 1942–43). He also commanded the Burma Area Army (1943–44) and headed the offensive into India (March–September 1944) that was defeated at Kohima and Imphal. Relieved of command for this failure, he returned to Japan. He then commanded Central District Army. Promoted general (1945), he served in the home islands as general director of the Army Air Forces until the end of the war.

Kawabe, Torashirō (1890–1960) Japanese general. The younger brother of Maskazu Kawabe, he graduated from the Military Academy (1912), the Artillery and Engineers School (1915), and Army Staff College (1921). He studied in Riga (then Latvia) (1926–28). Promoted major (1927), He taught at the Army Staff College (1928–29). He also served in the Operations Divison of the General Staff (1922–25 and 1929–32). He was military attaché in Moscow (1932–34) and then chief of intelligence for the Kwantung Army in Manchuria (1934–36). Promoted colonel (1935). he was involved in promoting Japanese control of Inner Mongolia. He commanded the Imperial Guards Division (1936–37) and then served on the General Staff (1937–38), when he tried to prevent a war with China following the July 1937 Marco Polo Bridge incident. Promoted major general (1938),

he was then military attaché in Berlin (1938–40).

Returning to Japan, Kawabe then held a series of commands in Manchuria and the Japanese home islands (1940–45). As vice chief of the General Staff (April–August 1945), he headed the team that traveled to Manila and arranged the details of Japan's surrender and the occupation of the home islands to end World War II (August 1945).

Kawaguchi, Kiyotake (1892–1961) Japanese general. A graduate of the Military Academy (1914) and Staff College (1922), Kawaguchi spent most of his military career in staff positions in Japan and China (1923–40). Promoted major general (1940), he commanded 35th Brigade (December) and led it in the invasion of Borneo (December 1941). He also participated in the latter stages of the Philippines invasions (March–April 1942). Sent from Rabaul to Guadalcanal, he landed there with some 3,500 reinforcements (August 1942). He then commanded some 6,000 Japanese troops on the island in attacks against American-held Henderson Field, which failed with heavy losses (September). Dismissed (November), he returned to Japan and was attached to the headquarters of the Eastern District Army. He was then relegated to the unassigned list (March 1943) and then the reserves (April). Recalled to active duty (March 1945), he commanded Tsushima Fortress. Tried and convicted of war crimes after the war, he was imprisoned during 1946–53.

Kawamura, Kageaki (1850–1926) Japanese field marshal. At age thirteen, Kawamura distinguished himself during the British bombardment of Kagoshima (15–16 August 1863). He fought against the Tokugawa Shogunate in the 1868 Boshin (Restoration) War. Joining the Imperial army as a sergeant (1871), he was commissioned (1872). He fought in the 1877 Satsuma Rebellion. Promoted major general (1891), at the beginning of the 1904–05

Russo-Japanese War he commanded a brigade of the Imperial Guards Division. Promoted major general (1904), he commanded the Yalu Army and fought with distinction in the Battle of Mukden (February–March 1905). Made a viscount after the war, he headed the Imperial Military Reserve Association from 1919.

Kemal, Mustafa (Atatürk) (1881–1938) Turkish general and political leader. Kemal began his military education in 1893 and graduated from the Staff College as a captain (1905). He served with distinction in the 1911–12 Italo-Turkish War and the 1912–13 Balkan Wars. Posted to Sofia as military attaché, he was promoted lieutenant colonel (March 1914).

Following Turkey's entry into World War I (October 1914), Kemal took command of 19th Division, the principal Turkish reserve of Fifth Army commanded by German General Otto Liman von Sanders and defending the Dardanelles (February 1915), and played a key role in containing the Allied landings. Promoted colonel, he continued to distinguish himself in subsequent fighting. After the Allied withdrawal, he took command of XVI Corps (January 1916). When it was transferred to the Caucasus Front (February), he was promoted brigadier general (pasha). He then became deputy commander of Second Army (March) and had success against the Russians. He took command of Seventh Army in Syria, part of a force commanded by German General Erich von Falkenhayn (July 1917), but resigned when the government ignored his counsel to let the Arab provinces go in favor of defending in Europe. He took command of the Fourth, Seventh, and Eighth Ottoman Armies in Syria (August 1918). Outnumbered by the British, he abandoned most of the Arab provinces to defend Anatolia. At the end of the war he was the only undefeated Ottoman field commander.

After the war Kemal became inspector general of Ninth Army in Anatolia and organized a national resistance movement against the invading Allies, primarily the Greeks. Resigning from the army (July 1919), he established a nationalist government in Ankara, and then defeated Greek efforts to slice off part of Asia Minor (1920–23). Turkey then became a republic, with Kemal its first president (1924–38). Fittingly, he took the surname of Atatürk (Father of the Turks).

Keitel, Wilhelm Bodewin Johann Gustav (1882–1946) German field marshal. Keitel was commissioned in the army (1901) and during World War I served as both an artillery officer and a General Staff officer. After the war he remained in the German army and headed the Army Organization Department (1929–34) to plan for military expansion. An ardent Nazi, after Adolf Hitler came to power he was promoted brigadier general (April 1934). A bureaucrat rather than a commander, he then headed the Wehrmachtsamt (1935–38), serving as deputy to the war minister but in fact *de facto* commander of the armed forces. He was promoted major general (1936) and lieutenant general (1937). When Hitler eliminated the War Ministry and took over direct control of the military (February 1938), he became CofS of the *Oberkommando der Wehrmacht* (OKW, Armed Forces High Command). Promoted full general (November 1938), following the defeat of France he was advanced to field marshal (July 1940).

Keitel served as Hitler's military spokesman and chief military advisor, but he was a slavish supporter of Hitler and awed by the latter's perceived military genius. Entirely unable to resist Hitler, he became Hitler's willing puppet and signed many of his most repressive decrees.

Keitel remained loyal to the end. After the war he was tried by the International Military Tribunal at Nuremberg, found guilty of war crimes, and executed.

Kenney, George Churchill (1889–1977) U.S. air force general. Kenney graduated from Massachusetts Institute of Technology (1911). An engineer and surveyor, he joined the army when the United States entered World War I (April 1917). Assigned to the Signal Corps, he received flight training. In France he served in the 91st Aero Squadron, and during the war flew seventy-five missions and shot down two German planes.

After the war Kenney was on occupation duty in Germany (1918–19). He graduated from the Army Air Service Engineering School (1921), the Army Air Corps Tactical School (1926), the Army Command and General Staff College (1927), and the Army War College (1933). He served on the Army Air Corps staff (1935–36). An instructor at the Infantry School, Fort Benning, Georgia, he was promoted lieutenant colonel (1936). Promoted colonel (1938), he commanded the 97th Observation Squadron at Mitchell Field, New York (1938–40). Promoted brigadier general, he commanded the Army Air Corps Experimental Depot, Wright Field, Ohio (1941). Promoted temporary major general, he commanded Fourth Air Force (April 1942). He then commanded Fifth Air Force and all Allied air units in the Southwest Pacific (September). Promoted lieutenant general, he directed resupply of U.S. forces in Papua/New Guinea (July 1942–January 1943).

Kenney provided air support to all General Douglas MacArthur's Southwest Pacific Campaigns from New Guinea to the Philippines. He modified B-25s for low-level bombing and developed the highly effective technique of skip-bombing ships. Promoted general (March 1945), he commanded all Allied air forces in the Pacific, then the Pacific Air Command (1945–46). He was briefly representative to the United Nations military staff committee (1946) then commanded the Strategic Air Command (1946–48), then the Air University, Maxwell Air Force Base, Alabama (1946–51) until his retirement in August 1951.

Kesselring, Albert (1885–1960) German air force field marshal. Kesselring was commissioned in the Bavarian Army (1906) and served in World War I. He continued in the post-war Reichswehr and secured his reputation as a superb administrator. He transferred to the still-secret Luftwaffe (Air Force) (1933) and became its CofS with the rank of lieutenant general (June 1936).

Promoted full general (1937), Kesselring commanded Luftflotte (Airfleet) I in the invasion of Poland (September 1939). He commanded Luftflotte II in the invasion of France and Benelux (May 1940). Raised to field marshal (July 1940), he continued to command Luftflotte II in the Battle of Britain (1940) and invasion of the Soviet Union (June 1941).

Kesselring then went to Italy as CinC, South (December 1941–March 1945). His command encompassed the Mediterranean Basin, and he won the nickname "Smiling Albert" for his ability to get along with Italian leaders. He also won admiration for the skilful evacuation of Tunis (May 1943) and Sicily (August 1943) and the defense of Italy. Injured in a car accident (October 1944), he returned to his command (January 1945). He followed Field Marshal Gerd von Rundstedt as CinC, West (March–May). On the division of the Reich into two defensive zones, he briefly commanded the south. Tried after the war, he was sentenced to death (1947) for his role in the Ardeatine Caves Massacre but this was remitted to life in prison. He was released (1952) on grounds of poor health.

Keyes, Geoffrey (1886–1967) U.S. general. Keyes was commissioned in the cavalry on graduation from West Point (1913). He graduated from the Command and General Staff School (1926) and the French École Supérieure de Guerre

(1933). He then headed the Tactics Department at the Cavalry School (1933–36). He graduated from the Army War College (1937) and was then executive officer of 13th Cavalry Regiment, 7th Cavalry Brigade (1938–39). He was chief of the supply and transportation division of the War Department General Staff (1939–40). Then CofS of 2nd Armored Division (1940–42), he was promoted brigadier general (January 1942) and major general (June). He served as deputy commander of I Armored Corps in North Africa (November 1942–May 1943). He then commanded II Corps (1943–46) in much of the Italian Campaign and coordinated the First Battle of Cassino (January–February 1944). Promoted lieutenant general (April 1945), he commanded Seventh Army (1945) and Third Army (1946–47) before becoming representative to the Allied Council for Austria (1947). He retired in 1950.

Keyes, Roger John Brownlow, Baron Keyes of Zeebrugge and Dover (1872–1945) British admiral. Keyes entered the navy (1885) and, following a variety of assignments, was promoted commander (1900) for action during the 1900–01 Boxer Rebellion when he captured a Chinese destroyer. He was commodore of submarines (1912–15) and, during World War I, devised a plan that led to the Battle of Heligoland Bight (28 August 1914). He then became chief of staff in succession to Admirals Sackville Carden and John de Robeck at the Dardanelles (February 1915).

After the failure of the naval assault (18 March), Keyes reorganized the minesweeping service and pushed for another attempt, but to no avail. He remained convinced that a reorganized fleet would have driven Turkey from the war. He returned to the Grand Fleet (1916) then went to the Admiralty as director of plans (September 1917). He executed a partially successful operation to block the entrances to the canals at Zeebrugge and Ostend leading to the German submarine base at Bruges.

After the war Keyes commanded the battle cruiser squadron (1919–21), was deputy chief of Naval Staff (1921–25), CinC Mediterranean (1925–28), and CinC Portsmouth (1929–31). Promoted to admiral of the fleet (1930), he retired in 1935. During World War II he was recalled to active duty (September 1939) and served as liaison with King Leopold of Belgium. He was then director of Combined Operations (July 1940–October 1941) before retiring again. He was then named Baron Keyes of Zeebrugge and of Dover (1943).

Khozin, Mikhail Semenovich (1896–1979) Soviet general. Khozin was a junior officer in the Russian army before joining the Red Army and Communist party (1918). He held a variety of assignments and, by the time of the German invasion (22 June 1941), headed the Frunze Military Academy. He then commanded the Leningrad Front (October). Stalin demoted him after he promised and failed to save General Andrei Vlasov's Second Shock Army. He then headed Thirty-Third Army (June–October 1942). He briefly commanded Twentieth Army (December–January 1943), before disappearing from the war.

Kiggell, Sir Launcelot Edward (1862–1954) British general. Kiggell entered the army from Sandhurst (1882) and was commandant of the Staff College (1913–14). During World War I he initially served in the War Office. General Douglas Haig then appointed him his chief of staff (1915), and he recommended the tactic of successive waves for the 1916 Somme Offensive and fought for the battle's continuation despite heavy casualties. Promoted lieutenant general (1917), the next year he resigned for medical reasons. He then served as commander and lieutenant governor of Guernsey, and retired in 1920.

Kim Ch'aek (1903–51) Korean People's Army general. Kim went to Manchuria (1903) and joined the Chinese Communist Party there (1922). He participated in the 1930s anti-Japanese guerrilla movement, until he, Kim Il Sung, and others, were forced into exile in Siberia (1941). Trained by the Soviets, Kim returned to Korea with the Red Army (August 1945) and supported Kim Il Sung in power. He then headed the Pyongyang Military Academy and joined the presidium of the North Korean Worker's Party. On the creation of the Democratic People's Republic of Korea (September 1948), he became one of three vice presidents under Kim Il Sung. During the 1950–53 Korean War he succeeded Kang Kon, killed in action by a land mine (September 1950), as front-line commander of the Korean People's Army (KPA). He subsequently put together a 10,000-man guerrilla force from broken and retreating KPA units in order to harass United Nations Command (UNC) troops moving north. He died in a UNC bombing raid (January 1951). The city of Songjin was renamed Kim Ch'aek City for him.

Kim Il Sung (Kim Sung-ju) (1912–94) Korean nationalist and guerrilla leader, and head of the Democratic People's Republic of Korea (DPRK, North Korea). Kim Sung-ju took the name of Kim Il Sung, a legendary hero of the Korean independence movement. His family moved to Manchuria (1919) and from youth he was involved in anti-Japanese activities. He joined the Communist party (1931) and soon was leading guerrilla raids against the Japanese in Korea (1932). A Japanese crackdown led he and his followers to move to Siberia (1941).

Kim fought in the Soviet Army in World War II and by 1945 was a major in the force that took the Japanese surrender above the 38th Parallel. Designated by the Soviets to establish a provisional government in the North, he created the Korean People's Army (KPA)

and eliminated numerous opponents to establish the DPRK with himself in charge (September 1948).

As premier of the new state, Kim dedicated himself to unifying Korea. Securing the support of Joseph Stalin and Mao Tse-tung, he invaded the South (25 June 1950). He believed an uprising there would bring victory, and he personally led KPA troops in the early months of the war. Following United States and United Nations intervention, China took over direction of the war (November 1950). After the armistice (July 1953), Kim focused on consolidating power and rebuilding his shattered country, shutting the DPRK off from most of the rest of the world. The "Supreme Leader" Kim was one of the last Stalinist leaders to hold onto power after the end of the Cold War.

Kim Ung (c. 1910–?) Korean Democratic People's Republic general. Born c. 1910, Kim was a nationalist who fled to China to escape the Japanese occupation of his country. Trained at Whampoa Military Academy, China (late 1920s or early 1930s), he became a dedicated Communist, probably participating in the Long March to Yenan (Yan'an). During the late 1930s and 1940s he served with the Eighth Route Army in North China, reaching the rank of brigade or division commander.

Kim returned to North Korea after the war and was a member of the China-oriented "Yenan faction" within the North Korean Communist leadership. On the start of the Korean War (25 June 1950) he commanded the Korean People's Army (KPA) I Corps as a lieutenant general. In the fighting he was known as a harsh disciplinarian and demanding leader, but as one of the ablest Communist commanders. He succeeded Lieutenant General Kang Kon, CofS of the front-line commander of the KPA General Kim Ch'aek, when he was killed in action (September). He then succeeded Kim

Ch'aek (1951) and held the position of front-line commander of the KPA the remainder of the war.

After the war, Kim was vice-minister of defense. Purged by North Korean leader Kim Il Sung (1958), he was rehabilitated but was purged again (1978). Nothing is known of him afterward.

Kimmel, Husband Edward (1882–1968) U.S. admiral. Kimmel graduated from Annapolis (1904) and was commissioned (1906). He had a variety of assignments, principally aboard battleships. He served in the Great White Fleet in its 1907–09 circumnavigation of the globe, participated in the occupation of Vera Cruz and was wounded (1914), and was aide to Assistant Secretary of the Navy Franklin Roosevelt (1915). Following U.S. entry into World War I (April 1917), he served with the Grand Fleet.

After study at the Naval War College, he was promoted captain. He made rear admiral (November 1937) and commanded Cruiser Division 7 (1938), then cruisers in the Battle Force (1939–41). Promoted admiral (February 1941), he was appointed CinC of Pacific Command (CINCPAC) at Pearl Harbor.

Kimmel worked to prepare the fleet for war but was caught by surprise, along with most senior U.S. commanders, by the Japanese attack at Pearl Harbor (7 December). He received much blame for the disaster and was soon relieved of his command and demoted to his permanent rank of rear admiral, at which rank he retired (March 1942). He claimed he had been made a scapegoat and that President Franklin Roosevelt had maneuvered the Japanese into attacking Pearl Harbor to bring the United States into the war. There have been efforts, especially in recent years, to clear his name.

Kimura, Heitarō (1888–1948) Japanese general. Commissioned on graduation from the Military Academy (1908), Kimura graduated from the Army Staff College (1916). A division staff officer in the Siberian expedition (1918–19), he was resident officer in Germany (1922–25) and promoted major (1923). He was then on the Army General Staff (1925–29) and instructor at the War College. As a lieutenant colonel, he was a member of the delegation to the London Naval Conference (1930). He commanded a regiment (1931–32), held various staff positions, and was promoted major general (1936). Promoted lieutenant general (1938), he commanded 32nd Division (1939–40). He was then CofS of the Kwantung (Guangdong) Army, Manchuria (1940–41).

Kimura was army vice minister (1941–43). He then commanded the Burma Area Army of ten divisions (June 1944–May 1945) and fought General William Slim's British Fourteenth Army in central and south Burma, and General Joseph Stilwell's Chinese and U.S. forces in north Burma. He concentrated on Slim's force in central Burma first, but his plans failed to take into account Allied air superiority and ability to resupply by air. Outmaneuvered, he was defeated at Meiktila and Mandalay (February–March 1945). He skillfully evacuated Rangoon, but abandoned many stragglers in the jungle (May). He was then promoted full general. Tried and convicted after the war of war crimes in the treatment of Allied prisoners on the Thailand–Burma railroad, he was condemned to death and executed (1948).

Kimura, Masatomi (1891–1960) Japanese admiral. A graduate of the Navy Academy (1912), Kimura was trained in mine warfare. Promoted lieutenant commander (1936), he commanded destroyers (1926–33) and destroyer flotillas (1935–37). Promoted captain (1939), he then commanded cruisers. Promoted rear admiral (November 1942), he took command of 3rd Destroyer Squadron (February 1942). He was escorting Japanese transports in a convoy attempting to resupply the Japanese garrison at Lae when attacked in the Battle of the Bismarck Sea (March), during which he lost half his ships to U.S. Fifth Fleet carrier aircraft. As commander of 1st Destroyer Squadron, he carried out the difficult evacuation of Japanese forces from Kiska Island in the Aleutians (July). Commanding three cruisers and five destroyers, he attacked the American beachhead on Mindoro Island (December 1944). Promoted vice admiral (1945), he held staff positions at the end of the war.

King, Edward Postell, Jr. (1884–1958) U.S. general. A graduate of the University of Georgia with a degree in law (1903), King was commissioned in the National Guard field artillery (1908). He served with the 2nd Field Artillery in the Philippines (1915–17). He graduated from Command and General Staff School (1923) (where he was also an instructor (1930–35)), from the Army War College (1930), and from the Naval War College (1937). He was then director of the War Plans Section of the Army War College (1937–40). Ordered to the Philippines (1940), he was promoted major general (December 1941) and commanded General Douglas MacArthur's artillery units there.

Following the Japanese invasion of the Philippines (December 1941), King commanded the Northern Luzon Force and then, after MacArthur's departure, commanded all U.S. forces on Bataan (March 1942). Forced to surrender U.S. forces there (9 April), he remained a POW until his release in 1945. He retired in November 1946.

King, Ernest Joseph (1876–1956) U.S. admiral. King entered Annapolis (1897) and saw action as a midshipman during the 1898 Spanish–American War. After graduation (1901), he held a variety of assignments, including ordnance instructor at the Academy (1906–09) and service aboard battleships (1909–13). Promoted lieutenant commander (1913), he commanded destroyers and a destroyer squa-

dron. He was on the staff of the commander of the Atlantic Fleet when the United States entered World War I (April 1917). Promoted commander (1917), he was then a temporary captain (1918).

Following the war, King directed postgraduate education at Annapolis (1919–21) and sought as many varied experiences as possible. He commanded a submarine division and then the New London, Connecticut submarine base (1923). He also took flight training and qualified as a pilot (1927). He commanded the carrier *Lexington* (1930–32), headed the Aeronautics Board (1932), graduated from the Naval War College (1933), and was chief of the Bureau of Aeronautics (1933–36). Promoted vice admiral (1938), he commanded the five-carrier Aircraft Battle Force (1938–39), recommending that carriers act as independent task forces.

Promoted rear admiral (1939), King commanded the Atlantic Fleet as a full admiral (February 1941). Following Japan's attack on Pearl Harbor (7 December 1941), he commanded the U.S. Fleet (December) and then (March 1942) became chief of naval operations (CNO), the first time these two posts were combined in one individual. He held both for the duration of the war and thus was second only to General George Marshall in the U.S. military hierarchy. He was promoted fleet admiral (December 1944).

Brilliant and outspoken, King could also be arrogant and rude, but under his command the U.S. Navy grew to be larger than all the other navies of the world put together. In addition to his operational duties, he advised President Franklin Roosevelt at important wartime conferences. King retired after the war in December 1945.

Kinkaid, Thomas Cassin (1888–1972) U.S. admiral. Kinkaid graduated from Annapolis (1908) and was commissioned (1910). A variety of assignments followed, many involving naval gunnery. He graduated from the Naval War College (1930). Promoted captain, he commanded a cruiser (1937–38).

In 1941 Kinkaid was promoted rear admiral and took command of Cruiser Division 6. Following U.S. entry into World War II, he led it in the raids on Rabaul and New Guinea (March 1942). He fought in both the Battle of the Coral Sea (May) and the Battle of Midway (June). During the remainder of 1942, he commanded Task Force 16 and covered landing on Guadalcanal (August) and fought in subsequent naval battles in the Solomons. He then commanded the North Pacific Task Force and directed the recapture of Aleutian Islands taken by the Japanese (February–August 1943). Promoted vice admiral, he commanded Seventh Fleet and Allied naval forces in the Southwest Pacific (November 1943), covering U.S. landings on Leyte (October 1944). He warned of an impending Japanese attack and participated in the subsequent Battle of Leyte Gulf. He then supervised other landings in the Philippines. Promoted admiral (April), he directed landings by U.S. occupation troops in China and Korea.

After the war, Kinkaid commanded the Eastern Sea Frontier (1946) and the Atlantic Reserve Fleet until his retirement in May 1950.

Kirk, Alan Goodrich (1888–1963) U.S. admiral and diplomat. Kirk graduated from Annapolis (1909). While serving in China, he witnessed the 1911 Chinese Revolution. In the early 1920s he was executive officer of the presidential yacht under Presidents Woodrow Wilson and Warren Harding. After other assignments and promotions, as a captain he was U.S. naval attaché in London (June 1939). He then served as director of Naval Intelligence (1941) before commanding a destroyer division escorting Atlantic convoys and winning promotion to rear admiral (November 1941).

After the United States entered World War II (December 1941), Kirk returned to Britain as CofS to commander of U.S. naval forces in Europe Admiral Harold Stark (1942–43). Returning to sea duty (March 1943), he headed the Atlantic Fleet Amphibious Force, which participated in the invasion of Sicily (July). He took command (February 1944) of the Western Task Force in the Normandy invasion (6 June 1944), then commanded U.S. Navy forces in France (October) and was promoted vice admiral (November). He retired from the navy a full admiral (March 1946), then served as ambassador to Belgium and minister to Luxembourg (1946–49), ambassador to the Soviet Union (1949–51), and the Republic of China (1962–63).

Kitchener, Horatio Herbert, 1st Earl Kitchener of Khartoum (1850–1916) British field marshal. Kitchener studied at the Royal Military Academy, Woolwich, obtaining his commission (1871). Following routine assignments, he became commander of the Egyptian army (1892). A superb organizer, he led it in the 1896–98 invasion of the Sudan, defeating the Mahdi at Omdurman (September 1897), for which he was appointed governor general of the Sudan and made Earl Kitchener of Khartoum. In the 1899–1902 Boer war he was initially chief of staff to Field Marshal Lord Roberts, then his successor. He then commanded in India (1902–09).

Just before the start of World War I, Kitchener was appointed as minister of war (July 1914). On the outbreak of the war, he predicted a long and costly struggle that would require the training of thousands of new soldiers. As war minister, he presided over the mobilization and training of a British military force that grew from seven to seventy divisions. He was aboard the cruiser *Hampshire* bound for Archangelsk when she struck a German mine west of the Orkney Islands and quickly sank in rough seas. His body was never recovered.

Kleist, Paul Erwin Ludwig von (1881–1954) German field marshal. Kleist joined the army (1900) and rose to captain in the "Death's Head" Hussars (1914). He continued in the army after World War I and was a lieutenant general when forced to retire (1938) in Adolf Hitler's purge of the officer corps following the von Blomberg and von Fritsch affairs. Recalled to active duty (1939), he commanded XXII Panzer Corps in Fourteenth Army in the invasion of Poland (September). In the invasion of France and Benelux (May 1940), he commanded army-strength Panzergruppe Kleist of eight divisions. It spearheaded Army Group A's drive through the Ardennes and was poised to cut off the British Expeditionary Force from Dunkerque when Hitler issued his stop order (24 May). Commanding the same unit in the invasion of Yugoslavia (April 1941), he took Belgrade (13 April).

Kleist commanded First Panzer Army, spearheading Army Group South in the invasion of the Soviet Union (22 June 1941), achieving much with scant resources. He then led the drive into the Caucasus (1942) but was unable to cross the mountains as his resources were drained off to support operations against Stalingrad. Named commander of Army Group A (November 1942), he was a master in defensive operations. Staging an orderly withdrawal from the Caucasus, he was promoted field marshal (February 1943). He then completed a successful withdrawal from the Crimea (October 1943). His force redesignated Army Group Southern Ukraine, he withdrew into Romania. He then relinquished his command to Field Marshal Ferdinand Schörner and retired. Extradited to Yugoslavia for trial as a war criminal, he was sentenced in 1948 to fifteen years in prison but was then extradited to the Soviet Union, where he was sentenced to an additional term. He died in prison there.

Kluck, Alexander von (1846–1934) German general. Kluck joined a Westphalian infantry regiment as an officer aspirant (1865) and was soon commissioned. He participated in both the 1866 Austro-Prussian War and 1870–71 Franco-German War. He was promoted colonel (1896), major general (1899), and lieutenant general (1906). He commanded V Corps, and then I Corps. He became inspector general of VIII Army (1913), and was promoted full general and took command of First Army (1914).

At the start of World War I (August 1914) Kluck led his troops into Belgium, took Brussels, and defeated the British near Mons and at Le Cateau. He then abandoned the original plan of advance and wheeled east of Paris, in the process exposing German forces to envelopment. Although he defeated the French near Amiens, he failed to cover the flank of General Karl von Bülow's Second Army and instead crossed the Marne River, opening a 30-mile gap between the two principal German armies. Following the Battle of the Marne (September), Kluck was ordered to withdraw to the Aisne River.

Kluck was seriously wounded by shrapnel while inspecting his troops (March 1915) and was forced to yield command to General Max von Fabeck. He retired in 1916.

Kluge, Hans Günther von (1882–1944) German field marshal. Kluge joined the army as an artillery officer (1901). He was a staff officer in World War I and continued in the Reichswehr afterward, and was promoted major general (April 1933). He was purged for his support of General Werner von Fritsch in his dispute with Adolf Hitler.

Recalled from retirement on the outbreak of World War II, he led Fourth Army during the invasions of Poland (September 1939) and France and Benelux (May 1940). Raised to field marshal (July 1940), he led Fourth Army in the invasion of the Soviet Union (June 1941) and then commanded Army Group Center (December 1941–October 1943). Injured in a car accident (October 1943), he replaced Field Marshal Gerd von Rundstedt as CinC, West and command of Army Group B (July 1944). Aware of the plot to assassinate Hitler, he refused to participate but failed to report it. Following the bomb attempt (20 July), he came under increasing suspicion by the Gestapo. He led the German counterattack at Avranches (August), but on its failure was relieved of command by Field Marshal Walther Model that same month. Aware that he would be implicated in the conspiracy against Hitler and depressed by the military situation, he committed suicide.

Knox, William Franklin (1874–1944) U.S. secretary of the navy. Knox attended Alma College in Michigan but dropped out to enlist in the army during the 1898 Spanish-American War, and fought as a member of the "Rough Riders" at San Juan Hill. After the war he was a journalist and newspaper owner. Appointed secretary of the navy (July 1940), he held that post until his death. Lacking naval experience and expertise, he relied heavily on the advice of Chief of Naval Operations Admiral Harold Stark and the naval staff. He was a key figure in the Destroyers–Bases deal arranged with Britain (September 1940). He died in office.

Knudson, William Signius (1879–1948) U.S. director of World War II production. Born in Copenhagen, he came to the United States at age twenty. He became a close associate of Henry Ford at Ford Motor Company, but disagreements with Ford led him to join General Motors (1919) and he rose to be president of the company (1937). Appointed head of the seven-member National Defense Commission (1940), he then became director for production in the new Office for (Emergency) Production Management (January 1941). When the War Production Board replaced this office (January 1942), he became director of production in the War Department with the rank of lieutenant general (January 1942–June 1945). He played a key role in speeding up armaments production, especially aircraft. Knudson retired in May 1945.

Kodama, Gentarō (1852–1906) Japanese general. Kodama fought in the 1868 Boshin (Restoration) War, enlisted in the imperial army (1870), and was commissioned a lieutenant (1871). Following training as a staff officer, he was commandant of the Army Staff College (1887). Promoted major general (1889), he then held a number of military and civilian posts, including vice minister of the army, governor general of Taiwan (1898), army minister (1900–02), and army vice chief of staff and chief of staff (1891–1906). He directed planning for the 1904–05 Russo-Japanese War, then was chief of staff to Marshal Iwao Ōyama, who commanded Japanese forces in the field (1904–05). Realizing that Japan had exhausted its resources, he returned to Tokyo to urge the government to negotiate while it could still secure favorable terms. He died in Tokyo and was posthumously created a count.

Koenig, Marie Pierre (1898–1970) French general. Koenig volunteered for the army during World War I on obtaining his *baccalauréat* (1917). He ended the war as a temporary *sous-lieutenant* with the Médaille Militaire. After the war he served with the army of occupation in Germany. Promoted lieutenant (1920), he participated in the French occupation of the Ruhr (1923) and then was with occupation forces in the Rhineland (1923–29). From 1931 he served with the Foreign Legion in Morocco. Promoted captain (1932), he participated in pacification campaigns. After the start of World War II (September 1939), he left Morocco (February 1940) and fought in the 1940 Norwegian campaign. He then joined the Free French Forces of General Charles de Gaulle (June) and commanded a battalion. He fought against Vichy French forces in Africa and the Middle East (1940–41). His advance was rapid. He was promoted colonel (June 1941) and then temporary major general (August), commanding a Free French division in the Levant.

Koenig won renown for leading the 1st Free French Brigade Group in the Battle of Bir Hakeim against German General Erwin Rommel's Afrika Korps (May-June 1942) and refusing to withdraw until ordered to do so (night of 10–11 June). This stand established the Free French as a fighting force.

Koenig then went to Algiers, where he was promoted lieutenant general (May 1943) and became deputy CofS of the French Army (July). In early 1944 he was named commander of Free French forces in Britain, then commander of Free French Forces of the Interior (FFI) for the upcoming Normandy invasion (June 1944). He was then promoted full general (25 June).

After serving as military governor of Paris (August 1944), Koenig commanded the French zone of occupation in Germany (1945–49) and was promoted general of the army (1946). He retired from the army (1951) and was elected a deputy to the National Assembly. He then served as minister of defense (1954) but resigned in opposition to the government's policy toward Morocco (1955). He retired from politics (1958) and was posthumously promoted marshal (1984).

Koga, Mineichi (1885–1944) Japanese admiral. A graduate of both the Naval Academy (1906) and Naval War College (1915), Koga held a number of staff assignments ashore (1916–20). He was then resident officer in France (1920–22). Promoted captain (1926), he served as naval attaché in Paris (1926–28), then commanded the Yokosuka Naval Station. He commanded a cruiser, then a battleship (1930–31). Promoted rear admiral (1932), he headed the naval intelligence

division (1933) and was vice chief of the Naval General Staff (1937). He then commanded Second Fleet (1939).

Appointed commander of the China Area Fleet (September 1941), he participated in the capture of Hong Kong (December). Following the death of Admiral Isoroku Yamamoto (18 April 1943), he succeeded Yamamoto as commander of the Combined Fleet (May). He was unsuccessful in his Plan Z to draw the U.S. Navy into a battle that could turn the war in Japan's favor before the odds became hopeless. During the evacuation of Combined Fleet Headquarters from Palau, his plane crashed in a storm (April 1944). He was posthumously promoted admiral of the fleet.

Koiso, Kuniaki (1880–1950) Japanese general. Commissioned in the army (1901), Koiso rose rapidly. A company commander and captain (1905), he graduated from the War College (1910) and was then a staff officer. Promoted lieutenant general (1931), he was vice minister of war (1932), serving concurrently as Kwantung Army chief of staff. He then commanded 5th Division (1934) before becoming CinC of Japanese forces in Korea (1935). Promoted full general (1937), he retired (1938). He was then foreign minister (1939–40), and governor general of Korea (May 1942).

Kosio became prime minister following the overthrow of Hideki Tojo (18 July 1944). Failing in peace negotiations, he resigned (5 April 1945) and was replaced by Kantarō Suzuki. Convicted of war crimes (1948), he was sentenced to life in prison.

Kolchak, Aleksandr Vasilevich (1874–1920) Russian admiral. Kolchak graduated from the Russian Naval Academy in 1894. He took part in two polar expeditions, and during the 1904–05 Russo-Japanese War commanded a destroyer and then a battery at Port Arthur, where he was taken prisoner. On the outbreak of

World War I, Kolchak was captain of the flagship of the Baltic Fleet. He was then chief of operations of the Baltic Fleet (1915). He distinguished himself as commander of a destroyer flotilla in the Gulf of Riga (1916). Promoted rear admiral (April 1916), he commanded the Baltic Fleet's Destroyer Division. Promoted vice admiral (July 1916), he took command of the Black Sea Fleet, where he carried out effective offensive mine operations. He was probably Russia's most effective naval commander of the war.

After the March 1917 Revolution, Kolchak sought to halt revolutionary sentiment among the sailors and was forced to resign (June 1917). The provisional government then sent him to Washington to discuss naval cooperation; he was returning to Russia by way of Japan when the Bolshevik Revolution occurred.

Kolchak was determined to keep his country in the war against Germany. By November 1918 he had nominal command of anti-Bolshevik forces in Siberia, but was dependent on the Czech Legion and Allied support. His spring 1919 offensive collapsed, and in early 1920 he fell into Bolshevik hands at Irkutsk and, following a brief trial, was shot.

Komatsubara, Michitarō (1886–1940) Japanese general. A graduate of the Military Academy (1905), Komatsubara was an infantry officer who became expert in Russian affairs. He studied in Russia (1909–12) and was assistant military attaché (1919–25), then military attaché (1927–30) in Moscow. Promoted colonel (1929), he commanded a regiment in Japan (1930–32). Assigned to the Kwantung (Guangdong) Army in Manchuria, he headed the Harbin Special Service Agency (1932–33) and was promoted major general (1933). After command of brigades (1933–37), he was promoted major general (1937).

Assuming command of 23rd Division (1938), Komatsubara ordered it to attack Nomonhan near the Khalkin Gol River,

territory claimed by Japan on the Manchurian – Mongolian border but occupied by the Russians (28 May 1939). This began the Nomonhan Incident (May–September). Initially successful, his division and Japanese reinforcements were ground down by larger Russian forces commanded by General Georgi Zhukov. In the purge of officers in the Kwantung Army held responsible for the debacle, he was placed on the reserve list (January 1940) and died soon thereafter.

Komer, Robert W. (1922–2000) U.S. coordinator of pacification efforts during the Vietnam War. Following graduation from Harvard University (1942), Komer served in the Army in World War II. He then graduated from Harvard Graduate School of Business (1947) and joined the Central Intelligence Agency (CIA) (1947–60), then was a senior staff member in the Kennedy administration's National Security Council (NSC) (1961–65). He was deputy special assistant (1965–66), then special assistant to the President for national security affairs (1966–67) and became increasingly involved in pacification efforts in the Vietnam War. President Lyndon Johnson appointed him his special assistant for Vietnam to coordinate pacification activities (1966).

Komer believed that Military Assistance Command, Vietnam (MACV) commander General William Westmoreland concentrated too much on search-and-destroy big-unit operations, to the detriment of population control and security. Following a trip to Vietnam (June 1966), he reported that the pacification effort was failing and proposed that it be concentrated in the U.S. military with a civilian to run it. This resulted in establishment of the Civil Operations and Revolutionary Development Support (CORDS), with himself running it as Westmoreland's deputy (March 1967) and the rank of ambassador, equivalent to lieutenant general.

Known as "Blowtorch Bob" for his

abrasive, no-nonsense approach to problem-solving, Komer was also sensitive to Johnson's desires and projected optimism, buttressed with an impressive array of statistics. He led a village-by-village effort to "win the hearts and minds" of the people, worked to build up territorial forces, and pulled together disparate elements of the U.S. advisory effort. For various reasons, this effort was a mixed success. Komer was then ambassador to Turkey (1968–69), worked at the Rand Corporation, and was then undersecretary of defense for policy (1979–81).

Komura, Keizō (1896–1978) Japanese admiral. Komura graduated from the Naval Academy (1917) and studied at the Naval Staff College (1927–29). Promoted commander (1929) and captain (1931), he commanded destroyers. He was then deputy naval attaché in Britain (1932–34). He then taught at the Naval Staff College (1934). In 1937 he became CinC of 2nd Destroyer Squadron.

Rear Admiral Komura commanded the heavy cruiser *Chikuma* at Pearl Harbor (7 December 1941) and at the Battles of Midway (June 1942) and Santa Cruz (October). He was Admiral Ozawa's chief of staff in the Battle of the Philippine Sea (June 1944) and commanded 1st Carrier Division at Leyte Gulf (October 1944). While commanding Destroyer Squadron 2, he survived the sinking of his flagship, light cruiser *Yahagi*, escorting the battleship *Yamato* toward Okinawa in April 1945.

Kondō, Nobutake (1886–1953) Japanese admiral. A graduate of the Naval Academy (1907), Kondō was promoted lieutenant commander after graduation from the Naval Staff College (1919). A resident officer in Russia (1919–20), he was aide to the Imperial Prince (1920–23), then a staff officer in the Combined Fleet (1926). Promoted captain (1927), he was an instructor at the Naval Staff College and captain of a battleship (1932). Promoted

rear admiral, he was president of the Naval Staff College (1933). CofS for the Combined Fleet (1935), he was promoted vice admiral (1937), and became vice chief of the Naval General Staff (1939).

Kondō was commander of Second Fleet (1941–43) when his aircraft sank Force Z, the British capital ships *Prince of Wales* and *Repulse*, off Malaya (10 December). He also carried out landings in the Philippine Islands. In the Battle of Midway (3–6 June 1942) he commanded the support force.

Kondō played a major role in the long-running Battle of Guadalcanal (August 1942–February 1943). He was unsuccessful in efforts to lure the U.S. Navy into a trap in the Battle of the Eastern Solomon Islands (24 August 1942). In the Battle of Santa Cruz (October 1942), his naval units provided fire support in the effort to retake Henderson Field and scored a tactical victory, crippling U.S. carrier *Hornet*, which was eventually sunk. In naval actions off Guadalcanal (12–15 November), he suffered tactical defeat with the loss of the battleship *Kirishima* and withdrew, sealing the fate of the Japanese on Guadalcanal. He then oversaw the well-executed withdrawal of survivors.

Kondō was promoted full admiral (April 1943) and appointed a naval advisor (August 1943). Appointed CinC of the China Fleet (December 1943), he was again appointed a naval advisor in May 1945.

Konev, Ivan Stepanovich (1897–1973) Soviet marshal. Drafted into the Russian army (1916), Konev fought on the Galician Front in World War I and was commissioned (1917). He joined the Red Army and Communist Party (1918) and commanded a division at the end of the 1918–20 Civil War. He played a notable role in crushing the Kronstadt mutiny (March 1921).

Konev transferred to the regular army and graduated from the Frunze Military Academy (1927). He commanded a corps, first in the Belorussian Military District (1937), then in Outer Mongolia. In the course of fighting against the Japanese (1939), he developed a bitter rivalry with Georgi Zhukov. His presence in the Far East and his political acumen helped him survive Stalin's purges. Promoted lieutenant general, he took command of the North Caucasus Military District (January 1941).

Appointed to command Nineteenth Army as the Germans invaded (22 June 1944), Konev came to be regarded as one of the top Russian field commanders of the war and took part in fighting around Smolensk (July). Promoted colonel general, he commanded the Western Front (September). When he failed to stop the German advance, Stalin replaced him with Zhukov (October) and sent him to command the newly created Kalinin Front. He then commanded the Steppe (later designated 2nd Ukrainian) Front (summer 1943), and later the 1st Ukrainian Front. Promoted marshal (February 1944), during the drive on Berlin Stalin diverted his forces to the Elbe to seal off the possibility of an Allied push into eastern Germany. He then turned south and took Prague.

After the war Konev commanded Russian occupation forces in Austria (1945–46), and then forces in Germany (1946). He next commanded Soviet ground forces (1946–50). He held a succession of senior posts before being named CinC of Warsaw Pact forces (1956–60) and was then inspector general of the ministry of defense, save for a brief period in command of Soviet forces in Germany (1961–62).

Kornilov, Lavr Georgievich (1870–1918) Russian general. Kornilov graduated from the Artillery College (1892) and the General Staff Academy (1898). He fought in the 1904–05 Russo-Japanese War and was then Russian military attaché in China (1907–11). At the beginning of World War I, he was a brigade commander in General Aleksei Brusilov's Eighth

Army. He commanded 48th Division during the Austro-German Gorlice Offensive (May 1915), but failed to withdraw his unit and was trapped and taken prisoner. He spent nearly a year in a prison camp but escaped from Hungary to return home a hero and receive command of XXV Corps.

Kornilov accepted the March 1917 Revolution, and the provisional government appointed him commander of the Petrograd Military District. Not permitted forceful measures to curb dissent, he resigned to command Eighth Army. It performed well in the unsuccessful July offensive, and he was promoted general of infantry. Premier Aleksandr Kerensky then appointed him CinC of the Russian Army with instructions to restore discipline.

Kornilov soon clashed with Kerensky and attempted a *coup d'état* (September 1917) but his troops deserted him on a march to the capital. He was jailed briefly but was released by sympathizers. Following the Bolshevik Revolution, he fled to the Don area to organize an anti-Bolshevik military force with the hopes of bringing about Russian re-entry in the war against Germany. He was killed in a skirmish with Bolshevik Red Guards.

Kövess von Kövesshaza, Baron Hermann (1854–1924) Austro-Hungarian field marshal. Kövess entered the army in 1872 after attending the Technical Military Academy. He studied at the War Academy and had a long tenure on the General Staff. Promoted major general (1902), he commanded XII Corps in Transylvania (1911) but was scheduled to retire late in 1914.

On the outbreak of World War I, Kövess led XII Corps in fighting in East Galicia. He commanded Third Army against Serbia (1915) and captured Belgrade (October). His forces went on to occupy Montenegro and Northern Albania. His army then fought on the Italian Front (1916) and he commanded Seventh Army and helped drive the Russians from East Galicia

(1917). Emperor Charles promoted him to field marshal (August 1917).

Kövess then headed an army group of First and Seventh Armies on the Eastern Front (January–April 1918). He then commanded all Austro-Hungarian troops in the Balkans (army group "West Balkans") (September) but could not stop the Allied advance. He became the last CinC of the dissolving Austro-Hungarian Army (3 November 1918).

Kozhedub, Ivan Nikitovich (1920–91) Soviet air force general. Kozhedub completed chemical engineering school (1940) and immediately afterwards joined the air force. Graduating from the Aviation School for Pilots (1941), he was then a pilot instructor until the end of 1942.

Kozhedub saw combat while assigned to the Voronezh, Steppe, 2nd Ukranian, and 1st Belorussian Fronts (March 1943–May 1945). During this period, flying LA-5s and LA-7s, he flew 330 combat missions and was credited with sixty-two air-to-air kills in 120 dogfights, making him the leading Soviet and Allied ace of the war. He was three times a Hero of the Soviet Union, and commanded a squadron and then was deputy commander of a fighter wing.

Kozhedub remained in the service after the war. He commanded 324th Fighter Air Division during the 1950–53 Korean War and graduated from the Military Academy of the General Staff (1956). He was then inspector of flight training (1956–66). As a colonel general, he was first deputy commander of aviation for the Moscow Military District (1964). Promoted marshal of aviation, he was a member of the Group of Military Inspectors (1978–85).

Krebs, Hans (1898–1945) German general. Krebs joined the army (September 1914) and by the end of World War I was a regimental adjutant. He remained in the army after the war and continued in staff positions during his entire career, includ-

ing several postings to Moscow as a military attaché (1933–34, 1939, 1941).

As a colonel at the start of World War II, Krebs was two years chief of staff of the Bavarian IX Corps. He then became CofS of Ninth Army on the Russian Front (1942), then CofS of Army Group Center (1943–44) under Field Marshals Günther von Kluge, Ernst Busch, and Walter Model. When Model transferred to the Western Front as commander of Army Group B and CinC West (August 1944), Lieutenant General Krebs accompanied him as his CofS. Assigned to the Army high command (February 1945), he was selected by Adolf Hitler as "Interim" chief of the general staff (March 1945), replacing General Heinz Guderian. Following Hitler's suicide, he personally negotiated with General Vasily Chuikov the surrender of the Berlin garrison. He then returned to the chancellory bunker and shot himself.

Kretschmer, Otto August Wilhelm (1912–) German naval officer. Kretschmer entered the naval training program (1930). During World War II he was the first submarine commander to sink 250,000 tons of shipping, and was the most successful U-boat commander of the war, ultimately sinking over 350,000 tons, most in *U-99*. He employed bold innovative tactics, including firing torpedoes at very close range, usually at night on the surface, and often inside the surface escort screen. Greatly concerned for the welfare of his men, he was idolized by them in return. He believed in loyalty to the government but eschewed efforts to propagandize his achievements.

Captured with about fifty of his crew during a running convoy battle (March 1941) when *U-99* was sunk by a British destroyer, he was held prisoner in Canada for the remainder of the war. Released (1947), he joined the Federal Republic of Germany navy (1955) and rose to rear admiral before he retired in 1970.

Krobatin, Alexander Freiherr Baron von
(1849–1933) Austro-Hungarian field marshal and minister of war. Krobatin graduated from the Artillery Academy (1869)
and took additional studies in that field,
enabling him to be an instructor at the
Technical Military Academy (1877–82).
As a major he headed the Artillery Cadet
School in Vienna, and after 1896 was in
the War Ministry. He was promoted
major general (1900) and appointed minister of war (1912).

After the outbreak of World War I,
Krobatin's main focus was increasing
arms and ammunition for the army. In
two years he tripled the amount of artillery at divisional level. After repeated
requests for field command, he headed
Tenth Army (April 1917) and took part in
the Caporetto offensive against Italy (October). His army captured two Italian
divisions, and this success brought his
elevation to field marshal (November). In
1918 his forces, which came to include
Eleventh Army, were routed at Vittorio
Veneto (November 1918). He retired at
the end of the war.

Krueger, Walter (1881–1967) U.S. general. An immigrant from Germany at age
eight, Krueger left school to join the army
on the outbreak of the 1898 Spanish-
American War. He saw combat in Cuba,
joined the regular army (1899), and
fought in the Philippines (1899–1903),
including the 1900–02 Philippine-American War. Commissioned (1901), he graduated from the Infantry and Cavalry
School (1906) and the Command and
General Staff School (1907) and was a
faculty member of the Army Service
School (1909–12). As a captain, he participated in the 1916–17 Punitive Expedition into Mexico.

Krueger fought in France during World
War I with the AEF. He arrived there in
February 1918 and ended the war as CofS
of the Tank Corps in the Meuse–Argonne
offensive. He was then CofS first for VI

Corps in France, then IV Corps in Germany.

Krueger graduated from the Army War
College (1921) and Naval War College
(1926), where he then taught (1928–32).
Promoted colonel (1932) and brigadier
general (1936), he commanded 16th Brigade (1938). Promoted major general
(1939), he commanded 2nd Division, then
VIII Corps. Promoted temporary lieutenant general (1941), he assumed command of the new Sixth Army, which he
took to Australia (January 1943) and led
in a long series of operations, including
assaults on New Britain, the Admiralty
Islands, and the Philippines (where he
directed landings on Leyte and Luzon).
Promoted full general (March 1945), after
the war he took his army to Japan for
occupation duty. A meticulous planner,
his operations were marked by low ca-
sualty rates and his concern for his men.
He retired in July 1946.

Kuribayashi, Tadamichi (1891–1945) Japanese general. A graduate of the Military
Academy (1914) and the Army Staff
College (1923), Kuribayashi trained as a
cavalry officer. He was in the United
States (1927–30) and then was military
attaché to Canada (1931–33). Promoted
lieutenant colonel (1933), he took command of a cavalry regiment (1936–37).
Promoted major general (1940), he commanded brigades (1940–41).

At the beginning of World War II,
Kuribayashi was CofS of Twenty-third
Army in China (1940–43). As commander
of the 103rd Division, he was entrusted
with defending the Island of Iwō Jima
(1944–45) with 14,000 army and 7,000
navy personnel. He prepared a skillful
interlocking defensive system of concealed
strong points, caves, and tunnels, most of
which remained undetected until the U.S.
Marines came ashore. The resultant fighting (February–March 1945) was exceed-
ingly costly for both sides. Marine
casualties totalled 6,891 killed and
18,070 wounded. Only 212 Japanese

surrendered; more than 21,000 were counted dead, Kuribayashi among them.

Kurita, Takeo (1889–1977) Japanese admiral. A graduate of the Naval Academy (1910), he held a number of destroyer commands (1920s). Promoted commander, he was an instructor at the Torpedo School (1928–34, 1935–37), then commanded a cruiser (1934–35) and a battleship (1937–38) and was promoted rear admiral (1938). He then commanded destroyer squadrons (1938–40). Promoted vice admiral (May 1942), he commanded the Close Support Group in the Battle of Midway, losing half his force to U.S. naval air power (June 1942). He then commanded Second Fleet (August 1943).

In the Battle of Leyte Gulf (October 1944) he commanded 1st Strike Force in Operation SHO-1 with the bulk of Japanese strength, including giant battleships *Yamato* and *Musashi*. The plan called for his force to pass through San Bernardino Strait and meet up with C Force coming through Surigao Strait under Vice Admiral Shoji Nishimura. They were to converge on the American landing beaches while the covering warships were drawn off to the northeast by a decoy force under Vice Admiral Jisaburo Ozawa.

Nishimura's force was destroyed and Kurita's force was discovered and *Musashi* sunk. Kurita then reversed course but, unknown to the Americans, turned back again. As Admiral William Halsey rushed off with the bulk of his warships after Ozawa, Kurita's force surprised the virtually undefended American transports and their weak escorts off Leyte. He failed to press his advantage, however, withdrawing before striking the transports. He then returned to Japan and commanded the Naval Academy in 1945.

Kuroki, Tamemoto (1844–1923) Japanese general. Kuroki fought in the Boshin (Restoration) War (1868) and joined the Imperial Army as a captain (1871). As a lieutenant colonel, he commanded a regiment in the 1877 Satsuma Rebellion. As a lieutenant general, he commanded 5th Infantry Division in the 1894–95 Sino-Japanese War. Promoted full general (1903), he commanded First Army in the 1904–05 Russo-Japanese War. He was victorious in the Battle of the Yalu River (April–May 1904), and his army then played prominent roles in the Battles of Laioyang (August–September) and Sha Ho (October), each time turning back Russian attacks. He commanded the Japanese right wing in the largest battle of the war, at Mukden (February–March 1905). Upon retirement from the army (1909) he was made a count. He served as privy councelor (1917–23) until his death.

Kuropatkin, Aleksei Nikolaevich (1848–1925) Russian general. Kuropatkin graduated from the Pavlovsky Military School (1864) and distinguished himself in the conquest of Samarkand (1868) and Kokand (1876). During the 1877–78 Russo-Turkish War, he was CofS of an infantry division and fought in the Third Battle of Plevna (Pleven) (September 1877) and Senova (January 1878). Promoted major general (1882), he commanded Russian forces in Transcaucasia (1890–98).

Appointed minister of war (1898–1904), Kuropatkin supported an expansionist policy in the Far East; but, alarmed by Japanese military preparations, he counseled withdrawal (1903). After the outbreak of the 1904–05 Russo-Japanese War (February), he commanded the Manchurian Army (April) and eventually all forces in the Far East. Although he came close to success on many occasions, he was relieved for repeated defeats, including the Battle of Mukden (February–March 1905). He then published a book on his experiences.

During World War I, in late 1915 Kuropatkin took command of the Grenadier Corps. He then commanded Northern Army Group (February–July 1916). He and General A. E. Evert mismanaged the offensive in the Lake Naroch (Narocz) area and failed to support General Aleksei Brusilov's offensive to the south.

Kuropatkin was then sent to Turkestan as governor in chief. Local authorities arrested him and sent him to Petrograd, but he was released by the Provisional government (April 1917). He then retired.

Kusaka, Ryūnosuke (1892–1971) Japanese admiral. A specialist in naval aviation, Vice Admiral Kusaka helped plan key naval operations in World War II. As CofS to Admiral Chuichi Nagumo, he helped develop plans for the attack on Pearl Harbor (7 December 1941) and the offensive that led to the Battle of Midway (June 1942). He then served as CofS to Commander of the Combined Fleet Admiral Soemu Toyoda and sought unsuccessfully to bring the U.S. Navy into a decisive battle to tip the war in Japan's favor. Kusaka was CinC, Fifth Air Fleet, based in Kyūshū during the April–June 1945 Okinawa Campaign.

Kuznetsov, Nikolai Gerasimovich (1902–74) Soviet admiral. Kuznetsov joined the navy (1919) and fought in the 1918–20 Civil War; he attended the Naval Academy (1926) and the Naval College (1932).

He was naval attaché to Spain during its 1936–39 Civil War. He was deputy commander, then commander, of the Pacific Fleet (1937–39) before becoming people's commissar (minister) and CinC of the navy (1939) and a full admiral (1940).

As a member of the High Command (Stavka), Kuznetsov was primarily involved in strategic and policy decisions rather than operational matters. Kuznetsov stressed readiness for war and actually placed the navy on combat alert just before the German attack. One of his chief accomplishments was to convince Stalin of the need to develop a naval air arm. He also built up the numbers of Soviet cruisers and submarines. Known as the father of the modern Soviet navy, he was promoted admiral of the fleet (May 1944).

Kuznetsov was then deputy minister of defense and commander of the navy (1946–47); he was next minister of the navy (1951–53) and first deputy minister of defense and commander of naval forces (1953–55). Promoted admiral of the fleet of the Soviet Union (1955), after the battleship *Novorossiisk* blew up at Sevastopol late that same year, he was removed from his posts and demoted to vice admiral.

L

Laborde, Jean Joseph (1878–1977) French admiral. Laborde entered the Naval Academy (1895). On graduation he had a variety of assignments. While in the Far East he became interested in aviation and learned to fly. During World War I he distinguished himself in command of bomber squadrons and then commanded the naval aviation center at Dunkerque. After the war he commanded the naval aviation center at Saint-Raphaël (1919). Promoted captain (1923) and appointed head of the Central Service of Naval Aviation, he pushed construction of the *Béarn*, France's first aircraft carrier, of which he took command (1926) and developed air doctrine. Promoted rear admiral (1928), he commanded 2nd Squadron (1930). He was promoted vice admiral and became maritime prefect of Bizerte (1932–34). Promoted full admiral (1938), he took command of the French Atlantic Fleet (1939), carrying out joint maneuvers with the British, who regarded him highly. On the collapse of France (June 1940), the self-proclaimed anglophile Laborde ordered his ships to British ports, but Admiral Jean Darlan prevailed on him to honor the naval clauses of the armistice agreement (22 June). He then commanded the largely disarmed French fleet at Toulon.

Following the Allied landings in North Africa (8 November 1942), the Toulon fleet became a significant military prize.

Darlan, having reached accommodation with the British and Americans, "invited" Laborde to bring the fleet to North Africa, but he refused, announcing that he would defend his base and sacking senior officers who refused to obey him. The Germans launched a surprise attack (27 November) and he ordered his ships scuttled, the plan for which had long been in effect (June 1940). This decision resulted in the loss of three battleships, eight cruisers, seventeen destroyers, sixteen PT boats, sixteen submarines, and some sixty transports. Five submarines braved German mine fields and three of these escaped.

Critics argued that Laborde should have fought his way out, but the Germans had placed extensive mine fields and their aircraft controlled the skies. Stripped of his pension at the end of the war (1945), he was condemned to death (1947), a sentence reduced to fifteen years in prison. Freed in 1951, he was amnestied in 1959.

Lacaze, Marie Jean Lucien (1860–1955) French admiral. Lacaze entered the Naval Academy (1877). He took part in the French seizure of Tunis (1881) and held a number of overseas assignments. He commanded a cruiser (1903) and was naval attaché at Rome (1905). Promoted captain (1906), he commanded a battleship. Promoted rear admiral (1911), he was chef du cabinet to Naval Minister Théophile Delcassé (1911–13) and pushed for Anglo-French naval cooperation.

During World War I Lacaze was naval commander at Marseille. He was then naval minister (October 1915–August 1917). He would have supported another attempt to force the Dardanelles, and he actively pushed anti-submarine warfare, ordered additional ships, reorganized administration, and pushed development of naval aviation.

Criticized for French ship losses to German submarines, Lacaze was forced to resign (August 1917). Promoted vice admiral (September), he was then maritime prefect of Toulon and commanded French patrols of the Mediterranean. He retired from active service in June 1922.

Lake, Sir Percival (1855–1940) British general. Lake joined the army (1873) and fought in the 1878–79 Second Afghan War. He later graduated from the Staff College and served in the Intelligence Department of the War Office, with the army in India, and with the Canadian militia. He was also chief military advisor to the Canadian government (1908–10).

During World War I Lake was sent to Mesopotamia to guard British interests in the oil fields (1915). He replaced General Sir John Nixon as CinC in Mesopotamia (January 1916) and was directed to make a second attempt to relieve General Charles Townshend and 13,000 British troops besieged at Kut.

Three attempts to relieve Kut failed, with Townshend forced to surrender. Lake returned to England to testify before the Mesopotamia Commission and then was posted to the Ministry of Munitions (May 1917). He retired after the war in November 1919.

Langle de Cary, Fernand Armand Marie de (1849–1927) French general. Langle de Cary graduated from St. Cyr (1869) and served with distinction in the 1870–71 Franco-German War. Thereafter, he held a

variety of posts with a culminating appointment as a member of the Supreme War Council (1912). He retired from the army as lieutenant general (July 1914).

Recalled to active duty to command Fourth Army on the outbreak of World War I (August 1914), Langle de Cary attacked into the Ardennes. Superior German numbers and artillery stopped his advance and he ordered his army back behind the Meuse. For the next two weeks his army carried out a fighting retreat. In the Battle of the Marne (September) his army took the full brunt of the German Fourth Army's attack. His chief concern was to prevent German exploitation of gaps on his flanks and, in three days of savage fighting, he contained the German advance.

Langle de Cary continued to command Fourth Army until appointed commander of Center Army Group from Verdun through Champagne (December 1915). Made a scapegoat for the inadequacy of French fortresses following the German attack at Verdun (February 1916), he was removed from command, ostensibly because of his age, and sent on an inspection tour of North Africa (March). He was retired altogether in December 1917.

Langsdorff, Hans (1894–1939) German navy officer. Langsdorff joined the Imperial German Navy as a cadet (1912) and was commissioned (1915). During World War I he served on a variety of vessels. He continued in the navy after the war and was promoted captain (1937). A consummate professional, he commanded pocket battleship *Admiral Graf Spee* (1938), then flagship of the fleet.

When World War II began, Langsdorff and the *Graf Spee* were already at sea. Ordered on a commerce-raiding mission in the South Atlantic, in three months his ship sank 50,000 tons of merchant shipping. Cornered off the Rio de la Plata, he fought a battle with the British cruisers *Ajax*, *Achilles*, and *Exeter* (13 December 1939) and put into Montevideo for repairs.

Tricked into believing that a superior British force now opposed him, he scuttled his ship (17 December) and then committed suicide.

Lanrezac, Charles Louis Marie (1852–1925) French general. Lanrezac left St. Cyr (1870) to fight in the 1870–71 Franco-German War. Promoted colonel (1902), he was a professor at the War College and a brigadier general (1906).

On the eve of World War I, Lanrezac commanded Fifth Army, which was to support an offensive by Third and Fourth armies into the Ardennes. He warned French Army commander General Joseph Joffre that this left much of the French–Belgian border uncovered and subject to envelopment. When German troops crossed the Meuse, Joffre ordered him to move part of his army northwest and hold while the remainder of his troops supported the main French offensive through the Ardennes. Lanrezac was outnumbered two to one, and Joffre finally authorized a retreat.

Joffre then ordered Lanrezac to counterattack northwest against the German First Army. He reluctantly obeyed, and this counterattack caused the Germans to abandon their plan for a wide sweep west of Paris. Taking heavy losses and threatened by envelopment, he again retreated to bring his army into line with other retreating French armies. On the eve of the Battle of the Marne (5 September), Joffre replaced him with General Louis Franchet d'Esperey. He refused a new command (1917) and, after the war, published a scathing critique of Joffre's conduct of the August 1914 campaign. Marshal Henri-Philippe Pétain decorated him (1924), which act for many vindicated his role early in the war.

Lawrence, Thomas Edward (1888–1935) British army officer. Educated at Jesus College, Oxford, Lawrence traveled to the Middle East (1909), where he worked and lived with Arabs. At the start of World War I (August 1914), he failed to meet the height requirement to join the army and was assigned to the Geographical Section of the War Office. When Turkey joined the war he became an intelligence officer in British Headquarters, Cairo.

With the Arab revolt against Turkey, Lawrence was posted as liaison to Emir Faisal's army and argued for using tribal warriors as guerrillas. Against orders, he convinced Faisal to cut Turkish rail communications and capture the vital port of Aqaba. He led a small camel force in a 500-mile ride across the desert, taking Aqaba from the rear (August 1917).

Major Lawrence convinced the new British commander in Egypt, General Edmund Allenby, to use the Arab forces as the right flank of his advance through Palestine to Damascus. Lawrence wanted that city as capital of an independent, free Arabia. Told not to advance on Damascus, he again violated orders. He, Faisal, and their men entered the city (1 October 1918), just ahead of Allenby's forces.

Lawrence, now a colonel, resigned at the end of the war and attempted at the highest levels to secure independence for the Arabs. The peace settlement was a bitter disappointment. He then wrote his memoirs and was briefly at All Souls College and the Colonial Office. He then enlisted in the RAF under a false name but, when his identity was learned, was cashiered. He joined the Tank Corps (1923) but was permitted back into the RAF (1925), where he served until 1935. He died following a motorcycle accident.

Leahy, William Daniel (1875–1959) U.S. admiral. Leahy graduated from Annapolis (1897). He participated in the 1898 Spanish-American War and in forces sent to rescue the Foreign Legations in Peking during the 1900–01 Boxer Rebellion. An instructor at Annapolis (1907–09), in World War I he commanded several ships and was promoted captain (1918). Promoted rear admiral (1927), he commanded the Bureau of Ordnance. As a vice admiral (1935), he commanded battleships in the Battle Force. He was then advanced to admiral and made chief of naval operations (January 1937).

Following his retirement from the navy (August 1939), his friend President Franklin Roosevelt appointed him governor of Puerto Rico (1939–40). He was then ambassador to Vichy France (1940–42), before returning to active duty as CofS to Roosevelt. He was, in effect, chairman of the Joint Chiefs of Staff and presided over its meetings. He also chaired meetings of the Combined Chiefs of Staff when the U.S. was host. He was an important advisor and confidant to Roosevelt, who secured his promotion to fleet admiral (December 1944). After Roosevelt's death (April 1945), Leahy advised President Harry S Truman. He played a major role in the formulation of the post-war 1947 National Security Act and reformation of the national defense establishment. He retired again in 1949, one of the longest serving naval officers in U.S. history.

Leclerc, Jacques Philippe (1902–57) French general. Born into an aristocratic family, the Count de Hauteclocque took the *nom de guerre* of Leclerc during World War II to avoid reprisals against his family in France. After his being commissioned in the infantry upon graduation from St. Cyr (1924), he fought in the Rif War in Morocco. He also taught at St. Cyr.

During World War II Leclerc was wounded in the Battle for France and taken prisoner (June 1940). Despite his wounds, he escaped and joined Charles de Gaulle's Free French in London. After recuperation he went to Africa. Beginning with a very small force, he won control first of Cameroon, and then of all French Equatorial Africa. As a colonel, he commanded the Desert Army in a 2,000-mile march to join the British Eighth Army in Tripoli (January 1943). In command of the French 2nd Armored Division, Leclerc

had the honor of liberating Paris (August 1944).

Appointed to command the French Expeditionary Corps in Indo-China (June 1945), Leclerc signed the Japanese surrender agreement for France and then went on to Saigon (October). Although his forces re-established French control in the populated areas, he believed the Viet Minh was a nationalist movement that could not be subdued militarily and favored negotiations and a political solution. His work undermined by High Commissioner Admiral Georges Thierry d'Argenlieu, he was relieved at his own request. Named inspector general of French forces in North Africa and promoted full general (July 1946), he died in a plane crash in Algeria.

Lee, John Clifford Hodges (1887–1958) U.S. general. A West Point graduate (1909), Lee was commissioned in the engineers. After the United States entered World War I (April 1917), he served in France as a staff officer and was promoted temporary colonel. Known in the army for his ego, he was nicknamed by his initials J.C.H. as "Jesus Christ Himself." He was promoted brigadier general (October 1940). Appointed to command 2nd Infantry Division at Fort Sam Houston, Texas (November 1941), he was promoted major general (February 1942).

When he failed to get the command he wanted, Lee became logistics chief for General Dwight D. Eisenhower (April). His Services of Supply (SOS) performed superbly and he was promoted lieutenant general (February 1944) and named deputy U.S. theater commander with special responsibility for administration and supply. Following the Normandy invasion (6 June 1944), he set up the Communications Zone, European Theater of Operations, replacing SOS (July). Although accused of empire building and flouting Eisenhower's directives, he remained in command.

Lee then commanded the Mediterranean

Theater of Operations (December 1945), but was accused by the American press of living too well in Rome and neglecting the needs of his enlisted men. Eisenhower, then army CofS, refused him permission to issue a rebuttal. He retired in December 1947.

Lee, Willis Augustus, Jr. (1888–1945) U.S. admiral. A graduate of Annapolis (1908), Lee served aboard warships in the Caribbean and China. He took part in the landing at Vera Cruz (1914) and served on destroyers in the North Sea at the end of World War I. He then operated with former German U-boats in the Atlantic (1919–20) and commanded destroyers and had shore assignments (1920–28). Following graduation from the Naval War College (1929), he held other assignments, including service with the Division of Fleet Training. Promoted captain (1936), he commanded a cruiser (1936–38) and then directed the Division of Fleet Training (1941–42) and was promoted rear admiral (January 1942).

Lee took command of Battleship Division 6 (August 1942) and won the second night fleet action off Guadalcanal (14–15 November), sinking a Japanese battleship and destroyer while losing only two destroyers. More importantly, he prevented the Japanese from bombarding Henderson Field. He then commanded the battleships in the Pacific Fleet (April 1943) and for the rest of the war led the fast battleship task force accompanying carriers of Third/Fifth Fleet in operations against the Japanese. Promoted vice admiral (March 1944), he commanded Battleship Squadron 2 (November). He returned to the United States (June 1945) to develop anti-*kamikaze* tactics at Casco Bay, Maine, where he died in August.

Leeb, Werner Ritter von (1876–1956) German field marshal. Leeb joined the Bavarian Army (1895) and was a staff officer in World War I. He then served in the Reichswehr. Promoted brigadier gen-

eral, he commanded Military District VII (1929–33). Promoted lieutenant general, he took command of Army Group II (1934).

A devout Catholic, Leeb detested the National Socialists and was among the high-ranking generals who were retired (1938) following the Blomberg–Fritsch crisis. He was recalled that same year to command in the Sudetenland during the crisis with Czechoslovakia. Considered an expert in defensive strategy, during the German invasion of Poland (September 1939) he commanded army units left in the west to defend against a French attack. As early as October, he urged negotiations to end the war. He commanded Army Group C in the invasion of France and Benelux (May 1940). His opposition to Hitler was well known, and he was under constant surveillance. Following the German victory over France, he was promoted field marshal (July).

Although he protested that the army was unready, Leeb commanded Army Group North in the invasion of the Soviet Union (22 June 1941). When he urged withdrawal to more easily defendable lines, Hitler removed him from command for his "defeatist mentality" (January 1942). Following the war, he was sentenced to three years imprisonment on war crimes but was released for time served awaiting trial.

Leese, Oliver William Hargreaves (1894–1978) British general. Commissioned in the army, Leese fought in World War I on the Western Front. He held a variety of assignments after the war and advanced steadily in rank. At the beginning of World War II he was deputy CofS of the BEF in France and was evacuated from Dunkerque (June 1940). He commanded the Guards Armored Division (1941) and, at General Sir Bernard Montgomery's request, took command of XXX Corps of Eighth Army in North Africa as a lieutenant general (1942). Leading the breakout at El Alamein, he participated in the subsequent North African campaign, the invasion of Sicily (July 1943) and the invasion of Italy (September). When Montgomery was recalled to Britain to direct the land invasion of France, he took over command of Eighth Army (December 1943–October 1944).

Transferred to the Pacific Theater, Leese commanded Allied Land Forces, Southeast Asia for the reconquest of Burma (1944–45). Following a clash of personalities, he decided to replace General Sir William Slim, commander of Fourteenth Army and one of the best British generals of the war. In the ensuing uproar over this action, General Louis Mountbatten then relieved Leese himself (August) and replaced him with Slim. Leese returned to Britain as CinC of the Eastern Command and then retired (1946).

Leigh-Mallory, Sir Trafford (1892–1944) British air marshal. Educated at Magdalene College, Cambridge, Leigh-Mallory joined the army (1914), then the Royal Flying Corps (1916), and the Royal Air Force (1918). During World War I he served on the Western Front. After the war he graduated from the RAF Staff College and the Imperial Defense College and was an instructor at the Army War College. He was promoted air commodore (1936) and air vice marshal (1938).

On the outbreak of World War II (September 1939), Leigh-Mallory commanded Number 12 Fighter Group. During the 1940 Battle of Britain 12 Group provided protection for the industrial centers and shipping lanes. Resenting his secondary role to Air Vice Marshal Keith Park's Number 11 Group, he clashed with the head of Fighter Command, Air Chief Marshal Sir Hugh Dowding. In actions bordering on insubordination, he boasted he would secure Dowding's removal. Throughout his career he had stormy relationships with others.

Leigh-Mallory favored the "big wing" concept of massing fighter formations in attacks on German bombers. Dowding

resisted this until Leigh-Mallory convinced the air staff of the concept's superiority. Following victory in the Battle of Britain, when Air Marshal William Sholto Douglas replaced Dowding (25 November 1940), Leigh-Mallory assumed command of Park's 11 Group and instituted the "big wing." Sacrificing surprise, the concept was only marginally successful. 11 Group also provided support for bomber raids into France and the cross-channel Dieppe Raid (19 August 1942).

Promoted acting air marshal (July 1942), Leigh-Mallory then headed Fighter Command (November). He was made air CinC designate for the invasion of Europe and knighted (1943). His "Transportation Plan" was a coordinated effort to isolate the landing areas in France prior to the Normandy invasion, and it was at his urging that Bomber Command was used in tactical support of ground troops. For the landing itself (6 June 1944), he commanded 9,000 aircraft.

Reassigned as Allied air commander for Southeast Asia, Leigh-Mallory was killed when his plane crashed in France in November 1944.

Lejeune, John Archer (1867–1942) U.S. Marine Corps general. A graduate of Annapolis (1888), Lejeune was commissioned in the Marines (1890). Over the next three decades he fulfilled a variety of routine ship and shore assignments. The first Marine officer to attend the Army War College (1909), he commanded a regiment during the 1913 Advance Base Maneuvers on Puerto Rico and there began re-evaluating the tactical Marine mission. He then became aide to Marine General Commandant George Barnett (1916).

During World War I Lejeune was the first Marine Corps officer nominated to command an infantry division. He fought in the 1918 St. Mihiel and Meuse–Argonne offensives and emerged from the war as one of its most decorated American officers.

Lejeune became commandant of the Marine Corps (June 1920) and served an unprecedented three terms. His tenure was marked by unceasing efforts to upgrade the educational standards of the Corps. He also instituted modern amphibious assault tactics and technology, and he established aviation units. He retired from the Marine Corps (1929) to serve as superintendent of the Virginia Military Institute.

Leman, Gérard (1851–1920) Belgian general. Leman was commissioned from the École Militaire at Brussels and later headed that school before being appointed commander of the ring-fortress of Liége (January 1914). The twelve forts of the fortress were athwart the Maastricht–Ardennes gap through which the Germans would funnel two armies at the start of World War I (August 1914). The obsolete forts were soon reduced by heavy Krupp howitzers.

Leman himself was captured, wounded and unconscious, in the ruins of Fort Loncin (15 August). After the war he returned to Belgium a hero.

LeMay, Curtis Emerson (1906–90) U.S. Air Force general. LeMay was commissioned in the army (1928) through the Reserve Officer Training Corps program at Ohio State University. He then became both a navigator and pilot. Promoted lieutenant colonel (January 1942) then colonel (March), he took command of the 305th Bombardment Group (April) and went with it to Britain where he developed new bombing tactics. He then commanded 3rd Bombardment Division (June 1943). Promoted major general (March 1944), he commanded 20th Bomber Command in China. He then took command of 21st Bomber Command on Guam (January 1945) and developed new tactics for B-29 raids against Japanese cities. He then took command of Twentieth Air Force (July).

After the war, LeMay was promoted lieutenant general in the new Air Force and played a key role in the Berlin Airlift. Promoted full general (1951), he headed the Strategic Air Command (1948–57). He became Air Force vice CofS (1957), then CofS (1961). He held the latter post until his retirement (1965).

LeMay was often at odds with the Kennedy and Johnson administrations over a variety of issues, including conduct of the Vietnam War. He favored massive bombing of the Democratic Republic of Vietnam (North Vietnam) and believed that victory could be achieved through strategic bombing. He ran unsuccessfully for vice president of the United States in 1968.

Lemnitzer, Lyman Louis (1899–1988) U.S. general. Commissioned in the coast artillery on graduation from West Point (1920), Lemnitzer taught at West Point (1926–30, 1934–35) and graduated from the Command and General Staff School (1936) and Army War College (1940). Promoted colonel (1941), he joined the General Staff in Washington.

Promoted brigadier general (June 1942), Lemnitzer commanded the 34th Anti-Aircraft Brigade. After helping plan the North African invasion, he led the 34th through the invasion of Sicily. He was then CofS of the Allied Fifteenth Army Group and was promoted major general (1944).

Lemnitzer was the senior army representative to a planning group to develop what became the North Atlantic Treaty Organization (NATO) (1946–47). He was deputy commander of the Army War College (1947–49) and then took parachute training (1950) and commanded the 11th Airborne Division. He was then in Korea commanding the 7th Infantry Division (1951), and the next year was promoted lieutenant general and named deputy army CofS for plans and research. Promoted general (1955), he commanded Eighth Army and all army forces in the Far East, then the entire Far East Command. He was then vice CofS of the Army (1957–59), army CofS (1959–60), and chairman of the Joint Chiefs of Staff (1960–62). He was then supreme allied commander, Europe (1963–69), until he retired in July 1969.

Leopold III, King of the Belgians (1901–83) Leopold succeeded his father King Albert as King of the Belgians in 1934. After the German remilitarization of the Rhineland (1936), Belgium declared its neutrality, but there was informal cooperation between that country and France and Britain thereafter. When the Germans invaded France and Benelux (10 May 1940), Leopold assumed command of his army and promised that Belgium would not quit the fight unilaterally. He did just that, surrendering (28 May) after a brief stand and rendering the BEF position in Belgium impossible and evacuation at Dunkerque all but inevitable. The king also refused to go abroad with his ministers in a government-in-exile. Suspected of both German sympathies and authoritarian preferences, he compounded his unpopularity by remarrying in wartime, and to a commoner.

Leopold was held in Germany when Belgium was liberated (fall 1944) and his brother Prince Charles, Count of Flanders, became regent. After the war the question of the monarchy hung fire, and not until a referendum (March 1950) gave him a 58 percent favorable vote did he attempt to regain his throne. His arrival precipitated such a crisis that he relinquished control of affairs to his son; and when Baudouin reached the age of majority in 1951, Leopold abdicated.

Lettow-Vorbeck, Paul Emil von (1870–1964) German general. Lettow-Vorbeck was commissioned (1899) on graduation from the Kriegsakademie. He served in China during the 1900–01 Boxer Rebellion, saw action in Southwest Africa during the 1904–08 Hottentot and Herero Rebellions, and was appointed commander of forces in German East Africa and promoted lieutenant colonel (1914).

Lettow-Vorbeck worked diligently to prepare his German troops and native askaris for the war. A proponent of the offensive, at the start of World War I he raided the British in Kenya to tie down as many Allied troops as possible and prevent their use in Europe (August 1914). Cut off from supplies from Germany, he improvised. He made certain that Africans were treated with justice, and his native askaris showed great loyalty to him and fought well against British Empire troops who discounted their fighting abilities.

With never more than 3,000 German and 11,000 askari troops, Lettow-Vorbeck diverted over 130,000 Allied troops from use on the Western Front. Driven from East Africa, his men continued the fight. He invaded Portuguese Mozambique and then moved into Rhodesia, proving himself a master of guerrilla warfare. Upon learning of the armistice in Europe, he negotiated the surrender of his undefeated army (25 November 1918). Upon his return to Germany (January 1919), he was lauded and promoted major general.

Levetzow, Magnus von (1871–1939) German naval officer. Levetzow received his commission and was an Admiralty staff officer during the European blockade of Venezuelan ports (1903). Promoted captain (1913), during World War I he commanded a battle cruiser in the Yarmouth and Hartlepool raids (November and December 1914) and at the Battle of the Dogger Bank (January 1915). At the Battle of Jutland (31 May–1 June 1916) he was chief of the Operations Division under Captain Adolf von Trotha, chief of staff to Vice Admiral Reinhard Scheer, commander of the High Seas Fleet.

In 1917 Levetzow helped plan Operation ALBION, the amphibious invasion of the Baltic Islands off the Gulf of Riga. Commodore Levetzow became chief of staff of Admiral Scheer's new Naval

Supreme Command (August 1918) and planned the last fleet sortie, which was prevented by mutiny. An ardent nationalist, he later joined the Nazi party.

Lewin, Sir Terence Thornton (1920–99) British admiral of the fleet. Lewin joined the navy (1939) and saw extensive naval combat in World War II. Raised to flag rank (1969), he was vice chief of the Naval Staff (1971–1973), CinC of the fleet (1973–75), and chief of the Naval Staff and first sea lord (1977–79).

As chief of the Defense Staff (1979–82), Lewin is credited with overseeing Britain's victory over Argentina in the 1982 Falklands War. He commanded the buildup of British naval forces and secured a change in the rules of engagement to allow an attack on the Argentine cruiser *General Belgrano*. In 1983 he was made a life peer and became Lord Lewin.

Li K'e-nung (Li Kenong) (1907–62) People's Republic of China general. Li joined the Chinese Communist party (CCP) (1926) and worked for its underground organizations as a spy against the Nationalist or Kuomintang (KMT, Guomindang) government (1930s). He became director of Internal Security Affairs for the CCP First Route Army (1932–33) and joined the 1934–35 Long March to north Shensi. He became director of the CCP's Foreign Affairs Department (1937), then was deputy director of the CCP Central Intelligence Department (1938). After World War II, with the Nationalist forces preparing to attack Yenan (1946), he represented the CCP on the Military Mediation Sub-Committee (1946–47).

Li was then director of the Military Intelligence Department, People's Liberation Army (PLA) General Staff and vice-minister of foreign affairs (1949–54). During the 1950–53 Korean War he headed the Chinese People's Volunteer Army (CPVA) negotiating team at the Korean armistice talks (1951–53) and was the key figure in formulating nego-

tiating strategies on the Communist side. He accompanied Foreign Minister Chou En-lai (Zhou Enlai) to the 1954 Geneva Conference. Appointed deputy CofS of the PLA with special charge of intelligence operations (1954), he was promoted full general (September 1955).

Li Tsung-jen (Li Zongren) (1891–1969) Nationalist Chinese general. Li Tsung-jen attended the Kwangsi (Guangxi) Military Academy and in 1916 was a platoon leader in the Kwangsi provincial army, which was defeated by the Nationalist or Kuomintang (KMT, Guomindang) Army (1922). Li then formed a new force, which came to dominate the province (1925). When Sun Yat-sen's (Sun Zhongshan) Canton government recognized his authority in Kwangsi, he joined the KMT. He took command of Seventh Army (March 1926) and played a key role in the 1926–28 Northern Expedition to crush the remaining provincial warlords. Li took Wuhan (1927) and commanded Fourth Army Group in the capture of Peking (Beijing) (1928).

Now a rival of Chiang Kai-shek (Jiang Jieshi), Li rebelled (1928) against the increasing centralization of government but was defeated. He then rebelled a second time (1936). After the start of war with Japan (1937), he rejoined the KMT, commanding Fifth War Area at Hsüchou (Xuzhou) and defeated the Japanese in the Battle of Taierhchwang (Taierzhuang) (April 1938). At the end of the war he helped liberate much of China, but Jiang did not trust him and held up his advance, refusing to give him any important command after 1947.

Elected vice president (1947), Li was briefly president (1949), when he made an effort to reach peace with the Communists. He then left China for the United States and exile. In 1965 he returned to mainland China to support Mao Tse-tung (Mao Zedong).

Liddell Hart, Sir Basil (1895–1970) British military historian and strategist. Liddell Hart left Cambridge to join the army as a lieutenant of infantry (December 1914). He was gassed in the Somme Offensive (1916) and spent the rest of the war in England training infantrymen. He wrote the army's infantry training manual (1920), which included his "expanding torrent" strategy evolved from World War I German infiltration tactics. He soon became a leading advocate of military reform through his "indirect approach" of dislocating an enemy and reducing his means of resistance.

Invalided out of the army because of a heart problem (1924), Liddell Hart retired as a captain (1927). He became a military correspondent for the *Daily Telegraph* (1925) and moved to *The Times* (1935). He published extensively on strategy and tactics, although the government strongly resisted his ideas to mechanize the army with tanks and anti-aircraft forces. He spent the war as a correspondent for the *Daily Mail*. His post-war writings often contradicted what he had said before the war, and seemed to show him as a lone Cassandra warning against the German danger.

Liggett, Hunter (1857–1935) U.S. general. Commissioned on graduation from West Point (1878), Liggett spent much of his early career with the 5th Infantry Regiment in the West, during which time he participated in Indian wars. He served in the 1898 Spanish-American War as a major of volunteers, then returned to the regular army. A decade later he attended the Army War College and then served as its director and president. Promoted brigadier general (1913), he commanded a brigade in the Philippines, then headed the Philippine Department (1916–17). Promoted major general (March 1917), after the United States entered World War I (April 1917), he took command of the 41st Infantry Division (September) and sailed with it for France.

Liggett was widely admired in the army and suited to high command. AEF commander General John J. Pershing made him his first corps commander. He took command of I Corps (January 1918), which played a key role in stopping the German Champagne–Marne Offensive (July 1918) and then participated in the St. Mihiel (September) and Meuse–Argonne Offensives (October–November). He commanded First Army (October) and was promoted temporary lieutenant general. He continued to command First Army in Germany until it was disbanded (April 1919). He then commanded Third Army, consisting of all U.S. occupation forces in Germany. He returned to the U.S.A. (July 1919) and retired in 1921.

Liman von Sanders, Otto (1855–1929) German general and Turkish field marshal. Liman joined the Hessian Life Guards (1874), then transferred to the cavalry (1879). After 1887 he held General Staff assignments. He commanded a cavalry brigade (1906) and was a lieutenant general commanding an infantry division (1911). Enobled (1913), he added the name of his deceased Scottish wife, Sanders, to his own.

Emperor William II sent Liman von Sanders on a special military mission to the Ottoman Empire (late 1913). Appointed inspector general of Turkish troops with the rank of field marshal, he did much to improve the army. On the outbreak of World War I, he worked to bring Turkey in on the side of the Central Powers. He took command of the Turkish First Army in the Bosporus (August 1914), then Fifth Army at Gallipoli (March 1915). Although outnumbered, his forces contained the Allied landings on the beachhead and ultimately forced their withdrawal.

Liman von Sanders received command of Army Group F (February 1918), consisting of three Turkish armies in Syria and Palestine. For a time he held the British advance north but, pressured by

Allied forces commanded by General Edmund Allenby, he withdrew most of his force to Aleppo. He retired from the German army in 1919.

Lin Piao (Lin Biao) (1907–71) Chinese general and politician. Lin joined the Chinese Communist Party (CCP) (1925), then graduated from the Nationalist party or Kuomintang (KMT, Guomindang) Whampoa Military Academy (1926). He took part in the abortive August 1927 Nanchang Uprising; he then marched his men to Fukien, then Tayu (1927–28) and undertook guerrilla operations in Tapai Mountain district, Kiangsi (1929). He commanded a regiment under Chu Teh (Zhu De) (1929) and then Fourth Red Army (1929–30). As commander of First Army Group (1932), he led it in the breakout against surrounding KMT troops and was one of the military leaders of the 1934–35 Long March. He ran the CCP military academy (1936–37). When the 1937–45 Sino-Japanese War began, he commanded 115th Division of Eighth Route Army. At the end of the war the 115th resembled a full army in size.

After World War II, Lin commanded the Northeast Democratic Joint Army and led 100,000 men into Manchuria but was defeated there by Nationalist generals Ch'en Ch'eng (Chen Cheng) and Tu Yuming (Du Yuming) (March–June 1946). Renewing the attack, he defeated Nationalist troops in Manchuria (May–November 1947). Commanding Northeast Liberation Army, then Northeast Field Army (1948), he was the architect of important Communist military triumphs, taking both Peking (Beijing) (January 1949) and Canton (October).

The logical choice to command Chinese troops in the 1950–53 Korean War, he reportedly opposed China's intervention, so that distinction fell to Marshal P'eng Te-huai (Peng Dehuai). He joined the Politburo (1955) and then became defense minister (1959). Officially designated Mao Tse-tung's successor, he died in a plane crash trying to escape China, supposedly after a failed coup attempt.

Lindbergh, Charles Augustus, Jr. (1902–74) U.S. Air Force reserve general and aviation pioneer. Lindbergh left college, learned to fly (1922), and joined a flying circus. He joined the Army Air Corps (1924) and then became an airmail pilot. Lindbergh was the first person to fly nonstop from New York to Paris. He made the 3,610-mile flight in 33.5 hours in *The Spirit of St. Louis* (1927). An instant celebrity, "Lucky Lindy" received the Medal of Honor.

Lindbergh and his wife Anne, who flew as his co-pilot and later became a well-known author, made a number of pioneering flights, but were again catapulted into the limelight on the kidnapping and death of their infant son (1932). Fleeing to England to escape the press, he returned from an evaluation of the German air force with a false sense of the Luftwaffe's superiority and as an admirer of Nazi Germany. His reputation was further stained by racial statements and his advocacy of isolationism as a spokesman for the America First Movement. President Franklin Roosevelt's sharp reproof caused him to resign his Army Air Corps reserve colonel's commission.

When the Japanese attacked Pearl Harbor (7 December 1941), Lindbergh urged an all-out war effort and sought reinstatement in the army, which Roosevelt blocked. He secured a position as a test pilot and traveled to the Pacific Theater of Operations, where he introduced important fuel economy techniques and flew combat missions as a civilian, shooting down at least one Japanese plane. Vindication came after the war with a commission as a brigadier general in the Air Force reserve.

Linsingen, Alexander von (1850–1935) German general. Linsingen joined the Prussian army (1868) and rose to command a division (1905) and then a corps

(1909). At the beginning of World War I (August 1914) his II Corps was part of First Army, but was transferred to the Russian Front (November). Linsingen took command of *Südarmee*, a mixed force of German/Austro-Hungarian troops that held a crucial sector in the front (January 1915). He then moved to central Poland as head of a newly formed Bugarmee (July) and then "Army Group Linsingen." The latter consisted of his own Bugarmee and the German Eleventh Army, and later the Austro-Hungarian Fourth Army. Following the Treaty of Brest-Litovsk, his army group was dissolved and he was promoted to full general with charge of Berlin and its environs. He resigned at the end of the war.

List, Siegmund Wilhelm (1880–1971) German field marshal. List served as a staff officer on the Western Front during World War I. He also saw service in the Balkans and with Turkish forces (1916–17). He joined the Reichswehr (1923) and rose steadily in rank and responsibility.

Following the *Anschluss* (March 1938), Adolf Hitler selected List to organize the new Army Group Five in Austria. He commanded Fourteenth Army during the Polish campaign (September 1939) and Twelfth Army in the Battle for France and Benelux (May 1940), where his troops pierced the Weygand Line and outflanked the Maginot Line. Promoted field marshal (July 1940), he was sent to the Balkans (February 1941), where he secured an agreement with Bulgaria allowing Germany to attack Greece through that country. The invasion of Greece (April) was another success for Twelfth Army. He served in Norway and then commanded Army Group A in the Soviet Union (June 1942), when Hitler directed him to take Rostov and the oilfields in the Caucasus. Overextended supply lines and resources diverted to the effort at Stalingrad prevented him from realizing all his objectives, which caused Hitler to dismiss

him (September). Sentenced at Nuremberg to life imprisonment (1948) for war crimes in the Balkans, he was released in 1952.

Litvak, Lilly (1922?–43) Russian pilot. Following the German invasion of the Soviet Union (22 June 1941), Russian woman aviator Martina Raskova organized several Red Air Force regiments of women pilots. Litvak, who had learned to fly before the war, joined one of these. On completion of training, she was assigned to the 586th Interceptor Regiment. She then fought with the 758th Fighter Regiment at Saratov near Stalingrad. Flying in a Yak-1, she shot down a German Ju-88 and several Do-17s. Transferred to the 73rd Fighter Regiment of the Guards Air Division (January 1943), she was commissioned a lieutenant and awarded the Order of the Red Banner (February). She then participated in air battles around Belgograd, Orel, and Kharkov and was wounded twice and forced to bail out once. She also shot down a German observation balloon. Last seen in her Yak "Yellow 44" chasing three Bf-109s (1 August 1943), she was credited with twelve kills, making her the world's leading woman ace.

Liu Chih (Liu Zhi) (1892–) Chinese Nationalist general. A graduate of the Paoting Military Academy (1914), Liu served in the armies of several warlords. Appointed instructor at Whampoa Military Academy under Chiang Kai-shek (Jiang Jieshi) (1924), he commanded First Route Army during the Nationalist or Kuomintang (KMT, Guomindang) 1926–28 Northern Expedition to reunify China. He commanded Second Army Group at the beginning of the 1937–45 Sino-Japanese War, directing the military effort in north China (1937–38). Thereafter he had command of the Chungking (Chongqing) garrison district. Promoted full general at the beginning of the 1946–49 Civil War, he commanded a half million KMT troops in the Huai-Hai campaign, but his forces were cut off and defeated (November 1948–January 1949). Relieved of command (January 1949), he left China and then joined the Nationalist government on Taiwan, where he was national security advisor to Chiang Kai-shek (1955–56).

Liu K'un-yi (Liu Kunyi) (1830–1902) Chinese general. Liu fought in the Hunan Army in the 1850–1864 Taiping Rebellion (from 1854) and advanced rapidly to general. After the defeat of the Taipings, he fought Nien rebels in north China (1864–68). Appointed commander of the Hunan Army (1872) he was also governor-general of Nanking, then of Kiangsi, Anhwei, and Kiangsu. He commanded in northern China on the border with Manchuria during the 1894–95 Sino-Japanese War and opposed the Chinese government decision to seek peace following defeat at sea by the Japanese (September–November 1894). He also opposed without success the Dowager Empress's deposition of the young reform emperor Kuang-hsü (Guang Xu) (1898). He chose not to obey the government's declaration of war against the Western powers during the 1900–01 Boxer Rebellion. He put down the rebellion in south China and urged the government to accept the Western powers' humiliating peace terms (1901), although he opposed peace with Russia because of the latter's occupation of Manchuria. Just before his death, he submitted a list of recommended reforms, which however were not implemented.

Liu Po-ch'eng (Liu Bocheng) (1892–1986) People's Republic of China marshal. Liu graduated from the Chengdu Military Academy and was commissioned in the provincial army. He took part in the 1911 revolution and joined the Nationalist or Kuomintang (KMT, Guomindang) Party in the early 1920s and was made a general, and joined the Communist party in 1926. He was a corps chief of staff in

the 1926–28 Northern Expedition. Liu took part in the August 1927 Nanchang Uprising. He escaped to study in the Soviet Union at the Frunze Military Academy. Returning to China (1930), he joined Mao Tse-tung (Mao Zedong) in southern Kiangsi Province and became chief of staff of the General Headquarters, Red Army (1921). He was chief of staff during the 1934–35 Long March to Yenan (Yan'an). He established the Red Army military academy (1935) and during the 1937–45 Sino-Japanese War commanded the 129th Division of Eighth Army (1937–40), and then forces operating in the Taihang Mountain region.

Renowned as a leader of guerrillas, Liu played a key role in the 1946–49 Civil War, first in cutting communications and then winning victories in southern Shantung province. He commanded the Shansi–Hopeh–Shantung–Honan Military Region (1947), then the Central Plains Field Army (1948) and Shansi–Hopeh–Shantung–Honan Field Army (1948–49). He played a major role in the final campaigns in south China. He commanded the East China Military Region (1949–50), and Second Field Army (1949). President of the Nanking (Nanjing) Military Academy (1951–58), he held a variety of political posts and was promoted one of ten marshals (September 1955).

Lockwood, Charles A., Jr. (1880–1967) U.S. admiral. An Annapolis graduate (1912), Lockwood began his long career in submarines when he commanded one in the Philippines (1914). He then commanded the 1st Submarine Division, Asiatic Fleet (1917–18). A succession of submarine commands followed, along with service in China in the Yangtse (Yangzi) River patrol force. Lockwood taught at Annapolis (1934–35) and then commanded Submarine Division 13. He held staff positions, including service with the office of the Chief of Naval Operations, before becoming naval attaché in London (1941–42).

Lockwood assumed command of submarines in the Southwest Pacific Force, based at Fremantle, Australia (February 1942), and then commanded submarines in the Pacific Fleet (February 1943–December 1945), based at Pearl Harbor. He pushed for changes in the design and manufacture of torpedoes and had charge of the campaign against Japan that saw the U.S. Navy become the most effective practitioner of submarine warfare in history. Following the war, Lockwood was navy inspector general (1946–47). He retired in 1947.

Löhr, Alexander (1885–1947) German general. An Austrian by birth, Löhr began his military career in a Hungarian infantry regiment. He continued in the Austrian army after World War I, eventually commanding its aviation branch. He transferred to the Luftwaffe after the March 1938 German absorption of Austria (*Anschluss*) and was appointed commander of the Fourth Luftflotte (Air Fleet) (1939). He led it in the invasions of Poland and the Balkans, the airborne assault on Crete (May 1941), and into southern Russia (June 1941).

Assigned to the Balkan theater (mid-1942), Löhr, A full general, commanded first Twelfth Army and then Army Group E (January 1943), with his authority restricted for much of the period (1942–44) to Greece and the Aegean Islands. He conducted a skillful fighting withdrawal through Yugoslavia (late 1944). Imprisoned in Yugoslavia (May 1945), he was later tried and convicted by a Yugoslav court on war crimes charges and was executed.

Loßberg, Friedrich von (1868–1942) German general. Commissioned in the army (1888), Loßberg headed the Kriegsakademie (1911). He was then chief of staff of XIII Württemburg Army Corps (1913). During World War I he was promoted colonel (1915) and directed and organized German defenses during the Battles of

Champagne (1915) and the Battle of the Somme (1916).

Loßberg allowed his subordinate commanders freedom to make important decisions and developed the defense in depth or "elastic" defense. In fall 1916 he took charge of Operation ALBERICH, the movement to the shorter, more easily defended *Siegfriedstellung* (Siegfried or "Hindenburg" Line). He directed the line's construction and saw that it incorporated advanced defensive techniques. He was then chief of staff for General Max von Boehn's army group (summer–November 1918). After the war he served on the staff of Army Quartermaster General Hans von Seeckt with responsibility for securing Germany's eastern border.

After the war Loßberg served in the Reichswehr, as chief of staff in Kassel (1920–1921) and commander of 6th Division. He retired (1927) as a lieutenant general.

Lucas, John Porter (1890–1949) U.S. general. Lucas was commissioned in the cavalry on graduation from West Point (1911). He served in the Philippines (1911–14) and in Pershing's 1916–17 expedition into northern Mexico. Following U.S. entry into World War I (April 1917), he fought in France with the 33rd Infantry Division, was promoted temporary lieutenant colonel, and was wounded (1918).

Lucas continued in the army after the war, reverting to captain. Transferring to the field artillery, he graduated from the Field Artillery School (1921), the Command and General Staff College (1924), and the Army War College (1932). Among other assignments, he taught at the Artillery School (1921–23) and was also an ROTC instructor at the University of Michigan (1919–20) and Colorado Agricultural College (1924–29).

Promoted brigadier general (October 1940), Lucas commanded 2nd Division Artillery (1940–41). Promoted major general (August 1941), he commanded and trained 3rd Infantry Division (July 1941–March 1942). He commanded III Corps in Georgia before serving as General Dwight Eisenhower's deputy ground commander (November 1942–August 1943). He commanded VI Corps in Fifth Army (September 1943) and led the Anzio landing to flank the German Winter line. Although this achieved tactical surprise (January 1944), his caution and the time needed to stabilize the beachhead allowed the Germans to reinforce and counterattack (February). Replaced by Major General Lucian Truscott, he then commanded Fourth Army, San Antonio (May 1944). After the war he was chief of the military advisory group to Nationalist China (1946–48), then deputy commanding general of Fifth Army, Chicago (1948–49).

Ludendorff, Erich (1865–1937) German general. Ludendorff was commissioned in the infantry (1883), attended the Kriegsakademie, and joined the General Staff as a captain (1895). He was briefly a company commander and then became chief of the mobilization and deployment section of the General Staff (1908). Although capable of great concentration, he was a narrow technical specialist whose entire life was focused on the army. As a colonel, he drafted the 1913 army bill that called for expanding the peacetime army by three corps, but the War Ministry refused to adopt it and transferred him to command of a regiment and then, as a brigadier general (1913), to a brigade.

On the outbreak of World War I, Ludendorff was deputy CofS of General Karl von Bülow's Second Army. On 8 August he won fame commanding 14th Infantry Brigade in the capture of the Belgian fortress of Liège. Transferred to the east as quartermaster general (CofS) to Paul von Hindenburg in East Prussia, he rose with Hindenburg in responsibility, becoming quartermaster of the German Army (August 1916).

Since Germany was now ruled by the army and in many ways he dominated Hindenburg, Ludendorff had vast political as well as military power. In early 1917 he endorsed the navy's plan for unrestricted submarine warfare, easily the worst German blunder of the war as it brought U.S. entry on the Allied side. Following an armistice with Russia, he transferred resources from the east and oversaw a series of five offensives, usually known as the Ludendorff Offensives (March–July 1918), to try to win the war in the west. These failed in part through his strategic miscalculations. One of the first to call for an armistice, he resigned (29 October) and went into exile in Sweden.

Ludendorff was then involved in a series of plots against the new Weimar Republic, most notably the Kapp Putsch (1920) and Hitler's Beer Hall Putsch (1929). He later turned against the Nazis.

Lütjens, Günther (1889–1941) German admiral. Lütjens entered the German Navy as a cadet (1907) and spent most of his early naval career in torpedo boats. He continued in the navy after World War I and became chief of the officer personnel branch (1935). Promoted rear admiral, he then commanded the torpedo boats (October 1937–October 1939). After the start of World War II, he commanded German destroyers (1939). A fervent Nazi, he was then promoted vice admiral (January 1940) and commanded Group I (battle cruisers *Scharnhorst* and *Gneisenau*) in the assault on Norway (April 1940), supporting the assault on Narvik and engaging HMS *Renown*.

Replacing Admiral Wilhelm Marschall as fleet commander (July 1940), Lütjens was posted aboard the battleship *Bismarck*. His frequent communications with naval headquarters during the ship's sortie (May 1941) helped the Royal Navy to locate and destroy the battleship. Lütjens went down with the ship.

Lyautey, Louis Hubert Gonzalve (1854–1934) French marshal. Lyautey graduated from St. Cyr (1875), then attended the staff college (1875–76), and served with a cavalry regiment (1877–80). He was then in Algeria (1880–82). Promoted captain (1882), he commanded a cavalry squadron in France (1887–91). Promoted major (1893), he was chief of staff of 7th Cavalry Division. In 1895 he went to Tonkin in Indo-China. Promoted lieutenant colonel, he worked closely with Joseph Galliéni and became a specialist in military pacification. He accompanied his chief to Madagascar (1896), where he was promoted colonel and pacified the southern part of the island. He returned to France (1902) and briefly commanded a regiment until posted to Algeria (1903).

He achieved success in putting down a rebellion and added to Algerian territory. Promoted brigadier general (1904), he became commandant of Oran. Recalled to France (1910), he commanded X Corps (1910–12). He then went to Morocco as resident general.

During World War I Lyautey was recalled to be minister of war (December 1916–March 1917), but he resigned when he was not consulted on the appointment of General Robert Nivelle as French Army commander, and over opposition to Nivelle's plans for an offensive. He returned to Morocco, was appointed marshal (1921), and crushed Abd-el-Krim's Rif Rebellion (1925). He then retired (September 1925).

M

MacArthur, Arthur (1845–1912) U.S. general. During the 1861–65 Civil War, MacArthur secured an appointment as a lieutenant of volunteers (1862). He saw combat in Kentucky (1862) and fought at Missionary Ridge (1863), and was belatedly awarded the Medal of Honor for his actions there (1890). At eighteen he was a major and later commanded a regiment. Badly wounded in the Battle of Franklin (1864), he was a brevet colonel at war's end.

After the war MacArthur became a second lieutenant in the regular army, rising to the rank of major (1889). During the 1898 Spanish-American War, he was a brigadier general of volunteers. As commander of 3rd Expeditionary Force, he helped take Manila and hold the city. Promoted major general there, he commanded the principal field force against Filipino guerrillas. He then became military governor of the islands (May 1900). A military observer in the 1904–05 Russo-Japanese War (1905–06), he was promoted lieutenant general (September 1906) and was the senior officer in the army. He retired in 1909.

MacArthur, Douglas (1880–1964) U.S. general. Son of General Arthur MacArthur, he graduated first in his class West Point (1903) and was commissioned in the engineers. MacArthur served in the Philippines and then as aide to his father

in Tokyo (1905–06). He was aide to President Theodore Roosevelt (1906–07), then an instructor at the General Service and Cavalry Schools (1903–12), and participated in the 1914 occupation of Vera Cruz.

When the U.S entered World War I, MacArthur transferred to the infantry (August 1917) and became CofS to the 42nd Division. Promoted brigadier general in France, he led the 84th Infantry Brigade in the St.-Mihiel (September 1918) and Meuse–Argonne (September–November) offensives. He commanded the 42nd Division at the end of the war.

After occupation duties in Germany, MacArthur was superintendent of West Point (1919–22), then a major general in command of a division in the Philippines (1922–25). He commanded the Department of the Philippines (1928–30). Promoted general, he served as CofS of the army (1930–35) and dispersed the Bonus Army outside Washington. He reverted to major general and returned to the Philippines to organize its defenses. Named field marshal by the Philippine government (1936), he retired from the U.S. Army (1937).

Recalled to active service in the U.S. Army as lieutenant general, he became commander, U.S. Army Forces, Far East (July 1941). Surprised by the Japanese attack, despite Pearl Harbor, he conducted a skillful withdrawal to the Bataan Peninsula. Ordered by President Franklin Roosevelt to Australia (March 1942), he was awarded the Medal of Honor and named supreme commander, Southwest Pacific Area. He initiated the system of island-hopping back to the Philippines (1942–44). The system of leap-frogging (bypassing Japanese strongpoints) was imposed by Washington, however. His reconquest of the Philippines was a brilliant operation. Promoted general of the army, he oversaw the formal Japanese surrender (2 September 1945).

Following the war, MacArthur commanded Allied occupation forces in Japan and, as a benevolent autocrat, oversaw its reconstruction and drafting of a new constitution. After North Korea attacked South Korea (25 June 1950), he commanded United Nations forces in Korea. His Inchon landing was brilliant, but after that his operations went awry, and his separation of Eighth Army and X Corps during the advance into North Korea had disastrous results when China entered the war. Frustrated by what he perceived to be undue restraints placed upon him, he began to vent this publicly and flout directives, leading President Harry S Truman to relieve him of command (11 April 1951).

McAuliffe, Anthony Clement (1898–1975) U.S. general. Commissioned in the artillery upon graduation from West Point (1919), McAuliffe held routine assignments. He graduated from the Command and General Staff School (1937) and the Army War College (1940). He was then involved in the development of new equipment and weapons.

Following U.S. entry into World War II (December 1941), McAuliffe was promoted brigadier general (August 1942) and had charge of artillery in the 101st Airborne Division. He parachuted into Normandy during the invasion of France (6 June 1944) and also took part in Operation MARKET-GARDEN, the Allied effort to secure Arnhem (September). He was recuperating with his division,

when the Germans began their Ardennes offensive (Battle of the Bulge) (December 1944). As acting division commander in the absence of Major General Maxwell Taylor and assistant division commander Brigadier General Gerald Higgins, McAuliffe commanded the 101st and secured Bastogne, an important road hub, which the Germans needed. Despite being completely surrounded by German forces, in one of the memorable quotes of the war, he rejected a call to surrender with the single word, "Nuts!" Promoted major general (January 1945), he commanded the 103rd Division, then 79th Division (January–September 1945), which he led from Alsace to the Siegfried Line and into Austria at the end of the war. After the war he headed the Army Chemical Corps (1947–53). He returned to Europe to command Seventh Army (1953–55), then U.S. Army forces in Europe (March 1955) until his retirement with the rank of general in May 1956.

McCain, John Sidney (1884–1945) U.S. admiral. McCain graduated from the Naval Academy (1906). He saw extensive sea service and, during World War I, convoy escort duty. He graduated from the Naval War College (1929), qualified as a naval aviator (1936), and commanded the carrier *Ranger*, then the Naval Air Station at San Diego (1939–41). Promoted rear admiral, he commanded all land-based naval aircraft in the South Pacific and directed them in early fighting on Guadalcanal.

Promoted vice admiral, McCain became deputy chief of naval operations (air) (August 1943). He then commanded Task Group 38.1 (August 1944) and fought in the Battle of Cape Engaño (October). He then helped direct final air strikes on Japan. He was posthumously promoted to full admiral.

McCain, John Sidney, Jr. (1911–81) U.S. admiral. The son of Admiral John S. McCain, McCain graduated from Annapolis

(1931) and was a submariner in World War II. In the 1950s he held a variety of posts, including director of Navy Undersea Warfare Research and Development and chief legislative liaison for the secretary of the navy. Promoted rear admiral (1958) and vice admiral (1963), as commander of the Amphibious Force, he led the U.S. intervention in the Dominican Republic (April 1965). Promoted full admiral (May 1967), he was CinC, U.S. Naval Forces Europe.

McCain was then appointed CinC Pacific Command (1968–72), commanding all U.S. forces in the Pacific including those in Vietnam. He was a hawk on Vietnam, seeing the war as part of a general Communist offensive in Asia. He urged President Richard Nixon to carry out a strong response to the Democratic Republic of Vietnam (DRV, North Vietnam) spring 1972 offensive and advocated mining of DRV ports, including Haiphong, and resumption of strategic bombing of the North. On retiring from the service (1972) he became president of the U.S. Strategic Institute. His son, Navy aviator Lieutenant Commander John McCain III, was shot down over Vietnam and became a POW, and was later a U.S. senator.

McCalla, Bowman Hendry (1844–1910) U.S. admiral. McCalla joined the navy as a midshipman (1861) and was promoted ensign (1866), master (1866), lieutenant (1868), lieutenant commander (1869), and commander (1884). He led the landing party of sailors and Marines that ended the disturbances at Panama City (1885). While in command of the *Enterprise*, he hit a mutinous sailor (1890), for which he was court-martialed and sentenced to suspension from service for three years. Recalled to duty early, however (1891), he commanded the cruiser *Marblehead* in the 1898 Spanish–American War during the action at Guantanamo Bay, Cuba (7 June). After shelling shore installations, he led a party of sailors and

Marines ashore to establish a naval base there for the remainder of the war. Guantanamo Bay has remained in U.S. hands ever since. Promoted to captain (1899) and awarded two Medals of Honor for his action there and in establishing contact with the Cuban rebels at Cienfuegos, he was also given a special Congressional medal.

During the 1900–01 Boxer Rebellion McCalla again led a landing party, which became part of the column to relieve the Western legations at Peking (Beijing). He was wounded three times. Promoted rear admiral (1903), he retired in 1906.

McConnell, John Paul (1908–86) U.S. Air Force general. McConnell attended Henderson Brown College and then graduated from West Point (1932). He completed pilot training (1933) and held a variety of assignments. Promoted major (July 1941), after the United States entered World War II he advanced to lieutenant colonel (January 1942) and served in the office of the chief of the Army Air Forces (AAF). Promoted colonel (December 1942), he became deputy CofS of the AAF Training Command in Fort Worth, Texas (1943). He then served in staff positions in India (1943–44), and, as a brigadier general (August 1944), in Ceylon.

Following the war, McConnell served in China with the Eastern Air Command (1945–47). He returned to the United States to serve in a staff position at Air Force headquarters (1947–50). He then commanded 3rd Air Division and Third Air Force in Britain (1950–51). Promoted major general (December 1950), he commanded 7th Air Division of the Strategic Air Command (SAC) in Britain (1951–52). He then commanded Third Air Force (1952–53) and was director of plans for SAC (1953–57). Promoted lieutenant general, he commanded Second Air Force (1957–61). He was then vice commander of SAC (1961–62) and deputy commander of the European Command (1962–64). Promoted full general, he was vice CofS

(1964) and CofS of the Air Force (1965–69). He retired in July 1969.

McCreery, Sir Richard Loudon (1898–1967) British general. Educated at Eton and Sandhurst, McCreery entered the army as a lieutenant with the 12th Lancers (1915). During World War I he served in France and was wounded. After the war he attended the Staff College, but spent most of the period between the wars with his regiment.

Promoted colonel (1938), at the beginning of World War II he commanded a mechanized brigade in the BEF in France. Following the Dunkerque Evacuation (May–June 1940), he commanded an armored division in Britain for two years. He then went to the Middle East as chief of staff to General Harold Alexander (1942), and received command of X Corps at Salerno during its long march north through Italy. He then commanded Eighth Army (November 1944), and at the end of the war had charge of British occupation troops in Austria. His last assignment before retirement was to command the British Army of the Rhine (1946–48).

McGrigor, Rhoderick (1893–1959) British admiral. During World War II McGrigor commanded the battle cruiser *Renown* in Force H protecting Malta convoys. He also participated in the pursuit of the *Bismarck* (May 1941). He then was assistant chief of the naval staff for weapons (1941–43). He commanded the naval assault on Pantellaria Island and an assault force in the invasion of Sicily (July 1943). Rear Admiral McGrigor then commanded 1st Cruiser Squadron and aircraft carriers in the Home Fleet, assisting in Arctic convoy escort and harassing German shipping in the North Sea.

McIndoe, Sir Archibald Hector (1900–60) Pioneering plastic surgeon. Born in New Zealand, McIndoe obtaining his medical degree from Otago University and studied in the United States at the Mayo Clinic, where he was regarded as an excellent surgeon. On arrival in Britain (1930), he specialized in abdominal surgery until he took up the new field of plastic surgery.

On the beginning of World War II (September 1939), McIndoe became a consultant to the Royal Air Force and also became involved in treating victims with facial wounds and burns resulting from German air raids. He built Victoria Hospital into a model center for the treatment of severely burned RAF personnel. He also secured improved pay and benefits for victims until they were rehabilitated, and insisted that the rule invaliding men out of military service after 90 days be abolished. He refused a commission because he said that would inhibit him from going to the highest echelons. He was knighted for his services (1947).

Mackensen, August von (1849–1945) German field marshal. Mackensen joined the army (1869) and served in the 1870–71 Franco-German War. He had experience on the General Staff and as aide to Count Alfred von Schlieffen. After extended service as a brigade and divisional commander, he was promoted lieutenant general (1908) and assumed command of XVII Corps at Danzig, which he led in the important early battles of World War I on the Eastern Front.

When Hindenburg took command of the Eastern Front (November 1914), Mackensen succeeded him as head of the Ninth Army. After fighting in Poland during the winter, Mackensen was reassigned to western Galicia. There he took charge of two armies and orchestrated the breakthrough at Gorlice-Tarnow (May 1915), which eventually pushed the Russians out of most of Galicia and all of Russian Poland.

Promoted field marshal (June), Mackensen directed German and Austro-Hungarian forces acting in conjunction with the Bulgarians against Serbia (September). After defeating the Serbs, his army group took up defensive positions in Macedonia. When Romania entered the war (August), his forces helped defeat that country. He then headed the army of occupation. At the end of the war he presided over the repatriation of his troops via Hungary (November 1918). Although he was sceptical about the Nazis, two of his sons became prominent figures in the Third Reich, one of them an army commander.

Mackensen, Eberhard von (1889–1969) German general. Son of August von Mackensen, he was commissioned in the cavalry (1908). Eventually Mackensen joined the General Staff. Promoted brigadier general (January 1939), when World War II began he was CofS to General Wilhelm List. Promoted major general (January 1940) and lieutenant general (August), he commanded III Corps (January 1941–November 1942) in the invasion of the Soviet Union, spearheading the drive into Ukraine and the Caucasus region. He then commanded First Panzer Army (November 1942–October 1943) and was promoted full general (July 1943). He then commanded the newly formed Fourteenth Army in Italy and, following the Allied landings at Anzio (January 1944), held them on the beachhead until May. Blamed by Adolf Hitler for German setbacks leading to the fall of Rome, he was removed from command (June 1944).

Following the war, General Mackensen was sentenced to death on war crimes charges in connection with the Ardeatine Caves Massacre. The penalty was then reduced to life imprisonment. He was released early (1952).

McLain, Raymond (1890–1954) U.S. general. McLain joined the Oklahoma National Guard (1912) and was commissioned in the infantry (1914). He served on the Mexican border during the 1916 National Guard callup. In World War I he commanded a machine gun company of

the 36th Infantry Division and fought with it in the Champagne–Marne (July 1918) and Meuse–Argonne offensives (September–November).

McLain left the Guard after World War I and returned to a career in banking. He rejoined the Guard (1921) and rose to be operations officer of the 45th Infantry Division, attending the Command and General Staff College (1938).

During World War II as a brigadier general, McLain commanded the 45th Division's artillery in Sicily (July–August 1943) and in Italy, most notably in the Anzio landing (January 1944). He transferred to the 30th Infantry Division (April) and commanded the 90th Infantry Division after the Normandy landings (June) and then took command of XIX Corps (October). At the end of the war (May 1945), his forces were across the Elbe at Magdeburg.

McLain was one of the few National Guardsmen to command a division and the only one to command a corps during the war. He remained in the army after World War II as comptroller of the Department of the Army, and retired as a lieutenant general in 1953.

McMorris, Charles Horatio (1890–1954) U.S. admiral. McMorris graduated from Annapolis in 1912 and took took part in the landing at Veracruz (1914). During World War I he served aboard destroyers in the North Atlantic. He then held a variety of assignments, including instructor at Annapolis (1925–27, 1930–33). Following graduation from the Naval War College (1938), he was operations officer for the Scouting Force (1938–41). Promoted captain, he joined the staff of commander of the Pacific Fleet (CINC-PAC), Admiral Husband Kimmel (January 1941–April 1942). He then commanded a cruiser and participated in operations in the Solomon Islands. While in command of a task force in the Aleutian Islands, he drove off a superior Japanese force under Vice Admiral Boshiro Hosogaya in the

Battle of the Komandorski Islands (26 March 1943). Then, as chief of the joint staff under CINCPAC Admiral Chester Nimitz (May 1944), he helped plan the Central Pacific offensives. Promoted temporary vice admiral (September 1944), he commanded the Fourth Fleet (1946).

McMorris then served on the General Board (1947–48). Promoted permanent vice admiral (June 1948), he commanded 14th Naval District and Hawaiian Sea Frontier until his retirement in September 1952.

McNair, Lesley James (1883–1944) U.S. general. Commissioned in the artillery on graduation from West Point (1904), McNair had a number of varied assignments, after which he took part in the 1916–17 Punitive Expedition into Mexico. Following U.S. entry into World War I (April 1917), he went to France with the AEF as a lieutenant colonel. He ended the war as a temporary brigadier general, the youngest U.S. general officer.

McNair graduated from the Army War College (1929) and was promoted again to brigadier general (March 1937). He then commanded an artillery brigade and was commandant of the Command and General Staff School. He then became chief of the General Headquarters (1940) and assumed responsibility for training and organizing the entire army under the overall command of General George C. Marshall. He was then chief of Army Ground Forces (March 1942).

McNair reorganized the military and substituted the three-regiment "triangular" division for the old four-regiment "square" division. He insisted on realistic and rigorous training and he set high standards for officers.

McNair was promoted to major general (1940) and lieutenant general (June 1941). He was in Normandy observing the Allied breakout when he was killed near St. Lo by a bomb that fell short. In 1945 he was promoted posthumously to general.

McNaughton, Andrew George Latta (1887–1966) Canadian general. McNaughton received a BS (1910) and MS (1912) from McGill University. An electrical engineer of genius, he secured a commission as a reserve officer. He served in the artillery in the Canadian Army in World War I and was regarded as one of the principal pioneers of scientific techniques in artillery. He remained in the army after the war, and was promoted major general and appointed chief of the Canadian general staff (1929). He served until 1935, when he became president of the National Research Council. Following the outbreak of World War II (September 1939) he was appointed CinC of Canadian troops in Europe (December 1939–December 1943). During his tenure, the size of the Canadian force grew from divisional to army strength.

McNaughton sought to have Canadian forces held together rather than be parceled out to other commands, a position that brought him into conflict with Canadian Minister of National Defense Layton Ralston. This, and British Chief of the Imperial General Staff General Sir Alan Brooke's pronouncement that McNaughton was incapable of field command, led to his resignation. He returned to Canada and retired with the rank of general (October 1944) but briefly served as minister of defense (November 1944–August 1945).

Maczek, Stanislaw (1892–1994) Polish general. Maczek was an officer in the Austro-Hungarian Army during World War I and fought on the Italian Front. After the war he joined the new Polish Army and fought in the 1920 Russo-Polish War. At the time of the German invasion (September 1939), he commanded the 10th Motorized Cavalry Brigade, fighting against General Paul von Kleist's XXII Panzer Corps.

With Poland on the verge of defeat, on government orders his brigade crossed into Hungary and was interned. On learning that Polish forces were being formed in France, he escaped Hungary (October) and reported to General Wladyslaw Sikorski, commander of Polish forces in exile. Promoted brigadier general, he had charge of a Polish army camp. He fought the invading Germans as commander of the Oikusg 10th Armored Cavalry Brigade in the Battle of France (May–June 1940), then escaped to Britain following the Polish defeat (October).

Promoted major general, Maczek formed the Polish 1st Armored Division in Scotland (February 1942) and commanded it as part of Canadian First Army in France following the Normandy invasion. His division helped close the Falaise Gap (August 1944) and then fought in the Netherlands. At the end of the war it occupied the German navy base at Wilhelmshaven. He was promoted lieutenant general (May 1945) and lived in Scotland after the war.

Madden, Sir Charles Edward (1862–1935) British admiral. Madden entered the Royal Navy as a cadet (1875). Primarily known for his expertise in naval technology, he was promoted to flag rank (1911). He served as CofS to Admiral Sir John Jellicoe when the latter commanded the Grand Fleet. Madden then commanded 1st Battle Squadron. Promoted admiral (1916), after the war he commanded the Atlantic Fleet. He was first sea lord and CofS of the Royal Navy (1927–30). In 1924 he was promoted admiral of the fleet.

Maginot, André Louis René (1877–1932) French politician and minister of war. After receiving a law degree (1897), Maginot entered the civil service. Elected to the Chamber of Deputies (1910), he was deputy minister of war (1914), but on the start of World War I he enlisted in the army, where, as a sergeant, he continued to be consulted on military policy. His knee was shattered in fighting at Verdun (November 1914).

Following the war, Maginot returned to public life as a member of the Chamber of Deputies, opposing the Versailles Treaty with Germany for its lack of guarantees for France. As minister of pensions (1920), he worked to assist veterans. He then became minister of war (1920–24) and sought to address the issue of fortifications in the east against Germany. Supporters included Premier Paul Painlevé and Marshal Henri Philippe Pétain. The chambers voted funding and work began when he returned as minister of war (1929–32). The resulting defensive system was named for him. Ultimately France expended seven billion francs on some 87 miles of the Maginot Line. It halted at Belgium and in any case was not solid but a series of forts, each within range of the other to provide connecting fire. Its largest guns were 135mm howitzers, and there were only 345 of these. There were no anti-aircraft positions. The line was never considered impregnable, and was to be backed up by troops to pinch off breakthroughs. For the money expended on the Maginot Line, however, France might have had twenty-five armored divisions or 10,000 fighter aircraft.

Magsaysay, Ramón (1907–57) Filipino soldier and president. Magsaysay attended the University of the Philippines (1927–31) and graduated from José Rizal College (1933). He then worked for a transport company. When World War II began, he joined the Philippine Army and fought as a captain on Luzon and at Bataan (December 1941–April 1942). Following the U.S. surrender, he became a guerrilla in Zambales province. After liberation by U.S. troops, Magsaysay was appointed military governor of Zambales (1945). He was elected to two terms in the Philippine Congress (1946–50) as a member of the Liberal party.

In 1950 President Elpidio Quirino appointed Magsaysay minister of defense and charged him with putting down the Hukbalahap (Huk) Rebellion. He had great success in this, using army personnel instead of the local constabulary and offering generous terms to those who surrendered; but he resigned (1953), believing the Liberal party too corrupt.

Joining the Nationalist party, Magsaysay won election to the presidency (1953) and served as his own secretary of defense until the Huk movement collapsed (1954). Although popular, he was criticized for his close U.S. ties. He had begun a land redistribution program when he was killed in a plane crash.

Mahan, Alfred Thayer (1840–1914) U.S. navy officer and propagandist. The son of influential West Point professor Dennis Hart Mahan, Mahan attended Columbia College for two years and then graduated from Annapolis (1859). During the 1861–65 Civil War he served with the South Atlantic Blockading Squadron. He then published a book on U.S. Navy operations during the war (1883) and was promoted captain and joined the faculty of the newly established Naval War College (1885); he was later its president (1886–88, 1892–93).

Mahan published many books, but by far his most important was *The Influence of Sea Power upon History, 1660–1783* (1890). It is a history of British naval development, a treatise on war at sea, and a strong defense of a large navy. The book had great influence in Britain and Germany, but his lectures and magazine articles on current strategic problems also won a widening audience in the United States.

Mahan argued that the U.S. needed a strong navy to compete for the world's trade. He also criticized traditional "single ship, commerce raiding" (*guerre de course*), which could not win control of the seas. He instead advocated building a seagoing fleet with its strength in battleships operating in squadrons. An important apostle of the new navalism, he retired from the Navy (1896) to devote himself full time to writing, but was

recalled during the 1898 war with Spain. President of the American Historical Association (1902), he was promoted rear admiral on the retired list (1906).

Maistre, Paul (1858–1922) French general. Maistre was commissioned in the army from St. Cyr and later taught tactics at the War College. In 1914 he was chief of staff of Fourth Army. After the Battle of the Marne (September), he took command of XXI Corps and fought with it at Vimy, Verdun, and the Somme. He then took over Sixth Army (May 1917), which had suffered terribly at the Chemin des Dames, and restored it to effectiveness. His carefully prepared attack at Malmaison (October) characterized General Henri-Philippe Pétain's policy of selective, limited attacks. Maistre briefly commanded French forces sent to Italy after the Caporetto disaster (October–November 1917). He returned to the Western Front to command Tenth Army, which slowed the German advance in the spring of 1918. He then commanded the Center Army Group in the Allied counteroffensive until the armistice.

Makarov, Stephan Osipovich (1848–1904) Russian admiral. Following Vice Admiral Heihachiro Togo's surprise attack on the Russian naval base of Port Arthur without declaration of war (8–9 February 1904), St. Petersburg sent out Vice Admiral Makarov to command the Russian 1st Pacific Squadron. An expert on torpedo warfare and an effective and energetic leader, he arrived at the base (8 March) and promptly initiated a series of harassing sorties against the Japanese cruisers, while avoiding contact with the Japanese battleships.

Both sides also laid minefields. Makarov's battleship *Petropavlovsk* and other ships of the squadron ran over a Japanese minefield (12 April). The flagship went down quickly, carrying to their deaths Makarov and 635 officers and men. His death was a serious blow to the Pacific

Fleet, to Russian morale, and to hopes of relocating the squadron's ships to Vladivostok.

Malinovsky, Rodion Yakovievich (1898–1967) Soviet marshal. Malinovsky enlisted in the Russian Army (1914) and fought in France during World War I with the Russian Expeditionary Corps. Returning to Russia (1918), he joined the Red Army (1919) and Communist party (1926). A graduate of the Frunze, he was also military advisor to the Republican side during the 1936–39 Spanish Civil War (1937–38), then returned to the Frunze as an instructor.

Major General Malinovsky took command of the XLVIII Rifle Corps on the Romanian border (March 1941). Following the German invasion (22 June 1941), he commanded Sixth Army in Ukraine (August). Promoted lieutenant general (November), he next commanded Southern Front (December). Relegated to rear area duties following the loss of Kharkov (June 1942), he took command of Sixty-Sixth Army (August 1942), then was deputy commander of the Voronezh Front (October), and commanded Second Guards Army (November). He played a key role in the Battle of Stalingrad, preventing the Germans from relieving Sixth Army (December). Promoted colonel general (February 1943), he commanded Southern Front (February) and Southwest Front (March). He was then promoted general of the army (April). His command was redesignated 3rd Ukrainian Front (October), then 2nd Ukrainian Front (May 1944). Following liberation of southern Ukraine, his forces pushed into Romania, Hungary, Austria, and Czechoslovakia.

Following the German surrender (May), Malinovsky commanded the Transbaykal Front in the Far East (July 1945), then the Far East Command (1947–53), and the Far East Military District (1953–56). Appointed deputy minister of defense (1956–57), he was

then minister of defense (1957) until his death in 1967.

Mangin, Charles Marie Emmanuel (1866–1925) French general. Mangin graduated from St. Cyr (1888) and spent his early military career primarily in the colonies, where he was wounded three times. He led the advance guard of Colonel Jean-Baptiste Marchand's expedition across Africa to the Nile at Fashoda (1898).

In World War I Mangin returned to France to command a brigade (1914). He combined an aggressive style with excellent technical ability. His recklessness with the lives of his troops was legendary. Often called "the butcher" or "eater of men," he was also fearless and was often seen inspecting his troops at the front, where he was wounded several times.

Promoted general of division (early 1915), Mangin commanded 5th Division, which recaptured Forts Douaumont and Vaux at Verdun (1916). He commanded Sixth Army during the ill-fated Nivelle Offensive on the Aisne (1917), but his troops failed to capture the Chemin des Dames. In an attempt to shift blame for the failed offensive, General Robert Nivelle relieved him of command.

Absolved, Mangin was brought back to command Tenth Army and halted the last of the Ludendorff Offensive (July 1918). He then launched the first counterattacks against the Germans. After the war he commanded French occupation troops in the Rhineland.

Mannerheim, Carl Gustav Emil (1867–1951) Finnish statesman and field marshal. Mannerheim began his military service in the Russian cavalry. He saw action in the 1904–05 Russo-Japanese War and then commanded cavalry units in Poland. During World War I he served on the Eastern Front against the Austrians. He commanded 12th Cavalry Division in the 1915 Galician campaign and participated in the 1916 Brusilov offensive. After

Romania joined the war, Mannerheim transferred to the Transylvanian Alps. Promoted lieutenant general (June 1917), he took command of VI Cavalry Corps.

After the Bolshevik Revolution, Mannerheim returned to Finland. During the 1918 War of Independence, he led the Finnish Defense Corps to victory against the Russians. He was then regent of Finland (1918–19) but resigned following adoption of a republican constitution. He was made field marshal (1933).

A master of defensive warfare, Mannerheim led Finland's vastly outnumbered forces against the Soviet Union in the 1939–40 Winter War and the 1941–44 Continuation War. Raised to the rank of marshal of Finland (1942), he was later president of Finland (1944–46).

Manstein, Erich Lewinski von (1887–1973) German field marshal. Manstein was commissioned in the army (1906). World War I interrupted his studies at the War Academy. He took part in the capture of Namur but was severely wounded on the Eastern Front and thereafter served in staff positions. He continued in the Reichswehr after the war and headed the Operations Section of the General Staff (1929). He commanded an infantry battalion (1933), was promoted colonel (1934), and was deputy to Chief of the General Staff General Ludwig Beck (1936). His opposition to Hitler's rearmament program led to his assignment to command 18th Infantry Division (1938). Already he was known as a superb tactician and planner.

Manstein was CofS of General Gerd von Rundstedt's Eastern Army Group in the invasion of Poland (September 1939), where he masterminded the decisive action on the Bzura River. He held the same post under Rundstedt in Army Group A for the invasion of the West (May 1940). Following the compromising of the original plan, he devised the *Sichelschnitt* strategy that brought swift victory. He

commanded XXXVIII Corps in that campaign.

After the fall of France, Manstein commanded LVI Corps (March 1941) for the invasion of the Soviet Union (22 June 1941) and then commanded Eleventh Army in the Crimea (July 1941). After his forces captured Sevastopol, Hitler promoted him field marshal (July 1942). Assigned to command Army Group Don (November 1942), he tried in vain to relieve Stalingrad. As commander of Army Group South, he captured Kharkov (March 1943). Disagreement with Hitler over strategy led to his relief from command (March 1944). Tried and convicted after the war, largely on Russian insistence (August 1949), he was sentenced to eighteen years in prison but was released in 1953. He then chaired a committee to advise the government of the Federal Republic on military reorganization (1955–56). Basil Liddell Hart called him the ablest German general of World War II.

Manteuffel, Baron Hasso Eccard von (1897–1978) German general. Manteuffel entered the army (1916) during World War I and saw action as a cavalry officer on the Western Front. He remained in the army after the war and joined the Panzer troops (1934). A lieutenant colonel on the outbreak of World War II, he held a range of staff positions under General Heinz Guderian. He distinguished himself during the invasion of the Soviet Union (22 June 1941) as a battalion and regimental commander in 7th Panzer Division. Transferred to North Africa (July 1943), he commanded "Division Manteuffel," which fought well until pinned at Bizerte. Evacuated, he was promoted brigadier general (May 1943). Given command of 7th Panzer Division in Russia, he was wounded shortly after taking up his command (August 1943). Promoted major general, he assumed command of the *Grossdeutschland* Division (March 1944).

Promoted lieutenant general (September), he commanded Fifth Panzer Army against General George Patton's U.S. Third Army in Lorraine. He opposed Hitler's larger plans for the Ardennes Offensive (Battle of the Bulge) (December 1944), in which his forces surrounded Bastogne before continuing to the Meuse River. He then commanded Third Panzer Army in the east (March 1945) and defended along the Oder, managing to surrender to the Americans (3 May 1945). Never intimidated by Hitler, he was one of Germany's best field commanders.

Mao Tse-tung (Mao Zedong) (1883–1976) Revolutionary war leader and leader of the People's Republic of China. Mao supported the 1911 Chinese Revolution, and following graduation from Hunan Normal School (1918), went to Peking (Beijing) and worked as a university librarian. He was one of the founders of the Chinese Communist Party (CCP) in Shanghai (1921). He disagreed with the party leadership and believed that revolution in China should originate with the peasants rather than the industrial workers, and he worked to organize the peasants in Hunan province. Nationalist Kuomintang (KMT, Guomindang) party leader Chiang Kai-shek (Jiang Jieshi) then purged the Communists and carried out a series of military campaigns against them. Forced to flee, Mao was one of the leaders of the 1934–35 Long March, establishing a new base at Yenan (Yan'an) in north China.

During 1937–45, Mao and his army fought the Japanese. He and his commanders developed "people's war": "The enemy advances, we retreat; the enemy camps, we harass; the enemy tires, we attack; the enemy retreats, we pursue." He forged the Red Army into a political weapon in which the soldiers lived and worked among the people and won their trust, "swimming among the people as fish swim in a sea."

After World War II, when Chiang renewed the struggle with the Communists, Mao and the Red Army were victorious (October 1949). He remained China's supreme ruler for more than a quarter of a century. He ordered Chinese troops into the Korean War (October 1950), and he was responsible for the effort to make China economically self-reliant, the disastrous Great Leap Forward (1959–61), as well as the bizarre 1966–69 Cultural Revolution. This visionary was one of history's deadliest tyrants; tens of millions of Chinese died as a direct result of his policies.

March, Peyton Conway (1864–1955) U.S. general. Commissioned in the artillery on graduation from West Point (1888), March held a variety of posts until the 1898 Spanish-American War. As a captain and battery commander, he participated in the occupation of the Philippines (1898). He returned there as a major of volunteers to fight in the 1900–02 Philippine-American War, and was promoted lieutenant colonel of volunteers (1900) and served as aide to General Arthur MacArthur. Discharged from volunteer service (1901), he served on the Army General Staff (1903–07) and was an observer in the 1904–05 Russo-Japanese War. Promoted major, he commanded a field artillery regiment, then served in the Adjutant General's Office (1911–16). Promoted colonel, he commanded 8th Field Artillery on the Mexican Border (1916).

Following U.S. entry into World War I, March was promoted brigadier general and given command of artillery in the AEF in France (June). He was promoted major general (September). Recalled to the U.S. as acting army CofS (March 1918), he assisted General Tasker Bliss and succeeded him as CofS (May) with the rank of general. A capable administrator, he streamlined procedures and oversaw the organization, training, and movement of U.S. forces to fight in France. Following the war, he directed the demobilization of U.S. forces, then retired (1921) as a permanent major general, but in 1930 was promoted general on the retired list.

Marschall, Wilhelm (1886–1976) German admiral. A submarine commander during World War I, Marschall commanded German naval forces off Spain during the Spanish Civil War (1937–38), then was chief of the operations staff of the navy just before the start of World War II, with responsibility for wartime planning.

As fleet commander (October 1939), Vice Admiral Marschall sortied with the *Scharnhorst* and *Gneisenau* (November). Promoted admiral (1940), he was relieved from command by Grand Admiral Erich Raeder for not strictly following the operational plan in German operations against Norway (April–June 1940). Marschall held that a commander at sea had to have freedom of action. Appointed commander of Group West (1942), he was promoted to full admiral (February 1943) and then held posts ashore.

Marseille, Hans-Joachim (1919–42) German fighter pilot. During World War II, Marseille shot down more British aircraft than any other pilot in history. Some rate him the best fighter pilot of the war. Although a number of other German pilots surpassed his number of kills (158 victories between 10 May 1940 and 27 September 1942), most of theirs came over a longer time period and on the Eastern Front.

All but the first seven of Marseille's victories were in North Africa. Commander of 3rd Squadron in JG-27, the youngest squadron captain (*Staffel Kapitan*) of the war, he shot down seventeen British aircraft in one day (1 September 1942), a tally surpassed by only one other Luftwaffe pilot. He was killed when he hit the tail section of his plane while bailing out following aerial combat.

Marshall, George Catlett (1880–1959) U.S. general and statesman. Marshall graduated from the Virginia Military Institute (1901) and was commissioned in the infantry (1902). He held a variety of assignments, including in the Philippines, and attended the Infantry and Cavalry School, Fort Leavenworth (1907). He was an instructor at the Staff College (1907–08).

Marshall established his reputation as a brilliant staff officer during World War I. Sent to France (June 1917), he served on the staff of AEF commander General John J. Pershing and planned the American offensives at St. Mihiel (September 1918) and the rapid redeployment of men for the Meuse–Argonne Offensive (September–November).

After the war Marshall was aide to Army commander CofS General Pershing (1919–24). He served briefly in China and was then deputy commander of the Infantry School at Fort Benning (1927–32). Promoted brigadier general (1936), he was then deputy chief of staff of the army (1938). He was promoted major general (July). President Franklin D. Roosevelt advanced Marshall over many more senior officers to become CofS of the army with the rank of temporary general (September 38). Promoted to general of the army (November 1944) he continued in that capacity, earning the title of "Organizer of Victory," until his retirement (November 1945).

President Harry S Truman recalled Marshall to serve as special envoy to China (1945–47) and secretary of state (1947–49). He was serving as president of the American Red Cross when Truman again recalled him (September 1950) as secretary of defense to preside over the 1950–53 Korean War military buildup. He held that post until he retired altogether (September 1951). He was awarded the Nobel Prize for Peace (1953), the first soldier so honored.

Marshall, Samuel Lyman Atwood (1900–77) U.S. army reserve officer and writer. Commissioned a reserve officer (1917) and known by his initials as "Slam," Marshall spent sixty years as a reserve officer, writing about warfare. During World War II he was U.S. Army chief historian for the European Theater of Operations, recruiting many of the historians and initiating the work that led to the extensive series, *U.S. Army in World War II*.

Marshall emphasized the need for direct interviews with participants as soon as possible after the events occurred. His work led to *Men Against Fire* (1947), in which he pointed out U.S. infantry combat performance problems and suggested solutions; the army adopted many of the latter.

Marshall was an army historian during the 1950–53 Korean War. During the Vietnam War, as a retired brigadier general he traveled several times to the war zone. Among his half-dozen books on Vietnam is a lessons-learned manual written by he and Colonel David Hackworth, two million copies of which were printed by the army. Although in recent years there has been criticism of both inconsistencies in data and his collection methods, he had a profound impact.

Marshall, Sir William Raine (1865–1939) British general. Marshall attended Sandhurst and was commissioned in the Sherwood Foresters (1885). He served in Ireland and Malta and fought in wars in India and South Africa, receiving two brevet promotions.

During World War I Marshall was a battalion commander in France (1914–15). He led a brigade of the 29th Division at Gallipoli and was promoted major general (June 1915). He then commanded 42nd, 29th, and 53rd Divisions, respectively. He commanded 27th Division at Salonika and then III (Indian) Corps in Mesopotamia, leading it in the campaign that defeated the Turkish Army at Kut-el-Amara (February 1917) and the capture of Baghdad (March). After the death of General Frederick Maude (November), he commanded the Mesopotamia Expedi-

tionary Force and took the surrender of the Turkish Army on the Upper Tigris (30 October 1918). After the war he commanded Southern Command, India. He remained there until 1923, retiring in 1924.

Martel, Giffard le Quesne (1889–1958) British general. Educated at the Royal Military Academy at Woolwich, Martel was commissioned in the engineers (1909). He served in France during World War I but returned to Britain (1916) to train tank crews. He returned to France in the new Tank Corps.

After the war Martel was an advocate of armored warfare and designed a "tankette" (1925–26). When World War II began, he took command of the 50th Northumbrian Division of the Territorial Army. During the German invasion of France and Benelux (May 1940), his attack on the flank of General Erwin Rommel's 7th Panzer Division helped bring about the German stop order that subsequently allowed the BEF to escape at Dunkerque.

Martel then commanded the newly formed Royal Armoured Corps (December 1940–September 1942). Promoted lieutenant general (1942) but unhappy with a loss of authority, he left on a tour of British army units in India and Burma. On his return he headed a military mission to Moscow, but returned to Britain (February 1944) and was knighted. Shortly after his return he lost an eye to a German bomb on London. He retired (1945) and wrote a controversial book, *Our Armoured Forces*.

Marwitz, Georg von der (1856–1929) German general. Marwitz was commissioned in the army (1875). He later attended the War Academy and held a variety of staff and command positions. He commanded a cavalry regiment (1900–05), then was CofS of XVIII Corps. Promoted brigadier general (1908) and major general (1911), he was inspector-general of all cavalry (from 1912).

At the start of World War I, Marwitz assumed command of a group of cavalry divisions and was soon thereafter promoted lieutenant general. After participating in a number of battles in Belgium and France, his cavalry group was dissolved (December 1914), and he was sent to the Eastern Front to command the new XXXVIII Reserve Corps. He fought in the Second Battle of the Masurian Lakes (February 1915), then was sent to the Carpathians to command a corps and again distinguished himself.

Marwitz took command of VI Corps on the Western Front (November 1915). Transferred to the East (summer 1916), he and his troops helped contain the Brusilov Offensive. At the end of the year he returned to France to command Second Army, which saw heavy fighting in the British attack at Cambrai (November 1917). His army then participated in the Spring 1918 Ludendorff Offensive, but failed to take Amiens. Attacked by British forces, his army suffered a major reverse (8 August) in what General Erich Ludendorff called "the black day of the German Army." He retained his command, but six weeks later was reassigned to Fifth Army in the Verdun sector. He retired in December 1918.

Massu, Jacques (1908–) French general. Massu entered the army and distinguished himself as a colonel in fighting in Indo-China and, as a general, commanded the elite 10th Parachute Division during the abortive 1956 Suez Invasion. Governor General of Algeria Robert Lacoste, faced with a general strike proclaimed in Algiers by the rebel National Liberation Front (FLN), invested Massu with civil power and ordered him to break the strike at any cost and by any means (January 1957). Operating with a ruthlessness that included torture of suspects, he and his paras won the so-called Battle of Algiers (January–March). Probably the most dra-

matic episode of the Algerian War, it ended with the paras in command of the city and the casbah, and the FLN terrorist cells broken.

When the French Army and European Algerians were convinced that the Paris government was about to give Algeria independence, Massu took the lead in the formation in Algiers of a committee of public safety (13 May 1958). This led to the end of the Fourth Republic and the return to power of Charles de Gaulle.

In December 1959 Massu made critical remarks to a journalist regarding de Gaulle, complaining that perhaps the army had made a mistake in bringing him back to power. When these became public, de Gaulle immediately recalled Massu to France and chastised him, but eventually gave him command of the army garrison at Metz. Massu remained a loyal Gaullist and refused to lend support to the January 1960 and April 1961 insurrections in Algiers, which were designed to force de Gaulle's hand and keep Algeria part of France.

Matsui, Iwane (1878–1948) Japanese general. Matsui graduated from both the Military Academy (1897) and Army Staff College (1904). He fought in Manchuria during the 1904–05 Russo-Japanese War, and then was a resident officer in China (1907–12; 1915–19) and France (1914–15). Promoted colonel (1918), he commanded a regiment (1919–21), then was a staff officer in the Siberian Expeditionary Army (1921–22). He served in Kwantung Army Headquarters in Manchuria (1922–24) and was promoted major general (1923). He then commanded a brigade (1924–25) and was chief of the Intelligence Division, Army General Staff (1925–28). Promoted lieutenant general (1927), he commanded 1st Division (1929–31). After serving as a delegate to the Geneva Disarmament Conference (1931–33), he was promoted general (1933).

In semi-retirement, Matsui served on the Supreme War Council (1924–35).

Recalled to active duty during the 1937–45 Sino-Japanese War, he commanded the Shanghai Expeditionary Army and took Shanghai (August–November 1937) and Nanking (Nanjing) (November–December). He then commanded Central China Army (December 1937–38). Returning to Japan (1938), he was a cabinet councillor (1938–40) and then retired. After the war he was tried on war crimes charges for having overall command of Japanese troops who killed an estimated 200,000 Chinese civilians in the "Rape of Nanking." Found guilty, he was executed.

Matsumoto, Yawara (1860–*c*.1925) Japanese admiral. Matsumoto graduated from the Naval Academy (1880) and the Naval Staff College (1889), then served with the navy General Staff (1892–96) and held various staff and command positions (1896–1904). In the 1904–05 Russo-Japanese War he commanded the battleship *Fuji* off Port Arthur, in the Battle of the Yellow Sea (10 August 1904), and in the Battle of Tsushima, when his ship fired the last salvos that sank the Russian battleship *Borodino* (27 May 1905).

Matsumoto was commanding Kure Naval Base when it was revealed (January 1914) that he had accepted a large bribe in conjunction with the order for the battleship *Kongō* from the British firm of Vickers (known in Japan as the Siemens scandal). Court-martialed, he was convicted and sentenced to prison as well as being stripped of his rank and decorations.

Maude, Sir Frederick Stanley (1864–1917) British general. Maude was educated at Eton and Sandhurst and joined the army (1884). He attended the Staff College, Camberley, and fought in the 1899–1902 Boer War. He then served as military secretary to the governor general of Canada (1901–05).

On the outbreak of World War I, Maude joined the staff of III Corps. He

was promoted to major general (June 1915) and took command of 31st Division. He then went to Gallipoli to command 13th Division (August 1915) and took it to Egypt after the evacuation. The division then went to Mesopotamia to take part in the aborted relief expedition to Kut-al-Amara (1916), then remained on the Tigris confronting the Turks. He then took command in Mesopotamia (September 1916) and spent the remainder of the year reequipping and training his troops. With a considerable numerical advantage, he went on the offensive (December) and drove the Turks back, recapturing Kut-al-Amara. He continued the advance and took Baghdad (March 1917). Promoted lieutenant general, he paused to consolidate but was stricken with cholera and died in November.

Maud'huy, Louis Ernest de (1857–1921) French general. Maud'huy entered the army (1879) and rose to serve on the General Staff, and was a general by 1912. At the beginning of World War I he commanded four divisions of I Cavalry Corps north of Arras. These soon came under heavy pressure from three German corps, but General Ferdinand Foch insisted that his newly named Tenth Army "hang on like lice." The army managed to repulse the German attack and even take the offensive for a time (September–December 1914).

Maud'huy then took command of the Vosges Army (April 1915). Here he oversaw a series of indecisive attacks and retreats along a limited front (summer 1915). He next commanded XV Army Corps and led it at Verdun (1916). Transferred to XI Army Corps (1917), he was its commander in fighting along the Aisnes River (May 1918). While faring no worse than most other French commanders in the face of a German offensive that advanced thirteen miles on its first day, he was sacked (June 1918). His military career closed in his hometown of

Metz, where he was appointed military governor of the city after the war.

Maunoury, Michel Joseph (1847–1923) French general. Maunoury graduated from the École Polytechnique and fought with distinction in the 1870–71 Franco-German War. He advanced steadily and was promoted brigadier general (1901) and major general (1906). He was serving as military governor of Paris and as a member of the Supreme War Council when he retired (1912).

Recalled to active duty at the start of World War I, Maunoury took command of the new Army of Lorraine of seven reserve divisions (mid-August). Designated Sixth Army, this force fought north of Paris but was pushed back into the city's defenses and came under command of Military Governor of Paris, General Joseph Galliéni, who urged an attack on Alexander von Kluck's right flank as the German First Army passed east of Paris. French Army commander General Joseph Joffre accepted this plan (5 September). Sixth Army then struck the German flank along the Ourcq River to open the Battle of the Marne. When the Germans began their retreat to the Aisne (9 September), Sixth Army joined the pursuit.

Maunoury's battlefield career ended (March 1915) when he was wounded while touring his front lines. Partially blinded, he served as military governor of Paris until he retired again in 1916.

Maxse, Sir Frederick Ivor (1862–1958) British general. Maxse joined the army in the infantry and saw service as a staff officer during the 1899–1902 Boer War. He worked his way up through the Coldstream Guards to command of the 1st Guards Brigade (1914).

Promoted major general (1915), Maxse took command of 18th Division. He insisted on thorough preparation and training, and his division had considerable success in the Battle of the Somme (July–November 1916). He then commanded

XVIII Corps. He became Inspector-General (Training) of British forces in France (early 1918) and advocated the new techniques of infiltration and maneuver. Maxse was promoted full general (1923) and retired in 1926.

Maxwell, Sir John Grenfell (1859–1929) British general. Maxwell was commissioned in the British Army from Sandhurst (1879). He served in Egypt and was military governor of Pretoria. Promoted major general (1906), he commanded British troops in Egypt (1908–12).

On the outbreak of World War I, Lieutenant General Maxwell headed the British military mission in France. Following the Battle of the Marne (September 1914), he resumed command of British forces in Egypt and repelled an attack by the Senussi in the Western desert (January 1916). Called home at his own request (March), he shortly thereafter took command in Ireland and helped crush the Easter Rebellion. Promoted general (June 1919), he retired in 1922.

Mayo, Henry Thomas (1856–1937) U.S. admiral. Mayo graduated from the Naval Academy (1876) and was promoted ensign (1879). He worked with U.S. Coast and Geodetic Survey and then participated in the 1883 Greely relief expedition to the Arctic. As navigator of the hydrographic survey ship *Bennington* (1895–98), he helped carry out the first survey of Pearl Harbor. Promoted to lieutenant commander (1899), commander (1905), and captain (1908), he then served on the Lighthouse Board.

As commander of divisions of the Atlantic Fleet (1913), he demanded a public apology, disciplinary action against those responsible, and a salute to the U.S. flag following an incident in which Mexican authorities seized an unarmed party of American sailors ashore at Tampico (9 April 1914). The Mexican government's refusal to comply with these demands led President Woodrow Wilson to order seizure of the customs house at Vera Cruz, ultimately forcing from power the reactionary dictator of Mexico, General Victoriano Huerta.

Appointed to command the Atlantic Fleet with the rank of vice admiral (1916), Mayo held this key post during World War I. He then chaired the navy's General Board until his retirement from the navy (1920). He was advanced to admiral on the retired list in 1930.

Mazaki, Jinzaburō (1876–1956) Japanese general. A graduate of the Military Academy (1897) and Army Staff College (1907), Mazaki was trained as an infantry officer. Following study in Germany (1911–14), he served with the Inspectorate General of Military Education (1916–20). Promoted colonel (1918), he served in the Army Ministry (1920–21). Commander of the 1st Imperial Guards Regiment (1921–22), he was then promoted major general (1922) and commanded a brigade (1922–23). He was first on the staff of the Military Academy (1923–24), then its commandant (1925–27). Promoted lieutenant general (1927), he commanded 8th Division (1927–29), then 1st Division (1929–31). He was then vice chief of the General Staff (1933–44). Promoted general (1933), he became inspector general of military education (1934–36). Identified with the army ultranationalist Imperial Way faction, he was forced into retirement (1936) by Control Faction leader General Tetsuzan Nagata, an event that led to Nagata's assassination and the Young Officer's Rebellion (26 February 1936).

Mellenthin, Friedrich-Wilhelm von (1904–97) German general. Mellenthin enlisted in the 7th Cavalry Regiment (1924) and was commissioned in the cavalry (1928). He attended the War Academy (1935–37), and held principally staff positions.

When World War II began, Mellenthin was an intelligence officer assigned to III Corps. He then served on Rommel's staff

in North Africa and was on the Eastern Front as chief of staff for XLVIII Panzer Corps. When his commander, General Hermann Balck, took command of Fourth Panzer Army, Colonel Mellenthin accompanied him as his chief of staff (August 1944). He again went with Balck to Lorraine when the latter took over Army Group G (September). A run-in with the army high command led to Mellenthin's assignment to the front as a regimental commander.

Brigadier General Mellenthin was CofS of Fifth Panzer Army (March 1945). He was captured while trying to escape the Ruhr pocket in May. Held prisoner for two years after the war, following his release he became a businessman and emigrated to South Africa. Among his books are *Panzer Battles* and *German Generals of World War II*.

Meretskov, Kirill Afanasyevich (1897–1968) Soviet marshal. Meretskov joined the Communist Party (1917); he led units in the 1918–20 Civil War and was wounded. He then attended the Frunze Military Academy and was an advisor in Spain during the 1936–39 Civil War. During the 1939–40 Russo-Finnish War his forces failed to breach the Mannerheim Line and Josef Stalin appointed Semen Timoshenko over him. He became chief of the General Staff (1940), but was soon removed to head combat training, where he stressed armor and mechanized forces patterned after those of Germany.

Following the German invasion (22 June 1941), Meretskov took command of the Volkhov Front with the task of raising the siege of Leningrad, but was unsuccessful. He was then downgraded to command Thirty-Third Army before being reinstated to command the Volkhov Front. Following the lifting of the siege (January 1944), he was given charge of driving Finland from the war. On accomplishing this, he was promoted to marshal (October). He ended the war as commander the 1st Far Eastern Front that forced the surrender of the Japanese Kwantung Army in Manchuria.

Merrill, Frank Dow (1903–55) U.S. general. Merrill enlisted in the army and served in Panama (1922–25). He was commissioned in the cavalry on graduation from West Point (1929). He attended the Ordnance School (1931–32) and the Cavalry School (1934–35), and then was an instructor at the latter (1935–38). He was then assistant military attaché in Tokyo (1938–40). Promoted temporary major (October 1941), he served on the intelligence staff of General Douglas MacArthur in the Philippines. He was on assignment in Burma when the Japanese attacked Pearl Harbor (7 December 1941).

Merrill remained in Burma on the staff of Lieutenant General Joseph Stilwell and retreated with him to India in the first Burma campaign (May 1942). Promoted temporary lieutenant colonel (May), he organized and commanded the 5307th Composite Force, more commonly known as "Merrill's Marauders." Trained in jungle warfare in India, it was to be used for long-range pentrations. Heart problems prevented him from actually commanding it for long during the effort to reopen the Burma Road (February 1944).

Transferred to head a liaison group to the Southwest Asia Command in Ceylon (August 1944), Merrill was promoted major general (November). He was then CofS of Tenth Army on Okinawa (April–October 1945). After the war he was CofS of Sixth Army at San Francisco (1946–47) and then headed a military advisory mission to the Philippines (February 1947). He retired in July 1948.

Messerschmitt, Wilhelm (1898–1978) German aircraft designer. Trained at the Munich Technical College, "Willi" Messerschmitt learned to fly at fifteen and became a designer for the Bavarian Aircraft Works. He then founded in Augsburg the Messerschmitt Aircraft Company (1923). The company at first built sport planes and produced the first German all-metal aircraft (1926). Munich's Technical College awarded him the honorary title of professor of aircraft construction (1930).

A major element in the growth and development of the German Luftwaffe (air force), Messerschmitt designed many aircraft that saw combat in World War II. His most successful by far was the Me-109 (also known as the Bf-109 for the production firm). First produced in 1935, it was easily the most important German fighter of World War II. More of this aircraft (35,000) were built than any other fighter of the war (the Russian Yak-1 was second at 30,000). The Me-109 set a record for speed (some 468 mph) that stood until 1969. Among other Messerschmitt designs were the Me-210, Me-410, and the first jet fighter, the Me-262. After the war a German court convicted him as a Nazi "sympathizer" (1948). Eight years later he was designing aircraft for the German Air Force and NATO (1956).

Metaxas, John (1871–1940) Greek general and dictator. Commissioned in the army on graduation from the Greek Military Academy (1890), Metaxas studied at the Military Academy of Berlin and served on the Greek General Staff during the 1912–13 Balkan Wars. He then became army CofS (1913).

At the beginning of World War I, Metaxas favored an alliance with the Central Powers. He left Greece following the forced abdication of Constantine (1917) and returned with the King (1920). In 1936 he seized power and became dictator, with the justification of preventing a Communist takeover. During his rule the Greeks successfully repelled the 1940 Italian invasion. Metaxas died (January 1940) before Germany intervened.

Methuen, Paul Sanford, 3rd Baron Methuen (1845–1932) British general. Educated at Eton, Methuen was commissioned (1864). He served as a staff officer in the 1873–74 Second Ashanti War and 1882 brief war with Egypt. Following additional African service, he went to India. A competent staff officer, he proved hopelessly inadequate in command of troops. As a major general, he commanded 1st Division in the Indian corps sent to South Africa under General Sir Redvers Buller (November 1899) in the 1899–1902 Boer War. His efforts to clear the railroad to Kimberley and relieve its besieged garrison in frontal attacks were repulsed (late November–December). When his forces were then immobile for two months, General Lord Roberts reduced him in rank to brigadier general (February 1900). Following the taking of Pretoria and Johannesburg (May–June), he commanded forces trying to chase down Boer commandoes. Failing in an attempt to take Christiaan De Wet's forces, he was surprised by Jacobus de la Rey. His own newly recruited troops panicked and left him wounded on the field to be captured (7 March 1902), the only British general taken prisoner in the war.

Methuen was later CinC, South Africa (1909–15), governor of Malta (1915–19), and governor and constable of the Tower of London until his death.

Meyer, Kurt (1911–61) German SS general. Meyer, a policeman, joined the SS (1931) and the *Leibstandarte Adolf Hitler* (LAH) (1934). During World War II he fought with distinction in the invasion of Poland (September 1939) and received command of the LAH motorcycle reconnaissance battalion. Known for his aggressive and resolute command style, he participated in the invasions of France and Benelux (May 1940) and Greece (April 1941). He fought in the invasion of the Soviet Union (22 June 1941) as a regimental commander. In Normandy (1944), he led 12th SS Panzer (*Hitlerjugend*) Division, the youngest *SS-gruppenführer* (major general) and division commander. Known for its fanaticism

and refusal to surrender, the division played a key role in holding the northern edge of the Falaise Pocket long enough to allow much of the German Seventh Army to escape east.

After the war Meyer was tried and convicted of the deaths of sixty-four British and Canadian POWs (December 1945). The sentence was commuted to life in prison, and he was released because of poor health (1954).

Michaelis, John Hersey (1912–88) U.S. general. Michaelis served in the army for a year before attending West Point. On graduation (1936), he was commissioned in the infantry. Among other assignments, he served in the Philippines. During World War II he served with the 502nd Parachute Infantry Regiment and the 101st Airborne Division, which he ultimately commanded (1944). Wounded in the Battle of the Bulge (December 1944), on recuperation he was promoted colonel and appointed CofS to 101st Division commander, Major General Maxwell Taylor.

After the war Michaelis reverted to lieutenant colonel. Assigned to Washington (1945), he was then aide to Army CofS General Dwight D. Eisenhower (1946–48), then assigned to Eighth Army headquarters in Japan. At the start of the 1950–53 Korean War, he took command of the 27th Infantry Regiment, which soon had the reputation as one of the best combat units in Korea. Promoted colonel, "Iron Mike" was then advanced to brigadier general (February 1951) and assistant commander of the 25th Infantry Division. At age thirty-eight, he was the youngest U.S. Army general.

Michaelis became commandant of cadets at West Point (1952). He subsequently commanded U.S. Army Alaska, V Corps, Allied Land Forces, Southeast Europe, and Fifth U.S. Army. He then commanded the United Nations Command and U.S. forces in Korea (1969–72). He retired in 1972.

Michel, Victor (1850–1937) French general. Michel held several field positions before his appointment to the Supreme War Council (1907). He then became its vice president and commander-in-chief designate (January 1911). Anticipating the German Schlieffen plan, he rejected French plans to concentrate against Alsace and Lorraine. He wanted to reduce French forces there in favor of additional forces along the entire Franco-Belgian border. To obtain the manpower, Michel sought to utilize reserves on the front lines.

Much of the High Command rejected these proposals, and Michel was forced to resign (December 1911). He served the next two years as military governor of Paris but failed to prepare the city adequately for the expected German onslaught. He was then relieved of his command and placed in the inactive reserve.

Micheler, Joseph Alfred (1861–1931) French general. Micheler commanded the French Tenth Army in the Battle of the Somme (July–November 1916). His performance there earned him command of the Reserve Army Group. During the planning stages for General Robert Nivelle's 1917 Champagne offensive, he and some other French generals questioned its prospects of success. When Nivelle threatened to quit, the opposition collapsed and the offensive went forward to defeat.

When the Reserve Army Group was dissolved (May), Micheler commanded Fifth Army. He then criticized French Army commander General Henri-Philippe Pétain's "inertia" and orders for a defense in depth (Autumn 1917). The result was nearly a disaster. When the Ludendorff Offensive opened (March 1918), the German First and Seventh Armies attacked his Fifth Army and General Denis Duchêne's Sixth Army along the Chemin des Dames. The early German success was in large part because most French troops there were forward in shallow trenches.

Micheler and Duchêne were then both dismissed.

Middleton, Troy H. (1889–1976) U.S. general. Middleton graduated from Mississippi A&M College (1909) and enlisted in the army (1910). He was then commissioned in the infantry (1912). When World War I began he was assigned to training but, following U.S. entry into the war (April 1917), he was promoted major and sent to France (May), where he was appointed a battalion commander (July 1918). He swiftly proved his ability under fire and was promoted to temporary lieutenant colonel and colonel.

Following the war Middleton briefly served with the occupation forces in Germany. Reduced to the permanent rank of captain, he was then instructor at the Infantry School at Fort Benning. He graduated from the Advanced Infantry Course, the Command and General Staff School, and the Army War College. He retired from the army in 1937.

Middleton returned to active duty (1941) as assistant division commander of the 45th Infantry Division and then its commander. He fought with it in the 1943 invasions of Sicily and Salerno, Italy. Following leave for a knee injury, he returned to command VIII Corps after D-Day and enjoyed success in Operation COBRA and in clearing the Brittany Peninsula. One of the most effective U.S. corps commanders of the war, he was absolutely unflappable. VIII Corps bore the brunt of fighting in the Battle of the Bulge (December 1944–January 1945), and it was his decision to hold the road hub of Bastogne. He retired as a lieutenant general in August 1945.

Mihailović, Draža (1893–1946) Yugoslav general. Following the rapid German occupation of Yugoslavia (April 1941), Colonel Mihailović, who had been inspector general for fortifications, organized a guerrilla force composed of some Yugoslav military units and other fighters.

These called themselves Čhetniks, a term originally used by Serbian rebels against the Turks.

King Peter's government-in-exile promoted Mihailović full general and named him minister of war (December 1941). His conservative views and desire to restore the previous regime, however, led many Yugoslavs to support a second, rival underground in Yugoslavia: the Partisans, led by Josip Broz, known as Tito. His followers were not unwilling to risk reprisals by the Germans on the Yugoslav population. The two rival resistance groups frequently fought each other. In part because of greater Partisan willingness to engage the German occupiers, the British, who provided all military aid to the Yugoslav resistance, shifted this to the Partisans (1943), a key factor in the latter's ability to liberate much of Yugoslavia at the end of the war.

Captured by the Partisans after the war, Mihailović and other leading Čhetniks were brought to trial on trumped-up charges of collaboration with the Germans and Italians. Despite vigorous Western protests, they were condemned and executed in July 1946.

Mikawa, Gun'ichi (1890–1981) Japanese admiral. A graduate of the Naval Academy (1910) and Naval Staff College (1917, 1924), Commander Mikawa was part of the Japanese delegation to the League of Nations (1929–30). Promoted captain (1930), he was naval attaché in Paris (1930–31), taught at the Naval Academy (1931), and held cruiser and battleship commands (1931–36). Promoted rear admiral, he was CofS of the Combined Fleet (1936). Appointed commander of 3rd Battleship Division (September 1941), he had charge of the Support Force of 3rd Battleship and 8th Cruiser Divisions for the attack on Pearl Harbor (December 1941).

Mikawa then commanded the newly formed Eighth Fleet and Outer South Seas Force at Rabaul (July 1942). He thus had command of Japanese naval forces in the battles off Guadalcanal (August–November), and he inflicted the worst defeat in U.S. Navy history in the Battle of Savo Island (8–9 August), sinking three U.S. and one Australian heavy cruiser and a destroyer, with none of his own ships lost. He commanded the covering force for the Japanese carriers in the Battle of the Eastern Solomons (23–25 August). After the Japanese were forced to withdraw from the Solomons, he commanded the Southwest Area Fleet and Thirteenth Air Fleet at Manila (June 1944). Concurrently commander of the Southern Expeditionary Fleet (August–November 1944), he was attached to the Naval General Staff until he transferred to the reserves in May 1945.

Milch, Erhard (1892–1972) German air force field marshal. Milch was an artillery lieutenant at the beginning of World War I but became an air observer. Although not a pilot, he came to command a fighter squadron as a captain (October 1918). He left the military (1921) for a career in civil aviation and became chief executive of the national airline, Deutsche Lufthansa (1929). A close associate of Hermann Göring, when the National Socialists came to power he became state secretary of the Air Ministry (1933).

Göring was nominal head of the Luftwaffe (air force), but Milch was its true architect. His long experience in civil aviation and organizational skills were invaluable in rapidly building the world's most powerful air arm (1939). Named inspector general of the Luftwaffe (1939), his only operational command was Air Fleet Five during the Norwegian campaign (1940). Promoted field marshal (July 1940), following the suicide of Ernst Udet (1941) he became director of Air Armament, tripling aircraft production and improving maintenance. He was, however, increasingly estranged from Göring and Hitler, who refused to believe his realistic assessments. They also rejected his conclusion that the key to Germany's survival was an umbrella of fighter air-craft to protect industrial production.

Milch pushed development of the V-1 flying bomb and the Me-262, which he wanted as a fighter rather than a bomber. Removed from most of his posts by Göring (July 1944), after the war he was sentenced to life in prison for war crimes (1947), mainly the utilization of forced labor, but he was released in 1955.

Milne, Sir Archibald Berkeley (1855–1938) British admiral. The only surviving son of then Admiral of the Fleet Sir Alexander Milne, Milne briefly attended Wellington College and then entered the navy (1869). He lacked ambition, but he was an intimate at court and owed his promotions primarily to connections. Promoted rear admiral (1904), vice admiral (1908), and admiral (1911), he was appointed CinC in the Mediterranean (November 1912).

Just before World War I began (August 1914), the Admiralty ordered Milne to watch for two German warships commanded by Admiral Wilhelm Souchon, the battle cruiser *Goeben* and light cruiser *Breslau*. Assuming they would head west, Milne sent his own battle cruisers *Indomitable* and the *Indefatigable* to locate them. They were spotted on August 4, but neither side was technically at war until the expiration at midnight of the British ultimatum to the German government. Never suspecting the Germans might make for the Dardanelles, Milne failed to take decisive action and the two German ships then escaped to Constantinople. Their arrival there helped bring Turkey into the war on the side of the Central Powers.

The Admiralty exonerated Milne of any blame in the escape of the *Goeben* and *Breslau*, in part in recognition of its own failures in the affair, but press criticism was severe and Milne was never employed again by the Admiralty. He retired at the end of the war, and in 1921 published a book defending his actions.

Milne, George Francis, 1st Baron Milne (1866–1948) British field marshal. Milne graduated from the Royal Military Academy at Woolwich (1885) and Staff College at Camberley (1897). He directed artillery at the Battle of Omdurman (1898) and was a brevet lieutenant colonel on Kitchener's intelligence staff during the 1899–1902 Boer War.

Milne commanded 4th Division artillery (1913) and at the beginning of World War I participated in the Battles of Le Cateau, the Marne, and the Aisne. Promoted brigadier general (October 1914), he was advanced to major general on the staff of Second Army (1915). He was then appointed to command 27th Division in Salonika under overall Allied commander General Maurice Sarrail, and in January 1916 commanded all British forces under Sarrail and later General Franchet d'Esperey. He had only a small force decimated by sickness, and Chief of the Imperial General Staff Sir William Robertson would not permit him to undertake offensive action until April 1917. His troops suffered heavy losses in fighting near Lake Dorian, and did not advance again against Bulgaria until 1918.

After the war Milne's troops occupied Constantinople. He remained in Turkey until 1920, when he was promoted general. He took over the Eastern Command (1922) and was appointed chief of the Imperial General Staff (1926). Promoted field marshal (1928), he retired in 1933 as Baron Milne of Salonika and Rubislaw, county of Aberdeen. He was active in the Home Guard during World War II.

Mišić, Živojin (1855–1921) Serbian field marshal. Mišić fought in the 1877 Serbian-Turkish War, the 1885 Serbian-Bulgarian War, and the 1912–13 First and Second Balkan Wars. He was on General Radomir Putnik's staff during the 1908–09 Bosnian annexation crisis. He commanded First Army defending against Austro-Hungary (November 1914) and won the decisive Battle of Rudnik (December

1914) that forced the withdrawal of Austro-Hungarian troops from Serbia. In the winter of 1915 he participated in the epic retreat of the Serbian Army to the Adriatic coast.

Following his relocation to Corfu with the remnants of the Serbian Army, Mišić performed staff and political duties. He then commanded First Army at Salonika (August 1917–June 1918) until he became CofS and commander of the Serbian armed forces. He received the support of new French commander, General Franchet d'Esperey, for an offensive against the Bulgarian line and smashed it in mid-September, leading to Bulgaria's capitulation that same month. The Serbian army re-entered Belgrade (1 November). After the war he aggressively promoted Yugoslav nationalism.

Misu, Sōtarō (1855–1921) Japanese admiral. Misu entered the Naval Academy (1871) and as a cadet participated in the 1874 expedition to Taiwan and suppression of the 1877 Satsuma Rebellion. Following graduation from the academy (1878), he held assignments both ashore and afloat; by the 1894–95 Sino-Japanese War he had charge of the navy's personnel section. Promoted captain (late 1894), he commanded cruisers, then a battleship. Promoted rear admiral (1901), during the 1904–05 Russo-Japanese War he commanded 1st Battle Division, First Fleet and saw action in the blockade of Port Arthur (February–June 1904) and battles of the Yellow Sea (10 August) and Tsushima (27 May 1905). Wounded at Tsushima, he lost an eye and was thereafter known as the "One-Eyed Dragon." Promoted vice admiral (January 1905), after the war he held posts ashore, including vice chief of the Navy General Staff (1906–09). He was then made a baron (1907). Promoted admiral (1913), he retired in 1914.

Mitchell, William Lendrum (1879–1936) U.S. general. Mitchell fought in the 1898

Spanish-American War as a private and then became a Signal Corps lieutenant. He joined its Aviation Section as a pilot (1915), then was sent to France as an observer in World War I (1916). When the United States entered the war (April 1917), he became air officer for the AEF as a lieutenant colonel. Promoted colonel (May 1918), he had charge of air operations in the Meuse–Argonne Offensive (September–November) as a brigadier general and led several hundred bombers in attacks behind German lines. He was convinced that aviation would be decisive in future wars.

As assistant chief of the Air Service (March 1919), Mitchell was a vocal proponent of military aviation and crusader for an independent air force, which alienated many in the army and navy. Off the Virginia Capes, his bombers sank the former German battleship *Ostfriesland* (21 June 1921), the first time a battleship had been sunk from the air.

Mitchell's uncompromising and strident advocacy of air power led to his demotion to colonel (April 1925). When the navy airship *Shenandoah* crashed in a storm (3 September), he publicly accused the Navy and War Departments of "criminal negligence." This brought his court martial and conviction for insubordination (December), and he chose to resign (February 1926). Over the next decade he published three books and gave frequent speeches in support of air power. He is considered by many to be the founder of the U.S. Air Force.

Mitscher, Marc Andrew (1887–1947) U.S. admiral. Mitscher graduated from Annapolis (1910) and then served in the Pacific and Caribbean. He became a pilot (1916) and thereafter was identified with the development of U.S. Navy aviation. After a variety of assignments, he served on the carriers *Langley* and *Saratoga*. He commanded the carrier *Hornet* in the raid on Tokyo (April 1941) and Battle of Midway (June). Promoted vice admiral (July

1942), he commanded aircraft in the Guadalcanal campaign and all Allied aircraft in the Solomons. He took command (January 1944) of Fast Carrier Task Force (TF 58 or 38) in operations in the Marshall Islands, Truk, and New Guinea. Promoted vice admiral (March 1944), he directed carrier operations in the Battle of the Philippine Sea (June). His carriers also participated in the Battle of Leyte Gulf (October) and the Iwo Jima (February–March 1945) and Okinawa (April–June) campaigns. He was probably the top carrier admiral of the war. Appointed deputy chief of naval operations (Air) (July 1945), he was promoted admiral (March 1946) and commanded Eighth Fleet and the Atlantic Fleet until his death.

Miyazaki, Shigesaburo (1895–1965) Japanese general. Known as perhaps the most skillful and tenacious tactical commander in the Imperial Japanese Army, Miyazaki commanded 16th Regiment in the 2nd Division and executed the successful final tactical night offensive against Soviet forces in the Nomonhan Incident (early September 1939).

Miyazaki then commanded a regiment of the 31st Division under Sato Kotoku. He fought in the siege of Kohima (spring 1944), and his unit was the last to evacuate the area, guarding the rear of the withdrawing Fifteenth Army.

Miyazaki's final post was CinC of 54th Division of Twenty-Eighth Army in southern Burma, where he had several tactical successes against numerically superior forces and was able to extract half of his division in the Sittang River breakout (March–April 1944).

Model, Walther (1891–1945) German field marshal. Model joined the army (1909) and ended World War I as a captain. Continuing in the Reichswehr, he joined the Nazi party. Promoted brigadier general, March 1938), he commanded IV Corps in the invasion of Poland (Sep-

tember 1939). Promoted major general (April 1940), he led 3rd Panzer Division in the invasion of France and Benelux (May 1940). Promoted lieutenant general (October 1941), he commanded XXXI Panzer Corps. Promoted full general (February 1942), he then commanded Ninth Army.

Extremely capable, Model was one of Adolf Hitler's favorite generals and became known as "Hitler's Fireman." Slavishly loyal to Hitler throughout the war, he nonetheless convinced him to delay Operation CITADEL, which resulted in the Battle of Kursk (July 1943). The delay allowed the Russians time to reinforce.

Model briefly commanded Army Group North (January–March 1944). Promoted field marshal (March 1944), he commanded Army Group Center. Hitler then appointed him commander of Army Group B and CinC (August 1944). In September he reverted to command Army Group B only and blunted the drive to take Arnhem. He commanded the Ardennes Offensive (Battle of the Bulge) (December 1944–January 1945), but his army group was caught in the Ruhr pocket and forced to surrender (March 1945), where he committed suicide.

Moffett, William A. (1869–1933) U.S. admiral. Moffett graduated from Annapolis (1890) and had a variety of assignments. During the 1898 Spanish-American War he participated in the capture of Guam and bombardment of Manila. As captain of the cruiser *Chester*, he took part in the 1914 occupation of Vera Cruz and was awarded the Medal of Honor. During World War I he established training procedures for naval recruits.

Appointed director of naval aviation (1921), Moffett became chief of the new Bureau of Aeronautics (July). He held that post for three consecutive four-year tours and is often known as the Father of U.S. Naval Aviation. As a rear admiral, he logged sufficient flying time to qualify as a naval observer. He died in the crash of the airship *Akron* off Lakehurst, New Jersey on 4 April 1933.

Mola Vidal, Emilio (1887–1937) Spanish general. Graduating from the Toledo Military Academy (1909), he joined the army in Morocco. During fighting in North Africa, he was promoted colonel (1926), then brigadier general (1927). He served as director of state security under King Alfonso XIII and then was military commander of Pamplona.

Mola was one of the chief organizers of a rightist effort to overthrow the legitimately elected Republican government of Spain. On outbreak of the rebellion (July 1936), he took command of rebel (Nationalist) forces in northern Spain and carried out atrocities against those supporting the Republican cause.

In advancing on Madrid, Mola coined the term "fifth column," when he announced that he had four armed columns marching on the capital and that a fifth column would rise up from within the city. Failing to take Madrid in a speedy advance on the outset of the rebellion, which would have ended the Civil War much more quickly, he then concentrated on the northern front, especially in the Basque region. He was killed when his plane crashed during a flight from Burgos to Salamanca.

Mölders, Werner (1913–41) German air force general. Mölders joined the Luftwaffe in 1935. Initially a flight instructor, he led a squadron of Fighter Group JG-88 in the Condor Legion during the 1936–39 Spanish Civil War. He was the leading German ace in Spain with fourteen kills.

On the outbreak of World War II (September 1939), Mölders served in JG-53 in the invasion of Poland (September 1939), and JG-51 in the invasion of France and Benelux (May 1940) and Battle of Britain (1940). An expert in air tactics, he developed the *Schwarm* "Finger Four" flying formation used by the Ger-

mans and, later, the Royal Air Force. He was credited with fifty-eight kills in the Battle of Britain. He commanded JG-51 in the invasion of the Soviet Union (June 1941) and was ultimately credited with 115 kills, the first pilot in history with more than 100 aerial victories. Promoted at only age twenty-eight to lieutenant general and appointed inspector of fighter aircraft, he directed air operations over the Crimea. He died on his way to the funeral of General Ernst Udet when the plane in which he was a passenger developed engine problems and crashed (November 1941).

Moltke, Graf Helmuth Johannes Ludwig von (1848–1916) German general. Nephew of Helmuth von Moltke ("the Elder"), who led Prussian armies to victory over Austria and France, Moltke joined the Prussian Army (1869) but showed little of his uncle's innovative genius. He was adjutant to his uncle and the Kaiser and held a variety of field commands. Promoted colonel (1895) and brigadier general (1899), in 1900 he was a major general commanding the 1st Guards Division. He was then quartermaster general (1904). Kaiser William II named him chief of the General Staff, succeeding General Alfred von Schlieffen (1906). Moltke accepted the post with reservations, knowing he was incapable of quick decisions.

As German Army CofS, Moltke believed war with the Entente powers was inevitable, and pushed for war sooner rather than later. His major contribution to World War I was his ill-conceived revisions of the Schlieffen Plan. Because he feared a French thrust into Alsace and Lorraine, he strengthened the German left wing at the expense of the right. This made it much more difficult for the right wing's encircling movement to succeed. Then, with the offensive already under way, Moltke exacerbated matters by taking two corps and a division from the right wing and sending them east against the Russians (25 August 1914). He exercised little leadership during the fighting and, following the critical Battle of the Marne, was relieved of his post and demoted to deputy CofS on 14 September.

Monash, Sir John (1865–1931) Australian general. Monash graduated from Melbourne University (1891). As an engineer he pioneered construction of reinforced concrete bridges. He also served as a militia officer, reaching the rank of colonel. When World War I began, he joined the Australian Imperial Force (AIF). He commanded the 4th Infantry Brigade at Gallipoli (April 1915–January 1916) and took part in the British advance across the Sinai (January–September 1916). He then commanded the 3rd Australian Division in France (1916–1918). Promoted lieutenant general, he replaced General Sir William Birdwood as commander of the Australian Army Corps (March 1918). He earned praise for careful planning, organization, and leadership, especially in the last battles of the war when he helped plan the final British offensive.

Called "the most outstanding Australian general" of the war and "the greatest Jewish soldier of modern times," after the war he was active in Zionist organizations. Monash University in Melbourne is named for him.

Monro, Sir Charles Carmichael, baronet (1860–1929) British general. Monro joined the army (1879) and saw service in various colonial actions. A major during the 1899–1902 Boer War, he served on the army staff. He then became commandant of the Hythe School of Musketry (1901–07), where he was promoted to colonel (1903).

Promoted major general (1910), Monro went to France at the beginning of World War I in command of 2nd Division in I Corps. He took part in the retreat from Mons and the First Battle of Ypres. Promoted lieutenant general (December) and given command of I Corps, which he

led with distinction in the Battles of Aubers Ridge, Festubert, and Givenchy, he then took command of the newly formed Third Army (July 1915).

Sent to command of the Mediterranean Expeditionary Force (October 1915), on arrival Monro immediately recommended evacuation of Allied forces from Gallipoli. Winston Churchill said, "He came, he saw, he capitulated." Monro's evacuation plan was brilliantly executed.

Monro returned to the Western Front to command First Army. He then became CinC India (October 1916) and increased the number of Indian forces fighting in the war. Created a baronet (1921), he was then governor and commander of Gibraltar (1923–28).

Montgomery, Alfred Eugene (1891–1961) U.S. admiral. Montgomery graduated from Annapolis (1912) and was commissioned (1914). He transferred to submarines (1915) and became a naval aviator (1922). He commanded naval air stations at Seattle (1930–32) and San Diego (1938–39), and then took command of a carrier (1940). Promoted rear admiral (May 1942), he then commanded the naval air station at Corpus Christi, Texas.

Montgomery took command of Carrier Division 17 in Task Force 50 (August 1943) and carried out strikes on Wake Island and Rabaul. He also supported U.S. landings at Tarawa and in the Marshall Islands. His units also made the first attacks on Truk. As commander of Carrier Division 3 in Task Force 58, he participated in the Marianas Campaign and the Battles of the Philippine Sea (June 1944) and Leyte Gulf (October). In early 1945 he returned to the United States and headed Fleet Air West Coast until the end of the war.

Promoted vice admiral, Montgomery commanded Fifth Fleet (1946–49), then the Naval Operating Base Bermuda, until his retirement in June 1951.

Montgomery, Sir Bernard Law, 1st Viscount Montgomery of Alamein (1887–1976) British field marshal. Montgomery graduated from Sandhurst (1908) and joined the Royal Warwickshire Regiment. During World War I he was badly wounded in the First Battle of Ypres (October–November 1914). Following recovery, he was on training duty in Britain but returned to France as a major for the Battle of the Somme (July–November 1916). He held other assignments, ending the war as a staff officer in the 47th Division.

Following occupation duty in Germany, Montgomery graduated from the Staff College at Camberley (1921) and was instructor there (1926). In 1929 he rewrote the infantry training manual. He was then stationed in the Middle East, commanded a regiment, was chief instructor at the Quetta Staff College (1934–37), and commanded 9th Brigade (1937–38). He was then in Palestine commanding the 8th Division (1938–39).

When World War II began, Montgomery took command of the 3rd Division and distinguished himself in rearguard actions during the retreat to Dunkerque and evacuation (May–June 1940). He then commanded V Corps (July), XII Corps (April 1941), and Southeastern Army (November). He helped plan the disastrous Dieppe raid (19 August 1942). He left to command First Army in the invasion of North Africa, but instead took command of Eighth Army in Egypt following the death of General W.H.E. Gott (August) and repulsed General Erwin Rommel's attack at Alam Halfa (August–September 1942).

Montgomery rebuilt Eighth Army's morale. Known for his concern for his men's welfare, he was also deliberate as a commander, rather than bold and daring. In the Second Battle of El Alamein (October–November), his superior forces defeated German and Italian forces under General Erwin Rommel, driving them west. He was promoted general (November), but his less-than-rapid advance allowed the bulk of Axis forces to escape. Following the Axis surrender in Tunisia (May 1943), he led Eighth Army in the invasions of Sicily (July) and Italy (September). He returned to Britain to assume command of land forces in the Normandy invasion (6 June 1944) until General Dwight Eisenhower moved his headquarters to France (September). Promoted field marshal (September), he sought to end the war by the end of the year with an invasion of Germany at Arnhem, Operation MARKET-GARDEN, which however failed (September). He defended the north shoulder in the Battle of the Ardennes (Battle of the Bulge) (December 1944) and then directed the drive into northern Germany.

After the war Montgomery commanded British occupation troops in Germany (May 1945–June 1946), and then was chief of the Imperial General Staff (1946–48), chairman of the Western European commanders-in-chief (1948–51), and commander of NATO forces in Europe and deputy supreme commander (1951–58). He retired in September 1958.

Moreell, Ben (1892–1976) U.S. admiral. Moreell graduated with a civil engineering degree from Washington University, St. Louis (1913). He joined the navy's Civil Engineering Corps as a lieutenant (jg) (1917) and spent World War I in the Azores. He then served in the Bureau of Yards and Docks (1926–30, 1935–37). Appointed chief of the Bureau of Yards and Docks and chief of the Civil Engineering Corps of the navy as a rear admiral (1939), he held both posts until the end of World War II.

Following U.S. entry into World War II (December 1941), Moreell created the Naval Construction Battalion, known as the "Seabees." Initially, these were engineers and construction workers on U.S. Pacific islands who received some weapons training. The number of Seabees grew from some 3,000 in early 1942 to

250,000 at war's end, and they oversaw the construction of roads, docks, airfields, bridges, and many other facilities, often in the midst of fighting.

Moreell was the first Civil Engineering Corps officer to attain vice admiral (February 1944), and the first staff officer to reach the rank of admiral (June 1946).

Morgan, Frederick (1894–1967) British general. Morgan graduated from the Royal Military Academy, Woolwich (1913) and was commissioned in the artillery. During World War I he served in France with the Canadian Corps. A logistician, he headed supported services for the 1st Armoured Division (1938) and fought with it in France at the beginning of World War II.

Returned to Britain with the Dunkerque evacuation (May–June 1940), Morgan held a variety of staff posts. As assistant to U.S. Army General Dwight Eisenhower (October 1942), he was involved in planning Operation TORCH (November). Appointed CofS to the supreme allied commander (COSSAC) for the invasion of Europe (April 1943), he was principal planning officer for Operation OVERLORD. His plan selected Normandy for a three-division landing on a twenty-five-mile front and the use of Mulberries, or artificial harbors. U.S. General George C. Marshall and British General Bernard Montgomery criticized the plan and Morgan was in effect "kicked upstairs". Eisenhower then expanded the plan, to a five-division assault on a fifty-mile front. Morgan served as Eisenhower's deputy CofS until the end of the war.

After the war, Morgan headed the United Nations Relief and Rehabilitation Administration in Germany and then supervised development of the British atomic energy program from 1951–56.

Morison, Samuel Eliot (1887–1976) U.S. naval officer and historian. A distinguished historian at Harvard University,

Morison was also a sailor. He suggested to President Franklin D. Roosevelt, and Secretary of the Navy William F. Knox approved, that he be commissioned (May 1942) in order to obtain first-hand experience to write an official history of the navy in the war. Promoted captain (1945), he resigned his commission (1946) but retained a sizeable staff to write the fifteen-volume official history of the U.S. Navy in World War II. He retired from the navy a rear admiral (1951). Morison was presented the Presidential Medal of Freedom (1964) for his writing.

Moskalenko, Kirill Semenovich (1902–85) Soviet general. Moskalenko joined the Red Army as a cadet (1920) during the Civil War and became a battery commander that same year. He joined the Communist party (1926) and, following routine military assignments, commanded a mechanized brigade in the Far East (1935). He fought in the 1939–40 Russo-Finnish War as an artillery commander in a rifle division and was promoted brigadier general.

Promoted major general of artillery (June 1940), at the time of the German invasion of the Soviet Union (22 June 1941) Moskalenko commanded the 1st Artillery Antitank brigade at Kiev. As commander of XV Rifle Corps, he managed to break out of the Kiev encirclement (September), fought in the counteroffensive that saved Moscow (December), then commanded Thirty-Eighth Army (March–July 1942) of the Northern Attack Group on the north Donets River. He then commanded First Tank Army (July–August) and was engaged in heavy fighting along the lower Don River. He led First Guards Army in counterattacks in the Battle for Stalingrad (August–September), then took over Fortieth Army on the Voronezh Front (October). Promoted lieutenant general (January 1943) and colonel general (September), he commanded the reconstituted Thirty-Eighth Army in Ukraine (October 1943) until the end of the war. His forces liberated Kiev and then helped smash German Army Group South, driving the Germans back through the Carpathian Mountains. At the end of the war, his forces were in Czechoslovakia, driving on Prague. After the war he commanded the Moscow Air Defense District and made the initial arrest of Lavrenty Beria. A protégé of Soviet leader Nikita Khrushchev, he was promoted marshal in 1955.

Mountbatten, Louis Francis Albert Victor Nicholas, Earl Mountbatten of Burma (1900–79) British admiral and administrator. Related to the British royal family and son of first sea lord Prince Louis Battenberg, Mountbatten joined the navy as a cadet (1913). Educated at Dartmouth and the Royal Naval College, Devonport, he graduated first in his class (1916). He served on battleships in World War I. After the war he studied at Cambridge for a year, then accompanied his cousin the Prince of Wales (the future Edward VIII) on royal tours in Asia (1920–22). He then held a variety of assignments and commands. At the beginning of World War II Mountbatten took command of 5th Destroyer Flotilla (September 1939). He participated in the evacuation of Norway and Crete, and survived the sinking of his own ship, the *Kelly*, by a German dive bomber (May 1941). Promoted vice admiral and appointed to the new post of chief of Combined Operations (1942), he had overall responsibility for the successful commando raid on St. Nazaire (March) and the costly failure at Dieppe (19 August). He made significant contributions in the early planning for the invasion of France, Operation OVERLORD, including suggestions for harbors ("mulberries") to be floated across the channel and sunk in place and an underwater oil pipeline.

Appointed by Prime Minister Winston Churchill as supreme Allied commander Southeast Asia (August 1943), his forces by the end of the war had reconquered Burma and were ready to invade Malaya. He then carried out the difficult task of reinstalling civilian governments in his area of operations.

Prime Minister Clement Attlee persuaded Mountbatten to become the last British viceroy of India (1947). Made an earl (1947), he returned to India as governor-general (1947–48) but, while resolving some disputes, he was unable to prevent the bloodshed that marked the division of the subcontinent between India and Pakistan. He returned to the navy as fourth sea lord (1950–52), commanded the Mediterranean Fleet (1952–54), and then took his father's former post of first sea lord (1956–59). Promoted admiral of the fleet (1956), he was chief of the defense staff and chairman of the Chiefs of Staff Committee (1965–69). He retired in 1965, and was killed by a bomb planted by IRA terrorists.

Mueller, Paul John (1892–1964) U.S. general. Commissioned in the infantry on graduation from West Point (1915), Mueller served with the AEF in France in World War I, ending in command of a battalion of the 64th Infantry. Following the war he was on occupation duty at Coblenz in Germany (1920–22).

Mueller graduated from Command and General Staff School (1923) and the Army War College (1928). He then served in the War Plans Division of the War Department General Staff (1931–34) and as an instructor at the Command and General Staff College (1935–40). He then headed the training division of the chief of infantry (1940–41).

In 1941 Mueller became CofS of Second Army and was promoted brigadier general (October). Promoted major general (September 1942), he commanded the 81st Division (1942–46), leading it in the Pacific Theater of Operations in the Western Carolines and Philippine Islands campaigns.

Following World War II, Mueller commanded the 86th Division (1946) and was then CofS, GHQ, Tokyo (1946–49). He was then deputy commander of Third Army (1949–50). He headed the Career Management Division before retiring in September 1954.

Müller, Georg Alexander von (1854–1940) German admiral. Müller joined the navy (1871) and held numerous shore and shipboard commands, several of them overseas. Originally a protégé of Admiral Alfred von Tirpitz and elevated into the Prussian nobility (1900) while still a captain, Müller adopted views considerably more elastic and reform-oriented than those of his mentor. Appointed chief of the Naval Cabinet and Kaiser William II's principal advisor in naval matters (1906), he became an admiral (1910).

During World War I Müller shared the Kaiser's desire not to risk the fleet against superior British forces. He also opposed introduction of unrestricted submarine warfare and sought to liberalize the "feudalized" naval officer corps. While retaining the Kaiser's trust, he gradually lost the support of frontline officers. He retired at the end of the war.

Murphy, Audie L. (1924–71) U.S. army officer. Born into poverty, Murphy received only a fifth-grade education. The military offered a way out. After the Marines rejected him as too small physically, the army accepted him when he reached eighteen (June 1942). He proved an exemplary soldier. Assigned to the 15th Regiment of Major General Lucian K. Truscott's 3rd Infantry Division, he fought in Sicily, at Salerno, the Volturno River, Anzio, and the march on Rome. He then participated in Operation DRAGOON (August 1944), the invasion of southern France, and was awarded a battlefield commission for distinguishing himself in fighting in the Colmar Pocket. He won the Medal of Honor for single-handedly breaking up a German attack near Strasbourg that included 250 infan-

try and a half dozen Tiger tanks (16 January 1945).

With twenty-four medals in only twenty-eight months of combat, Murphy was the most decorated U.S. soldier of the war. Following the war he became an author and movie actor, starring in some forty feature films. He died in a plane crash.

Murray, Sir Archibald James (1860–1945) British general. Murray was educated at Sandhurst and joined the army (1879). He served in Hong Kong, Singapore, and the Cape Colony, and attended the Staff College (1897–99). He served in the 1899–1902 Boer War, then held a series of positions, including director of military training at the War Office (1907–12), inspector of infantry (1912–14), and commander of 2nd Division of the BEF (1914).

Murray was then CofS to BEF commander General Sir John French and participated in the Battles of Mons, Le Cateau, the Marne, Aisne, and First Ypres. He returned to England (1915), suffering from illness and exhaustion. He was appointed deputy chief of the Imperial General Staff (February 1915), then its chief (September). He then took command of the Egyptian Expeditionary Force (December 1915). Murray's capabilities were reduced early in 1916 by the transfer of ten of his fourteen divisions to other theaters. He prepared defenses along the Suez Canal and defeated the Turks there at Români (August 1916). His attack at Gaza (26–29 March 1917) ended in defeat; he attacked and again failed there (17–19 April). Replaced by General Edmund Allenby (June), he returned to the command at Aldershot (1917–19). Promoted to general (August 1919), he retired in 1922.

Mussolini, Benito Amilcare Andrea (1883–1945) Italian dictator. A high school graduate, he became a militant socialist and nationalist. As editor of the socialist newspaper *Avanti!* (1912), he became the leader of the Socialist Party's revolutionary wing. He disagreed with the Italian government position that Italy should remain neutral in World War I, and argued for intervention on the Entente side. He began his own newspaper, *Il Popolo d'Italia*, to advance this position. After Italy joined the war (May 1915), he volunteered for service and fought in the trenches until wounded and honorably discharged (1917), having risen to corporal.

After the war Mussolini founded the *Fasci di combattimento* (combat groups) (1919), which included a large number of veterans. The Fascists clashed openly with the Communists and Socialists, and a veritable civil war raged. Pledging allegiance to crown and church, he took power under the threat of force (October 1922) and held it through establishment of an authoritarian state. His efforts to make Italy the fulcrum of European politics became impossible after Adolf Hitler came to power in Germany. A champion of action, even war, he invaded Ethiopia (October 1935) and Albania (April 1939) but shrank from joining Hitler at the beginning of World War II. With the collapse of France, he was convinced that Germany had won and joined Hitler (June 1940). His insistence on Italian participation in the 1940 Battle of Britain consumed scant Italian air assets that might have been used better in North Africa. His campaign in North Africa and invasion of Greece (October 1940) went badly, forcing Hitler to come to his rescue and postponing the German timetable to invade the Soviet Union. Italian troops also participated in the invasion of Russia.

Mussolini was overthrown by his own Fascist Grand Council (July 1943) and imprisoned. Rescued by German commandos, he became the figurehead ruler of a puppet state in northern Italy under German control. Captured by partisans while trying to escape to Germany at the end of the war, he was executed.

Mutaguchi, Ren'ya (1888–1966) Japanese general. Mutaguchi graduated from the Military Academy (1910) and Army Staff College (1917). Trained as an infantry officer, he served on the staff of the Siberian Expeditionary Army (1920–21). Promoted major (1926) and colonel (1930), he headed the Military Affairs Section, Army General Staff (1933–36). While commanding the 1st Infantry Regiment of the China Garrison Army in Beijing (1936–38), he helped provoke the Marco Polo Bridge Incident that began the 1937–45 Sino-Japanese War (July 1937). Promoted major general, he was assigned to Kwantung Army headquarters (1938).

As a lieutenant general (1940), Mutaguchi commanded 18th Division in the Malaya Campaign (December 1941–February 1942), then Fifteenth Army in northern Burma (1943). On his urging, the commander of Burma Area Army, General Masakazu Kawabe, authorized him to carry out Operation U-GO, an offensive against Imphal and Kohima. While he achieved initial success (March–April 1944) and besieged both places, British General William Slim utilized superior Allied firepower and resources to force him into retreat, and he returned to Burma with only 35,000 of his 100,000-man force. Relieved of command (August), he was assigned to staff duties until the end of the war.

Mutō, Akira (1892–1948) Japanese general. Commissioned in the army (1913), Mutō served in a succession of increasingly important staff positions, including inspector general of military training. He was a member of the Control Group, and had a prominent role in bringing on the 1937–45 Sino-Japanese War. Promoted major general (March 1939), he was chief of the military affairs bureau of the War Ministry (1939–43) when Prince Konoye was prime minister (1937–41).

Promoted lieutenant general (October

1941), Mutō disapproved of General Hideki Tōjō's policies and urged his removal from office. Exiled to command the 2nd Imperial Guards Division in Sumatra (June 1943), he then became CofS to General Tomoyuki Yamashita in the Philippines (October 1944) and was his chief's most eloquent defender. He himself was also tried, convicted, and hanged as a war criminal.

Mutō, Nobuyoshi (1866–1933) Japanese field marshal. A graduate of the Military Academy (1892) and Army Staff College (1899), he fought in the 1894–95 Sino-Japanese War. A specialist in Russia, he was resident in Vladivostok (1900–01) and Odessa (1902–03). He fought in the 1904–05 Russo-Japanese War, was a military attaché in St. Petersburg (1906–08), and traveled extensively in Siberia during the early period of Japanese intervention there (1918–20). Promoted lieutenant general (1920), he commanded 3rd Division (1921–22), then the Kwantung Army in Manchuria (1926–27). He was inspector general of military education (1927–32), then again commanded the Kwantung Army and was governor of the Kwantung Leased Territory (1932–33). He died on active duty, and was posthumously made a baron.

N

Nagano, Osami (1880–1947) Japanese admiral. Nagano graduated from the Naval Academy (1900) and steadily advanced in rank and positions, serving mostly in staff assignments. He did, however, head a land-based navy heavy gun unit supporting the army during the siege of Port Arthur during the 1904–05 Russo-Japanese War. Naval attaché in Washington, DC (1920–23), he visited the United States again (1927, 1933), was promoted to rear admiral (1928), and commanded the Naval Academy (1928–29). He headed the Japanese delegation to the second London Naval Disarmament Conference (1935–36). Appointed Japanese Navy minister (1935–36), he then commanded the Combined Fleet (1936–37).

Nagano was chief of the Naval General Staff (April 1941–February 1944) and had a major role in the development of strategy during World War II in the Pacific. Originally opposed to the army's plans for war with the United States on the assumption that more powerful U.S. economic might would in the long run wear down Japan, he later came to support the preemptive strike at Pearl Harbor (7 December 1941). Promoted to fleet admiral in June 1943, he died in prison while awaiting trial for war crimes.

Nagumo, Chūichi (1886–1944) Japanese admiral. Nagumo graduated from the Imperial Naval Academy (1908) and the Naval Staff College (1920). He held cruiser commands and then led a destroyer squadron. He took command of the First Air Fleet (April 1941), and was then tasked with the strike on Pearl Harbor (7 December 1941). His fleet then carried out successful strikes against British assets in the Indian Ocean.

Nagumo suffered his first major defeat in the Battle of Midway (June 1942), where the plan and his decisions led to the loss of all four of his fleet carriers. He next directed carriers during the Guadalcanal campaign, where his forces were also defeated. However, he was victorious in the Battle of Santa Cruz (October 1942), sinking the U.S. carrier *Hornet*. Entrusted with the defense of the Marianas as CinC of the Central Pacific Fleet, Nagumo was on Saipan during the U.S. invasion (June 1944), where he committed suicide rather than surrender.

Nakagawa, Kunio (1898–1944) Japanese army officer. Nakagawa commanded 2nd Regiment of 14th Division based on Pelelieu in the Palau Islands. He inflicted heavy casualties on invading U.S. Marines and held the island for nearly three months. He committed ritual suicide at the end of the battle, and was posthumously promoted lieutenant general.

Nam Il (1913–1976) Korean People's Army general and political leader. Nam grew up in Russia, his family having fled Korea to escape the Japanese. Graduating from a teacher's college in Tashkent, he then attended Smolensk Military School. During World War II he fought in the Red Army as an officer and by the end of the war was CofS of a division.

Nam returned to North Korea (August 1946) and joined the Democratic People's Republic of Korea (DPRK, North Korea) government. He helped plan the attack on the Republic of Korea (South Korea) (25 June 1950) and then became vice CofS of the Korean Peoples Army (KPA, North Korean Army). When Kang Kon was killed in battle during the 1950–53 Korean War, he replaced him as CofS with the rank of lieutenant general (December 1950).

When armistice negotiations opened (July 1951), he headed the DPRK delegation, although he was clearly subordinate to Chinese representative, Xie Fang. Shortly before the armistice was signed (July 1953), he was promoted full general so as to outrank U.S. Lieutenant General William K. Harrison, Jr., who signed for the United Nations Command. Nam then became DPRK foreign minister (August 1953–59) and vice president (1957–76).

Nasser, Gamal Abd-al (1918–70) Egyptian army officer and political leader. A graduate of the Egyptian military college (1936), he became politically active and a leader of nationalist Egyptian officers. He fought in the 1948–49 Israeli War of Independence and was seriously wounded. Disillusioned with the monarchy of King Farouk, he led a coup that overthrew it (July 1952).

While Major General Mohammed Naguib was the titular head of state, Nasser was the real authority. Following an attempt on his life, he replaced Naguib (1954). He secured the withdrawal of British troops from the Suez Canal (1954), but his nationalization of the canal (July 1956) touched off a new war with Israel, joined by Britain and France

(October–November 1956) Although Egyptian forces were soundly defeated, Nasser's defiance of the West and his aggressive pan-Arabism won him the support of his people and the Arab world.

A Nasser-secured union between Egypt and Syria, the United Arab Republic, collapsed in 1961. Following provocative Egyptian military preparations, Israel staged a pre-emptive strike to begin the 1967 Six-Day War (5–11 June), decisively defeating Egyptian, Syrian, and Jordanian forces. Nasser's policy of artillery strikes (1969–70) provoked Israeli military response, but also a UN-brokered agreement whereby Israel returned the Sinai peninsula (1970).

Navarre, Henri Eugène (1899–1983) French general. Navarre enlisted in the French Army (1916) during World War I, attended St. Cyr, and was commissioned (November 1918). Following the war he served in Syria, Morocco, and Germany (1922–26). After study at the Cavalry School at Saumur, he transferred to armor. He fought in the 1925–26 Rif War in Morocco, attended the École Supérieur de Guerre, and headed the German section of the Deuxième Bureau (Army Intelligence) (1936–39).

After the French defeat in World War II, Navarre organized military intelligence in occupied France and North Africa (1940–42). He commanded a heavy cavalry regiment, but was recalled to France (November 1942) to organize Resistance intelligence operations. Joining Allied forces invading southern France (late 1944), he was promoted colonel and commanded a regiment of Moroccan Spahis. He was then CofS to the French military commander in Germany and, as a brigadier general (October 1945), inspector general. He commanded a division in Algeria (1948) and attended the Institute of Advanced Studies for the National Defense. Promoted major general, he returned to Germany to command the 5th Armored Division (1950–52). Promoted lieutenant general (1952), he was CofS to commander of NATO Central European forces, Marshal Alphonse Juin.

Named commander of French Union forces in Indo-China (May 1953), Navarre instituted fluid offensive operations. Determined to take the war to the Viet Minh, he created the airhead at Dien Bien Phu to lure the Viet Minh into a set-piece battle, resulting in a disastrous defeat (May 1954) and the end of French rule in Indo-China. Embittered, he retired (1956) to write his memoirs, blaming French politicians for the loss of Indo-China.

Neame, Sir Philip (1888–1978) British general. Neame joined the army and rose to brevet major in the Tank Corps during World War I. After a variety of assignments, he was deputy CofS of the BEF in France (1939–40). He then took command of the Indian 4th Division in Egypt (early 1940). Promoted lieutenant general (August) he commanded forces in Palestine, Trans-Jordan, and Cyprus. When General Archibald Wavell's forces were stripped away to go to the aid of Greece, he took command of the British Desert Force in Cyrenaica (February 1941), one of his actions being to strengthen Tobruk. He and his predecessor, General Richard O'Connor, then commander in Egypt, were captured by a German patrol (6 April). They escaped together from a POW camp in Italy (March 1943) and got back to Britain. Neame spent the rest of the war as lieutenant governor and commander of Guernsey and its dependencies. Knighted (1946), he retired in 1947.

Nehring, Walther Kurt (1892–1983) German general. Joining the army as an officer candidate (1911), Nehring was commissioned (1914) and fought in World War I. He continued in the Reichswehr after the war and was selected for General Staff training. A close associate of General Heinz Guderian, he assisted in developing German armor formations and was a colonel on Guderian's staff during campaigns in Poland (September 1939) and France (May–June 1940). Promoted brigadier general (August 1940), he commanded the new 18th Panzer Division (October) and led it as part of Panzer Group Guderian in the invasion of the Soviet Union (June 1941). Promoted major general (February 1942), he took command of the Afrika Korps (May). Promoted lieutenant general (July 1942), he directed the German effort in the Battle of Alam Halfa (August–September 1942). Seriously wounded in an Allied air attack (31 September) he was in Germany recovering when the Allies invaded northwestern Africa (8 November). Immediately ordered to Tunisia to hold there pending reinforcements from Sicily, he set up blocking positions and held until the arrival of 10th Panzer Division allowed him to launch a counteroffensive that ended the Allied "race for Tunis." Regarded as pessimistic, he was replaced by Hans von Arnim (December).

A capable Panzer leader, Nehring then held a succession of important commands in Russia: XXIV Panzer Corps (February 1943–June 1944), Fourth Army (June–August 1944), and XLVIII Panzer Corps (August 1944), then XXIV Panzer Corps again. He briefly commanded First Panzer Army (March 1945).

Nicholas II (1868–1918) Tsar of Russia, 1894–1917. Determined to preserve the monarchy, he nonetheless felt compelled to support Serbia against Austrian reprisal and ordered the mobilization that committed Russia to war. He had done little to prepare Russia to fight and his government was incapable of carrying out a sustained war effort. Despite opposition from his ministers, he removed his uncle, the capable Grand Duke Nikolai as commander of the army (August 1915), and took that post himself in the mistaken belief that he could rally the army to victory. Following Russian military disasters, he was forced to abdicate in the March 1917 Revolution.

Nieh Jung-chen (Nie Rongzhen) (1899–1997) People's Republic of China marshal. Nieh participated in the May 4th Movement (1919), then was in France and Belgium on a work study plan (1920–23). He joined the Chinese Communist party (CCP) (1923), then went to the Soviet Union for military studies (1924–25). Returning to China, he was an instructor at Whampoa Military Academy (1925–26). He participated in the Northern Expedition (1926–27), and then the unsuccessful 1927 Nanchang and Canton uprisings. Escaping to Hong Kong, he made his way to Kiangsi and became a Red Army political commissar (1931). He participated in the 1934–35 Long March as political commissary for I Army Corps.

During the 1937–45 Sino-Japanese War, Nieh was first the deputy commander of 115th Division, Eighth Route Army, then its commander, conducting guerrilla operations in the Shansi–Chahar–Hopeh Border Region. He commanded the Shansi–Chahar–Hopeh Army (1937–47) and the North China Military Region in the 1946–49 Civil War (1948). He was CCP representative in negotiations with the Nationalist Kuomintang (KMT, Guomindang), then commanded the Peking-Tientsin Garrison Force and then the North China Military Region, and was deputy CofS of the People's Liberation Army (PLA) (1949). He held a variety of other diplomatic and political posts and was promoted marshal in September 1955.

Nieh Shen-ch'eng (Nie Shenqeng) (?–1900) Chinese general. Following a distinguished military career in the Imperial army, Nieh commanded the Wuyi army in Chihli province around Peking (Beijing) (c.1897). He conducted military operations against Boxer guerrillas in the 1900–01 Boxer Rebellion, and also re-

pulsed a British force in the first Western effort to relieve the foreign legations at Peking (26 June 1900), but was killed shortly thereafter in July.

Nikolai Nikolaevich Romanov, Grand Duke (1856–1929) Russian general. Nikolai entered the army (1872) and held a variety of posts. A capable administrator with an interest in new methods, he took command of the Russian Army (July 1914) on the eve of Russian mobilization, appointed by his nephew Tsar Nicholas II. Under his overall command, in 1914 Russian forces were defeated in East Prussia but were able to repulse a German thrust towards Warsaw and achieve success in the Galician offensive against Austria-Hungary. The 1915 campaigns, however, produced massive casualties and the eventual retreat of Russia's armies. The tsar removed Nikolai (August 1915) and took personal command of the army, assigning him command of the Caucasus region. There Nikolai injected new spirit in the Russian forces, and fighting on that front was on the whole favorable to Russia, leading in 1916 to the invasion of Armenia and the capture of Turkish territory.

During the March 1917 revolution, Nikolai was for one day again commander of the army and was instrumental in persuading Nicholas II to abdicate. He emigrated in March 1919.

Nimitz, Chester William (1885–1966) U.S. admiral. Upon graduation from Annapolis (1905), Nimitz saw service in the Pacific and was commissioned (1907). He commanded submarines and promoted the use of diesel engines, which he then studied in Germany. He supervised construction of the first U.S. Navy diesel ship engine, and helped to pioneer underway refueling.

During World War I Nimitz was CofS to the commander of U.S. submarines in the Atlantic. Promoted commander, he graduated from the Naval War College

(1923). He organized the first NROTC unit at the University of Califormia (1926–29) and was promoted captain (1927). He then commanded a submarine division and a cruiser. Promoted rear admiral (1938), he commanded a battleship division.

Promoted admiral, Nimitz replaced Admiral Husband Kimmel as commander of the U.S. Pacific Fleet (31 December 1941). Benefiting from code-breaking, he turned back Japanese forces in the Battle of the Coral Sea (May 1942) and Battle of Midway (June). He left tactical control with subordinates, but beginning in 1943 he directed U.S. operations to secure Japanese-held islands in the Central Pacific, culminating with the capture of Okinawa (April–June 1945) and naval operations against the Japanese home islands. He was promoted to the newly created rank of fleet admiral (December 1944). Surrender ceremonies were held aboard his flagship, the battleship *Missouri*, in Tokyo Bay (2 September 1945).

Appointed chief of naval operations (CNO) (December), Nimitz oversaw the downsizing of the navy. He also promoted the development of nuclear submarines. Upon retirement (December 1947), he served as a special assistant to the secretary of the navy (1948–49), then UN commissioner for Kashmir (1949–51).

Nishimura, Shōji (1889–1944) Japanese admiral. A graduate of the Naval Academy (1911), Nishimura was promoted lieutenant commander (1914) and held a variety of destroyer commands (1926–29). While in command of destroyer squadrons (1931–36), he was promoted captain (1934). He commanded a cruiser, then a battleship (1937–40). Promoted rear admiral, he commanded Destroyer Squadron 4 (November 1940), which participated in the conquest of the Philippine Islands (December 1941–May 1942), the capture of Balikpapan, Borneo (January 1942), and the Battle of the Java Sea (February). He then took command of

Cruiser Division 7 (June) and participated in naval battles off Guadalcanal (August 1942–February 1943). Promoted vice admiral (1943), he commanded C Force, Southern Force, in the Sho Plan, in an attempt to reach the Leyte landing beaches through Surigao Strait, part of the Battle of Leyte Gulf (October 1944). In the Battle of the Surigao Strait (night 24–25 October) his force was savaged by Admiral Jesse Oldendorff's Seventh Fleet Fire Support Force of destroyers, torpedo boats, and six old battleships. In the battle he lost two battleships, a cruiser, and four destroyers. Nishimura died when his flagship, the battleship *Yamashiro*, capsized.

Nivelle, Robert (1856–1924) French general. A graduate of the École Polytechnique (1878), he entered the artillery. Promoted colonel (1911) and then brigadier general (October 1914), he commanded III Corps at Verdun and developed tactics that won him prominence. These consisted of training selected units to assault objectives in small groups. Attacks would be preceded by deception barrages that would be halted to encourage the Germans to reveal their artillery positions. With enemy guns silenced, attacks would then resume.

Because of his Verdun success, Nivelle was named CinC of the French Army (December 1916), replacing General Joseph Joffre. His fluent English helped him secure approval from Prime Minister David Lloyd George for a plan to secure victory. The focus of the attack was in Champagne, and the key to success would be the "Verdun" formula, despite the difficulty of applying these tactics at the army level.

The "Nivelle Offensive" (16 April–9 May) produced only minimal gains and 130,000 French casualties. It led to widespread mutinies in the army and to Nivelle's replacement as CinC by General Henri-Philippe Pétain (May). He declined command of an army group and submitted to review by a military inquiry (October) that whitewashed him. He spent the remainder of the war in North Africa and retired soon thereafter.

Nixon, Sir John Ecces (1857–1921) British general. Educated at Wellington College and Sandhurst, he joined the 75th Foot (1875) and fought in Afghanistan (1879–80) and in the 1899–02 Anglo-Boer War (1901–02). He then served in India. Promoted major general (1904), then lieutenant general (1909), he was promoted general (1914) and given command of the Northern Army of India.

During World War I Nixon received command of British forces in Mesopotamia (April 1915). London wanted a defensive strategy to protect the oil fields, but he instructed his field commander, Major General Charles Townshend, to advance on Baghdad. At first Townshend was successful, taking Amara (3 June) and Kut-el-Amara (29 September). Nixon then received approval for a drive on Baghdad, provided it could be held, but the Turks halted the British advance at Ctesiphon (November), and Townshend fell back to Kut, where he was besieged by the Turks and forced to surrender (April 1916), two divisions promised from France having failed to arrive.

Nixon gave up his command ostensibly for health reasons (January 1916) and appeared before a commission investigating the disaster. It found he bore the "weightiest share of responsibility." Plans to bring him before a special court of inquiry were overtaken by the end of the war, but his career had been ruined.

Njegovan, Maximilian (1858–1930) Austro-Hungarian admiral. Njegovan graduated from the Austro-Hungarian Naval Academy at Fiume (1877). He then served in a variety of posts and from 1893 held various fleet commands. Promoted captain (1907), he was a squadron commander (1907–09). He was then chief of the operations chancellory in the Naval Secre-

tariat (1909–10). Promoted rear admiral (1913), he commanded naval units during the international blockade of Montenegro.

At the beginning of World War I, Njegovan assumed command of the 1st Squadron of the fleet at Pola and undertook the naval bombardment of Ancona (May 1915). Following the death of Admiral Anton von Haus (February 1917), he commanded the Austro-Hungarian fleet and continued his predecessor's policy of seeking to preserve the capital ships.

Njegovan was promoted full admiral (1917) and made chief of the Naval Section. During his period in command, the Italians deployed their MAS torpedo boats and inflicted heavy losses on Austro-Hungarian coastal defense ships. He also had the misfortune of commanding when war-weariness was rampant, leading to mutinies (November 1917 and February 1918, especially at Cattaro). Shortly after the latter was quelled, he retired (March 1918), replaced as fleet commander by Rear Admiral Miklós Horthy.

Noble, Sir Percy Lockhart Harnam (1880–1955) British admiral. Noble joined the Royal Navy and during World War I served on cruisers. Following assignments afloat and ashore, he commanded the China Station (1937–40). During World War II he was CinC, Western Approaches (February 1941–November 1942) with headquarters at Liverpool.

Noble helped pave the way for eventual Allied victory in the 1939–45 Battle of the Atlantic by laying the foundations for successful anti-submarine warfare. He stressed training and began schools for that purpose. He also improved effectiveness of convoy escorts by establishing them as permanent groups.

Noble then headed the British Admiralty delegation to Washington (1942–43), where he worked to maintain close Anglo-American naval cooperation. He was then principal aide-de-camp to King George VI (1943–45). He retired in January 1945.

Nogi, Maresuke (1843–1912) Japanese general. Nogi fought as a member of the Chōshā Clan during 1868 Boshin (Restoration) War against the Tokugawa shogunate and became a major in the new imperial army (1871). He fought in the 1877 Satsuma Rebellion. As a major general (1885), he studied in Germany (1885–86). He commanded a brigade in the 1894–95 Sino-Japanese War and fought in the siege of Port Arthur (October–November 1894) and Battle of Yingkow (March 1895). He commanded Third Army during the 1904–05 Russo-Japanese War, directing siege operations against Port Arthur (June 1904–January 1905), which claimed 100,000 Japanese casualties, including both his own sons. He played a key role in the Battle of Mukden, turning the Russian right flank (February–March 1905). He and his wife committed suicide on the death of the Emperor Meiji (30 July 1912), making Nogi something of a spiritual icon in the Japanese military ethos.

Noguès, Charles Auguste Paul (1876–1971) French general. Commissioned in the artillery on graduation from the École Polytechnique (1899), Noguès served in North Africa, first in Morocco as a cartographer, then in Tunisia and Algeria. He worked closely with General Louis Lyautey, both in North Africa and when the latter was minister of war (1917). He served on the Western Front during World War I, ending up in command of an artillery regiment.

After the war Noguès held staff positions in Paris before returning to Morocco, where he fought to put down the 1923–26 Rif Rebellion. A capable colonial administrator, he was inspector general of troops in North Africa, then resident general (a post held since 1925 by a civilian) and CinC of troops in Morocco (1936).

When World War II began (September 1939), Noguès was CinC, North African Theater of Operations with headquarters in Algiers. He obeyed government orders to arrest officials reaching Morocco who objected to the armistice and wished to continue the fight. He reverted to his Moroccan post when General Maxime Weygand took overall command in North Africa. When he reached mandatory retirement age, he retired from the military but kept his civilian position. Although anti-German, he pursued a neutralist position and strictly enforced Vichy policies. He ordered resistance to the Allied invasion (8 November 1942) and agreed to a ceasefire (11 November) only on the basis that further resistance was useless. He was then deputy high commissioner for French North Africa until General Charles de Gaulle replaced him (June 1943), whereupon he fled to Portugal. A French court sentenced him in absentia (1947) to twenty years of hard labor and national indignity for obeying orders to resist the Allied landings.

Norden, Carl Lukas (1880–1965) American inventor. Born in the Netherlands, Norden emigrated to the United States (1904). Working for the Sperry Gyroscope Company (1911), he helped perfect the gyroscope for the navy. He also worked to develop stable gun platforms and radio-controlled aircraft as guided bombs. After World War I at the behest of the navy, he and two associates, Theodore Barth and Frederick Entwhistle, developed the Norden bombsight, which was used extensively by U.S. forces in World War II. The bombsight was closely guarded and the Army Air Corps used it as justification for its plan to conduct pinpoint daylight strategic bombing, but combat conditions were quite different from those during tests.

Among other inventions, Norden also developed catapults and arresting gear for use aboard aircraft carriers and the first hydraulically controlled landing gear.

Norstad, Lauris (1907–88) U.S. Air Force general. Norstad was commissioned in the cavalry on graduation from West Point (1930). He transferred to the Air Service (1931) and commanded 18th Pursuit Group in Hawaii (1933–36). He attended the Air Corps Tactical School (1938–39), and was then assistant CofS for intelligence at GHQ Air Force at Langley Field (1940–42). Following brief service on the staff of commander of Army Air Forces General Henry Arnold, he was assistant CofS of Twelfth Air Force (October 1942), accompanying it to North Africa. Promoted brigadier general (March 1943), he directed operations in the Mediterranean Allied Air Forces. He returned briefly to the United States as CofS for Twentieth Air Force (August 1944). Promoted major general (June 1945), he helped plan the atomic bomb raids against Japan (August).

In the immediate postwar period, Norstad helped draft the National Security Act (1947) that created an independent U.S. Air Force. Promoted lieutenant general, he commanded U.S. Air Forces, Europe (October 1950), and also Allied Air Forces in Central Europe (April 1951). Promoted general (July 1952), he was air deputy to NATO's supreme Allied commander, first General Matthew Ridgway and then General Alfred Gruenther (1953–56). He succeeded Gruenther (November 1956) until his own retirement in January 1963.

Novikov, Aleksandr Aleksandrovich (1900–76) Soviet air force marshal. Novikov joined the Red Army (1919) and the Communist Party (1920), fought in the 1918–20 Civil War, and attended the Higher Infantry School. He transferred from the infantry to the air force (1933) and, following study at the Frunze, was CofS of the 450th Aviation Brigade. He was CofS of the Karelian Front during the 1939–40 Soviet–Finnish Winter War, then commanded aviation in the Leningrad Military District, which became the Northern Front after the German invasion of the Soviet Union (22 June 1941).

Lieutenant General Novikov became deputy commander of the Air Forces of the Soviet Army (February 1942), then commander (April 1942–March 1946). In the latter post he was responsible for coordinating Russian air assets at Stalingrad, Kursk, and Belorussia. Promoted colonel general (1943), he was the first Soviet marshal of aviation and one of only two officers to be made chief marshal of aviation in the war. Following the defeat of Germany, he directed air actions against the Japanese Kwantung Army in Manchuria.

Arrested after the war in a purge of the military (March 1946), he was held under strict confinement (1946–53), but released after Josef Stalin's death. Rehabilitated, he held a succession of important posts, including commander of long-range aviation units and deputy CofS of the now-independent Soviet Air Force (1954–55).

Nozu, Michitsura (1841–1907) Japanese field marshal. Nozu participated in the 1868 Boshin (Restoration) War that overthrew the Tokugawa shogunate. Commissioned a major in the new imperial army (1871), he was a colonel and CofS of the 2nd Infantry Brigade during the 1877 Satsuma Rebellion and traveled in the United States and Europe in the 1870s and 1880s.

Nozu commanded 5th Infantry Division in the 1894–95 Sino-Japanese War and played a major role in the Japanese victory in the Battle of Pyongyang, Korea (September 1894). When Marshal Aritomo Yamagata fell ill, he succeeded him as CG of First Army (December). Promoted general (1895), he commanded Fourth Army in the 1904–05 Russo-Japanese War. He directed the landing at Kushan (May 1904) and fought in the battles of Liaoyang (August–September), Sha Ho (October), Sandepu (January 1905), and Mukden (February–March).

In recognition of his services, he was promoted field marshal (January 1906).

Nuri as-Said (Nuri al-Sa'id Pasha) (1888–1958) Arab general and Iraqi political leader. Commissioned in the Turkish army (1909), Nuri fought against Bulgaria in Thrace during the 1912–13 First and Second Balkan Wars. He became active in Arab nationalist societies while stationed in Cairo and Basra (1913–14). Following a year's forced residence in India, British authorities secured his return to join the Arab Revolt in the Hejaz (1916–18), where he served as staff officer and adviser to Emir Faisal. He continued with Faisal until the French drove the latter out as ruler of Syria (July 1920), then fled with Faisal to Iraq and continued as his close advisor there after the latter's proclamation as king (August 1921) until his death (September 1933).

Nuri was prime minister thirteen times. Known as pro-British and pro-Turkish, he opposed the pro-German policy of the new government of Rashid Ali al-Gailani, which went to war against Britain in a short-lived effort (May 1941). He worked to support the Allied war effort. He helped found the Arab League (1945) and committed Iraqi forces to the 1948–49 Israeli War of Independence. A staunch anti-Communist, he also abolished all political parties. He helped arrange the short-lived union of Iraq and Jordan (February 1958) but was murdered when the army overthrew the monarchy (July).

O

Obata, Hideyoshi (1880–1944) Japanese general. Obata graduated from the Military Academy (1911) and Army Staff College (1919). He taught at the latter three times (1921–23, 1926–27, 1930–31). Resident officer in Britain (1923–26), he was promoted major (1926) and colonel (1934). He served briefly on the Army General Staff (1930) and the General Staff (1934–35). Following command of a regiment (1935–37), he was promoted major general (1938) and appointed commander of Akeno Army Air School (1938–40). Promoted lieutenant general, he then commanded 5th Air Group (1940–43).

During World War II Obata commanded Third Air Army in New Guinea and New Britain islands (1943). He then took command of Thirty-First Army in the Marianas at Saipan (February 1944). Declaring to his troops, "I will leave my bones as a bulwark of the Pacific," he was killed early in the U.S. invasion in August.

O'Connor, Sir Richard Nugent (1889–1981) British general. Commissioned on graduation from Sandhurst (1909), O'Connor served with distinction in World War I. Assigned to India (1936), he commanded the Peshawar Brigade on the northwest frontier and was promoted major general (1938).

At the beginning of World War II, O'Connor commanded 7th Division and was military governor of Jerusalem. He took his division to Egypt (June 1940), and as temporary lieutenant general commanded the small Western Desert Force during Marshal Rodolfo Graziani's invasion (September). He and CG of Middle Eastern Command General Sir Archibald Wavell planned a masterful counterstroke, Operation COMPASS (December), against the Italian forces. Facing heavy numerical odds and with never more than two divisions, O'Connor expelled the Italians from Egypt and pushed deep into Libya and took Tobruk (January 1941) and Beda Fomm (February). In 10 weeks, with fewer than 2,000 casualties, his forces inflicted 12,000 killed and missing and took 138,000 prisoners, including five generals, and 400 tanks and 850 guns.

Following the arrival of the German Afrika Korps (February), General Erwin Rommel launched a counterattack (March), successful in part because many of the Western Desert Force had been stripped of units to fight in Greece. O'Connor was then commanding British troops in Egypt, but Wavell sent him to the front to serve as advisor to his successor, General Philip Neame. O'Connor and Neame were captured by a German patrol (April). Both men escaped from a POW camp in Italy (September 1943) and reached Britain.

O'Connor commanded VIII Corps from the Normandy invasion (6 June 1944) but returned to India (1945) to head first Eastern and then Northwestern Command, when he was promoted full general. He then served on the Army Council (1946–47) and was knighted. He retired in 1948.

O'Daniel, John Wilson (1894–1975) U.S. general. O'Daniel joined the regular army from the Delaware National Guard while still a student at the University of Delaware and saw service in the guard on the Mexican border. Commissioned in the infantry (1917), he served in France with the AEF in World War I.

Known as "Iron Mike" for his tough appearance and commanding voice, as a colonel in World War II, he led the 168th Regimental Combat Team of the 34th Infantry Division in Operation TORCH, landing at Algiers (8 November 1942). Promoted brigadier general (November), he helped train Fifth Army for the landing on Sicily (July 1943) and was assigned to 3rd Infantry Division.

After taking part in landings on Sicily and at Anzio (January 1944), he succeeded General Lucian Truscott as commander of the 3rd Division (February). Promoted major general, he helped lead the Anzio breakout (May). After the fall of Rome (June), he helped train his division and others for the invasion of southern France, Operation DRAGOON (August 1944). Following the linkup with forces in northern France, he drove on Strasbourg (November), helped cut off the Colmar Pocket (January), breached the Siegfried Line, crossed the Rhine (March), and drove into south Germany and Austria by war's end.

O'Daniel then commanded the Infantry School (July 1945–July 1948). Promoted lieutenant general, he was military attaché in Moscow (1948–50). He commanded I Corps in the 1950–53 Korean War. His final duty assignment was chief, Military Assistance and Advisory Group (MAAG) to the Republic of Vietnam (1954–55).

Oesch, Karl (1892–1978) Finnish general. During the November 1939–March 1940 Russo-Finnish War, Oesch was chief of the General Staff. At the end of the war he commanded the Coastal Group that repulsed the Russians and pushed them back across the Gulf of Viipuri. During the so-called War of Continuation (1941–44) when Finland entered World War II against the Soviet Union to take back the territory taken from it the year before, he commanded IV Corps and retook Viipuri. In 1944 he commanded forces in the Karelian isthmus and was forced under Soviet pressure to give up Viipuri.

Oikawa, Koshirō (1883–1958) Japanese admiral and political leader. A graduate of the Naval Academy (1903), Oikawa was naval aide to Crown Prince Hirohito (1915–22). Promoted vice admiral (1938), he commanded the China Fleet (1938–40). Promoted full admiral (1939), he was minister of the navy (September 1940–October 1941). In this capacity he made many concessions to the army, including consent for the Tripartite Pact with Germany and Italy in September 1940. He thus greatly aided the army leadership in its determination to go to war with the United States, for which he was bitterly criticized by Admiral Isoroku Yamamoto.

Oikawa was then on the Military Council until November 1943, when he headed the new Grand Escort Command Headquarters, with four escort carriers and a naval air group to protect merchant shipping against U.S. submarine attack. He was chief of the naval staff (August 1944–April 1945) until mounting defeats, culminating in the U.S. invasion of Okinawa, led to his replacement.

Okamura, Yoshiji (1884–1966) Japanese general. Okamura graduated from the Military Academy (1904) and Army Staff College (1913), He served on the Army General Staff (1914–17, 1923–25, 1928) and was promoted major (1919). He studied in Europe (1921–22). After being resident officer in Shanghai (1925–27), he was promoted colonel and commanded a regiment (1927–28). He was then vice CofS, Kwantung Army and helped plan the takeover of Manchuria (1931–32). He was next deputy CG of the Shanghai Expeditionary Army (February 1932), sent to break the boycott of Japanese goods following the takeover of Manchuria. Promoted major general (1932), he was vice CofS of the Kwantung Army in Manchuria and military attaché to the puppet Japanese state of Manchukuo (Manchuria) (1933–34). He was then chief of the intelligence division, Army General Staff (1935–36). Promoted lieutenant general (1936), he commanded 2nd Division (1936–38), then Eleventh Army (1938–40).

Promoted general (1941), Okamura commanded North China Area Army (1941–44) and began the Three All Policy ("Kill All, Burn All, Take All"). As commander of the all Japanese forces in China, the Chinese Expeditionary Army (1944), he began the ICHI-GO offensive in southern China, capturing most U.S. bomber fields (May–December 1944). He retired after the war (September 1945) and escaped punishment for war crimes by serving as leader of the *Pai-dan* (White Company), the Japanese military advisers to Nationalist Chinese forces (1946–48).

O'Kane, Richard Hetherington (1911–94) U.S. admiral. O'Kane graduated from Annapolis (1934). Following routine assignments, at the beginning of World War II he was executive officer of submarine *Wahoo*, which sank sixteen Japanese vessels totalling 45,000 tons by July 1943. He then took command of submarine *Tang*, and made five voyages in her, during which time he became the leading U.S. submarine commander of the war, sinking more than thirty-two ships totalling 227,800 tons. The *Tang* also rescued U.S. and Allied airmen.

Attacking a Japanese freighter, the *Tang* was sunk by one of its own torpedoes, which circled out of control and returned to hit the submarine (night of 24–25 October 1944). O'Kane and seven others survived but were taken prisoner by the Japanese and spent the rest of the war as POWs. After the war he commanded submarines and submarine squadrons, retiring as a rear admiral in 1957.

Oktyabrsky, Filip Sergeyevich (1899–1969) Soviet admiral. Oktyabrsky joined the Red Navy (1918) and the Communist party (1919). Following routine assignments, he commanded the Amur Military Flotilla (February 1938), then the Black Sea Fleet (March 1939–May 1943). He was promoted rear admiral (June 1940) and then vice admiral (June 1941).

Oktyabrsky directed Odessa's land defenses (July–October) and carried out a masterly evacuation of Odessa (night of 15–16 October). He then directed the defense of Sevastapol against German attack (November 1941–June 1942), being evacuated on orders from Moscow by submarine at the last moment (30 June). He headed the Amur Military Flotilla (June 1943–March 1944), then again commanded the Black Sea Fleet as a full admiral.

Continuing as commander of the Black Sea Fleet, Oktyabrsky was also first deputy CinC of the Navy until 1950. His criticism of naval policy led to his retirement that year, but he re-emerged to head the Black Sea Higher Naval School (1957). He then joined the General Inspector's Group (1959).

Oku, Yasukata (1846–1930) Japanese field marshal. Oku was a samurai of the Kokura clan. Unlike many other Japanese generals, he lacked political connections and advanced on his own merit. He joined the new Imperial army (1871) and distinguished himself in the 1877 Satsuma Rebellion, and enjoyed rapid promotion to major general (1885). He took a military tour of Europe (1893–94) and then returned to Japan to command 5th Division in the 1894–95 Sino-Japanese War.

Oku won renown during the 1904–05 Russo-Japanese War when he commanded Second Army in the landing on the Liao-tung (Liaodong) peninsula (May 1904), began the siege of Port Arthur, and took Dairen (Luda). He drove back the Russians at Telissu (Wafangkou) then fought in the Battles of Liaoyang (August–September 1904), the Sha Ho (October), and Mukden (February–March 1905).

After the war Oku was army CofS (1906–12). He was made a viscount (1907) and promoted field marshal (1911). After 1912 he was on the reserve list.

Oldendorf, Jesse Bartlett (1887–1974) U.S. admiral. Oldendorf graduated from Annapolis (1909) and was commissioned (1911). During World War I he served in Atlantic convoy escort duty. After the war he held a variety of assignments, including command of a destroyer (1924–27). He then attended the Army as well as the Naval War Colleges (1928–30) and taught at Annapolis. Promoted captain (1938), he commanded a cruiser and then joined the Naval War College staff (1941).

After the Japanese attack on Pearl Harbor (7 December 1941), Oldendorf was promoted rear admiral. He held Caribbean commands (January 1942–April 1943) and then led an Atlantic Fleet task force. He transferred to the Pacific as commander of Cruiser Division 4 (January 1944), participating in operations in the Marshall Islands and Truk (January–February), the Marianas (June–August), Peleliu (September), and the Leyte Gulf landings in the Philippines (October).

In the Philippines, Oldendorf commanded Seventh Fleet's Fire Support Force of six old battleships, three heavy and five light cruisers, twenty destroyers, and some forty PT boats. With this force he laid an ambush for a Japanese force that attempted to pass through Surigao Strait to attack U.S. shipping in Leyte Gulf,

sinking two Japanese battleships, two of four cruisers, and four of eight destroyers in a night battle (24–25 October) that was the last major action between battleships. Promoted vice admiral (December 1944), he commanded Battleship Squadrons 1 and 4, supporting landings at the Lingayen Gulf. He commanded Task Force 95 at Okinawa (June–November).

Following the war, Oldendorf commanded the 11th Naval District and San Diego Naval Base (January 1946) and then the Western Sea Frontier and the "mothball" fleet at San Francisco (1947–48). On his retirement (September 1948) he was promoted admiral.

Ōmori, Sentarō (1894–?) Japanese admiral. Ōmori graduated from the Naval Academy (1913) and the Torpedo School (1920). An instructor at the Torpedo School (1924–30, 1932–34, 1937–39), he was promoted lieutenant commander (1925). He held destroyer (1931–32) and battleship commands (1939–40) and was promoted captain (1939).

Promoted rear admiral (1940), Ōmori commanded 1st Destroyer Squadron (1940–41), part of the Pearl Harbor Task Force (December 1941). He commanded the Attu Occupation Force in the Aleutian Islands (June 1942). As commander of Cruiser Division 8 (November), he led the night attack to interfere with U.S. landings in Empress Augusta Bay, Bougainville (2 November 1943). His force of four cruisers and six destroyers was repulsed by U.S. Rear Admiral Stanton A. Merrill's flotilla of four cruisers and eight destroyers. U.S. radar was an important factor and in the battle Ōmori lost a light cruiser and a destroyer and most other ships damaged. Merrill had only one destroyer badly damaged.

Ōnishi, Takijirō (1891–1945) Japanese admiral. A graduate of the Naval Academy (1912), Ōnishi was one of the first Japanese military aviators. Resident officer in Britain and France (1918–20), he was promoted lieutenant commander. Instructor at the Kasumiga Ura Naval Air School (1925), he then commanded the Sasebo Naval Air Unit (1926). He commanded an air wing aboard a light carrier (1928) and was promoted commander (1929). On the staff of Third Fleet Headquarters, Shanghai (1932), he helped plan air strikes on that city (February–March). Promoted captain (1933), he held shore assignments and pushed for construction of aircraft carriers.

Promoted rear admiral (1939), Ōnishi became CofS of Eleventh Air Fleet (January 1941). Although he had initially opposed it, he helped plan the Japanese attack on Pearl Harbor (7 December 1941). He then led the air assault on the Philippines (December).

Promoted vice admiral (1943) and appointed CG of First Air Fleet on Luzon, the Philippines, Ōnishi was ordered to support the naval attack on American vessels, culminating in the Battle of Leyte Gulf (October 1944), but with only 150 aircraft available he formed suicide units. The relative success of these (beginning 25 October) led to the creation of other *kamikaze* units. Appointed vice chief of the Navy General Staff (May 1945), he insisted on fighting to the last man. Ōnishi committed suicide after the emperor's surrender broadcast.

Ōsako, Naotoshi (1844–1927) Japanese general. Ōsako fought against the British in the 1863 Satsuei War and against the Tokugawa shogunate in the 1868 Boshin (Restoration) War. He joined the imperial army (1871) and helped repress the 1877 Satsuma Rebellion. A major general during the 1894–95 Sino-Japanese War, he commanded an infantry brigade and saw fighting at Haicheng (December 1894).

Vice chief of the Army General Staff (1898–1900), Ōsako fought in the 1904–05 Russo-Japanese War as a lieutenant general commanding 7th Division. He participated in the siege of Port Arthur (May 1904–January 1905) and his divi-

sion captured a key hill in costly fighting. He also fought in the Battle of Mukden (February–March 1905). Promoted general (1906), he was made a viscount the year he retired (1908).

Ōshima, Hiroshi (1885–1975) Japanese general and diplomat. Ōshima graduated from both the Military Academy (1906) and Army Staff College (1915). He participated in the Siberian expedition (1918–19) and began his identification with Berlin as assistant military attaché there (1921–23) and was promoted major (1922). He was then military attaché to both Vienna and Budapest (1923–24). He taught at the Heavy Field Artillery School (1926–28) and was then on the Inspectorate General for Artillery (1928–30). Promoted colonel (1930), he commanded a regiment (1930–32), then was in the Operations Division of the Army General Staff (1931–34).

Ōhima returned to Berlin as military attaché (1934–38). A strong supporter of German–Japanese cooperation, he worked to secure the 1936 Anti-Comintern Pact. Promoted major general (1935) and lieutenant general (1938), he went on reserve status to become ambassador to Germany. Save for two short periods in 1939 and 1940, he served in this post during 1938–45. His messages sent to Tokyo were targeted by Allied code-breakers and became a source of important information concerning German–Japanese relations and strategies.

Ōshima helped negotiate the 1940 Tripartite Pact with Germany and Italy. After the war he was tried and convicted by Allied authorities in Japan as a war criminal. Sentenced to life in prison, he was released in 1955.

Ōshima, Hisanao (1848–1928) Japanese general. Ōshima fought in the 1868 Boshin (Restoration) War and was commissioned a lieutenant in the new imperial army (1871). He commanded a battalion in the repression of the 1877 Satsuma

Rebellion. During the 1894–95 Sino-Japanese War he commanded a brigade and, in the 1904–05 Russo-Japanese War, 9th Division. He was one of few Japanese generals who emerged from the long siege of Port Arthur (May 1904–January 1905) with his reputation intact. His division played a key role in the seizure of 203 Meter Hill (November–December 1904). Promoted general, he commanded the Guards Division (1906–08) and was inspector general of military training (1908–11). He was a military councillor (1911–13) before retiring in 1913.

Ōshima, Yoshimasa (1850–1926) Japanese general. A graduate of the Osaka Youth School (later the Military Academy), Ōshima was commissioned a captain in the new imperial army (1871). He commanded a battalion in the repression of the 1877 Satsuma Rebellion. During the 1894–95 Sino-Japanese War he commanded the 9th Mixed Brigade and was involved in fighting at Asan (June 1894) before the formal declarations of war. He fought in the Battle of Pyongyang (September) and in the Manchurian campaign (October 1894–January 1895). Promoted lieutenant general (1898), he commanded 3rd Division in Second Army during the 1904–05 Russo-Japanese War and fought in the battles of Liaoyang (August–September 1894), the Sha Ho (October), Sandepu (January 1905), and Mukden (February–March). Promoted general at the end of the war, he was the first governor-general of the Kwantung Leased Territory (1905–11). He was a military councillor (1911–15) before retirement.

Österman, Hugo (1892–1972) Finnish general. During the November 1939–March 1940 Russo-Finnish War, Österman commanded the Kannas Army defending the Karelian isthmus. He held the Soviet offensive at the Mannerheim Line (February 1940) until superior Soviet numbers overwhelmed the Finnish defenses. During the so-called War of Con-tinuation (1941–44) when Finland entered World War II against the Soviet Union to take back the territory taken from it the year before, he was inspector general of infantry. For a brief time (1944), he was Finnish representative to the German High Command.

Ōyama, Iwao (1842–1916) Japanese field marshal. A member of the Satsuma clan, Ōyama fought in the 1868 Boshin (Restoration) War. He then studied in Europe, especially France (1870–74). He fought to put down the 1877 Satsuma Rebellion, then held a number of important posts, including vice chief of the Army General Staff, minister of the army, and minister of the navy. One of Japan's most effective modern generals, during the 1894–95 Sino-Japanese War he commanded Second Army in the successful siege of Port Arthur (October–November 1894). During the 1904–05 Russo-Japanese War, he commanded Japanese forces in Manchuria and won the battles of Liaoyang (August–September 1904), the Sha Ho (October), Sandepu (January 1905), and Mukden (February–March). He retired in 1906.

Ozawa, Jisaburō (1866–1966) Japanese admiral. Ozawa graduated from both the Naval Academy (1909) and Naval Staff College (1921). He served in destroyers (1918–21). As a lieutenant commander (1921), he commanded destroyers (1924–25) and was a Torpedo School instructor (1927). Promoted captain, he commanded a destroyer squadron (1930–31). He taught at the Naval Staff College (1931–34), then commanded a cruiser, and then a battleship (1934–35). Promoted rear admiral, he was CofS of the Combined Fleet (1937). He then commanded the Torpedo School (1938), then 1st Naval Air Group (1939). Despite a lack of training in naval aviation, he advocated using carriers offensively. Promoted vice admiral, he was president of the Naval Staff College (September 1941).

At the start of World War II Ozawa commanded Southern Expeditionary Fleet and directed invasions of the Dutch East Indies (Indonesia) and Malaya (December 1941–March 1942). Appointed commander of Third Fleet (November 1942), he concurrently commanded it and First Mobile Fleet (March 1944). He led them against Admiral Raymond Spruance's Fifth Fleet in the Battle of the Philippine Sea (June), but suffered heavy losses in planes and aircraft carriers. He led the decoy force in the SHO-1 plan against Leyte. While he drew Admiral William Halsey's Third Fleet north away from the U.S. landing site as planned, the lack of aircraft cost him four carriers and a destroyer in the Battle of Cape Engaño (25 October). He then served concurrently as vice chief of the Naval General Staff and president of the Naval Staff College (November). He then commanded both the Combined Fleet and Escort Forces (May 1945), retiring after the Japanese surrender.

P

Paek In-yop (1922–) Republic of Korea general. The younger brother of Republic of Korea Army (ROKA) General Paek Son-yop, Paek graduated from the Japanese Military Academy (1945) and was commissioned a lieuteuant in the Japanese Army. After World War II he became a colonel in the ROK National Constabulary, and then commanded 17th Regiment in the Ongjin Peninsula and was a key participant in border fighting between North and South Korea (1948–49). His regiment was long identified with the "Haeju Attack" theory regarding the beginning of the 1950–53 Korean War. Since proven false, this theory held that the war was initiated by ROK forces.

Paek's 17th Regiment was forced to withdraw, with the remainder of the ROK Army, following the North Korean invasion (25 June 1950). He then commanded the Capital Division (August) and distinguished himself in later fighting. He studied at the U.S. Army War College (1953), was promoted lieutenant general, and commanded VI Corps. He retired from the military in 1964.

Paek Sŏn-yŏp (1920–) Republic of Korea general. Paek graduated from the Japanese Manchurian Military Academy (1941) and was a lieutenant in the Japanese Army during World War II. He returned to Korea after the war and graduated from the U.S. military government's Military English Language School, joining the Korean constabulary as a company commander.

When the Korean People's Army (KPA, North Korean Army) invaded South Korea (25 June 1950), Paek commanded the Republic of Korea Army (ROKA) 1st Division, which held for three days south of the Imjin River. He quickly established a reputation as one of the best ROKA generals of the 1950–53 Korean War. His division played an important role in the Defense of Taegu and subsequent drive into North Korea, taking the North Korean capital of Pyongyang. Promoted major general (April 1951), he then commanded ROKA I Corps. On the opening of armistice talks (July) he became one of the United Nations Command representatives. He then commanded Task Force Paek (November 1951–April 1952) in Operation RATKILLER, wiping out Communist guerrillas in South Korea. Promoted lieutenant general (January 1952), he commanded II Corps. He served twice as ROKA CofS (1952–54 and 1957–59). He was the first ROKA officer promoted to full general (January 1953) and was chairman of the Joint Chiefs of Staff (1959–60). He then retired (1960) from the military but served as both ambassador and cabinet minister.

Paget, Sir Bernard Charles Tolver (1887–1961) British general. Paget graduated from Sandhurst and was commissioned in the Oxfordshire and Buckinghamshire Light Infantry (1907). He served in India and fought on the Western Front as a captain in World War I. He was wounded twice, permanently crippling his left arm. Following recovery, he was a staff officer in BEF headquarters. After the war he graduated from the Staff College (1920) and served in a number of instructional posts, including commandant of the Quetta Staff College, India (1937) and commandant at Camberley (1938–39).

During World War II, General Paget took command of 18th Division (November 1939) and was promoted major general. He had only one brief field command in the war, of British troops in Norway (April 1940). Within days, London ordered an evacuation. Paget, who had performed well, was known as the "Hero of Trondheim" for extricating his troops from a hopeless situation.

Briefly CofS of Home Forces and head of Southeastern Command, he was promoted lieutenant general (1941). He then commanded Home Forces (December 1941–June 1943). Knighted (1942) and promoted general, he played a key role in training the British army, revising procedures and setting up new schools. Forming Twenty-First Army Group of fifteen divisions, he prepared it for the Normandy invasion until that command went to General Bernard Montgomery (December 1943). A disappointed Paget then served as CinC, Middle East (January 1944–October 1946), until he retired at his own request.

Pai Ch'ung-hsi (Bai Chonhxi) (1893–1966) Nationalist Chinese general. An officer in the provincial Kwangsi army until it was destroyed (1921), Pai then fled into the mountains and worked with other former Kwangsi officers, especially Li Tsung-jen (Li Zongren), in order to regain control of the province (1922–25). He joined the Nationalists or Kuomintang (KMT, Guomindang) (1925) and helped develop a strategy for reunifying China in the Northern Expedition (1926–28), while at the same time maintaining his power base at Kwangsi. A fine general, he defeated warlord Sun Ch'uan-fang (Sun Quanfang) at Lungt'an (1927). He supported Chiang Kai-shek (Jiang Jieshi) in his purge of Communists (CCP) within the KMT (1927), but he and Li then rebelled against Chiang for his concentration of power. The resulting military contest ended in stalemate. He and Li then worked to create a reformist provincial government (early 1930s), abandoning a second revolt (1937) to join forces with Chiang against the Japanese.

In the 1937–45 Sino-Japanese War, Pai was vice CofS for training (1937–44). He argued for keeping Chinese forces intact, then striking against extended Japanese army supply lines, and he opposed the stand at Nanking (Nanjing) (October–November) and loss of so many KMT troops. His strategy was ultimately adopted, and he took command of forces facing the Japanese in the ICHIGO offensive in south China (May–November 1944).

After the war, Pai directed the KMT occupation of Manchuria (October 1945–June 1946) and became Minister of War (1946). During the Civil War with the CCP (1946–49), he grew frustrated by Chiang's refusal to yield any authority and resigned (1948). He returned to command an army group in central China (1948) and opposed Chiang's plans for the disastrous Huai-hai campaign (November 1948–January 1949). He then tried to withdraw his remaining forces to Hainan Island but was blocked by Red Army forces, and fled abroad where he died in exile.

Palmer, Bruce, Jr. (1913–) U.S. general. Palmer graduated from West Point (1936). During World War II he rose to be CofS of the 6th Infantry Division in the Pacific Theater. He then commanded 63rd Infantry Regiment in Korea. Promoted lieutenant general, he commanded Task Force 120 and led U.S. land forces in the intervention in the Dominican Republic. He then commanded XVIII Airborne Corps at Fort Bragg (1965–67).

During the Vietnam War, Palmer commanded II Field Force (March–July 1967), the largest U.S. Army combat command in Vietnam. As deputy CofS of army forces in Vietnam (July 1967–June 1968), he had operational command of daily operations. Promoted full general, he was army vice CofS (August 1968–June 1972), then acting CofS (June–October). He commanded the Army Readiness Command until his retirement (September 1974). He then wrote a perceptive and critical book, *The 25-Year War: America's Military Role in Vietnam*, in which he concluded that the U.S. failure in Vietnam was shared by military and political leaders.

Palmer, John (1870–1955) U.S. general. Commissioned in the infantry on graduation from West Point (1892), Palmer served in the 15th Infantry and helped suppress the Chicago railroad strike riots (1894). He was in Cuba during the 1898 Spanish–American War and served in the China Relief Expedition during the 1900–01 Boxer Rebellion. An instructor at West Point (1901–06), he then served in the Philippines (1906–08) and was on the War Department General Staff (1908–10). Assigned to Tientsin, China (1910), he went to the Philippines (1914–16), then returned to the General Staff (1916).

Upon U.S. entry into World War I (April 1917), Palmer helped prepare draft legislation and plans for U.S. troops sent to France. AEF CG John J. Pershing then selected him as assistant CofS for training. He left that post because of illness, then set up training schools in France. As a colonel, he commanded 58th Brigade of 29th Division in the last month of the war.

After the war, Palmer helped draft the National Defense Act (1920). He was special assistant to Army CofS General Pershing (1921–23) and was promoted brigadier general (1922). After commanding a brigade in Panama (1924–26), he retired (1926) and wrote a number of books on military affairs.

During World War II, Palmer was recalled to active duty (1941–46) as special adviser to Army Chief of Staff George C. Marshall on military policy, and he helped draw plans for the post-war army.

Papagos, Alexandros (1883–1955) Greek general and political leader. Papagos studied at the Greek and Belgian military academies and was commissioned in the army (1906). He fought in the 1912–13 Balkan Wars and in the 1919–22 war against Turkey, commanding first a battalion and then a regiment. In 1935 he was minister of war. He became army CofS under General John Metaxas when the latter seized power and became dictator (1936).

Papagos commanded Greek forces during the war with Italy from October 1940, halting the invasion and then going on the offensive. He adroitly confined operations to the mountain areas where the Italians could not exploit their technological advantage. His forces defeated the Italian Ninth Army and invaded Italian-held Albania; they fought bravely in the German invasion (April 1941), but he was slow to withdraw them to the Aliakmon Line and, even with British assistance, was unable to halt the Germans. Taken prisoner, he was sent to Germany and imprisoned at Dachau.

Released by U.S. troops in 1945, Papagos returned to Greece and utilized American aid to defeat Communist insurgents in the ensuing Civil War. Advanced to field marshal (October 1949), he resigned his military posts in May 1951. He then formed the conservative Greek Rally Party, which won the 1952 elections. Elected prime minister in 1952, he served in that post until his death.

Papoulas, Anastasios (1859–1935) Greek general. Active in politics from an early age, Papoulas was an avid supporter of King Constantine. Appointed by the king to command the Greek Army in Anatolia (late 1920), he began an offensive that was stopped by the Turks in the first battle of Inönü (January 1921). Building up his army to 100,000 men, he renewed the offensive, only to be halted in the second battle of Inönü (March 1921). When Constantine took over the army in person, he remained in the field and helped keep the army together during its retreat before the advancing Turks.

Papoulas subsequently opposed the monarchy and supported the government of Eleutherios Venizelos (1928–32, 1933). He then led a revolt in support of Venizelos (1935). On its failure, he was captured, tried, and executed.

Park, Sir Keith Rodney (1892–1975) British air marshal. Born in New Zealand, Park studied mining at Otago University. During World War I he joined the New Zealand Expeditionary Force, secured an artillery commission, and served in France. Wounded at the Somme, on his recovery he joined the Royal Flying Corps and then the Royal Air Force (1918), becoming a captain. After World War I he was a flying instructor, fighter station commander, and served in Argentina. As senior air staff officer to Air Marshal Sir Hugh Dowding (1938–40), Park was staunchly loyal to his chief. Appointed to command Fighter Group 11 (April 1940), he was promoted air vice marshal (July). His group provided cover during the Dunkerque evacuation (May–June), then defended the most vital area of the country during the Battle of Britain (July–October). He flew his own Hurricane fighter to evaluate the situation. His strategy was to try to avoid fighter-to-fighter combat but to disrupt the German bomber formations before they could reach their targets.

Park and Dowding rejected 12 Group commander Air Vice Marshal Traford Leigh-Mallory's "big-wing" concept for concentrating aircraft. When the air staff agreed to Leigh-Mallory's ideas (mid-November), Air Marshal William Sholto Douglas replaced Dowding and Leigh-Mallory replaced Park at 11 Group.

Park then commanded air defenses on Malta (1942–43). He was supreme air commander in the Middle East (1944), then went to Southeast Asia to support the reconquest of Burma (1945). Knighted (1945), he retired in 1946.

Parker, George Marshall, Jr. (1889–1968) U.S. general. Parker graduated from the Shattuck School (1909) and was commissioned (1910). He served in the Philippines, Panama Canal Zone, and along the Mexican border as well as participating in the 1916–17 Punitive Expedition into nothern Mexico. He did not see combat in World War I.

Parker graduated from the Command and General Staff School (1923) and the Army War College (1925). He was promoted lieutenant colonel (1934), colonel (1939), and then brigadier general (April 1941). He was then ordered to the Philippines where he commanded the Southern Luzon Force. He was promoted major general shortly after the U.S. entered World War II. Following the Japanese landings he took charge of the defense of Bataan, then II Corps. Forced to surrender (April 1942), he was held as a POW until the end of the war, when he was released in Manchuria. He retired from the army in September 1946.

Patch, Alexander McCarrell, Jr. (1889–1945) U.S. general. Patch attended Lehigh University for a year before graduating from West Point (1913). Commissioned in the infantry, he participated in the 1916–17 Punitive Expedition into Mexico and, on U.S. entry into World War I, directed the Army Machine Gun School in France. He participated in the Aisne–Marne, St. Mihiel, and Meuse–Argonne offensives, and ended the war a temporary lieutenant colonel and battalion commander.

Following occupation duty in Germany, Patch returned to the U.S. as a captain. An instructor at the Staunton (Virginia) Military Academy (1925–28, 1932–36), he graduated from the Command and General Staff School (1925) and the Army War College (1932), and he served on the Infantry Board that instituted the triangular division (1936–39).

Promoted colonel (August 1939), Patch commanded the 47th Infantry Regiment. Promoted brigadier general (1941), he commanded U.S. troops on New Caledonia (1942) and was promoted major general (March 1942). He led these troops, which became the Americal Division, in relief of the 1st Marine Division on Guadalcanal (December 1942–January 1943), and he commanded XIV Corps there (January–April 1943). Recalled to the U.S., he commanded IV Corps at Fort Lewis, Washington, and was involved in training (1943–44).

Patch then commanded Seventh Army in Sicily (March 1944), and led it as a lieutenant general in Operation DRAGOON (15 August 1944), the invasion of southern France. His forces pushed up the Rhone Valley, linking up with Third Army at Dijon. Seventh Army captured Strasbourg (November) and was involved in hard fighting in the Colmar Pocket (February 1945). His forces then advanced into Austria, linking up with Fifth Army at the Brenner Pass.

Following the defeat of Germany, Patch received command of Fourth Army in Texas in preparation for the invasion of Japan. When the war ended he was given charge of planning army reorganization, but died at the end of 1945. A strict disciplinarian with great concern for his men, he was an exceptionally fine trainer. He was posthumously promoted to general in 1954.

Pate, Randolph McCall (1898–1961) U.S. Marine Corps general. Pate graduated

from the Virginia Military Institute (1921) and was commissioned into the Marine Corps. He experienced a variety of assignments and was promoted lieutenant colonel (1942) and assigned to the 1st Marine Division on Guadalcanal. Promoted colonel (1943), he served as deputy CofS of the V Amphibious Corps and participated in the World War II Iwo Jima and Okinawa campaigns.

After the war Pate was stationed in Washington as director of reserves. He was then CofS of Marine Corps Schools at Quantico (1947). Promoted brigadier general (1948) and then major general (1952), he commanded 2nd Marine Division at the end of the 1950–53 Korean War (1953). He returned to the United States (1954) as assistant commandant of the Corps with the rank of lieutenant general. Promoted general (1956), he replaced General Lemuel Shepherd as Marine Corps commandant (1956–59). He retired in December 1959.

Patrick, Mason Mathews (1863–1942) U.S. general. Patrick was commissioned in the engineers on graduation from West Point (1886). He graduated from the Engineers School of Practice (1889), taught at West Point (1892–95, 1903–06), and worked on the Mississippi River improvement project (1897–1901). Promoted major (1904), he was chief engineer for the army in Cuba (1907–09), then worked on river control projects in the United States (1909–16). Promoted lieutenant colonel (1916), he served with U.S. forces mobilized along the Mexican border (1916–17).

Patrick went to France with the AEF following U.S. entry into World War I (April 1917). Promoted brigadier general (August), he was chief engineer of the lines of communication (September). Appointed commander of the combined air service of the AEF (May 1918), he was promoted major general (June). He returned to the U.S.A. and resumed engineer duties (July 1919). Assistant chief of engineers (1920–21), he was then chief of the Air Service (October 1921). He learned to fly, established an experimental facility at Wright Field Ohio, sat on the court-martial of Brigadier General William Mitchell (1925), and helped secure reorganization of the Air Service as the Air Corps (1926). After retirement (1927), he published a book, *The United States in the Air* (1928).

Pattle, Marmaduke T. St. John (1914–41) South African pilot. RAF Squadron Leader Pattle from South Africa is generally regarded as the leading Allied ace of World War II. His tally is variously assessed at between forty-one and fifty-one victories. He was shot down and killed over Athens, Greece (20 April 1941). The problem in assessing the exact total is that many of his kills came in remote areas, over the Western Desert flying in a Gladiator and over Greece in a Hurricane. Records were also lost in the BEF evacuation from Greece. His total is all the more impressive in that it occurred over a relatively short space of time. U.S. Major Richard Bong is credited with 40 victories, followed by RAF Group Captain J. E. Johnson with 38.

Patton, George Smith, Jr. (1885–1945) U.S. general. Patton attended the Virginia Military Institute and graduated from West Point (1909), being commissioned in the cavalry. An expert horseman, he participated in the Olympic Games (1912). He took part in the 1916–17 Punitive Expedition into Mexico. Following U.S. entry into World War I (April 1917), he was an aide to AEF commander General John J. Pershing but transferred to the Tank Corps and headed the U.S. tank training center in France at Langres before commanding the 304th Tank Brigade as a temporary lieutenant colonel. Wounded in the St. Mihiel offensive (September 1918), he won promotion to colonel and participated in the Meuse–Argonne offensive (September–November).

After the war Patton reverted to the permanent rank of captain. An ernest champion of armored warfare, he graduated from the Command and General Staff School (1924) and the Army War College (1932). He returned to armor and was promoted temporary brigadier general (October 1940) and then temporary major general (April 1941) commanding the 2nd Armored Division. He commanded I Corps, and then the Desert Training Center.

Patton commanded the Western Task Force in the Allied invasion of North Africa (8 November 1942). Following the U.S. defeat at the Kasserine Pass, he took command of II Corps (March 1943) and was promoted temporary lieutenant general. He then commanded Seventh Army in the invasion of Sicily (July 1943). A disciplinary incident there almost ended his career. Finally given command of Third Army (January 1944), he landed with it in France (August 1944) and conducted a brilliant campaign across France and into Germany. Forces under his command relieved Bastogne during the Battle of the Bulge (December 1944), crossed the Rhine (March 1945) and reached into Czechoslovakia. His army had covered more ground and taken more prisoners than any other Allied force. Promoted general (April 1945), Patton then commanded U.S. occupation forces in Bavaria. He died of complications following injuries received in an automobile accident.

Pau, Paul Marie César Gerald (1848–1932) French general. Pau graduated from St. Cyr (1869) and lost a hand during the 1870–71 Franco-German War. He continued in the military and rose to lieutenant general (1903).

French Army commander General Joseph Joffre recalled Pau from retirement (August 1914) to command the newly formed Army of Alsace. Tasked with covering the right flank of the First Army's drive to recover that province, his three corps won several victories before reversals ended the French offensive. His army was then dissolved and its troops transferred to Sixth Army. Pau later served as a member of the Council of War and headed several missions abroad during the war.

Paulus, Friedrich (1890–1957) German field marshal. Paulus joined the army as an officer cadet (1910) and was commissioned (1911). He fought in most of the big Western Front battles of World War I and ended the conflict as a captain in the Alpenkorps, stationed in Serbia. Paulus remained in the army after the war and held a succession of staff assignments, in which he was known for his attention to detail.

Promoted brigadier general in 1939, Paulus was CofS of Tenth (later Sixth) Army and fought with it in Poland and then Holland. He was then director of operations at army general headquarters where he helped develop plans for the invasion of the Soviet Union. He replaced General Walter von Reichenau as commander of Sixth Army (January 1942), which defeated the Russians in the Battle of Kharkov (February 1942) and then drove into southern Russia.

As German commander in the Battle of Stalingrad, Paulus slavishly followed Hitler's orders, dooming his army to a slow death. Promoted field marshal (15 January 1943), he surrendered two weeks later. He was kept prisoner in the Soviet Union until 1953, when he was allowed to live in East Germany.

Pavelić, Ante (1889–1959) Croatian nationalist and leader of the Fascist Ustašas. An extreme right-wing deputy in the Yugoslav parliament, Pavelić emigrated to set up his organization in exile following King Alexander's suspension of the constitution (1934). Supported by the Italian and Hungarian government, his Ustašas carried out the assassination of King Alexander and French Foreign Minister Louis Bathou at Marseille (1934).

Following the collapse of Yugoslavia after the German invasion (April 1941), he became *Poglavmik* ("Leader") of an "independent" Croatia under German control. He was a militant Catholic and fiercely anti-Serb.

Although the state had its own military, Pavelić relied primarily on the Ustašas militia, equivalent to the German SS, which executed hundreds of thousands of Jews, Orthodox Serbs, and other minorities within Croatia. He remained slavishly loyal to Hitler. After the war he managed to reach Argentina, where he survived an assassination attempt. He then settled in Spain.

Pavlov, Dimitri Grigor'evich (1897–1941) Soviet general. Pavlov fought in World War I and was taken prisoner by the Germans. He joined the Red Army after the war. A cavalry officer, he graduated from the Frunze Military Academy (1928) and the Military-Technical Academy (1931). He then commanded the 4th Mechanized Brigade, one of the Red Army's first mechanized units. He then headed the Armored Directorate (1937). He led armor advisors sent to assist the Republican side in the 1936–39 Spanish Civil War and concluded, falsely, that there was no future for large armor formations. Although this decision was shared, such thinking helped bring the disbandment of the Soviet mechanized corps (late 1939).

As a colonel general, Pavlov was appointed to the Main Military Council (July 1940). Promoted general of the army (February 1941), he received command of the Western Front (6 June) just prior to the German invasion (22 June). Facing German Army Group Center, he placed three of his armies forward and only one in reserve.

A week after the German invasion of the Soviet Union and the collapse of his sector of the front, Pavlov and his chief of staff were ordered to Moscow. Arrested (22 July), he was made the scapegoat for

Soviet military disaster, accused of collaboration with the Germans, and shot.
Also executed were his chief of staff
Major General V. Y. Klimovskikh, Fourth
Army commander General A. A. Korob-
kov, and several divisional commanders
and commissars.

Peiper, Joachim (1915–76) German SS
officer. Peiper joined first the Hitler
Youth, then the SS. Commissioned in the
SS (1936), he served on Heinrich Himmler's personal staff but sought a combat
command and fought as a company commander in the elite SS *Leibstandarte Adolf
Hitler* (LAH) in the invasion of France
and Benelux (May 1940) and led an
abortive effort to seize bridges over the
Meuse. He served in the LAH in the
invasion of the Soviet Union (June 1941)
and in Italy. In Italy his troops destroyed
the town of Boves and murdered its
inhabitants (September 1943). After LAH
transferred to France, he studied techniques for night movements that were later
employed with great effectiveness in the
Ardennes Offensive (Battle of the Bulge,
December–January 1944). In that offensive his unit, *Kampfgruppe* Peiper, was
responsible for the murder of U.S. prisoners at Malmédy (17 December 1944).
Tried and condemned after the war, he
was imprisoned but later released. He
died in mysterious circumstances while
living in France.

P'eng Te-huai (Peng Dehuai) (1898–1974)
People's Republic of China marshal. P'eng
joined the Chinese Communist party
(1928). During the 1935 Long March, he
became one of Mao Tse-tung's (Mao
Zedong) closest lieutenants and was duly
appointed vice-commander of the army
(April 1937).

P'eng commanded the Eighth Route
Army (1937–46). His record as a field
general through the civil war was at best
spotty. Of twenty-nine battles he directed
to 1949, fifteen were victories and fourteen were defeats. At the start of the

1950–53 Korean War, he commanded the
First Field Army and also retained his
post as deputy CinC of the People's
Liberation Army (PLA). He commanded
Chinese forces in Korea (the Chinese
People's Volunteer Army) (October 1950–
September 1954) and signed the Armistice
Agreement (July 1953).

The Korean War convinced P'eng of the
need for China to modernize its forces,
which he endeavored to carry out as
minister of defense (1954–1959). He was
promoted marshal (1955). Dismissed by
Mao (1959) for leading an "anti-Party
clique," he was arrested and imprisoned
during the 1966–69 Cultural Revolution.
Mao ordered that he receive no medical
care and he died of complications from
torture. He was posthumously rehabilitated in 1978.

Percival, Arthur Ernest (1887–1966) British general. He began his military career
as a private and worked his way up
through the ranks. He served in Malaya
(1936–38), and at the beginning of World
War II he commanded the 43rd Division
of the BEF in France. Following the
Dunkerque Evacuation (May–June 1940),
he commanded the 44th Division in Britain. Appointed CG, Malaya (July 1941)
largely on the strength of his previous
service there, he understood there were
major shortcomings in the defenses of
both Malaya and Singapore (Europe received priority) but he did little to rectify
these, especially in training.

When the Japanese invaded, Percival's
opponent, Japanese General Tomoyuki
Yamashita, had better trained and
equipped troops and air and naval superiority, but he had only half the number of
men and many of these were sick. His
ammunition was also running out when
he bluffed Percival into surrendering Singapore, "the Gibraltar of Asia" (15 February 1942). In the whole Malaya
campaign the British sustained 138,700
casualties, mostly captured; the Japanese
lost only 9,824. British prestige in Asia

never recovered from the blow of what was probably the worst defeat in national history.

Kept as a POW in Manchuria the remainder of the war, Percival attended the formal Japanese surrender ceremony in Tokyo Bay (2 September 1945).

Pershing, John Joseph (1860–1948) U.S. general. Commissioned in the cavalry on graduation from West Point (1886), Pershing saw service in Indian campaigns before becoming professor of military science at the University of Nebraska (1891–95). He served with the 10th Cavalry (the Buffalo Soldiers) (1895–96), from which he gained his nickname "Black Jack." During the 1898 Spanish-American War he fought in Cuba and then went to the Philippines. He was a military attaché in Japan and an observer during the 1904–05 Russo-Japanese War, and was promoted to brigadier general (1906). He then served again in the Philippines. He commanded the 1916–17 Punitive Expedition into northern Mexico in an unsuccessful search for Pancho Villa.

When the United States entered World War I, Pershing was a major general commanding the Southern Department. Selected (May 1917) to command the American Expeditionary Force (AEF) in France, Pershing proved an excellent choice. A strict disciplinarian, he insisted on excellence in his subordinates. Promoted general (October 1917), he sought to preserve the independence of U.S. forces and directed the St. Mihiel Offensive (September 1918), but he was overruled by Marshal Ferdinand Foch in his desire to push an offensive toward Metz. He then led U.S. forces in the Meuse–Argonne offensive (September–November 1918). Promoted general of the armies (six stars) (July 1919), Pershing was army CofS (1921–24) before retiring (September 1924). He was later ambassador to Peru and served on the American Battle Monuments Commission.

Pétain, Henri-Philippe (1856–1951) French marshal. Pétain entered St. Cyr (1876) and without World War I would have retired as a colonel. He held that new machine weapons gave the defense superiority. When World War I began, he saw that it would be a struggle of attrition and he argued for wearing out the Germans along the entire front and only then mounting a "decisive effort."

At the start of the war Pétain was temporarily commanding a brigade. He commanded a division (September), then an army corps (November), and was then a full general in command of Second Army (June 1915). When the Germans mounted their offensive at Verdun (February 1916), he was placed in charge, reorganizing its defenses and transforming logistics so that supplies ran smoothly to the front. His leadership there made him a national hero.

Following the disastrous Nivelle Offensive (April–May 1917), Pétain was called on to deal with widespread mutinies in the French Army. Made commander of the French Army, he improved conditions and morale and promised the men that he would not waste their lives needlessly.

Pétain remained commander of the French Army until 1931. He supported construction of the Maginot Line and served as War Minister (1934). Appointed ambassador to Spain (1939), he was recalled to be the last premier of the Third Republic (June 1940) and negotiated the surrender to Germany.

Following the granting of emergency powers, Pétain set up an authoritarian government in southern, unoccupied France at Vichy that accepted collaboration with Nazi Germany. Tried as a war criminal after the war, he was convicted and sentenced to death, which was commuted to life in prison.

Petlyakov, Vladimir Mikhaylovich (1891–1942) Russian aircraft designer. Petlyakov worked for "Father of Russian Aviation" Nikolay Zhukovisky (1917–18) and then under Andrei Tupolev in the Central Aerodynamic Institute. A graduate of the Moscow Higher Technical School (1922), his four-engine, long-range TB-7 (renamed Pe-8) carried five tons of bombs (1936), but only 79 of this plane were produced. He ran foul of the 1930s Great Purges, but was allowed to continue working under special arrest.

Petlyakov designed the principal Soviet light bomber of the war, the two-engine Pe-2, counterpart to the Ju-87 Stuka dive bomber, U.S. A-20, and British Mosquito. With some 11,000 produced, it made up two-thirds of Soviet bomber production in World War II. Petlyakov was killed in a plane crash during the war.

Petrov, Ivan Efimovich (1896–1958) Soviet general. Petrov was commssioned out of military school in 1917 and entered the Red Army (1918). He fought in the 1918–20 Civil War as a platoon leader, rising to political commissar in a cavalry regiment. In the 1930s he commanded a cavalry regiment and cavalry brigade, and then the Tashkent Military Academy.

During World War II Petrov served mainly in the Crimea and Caucasus. Following the German invasion (22 June 1941), he was promoted major general and commanded 2nd Cavalry Division before Odessa. As commander of the Special Maritime Army in the Crimea (August–October 1941), he was forced to withdraw to the Crimea where he commanded Sevastopol's land defenses and escaped with other senior commanders on a submarine (June 1942). He then commanded Forty-Fourth Army in the Crimea (October). Promoted lieutenant general, he was CofS of the North Caucaus Front.

Promoted colonel general (August 1943), Petrov led the Novorossisk–Taman Offensive (September–October 1943) and was promoted general of the army. Following command differences, he was demoted to colonel general and removed from his post (January 1944). In March

1944 he commanded Thirty-Third Army, then Fourth Ukrainian Front (August), regaining the rank of full general. He led the Western Carpathian Offensive (January–February 1945), but was removed following a failed offensive (March). At war's end he was CofS of the 1st Ukranian Front. After the war he held a variety of posts and headed the Tashkent Military District until 1952.

Pflanzer-Baltin, Karl Freiherr von (1855–1925) Austro-Hungarian general. Pflanzer-Baltin graduated from the Theresa Military Academy (1875) and attended the War Academy (1879–80). He held a variety of field assignments, served on the General Staff, and was an instructor at the War Academy before becoming CofS of XII Corps. In 1911 he was in line to command a corps, but poor health caused him to be sent to Vienna as inspector general of Corps Officer Schools. In June 1914 he requested early retirement.

Pflanzer-Baltin was reactivated for service during World War I (October 1914) and led troops against the Russians in the eastern Carpathians and Bukovina. Promoted general of cavalry, he took command of an army corps, redesignated (May 1915) Seventh Army. A successful improvisor, Pflanzer-Baltin was one of the more successful Austro-Hungarian army commanders of the war. In June 1916, however, Seventh Army was overwhelmed and forced out of East Galicia during the Brusilov offensive. He then had his army placed under "German guardianship," as he put it, when German General Hans von Seeckt was made his "supreme chief of staff." He was relieved of his command entirely (September).

Recalled and given charge of training of all new recruits (March 1917), Pflanzer-Baltin received command of Austro-Hungarian forces in Albania (July 1918). Here he not only held his position but also directed the last successful offensive of the Central Powers before the end of the war.

Phillips, Sir Tom Spencer Vaughan (1888–1941) British admiral. Phillips entered the navy (1903) and, following routine assignments, was assistant director (1932–33), then director (1935–38) of the Plans Division at the Admiralty. Promoted rear admiral, he was appointed vice chief of the naval staff (1939–41). He was then promoted again to acting vice admiral (February 1940). On the instigation of his chief, Admiral Sir Dudley Pound, he was appointed CinC of the embryo Eastern Fleet (May 1941), the creation of which he had urged, to consist of six capital ships, a modern aircraft carrier, and appropriate light forces.

Promoted acting admiral on the instigation of Prime Minister Winston Churchill, Phillips was ordered to Singapore with the new battleship *Prince of Wales* and battle cruiser *Repulse*, the only capital ships the Allies would have in the western Pacific. This proved a major blunder on the part of the War Cabinet. The new aircraft carrier *Indomitable*, which was to have accompanied the two capital ships, ran aground off Jamaica and required repairs.

Phillips's Force Z of the two capital ships and four destroyers, was then intercepted by Japanese aircraft off the coast of Malaya (10 December) and the two capital ships were sunk. Although the destroyers rescued 2,081 of 2,921 crewmen, Phillips went down with his ship. This event proved that ships would have to have aircraft protection if they were to survive enemy air attack.

Pick, Lewis A. (1890–1956) U.S. general. Pick graduated from the Virginia Polytechnic Institute (1914), and then worked as a civil engineer. Following U.S. entry into World War I, he completed officers' training and was commissioned in the Corps of Engineers (August 1917). He went to France as an engineer company commander in the AEF (March 1918), participating in the Meuse–Argonne Offensive (September–November).

Demobilized after the war (1919), Pick applied for and received a regular army commission as a second lieutenant of engineers (1920). He then commanded a company in the Philippines, organizing the first Philippine engineer regiment (1920–23), graduated from the Engineer School, Fort Belvoir (1924), was an ROTC instructor at Alabama Polytechnic Institute (1924–25), was in the New Orleans Engineer District (1925–27), and organized the ROTC unit at Texas A&M College (University) (1928–32). He then attended, and was an instructor at, the Command and General Staff College, Fort Leavenworth (until 1938). He graduated from the Army War College (1939).

Promoted colonel after the U.S. entered World War II, Pick oversaw construction of military equipment from Missouri to Montana, including fifty-six airfields and hundreds of army camps. His major accomplishment came in North Burma (1943–45): the construction of the Ledo Road ("Pick's Pike") to connect with the old Burma Road from Ledo, India to Bhamo, Burma. The new 478-mile road ran through jungles, over mountains, and across ten rivers. Construction took twenty-five months.

Promoted brigadier general (February 1944) and major general (March 1945), Pick was Missouri River division engineer (1945–49), then chief of engineers (March 1949) until his retirement in February 1953.

Piłsudski, Józef Klemens (1867–1935) Marshal of Poland and statesman. An ardent patriot, Piłsudski was early involved in anti-Russian activity and exiled to Siberia. He favored collaboration with Austria-Hungary and Germany during World War I in order to secure independence for his homeland.

Piłsudski organized the Polish Legion to fight on the side of the Central Powers against Russia. Although he was minister of war in the provisional Polish government, he soon withdrew his support from the Central Powers because they refused to commit themselves on Poland's future.

Following World War I, Piłsudski guided the revived Polish state through particularly turbulent times. He commanded Polish forces during the 1920 Russo-Polish War, and he defeated the Russians in the Battle of Warsaw (August 1920). Concerned over the decay in his country, he seized power in a march on Warsaw (May 1926) with the intention of ending the divisions and strengthening the state. He then recast the constitution and ruled as de *facto* dictator until his death.

Plumer, Herbert Charles Onslow, Viscount (1857–1932) British general. Plumer was commissioned directly into the army (1876). He then served in a variety of assignments. Promoted to brigadier general (1903), then major general and quartermaster general of the Army Council, he then commanded 5th Division in Ireland (1906–09). Promoted to lieutenant general (1910), he was made CinC at York.

Early in World War I, Plumer received command of II Corps (December 1914). In 1915 he commanded V Corps in Smith-Dorrien's Second Army in the Second Battle of Ypres and afterward assumed command of the Second Army. A methodical planner, he was one of the best British generals of the war. Following the abortive Nivelle Offensive (April 1917), the British attempted an offensive while the French rebuilt their shattered forces. After careful preparations and employing mines, he took and held the high ground at Messines (June 1917). He then took over command of operations toward Passchendaele (August) and captured the high ground there (November) after eight great battles. Dispatched to Italy following the Italian defeat at Caporetto (October–November 1917), he commanded five British and six French divisions there. Returned to Flanders just prior to the start of Ludendorff's spring 1918 offensives, his army was forced back but held

the Ypres salient until the German drive stalled.

After the war Plumer commanded British forces in Germany. Promoted field marshal (1919), he was then made a baron. He was governor of Malta (1919–24) and then high commissioner in Palestine (1925–28). He was made viscount in 1929.

Pohl, Hugo von (1855–1916) German admiral. Pohl joined the Imperial Navy (1870s) and gained distinction in the 1900–01 Boxer Rebellion, when in command of battle cruiser *Hansa* he led a multi-national assault against Fort Taku. He then commanded battleship squadrons. Ennobled and promoted full admiral, he became chief of the Admiralty Staff (1913).

When World War I began, Pohl favored limited rather than full-scale fleet operations. He also advocated more aggressive U-boat warfare and accelerated naval building programs. After the Dogger Bank fiasco (January 1915), he succeeded Admiral Friedrich Ingenohl as chief of the High Seas Fleet. His year-long tenure predictably brought no noteworthy operations in the North Sea but some actions in the Baltic against the Russian Navy.

Pohl persuaded Kaiser William II to step up submarine activities by declaring a war zone around the British Isles. This policy soon had to be reversed after the sinking of the *Lusitania* (7 May 1915). Pohl revealed he was dying from liver cancer (January 1916), whereupon he was replaced by Reinhard Scheer.

Pol Pot (Saloth Sar) (1928–98) Cambodian military leader and head of state. Born into a prosperous family, Pol Pot attended high school in Cambodia and then a technical school in Paris, where he joined the French Communist party. Returning to Cambodia (1953), he was active against the French and later led the Khmer Rouge guerrilla movement against the Lon Nol government, seizing power by force of arms (April 1975). The Khmer Rouge changed the country's name to Kampuchea and instituted a reign of terror in an effort to produce a classless Marxist agricultural society. Up to two million Cambodians were killed and the rest of the population toiled under terrible conditions. Following border incidents between Kampuchea and the Socialist Republic of Vietnam (SRV), the SRV invaded and occupied the country (1978). Pol Pot and the Khmer Rouge then conducted guerrilla warfare against the Vietnamese.

Pol Pot surfaced again when he was tried by the Khmer Rouge and sentenced to life under house arrest (1997). He died in mysterious circumstances.

Popov, Markian Mikhailovich (1902–69) Soviet general. Popov graduated from a teachers' seminary (1913), became an ensign in the Russian army (1916), and fought in World War I. After the war he joined the Red Army and the Communist party. A divisional CofS during the 1918–20 Civil War, he graduated from the Military Political Academy (1931).

Popov was CofS of the First Special Red Banner Army in the Far East (1938–39). He then took command of the Leningrad Military District (January 1941) and held a succession of commands there following the German invasion (22 June).

Popov commanded Sixty-First Army in the Bryansk Front (November 1942-June 1942), then in succession Fortieth Army, Fifth Strike Army, Forty-Fifth Tank Army, and the Reserve Front (1942–43). Promoted general colonel, he directed the Bryansk Front (June 1943), until promoted general of the army and given command of the Baltic Front, which became the Second Baltic Front (October 1943). In this capacity he helped liberate Leningrad (January 1944).

A cautious commander, Popov was criticized for moving too slowly. When his forces failed to take Riga, he was removed from command, reduced in rank,

and made CofS of the Leningrad Front and the Second Baltic Front (1944–45). After the war he headed various military districts, was restored to the rank of general of the army (1953), and was appointed to the military inspectorate (1962).

Portal, Charles Frederick Algernon, Viscount Portal of Hungerford (1893–1971) British air marshal. Educated at Christ Church, Oxford, Portal qualified for the bar but enlisted in the Royal Engineers on the outbreak of World War I (August 1914) and was soon commissioned. He joined the Royal Flying Corps (1915) and was first an observer and then a pilot. By war's end he was a lieutenant colonel and had flown 900 missions. He remained in the Royal Air Force after the war and became a flying instructor. Also a fine administrator, he advanced rapidly. He commanded British forces in Aden (1934–35), then joined the staff of the Imperial Defense College. Promoted air vice-marshal (July 1937), he was then at the Air Ministry, where he pushed training and established thirty new airfields.

On the outbreak of World War II (September 1939), Portal was promoted air marshal. Reassigned to head Bomber Command (April 1940), he recommended striking targets within Germany, which had the support of Prime Minister Winston Churchill. Although the raids had little practical effect, they did cause Adolf Hitler to shift German targeting to London, which was decisive in the Battle of Britain.

Portal then was chief of the air staff (October 1940–January 1946) until his retirement. Widely regarded as Britain's leading airman and one of the key strategic planners of the war, he supported the U.S. position of daytime bombing, which Churchill opposed. His own program of area bombing of German industry, while controversial, inflicted great damage on the German war effort. Knighted (1940), he was made a baron (1945) and 1st Viscount Portal of Hungerford (1946)

Potiorek, Oskar (1853–1933) Austro-Hungarian field marshal. Potiorek became deputy chief of the General Staff. He was then commander of III Corps (1907) and inspector general of the Habsburg armies (1910). He was then governor of Bosnia-Herzegovina (1911).

Potiorek believed only a heavy hand could maintain Habsburg control, and he had no interest in reconciling even the more conservative Serb elements to Austrian rule. His repressive measures helped foster the very discontent they were designed to stamp out and they were often at cross-purposes with the directives of the civil administration in Vienna, which favored a more conciliatory approach. He took no special security precautions at the time of the Archduke Franz Ferdinand's visit to Sarajevo, where the latter was assassinated (28 June 1914), touching off the chain of events that led to World War I.

Condemned for his negligence, Potiorek nonetheless on 28 July received command of Habsburg forces to invade Serbia. Despite having Fifth and Sixth Armies (19 divisions) at his disposal, his repeated offensives all failed, and he was relieved of his command (December 1914).

Pound, Sir Dudley (1877–1943) British admiral. Pound joined the Royal Navy in 1891 as a cadet. He rose rapidly in rank and was promoted captain at the beginning of World War I. He commanded battleship *Colossus* in the Battle of Jutland (31 May–1 June 1916). He then served on the Admiralty staff, but returned to sea in the 1920s to command the battle cruiser *Repulse*. Appointed commander of the Mediterranean Fleet with the rank of admiral (1936), he was serving in that capacity when First Sea Lord Sir Roger Backhouse died, and he

was recalled to London to head the Royal Navy (June 1939).

Promoted admiral of the fleet (July), as first sea lord and chief of the naval staff, Pound's main duties were to advise Prime Minister Neville Chamberlain concerning strategy and to command the navy. He also served (until March 1942) as chairman of the Chiefs of Staff Committee and was a member of the Anglo-American Chiefs of Staff Committee. A capable administrator, he was not always successful in operational matters during World War II, as when he ordered Northern convoy PQ 17, bound for the Soviet Union (July 1942), to scatter because he believed a powerful German surface force was about to attack it. As a result, twenty-four of thirty-seven merchant ships were lost. He got on well with Prime Minister Winston Churchill and was able to counter some of his schemes. He also succeeded in having the Battle of the Atlantic receive top priority (1942–43). During his tenure, his health progressively deteriorated and, after several strokes, he resigned (September 1943) and died the next month.

Powell, Colin Luther (1937–) U.S. general. Powell graduated from the City College of New York (1958) and was commissioned in the infantry. Following a tour in Germany (1959–62), he served two tours in Vietnam, as an advisor (1962–63) and with the 23rd Division (1968–69). He attended the Command and General Staff College (1968) and earned a master's degree in business administration at George Washington University (1971).

Powell was a White House Fellow (1972–73) and thereafter began a steady rise in responsibility and rank. He attended the National War College (1976) and, as a colonel, commanded a brigade of the 101st Airborne Division (1976–77). He had several assignments with government agencies and became senior military assistant to the secretary of defense

(1983–86). He commanded V Corps in Germany as a lieutenant general (1986–87). He was then assistant to the president and assistant for National Security Affairs (1987–89). Promoted general (the first African American to hold that rank), he commanded U.S. Army Forces Command (January 1989). He was then appointed chairman of the Joint Chiefs of Staff (1989), the youngest man and the first African American to hold that position. He played a major role in the invasion of Panama (1989) and the war against Iraq (January–February 1991). He retired in 1993. In 2001 he became U.S. secretary of state.

Prezan, Constantine (1861–1943) Romanian general. Prezan received military training in Bucharest and in France. Commissioned (1880), he served on the General Staff and as adjutant to King Ferdinand. When Romania declared war on Austria-Hungary (August 1916), Prezan's Fourth Army crossed the Carpathians into Transylvania but met stiff resistance from General Arthur Baron Arz von Straussenburg's First Army. He was forced to divert forces from Transylvania, after Field Marshal August von Mackensen invaded the Dobrudja from Bulgaria in the south. General Erich von Falkenhayn's Ninth Army then crossed into Wallachia. The two German armies then converged on the capital. By January 1917 Romanian armies had been driven to the Sereth.

As Romanian CinC after the war, Prezan occupied Transylvania, which was taken from Hungary (1919). He retired from the army in 1920. The 1930 political crisis around the return of King Carol II led to his temporary return to military service. Promoted field marshal, he was asked to form a non-party government but failed and again retired.

Prien, Günther (1908–42) German naval officer and submarine commander. Prien was in the merchant marine (1923–31)

and joined the German Navy (1933). On the outbreak of World War II, German submarine commander Admiral Karl Dönitz assigned Prien and his *U-47* perhaps the most dangerous mission for any submarine during the war: attacking the Royal Navy base of Scapa Flow. Prien succeeded in penetrating the base and sank the battleship *Royal Oak* (14 October 1939). This daring feat made him an instant hero in Germany. He disappeared at sea (March 1941) with the *U-47*, credited with thirty-one Allied ships sunk.

Prittwitz und Gaffron, Maximilian von (1848–1917) German general. Prittwitz joined the army on the eve of the 1866 Austro-Prussian War. After attending the Kriegsakademie, he rose through a broad range of staff and command postings. Promoted brigadier general (1897), he was than a division commander (1901). He then took over XVI Corps at Metz (1906).

Although the Chief of the German General Staff, Colonel General Helmuth von Moltke, and some of his associates doubted Prittwitz's leadership qualities, he commanded Eighth Army in East Prussia at the beginning of the war. Faced with the difficult task of holding that area against numerically superior Russian forces, his work was more difficult thanks to the headstrong ways of corps commander General Hermann von François. It was partly under François's influence that Prittwitz agreed (19 August) to launch a frontal assault against the Russian First Army. In the ensuing Battle of Gumbinnen, elements of Eighth Army incurred heavy losses, and he ordered a general withdrawal (20 August). He then informed German army headquarters that the situation was critical and that it might become necessary to retreat all the way to the Vistula River. Moltke replaced him and his deputy General George Count von Waldersee (22 August) with General Paul von Hindenburg and Major General Erich

Ludendorff. He did not again hold command.

Puller, Lewis Burwell (1898–1971) U.S. Marine Corps general. Puller left the Virginia Military Institute to enlist in the Marines (August 1918) but did not see fighting in World War I. Commissioned (1919), he was caught in the post-war force reduction and re-enlisted as a corporal. He served in Haiti (1919–24) and was again commissioned (1924). He then had a variety of assignments, including that of instructor at the Marine Basic School (1936–39) and with the 4th Marines in Shanghai, China (1940–41), where he was promoted major and battalion commander. He then served with the 7th Marines at Camp Lejeune, North Carolina, and helped pioneer jungle training. During World War II, Puller distinguished himself with the 7th Marines on Guadalcanal. Promoted lieutenant colonel, he commanded battalions on New Britain and the 1st Marine Regiment on Peleliu (September 1944). Returning to the U.S. for training duty, he was promoted colonel.

During the 1950–53 Korean War, "Chesty" Puller commanded the 1st Marine Regiment in the Inchon landing and recapture of Seoul (September 1950). He won his fifth Navy Cross, the most in Marine Corps history, for his leadership in the Changjin Reservoir withdrawal. Promoted to brigadier general, he was briefly assistant divisional commander of the 1st Marine Division. He then commanded the 3rd Marine Division in the U.S. Promoted major general (September 1953), he commanded 2nd Marine Division until his retirement for disability with the rank of lieutenant general in November 1955.

Pulkowski, Erich (1877–?) German army officer. An artillery officer in World War I, Pulkowski developed (1917) a system of predicting artillery registration corrections without having actually to fire the guns, substantially increasing surprise in an attack. Registration corrections were derived from weather data, combined with previously measured muzzle velocity errors from individual guns. He became closely associated with Colonel Georg Bruchmüller and assisted him in the great artillery preparations of the last German offensives of the war. The Pulkowski Method (*Pulkowski Verfahren*), as it was known in the German Army, was employed in all five Ludendorff offensives. The same basic system continues to be utilized in most Western armies today. Not retained in the post-war Reichswehr, Pulkowski retired as a major. His date of death is unknown.

Putnik, Radomir (1847–1917) Serbian field marshal. Educated at the Serbian Artillery School and commissioned (1866), Putnik fought against Turkey (1876–78) and Bulgaria (1885–86). He graduated from the Army Staff College (1889). He rose steadily in rank to general and CofS of the army (1903). He also served three times as minister of war and did much to modernize the army. In the 1912–13 First Balkan War he was promoted to field marshal after leading the army to victory at Kumanovo (October 1912).

When World War I began Putnik was recuperating from illness in Austria-Hungary. Austro-Hungarian Chief of Staff Franz Conrad von Hötzendorf allowed him to return home to assume command. Putnik conducted the successful Serbian defense against the Austro-Hungarian 1914 invasions. In 1915 he directed fighting against the combined German, Austro-Hungarian, and Bulgarian invasion and supervised the epic Serbian retreat across the Albanian mountains. After surviving Serbian forces reached safety on Corfu (1916), Putnik was relieved of command, ostensibly because of illness but in reality as a scapegoat for the defeat.

Pyle, Ernest Taylor (1900–45) American war correspondent. Pyle studied journalism at Indiana University, becoming a syndicated columnist (1935). In World War II he reported from London during the Battle of Britain and covered subsequent Allied campaigns in North Africa, Sicily, Italy, and then in the Pacific Theater. His interest in the common soldiers, with stories that included their names and hometowns, made him popular. He won the Pulitzer Prize (1944). He also helped bring about combat pay supplements and the uniform sleeve stripe that indicated six months of overseas service.

"Ernie" Pyle believed in honesty in reporting and in covering the story from the front. The latter cost him his life when he was killed by a Japanese sniper during the Okinawa Campaign (April–June 1945).

Q

Quesada, Elwood Richard (1904–93) U.S. Air Force general. Quesada attended the University of Maryland and Georgetown University. He enlisted in the army (1924), became a flight cadet, and received his commission on graduation. In a test of refueling techniques, he helped set a world record of 151 hours in the air (1929). He held a succession of staff and command assignments and helped create the general headquarters staff of the Army Air Corps. He became General Henry "Hap" Arnold's foreign liaison chief (1940) and went with him to London (April 1941) to set up Lend Lease there.

When the U.S. entered World War II, "Pete" Quesada was a major commanding the 33rd Pursuit Group. Promoted brigadier general (December 1942), in early 1943 he went to North Africa to head XII Fighter Command during campaigns in Tunisia, Sicily, and Italy. He then headed IX Fighter Command (later IX Tactical Air Command) in Britain (October 1943). Promoted major general (April 1944), he took over 9th Tactical Air Command to provide support for the invasion of France. Among his innovations were ordering FM radios to replace the AM radios in aircraft and insisting that radios also be installed in tanks on the ground. He coordinated air activities during the Battle of the Ardennes (Battle of the Bulge) (December 1944–January 1945).

Quesada became air force chief of intelligence (1945–46). He then headed the Tactical Air Command (TAC) (1946–48) and directed the Eniwetok hydrogen bomb tests. He retired as a lieutenant general (1951) but returned to government (1955–61) as first director of the Federal Aviation Administration.

R

Rabin, Yitzhak (1922–95) Israeli general and political figure. Born in Palestine of Russian immigrant parents, Rabin studied at agricultural school and joined the Jewish armed underground force, the Haganah (1941) and then its elite strike force, the Palmach (1943). He fought in the 1948–49 Israeli War of Independence, commanding a brigade in the Jerusalem corridor.

Rabin attended the British Staff College at Camberley (1953). He headed Northern Command (1956–59) but did not see action in the 1956 Sinai War. After heading the manpower branch of the army (1959–60), he was then deputy chief of the General Staff (1960–64). As CofS (1964–68), he played a key role in the June 1967 Six-Day War.

Rabin resigned from the army (1968) to become Israeli ambassador to the U.S. (1968–73). He then won election to the Knesset (parliament) on the Labor party ticket (December 1973) and became minister of labor (March 1974). He succeeded Golda Meir as prime minister (June), the first native-born Israeli to hold that post, but resigned (December 1976) following a scandal over accounts while he was in Washington. He was defense minister (1984–90), then again prime minister (1990–95), dedicating himself to achieving a comprehensive peace settlement with the Palestinians and Israel's neigh-

bors until his assassination by a Jewish extremist in November 1995.

Radford, Arthur William (1896–1973) U.S. admiral. Radford graduated from Annapolis (1916) and served on a battleship during World War I. He completed flight training at the Naval Air Station, Pensacola (1920) and held a variety of assignments before being promoted captain (January 1942).

Promoted rear admiral (July 1942), Radford commanded Carrier Division 11. He participated in operations in the Gilbert and Marshall Islands and then returned to Washington to serve on the staff of the chief of naval operations (1943–44). He returned to the Pacific to command Carrier Division 6 (November 1944) and participated in the invasions of Iwo Jima (February–March 1945) and Okinawa (April–June) and strikes against Japan.

Promoted vice admiral (January 1946), Radford became deputy chief of naval operations (CNO) for air. He then commanded Second Fleet (1947). Promoted admiral, he became vice CNO (January 1948). He then commanded the Pacific Fleet (1949) and helped lead the "Revolt of the Admirals" (1949) to protest plans to unify the U.S. defense establishment. He served two terms as chairman of the Joint Chiefs of Staff (1953–57), after which he retired.

Radzievskiy, Aleksei Ivanovich (1911–78) Soviet general. Drafted into the Red Army (1929), Radzievskiy graduated from the Red Commanders' Cavalry School (1931), served as a cavalry unit commander, and then was a staff officer with the 18th Mountain Cavalry Division (1934). He graduated from the Frunze (1938) and the Voroshilov General Staff Academy (1941).

Following the German invasion of the Soviet Union (22 June 1941), Radzievskiy fought in the battle for Moscow (November–December 1941), in the German Stalingrad–Caucasus offensive (June–November 1942), at Kharkov (February–March 1943), Kiev (October–November), and, as a major general, at Zhitomir (December 1943–January 1944). Appointed CofS of Second Tank Army (February 1944), he fought in central Poland (1944) and in the advance into Germany leading to the capture of Berlin (April–May 1945).

After the war Radzievskiy commanded armor formations and was superintendent of first the Voroshilov Academy (1958–69) then the Frunze (1969–78). He also wrote several books on armored warfare.

Raeder, Erich (1876–1960) German admiral. Raeder joined the navy (1894) and was commissioned (1897). Promoted commander (1911), during World War I he held a variety of staff and command positions. He remained in the navy after the war, wrote a book on cruiser warfare, and was promoted vice admiral and assigned to the Naval Office (1925). Promoted admiral and chief of the Naval Command (1928), he became CinC of the Kriegsmarine and full admiral (1935). Hitler then raised him to the rank of grand admiral (1939).

As architect of the World War II German navy, Raeder planned to transform it from a modest coast defense force into a major ocean-going navy. He aimed to accomplish this through the Z Plan for a balanced fleet, including aircraft carriers.

This was based on the presumption that war would not come before 1944, and thus Germany had the wrong navy when fighting began (September 1939).

Raeder saw much of his surface fleet destroyed in the invasion of Norway (April 1940). He clashed with the other service chiefs over resources and with Hitler over the employment of the navy and grand strategy in the war. When Hitler ordered the decommissioning of major surface units, he resigned (January 1943) and became navy inspector general.

Raeder's role in the coming of the war led to his trial, conviction, and life sentence by the International Military Tribunal at Nuremberg (1946), but he was released for reasons of health in 1955.

Ramsay, Sir Bertram Home (1883–1945) British admiral. Ramsay joined the navy (1893) and commanded both a monitor and a destroyer during World War I. Promoted captain (1923), he commanded cruisers and then a battleship, winning promotion to rear admiral (1935) and the position of CofS of the home fleet. Placed on half pay, he retired as a vice admiral (early 1939).

When World War II began (September 1939), Ramsay returned to duty as flag officer, Dover. It thus fell to him to plan and organize Operation DYNAMO, the evacuation of the British Expeditionary Force and some French troops from Dunkerque (May–June 1940). Selected (March 1942) to plan Operation TORCH, the Allied invasion of North Africa, he was also chief planner for Operation HUSKY, the invasion of Sicily (July 1943). Promoted admiral, he was then given charge of the Allied naval force for the cross-channel invasion of France. The naval phase, Operation NEPTUNE, was highly successful. His final amphibious operation was at South Beveland and Walcheren Island (October–November 1944), vital in controlling the Scheldt River and access to Antwerp. He died in a plane crash on his way to meet with General Bernard Montgomery.

Rawlinson, Sir Henry Seymour, 1st Baron Rawlinson (1864–1925) British general. Rawlinson graduated from Sandhurst and joined the King's Royal Rifles in India (1884). In the 1899–1902 Boer War he established his reputation as one of the most able and energetic of younger British commanders. Promoted brigadier general and made commandant of the Staff College, Camberley (1903), he was promoted major general (1909) and then commanded 3rd Division (1910–14).

Rawlinson commanded two divisions landed in Belgium for the relief of Antwerp (October 1914), but was not in time to prevent the fall of that city to the Germans. He then fell back on Ypres and his divisions were absorbed into General Sir Douglas Haig's I Corps. He was then given command of IV Corps. At the end of 1915 he was promoted lieutenant general and given Fourth Army, which he commanded in the Battle of the Somme (July–November 1916). Promoted general (1917), his successful attack on Hamel (July 1918) was one of the first examples of infantry/tank cooperation. Rawlinson supervised the evacuation of the Allied force from Archangelsk (end of 1919) and took command in India (1920). His reforms there included Indianizing the officer corps.

Reeves, Joseph Mason (1872–1948) U.S. admiral. Reeves graduated from Annapolis (1894) and was commissioned (1896). He was then assistant engineer on the battleship *Oregon* through the 1898 Spanish-American War. He was instructor at Annapolis (1906–08) and during World War I commanded battleships in training duties. After the war he was naval attaché to Italy (1919–21). He graduated from the Naval War College (1925), then qualified as an observer following training at Pensacola Naval Air Station (1925). Promoted rear admiral (June 1927),

Reeves was an advisor to the U.S. delegation at the 1927 Geneva Disarmament Conference. He then commanded the Battle Fleet's aircraft squadrons, based aboard the U.S. Navy's first aircraft carrier, the *Langley*. He developed the navy's tactical aircraft doctrines (1927–31), carying out a successful mock attack with aircraft launched from carriers against the Panama Canal (1929).

Promoted full admiral, Reeves commanded the Battle Fleet (1933–34), then was CinC, U.S. Fleet (June 1934–December 1936). Recalled from retirement (May 1940), he served on various boards, including that investigating the Pearl Harbor attack, and was chief liaison officer for the Lend Lease program until late 1945. He retired for a second time in 1946.

Reichenau, Walther von (1884–1942) German general. Reichenau joined the army (1903) and was commissioned in the field artillery. He joined the German General Staff, and following World War I headed the Reichswehr chancellory. An aristocrat, he broke with his class to embrace the Nazis and Adolf Hitler. He was in part responsible for Hitler's selection of General Werner von Blomberg as minister of war, and was Blomberg's deputy. Promoted brigadier general, he worked to overcome army resistance to Hitler.

Reichenau assumed command of VII Corps (October 1935). Excluded by his fellow generals from an important post in Berlin, he was an effective field commander, leading from the front and known for close contact with his men. Promoted lieutenant general, he led Tenth Army (later designated Sixth Army) in the invasion of Poland (September 1939). His opposition to the violation of Belgian and Dutch neutrality in an invasion of the West and protests against atrocities in Poland alienated him permanently from Hitler.

Promoted full general on assumption of command of Sixth Army, he led his army through the Netherlands and northern

Belgium (May 1940), diverting Allied attention from the main southern thrust through the Ardennes. His army took Paris (14 June) and he was promoted field marshal (July). In the invasion of the Soviet Union (22 June 1941), he led Sixth Army in Ukraine and supported Hitler's plan to execute Red Army commissars. He died of a heart attack shortly after replacing Field Marshal Gerd von Rundstedt as commander of Army Group South.

Reinhardt, Georg-Hans (1887–1963) German general. Commissioned in the army (1908), after World War I Reinhardt held a number of staff positions. He took a training course in the Reichswehr's secret armor training school in the Soviet Union. He then commanded 1st Assault Brigade (1937). Promoted brigadier general, he commanded the 4th Panzer Division from its formation (November 1938) and in the invasion of Poland (September 1939). Promoted major general (October), he commanded XLI Panzer Corps with distinction in the invasions of France and Benelux (May 1940) and of Yugoslavia (April 1941). Promoted lieutenant general (June), he led his corps as part of General Wilhelm Leeb's Army Group North in the invasion of the Soviet Union (22 June 1941), penetrating Leningrad's defenses. He then took over General Hermann Hoth's Panzer Group Three (redesignated Third Panzer Army) in the drive on Moscow (October 1941). Promoted full general (February 1942), he played a major role in the defensive fighting that followed.

Remaining on the Eastern Front, Reinhardt succeeded Field Marshal Walther Model as commander of Army Group Center (August 1944) but was unable to stem the Soviet summer offensive and had to fall back to East Prussia. After suffering a serious head wound and disputes with Hitler, he was relieved of his command (January 1945). Tried by the Americans after the war, and sentenced to fifteen years' imprisonment, he won early release.

Reitsch, Hanna (1912–79) German test pilot. Reitsch set a number of gliding records in the 1930s and also after World War II. She was also a leading stunt pilot. General Ernst Udet appointed her flight captain (1937). She performed all manner of test flights, from fixed wing aircraft to helicopters and even jet aircraft. At the end of April 1945, Reich, a fervent Nazi who was also incredibly brave, made a daring flight into and out of Berlin under heavy Soviet anti-aircraft fire, carrying General Robert von Greim to a meeting with Adolf Hitler and landing on a shell-cratered Berlin avenue. She wanted to stay to share Hitler's fate, but was ordered to fly Greim back out of the city.

After the war Reitsch was confined for fifteen months. She was then a pilot and flight instructor in other countries, including India and Ghana.

Remarque, Erich Maria (1898–1970) German soldier and writer. Remarque held a succession of jobs before World War I, when he served on the Western Front and was badly wounded. After the war he taught for a time and was a magazine editor before becoming a writer. *All Quiet on the Western Front*, his classic depiction of warfare in World War I, appeared first in serial form (1928) and then as a book (1929). It was translated into many languages and made into films. When Adolf Hitler came to power in Germany, Remarque's works were banned and he himself was obliged to move abroad. He wrote many other novels, but none had the impact of his first book, perhaps the most influential anti-war novel ever written.

Rendulic, Lothar (1887–1971) German general. Member of an old Austrian military family, he joined the Austro-Hungarian Army (1910) and served on the Russian and Italian Fronts during

World War I. After the war he earned a doctorate in law and served in Paris as Austrian military attaché. Membership in the Nazi party forced his resignation, but he returned to service following Germany's absorption of Austria (*Anschluss*) (March 1938).

During World War II Rendulic proved himself a capable commander. One of the war's least known German generals, he participated in the invasion of Poland (September 1939) and was promoted brigadier general (December 1939) and given command of 14th Infantry Division, which he led in the Battle for France (May–June 1940). He led 52nd Infantry Division in Fourth Army of Army Group Center in the invasion of the Soviet Union (22 June 1941), then commanded XXXV Corps and was promoted major general. He then served in Yugoslavia as commander of Second Panzer Army against the resistance (August 1943–June 1944) and was promoted full general (April 1944). At the end of the war he held a succession of commands. Sent to Finland (June 1944), he withdrew Twentieth Mountain Army into Norway. He then commanded Army Group North in East Prussia (January 1945), Army Group Center (January), Army Group Kurland (March), and Army Group South in Ostmark (Austria) (April). Surrendering to U.S. forces at the end of the war, he was tried and convicted of war crimes and sentenced to twenty years in prison but was released early (1951).

Rennenkampf, Pavel Karlovich von (1854–1918) Russian general. A graduate of the Helsingfors Infantry Cadet School (1873), Rennenkampf commanded a cavalry division during the 1904–05 Russo-Japanese War. Appointed commander of First Army at the begnining of World War I, he was to advance into East Prussia in connection with General Aleksandr Samsonov's Second Army to his south. Moving with glacial speed, Rennenkampf failed to take advantage of the temporary German weakness on his front and also failed to support Samsonov's army. He and Samsonov were bitter rivals.

Decisively defeated in the subsequent Battle of the Masurian Lakes (September 1914), Rennenkampf managed to escape a double envelopment and extract much of his army. In a subsequent inquiry, he was exonerated. He also commanded in the Russian defeat at Lodz (1915). Then governor of St. Petersburg, he commanded the Northern Front (1916). He was shot by the Bolsheviks.

Reuter, Ludwig von (1869–1943) German admiral. Reuter joined the German Navy and rose to command a battle cruiser in World War I. He shelled Scarborough (December 1914) and fought at the Dogger Bank (January 1915). In the Battle of Jutland (31 May–1 June 1916) he led a group of light cruisers. Then assigned to operations in the Baltic, he returned to North Sea waters for the second battle of Heligoland (1917). When Admiral Franz von Hipper took over the High Seas Fleet, he succeeded him as leader of Scouting Forces.

Following the armistice, Reuter delivered the High Seas Fleet into internment at Scapa Flow in the Orkney Islands. He prepared clandestine orders to scuttle his ships to prevent them from falling into Allied hands. He then executed his scheme (21 June 1919). Some sixty-six major warships went down with the loss of nine German lives. Seen as heroes for having restored the honor of the German Navy, Reuter and his men received a triumphant reception on their return to Germany in 1920.

Richardson, Robert C. (1882–1954) U.S. general. Commissioned in the cavalry on graduation from West Point (1904), Richardson fought in the Philippines against the Moros (1904–05) and was wounded. Following other assignments he taught at West Point (1908–11). With U.S. entry into World War I, he served in France on the staff of AEF commander General John J. Pershing (1917–19) and helped plan the

U.S. role in the war's later offensives. He briefly served in the army of occupation in Germany after the war (1919) before returning to the U.S. to serve on the General Staff of the War Department (1919–21). He then served again in the Philippines and attended the French École Supérieure de Guerre (1924–25) and was military attaché in Rome (1926–28). He returned to West Point (1928–29) and was commandant of cadets (1929–33). He graduated from the Army War College (1934) and commanded 2nd Cavalry Brigade at Fort Bliss, Texas (1938–39) and the 1st Cavalry Division there (1939–41).

When the United States entered World War II, Richardson commanded VII Army Corps in the U.S. (1941–43). He took command of the Hawaiian Department and was military governor there (June 1943), then became commanding general of U.S. Army Forces in the Central Pacific Area (August). He was then commanding General of U.S. Army forces in the Pacific Ocean Areas. He retired in October 1946.

Richthofen, Manfred Albrecht, Baron von (1892–1918) German army officer and pilot. Richthofen joined the cavalry (1912) and when World War I began was in the 1st Uhlan Regiment near the Russian border. After his regiment was posted to infantry duties, he transferred to the Air Service (May 1915). He flew first as an observer and then as a bomber pilot on the Eastern Front.

Oswald Boelcke invited Richthofen to join his new fighter squadron, Jagdstaffel 2. Under Boelcke's tutelage, he became a proficient fighter pilot, scoring his first victory (September 1916). He then commanded his own squadron, Jagdstaffel 11 (January 1917) and was promoted captain (April 1917). His squadron was expanded to become the first independent wing, Jagdgeschwader 1, of three squadrons. It was known as "Richthofen's Flying Circus" for its brightly painted aircraft.

In his red Fokker triplane, the "Red Baron" was easily the most famous ace of the war and, despite his reclusive nature, one of its most enduring combatants. He died while pursuing an opponent at low altitude over enemy lines (21 April 1918). Either Canadian pilot Roy Brown, credited with the victory, or Australian ground gunners fired the fatal shot. With eighty victories, Richthofen was the highest-scoring fighter pilot of the war.

Richthofen, Wolfram, Baron von (1895–1945) German air force field marshal. Richtofen joined the army as an officer cadet (1913) and was commissioned (1914). He fought on both fronts in World War I. Qualifying as a pilot (1918), he was assigned to the squadron first commanded by his cousin Manfred von Richtofen. After studying engineering (1919–22), he joined the Reichswehr and worked to develop the illegal German air program. He was then in the Reich Air Ministry Technical Division (1933–36). Appointed CofS of the Condor Legion, air units sent to aid the Nationalists in the 1936–39 Spanish Civil War (1936), he there developed the tactics and close air support techniques, including air officers serving with grounds troops, so important in World War II. Promoted brigadier general (September 1938), he then commanded the Condor Legion.

Richtofen returned to Germany (May) and commanded VIII Air Corps in the invasion of Poland, directing the aerial destruction of Warsaw. In the invasion of France and Benelux (May 1940) he commanded three Stuka squadrons providing flying artillery support for Sixth Army. Promoted lieutenant general (May 1940), he commanded VIII Air Corps in the Battle of Britain and in the invasions of Greece and Crete. In 1942 he took command of Fourth Air Fleet (Luftflotte) supporting German armies in South Russia and in the Battle of Stalingrad. The youngest German field marshal (February 1943), he commanded Second Air Fleet in Italy. A brain tumor forced his retirement (November 1944) and led to his death.

Rickenbacker, Edward Vernon (1890–1973) U.S. army officer. One of the world's top racing car drivers, Rickenbacher enlisted in the army on U.S. entry into World War I (April 1917). He was a sergeant driver on the staff of AEF commander General John J. Pershing. A chance meeting with Colonel William Mitchell secured Rickenbacker's transfer to military aviation (August 1917). Although he was over the age limit to fly, he joined the 94th Aero Pursuit Squadron (March 1918) and shot down his first German plane. At the end of the war he was the leading U.S. ace with twenty-six victories. Later he was awarded the Medal of Honor for his 25 September 1918 attack on seven German planes, downing two of them.

Rickenbacker left the army at the end of World War I and formed his own automobile company. In 1935 he became general manager for Eastern Airlines.

During World War II Rickenbacker served as a representative of the secretary of war to survey aircraft installations and report on their status. He then returned to Eastern Airlines.

Rickover, Hyman George (1900–86) U.S. admiral. Rickover immigrated as a boy to the U.S.A. from Russian Poland. Overcoming anti-Semitism, he graduated from Annapolis (1922) and earned a master's degree in electrical engineering at Columbia University (1929), before beginning his long association with submarines. His only ship command was a minesweeper (1937).

During World War II Rickover headed the Electrical Division of the Bureau of Ships. He studied nuclear technology at the Oak Ridge Laboratory (1946) and became an advocate of nuclear power for warships. He then headed the nuclear power division of the Bureau of Ships (1948) and liaised with the Atomic Engery Commission. His efforts culminated in the first nuclear-powered craft, the attack submarine *Nautilus* (1954).

Promoted rear admiral, Rickover assumed greater influence over the nuclear program in the navy and personally interviewed all officers assigned to it. Facing mandatory retirement because of age, he used political connections in Congress to secure exemption. As deputy commander for nuclear propoulsion, Naval Seas System Command, he also helped develop the Polaris missile system. Transferred to the retired list (1964), he remained on active duty until age eighty-one (1981). He is considered to be the father of the U.S. nuclear navy, and his sixty-four years on active duty is the longest in U.S. Navy history. Even in retirement Rickover remained controversial and outspoken.

Ridgway, Matthew Bunker (1895–1903) U.S. general. Commissioned in the infantry on graduation from West Point (1917), Ridgway spent World War I on the Mexican border. Fluent in Spanish, he became an instructor at West Point (1918). He attended the Infantry School (1925) and held a number of overseas assignments. In the 1930s he attended the Command and General Staff School and the Army War College. A protégé of General George Marshall, he was advanced to temporary brigadier general and assistant commander of the 82nd Infantry Division (January 1942) and then its commander (June).

Ridgway oversaw the conversion of the 82nd to an airborne division and completed parachute training himself. He commanded the division in the drop into Sicily (July 1943) and led elements of it in fighting at Salerno. He jumped into Normandy preceding the D-Day invasion. He then commanded the XVIII Airborne Corps (August) and led it in the MARKET-GARDEN offensive (September) and along the Rhine. He was promoted lieutenant general (June 1945).

Appointed army deputy CofS (August 1949), Ridgway replaced Lieutenant General Walton Walker as commander of Eighth Army in Korea when the latter died in a jeep accident (December 1950). He restored morale and launched a series of counter-offensives. When General Douglas MacArthur was relieved as Far East and UNC commander (April 1951), Ridgway replaced him. Promoted full general (May 1952), he returned to the U.S. (October 1953) and became army CofS where he fought cuts in conventional forces. He retired in June 1955.

Ritchie, Sir Neil N. (1897–1983) British general. Educated at Lancing College and Sandhurst, Ritchie was commissioned (1914). During World War I he fought in France and Mesopotamia. Promoted major (1936), at the beginning of World War II he was brigadier general and CofS of II Corps of the BEF in France. After the Dunkerque evacuation (May–June 1940) he held the same post under Major General Claude Auchinleck in Southern Command. He was then a major general and deputy to Auchinleck when the latter commanded in the Middle East.

When Auchinleck relieved Lieutenant General Alan Cunningham as commander of Eighth Army in the midst of Operation CRUSADER (November 1941), he named Ritchie as his "temporary" replacement. He raised the siege of Tobruk and smashed into Cyrenaica to the El Agheila Line, whereupon his appointment was made permanent. German General Erwin Rommel then initiated a counteroffensive (January 1942) earlier than the British anticipated, shattering Eighth Army and pushing it back to the Gazala Line (February). When Ritchie lost control of the battle and most of his army's armor, Auchinleck relieved him (June).

Ritchie then commanded 52nd Division in the United Kingdom. He led XII Corps of Second Army as a lieutenant general in Field Marshal Bernard Montgomery's Twenty-first Army Group following the Normandy invasion (June 1944). Knighted (1945), he headed Scottish Command and was promoted general and made CinC, Far East Land Forces at Singapore

(1947–49). He next served on the Joint Service Commission in Washington and retired (1951).

Roberts, Sir Frederick Sleigh, Baron Roberts of Kandahar, Earl Roberts (1832–1914) British field marshal. Much of Roberts's service was in India. Commissioned in the Bengal Artillery (1851), he fought in the 1857–59 Sepoy Rebellion, winning the Victoria Cross. He served in the 1867–68 Abyssinian expedition and in the 1871–72 Lushai expedition in southern Assam. He commanded the Punjab Frontier Force and fought with distinction in the 1878–80 Second Afghan War, winning the Battle of Qandahar (1 September 1880) and, in effect, the war.

Sent to South Africa following the British defeat at Majuba Hill (February 1881), he arrived after peace had been arranged and returned to India to command the Madras army (1881–85) and then be CinC in India (1885). He was made Baron Roberts of Kandahar (Qandahar) (1892). Returning to England (1893), he was promoted field marshal (1895) and commanded in Ireland.

Following early British reversals in the 1899–1902 Boer War, Roberts was sent out to take command with Horatio Kitchener as his CofS (December 1899). The two men revitalized the war effort. He took Bloemfontein in the Orange Free State (March 1900) and Johannesburg (May), then the rest of the Transvaal. He returned to Britain (December) and was created earl. He was then CinC of the British Army (1901–04) and advocated conscription. Early in World War I he visited Indian divisions in France, but fell ill there and died.

Robertson, Sir Horace C.H. (1894–1960) Australian general. Educated at the Royal Military College, Duntroon, Robertson served with distinction during World War I in both the Gallipoli campaign and in Palestine. After the war he attended the

Royal Military College, Camberley, and held staff and instructor positions in the Australian Army.

During World War II Robertson commanded the 19th Australian Brigade in Libya before leading Australian troops in the Southwest Pacific. After the war he was named to head British Commonwealth occupation forces in Japan (April 1946). He was the first Dominion officer ever to command a British Commonwealth force that included British troops. When the 1950–53 Korean War began, Lieutenant General Robertson became administrative CinC of British Commonwealth Forces there, with responsibility for providing logistical and administrative support to the Commonwealth Division. Although his relations with London were often strained, he got on well with the U.S. commanders, which enhanced the image of Australia as a loyal ally of the United States and assisted in the 1951 ANZUS (Australia–New Zealand–United States) security pact. Robertson returned to Australia (December 1951) to become director general of recruiting. He retired in 1954.

Robertson, Sir William (1860–1933) British field marshal. Robertson joined the army (1877) and was commissioned (1888). He attended the Staff College at Camberley (1896–97), the first officer from the ranks to do so. He was promoted colonel (1903) during an assignment with the War Office (1901–07). As a major general, he was appointed to command the Staff College (1910), then was director of military training (1913).

At the onset of World War I, Robertson was quartermaster-general of the BEF. He replaced Field Marshal Lord Kitchener as chief of the Imperial General Staff (CIGS) (January 1915). Hardworking and an able staff officer, he emphasized concentrating Allied forces on the Western Front and opposed campaigns, as in the Balkans, where Britain had no vital interests. Following a difficult command conference at

Versailles in early 1918, he resigned as CIGS. He took over the Eastern Command in Britain and then command of Home Forces (June). After the war, he was made a baronet and commanded British occupation forces in the Rhineland (1919–20). He was promoted field marshal on his retirement (March 1920).

Rogge, Bernhard (1899–1982) German admiral. In the German merchant marine during and after World War I, Rogge was then appointed to command a German navy sail training ship (early 1939). Promoted captain (July), during World War II he commanded the commerce raider *Atlantis*. Over a twenty-month span (March 1940–November 1941), he sank twenty-two ships totaling 145,968 tons. The most successful armed merchant cruiser of the war, the *Atlantis* set a record for sea endurance of 622 continuous days at sea, sailing more than 102,000 nautical miles.

Rogge survived the sinking of his ship by a British cruiser (November 1941), made it back to Germany, and was appointed inspector general of training establishments directorate and commander of fleet training formations (1942). Promoted rear admiral, he then commanded Battle Group Rogge and was promoted vice admiral.

Because of his chivalrous treatment of crews of vessels he had sunk while captain of the Atlantis, Rogge was not brought to trial by the Allies after the war. When it was formed, he joined the navy of the Federal Republic of Germany as a vice admiral (1955). His last post was commander of the 1st Defense Area.

Rokossovsky, Konstantin Konstantinovich (1896–1968) Marshal of the Soviet Union. Born a Pole, Rokossovsky was drafted into the Russian army (1914) and, during World War I, rose to the rank of sergeant. He became close friends with Georgi Zhukov, joined the Red Army (1918), and fought against the Whites in the Civil War, advancing to command a regiment.

Rokossovsky graduated from the Frunze Military Academy (1929). Arrested on charges of treason in Stalin's purge of the army while commanding a corps in Manchuria (1937), he was imprisoned and tortured. Released largely on the behest of Zhukov (1940), he commanded IX Mechanized Corps in Ukraine in the German invasion of the Soviet Union (22 June 1942), where he temporarily halted the German advance and helped organize the breakout of Russian units at Smolensk (August 1941).

Given command of Sixteenth Army, Rokossovsky assisted in the successful defense of Moscow (December). He commanded the Don Front in the decisive defeat of the German Sixth Army at Stalingrad (December 1942–January 1943), then Central Front where he helped halt the Germans at Kursk (July 1943). His command was then redesignated the Belorussian Front and spearheaded the drive on Poland, taking Lublin and Brest-Litovsk. Advancing to Warsaw, he halted while the Polish resistance was destroyed and thousands were killed in the Warsaw Uprising. In January 1945 he commanded the 2nd Belorussian Front, taking Warsaw and then Danzig (March), before destroying German forces in East Prussia and Pomerania. After the war he served as Poland's minister of defense and was the real power in the country (1949–56). He ended his career as Soviet deputy minister of defense (1956–62).

Rommel, Erwin Johannes Eugen (1891–1944) German field marshal. Rommel joined the army (1909). During World War I he was wounded in France (September 1914). Following recuperation, he won renown on the Romanian and Italian fronts, especially in the Battle of Caporetto (October–November 1917) when he and his men captured more than 9,000 Italian troops and eighty-one guns, whereupon he was promoted captain.

Rommel continued in the Reichswehr after the war and became an instructor at the Infantry School at Dresden (1929), where he wrote *Infantry Attacks*, a textbook on infantry tactics. He commanded a battalion of the 17th Infantry Regiment (October 1935), the War Academy (1938), and then Adolf Hitler's bodyguard (1938–39). Assuming command of the 7th Panzer Division (February 1940), he played a key role in the Battle for France (May–June 1940). Promoted lieutenant general, he commanded forces in Libya (the Africa Korps) (February 1941) and became known as the "Desert Fox" for his skilful generalship. He was promoted full general (1942) and then field marshal following the British surrender of Tobruk (June 1942). He was defeated by General Bernard Montgomery's Eighth Army in the Battle of El Alamein (October–November 1942) and recalled (March 1943). He then commanded Army Group B in Northern Italy and had charge of coastal fortifications in France (November 1943).

Rommel then commanded German forces in northern France and Benelux (January 1944) but failed to stop the Allied invasion at Normandy, in part because of Hitler's interference. Wounded in an air attack (July), he was implicated marginally in the attempt to assassinate Hitler. Given the choice of a trial or committing suicide, he chose the latter.

Roosevelt, Franklin Delano (1882–1945) President of the United States (1932–1945). Roosevelt graduated from Harvard and Columbia Law School. He served as assistant secretary of the navy (1913–20) and did much to prepare the fleet for World War I. Governor of New York state (1928–32), he was elected president of the United States on the Democratic ticket (November 1932) and held the office until his death.

Although preoccupied with the economic depression, Roosevelt sought a more interventionist role for the United

States abroad. After the start of World War II he hoped to keep Britain fighting in Europe in order to gain time for American rearmament, and to restrain Japan by diplomacy and naval deterrence. Basing the Pacific fleet at Pearl Harbor was a part of that strategy.

Once the United States was in World War II, Roosevelt worked closely with British Prime Minister Winston Churchill. For the most part, he merely followed the advice of his military chiefs. His primary goal was to complete the war as quickly as possible at the least cost in American lives. He believed in maintaining peace in the post-war world through Soviet–U.S. cooperation and hoped that he had developed an entente with Soviet leader Josef Stalin toward that end, but he died knowing that the gambit had failed.

Roosevelt, Theodore (1858–1919) U.S. soldier and politician. Roosevelt graduated from Harvard University (1880) and became active in politics. Interested in the navy, he published *Naval History of the War of 1812* (1882). After service in the New York legislature, he entered national politics (1889) and was appointed assistant secretary of the navy (1897), helping to prepare the navy for the 1898 Spanish-American War. On the outbreak of war, he resigned his position to organize and lead a regiment, the 1st Volunteer Cavalry (the "Rough Riders"), which fought in Cuba in the key Battle of San Juan Ridge (1 July), charging on foot up Kettle Hill. This battle made him a national figure.

Elected vice president of the United States (1900), he succeeded to the presidency on the assassination of President William McKinley (1901). As president (1901–09), he advocated an increased role for the United States in world affairs and pushed naval expansion to further that end. He was the driving force behind the Panama Canal, helped settle the 1904–05 Russo-Japanese War (for which he was awarded the Nobel Peace Prize), and sent the Great White Fleet on its around-the-world cruise (1907–09).

Roosevelt, Theodore, Jr. (1887–1944) U.S. general. The son of President Theodore Roosevelt, Theodore Jr. also graduated from Harvard University (1908) and volunteered for World War I. He served in the 26th Regiment, 1st Infantry Division as a major, and was wounded in the St. Mihiel offensive (September 1918). Following the war he helped organize the American Legion, was assistant secretary of the navy, and served as governor of Puerto Rico, then the Philippines. He also wrote or co-authored nine books.

When the United States entered World War II, Roosevelt was recalled to command the 26th Regiment as a colonel. Later he was assistant commander of the 1st Infantry Division under Major General Terry de la Mesa Allen and fought in North Africa and Sicily. He and Allen ran afoul of Corps Commander Major General Omar Bradley, who relieved both from command. He became liaison officer for Fifth Army, then was assigned to headquarters, First Army (1944) and became assistant commander of the 4th Infantry Division for Operation OVERLORD, the Normandy invasion (6 June).

Brigadier General Roosevelt insisted on going ashore in the first wave on Omaha Beach, despite arthritis that caused him to walk with a cane, and he was the only general there. Despite constant German fire, he rallied his troops and led them inland over the sea wall. He died of a heart attack (12 July), the day he was to assume command of the 90th Infantry Division. Posthumously awarded the Medal of Honor for his valor on D-Day, he is buried at the American Cemetery at Colleville-sur-Mer.

Root, Elihu (1845–1937) U.S. secretary of war and military reformer. Root graduated from Hamilton College (1864) and from New York University Law School (1867). He practiced law in New York

City, where he became a close friend of Theodore Roosevelt.

President William McKinley appointed Root secretary of war (1899–1904) with instructions to place the U.S. army on a modern basis. With no experience of military affairs when he took office, Root came up with a comprehensive plan of army reorganization and brought the military managerial revolution to the United States.

Root did much to promote just administration of the territories taken from Spain, and under him the army was increased in size, the Army War College was established (1901), the general staff system came into being (1903) and the position of CofS of the army replaced that of commanding general. Root served as secretary of state under Theodore Roosevelt (1905–09) and did much to promote international cooperation. In 1912 he was awarded the Nobel Prize for Peace.

Roques, Pierre Auguste (1856–1920) French general. Roques commanded XII Corps in the Fourth Army during World War I. The French High Command had designated Fourth Army to undertake the principal offensive action against Germany. It attacked into the Ardennes forest with the mission of taking Neufchâteau (22 August 1914). XII Corps was to support the left flank of the main striking force, the Colonial Corps. Much of the Colonial Corps was surrounded and slaughtered at Rossignol, south of the Neufchâteau. Roques immediately stopped his advance, with the result that XVII Corps, just to the left, was exposed to a German attack and took heavy casualties, forcing Fourth Army to withdraw (24 August).

Although Roques received command of First Army (January 1915), it was as war minister (1916) that he had his greatest impact on the war by becoming involved in the removal of General Joseph Joffre as CinC of the French Army. Premier Aristide Briand dismissed Roques (December). He then commanded Fourth Army and held technical positions within the military administration.

Rotmistrov, Pavel Aleksevich (1901–82) Soviet marshal. Too young for World War I, Rotmistrov joined the Red Army (1919) and graduated from the Frunze. Promoted major general (June 1940), at the beginning of World War II he was chief of staff of III Motorized Corps. Promoted lieutenant general, he commanded a tank corps during the Battle of Stalingrad and helped prevent the Germans from relieving Sixth Army there.

A keen student of the use of armor in other nations, Rotmistrov himself proved a master in the imaginative employment of tanks. He demonstrated this in the greatest tank battle of the war at Kursk (July 1943), when he commanded the Fifth Guards Tank Army, the reserve in Marshal Ivan Konev's Steppe Front (army group). His own T-34 tanks were outgunned by German armor with 88mm guns, but he helped neutralize this advantage by ordering his crews to get as close as possible before engaging. Promoted colonel general (October 1943), he was the first marshal of armored troops (February 1944). At the end of the war he helped encircle Berlin from the south.

After the war, Rotmistrov became the first chief marshal of armored troops (April 1962). He also wrote several excellent military studies.

Rowecki, Stefan (1895–1944) Polish general. At the time of the German invasion of Poland (September 1939), Rowecki commanded the Warsaw Armored-Motorized Brigade in defense of the middle Vistula area. He remained in Poland in hiding after the defeat and was commander of the Armia Krajowa (Home Army), which he built into perhaps the most formidable underground army of Europe. It gathered intelligence information, conducted sabotage, and raided German lines of communications. Captured (1943) by the German Gestapo (secret police), Lieutenant General

Rowecki was shot (August 1944) in the first days of the Warsaw Uprising.

Rozhestvensky, Zinovy Petrovich (1848–1909) Russian admiral. Rozhestvensky joined the navy (1865), attended the Naval School (1870), and distinguished himself during the 1877–78 Russo-Turkish War. He then helped organize the Bulgarian Navy and served as attaché in London before gaining appointment as gunnery officer of the Baltic fleet. He was promoted to rear admiral (1902).

Following the Japanese success in their pre-emptive attack at Port Arthur that began the 1904–05 Russo-Japanese War, the Russian naval high command ordered Rozhestvensky to assume command of the Baltic Fleet and lead it on a 20,000-mile voyage to Vladivostok (July 1904). He departed St. Petersburg for the Far East (October) with his renamed 2nd Pacific Squadron of fifty ships of uneven quality and age. Mistaken shelling of the English fishing fleet off the Dogger Bank almost brought war with Britain, and his task was further complicated by a lack of proper coaling facilities. Despite his considerable ingenuity in keeping the 2nd Pacific Squadron intact during its eight-month voyage, his ships reached Asian waters (May 1905) with dispirited crews and in poor condition. Admiral Heihachiro Togo's ships engaged and defeated his squadron in the decisive Battle of Tsushima (27 May). Badly wounded in the action, he was taken prisoner. Exchanged after the war and subsequently exonerated in a court-martial, his active naval career nonetheless was ended.

Rudel, Hans-Ulrich (1916–82) German air force officer. Rudel joined the Luftwaffe (1936) and trained as a dive-bomber pilot. He took part in the initial invasion of the Soviet Union (22 June 1941) and the attack on the Russian fleet at Kronstadt, and is credited with sinking the battleship *Marat*. Of great determination, he continued to fly despite amputa-

tion of his right foot. He flew 2,530 sorties and had eleven aerial victories.

A master at "tank busting," Rudel introduced a 37mm gun on a Ju-87G Stuka aircraft (April 1943) and used this type of aircraft to destroy an incredible 532 tanks in the last two years of the war. Shot down (March 1944), he made it through Russian lines to safety. The most highly decorated German of World War II, he was the sole recipient of the Golden Oak Leaves to the Knight's Cross of the Iron Cross.

Ruge, Otto (1882–1961) Norwegian general. Army CofS (1933–38) and then inspector general of the infantry, Ruge was a colonel at the time of the German invasion of his country (9 April 1940). He stopped a German advance at Midtskogen (9 April) and, while Norwegian Army commander General Kristian Laake had no confidence in continued resistance, Ruge expressed determination to fight on. Appointed CinC of the Norwegian Army (10 April) and promoted general, he hoped to contain the German invasion along the southern coast and then slowly withdraw northwest to allow time for mobilization of the rest of the country and British intervention.

Ruge skillfully directed the Norwegian defense in a series of delaying positions. Not having been informed in advance of the British evacuation and with the end in sight, he steadfastly refused to abandon his men and capitulated only when King Haakon and the government had departed for London. He disbanded the 6th Division (9 June). The next day an armistice with the Germans was signed.

Rundstedt, Karl Rudolf Gerd von (1875–1953) German field marshal. Rundstedt was commissioned (1900), attended the War Academy (1902), and served on the General Staff. In World War I he held staff positions on both the Western and Eastern Fronts.

Following the war, Rundstedt continued in the Reichswehr. Promoted colonel (1923), he commanded 18th Infantry Regiment (1925–27) and, as brigadier general, 2nd Cavalry Division (1927). He was then promoted major general (1929), lieutenant general (1932), and full general (1938).

As head of First Army Command (1932–38), Rundstedt helped direct German rearmament. Disagreements with Adolf Hitler, including his support of non-Nazi generals, led to his retirement (October 1938).

Hitler recalled Rundstedt (June 1939) to command Army Group South, the main force in the invasion of Poland. Transferred to the Western Front, he approved and lobbied for the plan advanced by his CofS, General Erich von Manstein, for the invasion of France and Benelux (May 1940). He commanded Army Group A in the subsequent battle (May–June) and issued the fateful order to halt the Panzers (23 May), subsequently supported by Hitler, which allowed the BEF to organize its defenses and escape from France.

Promoted field marshal (July 1940), Rundstedt commanded the three armies that were to invade Britain (Operation SEA LION). In 1941 he commanded Army Group South in the invasion of the Soviet Union, which he opposed. His armies took the Crimea and Donetz Basin, and got as far as Rostov before being pushed back. He refused to obey Hitler's stand-fast order and resigned (December 1941) before Hitler could relieve him.

Recalled to service (March 1942), Rundstedt became CinC, West. Unlike General Erwin Rommel, he believed the Allies could be defeated in a mobile defense once they came ashore. After the Normandy invasion (6 June 1944) he met with Hitler to try to convince him to adopt a mobile defense and was then removed from command (6 July 1944). Recalled again as commander in the West (September 1944), he stabilized the front and directed Hitler's Ardennes offensive.

Following his recommendation that Hitler make peace, he was again relieved of command (March 1945). Known as *Der Alte Herr* (the old gentleman), he was widely respected by both friend and foe.

Rupprecht, Crown Prince of Bavaria (1869–1955) Bavarian field marshal. Son of King Ludwig III of Bavaria, Rupprecht was commissioned in the infantry (1886) and attended the Bavarian War Academy. He became a lieutenant general and commander of the I Bavarian Corps (1906). Promoted full general (1913), he oversaw inspection of Fourth Army.

When World War I began, Rupprecht commanded the Bavarian or Sixth Army and led it in early fighting in Lorraine and in the northern part of the front. Promoted field marshal (July 1916), he assumed command of the Northern Army Group with headquarters at Cambrai (early 1917). Ultimately he was responsibile for the entire northern section of the front. After a number of desperate defensive battles in Flanders, most notably Third Ypres (Passchendaele) and Cambrai, his army group launched the Somme offensive (March 1918). He then conducted a skillful retreat in the face of the British offensive (August). Following his father's abdication (November 1918), he retired to one of his estates.

Ruzsky, Nikolai Vladimirovich (1854–1918) Russian general. Ruzsky saw service in the 1877–78 Russo-Turkish War and was deputy CofS for the Kiev Military District (1896–1902) and CofS of Second Manchurian Army during the 1904–05 Russo-Japanese War.

In mid-September 1914 Ruzsky assumed command of the Northwest Front. He then took command of Sixth Army (March 1915), and in winter 1916 was given command of the Northern Front. He played a key role in pressuring Tsar Nicholas II into abdicating (March 1917). Following the March 1917 Revolution he was removed from command and subsequently fled to the Caucasus.

Ryan, John Dale (1915–83) U.S. Air Force general. Ryan graduated from West Point (1938) and became an aviator. Upon completion of pilot training at Kelly Field (1939), he remained there as an instructor for two years. A lieutenant colonel (1942), during 1944–45 he was involved in bombing operations in Europe, first in command of the 2nd Bombardment Group in Italy, then with 15th Bombardment Wing. He was promoted temporary colonel (August 1944).

Following the war Ryan had a succession of different assignments (1945–52) and was promoted to permanent colonel and to brigadier general (1952). He commanded several air divisions (1952–56) and was promoted to major general (October 1956). He took command of Sixteenth Air Force in Spain (1960), was promoted lieutenant general (1961), and took command of Second Air Force at Barksdale Air Force Base, Louisiana. He was inspector general of the Air Force (1963–64), then was appointed vice-commander of the Strategic Air Command (SAC) (August 1964). Promoted general (December 1963), he took command of SAC (1964–67); he then commanded the Pacific Air Force (1967–68). He was vice CofS of the Air Force (1968–69), then CofS of the Air Force (August 1969–August 1973) until he retired.

S

Saitō, Yoshitsugu (1890–1944) Japanese general. Saitō graduated from the Military Academy (1912) and the Army Staff College (1924). Commissioned in the cavalry, he was a member of the Inspectorate General for Cavalry (1932–33). Promoted lieutenant colonel (1933), he held cavalry commands (1933–36). Promoted major general (1939), he headed the Cavalry Remount Bureau (1941–44).

Sent to Saipan to command the army Northern Marianas District Group of Saipan and Tinian Islands (April 1944), Lieutenant General Saitō had the 43rd Infantry Division and the 47th Independent Mixed Brigade to defend against a U.S. invasion (15 June). He was junior to both Vice Admirals Chuichi Nagumo and Takeo Takagi, both of whom had headquarters on Saipan but few resources. He committed suicide during the war's largest *banzai* attack, when 3,000 Japanese troops in one of the last pockets of resistance perished (6–7 July 1944).

Sakai, Saburō (1916–2000) Japanese fighter pilot. Sakai began his combat career over China, then served in the Philippines and Java before being based at Rabaul in World War II. Attacked by an American aircraft during the long flight home after a mission over Guadalcanal (August 1942), he was badly wounded and lost one eye, and almost the other, but managed to return to base.

Following a long convalescence, he trained other pilots. Not authorized to fly combat missions again until mid-1944, he scored several more victories and was promoted ensign (late 1944). He survived the war and, with sixty-four victories over Allied aircraft, was one of Japan's greatest aces. The highest scoring ace in the IJN was his comrade on Rabaul, Lieutenant Hiroyoshi Nishizawa, killed in action in the Philippines in October 1944, and credited with some 100 kills.

In the post-war period Sakai was active as a pilot in Red Cross emergency rescue units.

Sakonjū, Naomasa (1890–1948) Japanese admiral. A graduate of the Naval Academy (1912), at the start of World War I, Sakonjū was a rear admiral and naval attaché in Thailand. Leaving that post (May 1942), he headed Transport Division 16 (July). He was in charge of efforts to reinforce Biak following the Allied landing there (May 1944). The reinforcements, however, never took place.

Following the U.S. landing on Leyte, Sakonjū headed Southwest Area Ground Force (transportation unit) of 2nd Striking Force with instructions to land 2,000 troops from Mindanao on the far side of that island at Ormoc on 26 October. His flagship, a cruiser, was disabled by a U.S. submarine outside Manila Bay, and he lost another cruiser and a destroyer in the Visyan Sea (26 October) but was able to carry out his mission and subsequently land other reinforcements on Leyte. Promoted vice admiral (December 1944), he commanded the China Area fleet. After the war he was tried, convicted, and executed for war crimes.

Sakuma, Tsutomu (1879–1910) Japanese naval officer. A Naval Academy graduate (1901), Sakuma served with the 15th Torpedo Boat Flotilla during the 1904–05 Russo-Japanese War and aboard a cruiser in the Battle of Tsushima (26 May 1905). Entering the submarine service (1907), he commanded submarine *No. 6*, a Holland-type boat built in Japan. In a practice dive in the Inland Sea, his boat went down with the loss of all men aboard (19 April 1910). His notebook, recovered in salvage operations, detailed the causes of the sub's sinking and contained an apology to the emperor for the loss of the submarine and its crew. Press reports transformed him into a national hero and role model.

Sakurai, Seizō (1889–1985) Japanese general. Sakurai graduated from the Military Academy (1911) and the Army Staff College (1919). Commissioned in the infantry, he became a specialist in transportation and was a member of the Maritime Transportation Unit, Army General Staff (1921–24, 1929–30), then resident officer in France (1924–26). Promoted colonel (1934), Sakurai commanded a regiment (1934–36). Promoted major general, he was on the staff of the Army Transportation Bureau (1938). Commander of an infantry brigade (1938–40), he was CofS of Thirteenth Army in China (1940–41). Promoted lieutenant general (1940), he commanded 33rd Division and led it in the invasion of Burma (January 1942). He was then chief, Mechanized Warfare Division, Army General Staff (1943–44). He returned to Burma to command Twenty-Eighth Army, launching Operation HA-GO (January 1944), then skillfully

directing a retreat across the Sittang River (March–April 1944).

Samson, Charles Rumney (1883–1931) British naval aviation pioneer. Samson conducted seaplane experiments, cross-country night flights, flights from ships, and air bombardment. During World War I he contributed much to development of tactical aviation. He commanded a variety of reconnaissance and bombing missions and also aircraft in the 1915–16 Gallipoli campaign. Later he conducted anti-submarine and reconnaissance patrols in the eastern Mediterranean and Indian Ocean. He then had charge of anti-submarine and anti-Zeppelin operations over the North Sea (1917) and conducted experiments with aircraft taking off from vessels.

Samson transferred to the new Royal Air Force (1919). Promoted air commodore (1922), his major postwar achievement was a round-trip flight of bombers from Cairo to Capetown. He retired in 1929.

Samsonov, Aleksandr Vasilevich (1859–1914) Russian general. Samsonov commanded a brigade and then a division in the 1904–05 Russo-Japanese War. After 1909 he was governor of Turkestan. When World War I began he took command of Second Army. He and First Army commander Pavel Rennenkampf, who were enemies, were to carry out a pincer movement against the German forces in East Prussia to meet west of the Masurian Lakes. Although Samsonov's units reached their initial goal, his northernmost units were unable to establish contact with Rennenkampf to the north. The Germans then struck Samsonov's exposed northern flank (26 August 1914) and then his southern flank. Rennenkampf never answered his pleas for assistance. As the German pincers closed around Second Army, Samsonov committed suicide on 30 August.

Sano, Tadayoshi (1889–1945) Japanese general. Sano graduated from the Military

Academy (1911), Artillery and Engineers School, (1914) and Army Staff College (1922). A resident officer in Britain (1927–28), he was promoted colonel (1935) and commanded a regiment (1935–37). Promoted major general (1938), he commanded a brigade (1938–40) and was then commandant of the Field Artillery School (1940–41).

At the beginning of World War II, Sano commanded 38th Infantry Division in the capture of Hong Kong (8–25 December 1941) and also assisted in the capture of Sumatra (February 1942). Sent with his division to reinforce Guadalcanal (October 1942), he and its remnants were subsequently evacuated (February 1943). He commanded Thirty-Fourth Army (September 1944). Attached to the China Expeditionary Army (January 1945), he died that same year.

Sarrail, Maurice Paul Emmanuel (1856–1929) French general. Sarrail graduated from St. Cyr (1877) and became an infantry officer in North Africa. During 1900–07 he served in the War Ministry, commanded the infantry school at St. Maixent, and took charge of the military guard at the Chamber of Deputies. He was then director of infantry at the War Ministry (1907–11). By 1914 he was a major general commanding VI Corps.

At the beginning of World War I, Sarrail's corps, which was part of Third Army, participated in a counterattack against the Germans in the Ardennes (August 1914). This was unsuccessful, but French Army commander Joseph Joffre elevated Sarrail to command First Army. As such, he played a distinguished role during the First Battle of the Marne (September).

In July 1915 Sarrail was less fortunate. Joffre dismissed him because of minor setbacks in the Argonne. But as the favorite general of the French left, his political supporters demanded he receive a prominent command. He was thus appointed commander of the newly cre-

ated Eastern Army with the mandate to open a new campaign in the Balkans. His major accomplishment in the Balkans was the capture of Monastir (1916). His inability to advance further led to his recall (1917) and an end to any military role in the war.

Sasaki, Minoru (1893–1961) Japanese general. Trained in the cavalry, Sasaki rose to major general (1939) and CG of 4th Cavalry Brigade, then CofS, Sixth Army. Appointed head of the Army mechanized department (August 1942), he commanded Southeast Detachment at Munda, New Georgia Island. Surprised by the U.S. landing a few miles away on Rendova Island (30 June 1943), he nonetheless was able to prevent the initial U.S. effort to take Munda Airfield (7 July). Despite reinforcements in July and a valiant effort, he was forced to give up Munda (4 August). Reassigned to Eighth Army Area headquarters, he was promoted lieutenant general.

Satō, Kōtoku (1893–1959) Japanese general. Satō graduated from the Military Academy (1913) and Army Staff College (1921). He served on the Army General Staff (1930–31), was promoted colonel (1937) and commanded a regiment (1937–38). During the border clash with the Russians at Changkufeng (July–August 1938), he led a night attack on the Russian positions. Promoted major general, he commanded an infantry brigade in further fighting with the Russians at Nomonhan (May–August 1939).

Promoted lieutenant general (1942), Satō commanded 31st Infantry Division in Burma (1943) and participated in the offensive against Imphal and Kohima (March–July 1944). After his first attack at Kohima failed with heavy casualties, he refused to allow a second. He pulled out his division from Kohima without General Ren'ya Mutaguchi's authorization, creating serious tension in Fifteenth Army. Satō was ordered to stand trial for insubordination and cowardice, but this never occurred because the Japanese command feared that a trial would reveal the inadequate preparations for the offensive. Satō spent the remainder of the war in staff posts in Burma, Java, and Japan.

Satō, Tetsutarō (1866–1942) Japanese admiral. Satō graduated from the Naval Academy (1887). During the 1894–95 Sino-Japanese War he fought in the Battle of the Yalu (September 1894) and was wounded. He served in the Naval Affairs Department of the Navy Ministry (1896–97). After studying naval strategy in the United States (1899–1902), he was an instructor at the Naval Staff College (1902–03) and wrote a book, *On the Defense of the Empire*, the first thorough Japanese statement of navalism.

In the 1904–05 Russo-Japanese War, Satō served on the staff of Second Fleet and participated in the battles of Ulsan (August 1904) and Tsushima (27 May 1905). After commanding a gunboat, he was an advanced student at the Naval Staff College, then an instructor (1906–08). Promoted captain (1907), he published several books calling for imperial expansion south into the Netherlands Indies and advocating that Japan maintain at least 70 percent of U.S. capital ship strength. Promoted rear admiral (1912), he held assignments at sea and at the Staff College and was then vice chief of the Navy General Staff (1915) and president of the Staff College (1915–20). Promoted vice admiral (1916), he commanded the port of Maizuru and then went on the inactive list (1922). In retirement he spoke against naval limitation treaties. He was named a member of the House of Peers (1934).

Sauken, Dietrich von (1893–1980) German general. Sauken was wounded seven times during World War I. At the beginning of World War II he led a regiment, first in Poland (September 1939), then in the invasion of France and Benelux (May 1940). As a colonel he was acting com-

mander of the 4th Panzer Division in the Soviet Union (December 1941–January 1942). Promoted brigadier general (January 1942) and major general (April 1943) he continued in command of the division (May 1943–January 1944; March–April 1944). Promoted lieutenant general (April 1944), he commanded first a corps, then Second Army. In fighting around Danzig, he was CinC of the Special Army Command. Surrendering to the Red Army at the end of the war, he was not released until 1955.

Saunders, Laverne George (1903–88) U.S. Air Force general. A graduate of the University of South Dakota (1924), Saunders was commissioned in the infantry on graduation from West Point (1928). He then transferred to the Air Corps and became a pilot at Kelly Field, Texas (1929). He was an instructor and assistant football coach at West Point (1931–39). He took command of the 23rd Bomb Squadron (1940) and 11th Bomb Group (1940–43).

Saunders' 11th Bomb Group of B-17s was the first Army Air Force unit to serve in the Guadalcanal campaign. Promoted brigadier general (December 1942), he was badly wounded when his crippled B-17 went down near the Shetland Islands (December 1942). He was commanding general of 7th Bomber Command (January–March 1943), then CofS of Seventh Air Force (March–June 1943). He then commanded 58th Bomb Wing of B-29 Superfortresses (June 1943–July 1944), then 20th Bomber Command in the China–India–Burma Theater (1944–45). After the war, he was retired on grounds of physical disability (February 1947).

Scheer, Reinhard (1863–1928) German admiral. As a young officer, Scheer gained recognition as a leader of torpedo boats. He commanded 2nd Battle Squadron (1913), then in World War I took command of 3rd Battle Squadron (December 1914).

Appointed chief of the High Seas Fleet, replacing Admiral Hugo von Pohl (1916),

Scheer favored aggressive action to reduce the British Grand Fleet piecemeal through carefully prepared surprise raids and to bring about an encounter that the Germans stood a good chance of winning.

Under pressure to do something while the German Army was locked in battle at Verdun, Scheer took the High Seas Fleet out (31 May 1916) on a sweep of the North Sea to lure a portion of the British Home Fleet into action. In the resulting Battle of Jutland, Scheer soon lost the initiative and finally ordered torpedo boat and battle cruiser attacks and used night to make good his retreat. He then experimented with units of dreadnoughts and fast battle cruisers in bombardment operations against the English coast (August).

When the German naval high command was reorganized (August 1918), Scheer was appointed its head. Apart from ordering massive U-boat construction, he could do little to influence events at sea. His plan for a last-ditch all-out naval effort at the end of the war produced a general mutiny in the fleet. He retired soon afterward.

Schepke, Joachim (1912–41) German navy officer. A U-boat commander in the Battle of the Atlantic during World War II, Schepke was responsible for sinking 39 Allied ships aggregating 159,130 tons. He preferred surface attacks at night and, on one occasion in *U-100*, he sank seven ships totalling more than 50,000 total tons in one Allied convoy (September 1940).

Detected by radar while surfaced and approaching a convoy, his submarine was rammed by the British destroyer *Vanoc* (15 March 1941) and sunk. Only seven crewmen survived. Schepke was among those who died.

Schlieffen, Count Alfred von (1833–1913) German general. After studying law, Schlieffen joined the Prussian Army and was commissioned (1854). He graduated from the Kriegsakademie and was a staff officer in the 1866 Austro-Prussian War and 1870–71 Franco-Prussian War. He commanded a cavalry regiment (1876–83), then began a series of assignments with the General Staff. Promoted to brigadier general (1886), he was then advanced to major general (1888).

Schlieffen became chief of the German General Staff (1891) and was promoted to lieutenant general (1893). Sensing the inevitability of a two-front war as a consequence of the 1894 Franco-Russian alliance, Schlieffen originated a comprehensive war plan that came to bear his name. It called for the bulk of German resources to be committed in the West in a sweeping movement with a strong right wing. There would be an invasion of neutral Belgium in order to defeat France quickly and enable Germany to then shift its resources to deal with a slow-moving Russia. Schlieffen was tireless in introducing refinements to maintain the German combat edge in the opening weeks of a war.

Schlieffen retired in 1906. His plan, which suffered from logistical shortcomings and rigidity, was in any case fatally modified by his successor, Helmuth von Moltke.

Schmid, Anton (1900–42) German army sergeant. Born in Vienna, Schmid was drafted into the army shortly after the 1938 *Anschluss*. Stationed near Vilnius as a sergeant (fall 1941), he witnessed Jews being herded into ghettos and the shooting of others in nearby Ponary. Shocked by what he saw, he resolved to do what he could to assist. He ultimately saved the lives of more than 250 Jews by hiding them. He also supplied forged papers and matériel to the Jewish underground.

Arrested (January 1942), Schmid was tried by a military court (February) and shot (13 April). In 2000 a German army barracks at Rendsburg was renamed in his honor.

Schmidt von Knobelsdorf, Constantin (1860–1936) German general. Schmidt joined the army (1878), attended the War Academy, and served on the General Staff. A battalion commander (1901), he was then promoted colonel and became CofS of X Corps (1904). He commanded a regiment (1908) and as a major general was CofS to the Guards Corps (1911). Then deputy chief of the General Staff (1912), he was promoted lieutenant general (January 1914).

At the beginning of World War I, Schmidt was CofS to Crown Prince Wilhelm's Fifth Army at Saarbrücken. He was largely responsible for victories at Longwy–Longuyon (August 1914) and Varennes–Montfaucon (September). Despite orders to stand in place, he advanced as far as Verdun. Following the German defeat on the Marne (September), he withdrew the army to Varennes, where the front stabilized. When Crown Prince Wilhelm took command of Third Army (September 1915), he temporarily commanded VIII Reserve Corps.

As CofS of new Army Group Prince Wilhelm, Schmidt began the Battle of Verdun (21 February 1916). Pushing for victory at any cost and supported by German Army CofS General Erich Falkenhayn, he refused to abandon the battle. He had a bitter falling out with Crown Prince Wilhelm over blame for the debacle, and he was removed as CofS (August) and given command of X Corps, which was sent to the Eastern Front to halt a Russian advance near Kovel. Thereafter it served in Alsace. Promoted lieutenant general (October 1918), he headed X Corps during the demobilization and retired in September 1919.

Schörner, Ferdinand (1892–1973) German field marshal. Schörner served in the Bavarian army before attending the universities of Munich, Lausanne, and Grenoble. Commissioned (October 1914), his specialty was mountain warfare. He served on both the Italian and Western Fronts and was wounded. After World War I he fought with the Freikorps before joining the Reichswehr. He served on the General Staff but much preferred line service.

Lieutenant Colonel Schörner took command of the 98th Mountain Regiment (1937). Promoted colonel (1939), he commanded his unit in the invasion of Poland (September 1939). He then commanded 6th Mountain Division in the invasion of France and Benelux (May 1940). Promoted brigadier general (August), he commanded the same unit in the invasion of Greece (April 1941). His division was then transferred to the Arctic (1941–1942). He took command of Mountain Corps Norway (January 1942) as a major general. Promoted to lieutenant general, his command was reorganized as XIX Mountain Corps (June 1942). Transferred to South Russia (October 1943), he commanded Army Detachment Nikopol. Following a brief stint in staff work with the High Command (March 1944), he was promoted full general and commanded Army Group South Ukraine (March–July 1944), then Army Group North (July–January). He then commanded Army Group Center (January–May 1945). Promoted field marshal (April) and named in Adolf Hitler's testament to succeed him as head of the Wehrmacht, he had a number of his own men executed for cowardice. He was one of the most unpopular and brutal German Army commanders.

Schwarzkopf, H. Norman (1934–) U.S. general. Commissioned in the infantry on graduation from West Point (1956), Schwarzkopf earned a master's degree in missile electronics from the University of California (1964) and then served two tours in Vietnam: the first (1965–66) as an advisor and the second (1969–70) as a battalion commander in the 23rd Division. He held a variety of other assignments, including teaching at West Point (1966–68) and attended the Command

and General Staff College and the Army War College.

As a major general (1988), Schwarzkopf commanded the 24th Mechanized Infantry Division (1983–85) and was an advisor for the joint task force that invaded Grenada (1983). As a lieutenant general (1986), he commanded I Corps at Fort Lewis, Washington (1986–87). Promoted general (1988), he headed Central Command and had responsibility for the U.S. and Allied (twenty-seven other countries) military buildup (code-named DESERT SHIELD) against Iraq, following that country's August 1990 invasion of Kuwait. He then orchestrated Operation DESERT STORM, the largest mechanized combat operation since 1945, beginning (17 January 1991) with a forty-day air war and then a 100-hour ground war. He retired in August 1991.

Scott, Hugh Lenox (1853–1934) U.S. general. Scott graduated from West Point (1876) and served in the cavalry in the American West, where he demonstrated diplomatic skills in dealing with the Indians. He trained troops during the 1898 Spanish-American War and afterward was governor of Sulu Archipelago in the Philippines. Superintendent of West Point (1906–11), he commanded a cavalry regiment (1912) and was promoted brigadier general. When trouble began with Mexico, he commanded American troops on the border and became involved in diplomatic efforts to reduce tensions between the United States and Mexico.

Scott was army CofS (1914–17) and remained on active duty past retirement age. He served as commander of Fort Dix until 1918.

Scott, Sir Percy Moreton (1853–1924) British admiral. Scott joined the navy as a cadet (1866). He attended the Royal Navy Gunnery School HMS *Excellent* (1878) and soon established his reputation as a gunnery expert. Promoted commander (1886), he returned to command the

Excellent (1890) and began reforms. Promoted captain (1893), he was appointed to the Ordnance Committee. Scott put his gunnery ideas into practice while in command of the cruiser *Scylla* in the Mediterranean. In the 1899 gunnery competition, where the average was 30 percent hits, *Scylla* scored a staggering 80 percent. He also introduced salvo firing. He was knighted for his conversion of naval guns to land use during the 1899–1902 Boer War.

After service in the 1900–01 Boxer Rebellion, Scott, known as "the Pocket Hercules," continued to improve fleet gunnery, inventing a number of devices to enhance both accuracy and rate of fire. Promoted rear-admiral, he was appointed inspector of target practice. He took command of 1st Cruiser Squadron of the Channel Fleet (July 1907). After being sent to South Africa and on a cruise in South America, he was placed on half-pay.

Promoted vice admiral (1908) and admiral (1913), Scott retired from the navy but worked with Vickers to develop what became the director fire control system: a telescopic sight and the means of laying and firing a battleship's guns electronically. Recalled to active duty in World War I, he realized that the big battleship had become obsolete and advocated greater emphasis on submarines and naval aircraft.

Seeckt, Hans von (1866–1936) German general. Seeckt entered the army (1885) and was a lieutenant colonel at the beginning of World War I and chief of staff for III Corps. His achievements secured him promotion to major general and the post of chief of staff of the new Eleventh Army on the Eastern Front. He helped secure the breakthrough at Gorlice (May 1915) and served as CofS for General August von Mackensen's army group in the Balkans during the conquest of Serbia (1915), for Archduke Karl's Twelfth Army in Hungary and Rumania (1916), and for the Turkish Army (1917–18). At war's end he was promoted lieutenant general.

As Quartermaster General (CofS) of the Reichswehr (1919–26), Seeckt rebuilt the German Army and created a cadre force capable of rapid expansion. He supported the entente with Russia that allowed him to train units secretly in Russia. He failed to support the government during the 1920 Kapp Putsch but remained as head of the Reichswehr until forced to resign (1926). He later served in the Reichstag and aligned himself with the Nazis. Sent to China (1934), he helped modernize the Nationalist Army.

Senger und Etterlin, Fridolin Rudolf von (1891–1963) German general. After attending Eton, Senger volunteered to serve in the 76th Field Artillery Regiment (1910) before becoming a Rhodes Scholar at Oxford (1912–14). He rejoined the regiment on the start of World War I and was commissioned (1917). He was one of few reserve officers to serve in the Reichswehr after the war, joining the horse cavalry and becoming a world-class rider. After service at the Cavalry School in Hanover, the cavalry inspectorate in Berlin, and on the General Staff, he commanded the 3rd Cavalry Regiment (1938) as a colonel (March 1939).

Senger commanded his regiment in the invasion of Poland (September 1939), and a motorized brigade in the invasion of France and Benelux (May 1940). He was then chief German liaison officer with the Franco-Italian armistice commission. Promoted brigadier general (September 1941), he commanded 17th Panzer Division in the Soviet Union and participated in Fourth Army's failed attempt to link up with Sixth Army at Stalingrad on the Eastern Front. Promoted major general (May 1943), he was chief liaison officer with the Italian army in Sicily (June) and, following Italy's defection, successfully evacuated German forces from Corsica and Sardinia. He then commanded XIV Panzer Corps in Italy (October 1943).

Promoted lieutenant general (January 1944), he proved singularly adept in defensive warfare, especially in the battle for Monte Cassino. He was later involved in *SS-Obergruppenführer* Karl Wolff's efforts to surrender German forces in Italy.

Seversky, Alexander Prokofieff de (1894–1974) American aeronautical engineer. Born in Russia, Seversky graduated from the Naval Academy (1914) and saw sea duty at the start of World War I, but transferred to the Naval Air Service (1915). As a lieutenant and pilot, he was shot down during a night bombing mission in the Gulf of Riga (2 July) and lost a leg. Fitted with an artificial limb, he returned to active duty (1916) and shot down thirteen German aircraft. He experimented with both flying techniques and aerial refueling, and he invented a bombsight.

Sent to the United States as part of a naval aviation mission (summer 1917), Seversky volunteered his services to the U.S. government when Russia left the war. He then started a firm that sold his bombsight to the U.S. government (1922). He founded the Seversky Aircraft Corporation (1931), which pioneered all-metal cantilever-wing monoplane fighters for the U.S. Army Air Corps. Working with fellow Russian emigré Alexander Kartveli, he designed and built the first fighter powered by an air-cooled, supercharged engine for high-altitude combat. This became the P-47 Thunderbolt escort fighter-bomber.

A U.S. citizen (1927) and a major in the Army Air Corps Specialists Reserve, Seversky then embarked on a crusade to alert the American public to the realities of air power and the need to develop a strategic bombardment doctrine. His book *Victory through Air Power* (1942) showed how the United States could use air power to win World War II.

Seymour, Edward Hobart (1840–1929) British admiral of the fleet. Seymour entered the Royal Naval College (1852). As a midshipman, he fought in the 1856–60 Second Opium War with China. Promoted lieutenant (1860), he participated in the Anglo-French attack on the Taku Forts (August–September 1860), commanded a warship in operations on the Canton River, and took part in military action against the Taiping rebels (1862). Promoted commander (1866), he was wounded in operations in the Congo (1870). He commanded a battleship (1882–85).

Given command of the China station (1889), Seymour played a key role in the 1900–01 Boxer Rebellion. Early in the rebellion he put ashore 2,000 British and U.S. troops at Tientsin (Tianjin) in a failed Allied relief effort (June 1900). The troops encountered superior Chinese forces and withdrew to the ships, suffering 300 casualties. Promoted admiral (March 1901), he became admiral of the fleet (1905).

Shaposhnikov, Boris M. (1882–1945) Soviet marshal. Shaposhnikov joined the Russian Army (1901) and graduated from both the Moscow Military School and the General Staff Academy. During World War I he first held staff positions, then commanded a regiment (1917).

Joining the Red Army (1918), Shaposhnikov held a variety of staff positions. He then commanded military districts (1925–37) and was commissar of the Frunze Military Academy. He served on the investigative board that presided over Josef Stalin's purge of the military (1937). Appointed chief of the Soviet General Staff (1940), he advised Stalin to abandon forward troop positions in eastern Poland and consolidate Soviet forces behind the former borders. Dismissed for this suggestion, after the German invasion of the Soviet Union (22 June 1941) he was reinstated (July 1941).

Shaposhnikov became ill (November 1941) and was replaced by General Aleksandr Vasilevsky. He nonetheless helped plan the defense of Moscow and the Russian counterattack. In June 1942 he advised against the attack at Kharkov. Appointed deputy commissar of defense, he was commandant of the Voroshilov Military Academy (June 1943) until his death.

Sharon, Ariel (1928–) Israeli general and politician. Born in Egypt, he joined the Zionist Haganah and was an instructor in the Jewish Settlement Police. In the 1948–49 Israeli War of Independence he served in 3rd Brigade, as a platoon commander, intelligence officer, and then company commander. He led its reconnaissance unit (1949–50), then was an intelligence officer (1951–52). He studied at Hebrew University (1952–53), then commanded Unit 101, which retaliated for Arab terrorist raids (1953–57). He commanded 202nd Paratroop Brigade in the 1956 Sinai War, leading the linkup with the advance battalion that had seized Mitla Pass and then driving south to Sharm el-Sheikh.

Sharon studied in Britain at the Staff College, Camberley (1957–58), then was training director of the General Staff (1958), led the Infantry School (1958–59) and commanded an armored brigade (1962–64). He was then CofS for Northern Command (1964–66) and director of training for the Israeli Defense Force (1966–67). During the 1967 Six-Day War he commanded an armored division task force in the Sinai, defeating Egyptian positions around Abu Ageila. He was involved in the War of Attrition with Egypt (1969–70) and then retired from the army (July 1973).

Recalled on the outbreak of the 1973 October War, Sharon commanded an armored division in the Sinai, leading it with distinction in halting the Egyptian offensive (7–8 October), in the Battle of Chinese Farm (16–17 October), and in the strike across the Suez Canal into Egypt (17–19 October). Again resigning, he entered politics and was a founder of the conservative Likud bloc (September 1973). A member of the Knesset (parliament) from 1973, he held various cabinet posts. As defense minister (1981–83), he masterminded the Israeli invasion of Lebanon (June 1982) and siege of Beirut (June–August). Under mounting criticism for this and for massacres at refugee camps, he resigned. Sharon became Israeli prime minister in 2001.

Shepherd, Lemuel Cornick, Jr. (1896–1990) U.S. Marine Corps general. Shepherd graduated from the Virginia Military Institute (1917) and was commissioned in the Marine Corps. He led a platoon in World War I, saw action in a number of battles, including Belleau Wood, and was wounded three times.

Shepherd held a number of assignments after the war and graduated from the Naval War College (1937). Promoted brigadier general (July 1942), he was assistant commander of the 1st Marine Division and fought with it on Cape Gloucester. He then led a brigade in the invasion of Guam (July–August 1944). Promoted major general, he commanded the 6th Marine Division in fighting on Okinawa (April–June 1945).

After the war Shepherd became assistant commandant of the Marines (1946–48). He then was commandant of Marine Corps Schools (1948–50). Promoted lieutenant general (June 1950), he took command of Fleet Marine Force, Pacific. Promoted full general (January 1952), he was commandant of the Marine Corps (1952–55). He carried out administrative changes and advocated the use of helicopters in assault operations before his retirement in 1956.

Sherman, Forrest Percival (1896–1951) U.S. admiral. Sherman attended Massachusetts Institute of Technology before graduating from Annapolis (1917). During World War I he served in destroyers in European waters. He completed flight training at Pensacola (1922) and then

served in a squadron on an aircraft carrier (1923–24). He then returned to Pensacola as an instructor (1924–26). He graduated from the Naval War College (1927), and served on carriers and taught at Annapolis (1926–27). He then held a variety of assignments before serving in the War Plans division of the Office of the Chief of Naval Operations (1940–42).

Captain Sherman commanded the carrier *Wasp* (1942) and fought in battles off Guadalcanal. Following the loss of his ship to torpedo attack (September), he became CofS to the commander of Pacific Fleet Air Force. Promoted rear admiral (April 1943), he became deputy CofS and head of the War Plans Division for Pacific Fleet commander Admiral Chester Nimitz.

Sherman took command of Carrier Division 1 (October 1945) but was soon promoted vice admiral and made deputy chief of naval operations (CNO) (December), where he defined the navy's position in interservice rivalries following the war and was an architect of the National Security Act (1947). He then commanded naval forces in the Mediterranean, soon known as Sixth Fleet (1948–49). Promoted admiral, he became the youngest CNO (November 1949) and oversaw navy activities at the beginning of the 1950–53 Korean War. He died in office.

Sherman, Frederick Carl (1888–1957) U.S. admiral. Sherman graduated from Annapolis (1910) and then held a variety of assignments, including submarine commands (1916–19). He twice attended the Naval War College (1924–25; 1939–40), and was promoted captain (1938).

Sherman took command of the carrier *Lexington* (June 1940) and, when the U.S. entered World War II, undertook operations against Japanese-held islands in the south Pacific. His carrier was lost in the Battle of the Coral Sea (May 1942). Promoted to rear admiral that same month, he became assistant to Chief of Naval Operations Ernest J. King. He returned to the Pacific first as commander of Task Force 16, and then Carrier Division 2, supporting operations in the Solomon Islands.

Sherman then commanded Carrier Division I and undertook attacks on Rabaul and supported the Bougainville and Tarawa-Betio landings. He commanded West Coast Fleet Air (March–August 1944) but returned to sea to command Carrier Division 1 and Task Force 33.3/58/3 in the Battle of Leyte Gulf (October 1944) and in support of landings on Iwo Jima (February–March 1945) and Okinawa (April–June). As vice admiral he commanded Task Force 58 (July 1945).

Sherman took command of the First Fast Carrier Task Force and TF-58 (July 1945). After the war he commanded Fifth Fleet (1946). He retired in March 1947.

Shimada, Shigetarō (1883–1976) Japanese admiral. Shimada graduated from the Naval Staff College (1910). He was naval attaché in Italy (1916–19). In 1926 he became CinC of a submarine flotilla. As a captain, he commanded light cruiser *Tama*, then battleship *Hiei* (1928). Promoted rear admiral, he was CofS, Second Fleet (1929), then CofS of Combined Fleet (1930). He then directed the Submarine School (1931) and was CofS of Third Fleet (1932). From 1932 he held various posts on the Navy Staff, then was vice chief of the Navy General Staff (1935). He was CinC, Second Fleet (1937), and CinC, China Fleet (1940).

Promoted full admiral (November 1940), Shimada supported the army's expansionist policies. Reportedly for that reason, he was appointed minister of the navy in the government of Hideki Tōjō (October 1941), where he slavishly did Tōjō's bidding. When Tōjō took over Hajime Sugiyama's duties as chief of the Army General Staff, he ordered Shimada to take over Osami Nagano's duties as chief of the Naval General Staff (February 1944). Following the loss of Saipan, with great reluctance Tōjō ordered Shimada to

resign (July) and then had to resign himself.

Tried for war crimes after the war, Shimada was convicted and sentenced to life in prison but was released in 1956.

Shimanura, Hayao (1858–1923) Japanese admiral. Shimanura graduated from the Naval Academy (1880) and held staff positions as a junior officer. He then studied in Britain and served aboard Royal Navy ships (1888–91). On the staff of the Standing Fleet during the 1894–95 Sino–Japanese War, he fought in the Battle of the Yalu (17 September 1894) and was wounded. He then held staff positions before commanding a cruiser in the occupation of Tientsin (Tianjin) in the 1900–01 Boxer Rebellion.

Promoted rear admiral on the outbreak of the 1904–05 Russo-Japanese War, Shimanura was CofS of First Fleet. He commanded 2nd Battle Division of Second Fleet in the Battle of Tsushima (27 May 1905). After serving as president of the Navy Staff College (1908–09), he was chief of the Navy General Staff (1919–20). Promoted admiral (1915), he was posthumously promoted fleet admiral (1923).

Short, Walter Campbell (1880–1949) U.S. general. Short graduated from the University of Illinois (1901) and was commissioned in the infantry (1902). He held a variety of assignments, including service in the Philippines (1907) and participation in the 1916–17 Punitive Expedition into Mexico. After the United States entered World War I (April 1917), he went to France as a captain and served on the staff of AEF commander General John J. Pershing. As CofS of Third Army, he saw action in the 1918 Aisne–Marne, St. Mihiel, and Meuse–Argonne offensives. At the end of the war he was a temporary colonel.

Following the war, Short reverted to the rank of captain. An instructor at the Command and General Staff School (1919–22, 1928–30), he graduated from the Army War College (1925). He served in the Bureau of Indian Affairs at the War Department (1930–34). Promoted colonel (1934), he commanded the 6th Infantry Regiment. He was then assistant commandant of the Infantry School at Fort Benning (1936). Promoted brigadier general, he commanded a brigade of the 1st Division (1937), then commanded the division (1938–40). Promoted major general, he commanded I Corps (1940). He then took command of the Hawaiian Department (January 1941). A month later he was promoted temporary lieutenant general. Relieved from command following the Japanese attack on Pearl Harbor and reverting to his permanent rank of major general, he retired in February 1942.

Shoup, David Monroe (1904–83) U.S. Marine Corps general. Commissioned in the Marines on graduation from DePauw University (June 1926), Shoup held a variety of assignments, including sea duty, service with the 4th Marine Regiment at Peking and Shanghai (1934–36), as student and instructor at the Marine Corps School at Quantico, Virginia (1937–41), and service in Iceland (1941–42). He joined 2nd Marine Division (July 1942), was promoted lieutenant colonel (August), and served with the division in New Zealand (September 1942–November 1943). He saw action as an observer on Guadalcanal with the 1st Marine Division (October 1942) and with the 43rd Infantry Division on New Georgia (July–August 1943). Promoted colonel, he commanded 2nd Marine Regiment in the Tarawa invasion (November), for which he was awarded the Medal of Honor. Appointed CofS of 2nd Marine Division (December 1943), he fought in the invasions of Saipan (June–July 1944) and Tinian (July–August).

Returning to the United States, Shoup then served on the staff of Marine Corps headquarters (1944–47). He headed Service Command, Fleet Marine Force, Pacific (1947–49), then was CofS, 1st Marine Division (1949–50). He commanded the Marine Basic School, Quantico (1950–52), and then was fiscal director, Marine Corps Headquarters (1952–56). Promoted major general (September 1955), he was inspector general for recruit training (1956), then inspector general of the Marine Corps (1956–57). He commanded 1st Marine Division at Camp Pendleton, California (1957–58), then 3rd Marine Division on Okinawa (1958–59). He briefly commanded the Marine Corps Recruit Depot at Parris Island, South Carolina (1958) before being promoted lieutenant general and becoming CofS of the Marine Corps (1959). Promoted general, he was Marine Corps commandant (1960–63) until he retired.

Shtemenko, Sergei M. (1907–76) Soviet general. Shtemenko joined the Red Army (1926) and the Communist party (1930) and graduated from a number of service schools, including the General Staff Academy (1940). A member of the Operations Directorate of the General Staff (1941–43), he was chief of the Operations Directorate (May 1943–April 1946). Promoted colonel general before the end of the war, he was the consummate staff officer; he organized military activities, especially those of the Transcaucasus, Black Sea, and Northern Fronts, and he had a key role in planning the final assult on Berlin.

After the war Shtemenko was deputy chief of the General Staff. Promoted general of the army (November 1948), he was then chief of the General Staff. Demoted (December 1952), he became CofS of Soviet occupation forces in Germany. He then dropped from sight in the successionist struggle following the death of Josef Stalin (1953). He returned to public life (1956) as head of the General Staff Main Intelligence Directorate. Promoted back to colonel general, he was demoted again that same year (1957) and then commanded military districts

(1957–68). Again promoted general of the army and appointed CofS of Warsaw Pact forces (1968), he oversaw the largest military deployment in Europe since World War II, the Warsaw Pact invasion of Czechoslovakia (August).

Shumikov, Mikhail Stepanovich (1895–1975) Soviet general. Shumikov attended military school and was an ensign during World War I. He joined the Red Army (1918), and during the Russian Civil War he commanded a rifle regiment. He attended the Higher Infantry School (1929) and commanded a rifle corps in the 1939–40 Russo-Finnish War.

At the start of World War II Shumikov commanded another rifle corps but was soon promoted to deputy commander of Fifty-Fifth Army on the Leningrad Front. In 1942 he commanded Sixty-Fourth Army (later Seventh Guards Army) in the Battle of Stalingrad. He also fought in the Battle of Kursk (July 1943) and participated in the Soviet invasions of Hungary and Austria, attaining the rank of colonel general.

After the war Shumikov commanded various military districts and then became consultant to the group of inspectors general of the Ministry of Defense.

Sibert, Edward Luther (1897–1980) U.S. general. Commissioned in the field artillery on graduation from West Point (1918), he served in the AEF in France in the 2nd Infantry Division (1919). An ROTC instructor at Cornell University (1922–26), he also taught at the Field Artillery School (1927–31). He graduated from both the Command and General Staff School (1935) amd Army War College (1939). Appointed military attaché to Brazil (1940–41), following U.S. entry into World War II, he was CofS of the 7th Infantry Division (1942).

Promoted brigadier general (October 1942), Sibert then commanded the 99th Division Artillery (1942–43). He was intelligence chief for the Twelfth Army

Group (1944–45) and U.S. Forces, European Theater of Operations. He retired in January 1954.

Sibert, Franklin Cummings (1891–1980) U.S. Army general. Commissioned in the infantry on graduation from West Point (1912), he graduated from the Command and General Staff School (1925) and Army War College (1929). Promoted brigadier general (September 1941), he was then on Lieutenant General Joseph Stilwell's staff in the China–Burma–India Theater (1941–42) and made the retreat from Burma (1942)

Promoted major general (1942), he commanded 6th Infantry Division (1942–44), then X Corps (1944–46) in New Guinea (1943–44) and on Luzon in the Philippines (1945). He retired in June 1946.

Sikorski, Wladyslaw E. (1881–1943) Polish general. During World War I he rose to the rank of colonel commanding Polish troops serving with the Austrians. As commander of Fifth Army, he played a major role in the 1920–21 Russo-Polish War and later became chief of the general staff. He was then prime minister of Poland (1922–23) and minister of war (1924–25). He opposed Jósef Pilsudski's 1926 *coup d'etat* and was denied influence thereafter. Prevented any military role, he left Poland on the German invasion and headed the Polish government-in-exile in Paris (30 September 1939) as premier and CinC. He moved to London after the fall of France.

Following the German invasion of the Soviet Union, Sikorski signed an agreement with the Russians (30 July 1941) ending the state of war between Russia and Poland and providing for the creation of a Polish army to be raised in Russia from Polish POWs captured in 1939. In 1943 following the discovery of mass graves of Polish army officers in the Katyn Forest, he called for an International Red Cross investigation. This created a crisis in Russo-Polish relations, in the midst of which he died in a mysterious plane crash on Gibraltar.

Simonds, Guy Grenville (1903–74) Canadian general. Simonds came to Canada from England as a boy. A graduate of the Royal Military College of Canada, he was commissioned in the artillery. He served in Canada and graduated from the Staff College at Camberley (1937). He went overseas (December 1939) on the staff of the Canadian 1st Division. Rapidly promoted, he received command of the Canadian 1st Division (April 1943), leading it in the invasion of Sicily (July), where he won General Bernard Montgomery's admiration, and in Italy (September). He then led the 5th Canadian Armored Division before being promoted to command the Canadian II Corps (January 1944) of the Canadian Second Army.

II Corps joined the action in Normandy (July 1944) south of Caen, and Simonds developed innovative tactics to deal with the German defenses including the use of armored personnel carriers (Kangaroos). His forces helped invest the Channel ports and clear the Scheldt estuary and open access to Antwerp (September). He briefly commanded Canadian First Army in the absence of General Henry Crear (September–November) and was widely praised, especially for the reduction of Walcheren Island. He then returned to command II Corps, leading it in fighting in the Rhineland. Lieutenant General Simonds was one of the best Allied corps commanders of the war.

After the war Simonds failed to secure the post of chief of the General Staff. He then held appointments in the Imperial and Canadian National Defense Colleges before becoming chief of the General Staff (1951–56).

Simović, Dušan (1882–1962) Yugoslav general and politician. Simović fought in the 1912–13 Balkan Wars and in World War I. After the war he was commandant of the Officers' Military School, chief of the general staff (1939), and chief of the air staff (1940). Following Yugoslavian leaders signing a pact joining the Axis (25 March 1941), he was one of the leaders of a *coup d'état* that overthrew the regency for King Paul. The real power behind the coup, however, was General Borivoje Mirković.

As both premier and chief of the armed forces supreme command, Simović worked to smooth relations with Germany but was unable to prevent that country from invading Yugoslavia (6 April). He divided his forces into three main groups with the intention of fighting a delaying action, but the Germans managed to split and isolate these, cutting off contact with Greece.

After the fall of Belgrade (13 April), Simović resigned his posts and charged his successor to sue for an armistice. He then went into exile. He appointed Draža Mihailović as commander of resistance forces and retained the premiership in the government-in-exile until January 1942. In 1944 he urged the Yugoslav people to support Tito.

Simpson, William Hood (1888–1980) U.S. general. Commissioned in the infantry on graduation from West Point (1909), Simpson served in the Philippines (1910–12) and in the 1916–17 Punitive Expedition into Mexico. During World War I he went to France in the AEF as a staff officer in the 33rd Infantry Division (April 1918). Advanced to temporary lieutenant colonel, he saw action in the St. Mihiel (September 1918) and Meuse–Argonne (September–November) offensives.

Following the war, Simpson reverted to the rank of captain. He attended the Infantry School (1924), the Command and General Staff School (1925), and the Army War College (1927–28). Promoted colonel (1938), he commanded the 9th Infantry Regiment. Promoted brigadier general (October 1940), he was assistant commander of the 2nd Infantry Division. Promoted major general (September 1941), he commanded the 35th Infantry Division (1941–42), the 30th Infantry Division (1942), and the newly activated XII Corps (September).

Promoted lieutenant general (October 1943), Simpson commanded Fourth Army in California. He and his staff went to England to organize Eighth Army (May 1944), thereafter redesignated Ninth Army, which he led as part of General Omar Bradley's Twelfth Army Group in reducing the Fortress of Brest (August 1944), and then in Holland, Belgium, and fighting in the Ruhr. The Ninth was the first across the Elbe River, where it met Soviet troops, and was then in occupation duty in Germany.

After the war, Simpson headed the board that reorganized the army. He retired (November 1946) but was promoted full general on the retired list in July 1954.

Sims, William Snowden (1858–1936) U.S. admiral. Following graduation from Annapolis (1880), Sims held a variety of sea and intelligence assignments. Noting British improvements in naval gunnery, he helped secure similar changes in the U.S. Navy. An observer during the 1904–05 Russo-Japanese War, he was promoted captain (1911), then was instructor at the Naval War College (1911–12) and its president (1917). He was promoted rear admiral (1916).

Sims was in Britain carrying dispatches when the United States entered World War I (April 1917) and was immediately given charge of U.S. ships operating from British bases. Promoted vice admiral (May), he was made commander of U.S. naval forces operating in European waters. He was a strong supporter of the convoy system and the need to supply adequate resources for it. Promoted admiral (December 1918), he reverted to rear admiral at the end of the war and was again president of the Naval War College.

Sims was outspoken on the issue of naval preparedness and clashed with Se-

cretary of the Navy Josephus Daniels. He retired as a rear admiral (October 1922) and continued to speak out on naval issues. A strong advocate of naval aviation, he even declared battleships to be obsolete. He was later promoted admiral on the retired list in 1930.

Skoropadsky, Pavlo P. (1873–1945) Russian general and Ukrainian leader. During World War I Skoropadsky was promoted lieutenant general. When the tsarist regime collapsed (March 1917), he "Ukrainized" forces under his command and offered to place a 40,000-man corps at the disposal of the new Ukrainian national government. Suspicious of Skoropadsky, the government refused.

Subsequently Skoropadsky seized power in Ukraine in alliance with the German military (April 1918), taking the historic Cossack title of *hetman*. His socially conservative, dictatorial regime was badly compromised by its complete reliance on the Germans. When the Germans agreed to an armistice (November 1918), his government collapsed and he went into exile.

Skorzeny, Otto (1908–76) German SS officer. Skorzeny graduated from the Vienna Technical College (1931). Dueling scars there brought him the nickname "Scarface." He joined the Nazi party. Rejected by the Luftwaffe because of his age, he joined the SS *Leibstandarte Adolf Hitler* (LAH) Division (1939). He transferred to the SS *Das Reich* Division and fought in the Invasion of France and Benelux (May 1940). He participated as a lieutenant in the invasions of the Balkans (April–May 1941) and the Soviet Union (22 June). Promoted *SS-Hauptsturmführer* (captain), he organized and commanded commandos in a daring mission to rescue deposed Italian dictator Benito Mussolini from confinement in the Abruzzi (12 September 1943). Promoted *SS-Sturmbannführer* (major), he conducted other such operations, including the capture of Hungarian Regent Miklós Horthy (16 October 1944), which led to a Nazi government in Hungary. Promoted *SS-Obersturmbannführer* (lieutenant colonel) for this accomplishment, Skorzeny then organized Operation GREIF (Condor). With more than 3,000 English-speaking German soldiers, he created confusion behind U.S. lines during Adolf Hitler's Ardennes Offensive (Battle of the Bulge) (December 1944–January 1945). He fought briefly on the Eastern Front. Transferred back to the Western Front, he tried but failed to destroy the Remagen bridge over the Rhine (March 1945). Tried for war crimes, including involvement in the massacre of U.S. POWs at Malmédy, he was acquitted on this charge (1947) but was not released. Following an escape from prison (1948), he lived in Spain.

Slessor, Sir John Cotesworth (1897–1979) British air marshal. Crippled by polio in his legs as a child, Slessor nonetheless secured a Royal Flying Corps commission (1915). He flew in combat in the Middle East and in France and became a flight lieutenant to the new Royal Air Force.

An advocate of strategic bombing, he argued in his book *Air Power and Armies* (1936) for strategic bombing of civilian centers to break morale. As director of plans at the Air Ministry (1937–41), he went to the United States (1940) to coordinate plans for possible American entry in the war. He then took over 5th Group of Bomber Command (March 1941) and was promoted air vice marshal. He next was assistant chief of the air staff for policy (1941) and worked with U.S. officers to develop policies and procedures of a combined air offensive, especially the compromise agreement of the Casablanca Conference (January 1943).

Slessor then headed Coastal Command (1943). A fine administrator, he coordinated Allied naval and air assets effectively; his extensive use of land-based aircraft was a key in winning the Battle

of the Atlantic against German submarines. Promoted air marshal, he was also knighted (1943). He next headed the RAF in the Mediterranean and Middle East (1944–45) and was deputy commander of Allied air forces there.

Slessor headed personnel for the RAF (1945–48), then the Imperial Defense College (1948–50). Promoted to air chief marshal (1946), he succeeded Air Chief Marshal Arthur Tedder as chief of the air staff (1950–53) until he retired.

Slim, Sir William Joseph, 1st Viscount (1891–1970) British field marshal. Educated at Birmingham University, Slim had joined the Officer Training Corps. He volunteered as a private at the beginning of World War I but was soon commissioned. Sent to Mesopotamia, he fought in the 1915–16 Gallipoli campaign (July–August 1915), but was wounded and invalided out of the army. He managed to secure reinstatement (January 1916) and served on the Western Front and in Mesopotamia. Again wounded and declared unfit for duty, he won reinstatement.

After the war, Slim served with the Indian Army and graduated from Quetta Staff College (1920). He taught at the Staff College at Camberley (1934–36), was on the staff of the Imperial Defense College (1937), then was commandant of the Senior Officers School, Belgaum, India. Promoted brigadier general, he commanded 10th Indian Brigade in the Sudan (September 1939). Wounded in an Italian air raid (January 1941), he missed most of the subsequent campaign in Ethiopia and Eritrea. He joined General Orde Wingate's Middle East Command (March) and assumed command of 10th Indian Division (May) as a major general and campaigned in Iraq, Syria, and Iran.

Assigned to India as a lieutenant general, Slim became CG of British, Burmese, and Indian Army troops in Burma (March 1942). Outnumbered by the Japanese, he retreated to India (May) and assumed command of XV Corps in Calcutta. He worked to rebuild Imperial forces and undertook a limited offensive to capture Akyab, which failed (June 1942).

After Admiral Louis Mountbatten became supreme Allied commander Southeast Asia (August 1943), Slim took command of the new Fourteenth Army (his XV Corps along with XIV Corps). His second Akyab campaign was a success, and he was able to stop Japanese General Ren'ya Mutaguchi's U-GO offensive before Kohima and Imphal (March–July 1944).

Knighted in late 1944, Slim went on the offensive, directing the liberation of northern Burma (July–December). Utilizing new techniques of aerial resupply, he orchestrated the capture of Mandalay (March 1945) and Rangoon (May). Promoted general (July), he was then CG of Southeast Asian ground forces (August). An extraordinarily capable individual who put the well-being of his men first, he was one of the top British field commanders of World War II.

After directing the pacification of Malaya and Indonesia (August–November), Slim was commandant of the Imperial Defense College (1946–48), then chief of the Imperial General Staff (November 1948). Promoted field marshal (January 1949), he was then governor general of Australia (1952–60). He was raised to the peerage (1960) as 1st Viscount Slim.

Slovik, Edward D. (1920–45) U.S. soldier. The only U.S. soldier executed for desertion by the United States since the American Civil War, Slovak had landed in Normandy, France (August 1944). Terrified of combat, he ran away, but he then turned himself in. Found guilty by a military court (November), he was executed by firing squad (January 1945). The army made an example of Slovik in part because of desertions during the December 1944–January 1945 Ardennes Offensive (Battle of the Bulge). The U.S. Army sentenced forty-nine men to death for

desertion under fire during the war but only Slovik was executed. In contrast, the Soviet Union executed 157,000 people on charges of desertion or cowardice.

Śmigly-Rydz, Edward (1886–1941) Polish general. A protégé of Jósef Pilsudski, Śmigly-Rydz volunteered in World War I to fight for Polish independence on the German side. He commanded first a battalion, then a regiment of Pilsudski's I Legionary Brigade and distinguished himself in the battles of Anielin (October 1914), Konary (May 1915), and Kostiuchnówka (July 1916).

Following the summer 1917 crisis, when Pilsudski and his men refused to swear an oath of allegiance to Kaiser William II, Śmigly-Rydz resigned his commission. Then, in the absence of the imprisoned Pilsudski, he commanded the underground Polish Military Organization (*Polska Organizacja Wojskowa*).

Śmigly-Rydz commanded an army group in the 1920–21 Russo-Polish War. Following Pilsudski's death, as commander of armed forces, he was the real power in the country. Although he tried to modernize the Polish armed forces after 1935, his system of rigid centralized command worked against Poland during the German invasion. Along with the Polish government, he crossed into Rumania with the plan to go to France but was interned. He escaped to Hungary (1940) and made his way back to Warsaw where he died under an assumed name.

Smith, Charles Bradford (1916–) U.S. general. Commissioned in the infantry on graduation from West Point (1939), Smith was serving as an infantry company commander at Schofield Barracks, Oahu when the Japanese attacked Pearl Harbor (7 December 1941).

Smith served with the 25th Infantry Division, first as a staff officer (1942), then as a battalion commander on Guadalcanal (1943), and then as a staff officer again (until June 1944). He graduated from the Command and General Staff School (1945) and the Army and Navy Staff College (1946), then served in the Intelligence Division of the War Department General Staff (1946–49).

Promoted lieutenant colonel, Smith commanded the 1st Battalion, 21st Regiment, 24th Infantry Division in Japan. In June 1950 he was picked to lead the first U.S. combat unit to see action in the 1950–53 Korean War. "Task Force Smith" consisted of 540 men and 5 × 105mm howitzers. It went into action north of Osan, where it was overrun by Korean People's Army (KPA, North Korean) infantry and T-34 tanks (5 July 1950).

Smith subsequently took part in the defense of the Pusan Perimeter and the advance into North Korea. Following return to the United States (1951), he served with the 3rd Infantry Division. Promoted brigadier general (1963), he became CofS of Second Army (1963–64) and then assistant commander of the 5th Infantry Division (1964–65). He retired in 1965.

Smith, Holland McTyeire (1882–1967) U.S. Marine Corps general. Smith graduated from Alabama Polytechnic Institute (1901) and took a law degree from the University of Alabama (1903). He joined the Marine Corps as a second lieutenant (1905) and over the next decade fulfilled a variety of routine sea and land assignments, during which he acquired the nickname of "Howlin' Mad."

During World War I, Smith fought in France with the 5th Marine Regiment and then became adjutant of the 4th Marine Brigade. He participated in the 1918 Aisne–Marne, St. Mihiel, and Meuse–Argonne offensives. Graduating from the Naval War College (1921), he rose to brigadier general (1938) and became an aide to Marine Commandant General Thomas Holcomb and headed the Division of Operations and Training (1937–39), responsible for developing and new tactics, landing craft, and amphibious

tractors. He assumed command of the 1st Marine Brigade (1939). Promoted major general (1941), he commanded the Amphibious Force, Atlantic Fleet.

Smith was occupied with training duties until 1943. That June he took command of the V Amphibious Corps, containing the 2nd and 4th Marine Divisions. In November 1943 he planned and orchestrated the capture of Tarawa. Throughout 1944 his forces fought across the Central Pacific, capturing Kwajalein and Eniwetok (January–February), and Saipan, Tinian, and Guam (July–August). During the Saipan operation he relieved Army General Ralph K. Smith from command, a move that temporarily jeopardized Army–Marine operations. Promoted lieutenant general (August 1944) and appointed commander of the newly created Fleet Marine Force, Smith directed the invasions of Iwo Jima (February–March 1945) and Okinawa (April–June). Recalled to the United States (July), he commanded Camp Pendleton, California. He retired from active service in July 1946, only the third Marine Corps general to achieve four-star rank.

Smith, Julian Constable (1885–1975) U.S. Marine Corps general. Commissioned in the Marines following graduation from the University of Delaware (1909), Smith took part in the U.S. occupation of Veracruz (1914) and held varied assignments abroad and in the United States. A graduate of the Command and General Staff School (1928), he served in Nicaragua as chief of staff of its National Guard detachment (1930–33). He was then attached to the U.S. embassy, London (1938–41) and promoted brigadier general (March 1941).

Promoted major general on his return to the United States (1942), Smith commanded Fleet Marine Corps Training Schools in North Carolina. In 1943 he commanded 2nd Marine Division in the assault of Betio Atoll, the center of the defenses of Tarawa in the Gilbert Islands

(November 1943). As commanding general, Expeditionary Troops, Third Fleet, he took the southern Palaus and then Ulithi (September 1944). Returning to the United States (end of 1944), he commanded Parris Island Marine Base, South Carolina (1944–46), then retired as a lieutenant general in 1946.

Smith, Oliver Prince (1893–1977) U.S. Marine Corps general. A graduate of the University of California at Berkeley (1916), Smith was commissioned (1917) and assigned to Guam. He held a varierty of assignments. Graduating from the Infantry School, Fort Benning (1932), he was then instructor at the Quantico Marine Corps School (1932–33). He studied at the French École Supérieure de Guerre (1934–36). Promoted major, he taught amphibious warfare at Quantico (1936–39) and was promoted lieutenant colonel (1938). When the United States entered World War II (December 1941) he was with the 6th Marine Regiment in Iceland. Following staff duties in Washington (1942–44), he took command of the 5th Regiment of the 1st Marine Division (January 1944) and led it during the New Britain campaign. Promoted brigadier general (April), he became assistant commander of the 1st Division and fought with it on Peleliu. Later he was deputy chief of staff to Tenth Army and fought on Okinawa.

After World War II, Smith commanded Marine Corps Schools at Quantico. He then became assistant commandant of the Marine Corps (1948). Promoted major general, during the 1950–53 Korean War he took command of the 1st Marine Division (June 1950), leading it in the Inchon landing (September) and the epic retreat from the Changjin Reservoir (December). He briefly commanded IX Corps (1951), then returned to the United States (April) to command Camp Pendleton. Promoted lieutenant general (1953), he commanded the Fleet Marine Force

Atlantic. On his retirement (September 1955), Smith was promoted general.

Smith, Ralph Corbett (1893–1998) U.S. general. Commissioned in the infantry on graduation from Colorado State College (1916), Smith served with the AEF in France during World War I, participating in the Aisne–Marne (July–August 1918), St. Mihiel (September), and Meuse–Argonne offensives (September–November). He was an instructor at West Point (1920–23) and then the Infantry School (1924–27). He graduated from the Command and General Staff School (1928), then was an instructor there (1930–34). He also graduated from the Army War College (1935) and attended the French École Supérieure de Guerre (1935–37). He was then in the military intelligence division of the War Department General Staff in Washington (1938–42).

Promoted brigadier general (April 1942), Smith became assistant CG of the 76th Division and was promoted major general (October 1942). Following U.S. entry into World War II (December 1941), he took command of the 27th Division, a National Guard unit (November 1942), elements of which participated in the invasion of Makin in the Gilbert Islands (November 1943) and Eniwetok in the Marshalls (February 1944).

Smith commanded the entire division in the assault on Saipan in the Marianas (June–July 1944). The 27th was the floating reserve, but Japanese resistance forced its commitment (19 June). Its slow progress angered V Amphibious Corps commander Marine Lieutenant General Holland "Howlin' Mad" Smith, who then relieved Ralph Smith from command (June 24). This matter, largely the result of different tactical doctrines, remains a subject of controversy between army and navy. Smith then briefly commanded 98th Division in Hawaii (July–August) before becoming military attaché to Paris (1945). He retired in October 1946.

Smith, Walter Bedell (1895–1961) U.S. general and director of the Central Intelligence Agency (CIA). Smith briefly attended Butler University, then enlisted in the Indiana National Guard (1911). He secured a commission in the Guard and saw action in France in World War I as a lieutenant in the 39th Infantry. Badly wounded in the Aisne–Marne Battle (August 1918) he was returned home.

After the war Smith served in the Bureau of Military Intelligence (1918–20), gained a regular army commission (1920), and served in the Army Bureau of the Budget (1925). He graduated from the Infantry School (1932) and taught there (1932–33, 1935–36). Graduating from the Army War College (1937), he was promoted major (1939). Army Chief of Staff General George Marshall appointed him to the General Staff (1939). He was promoted lieutenant colonel (April 1941) and colonel (July). He was assistant secretary, then secretary, to the General Staff and secretary for the Joint Chiefs of Staff (JCS) and Combined Chiefs of Staff (1940–42). Promoted brigadier general (February 1942), he was CofS to General Dwight Eisenhower (September 1942–December 1945). He was promoted major general (November 1942) and lieutenant general (January 1944).

Smith was chief of the Operations and Planning Division of the JCS (1946). President Harry S Truman appointed him ambassador to the Soviet Union (1946–49), and he then commanded First Army (1950). Named director of the Central Intelligence Agency (CIA) (September 1950), he was advanced to full general (July 1951) and was undersecretary of state in the Eisenhower administration (1953–54).

Smith-Dorrien, Sir Horace Lockwood (1858–1930) British general. Commissioned in the 95th Foot after graduation from Sandhurst (1877), Smith-Dorrien fought in the 1879 Zulu War. He then fought in Egypt (1882) and was trans-ferred back to India where he was injured and invalided home (1883). He returned to service with the Egyptian Army (1884). He attended the Staff College (1887–88) and then began a decade of service in India (1889). He commanded a battalion in the Sudan in the Battle at Omdurman (September 1898) and served in General Kitchener's escort at Fashoda (November). Promoted major general during the 1899–1902 Anglo-Boer War, he subsequently had commands in India and became head of Southern Command at Salisbury (1912).

At the beginning of World War I, Smith-Dorrien took command of II Corps British Expeditionary Force in France. It suffered heavy casualties in fighting at Mons (August 1914) and was effectively left on its own. His three divisions fought the whole of General Alexander von Kluck's First Army, which tried to carry out a double envelopment. Although forced to retreat toward St. Quentin after eleven hours of fighting, his stand had given the BEF time to regroup.

Smith-Dorrien commanded Second Army in the Ypres salient (December 1914). He disagreed with BEF commander General Sir John French on conduct of operations, especially the latter's decision of a tactical withdrawal at the Second Battle of Ypres (April 1915). A long critical letter to his chief led to his being reassigned to Britain (May).

Smith-Dorrien commanded First Army for the home defense (November), then commanded an expedition against German East Africa (December), but pneumonia prevented this and further military assignment until he became governor of Gibraltar (September 1918). He served in that post until he retired in 1923. He was arguably one of the best British generals of the war.

Smuts, Jan Christiaan (1870–1950) Boer general and British field marshal. Smuts graduated from Christ's College, Cambridge, and then practiced law in Capetown. During the 1899–1902 Boer War he fought against the British as a general. A close ally of Louis Botha, after the war he helped draft the constitution of the Union of South Africa and sought accommodation with the British.

When World War I began, Smuts was defense minister under Prime Minister Botha. He headed the southern offensive that took control of Southwest Africa from the Germans. London made Smuts a general and selected him to command British operations in East Africa. Before the end of the war, Smuts had joined the British cabinet as minister of air and helped to organize the Royal Air Force. He represented South Africa during the Paris Peace Conference, where he supported the League of Nations and developed the mandate system.

On the death of Botha, Smuts became prime minister of South Africa (August 1919). In 1941 he was made a British field marshal, and in 1945 he was one of the founders of the United Nations.

Sokolovsky, Vasily Danilovich (1897–1968) Soviet marshal. Sokolovsky joined the Red Army (1918) and during the 1918–20 Civil War rose to command 32nd Rifle Division. He attended the Red Army Military Academy of the General Staff (1921) and served in Central Asia as deputy chief of the Operations Directorate of the General Staff. He then was CofS of a division and corps, commanded a division (1930–35), was deputy CofS of the Volga Military District, and CofS of the Urals and Volga Military Districts.

Promoted major general (May 1938) and lieutenant general (June 1940), Sokolovsky was deputy chief of the General Staff (February 1941), then CofS of the Western Front (mid-summer), responsible for defense of Moscow. Promoted colonel general (June 1942), he commanded Western Front (February 1943) in the Battle of Kursk (July 1943) and was promoted general of the army (August), just before the liberation of Smolensk (September).

The CofS of Georgi Zhukov's First Ukrainian Front (April 1944), he alternated between duties in the field and Moscow. In the last month of the war he was deputy commander of First Belorussian Front in the capture of Berlin.

After the war Sokolovsky was deputy to Zhukov as commander of the Soviet occupation forces in Germany and governor of the Soviet zone of Berlin. Promoted marshal (1946), he commanded Soviet occupation forces in Germany (1946–49). He was first deputy minister of war, then chief of the General Staff (1952–60). His final assignment was as general inspector and head of a group working to formulate Soviet nuclear war strategy, published as *Soviet Military Strategy* (1962).

Somervell, Brehon Burke (1892–1955) U.S. general. Somervell was commissioned in the engineers after graduation from West Point (1914). He took part in the 1916–17 Punitive Expedition into Mexico. During World War I he commanded supply depots and ended up as G-4 (logistics) officer of the 89th Division. He was then CofS of the army of occupation (1919–20). He graduated from the Engineer School (1921), the Command and General Staff School (1925), and the Army War College (1926). Other assignments included New York administrator with the Works Progress Administration (WPA) (1936–40). Among other projects, he supervised construction of La Guardia Airport. Recalled to active duty, he commanded the construction division of the Quartermaster Corps (1940–41) to meet needs caused by the rapid expansion of the army. He then became assistant CofS, G-4, of the War Department general staff, where he helped oversee mobilization and munitions and shipping production.

Lieutenant General Somervell became commanding general of Services of Supply (SOS) (March 1942), later the Army Service Forces (ASF). He was thus the army's chief logistics officer. He held this post through the end of the war and had responsibility for the vast army logistical net, handling its mobilization, production, and allocation of supplies. He retired from the army (January 1948) but was raised to general on the retired list later in 1948.

Somerville, Sir James Fownes (1882–1949) British admiral. Somerville joined the navy as a cadet (1897) and was commissioned (1904). A torpedo officer, he also played a role in developing long-range continuous-wave radio (1912). During World War I, he served in the Dardanelles Campaign (1915) and was a radio communications specialist in the Grand Fleet (1915–18). Promoted commander (1915), he served in a number of posts after the war, including instructor at the Imperial Defense College (1929–31). Promoted rear admiral (1933) and vice admiral (1937), he commanded the East Indies Station (1938–39) but was forced out of the navy because of tuberculosis.

Although Somerville recovered, the navy refused his return to active duty until World War II. He aided in the development of effective surface ship radar and assisted in the Dunkerque Evacuation (May–June 1940). Given command of Force H (June), he participated in Operation CATAPULT, the effort to secure the French fleet. When negotiations failed, he ordered bombardment of the French squadron at Mers-el Kebir, Algeria (3 July 1940), resulting in the sinking of two French capital ships and several destroyers and 1,650 French casualties.

Somerville's command played a key role in escorting the Malta convoys and also helped sink the German battleship *Bismarck* (May 1941). He then commanded the Eastern Fleet in the Pacific (1942–44), before heading the Admiralty Mission in Washington (1944–45). Promoted admiral of the fleet (May 1945), he retired in December 1945.

Sosabowski, Stanislaw (1892–1967) Polish general. Sosabowski studied econom-

ics at Krakow. During World War I he served in the Austrian Army, but after the war joined the newly formed Polish Army. He held various line and staff positions and was an instructor at the Army Staff College (1929–37), then commanded 9th Infantry Regiment (1937–39). He commanded 21st Infantry Regiment in the defense of Warsaw following the German invasion (September 1939).

Following the defeat, Sosabowski escaped to France through Hungary and then to Britain after the fall of France. He then organized and commanded the Polish 1st Independent Parachute Brigade. Promoted major general (June 1944), he was deeply skeptical about the chances of success of Operation MARKET-GARDEN but commanded his brigade in the assault of Arnhem (September 1944). Dropped late, it landed at Driel, and Sosabowski's attempts to cross the Rhine and link up with the British 1st Airborne Division failed. Under British pressure, he was removed from his post. After the war he settled in London.

Sosnkowski, Kazimierz (1885–1969) Polish general. Sosnkowski joined the Polish Socialist Party (1904) and helped Jósef Piłsudski found the Polish Rifle Union (1910), which during World War I became part of 1st Brigade of the Polish Legion. Promoted colonel (May 1916), he was chief of staff of the 1st Brigade but later that year was imprisoned by the Germans along with Piłsudki when they came to believe the Central Powers did not plan to resurrect an independent Poland.

After the war Sosnkowski was promoted lieutenant general in the Polish Army and became CG of the Warsaw Military District. He fought in the 1920–21 Russo-Polish War, then commanded VII Corps in Poznan (1925–26). Promoted full general, he commanded Southern Front around Lwow during the German invasion (September 1939), achieving one of the few Polish tactical successes of the campaign (14–16 September). Escaping Poland through Hungary, he made his way to France, where he commanded the Polish resistance army until 1940 when its command was transferred to Warsaw. He resigned as minister of state following his objection to an agreement between the Polish government-in-exile and the Soviet Union (1941).

As CinC of Polish armed forces (July 1943–September 1944), Sosnkowski worked hard to secure supplies for the Armia Krajowa (Home Army). His strong position on this and insistence that the Soviet Union not control Poland led to his forced resignation, under Soviet and British pressure. He subsequently lived in Canada.

Souchon, Wilhelm (1864–1946) German admiral. Souchon entered the navy (1881). He served on the Admiralty Staff (1902–04). In October 1913 he assumed command of the Mediterranean squadron of the new battle cruiser *Goeben* and light cruiser *Breslau*. He opened World War I hostilities in the Mediterranean by shelling Bône and Philippeville in Algeria (4 August 1914).

Souchon then succeeded in escaping the French and British and reaching Constantinople with his squadron, where he arranged a fictitious sale of *Goeben* to the Turks. Frustrated by Turkish neutrality, he entered into a conspiracy with pro-Central Powers members of the Turkish government. He then attacked Odessa and other sites along the Russian coast (29 October), thereby initiating war in the Black Sea as well.

Souchon left Turkey to command the 4th Battle Squadron of the High Seas Fleet (September 1917) and took part in ALBION, the successful German operation in the Gulf of Riga (October). He then commanded the Baltic Naval Station, and was governor of the Naval base at Kiel. Souchon retired in March 1919.

Souphanouvong, Prince (1909–95) Laotian revolutionary general and political leader. Son of viceroy Prince Bounkhong, Souphanouvong studied at Hanoi and Paris and was licensed a civil engineer. Returning to Indo-China (1936), he worked in Vietnam. At the end of World War II he traveled to Hanoi and met there with veteran Communist leader Ho Chi Minh, who sent him to Laos to rally anti-French forces there.

Arriving in Vientiane (October 1945), Souphanouvong became foreign minister of the new Laotian government and commander of its armed forces. Wounded in the re-establishment of French control (March 1946), he went to Thailand with the revolutionary government. He then split with his fellows (1949) and went to Hanoi to join Ho.

Souphanouvong established the Pathet Lao, a resistance movement allied with the Viet Minh that soon began to fight the French. The 1954 Geneva Agreement did not recognize his government and the struggle in Laos continued. He briefly formed coalition governments led by his half-brother Prince Souvanna Phouma (1957, 1962). Imprisoned (1959–60), he escaped and remained the most visible Pathet Lao leader and party spokesman in negotiations with the neutralists and royalists.

Pathet Lao control of much of eastern Laos was of immense help to the North Vietnamese in their Ho Chi Minh Trail logistics network into South Vietnam during the Vietnam War. When the Communists seized power in Laos (1975), Souphanouvong was elected by a people's congress as president of the Lao People's Democratic Republic. He retired following a stroke in 1986.

Spaatz, Carl Andrew (1891–1974) U.S. Army and Air Force general. Commissioned in the infantry on graduation from West Point (1914), "Tooey" Spaatz was assigned to the Aviation School at San Diego (1916) and became one of the army's first aviators. He participated in the 1916–17 Punitive expedition into northern Mexico. When the United States joined World War I (April 1917), he headed the aviation training center at Issoudon, France. During one nineteen-day period of temporary duty he shot down three German planes.

After the war Spaatz held normal peacetime assignments and helped set an endurance record of 150 hours aloft. As a colonel, he went to England as an observer during the 1940 Battle of Britain and concluded the British were winning when the Germans began night bombing. He headed the Air Matériel Command (September 1940–July 1941), then was promoted brigadier general and made CofS and deputy commander of the Army Air Forces.

Following U.S. entry into World War II (December 1941), Spaatz took over the Army Air Forces Combat Command. He then commanded Eighth Air Force (January 1942) to conduct strategic bombing of Germany. Shortly after his arrival in Britain (June), he was promoted major general. Following U.S. landings in North Africa (November), he established the Northwest Africa Air Command in Algiers (December), then took command of Western Desert Air Force (February 1943).

When Air Marshal Arthur Tedder established the Mediterranean Allied Air Forces, Spaatz became its CofS and deputy commander (December 1943). He then commanded U.S. Strategic Air Forces in Europe (December 1943) for Operation OVERLORD, the invasion of Normandy (6 June 1944). Promoted to general (March 1945), he established the U.S. Army Strategic Air Forces on Guam (July 1945) and directed the final air assault on Japan. Succeeding General Henry Arnold as commander of the Army Air Forces (1946), he was the first CofS of the independent U.S. Air Force from 1947–48.

Spears, Sir Edward Louis (1886–1974) British general and diplomat. Educated on the Continent, Spears was fluent in French. A junior officer in the army at the beginning of World War I, he served as a liaison officer between the French Fifth Army headquarters and BEF headquarters. Promoted brigadier general (1917), he headed the British military mission in Paris.

After the war Spears was a member of Parliament (1922–24, 1931–45). He also pursued business interests and wrote several books. Recalled to active service as a major general with World War II, he went to Paris as liaison officer to the French premier and minister of defense. The outspoken Spears was on the last British plane to leave Bordeaux following the French government decision to surrender and had as passenger Brigadier General Charles de Gaulle (17 June 1940). He helped convince Prime Minister Winston Churchill that de Gaulle was the most likely figure to rally French resistance.

Spears was later British minister to Syria and Lebanon (1942–44), where he was pro-Arab and anti-French. Knighted, he wrote several books on his wartime experiences.

Spee, Maximilian Johannes Maria Hubert Graf von (1861–1914) German admiral. Spee joined the navy (1878) and had a variety of assignments, including CofS of the North Sea Command (1908). He reached flag rank (1910) and was appointed commander of the German East Asian Cruiser Squadron (1912). He was then promoted vice admiral (1913).

On the outbreak of World War I, Spee's squadron consisted of two heavy cruisers and two light cruisers. Holding the advantage in both speed and guns, he defeated British Admiral Sir Christopher Cradock's 4th Cruiser Squadron off Chile in the Battle of Coronel (November 1914), one of the few big victories for the German navy during the war.

Spee then headed for Germany through the Atlantic. His decision to stop at the Falkland Islands to destroy the wireless station there was fateful. The situation at Coronel was now reversed. At Port Stanley Spee encountered a faster and more heavily gunned squadron under Admiral Sir Doveton Sturdee. Spee and his two sons all died in the resultant Battle of the Falkland Islands (8 December). Only one German cruiser, the *Dresden*, escaped.

Speer, Albert (1905–81) German architect and minister of armaments. Speer studied architecture at the Munich Institute of Technology and the Institute of Technology in Berlin-Charlottesburg, and obtained his architect's license (1927). An admirer of Adolf Hitler, he joined the National Socialist party (1931). His design of the party headquarters building in Berlin (1932) so impressed Hitler that he commissioned him to design other buildings. He designed the rebuilding of Nuremberg stadium to hold 400,000 people for party rallies. Hitler then ordered him to draw plans for rebuilding Berlin (1936) and to complete a new chancellory building (1938), which Speer did in record time. Their shared love of architecture made him a member of Hitler's inner circle.

After World War II began, Speer was increasingly drawn into designing facilities for the war. After the death of Minister of Armaments and Production Fritz Todt in a plane crash (February 1942), Hitler appointed Speer to replace him. He soon became expert on armaments production and restructured it to improve production. He urged conversion of industry to mass production, an austerity program (which Hitler opposed), and concentration of armaments production in his ministry. The latter led to clashes with many, including Hermann Göring of the Luftwaffe and Heinrich Himmler of the SS, who was trying to build his own industrial empire.

Speer was only partially successful in his efforts. With production falling off, Hitler finally gave him full authority over the war economy. Despite increasing Allied air raids, he met production quotas through decentralization. Toward the end of the war Germany achieved its highest levels of production in many areas. It was the destruction of the transportation system that ultimately defeated his efforts. At the end of the war Speer turned against Hitler and worked to circumvent his scorched-earth policy. Tried at Nuremberg for the use of slave labor, he was the only defendant to admit complicity and show remorse. Sentenced to twenty years in prison, he was released in 1966 and wrote his memoirs, which provide valuable insight on the period.

Speidel, Hans (1897–1987) German general. Commissioned in the army (1914), Speidel served on the Western Front in World War I. He graduated from the University of Tübingen with a doctorate in political economy and history (1925). He joined the General Staff (1930) and then was a military attaché in Paris (1933–35).

After additional staff service, Speidel became CofS to military governor of France General Karl von Stülpnagel (June 1940). He was then CofS to Army Group Center on the Eastern Front (1942–44). Promoted to brigadier general (1943) and major general (1944), he turned against Hitler. As CofS to General Erwin Rommel's Army Group B (January 1944), he arranged for Stülpnagel to meet with Rommel to draw the latter into the plot against Hitler. He escaped implication in the 20 July 1944 assassination attempt, but was arrested (25 August) for refusing to obey orders to destroy Paris. Imprisoned in Berlin, he was acquitted by a court martial (September 1944) but detained. He escaped and went into hiding.

After the war Speidel was a witness for the prosecution at the International Military Tribunal at Nuremberg. He was then a professor at the University of Tübingen (1949–50).

After the war, Speidel was military adviser to Federal Republic Chancellor Konrad Adenauer, helping to plan the revival of a German army. Promoted lieutenant general (1955), he headed the department of the joint armed forces of the Bundeswehr (1955–57). Promoted full general, he commanded NATO land forces in Central Europe (1957–63), retiring in 1964.

Sperrle, Hugo (1885–1953) German air force field marshal. Sperrle began his military career as an infantry officer (1904) but became a pilot in World War I. He then commanded a detachment of the Freikorps (1919). He continued in the Reichswehr after the war, reverting to the infantry. He helped establish the secret German air force as a colonel and was promoted brigadier general on the formal establishment of the Luftwaffe (1935). He went to Spain (1936) to head the Condor Legion, basically an air force formation that fought on the Nationalist side in the 1936–39 Spanish Civil War. Promoted lieutenant general (1937), he commanded Third Air Fleet at Munich.

Although Sperrle did not participate directly in the invasion of Poland (September 1939), his Third Air Fleet played a key role in the invasion of France and Benelux (May–June 1940), and he was promoted field marshal (July), bypassing full general. In France as air commander in the West (from April 1941), his forces were gradually whittled away until, by the Normandy invasion, the Allies outnumbered them 25 to 1. Adolf Hitler was unhappy with reports of his high-living in Paris and failure to contest the Allies in the sky and replaced Sperrle (August 1944). Tried after the war at Nuremberg on war crimes charges, he was acquitted.

Sprague, Clifton Albert Furlow (1896–1955) U.S. admiral. A graduate of Annapolis (1917), "Ziggy" Sprague served in the Mediterranean in World War I (1917–19). He passed flight training at Pensacola Naval Air Station (1920), then served on an airship tender (1922–23). Assistant air officer on carrier *Lexington* (1928–29), he commanded Patrol Squadron 1 (1931–

33). He helping outfit carrier *Yorktown* and was her air officer (1937–39), then commanded auxiliary vessels (1939–41) and was at Pearl Harbor during the Japanese attack (7 December 1941). He was CofS of the Gulf Sea Frontier (1942–43), then commanded Seattle Naval Air Station (1943). He commissioned carrier *Wasp* (November 1943) and led her in raids against Wake and Marcus Islands (May 1944), in the Saipan invasion (June), and in the Battle of the Philippine Sea (June).

Promoted rear admiral, Sprague commanded Carrier Division 25 (August), then Task Unit 77.4.3 ("Taffy 3") in the Leyte invasion (October). With six escort carriers, three destroyers, and three destroyer escorts, abandoned by Admiral William Halsey, who had steamed north against the Japanese decoy force, he confronted Japanese Admiral Takeo Kurita's battleships and heavy cruisers (25 October). "Taffy 3's" resistance threw off Kurita, who believed he was being attacked by Halsey's carriers and retreated.

Sprague then commanded Carrier Division 26 (February 1945) in the Iwo Jima (February–March) and Okinawa (April–June) invasions, then Carrier Division 2 (May). After the war he held a succession of commands, including the Alaskan Sea Frontier, before his retirement as a rear admiral (November 1951).

Sprague, Thomas Lamison (1894–1972) U.S. admiral. A graduate of Annapolis (1917), not related to Clifton Sprague, Sprague served in Atlantic convoy duty during World War I (1917–18), then aboard and in command of a destroyer (1918–20). After flight training at Pensacola Naval Air Station, he was on the staff of the Pacific Air commander (1921–23). His following assignments included service with observation and scouting squadrons, air officer aboard a carrier, and head of naval air training at Pensacola (1937–40). He was then executive officer on the carrier *Ranger* (1940–41).

He helped commission carrier *Charger* and commanded her on training missions (1942), then commissioned carrier *Intrepid* and commanded her in raids against the Marshalls and Truk (January–February 1944).

Promoted rear admiral (June), Sprague commanded Carrier Division 22, covering assaults on Guam (July–August) and Morotai (September). He commanded Task Group 77.4 ("Taffy 1") in the Battle of Leyte Gulf (24–25 October). After brief command of Carrier Division 11, he commanded Carrier Division 3 off Okinawa (April–June 1945), then Task Force 38.1 in operations against the Japanese home islands (July–August).

After the war Sprague headed the Bureau of Naval Personnel (1946–49). Promoted vice admiral (August 1949), he commanded Air Force Pacific Fleet (October) until his retirement (April 1952). He returned to active duty briefly (1956–57) to negotiate the status of U.S. bases in the Philippines.

Spruance, Raymond Ames (1886–1969) U.S. admiral. Following graduation from Annapolis (1907), Spruance had a variety of assignments, including teaching at the Naval War College (1931–1932). When the U.S. entered World War II, he commanded Cruiser Division 5 in the Pacific. He participated in the raids on the Marshall and Gilbert Islands (early 1942) and on Tokyo (April). On the eve of the Battle of Midway (June), he relieved Admiral William Halsey as commander of Task Force 16. Subordinate to Admiral Frank Fletcher, the non-aviator Spruance actually had charge of the battle, the turning point in the war in the Pacific.

Spruance then became CofS to Pacific commander Admiral Chester Nimitz and helped plan the drive across the Central Pacific. Promoted vice admiral (May 1943), he commanded the Central Pacific Area and Force. Promoted admiral (March 1944), he commanded Fifth Fleet, the largest assemblage of naval power in

history. He had overall command of the invasion of the Marianas and commanded during the Battle of the Philippine Sea (June 1944) that destroyed Japanese carrier aviation. He then oversaw the invasions of Iwo Jima and Okinawa and naval air strikes against Japan. After the war he commanded the Pacific Fleet (November–December 1945), then served as president of the Naval War College until his retirement in July 1948.

Stalin, Joseph (Iosif Vissarionovich Dzhugashvili) (1879–1953) Ruler of the Soviet Union. Stalin joined the Social Democratic party (1901) and, when it split (1903), its Bolshevik faction. He used a number of aliases, one of which was Stalin (Steel), while raising party funds through common crime. Arrested for a fourth time (1913), he was sent to Siberia. Released by the March 1917 Revolution, he went to Petrograd and became a leading figure in the November Bolshevik *coup d'état*.

Initially commissar for nationalities in the Bolshivek government, Stalin took an active role in the Civil War. After Lenin's death (1924), he used his position as party general secretary (1922–53) as a springboard to supreme power. By 1929 he had crushed his rivals.

In power, Stalin was utterly ruthless and paranoid. His policies brought the deaths of tens of millions of his citizens, including much of the senior army leadership in the Great Purges of the late 1930s. Although he did much to industrialize the Soviet Union, it was at great human cost. Anticipating eventual war with Nazi Germany, he entered into the Nazi–Soviet non-aggression Pact (23 August 1939) to buy time, fulfilling his part of the pact to the letter. Invading Finland, he refused to put sufficient resources into the initial effort, only to be embarrassed in the 1940–41 Winter War.

Despite repeated warnings from the West of an impending German invasion, he refused to allow his military commanders to take adequate precautions and was totally surprised by the German attack (22 June 1941). He bears great responsibility for the early Russian military disasters. Stalin then took personal charge of the conduct of the war with front commanders reporting to him (2 July). He grew to be a competent war leader, directing his country to victory in 1945.

Determined to hold on to Eastern Europe for ideological and security reasons, Stalin bore much responsibility for the coming of the Cold War and the 1948–49 Berlin blockade, and he personally approved the North Korean plan to reunify Korea by force.

Standley, William Harrison (1872–1963) U.S. admiral. A graduate of Annapolis (1895), Standley was commissioned an ensign (1897) and held a variety of assignments afloat and ashore. Promoted commander, he was assistant to the superintendent of Annapolis during World War I (1916–1919). Promoted captain (1919), he commanded a battleship (1919–20) and graduated from the Naval War College (1921). He held staff assignments, including heading the War Plans Division of the office of chief of naval operations (CNO) (1923–26). Following command of another battleship, he was promoted rear admiral (1927) and directed the Division of Fleet Training (1927–28). He was then assistant CNO (1926–30), commanded destroyers of the Battle Fleet (1930–31), and was commander of cruisers, scouting force, and cruisers, U.S. Fleet (1931–32). Promoted vice admiral (1932), he commanded the Battle Force (1933). Promoted admiral, he was CNO (July 1933) until his retirement (January 1937) and attended the 1935–36 London Naval Conference and signed the treaty on behalf of the United States.

Returned to active duty during World War II (February 1942), Standley was the naval representative on the Office of Production Management Planning Board and served on the Roberts Commission

investigating the Pearl Harbor attack. Ambassador to the Soviet Union (February 1942–September 1943), he was then again recalled to active duty to serve in the Office of Strategic Services (1944–August 1945).

Stark, Harold Raynsford (1880–1972) U.S. admiral. Stark graduated from Annapolis (1903) and was commissioned an ensign (1905). During World War I he oversaw transfer of a torpedo boat flotilla from the Philippines to the Mediterranean and then served as aide to Admiral William Sims (1917–19).

After the war, Stark served on battleships and then was a naval ordnance inspector. He served in the Battle Fleet and was aide to the secretary of the navy (1930–33), before commanding a battleship. Promoted rear admiral (1934), he headed the Bureau of Ordnance (1934–37), then commanded Cruiser Division 3 in the Battle Force. Promoted vice admiral (July 1938), he had charge of all cruiser divisions in the Battle Force. Promoted admiral, he became chief of naval operations (CNO) (August 1939) and was thus responsible for U.S. preparations for war. Criticized when the Pacific Fleet was caught off guard in the Japanese attack at Pearl Harbor (7 December 1941), he was removed as CNO (March 1942) and became commander of U.S. naval forces in Europe, including the additional command of the Twelfth Fleet (1943) until 1945. He retired (April 1946) and was eventually cleared of any misconduct over the Pearl Harbor attack.

Stauffenberg, Count Klaus Philip Schenk von (1907–44) German army officer. Stauffenberg joined the army as an officer cadet (1926). Commissioned (1930), he was picked to attend the War Academy (1936–38) and promoted captain. A logistics officer (1938), he was posted to the General Staff (1940). Although he approved of Adolf Hitler's expansionist policies short of war, he was disturbed by his purge of the generals and his policies toward the Jews. During World War II he distinguished himself as a staff officer with 6th Panzer Division in Poland (September 1939) and France (May–June 1940). Transferred to the Eastern Front, he became disillusioned by Nazi occupation policies in the Soviet Union and requested a transfer. Sent to North Africa (early 1943), he was badly wounded (April), suffering loss of his left eye, right hand, and two fingers on his left hand. While convalescing in Germany, he decided to join the conspiracy against Hitler and took the lead in a plot to assassinate him.

Appointed CofS to General Friedrich Fromm, commander of the Reserve Army (1 July), Colonel Stauffenberg had access to Hitler's conferences. He planted a bomb in Hitler's headquarters at Rastenburg, East Prussia (Ketrzyn, Poland) (20 July 1944). When it went off, he believed Hitler had been killed, but the briefcase containing the bomb had been moved and Hitler escaped death. The plotters, inept in any case, came out in the open and were quickly arrested. Staffenberg himself was shot that same night by a firing squad in Berlin, one of 7,000 arrests and 5,000 executions.

Steiner, Felix (1896–1966) German general. A junior officer in World War I, Steiner was one of the few who transferred from the army to what became the Waffen SS (Armed SS) (1935). During World War II He fought in the invasions of Poland (September 1939) and France (May–June 1940). As *SS-Gruppenführer*, he commanded SS Division *Wiking* in fighting in the Soviet Union. Promoted *SS-Obergruppenführer*, he took command of 3rd SS Panzer Corps (early 1944) on the Leningrad front. Late that year he was again promoted, to *General der Waffen-SS*. He then took command of Eleventh Army in the defense of Pomerania (early 1945) and, in the final defense of Berlin, Adolf Hitler ordered him to take elements

from scattered divisions and seal a gap through which Russian forces under General Georgi Zhukov were driving. With few men and little equipment available, he was unable to accomplish this task, and surrendered to the British on 3 May.

Steinhoff, Johannes (1913–94) German air force general. Steinhoff joined the Germany Navy (1934), but his love of flying led to his transfer to the Luftwaffe (1936). During World II he saw combat on all major fronts and was selected (1944) to command JG-7, the first all-jet fighter unit. Removed from that post because of involvement in a plot to unseat Hermann Göring as commander of the Luftwaffe, he was later assigned to JV-44 squadron. During a takeoff, his Me-262 jet fighter crashed and burned (18 April 1945), leaving him badly burned and disfigured.

On the establishment of the Army of the Federal Republic of Germany (1955), he was one of the founders of the new Luftwaffe and qualified for jets. Later he was commander of Allied Air Forces, Central Europe. He retired as inspector general of the air force and a full general (1972).

Stilwell, Joseph W. (1883–1946) U.S. general. Commissioned in the infantry from West Point (1904), Stilwell served in the Philippines and fought on Samar. He was an instructor at West Point (1906–11, 1913–16) and again served in the Philippines (1911–13). During World War I he served in France and rose to be deputy CofS of IV Corps, taking part in fighting at Verdun and in the Meuse–Argonne offensive (September–November 1918).

Stilwell was then in China (1919–23). He attended the Infantry School (1923–24) and the Command and General Staff School (1925–26). He returned to China as a battalion commander and was promoted lieutenant colonel (March 1928). He was training officer for IX Corps (1933–35) before returning to China as a colonel and attaché (1935–39). Promoted brigadier general (April 1939), he commanded 3rd Infantry Brigade in Texas. Promoted major general (September 1940), he commanded 7th Infantry Division in California (1940–42). Promoted lieutenant general (January 1942), he returned to China as CofS to Chinese leader Jiang Jieshi (Chiang Kai-shek) and commander of all U.S. troops in the China–Burma–India (CBI) Theater. He secured command of Chinese forces in Burma (March 1942), but the Japanese pushed these back into India (May 1942). Appointed deputy supreme Allied commander of CBI under Admiral Lord Louis Mountbatten (July 1943), he launched a new offensive into Burma (March–August 1944) that cleared the Japanese from the north. Promoted to temporary general (August 1944), he sharply disagreed with Chiang over the employment of Chinese troops against the Japanese and was recalled to the United States at the latter's insistence (October 1944).

Made commander of Army Ground Forces (January 1945), Strilwell then took command of Tenth Army on Okinawa (June 1945). After the war he headed the War Equipment Board and then commanded Sixth Army (1946).

Stirling, Sir Archibald David (1915–90) British army officer. Educated at Cambridge University, Stirling was training to climb Mount Everest when World War II began. After a short period in the Scots Guards, he went to Number 3 Commando in the Middle East. There he secured approval (July 1941) from General Claude Auchinleck to recruit and train L Detachment, Special Air Service (SAS) Brigade, initially sixty-six men, who would mount parachute raids against Axis airfields in Libya.

This was the beginning of the elite SAS, which grew to regimental size. The first attack ran into high winds and sandstorms, and only twenty-two men survived. Stirling then switched to specially equipped ground vehicles. His tactic was to make the final approach on foot, hit the target, and then move by vehicle deeper into enemy territory. In eighteen months his SAS destroyed 350 enemy aircraft. It also blew up ammunition dumps, supply depots, and trains.

The raids forced the Germans to divert resources to protect their rear areas. The Germans came to know Stirling as "The Phantom Major." Captured in Tunisia (10 January 1943), he escaped a number of times but was recaptured thanks in large part to his 6'5" height. He ended the war imprisoned at Colditz.

Stirling's force expanded into three regiments and remained in existence for the remainder of the war. Today, the SAS is recognized as one of the world's premier counter-insurgency forces. Stirling was knighted shortly before his death.

Stratemeyer, George Edward (1890–1969) U.S. Air Force general. Commissioned in the infantry on graduation from West Point (1915), Stratemeyer transferred to the Aviation Section of the Signal Corps (1916). During World War I he helped organize the School of Military Aeronautics at Ohio State University and was promoted to brigadier general.

Stratemeyer taught at West Point (1924–29) and attended both the Command and General Staff School and the Army War College. At the beginning of World War II he was on the staff of the chief of the Army Air Corps. Promoted major general, he became chief of air staff of the Army Air Forces (AAF) (June 1942). Later he commanded operations in the Burma–India sector. He headed Eastern Air Command (1943) and, as a lieutenant general, commanded the AAF in China and was deputy commander of U.S. forces there (1945).

Following the Japanese surrender, Stratemeyer supervised the redeployment of 200,000 Nationalist Chinese troops to eastern China. He then headed the Air Defense Command (1936), then the Continental Air Command (1948). In 1949 he took command of the Far East Air Force in Japan. In this position he had charge of the air effort in the 1950–53 Korean War. He supported General Douglas MacArthur's desire to extend the war into China, but he said that decision rested with the government, not field commanders. In May 1951 he suffered a heart attack, and retired in November 1952. About the Korean War, he told a Senate committee in 1954, "We were required to lose the war. We weren't allowed to win it."

Stroop, Jürgen (1895–1951) German SS general. Stroop joined the SS in 1934, and by 1939 was an *SS-Brigadeführer* (colonel). Given the assignment of putting down the Warsaw Ghetto uprising (April 1943), he planned to use 2,000 men to remove the 56,000 Jews in three days. It took three weeks, and thousands of Jews died in the process. The remainder were sent to extermination camps.

When all Greece came under German military rule (September 1943), Stroop took over SS command in Athens and implemented the Final Solution there. Brought to trial by the United States after the war, he was convicted of ordering the deaths of U.S. aviators taken prisoner in Greece. Extradited to Poland, he was retried there on war crimes, convicted, and hanged in Warsaw.

Student, Kurt (1890–1978) German air force general. Student was commissioned in the army (1911) and underwent pilot training (1913). On the outbreak of World War I he was testing aircraft armament. From 1916 he commanded a squadron on the Western Front, where he was wounded.

Student continued in the army after the war and was posted to the Central Flying Office, working with German air units in Russia. He then reverted to infantry (1928–33), where he was promoted major and was a battalion commander. He then

directed air training schools for the aviation ministry. Promoted full colonel, he headed the test center for aviation equipment. As a major general (1938), he commanded 7th Air Division of paratroops and glider-borne infantry. Thanks to his high standards, he soon commanded some of the finest infantry in the world.

Student directed these elite forces in the invasion of France and Benelux (May 1940), most notably in the reduction of Fortress Eben Emael in Belgium. Wounded in Holland, he went on leave. He then directed the successful airborne assault on Crete (May 1941), but heavy casualties there convinced Hitler that the days of parachute troops were over, although elements did rescue Mussolini (September 1943).

As lieutenant general, Student commanded First Parachute Army during the Normandy invasion (June 1944), and as full general he assisted in the defense of Holland during Operation MARKET-GARDEN (September 1944). He then commanded Army Group H (November 1944) in defense of the Rhine.

Stülpnagel, Karl Heinrich von (1886–1944) German general. Commissioned in the army (1904), Stülpnagel during World War I was a captain on the General Staff. After the war he held infantry commands and was promoted colonel (1932), then headed the foreign armies branch of the General Staff (1933–37). Promoted brigadier general (1936) and major general (1937), he was a close associate of Generals Ludwig Beck and Franz Halder and active in the conspiracy against Adolf Hitler. Promoted lieutenant general (April 1939), he was quartermaster and deputy chief of the General Staff (August 1938– May 1940). He commanded II Corps in the invasion of France (May–June 1940), then directed the Armistice Commission at Wiesbaden (June–February 1941). He commanded Seventeenth Army in the invasion of Russia (February–October 1941).

He replaced his cousin Otto von Stülpnagel as military governor of France and Paris (March 1942), where he enforced Nazi occupation policies, including execution of more than 29,000 hostages in an effort to deter resistance. Active in conspiracies against Hitler, and believing that the bomb assassination attempt (20 July 1944) had succeeded, he ordered the arrest of German security personnel in Paris. On learning the attempt had failed, he left Paris to drive to Berlin to face charges, but stopped at Verdun and attempted suicide by shooting himself in the head. Only blinded, he was taken to Berlin, condemned to death by the People's Court, and hanged (30 August).

Stülpnagel, Otto von (1878–1948) German general. Commissioned in the army (1908), Stülpnagel fought on the Western Front in World War I. After the war he was extradited to France for trial on charges of murder and theft against French civilians, but was acquitted.

Stülpnagel worked to destroy the Weimar Republic and initially strongly supported the Nazis. He headed the motor transport section in the army (late 1920s) and was promoted brigadier general (February 1929). He then joined what would later became the Luftwaffe and rose to the rank of lieutenant general, but returned to the army (1939).

Retired in Adolf Hitler's purge of general officers (1939), he was recalled at the rank of lieutenant general (1940) and assigned as military governor of France and Paris (November). Ordered by Hitler to implement harsh policies, including execution of hostages, in response to attacks against the Germans by the Resistance (from August 1941), he asked to be relieved of his command (early 1941). His cousin General Karl von Stülpnagel replaced him (March). After the war he was extradited to France on charges of war crimes. Following one failed suicide attempt, he succeeded in hanging himself in a Paris prison.

Stump, Felix Budwell (1894–1972) U.S. admiral. A graduate of Annapolis (1917), Stump was on Atlantic escort duty during World War I. He qualified as a naval aviator (1920) and earned a master's degree in aeronautical engineering from Massachusetts Institute of Technology. Among other assignments, he headed the maintenance division of the Bureau of Aeronautics (1937–40). He was executive officer of the carrier *Enterprise*, then commanded the carrier *Langley* (September 1941) and took her to Australia after the United States entered World War II (December). He headed American–British–Dutch–Australian Command (ABDA) combined operations center (January 1942), and then was air officer, Western Sea Frontier (March).

Captain Stump commanded the new aircraft carrier *Lexington* (February 1943) in operations that included Tarawa, Wake, the Gilberts, Kwajalein, Mille, and Palau (September 1943–April 1944). Promoted rear admiral, he commanded Escort Carrier Division 24 in the Marianas (June–August 1944) and the Leyte landings (October). In the Battle of Leyte Gulf (October), his six escort carriers played a key role in turning back Admiral Takeo Kurita's far superior Center Force. His division then supported landings at Mindoro, Lingayen Gulf, and Okinawa (April–May 1945).

After the war Stump headed Naval Air Technical Training. Promoted vice admiral (December 1948), he commanded Naval Air, Atlantic Fleet, then Second Fleet (1951–53). Promoted admiral (July 1953), he became CinC Pacific Area Command. He was then military advisor to the Southeast Asian Treaty Organization, and then again CINCPAC (February–August 1958), after which he retired.

Sturdee, Sir Frederick Charles Doveton (1859–1925) British admiral. Sturdee entered the Royal Navy (1871). Achieving flag rank (1910), he served as commander of the 2nd Cruiser Squadron (1912–13). At the outbreak of World War I, he was chief of the War Staff at the Admiralty. Appointed CinC of the South Atlantic Fleet, he sailed with two battle cruisers to meet Admiral Count Maximilian von Spee's East Asia Squadron and avenge the Battle of Coronel (November 1914). He arrived at Port Stanley in the Falklands on 7 December. Spee appeared off Port Stanley the next morning. With his superior speed and larger guns, Sturdee pursued and annihilated Spee's squadron in the Battle of the Falklands (8 December).

Appointed commander of 4th Battle Squadron of the Grand Fleet (January 1915), Sturdee participated in the Battle of Jutland (31 May–1 June 1916). He was promoted admiral of the fleet (1921), when he also retired.

Sueter, Sir Murray Fraser (1872–1960) British admiral and aviation pioneer. Before World War I, Sueter specialized in submarines, wireless, and aviation. Director of the new Air Department at the Admiralty (1912), during World War I he helped develop torpedo carrying float planes, small non-rigid airships for antisubmarine operations, the combat armored car, and the early tank, and he assumed responsibility for aircraft construction (1915). Sent to southern Italy to command Royal Naval Air Service units there (1917), he further damaged his relations with the Admiralty by writing directly to King George V to press the tank program.

After the war Sueter became involved in the development of air mail postal services and served as member of the House of Commons.

Sugiyama, Hajime (1880–1945) Japanese field marshal. Sugiyama graduated from the Military Academy (1900) and Army Staff College (1910). As a major (1913), he commanded a battalion (1913–14). He

was then resident officer in India (1915–18) and commanded 2nd Air Wing (1918–20). He was next on the General Staff as a liaison officer to the League of Nations (1920–22). Promoted colonel (1921), he was in Army Air Forces Headquarters (1922–23), then in the Army Military Affairs Section (1923–25). Promoted major general (1925), he again served with the League of Nations (1926–27). He was then chief of the Military Affairs Bureau of the Ministry of War (1928–30) and a leading member of the Control Faction. He commanded 12th Division (1930–32) and Army Air Headquarters (1933–34). Next vice chief of the General Staff and also president of the Army Staff College (1934–36), he took an active role in the February 1936 Young Officers' Revolt. Inspector general of military education (1936–37), he was promoted general (1937).

As minister of war (1937–38), Sugiyama was the chief architect of Japan's hard-line approach to China, claiming the latter could be speedily defeated. He commanded the China Area Army (1938–39), then was CofS of the army (1940–44) and was promoted field marshal (1943). A leading advocate of taking advantage of the preoccupation of the Western powers and Soviet Union with Germany in World War II to move into South Asia, he assured a skeptical Emperor Hirohito that Japan could realize her ambitions quickly. He opposed evacuation of Guadalcanal, convinced that willpower could overcome the Americans. Dismissed by Hideki Tōjō (February 1944), he was then again inspector of military education but became minister of war when Tōjō was ousted (July 1944–April 1945). CG, First General Army for the "defense to the death" of the Japanese home islands, he committed suicide following the surrender.

Sultan, Daniel Isom (1885–1947) U.S. general. Commissioned in the engineers on graduation from West Point (1907),

Sultan returned as a member of the staff and instructor (1912–16). Sent to the Philippines, he supervised construction of fortifications on Corregidor (1916–18). He was then on the War Department General Staff (1918–19) and held a succession of other engineer assignments. He graduated from the Command and General Staff School (1923) and Army War College (1926). He then had charge of an inter-oceanic canal survey and commanded U.S. troops in Nicaragua (1929–31). He commanded 2nd Engineers (1938–39) and was promoted brigadier general (December 1938). He commanded 22nd Infantry Brigade in Hawaii (January 1939–April 1941). Promoted major general (April 1941), he commanded 38th Infantry Division (May 1941–April 42), then VIII Corps (April 1942–November 1943).

Promoted lieutenant general (September 1943) and regarded as an excellent staff officer, Sultan was CofS to Lieutenant General Joseph Stilwell, commander of U.S. forces in the China–Burma–India Theater (November 1943–November 1944). He then replaced Stilwell as commander of U.S. forces, India–Burma Theater (November 1944–July 1945). He was inspector general of the army (July 1945–January 1947) until his death.

Summerall, Charles Pelot (1867–1955) U.S. general. Commissioned in the infantry on graduation from West Point (1892), Summerall transferred to the artillery (1893) and held a variety of assignments before seeing combat in the Philippine-American (1899–1900). During the 1900–01 Boxer Rebellion he distinguished himself in the China Relief Expedition during the assault on Peking (Beijing) (1900).

After assignment in Alaska, Summerall was an instructor in artillery at West Point (1905–11). As a major (1911) he commanded the 3rd Field Artillery Battalion. He was an instructor at the Army War College (1913–17) and was promoted to lieutenant colonel (June 1916).

Following U.S. entry in World War I (April 1917), he was advanced to colonel (May).

Promoted temporary brigadier general (August 1917), Summerall took command of the 1st Artillery Brigade of the 1st Infantry Division. Promoted temporary major general (June 1918), he received command of the 1st Division (July) and fought in the 1918 Aisne–Marne, St. Mihiel, and Meuse–Argonne offensives. In the midst of the last offensive, he received command of V Corps.

After the war, Summerall commanded in succession V Corps, IX Corps, and IV Corps in occupation in Germany. He returned to the United States to command 1st Division and was promoted permanent major general (April 1920). He served as CofS of the army with the rank of general (1926–1930). Upon retirement (March 1931), he was president of The Citadel in Charleston, South Carolina (1931–53).

Sung Che-yuan (Song Zheyuan) (1885–1940) Nationalist Chinese general. Closely identified with Feng Yü-hsiang (Feng Yuxiang), Sung was commissioned and served under Feng in the Left Route Army, which became the Metropolitan Guard Army (1913). After the reorganization of Feng's troops following the 1922 Chihli–Fengtien War, he commanded 11th Division (1924). He was then military governor of Jehol. He then fought with Feng against the forces of Chang Tso-lin (Zhang Zuolin) and Wu P'ei-fu (Wu Peifu) (1925).

Sung then joined forces with the Nationalists or Kuomintang (KMT, Guomindang) (1927) and received command of the Fourth Area Army (June 1927). He fought in the 1926–28 Northern Expedition to reunify China. He took command of Twenty-Ninth Army (1930) and when the Japanese orchestrated the September 1931 Mukden Incident to absorb all Manchuria, he issued a public telegram proposing war with Japan. Appointed governor of Chahar (July 1932), he was ordered to assist with his Twenty-Ninth Army in the defense of Jehol (January 1933). His army helped stem the Japanese advance but was then forced to retreat (April–May). Resistance ended only with the signing of a truce (31 May).

In 1935 Sung became Peiping–Tientsin garrison commander, coinciding with the signing of the Ho–Umezu agreement. He then chaired the Hopeh–Chahar Political Affairs Council and was also governor of Hopeh (December). On the start of the 1937–45 Sino-Japanese War, he took responsibility for the Chinese defeat in north China and submitted his resignation (July). Chiang Kai-shek (Jiang Jieshi) refused to accept this and named him CG of First Army Group, composed of Twenty-Ninth Army and other forces. Despite stubborn Chinese resistance, superior Japanese forces again pressured a retreat. His forces shattered, he again submitted his resignation. This time Chiang accepted his resignation but he appointed Sung to the Military Affairs Commission. Sung soon took leave of his post because of illness. He was posthumously promoted full general.

Sun Li-jen (Sun Liren) (1900–88) Chinese Nationalist general. Sun graduated from Tsinghuä (Qinghua) College (1923). He then studied civil engineering at Purdue University in the United States, graduating in (1923). He then studied at the Virginia Military Institute, where he graduated in 1927. After touring Europe and Japan to study their militaries, he returned to China and enrolled in the National Revolutionary Army as a corporal. By 1930 he had risen to regimental commander and the rank of colonel. He was then a regimental commander. Severely wounded in the 1937–45 Sino-Japanese War while leading his men at Shanghai (1937), he recuperated and organized a new unit (1938), which became the New 38th Division with him as commander (1942).

In the spring of 1942 Sun's division took part in the first Burma Campaign on the Irrawaddy front. Attacking the Japanese to relieve pressure on the British Burma division, his actions allowed the British to escape. When the Japanese then drove Allied forces out of Burma, he enhanced his reputation by effecting a skillful withdrawal and bringing out his division intact.

Sun then commanded the New First China Army (consisting of the 30th and 38th Divisions) of the Northern Combat Area Command (Burma) under Lieutenant Generals Joseph Stilwell and then Daniel Sultan. He experienced his first jungle victory at Taipha Ga (January 1944) and had a prominent role in the retaking of Ledo and liberating central Burma (1944–45).

Sun and his men returned to China in 1945. Invited by General Dwight Eisenhower, he toured European battlefields, then returned to China to lead his New First Army into Canton and accept the surrender of the Japanese Twenty-Third Army. He then fought in the 1946–49 Civil War in the northeast. He became deputy CinC of the Chinese Army and CinC of army training at Nanking (Nanjing) (July 1947–September 1948), when he became Taiwan defense commander.

After Chiang Kai-shek established the Nationalist government on Taiwan, Sun was made CinC of the Chinese Army (March 1950) and was promoted full general (May 1951). He lost a power struggle to Chiang's son, Chiang Chingkuo (Jiang Jingquo) and was removed from his posts (1954) and dismissed (1955) on charges of "negligence"in connection with an alleged "plot" by a subordinate against the government. Placed under house arrest, he later lived in retirement. To many Chinese he was known as "the ever victorious general."

Suzuki, Kantarō (1868–1948) Japanese admiral. Suzuki graduated from the Naval Academy (1887) and was promoted ensign (1889). He became a torpedo specialist after attending Torpedo School (1890–91). Promoted lieutenant (1892), he commanded a torpedo boat in the 1894–95 Sino-Japanese War, taking part in the attack on Weihaiwei (February 1895). He graduated from the Naval Staff College (1898) and served on the Navy General Staff (1898–99) and Navy Ministry (1899–1901). During study in Germany (1901–04) he was promoted commander (1903). He fought in the 1904–05 Russo-Japanese War and took part in the Battle of the Yellow Sea (10 August 1904) as executive officer of a cruiser. As commander of 5th Destroyer Flotilla, he participated in the Battle of Tsushima (27 May 1905) and was credited with sinking a Russian battleship. He taught at the Naval War College (1905–08) and was regarded as Japan's foremost expert on torpedo warfare. Promoted captain (1907), he commanded cruisers (1908–10), headed the Torpedo School (1910–11), and commanded a battleship and battle cruiser (1911–13).

Promoted rear admiral (1913), Suzuki was vice minister of the navy (1914–17) and president of the Naval Academy (1918–20). He held other commands and was promoted admiral (1923), commanded the Combined Fleet (1924–25), and then was chief of the Naval General Staff (1925–29). He then went on the reserve list, but held a succession of political posts. Made baron, he was badly wounded in the 1936 Young Officers' Revolt. President of the Privy Council during World War II (1944–45), he was then prime minister (April 1945–August 1946), when he arranged Japan's surrender.

Suzuki, Sōsaku (1891–1945) Japanese general. Suzuki graduated from the Military Academy (1912) and War Academy (1919). Resident officer in Germany (1922–25), he was promoted major (1927) and joined the Army Ministry's Military Affairs Section (1928–31). He was a staff officer in the Kwantung Army in Manchuria (1933–35). Promoted colonel (1935), he commanded a regiment (1935–37). Promoted major general (1938), he was deputy CofS of Central China Expeditionary Army (1938–39).

During World War II, Suzuki was CofS of General Tomoyuki Yamashita's Twenty-Fifth Army in the conquest of Malaya and Singapore (December 1941–February 1942). He held administrative posts (1943–44) and then commanded the new Thirty-Fifth Army in the southern Philippines, with headquarters at Cebu City (mid-1944), but was unable to stop the U.S. landings at Leyte (October) or defeat the invaders ashore. Committing his remaining troops to the defense of Mindanao, he was killed in the fighting there shortly after the U.S. invasion (April 1945). He was posthumously promoted full general.

Swift, Innis Palmer (1882–1953) U.S. general. Commissioned in the cavalry on graduation from West Point (1904), Swift participated as a major in the 1916–17 Punitive Expedition into Mexico. He was a lieutenant colonel in the 86th Infantry Division with the AEF in France during World War I, but did not see combat. He graduated from the Command and General Staff School (1923), the Army War College (1930), and the Army Industrial College (1931). He commanded 8th Cavalry Regiment (1936–39), then 2nd Cavalry Brigade (1939–40).

Promoted brigadier general (October 1940) and major general (April 1941), Swift was CG of 1st Cavalry Division when it captured Los Negros in the Admiralty Islands (February–March 1944). He commanded I Corps, Sixth Army in Luzon (1944–45) and retired in February 1946.

Swing, Joseph May (1894–1984) U.S. general. Commissioned in the field artillery on graduation from West Point (1915), Swing served in the 1916–17 Punitive Expedition into Northern Mexico. After U.S. entry into World War I

(April 1917), he was assigned to the 1st Infantry Division and fought at Noyon-Montdidier. He participated in the 1918 Aisne–Marne, St. Mihiel and Meuse–Argonne offensives.

After the war, Swing graduated from the Command and General Staff School (1927) and was an instructor at the Field Artillery School (1927–31). He was then in the war plans section of the office of the chief of field artillery (1933–34) and graduated from the Army War College (1935). He was CofS of 2nd Infantry Division (1938–40). He then commanded artillery in the 1st Cavalry Division (1941–42). Promoted brigadier general (February 1942), he then commanded the artillery of the 82nd Division (1942–43). Promoted major general (February 1943), he activated and commanded 11th Airborne Division (1943–47). He conducted the first airlift division of a complete division by planes and gliders and the first such mass landing at night, proving that such deployments were feasible.

After World War II Swing commanded I Corps (1948–49), the Army War College (1950–51), and then Sixth Army as a lieutenant general (1951–54). He retired in February 1954.

Swinton, Sir Ernest Dunlop (1868–1951) British army officer. Posted to the historical section of the Committee of Imperial Defence (1910), Swinton became its assistant secretary (1913). An official war correspondent in France at the beginning of World War I, he thought the deadlock of trench warfare might be broken by using an armored vehicle to roll over the trenches and suggested to the Committee of Imperial Defence converting Holt caterpillar tractors into fighting machines (October 1914). First Lord of the Admiralty Winston Churchill created a Landships Committee, and a prototype vehicle was produced (September 1915). An official demonstration of the tank (February 1916) went well, although Lord Kitchener thought that it would easily be destroyed by artillery fire. Swinton coined the generic word "tank" as camouflage when the vehicles were shipped to France.

Appointed commander of the new unit, Swinton protested against its premature use but was overruled when British commander General Sir Douglas Haig sought to break the deadlock in the Battle of the Somme. The tanks were first employed (15 September 1916) without great success. Swinton, meanwhile, had been "released" to his former duties in the War Cabinet secretariat and without direct association with the force he had fathered. After U.S. entry in World War I, he was promoted temporary major-general and traveled to America to speak on behalf of war bonds. In 1934 he became colonel-commandant of the Royal Tank Corps.

T

Tachibana, Kōichirō (1861–1929) Japanese general. A graduate of the Military Academy (1883) and Army Staff College (1889), Tachibana fought in the 1894–95 Sino-Japanese War. He studied in Austria-Hungary (1895–99) then was military advisor to General Yüan Shi-k'ai (Yuan Shikai) in China (1902–03). During the 1904–05 Russo-Japanese War he was CofS of Fourth Army in the siege of Port Arthur (May 1904–January 1905) and Battle of Mukden (February–March 1905). He attended the Portsmouth, New Hampshire Peace Conference ending the war and then remained in the United States as military attaché (1905–06). Promoted major general (1909), he served in Korea (1912–18) and was then first commander of the Kwantung Army in Manchuria (1919–21). He then commanded the Vladivostok Expeditionary Army to include its withdrawal from Siberia (1921–22).

Tai Li (Dai Li) (1895–1946) Nationalist Chinese general. Tai Li graduated from Whampoa Military Academy and joined the Nationalist or Kuomintang (KMT, Guomindang) forces. Quickly reaching general, he then headed the KMT intelligence and secret police service. In this capacity he worked to ferret out Communist party members and opponents of KMT leader Chiang Kai-shek (Jiang Jieshi) (1938). He established a joint intelligence operation with the Americans (1943–45), but was then killed in a plane crash.

Takagi, Sōkichi (1893–1979) Japanese admiral. Takagi graduated from the Naval Academy (1915), Navigation School (1922), and Naval Staff College (1927). Promoted lieutenant commander (1927), he was resident officer in France (1927–30). Then private secretary to the navy minister (1930–32), he was promoted commander and appointed instructor at the Naval Staff College (1933–36). Promoted captain (1939), he headed the Research Section of the Navy Ministry (1939–42). Opposing the decision to go to war with the United States, he was transferred to be CofS of Maizuru Naval Base (1942).

Promoted rear admiral (1943) and regarded by many as the navy's leading intellectual, Takagi undertook a study at the request of the Navy Minister Shigetarō Shimada of the lessons to be learned from the war. He went beyond the assigned task and concluded that Japan must make peace as quickly as possible and that the government of General Hideki Tōjō would have to be replaced. Reluctant to show the report to Shimada, he entered into an abortive plot to assassinate Tōjō. While in the Research Department of the Naval Staff College (1944–45), and with encouragement from new Minister of the Navy Mitsumasa

Yonai, he drew up a top-secret report on the best way for Japan to withdraw from the war.

Takagi, Takeo (1892–1944) Japanese admiral. Takagi graduated from the Naval Academy (1912) and Torpedo School (1918). He held submarine commands (1921–27), then taught at the Submarine School (1922). Promoted lieutenant commander (1923), he graduated from the Naval Staff College (1924). As a captain (1932), he commanded cruisers and a battleship (1933–38). Promoted rear admiral, he was CofS of Second Fleet (1938). He then headed the Intelligence Division, Naval General Staff (1939).

Appointed to command Fifth Fleet (September 1941), he had charge of support forces in the invasion of the Philippines (December 1941). Commanding the covering force in the invasion of Java, he crushed Rear Admiral Karel Doorman's ABDA (American, British, Dutch, Australian) Command cruisers and destroyers in the Battle of the Java Sea (27 February 1942). Promoted vice admiral (May), he commanded the carrier task force in Operation MO against Port Moresby but was intercepted by Rear Admiral Frank Fletcher's Task Force 15 in the Battle of the Coral Sea (May), the first naval battle when the two fleets remained out of sight of one another. Both his carriers were damaged in the battle, but he sank U.S. carrier *Lexington* and damaged carrier *Yorktown*. A tactical Japanese victory, the battle was a strategic U.S. victory, because Takagi's superior, Admiral Shigeyoshi Inouye, then called off the invasion of Port Moresby. Takagi later commanded Sixth Submarine Fleet in the Marianas (June 1943). He died in the U.S. invasion of Saipan (June–July 1944).

Tal, Israel (1924–) Israeli general. Born in Palestine, Tal served in the Jewish Brigade in the British Army in the Western Desert (1942–43) and Italy (1944–45). He was then in Haganah, the underground Jewish army in Palestine (1946). In the 1947–48 Israeli War of Independence he commanded a platoon, then a company. Sent to Czechoslovakia to purchase arms (1948), he returned to Israel and additional combat. After the war he commanded a battalion. Commandant of the Israel Defense Forces Officer School (1955), in the 1956 Sinai War he took over command of 10th Infantry Brigade at Agheila (October). After the war he commanded an armor brigade and was first the deputy commander, then commander, of the armored force (1956). In the 1967 Six-Day War he commanded an armored division task force that took El Arish and advanced to the Suez Canal. He then directed the Merkava tank project while also chief of the Planning Staff for the Defense Ministry (1969), where he played a major role in the 1968–70 War of Attrition, unsuccessfully opposing construction of the Bar Lev Line at the Canal. He headed the Operations Staff at the time of the 1973 October War (1972–73), then Southern Command (1973–75). He then became minister of defense (1976).

Tanaka, Giichi (1863–1929) Japanese general and prime minister. Tanaka fought in the 1894–95 Sino-Japanese War and the 1904–05 Russo-Japanese War. As prime minister (April 1928–July 1929), his name is associated with the "Tanaka Memorial" (1929). Allegedly the blueprint for Japanese imperialism, it was a report he made to the emperor for the Far Eastern Conference (1927) that was amended by army and navy leaders. Tanaka's original draft is believed to have urged the emperor to concentrate on economic rather than military expansion. No copy of the original exists and after the war, during the war crimes trials, it was held to be a Chinese forgery.

Tanaka's handling of the case involving the assassination of Chang Tso-lin (Zhang Zuolin) by a Japanese Kwantung Army officer (1928) infuriated Emperor Hirohito and led to Tanaka's resignation.

Tanaka, Raizō (1892–1969) Japanese admiral. Tanaka graduated from the Japanese Naval Academy (1913). With a specialty in torpedoes, he held a variety of assignments, culminating in battleship command (1939–41). Promoted rear admiral (1941), he commanded Destroyer Squadron 2 in the invasions of the Philippines (December 1941) and Dutch East Indies (January–February 1942). He commanded the screening force in the Battle of the Java Sea (February 1942) and escorts for the transports intended to assault Midway (June 1942).

Tanaka played a prominent role in the naval battles off Guadalcanal, when he commanded the Japanese resupply effort of the Eastern Solomons, "the Tokyo Express." He encountered and defeated a larger U.S. force in the Battle of Tassafaronga (November 1942). Removed from sea command in early 1943 following his outspoken statements regarding the loss of Guadalcanal, he served for a time on the Naval General Staff. He then commanded a naval brigade before being relegated to base command in Burma (1943). Promoted vice admiral (1944), he retired at the end of the war.

Tanaka, Shin'ichi (1893–1976) Japanese general. Commissioned in the infantry from the Military Academy (1913), Tanaka graduated from the Army Staff College (1923). Promoted major (1928), he was a resident officer in the Soviet Union (1928–31), then a staff officer with Kwantung Army in Manchuria (1931–32). He was chief of the Military Affairs Division of the Army Ministry (1936, 1937–39). Promoted major general (1939), he was CofS of the Mongolia Garrison Army (February 1939). Promoted lieutenant general (October 1941), he became chief of the military operations section at Imperial General Headquarters. He favored an all-out attack on the Soviet Union and later urged greater efforts to reinforce Guadalcanal. His insults of Premier Hideki Tōjō led to his posting to

Southern Army headquarters in Saigon (December 1942).

As commander of 18th Division in Burma (March 1943), Tanaka showed superior leadership in adversity, but his outnumbered forces were steadily driven back. Appointed CofS of the Burma Army (August 1944), he was virtual commander of that outnumbered force until he was wounded (May 1945). He ended the war as a staff officer in a regional command in Japan.

Tanaka, Shizuichi (1887–1945) Japanese army general. Tanaka graduated from the Military Academy (1907) and the Army Staff College (1917). Resident officer in Britain (1919–22), he studied at Oxford. He was then military attaché to Mexico (1926–30). Promoted colonel, he commanded a regiment (1930) before becoming military attaché to the United States (1930–34). Promoted major general (1934), he commanded an infantry brigade (1934–36) and was then provost marshal general (1938–39, 1940–41). He commanded 13th Infantry Division (1939–40), then Eastern District Army (1941–42).

Tanaka commanded Fourteenth Army in the Philippines (1942–43). Promoted general (1943), he was then president of the Army Staff College (1944–45). At the end of the war he commanded the Twelfth Area Army occupying central Honshu Island around Tokyo, and he played a key role in suppressing an attempted coup by fanatics who sought to take over the Imperial Palace and prevent Japan's surrender. He committed suicide shortly thereafter.

Taylor, David Watson (1864–1940) U.S. admiral. Taylor graduated at the top of his class from three institutions, Randolph-Macon College, Annapolis (1885), and Britain's Royal Naval College. Commissioned in the Constructor Corps, on his return from Britain Taylor assisted in the design of the first U.S. modern battleships, *Indiana*, *Massachusetts*, and *Oregon*.

Taylor helped secure funds and oversaw construction at the Washington Naval Yard of the nation's first model ship basin (1899). As director of the Experimental Model Basin (1899–1914), he introduced new technology such as the Sperry Gyroscope and the bulbous bow, and he assisted in early submarine development. He also had a wind tunnel built at the facility and helped pioneer early aviation technology and initiated production of the NC-type flying boat. He served two terms as naval constructor and chief of the Bureau of Construction and Repair, overseeing design and construction of more than 900 U.S. Navy vessels, plus many others for foreign governments. He retired from the service in 1923.

Taylor, Maxwell Davenport (1901–87) U.S. general. Commissioned from West Point (1922), Taylor went to Paris to learn French (1927) and returned to teach at West Point (1928–32). Graduating from the Field Artillery School (1933) and Command and General Staff School (1935), he was attached to the U.S. embassy in Tokyo to study Japanese and briefly in China. He graduated from the Army War College (1940) and held a variety of assignments before being promoted colonel and becoming CofS to General Matthew Ridgway's 82nd Infantry Division, soon the first U.S. airborne division.

Brigadier General Taylor accompanied the 82nd to North Africa (March 1943) where he helped plan the July Allied assault on Sicily, in which he participated. His subsequent mission behind German lines to Rome led to a negative assessment of prospects of an airborne assault there and cancellation of the operation. Ordered to Britain (March 1944), he took command of the 101st Airborne Division and jumped with it in the Normandy invasion (5–6 June 1944) and in the assault on Eindhoven as part of Operation MARKET-

GARDEN (September). He commanded the 101st the rest of the war.

As superintendent of West Point (1945–49), Taylor modified the curriculum. He was then CofS of U.S. forces in Europe and commander in Berlin. Deputy CofS of the Army (1951–53), he succeeded Lieutenant General Van Fleet as Eighth Army commander in Korea (February 1953) during the 1950–53 Korean War. Promoted general, he commanded U.S. Army forces in the Far East (August 1954). He was then Army CofS (1955–59), where he protested Eisenhower administration emphasis on nuclear as opposed to conventional forces.

Taylor retired from the army in 1959. His advocacy of the doctrine of "flexible response" won Kennedy administration notice, and President John F. Kennedy returned him to active service as chairman of the Joint Chiefs of Staff (1962). He was then ambassador to the Republic of Vietnam (1964), where he argued against a large U.S. military commitment that would encourage South Vietnamese forces to let Americans do the fighting. General William Westmoreland's call for massive U.S. reinforcements won out, and Taylor left his post (1965), although he continued to advise the Johnson administration.

Tedder, Sir Arthur Williams, 1st Baron (1890–1967) British air marshal. A graduate of Magdalene College, Cambridge (1913), Tedder was commissioned in the army (1914) and served in France during World War I. He transferred to the Royal Flying Corps (1916), flew bombing and reconnaissance missions, and quickly rose to command 70th Squadron (1917).

Tedder secured a permanent commission in the Royal Air Force (1919) and became a member of the RAF Staff College at Cranston (1929), where he was promoted to group captain. He headed the Air Armament School and then was director of training at the Air Ministry (1934–36). He was then air commander in the Far East at Singapore

(1936–38), being promoted to air vice marshal (1937). He returned to Britain to serve in the Air Ministry as director of research and development (1938–40).

In World War II Tedder was first deputy air commander for the Middle East (1940), then, after the debacles of Greece and Crete, its commander (1941). Husbanding and concentrating his resources for specific objectives, he won control of the air by the spring of 1942. He was knighted that same year. Made air commander for the Mediterranean (1943–1944), he directed air support of the invasions of Sicily (July 1943) and Italy (September 1943). His operations were noteworthy for the integration of air assets with sea and land resources. A fine strategist and administrator who eschewed the limelight, as deputy commander of the Allied Expeditionary Force (1944) he helped plan the Normandy invasion (Operation OVERLORD) (6 June 1944). He replaced Air Marshal Trafford Leigh-Mallory as commander of tactical air forces (November 1944) and signed the instrument of surrender in Berlin on behalf of General Dwight Eisenhower (8 May 1945). Made a baron (1946), he was chief of the air staff until his retirement (1946–50).

Templer, Sir Gerald Walter Robert (1898–1979) British field marshal. Educated at Wellington College and Sandhurst, Templer was commissioned in the Royal Irish Fusiliers (1916) and fought in France during World War I. After the war he served in Iran, Iraq, Egypt, and Palestine, where as a company commander he saw action in the 1936 Arab rebellion.

During World War II Templer was in France on the intelligence staff of the BEF (1939–40). Following the Dunkerque evacuation (May–June 1940), he held staff assignments in Britain and advanced to lieutenant general (1942), the youngest to hold that rank in the British army. To secure a combat command, at his own request he reverted to major general and

took command of the 1st Division in North Africa (1943), then the 56th Division in North Africa (1943), where he saw action at Anzio. Still in Italy, commanding 6th Armored Division, he was invalided home when his jeep struck a mine (1944).

On his recovery, Templer served as director of Civil Affairs and Military Government in the British zone in Germany (1945–46), then in the War Office as director of Military Intelligence and vice chief of the Imperial General Staff (1946–50). He was knighted in 1949. Heading Eastern Command (1950–52), he was sent to Malaya following the 1951 assassination of British High Commissioner Sir Henry Gurney, as both high commissioner and CinC (1952–54) to crush the Malayan Races' Liberation Army (MRLA) insurgency. He restored morale, continued the Briggs' Plan resettlement incentives begun by his predecessor, and became linked with the "hearts and minds" philosophy of counterinsurgency warfare. By the time of his departure he had largely brought the insurgency to an end. Templer completed his active service as chief of the Imperial General Staff (1955–58) and was promoted field marshal in December 1956.

Teng Hua (Deng Hua) (1910–80) Peoples' Republic of China general. Teng joined the Chinese Communist Party (1927) and participated in the 1935 Long March. He formed the Eastern Task Group (January 1949) that fought in the Pingjin Campaign, one of the most decisive of the 1946–49 Civil War. Closely associated with P'eng Te-huai (Peng Dehuai) and Lin Piao (Lin Biao), he supported Chinese military modernization. He supervised the attack on Hainan Island and returned to the mainland (1950) to become CofS of South China Military Region.

Teng commanded Fifteenth Army in the Chinese intervention in the Korean War. He believed that U.S. troops in Korea could be defeated because he considered them politically unmotivated, inferior in night fighting techniques and bayonet charges, and unable to endure hardship. He favored close combat tactics and night operations.

Commander of the Chinese People's Volunteer Army (CPVA) in Korea General P'eng Te-huai (Peng Dehuai) named Teng one of his deputy commanders. He was then first senior Chinese delegate to the armistice negotiations (July 1951–July 1953). In late spring 1953 he urged that Chinese forces launch offensive operations when armistice talks stalled.

After the war Teng commanded Shenyang Military Region until 1959, when he was demoted. He survived the 1966–69 Cultural Revolution and was rehabilitated to become vice president of the Academy of Military Science in Beijing.

Terauchi, Hisaichi (1879–1946) Japanese field marshal. The son of Field Marshal Masatake Terauchi, from whom he inherited the title of count (1919), he graduated from the Japanese Military Academy (1899) and fought in the 1904–05 Russo-Japanese War. He graduated from the Army Staff College (1909), joined the General Staff (1911), was an assistant military attaché in Vienna (1911–13), and studied in Germany (1913–14). Promoted colonel (1919), he commanded a regiment (1919–21), then was CofS of the Imperial Guards Division (1922–24). Promoted major general (1924), he commanded an infantry brigade (1924–26) and was CofS of the Korea Army (1927–29). Promoted lieutenant general, he commanded 5th Division (1930–32), then 1st Division (1932–34). He commanded the Taiwan Army (1934–35) and was promoted general (1935).

Terauchi was about to retire when a purge of the military after a coup attempt (February 1936) left him the senior army officer. He then became in succession war minister (March 1936), inspector general of military training (February 1937), and commander of the North China Area

Army (August). He commanded the Southern Expeditionary Army (November 1941), directing all Japanese Army operations in Southeast Asia from Saigon (February 1942). A skillful coordinator of his subordinate commanders, he allowed them unusual latitude. Given the honorary rank of field marshal (June 1943), he was the only senior general in the army to hold the same post throughout the war. He suffered a cerebral hemorrhage (1945) before Japan's surrender and died the following year.

Terauchi, Masatake (1852–1919) Japanese field marshal. Terauchi fought in the 1868 Boshin (Restoration) War, and joined the new imperial army as a sergeant (1871) and was commissioned (1871). He was badly wounded and lost the use of one arm in the Battle of Tabaruzaka in the 1877 Satsuma Rebellion. He advanced steadily in rank to major general (1894) and served on the joint staff during the 1894–95 Sino-Japanese War. As army minister (1902–11), he supervised military operations during the 1904–05 Russo-Japanese War and the 1910 annexation of Korea. As governor of Korea (1910–15), he completed the Japanese takeover of that country. Promoted field marshal (May 1916), he was prime minister from October until the rice riots of 1918.

Thaon di Revel, Paolo (1859–1948) Italian admiral. Revel entered the Naval School (1873) and rose to command 2nd Naval Division during the 1911–12 Italo-Turkish War. As chief of the Italian naval general staff (March 1913–October 1915, February 1917–November 1919), he was a conservative brake on Fleet commander Duke of the Abruzzi. After losses inflicted by submarines, Revel determined that the Italian fleet had to be preserved either to face the Austrians in a classic battle or as a diplomatic tool after the war.

Revel was forced from office (October 1915) when the minister of marine decided to combine the CofS position with his own office. This turned out to be an unsuccessful experiment, and Revel returned as CofS (February 1917) with the additional title of head of mobilized naval forces. He was a champion of Italian interests, and vetoed anyone but an Italian to command in the Adriatic. He thus bore much of the responsibility for the Allied failure to create a unified Mediterranean naval command. King Victor Emmanuel III promoted him from vice admiral to admiral (November 1918) and, a few years later, to grand admiral.

After the war Revel was technical advisor to the Italian delegation at the 1919 Paris Peace Conference and minister of marine in Mussolini's first cabinet (October 1922–May 1925). In May 1924 the king gave him the title of *Duca del Mare* (Duke of the Sea).

Theobald, Robert Alfred (1884–1957) U.S. admiral. "Fuzzy" Theobald spent a year at the University of California before graduating from Annapolis (1906). He commanded a destroyer landing force in Santo Domingo (1916) and during World War I was on a battleship serving with the British Grand Fleet. After the war he was executive officer of the Naval Post Graduate School, Annapolis (1919–21) and its commander (1924–27). He had various assignments afloat, then graduated from the Naval War College (1930) and became secretary of war plans, Navy Department and member of the Joint Army–Navy Planning Commission (1930–32). He was then CofS of Destroyers, Pacific Fleet (1932–34), in a planning position at the Naval War College (1934–37), and commanded a battleship (1937–39).

Captain Theobald was then CofS to CinC, U.S. Fleet, commanded Cruiser Division 3, and served on the Navy General Board (1939–40). Promoted rear admiral (September 1940), he commanded Destroyer Flotilla 1, Pacific Fleet. Following U.S. entry into the war he commanded destroyers in the Pacific

Fleet. Admiral Chester Nimitz then named him commander of the North Pacific Fleet (May 1942). Although he got on well with his army and air force counterparts, he and the aggressive army commander Major General Simon Bolivar Buckner were at loggerheads over strategy and this paralyzed operations. After repeated requests to be relieved, he was replaced (June 1943). He then commanded the 1st Naval District and Boston Navy Yard, retiring as a rear admiral in February 1945.

Thoma, Wilhelm Ritter von (1891–1948) German general. An officer candidate (1914) Thoma was commissioned in the infantry in 1914. Following World War I, he remained in the army and became a leading German armor warfare theorist in the 1930s, second only to Heinz Guderian. As a major he took command of the first German tank battalion (1934), then commanded all German ground troops during the 1936–39 Spanish Civil War. He briefly commanded a tank regiment before taking over a brigade of the 2nd Panzer Division (August 1939) and distinguishing himself in the invasion of Poland (September 1939). He then was director of Mobile Forces. Sent to North Africa (October) to recommend whether German reinforcements should be sent to help the Italians in North Africa, he submitted a highly critical report.

Brigadier General Thoma replaced General Hans-Jürgen von Arnim as commander of 17th Panzer Division (July 1941) in the Soviet Union and participated in the Smolensk and Kiev encirclements. He then commanded 20th Panzer Division in the Moscow region until June 1942. Advanced to command a corps in the Soviet Union and promoted major general, he shortly thereafter replaced General Walther Nehring in command of the Afrika Korps (September 1942). The next month, during the First Battle of El Alamein and following the death by heart attack of General Georg Stumme, he briefly commanded Panzerarmee Africa. Refused by Adolf Hitler permission to withdraw, he was captured (4 November) trying to halt General Bernard Montgomery's Eighth Army breakout in the Second Battle of El Alamein.

Thompson, Sir Robert Grainger Ker (1916–92) British counterinsurgency expert. Educated at Cambridge, Thompson joined the civil service in Malaya (1938). During World War II he joined General Orde Wingate's Chindits in Burma as RAF liaison officer, rising to the rank of wing commander. He returned to Malaya after the war and, as civil affairs advisor, helped develop the Briggs plan, named for Director of Operations General Sir Harold Briggs, which was the basis for defeating the ongoing insurgency. He held a succession of posts, culminating in secretary of defense (1959–61).

Thompson then headed the small British Advisory Mission to the Republic of Vietnam (RVN) (1961–65). Events and his reputation soon meant that his advice on counterinsurgency techniques was sought after by the Kennedy administration. Knighted (1965), he was a Rand consultant on Vietnam to the U.S. government (1965–68) and wrote extensively and critically on U.S. involvement there. He made regular visits to Vietnam for President Richard Nixon and sought to interest the Americans and RVN government in applying the lessons learned in putting down the insurgency in Malaya, the core of which was denying the guerrillas access to the people. Washington rejected his warnings about using excessive force and the South Vietnamese too readily embraced the program of population control in a system of fortified villages against the insurgents ("Strategic Hamlets"). His core ideas are contained in his book *Defeating Communist Insurgency* (1966).

Timoshenko, Semen Konstantinovich (1895–1970) Soviet marshal. Timoshenko

was drafted into the army (1915) and fought in World War I as a machine gunner, rising to NCO. Jailed for striking an officer (1917), he was freed by the Bolshevik Revolution (November). He joined the Red Army (1918) and fought in Crimea during the 1918–20 Civil War, winning distinction in fighting at Tsaritsyn (Stalingrad). At this time he developed close associations with both Josef Stalin and Gregori Zhukov. Although virtually illiterate when he began Soviet military schools, he graduated from the Frunze Military Academy (1922), from cavalry schools, and from the Lenin Political Academy (1930). He then held a succession of military commands. A member of the Supreme Soviet on its creation (1937), he remained so for life.

In the Soviet invasion of Poland (September 1939), he commanded the Ukrainian Front, moving on Lwow and later the Lublin area, and he concluded the 1939–40 Russo-Finnish War as commander of Soviet forces there. Promoted marshal (May 1940), he was however unsuited for high command. At the time of the German invasion of the Soviet Union (22 June 1941), he was commissar (minister) of defense and commander of the Western Front, and he thus must share blame with Stalin for the debacle accompanying the German attack. Initially he refused permission to Russian commanders to return fire. He did, however, take charge in the first week when Stalin seemed unable to act. When Stalin re-emerged (2 July), he took charge of Stavka and Timoshenko became deputy commissar of defense and went off to command the Western Front.

Transferred to command Southwestern Front (September 1941), he failed to prevent a German breakthrough to the Crimea and the disaster of the Kiev encirclement (September), which however could be blamed on Stalin's refusal to allow withdrawal. Transferred to the Finnish Front (January–May 1942), he was then back in Ukraine, where his offensive at Kharkov failed (May 1942). During the remainder of the war he served in lesser assignments and, at one point or another, commanded operations on the Northern Caucasus, 2nd and 3rd Baltic, and 2nd, 3rd, and 4th Ukrainian Fronts.

After the war Timoshenko commanded the South Ural (1946–149) and Belorussian Military Districts (1946, 1949–60).

Tirpitz, Alfred von (1849–1930) German admiral and state secretary of the Navy. Tirpitz joined the navy (1865) and by the 1880s was the navy's chief torpedo specialist. After service as naval CofS (1892–96), he commanded cruisers in the Far East (1896–97).

Tirpitz was promoted rear admiral (1895) and admiral (1903). Kaiser Wilhelm II then appointed him state secretary of the navy with instructions to make Germany a major naval power (June 1897). He was the architect of the rise of Germany's naval power and one of the most able naval ministers in history. He convinced Kaiser Wilhelm II to emphasize battleships rather than cruisers, and he pushed through the Reichstag a naval bill (1898) for the construction of nineteen battleships, eight armored cruisers, twelve large cruisers and thirty small cruisers in only six years. He then introduced a second Naval Bill (June 1890) doubling the size of the projected navy. He was a late convert to both submarines and naval airships.

Although by World War I Germany had the world's second largest navy, this was at heavy cost and took resources from the army. Britain's construction outstripped Germany, and despite Tirpitz's stated belief that Britain would be forced into concessions, Germany's naval construction in fact drove Britain to ally with France.

During World War I, Tirpitz advocated unrestricted submarine warfare against England (early 1916), but the Kaiser rejected this and he resigned. After the war he was elected to the Reichstag on the political right.

Tito (Josip Broz) (1892–1980) Leader of Communist resistance forces and president of Yugoslavia. Broz fought in the Austro-Hungarian army during World War I and was wounded and captured by the Russians (1915). Freed by the Bolshevik Revolution, he became an enthusiastic Communist and joined the Red Guard, fighting with it during the Civil War. Returning to Yugoslavia, he was active in organizing the Communist party there and became its secretary general (1939).

Following the German invasion of Yugoslavia (April 1941), Broz organized Communist resistance forces under the *nom de guerre* of Tito and successfully waged a war of liberation against the Axis occupiers and the rival conservative Chetnik Yugoslav resistance. He secured British recognition and military support, ultimately to the exclusion of the Chetniks, and his Partisans liberated much of the country at the end of the war. After the war he purged the rival Chetniks and, despite Western protests, executed its leaders. He also did away with the monarchy and became chief of state (November 1945).

Tito was dictator of Yugoslavia from the end of the war. He broke with Moscow (1948) and became president for life (1974). As long as he lived, Yugoslavia held together. His federated scheme for Yugoslavia was abandoned after the end of the Cold War, however, leading to the country's breakup.

Tōgō, Heihachirō (1848–1934) Japanese admiral. Tōgō joined the Satsuma domain navy (1866) and was a gunnery officer in the 1868 Boshin (Restoration) War. He entered the new Imperial Navy as a cadet (1871), then apprenticed with the Royal Navy and studied mathematics at Cambridge (1871–78). Promoted lieutenant commander (1879), he received his first ship command. Promoted captain (1888), he commanded the cruiser *Naniwa*, in which he began the 1894–95 Sino-Japanese War off Korea, sinking by torpedo the British-flag transport *Kowshing* carrying Chinese troops (25 July 1884). He participated in the Battle of the Yalu River (17 September) and commanded naval forces that seized Formosa. Promoted rear admiral (1895), he headed the Naval Technical Council and the Higher Naval College (1895–96). He commanded the Japanese squadron in the suppression of the 1900–01 Boxer Rebellion in China (1900). He then commanded the Standing and Combined Squadrons, virtually the entire fleet (October 1903).

Tōgō began the 1904–05 Russo-Japanese War with a surprise attack on the Russian Far Eastern Fleet at Port Arthur (7 February 1904) and then carried out a successful blockade. Promoted full admiral (June), he won the Battle of the Yellow Sea (10 August), repulsing an attempt by the Port Arthur Squadron to reach Vladivostok. He then annihilated Admiral Zinovy Rozhestvensky's 2nd Pacific Squadron, which had steamed halfway around the world, in the Battle of Tsushima Straits (27 May 1905), the only decisive fleet action in the history of the steel battleship. This brought Russia to the negotiating table and made Tōgō a national hero.

Tōgō became chief of the Naval General Staff (1905–09) and a count (1907). Although virtually retired, he was promoted admiral of the fleet (1913), then oversaw the studies of Crown Prince Hirohito. He formally retired (1921), although he continued to have considerable influence on naval policies. He also helped widen the split within the navy between the Treaty faction and the Fleet faction. Just before his death he became a marquis (1934).

Tōjō, Hideki (1884–1948) Japanese general and political figure. Tōjō entered the army in 1902, graduated from the Military Academy (1905), and served in Man-

churia at the end of the 1904–05 Russo-Japanese War. He graduated from Staff College (1915) and held staff positions during World War I and the intervention in Siberia. He was then military attaché to Switzerland, then Germany (1919–22).

Promoted major, Tōjō joined the faculty of the Military Staff College at Tokyo. He then headed the General Affairs Bureau of the War Office (1933–35) and commanded a brigade (1935). Promoted major general, he commanded the gendarmerie in the Kwantung Army in Manchuria (October) with responsibility for security. Promoted lieutenant general, he was CofS of the Kwantung Army (1937). On the renewal of fighting with China that year, he secured all of Inner Mongolia.

Tōjō was vice minister of war (May 1938) and then (December) inspector general of the air forces. Again minister of war (1941), he redirected Japanese expansion from Manchuria to South Asia. Appointed premier (October) and essentially Japan's dictator, he prepared for war with the United States with surprise attacks against U.S. and British Pacific bases to force those two powers to sue for peace. He simultaneously served as premier, war minister, and (after February 1944), chief of the army general staff. He resigned (15 July 1944) following the loss of Saipan. After the war, following a failed attempt at suicide (September 1945), he was tried and convicted of war crimes and hanged.

Tolbukhin, Fedor Ivanovich (1894–1949) Soviet marshal. Drafted into the Russian army, he rose to captain by the end of World War I. He joined the Red Army (1918) and was a divisional CofS in the Civil War. He attended service schools and graduated from the Frunze Military Academy (1934). He was CofS first of a division, then of a corps. He then became CofS of the Transcaucasian Military District (1938) and joined the Communist party.

Promoted major general (June 1941), Tolbukhin continued as CofS in what became the Transcaucasian Front following the German invasion. From late 1941 he was CofS of the Caucasian Front, then the Crimea Front. He commanded Fifty-Seventh Army at Stalingrad (July 1942). Promoted lieutenant general, he led the main effort in the Soviet counteroffensive. He then commanded Sixty-Eighth Army on the Northwestern Front (February 1943) then the Southern Front (March), and was promoted colonel general (April) and general of the army (September). His army was then redesignated the 4th Ukrainian Front (October).

Tolbukhin led, along with General Andrei Yeremenko, the Soviet offensive that retook the Crimea (May 1944). From May 1944 he commanded 3rd Ukrainian Front and liberated Bulgaria, Romania, Hungary, and Austria, and also pushed into Yugoslavia. At the end of the war he commanded the Southern Group of armies in Bulgaria and Romania. His final army assignment was to command the Transcaucasian Military District.

Tovey, Sir John Cronyn (1885–1971) British admiral. Tovey joined the navy as a cadet (1900) and made his reputation in destroyers. During World War I in the Battle of Jutland (31 May–1 June 1916) he distinguished himself in the destroyer *Onslow*. After service at the Royal Naval Staff College and the Admiralty Operations Division, he was promoted captain (1923). He then served in both staff positions and destroyer commands and was a destroyer flotilla commander (1925). Following attendance at the Imperial Defence College (1927), he was assistant to the second sea lord and then took command of the battleship *Rodney* (April 1932).

Promoted rear admiral (1935), Tovey returned to sea in command of destroyer flotillas in the Mediterranean (1938). Promoted vice admiral (May 1939), he headed all Allied light naval forces in the Mediterranean and was second-in-command of the Mediterranean Fleet. He distinguished himself against the Italian Navy in the Battle of Calabria (9 July 1940).

Tovey was made temporary admiral and given command of the Home Fleet (December 1940). He coordinated naval assets in the pursuit and sinking of the German battleship *Bismarck* (27 May 1941). As CinC of the Nore (July 1943), he was involved in preparations for the Normandy landings (6 June 1944). Promoted admiral (1942) and admiral of the fleet (1943), he was raised to the peerage and retired from the navy in 1946.

Towers, John Henry (1885–1955) U.S. admiral. Towers graduated from Annapolis (1906) and served on a battleship during the 1907–09 Great White Fleet's circumnavigation of the globe. He learned to fly the navy's first aircraft, the Curtiss A-1, and was the U.S. Navy's third aviator (1911). One of the pioneers of early naval aviation, he helped establish the navy's first air station on the Severn River across from Annapolis, Maryland, then was assistant naval attaché in Britain during the early period of World War I. He was then in the aviation branch of the office of the chief of naval operations and oversaw U.S. naval aviation in the war (1916–18).

After the war Towers commanded the squadron of Curtiss Flying Boats attempting a flight across the Atlantic (1919). Only one plane made it, and Towers was forced to ditch. Rigging a sail on his plane, he got it to the Azores. After service as naval attaché to various European states (1920s), he was chief of the Bureau of Aeronautics (1939). Promoted vice admiral, he was commander of Air Force, Pacific Fleet (October 1942–February 1944) and advised Pacific Fleet commander Admiral Chester Nimitz on aviation matters and oversaw air strikes in the Central Pacific. He was then deputy CinC, Pacific Fleet and Pacific Ocean

(February–July 1944). He then commanded 2nd Carrier Task Force (TF) of TF-38, then TF-38, then Fifth Fleet, but too late in the war to see significant action. Promoted admiral (late 1945), he commanded the Pacific Fleet (November 1945–December 1947) until his retirement.

Townshend, Sir Charles Vere Ferrers (1861–1924) British general. Commissioned in the army (1881), Townshend saw action in the Sudan, India, and South Africa. Promoted major general (1911), he was sent to Mesopotamia at the beginning of World War I. There he commanded the 6th Indian Division. British commander General Sir John Nixon ordered him to sail up the Tigris and drive northward. The fleet became known as "Townshend's Regatta."

Seizing Kut-al-Amara from the Turks, Townshend's Anglo-Indian force of 12,000 men continued toward Baghdad, urged on by both military and civilian leaders. Halted at Ctesiphon, he retreated back to Kut al Amara to await reinforcements. Turkish forces under General Nur-ud-din pushed him to Kut, where he was besieged in early December. The Turks repelled three British relief columns and inflicted heavy losses. Starvation and disease forced him to surrender his remaining force of 10,000 men (29 April 1916). Released from imprisonment (1918), he helped negotiate the armistice with the Turks signed that October.

Toyoda, Soemu (1885–1957) Japanese admiral. Toyoda graduated from the Naval Academy (1905) and Naval Gunnery School (1911). He then taught at the latter school and graduated from the Naval War College. He was a resident officer in Britain (1919–22) and was promoted captain. After commanding a cruiser, then a battleship, he was chief of Intelligence Group, Naval General Staff (1932), then CofS of the Combined Fleet (1933). Promoted vice admiral (1935), he

commanded Fourth Fleet (1937). Promoted admiral (September 1941), he had command of the Kure Naval Station. He joined the Supreme War Council (November 1942), and commanded the Yokosuka Navy Base (May 1943).

Toyoda succeeded Admiral Mineichi Koga as CinC of the Combined Fleet (May 1944), but his plans to lure the U.S. Navy into circumstances for a decisive Japanese victory ran awry first in the Battle of the Philippine Sea (19–20 June 1944) and then in the Battle of Leyte Gulf (23–26 October 1944). He took desperate steps in the form of *kamikaze* attacks to try to save Okinawa (April 1945), resulting in the loss of the battleship *Yamato*. He replaced Admiral Jisaburō Ozawa as navy chief of staff (May), which post he held to the end of the war. He opposed Emperor Hirohito's efforts to surrender. After the war he was tried but acquitted of war crimes.

Trân Văn Trà (1918–) Socialist Republic of Vietnam general. Trân quit his job as a railroad worker to join the Việt Minh resistance to the French and Japanese during World War II. He was soon a senior officer in South Vietnam leading guerrillas near the Laotian border.

In 1954 Trân became deputy chief of staff to Democratic Republic of Vietnam Defense Minister Vô Nguyên Giáp. He spent the next nine years in the North and studying in China and the Soviet Union. He then (1963) commanded a Việt Cong (Vietnamese Communist, VC) cadre group in the Mekong Delta of South Vietnam. He chaired the Military Affairs Committee, Central Office of South Vietnam (COSVN) (1964–76), directing the war against the Republic of Vietnam (RVN) and commanding the attack on Saigon during the 1968 Tet Offensive. He was then Minister of Defense in the Provisional Revolutionary Government of South Vietnam (1969–76).

Returning to Hanoi (March 1973), Tran planned and then carried out the final offensive against South Vietnam (August 1974). He also planned the assault on Saigon led by General Văn Tiên Dũng and four divisions. Following capture of the city (April 1975), he commanded the military occupation there (May 1975–January 1976) and then served on the Politburo of the Vietnamese Worker's Party. His five-volume history (1982) criticized DRV wartime policies, especially the 1968 Tet Offensive and the willingness of the North to sacrifice VC manpower needlessly. He was then dropped from the Politburo and placed under house arrest, and his book was banned.

Trenchard, Hugh Montague (1873–1956) British air force marshal. Trenchard entered the militia (1893) and served in the 1899–1902 Boer War and in Nigeria (1902–04). In 1913 he commanded the Central Flying School.

During World War I, Trenchard took charge of the 1st Wing in France (November 1914), where he installed radio and photographic equipment and experimented with tactical bombing. In the course of 1915, he went from lieutenant colonel to major general and commander of the Royal Flying Corps (August 1915). He stressed securing air superiority through an aggressive offense.

Trenchard then became the first CofS for the Royal Air Force (January 1918). In the post he became a staunch advocate of strategic bombing. He resigned (April), the result of conflicts with Air Minister Lord Rothermere. He then led the Inter-Allied Independent Air Force, a bombing group that struck German civilian and military targets.

Trenchard was reappointed air CofS when Winston Churchill became air minister (February 1919) and continued in that position until 1929. The first marshal of the RAF (1927) and the "Father of the Royal Air Force," he created its staff and support systems. His belief that civilian

morale might be shattered by bombing was disproved in World War II.

Trotha, Adolf von (1868–1940) German admiral. Trotha joined the navy (1886), served in the torpedo branch, attended the Navy Academy, and then was attached to the East Asia Cruiser Squadron. He was in the Navy Office under Admiral Alfred von Tirpitz (1901–06). After a period of fleet duty, he was in the Navy Cabinet (1910–13). He then received command of the dreadnought *Kaiser* (1913).

Trotha advocated both a decisive naval battle with the Royal Navy and unrestricted submarine warfare. As vice admiral he became Admiral Reinhard Scheer's CofS (January 1916) and pushed for resumption of unrestricted submarine warfare and Scheer's goal of a unified and independent supreme naval command. The two men succeeded in creating the Naval War Command (August 1918), forcing opponents such as Henning von Holtzendorff, Eduard von Capelle, and Georg von Müller into retirement.

Trotha miscalculated the mood among the sailors in the High Seas Fleet. When he pushed for a last sortie to satisfy the navy's honor (October 1918), the sailors rebelled. Their mutiny hastened the collapse of the empire. He served as chief of the Admiralty in the early Weimar Republic until his resignation in October 1920.

Trotsky, Leon Lev Bronstein (1879–1940) Russian revolutionary and military commander. One of the leaders of the 1905 Russian Revolution and the November 1917 Bolshevik *coup d'etat*, he was commissar of foreign affairs in the new Bolshevik government and negotiated an armistice with the Germans (December 1917), but favored revolutionary war rather than accepting the March 1918 Peace of Brest-Litovsk.

Trotsky then became commissar of war (March 1918). An excellent organizer and gifted revolutionary general, he created and led the Red Army to victory against the Whites in the 1918–20 Russian Civil War. Following the death of Vladimir Lenin, Joseph Stalin was able to force him from his leadership posts and strip him of party membership (1927), and then force him into exile, where he was murdered on Stalin's orders.

Troubridge, Sir Ernest Charles Thomas (1862–1926) British admiral. Troubridge entered the Navy (1875) and was a naval attaché in Tokyo during the 1904–05 Russo-Japanese War, and was chief of the Naval War Staff (1911–12). As commander of 1st Cruiser Squadron with four heavy cruisers in the Mediterranean at the beginning of World War I, he was unable to prevent the escape of the German battle cruiser *Goeben* and light cruiser *Breslau* to the Dardanelles. This failure led to his court-martial. Acquitted, he was not again employed at sea. He subsequently headed the British naval mission to Serbia and served on the personal staff of Crown Prince Alexander. Promoted to admiral (1919), he retired in 1921.

Truman, Harry S (1884–1972) President of the United States (1945–53). Truman sought admission to West Point but was turned down because of his poor eyesight. Family commitments prevented him from attending college. After the United States entered World War I (April 1917), he fought in France as a captain in the field artillery. Following the war he entered Democratic party politics and was elected U.S. senator from Missouri (1934). Chosen by President Franklin D. Roosevelt as his running mate in the 1944 elections, he was elected vice president. He succeeded Roosevelt on the latter's death (12 April 1945).

Truman was president at a momentous time and did not shrink from exercising responsibility. He attended the Potsdam Conference (July 1945) and made the decision to employ the atomic bomb against Japan (August 1945). Reacting to the beginnings of the Cold War, he proclaimed the Truman Doctrine to aid

Greece and Turkey (1947), and he supported the Containment doctrine, the Marshall Plan, the 1948–49 Berlin Airlift, and the formation of the North Atlantic Treaty Organization (1949). Re-elected president (1948), his most difficult foreign policy decision came in 1950 when he committed U.S. forces to the defense of the Republic of Korea following the North Korean invasion (June). He also recognized the State of Vietnam and extended direct military aid to the French during the 1946–54 Indo-China War. He was succeeded by President Dwight D. Eisenhower (January 1953).

Truscott, Lucian King, Jr. (1895–1965) U.S. general. Truscott taught school in Oklahoma for six years before enlisting in the army after U.S. entry into World War I (April 1917). Commissioned in the cavalry out of officer's training camp, he served in Hawaii (1919–21), then with the 1st Cavalry Regiment (1922–25). He was promoted major following graduation from the Cavalry School (1926), where he then taught (1926–31). Following service with 3rd Cavalry (1931–34), he was promoted lieutenant colonel and graduated from the Command and General Staff School (1936), where he then taught. He was then in the 13th Armored Regiment (1940) and IX Corps (July 1941). Promoted temporary colonel (December), then temporary brigadier general (May 1942), he was assigned to Lord Louis Mountbatten's Allied Combined Operations staff. He then created and trained a U.S. commando unit, the Rangers, leading them in the Dieppe raid (August 1942).

Promoted major general (October), Truscott then participated in Operation TORCH, the Allied invasion of North Africa (8 November). Briefly on General Dwight Eisenhower's staff, he commanded 3rd Infantry Division (March 1943) in North Africa, the invasion of Sicily (July), and to reinforce at Salerno, Italy (September). After additional combat in Italy, he led his division in the amphibious assault at Anzio (January 1944).

Truscott succeeded General John Lucas in command of VI Corps at Anzio (February) and took part in the liberation of Rome (May–June). His VI Corps then participated in Operation DRAGOON, the invasion of southern France (August 1944). Promoted lieutenant general (September), he commanded Fifth Army in Italy (December 1944–October 1945). He replaced General George Patton as commander of Third Army in Bavaria (October). He returned to the U.S. (May 1946) and retired (October 1947). He was promoted general on the retired list in July 1951.

Ts'ai O (Cai E) (1882–1916) Chinese warlord. Ts'ai fought in the Westernized armies of the late Chi'ng (Qing) period and rapidly advanced to command a brigade (1911). He was then an instructor at Yunnan Military Academy. A supporter of the 1913 Second Revolution, he was lured to Peking (Beijing) by General and Provisional President Yüan Shih-k'ai (Yuan Shikai) and arrested. He escaped (November 1915) and returned to Yunnan by way of Japan and Vietnam. He then formed an army to resist Yüan's attempt to become emperor, and he then proclaimed the independence of Yunnan from Yüan's government (December). He was joined in this effort by leaders in Kweichow (Guizhou) and Kwangsi (Guangxi) provinces when they refused to move against him (January 1916), whereupon Yüan gave up his efforts to become emperor. Ts'ai died shortly after he became governor of Szechwan (Sichuan) (1916).

Ts'ao K'un (Cao Kun) (1862–1928) Chinese general and political leader. Ts'ao joined the imperial armies and was selected for officer training. He was commissioned on graduation from the Paoting (Baoding) Military Academy. He then served in General Yüan Shih-k'ai's (Yuan

Shikai) Peiyang army near Peking (Beijing). As commander of 3rd Division (1906), he helped Yüan become president (1911–12). After Yüan's death (1916), as military governor of Chihli province he supported efforts by Feng Kuo-chang (Feng Guozhang) to reunite China under the Peiyang warlord clique. He supported Tuan Ch'i-ju's (Duan Qirui) successful overthrow of the brief restoration of Henry Pu-yi as emperor (July 1917) but opposed Tuan's decision to bring China into World War I (August 1918), splitting the Peiyang clique and bringing Tuan's resignation (November).

Ts'ao resigned as general but remained governor of Chihli, gaining the presidency of China through bribery (October 1923), which brought scattered fighting throughout China. He remained in power thanks to the support of former subordinate Wu P'ei-fu. When Wu's subordinate Feng Yü-hsiang mutinied, he was placed under house arrest (October 1924) but was released on the pledge that he retire from public life (1926).

Tsuji, Masanobu (1903–68) Japanese army officer. Tsuji graduated from the War College (1929) then was a Military Academy instructor. Posted to the Kwantung Army in Manchuria as a major, he saw action in fighting with the Soviet Union (1939). His over-attention to planning was a principal reason for the debacle at Nomonhan. He then joined the Eleventh Army staff at Hankow, China. Known as a brilliant staff officer, he was also notorious in his fanaticism and ruthlessness.

Tsuji became General Tomoyuki Yamashita's chief on Formosa (November 1940), helping to plan the brilliant Malaya campaign and winning promotion to colonel. Assigned to General Masaharu Homma's Fourteenth Army in the Philippines (February 1942), he issued orders to field commanders and played a key role in the conquest of Bataan. He is said to have countermanded Homma's orders and have been primarily responsible for the inhuman treatment of American POWs in the Bataan Death March.

Tsuji was then on Guadalcanal (October 1942) and had a key role in sending the 2nd Division there and in the failed counter-offensive. Recalled to Tokyo for staff duty (November), he returned to China (August 1943), then went to Burma to Thirty-Third Army (Spring 1944). At the end of the war he joined Masatake Terauchi's Southern Army headquarters in Saigon, but escaped to advise the Chinese Nationalists against the Communists. He returned to Japan (1949), was elected to the lower house of Parliament, wrote books, and then disappeared in North Vietnam (1961).

Tuan Ch'i-jui (Duan Qirui) (1865–1936) Chinese warlord. Tuan graduated from the Paoting (Baoding) Military Academy and fought in the 1894–95 Sino-Japanese War. He then joined General Yüan Shih-k'ai's (Yuan Shikai) Northern Army as a senior officer, married Yüan's adopted daughter, and ultimately commanded three of the army's six divisions. He helped secure the emperor's abdication (January 1912) and was war minister and then acting premier on Yüan becoming president (September). He helped suppress the 1913 Second Revolution but refused to support Yüan as emperor or to lead an army against Ts'ai O's (Cai E) National Protection Army (1916). Following Yuan's death (June), he was premier in President Li Yüan-hung's (Li Yuanhang) government (1916–18), helping to reunify China under the Peiyang generals. He brought about China's entry into World War I on the Allied side (August 1918). Subduing Hunan, he failed to reward 3rd Division commander Ts'ao K'un, creating a split in the Peiyang (Northern) clique. His efforts to create a Northern Army failed on defeat of his forces by Ts'ao and his supporter Wu P'ei-fu (Wu Peifu) July 1920). He was then forced to retire (1924) after the defeat of Wu P'ei-fu by

Chang Tso-lin (Chang Zuolin) and Feng Yü-hsiang (Feng Yuxiang).

Tukhachevsky, Mikhail Nicolaevich (1893–1937) Marshal of the Soviet Union. Commissioned on graduation from the Alexandrovski Military Academy in Moscow (1914), Tukhachevsky was taken prisoner in World War I (February 1915) but escaped and returned to Russia (1917). After the war he joined the Red Army, and, as a protégé of Leon Trotsky, commanded the First Army, then Eighth and Fifth Armies in the Civil War.

Appointed supreme commander in the west (April 1920), Tukhachevsky led the invasion of Poland in the 1920 Russo-Polish War. At a critical point in the Battle of Warsaw (August 1920), Josef Stalin withheld troops, allowing the Poles to defeat the offensive. Tukhachevsky then put down the Kronstadt Rebellion (March 1921) and was CofS of the army (1926–27). After a fall from favor, he became director of armaments (1931) and was promoted marshal of the Soviet Union (1935).

Tukhachevsky promoted development of combined arms warfare with mechanized and airborne forces operating in conjunction with aircraft. He saw clearly the nature of the German threat and called for a few areas to be lightly held with the bulk of the Red Army remaining back for subsequent deep penetration operations. Stalin disregarded his ideas. Arrested on charges of treason (June 1937), he was tried and executed the same day. A 1956 investigation concluded that the charges against him were fabricated. His tank corps organization was done away with on his death but was revived after the German invasion and became the basis of Soviet fighting doctrine in World War II and beyond.

Tunner, William Henry (1906–83) U.S. air force general. Commissioned on graduation from West Point (1928), Tunner became an army aviator (1929). At the beginning of World War II he commanded the Ferry

Division, Air Transport Command (ATC), ferrying planes to Europe (January 1942). Promoted brigadier general (1943), he then commanded the India-China Division of ATC and was responsible for the resupply of China from India over the "Hump" (1943–45).

After the war, Tunner commanded the Continental, then the Atlantic Divisions of ATC (1946–48). As an Air Force major general, he was deputy commander of the Military Air Transport Service (MATS) and was temporarily assigned to command the 1848–49 Berlin Airlift. At the beginning of the 1950–53 Korean War, he had charge of Combat Air Command, with responsibility for the aerial resupply of U.S. and other United Nations forces in Korea (1950–52). He briefly commanded Air Matériel Command (1952), then was CinC, U.S. Air Force in Europe (1952–57). He commanded MATS (1958–60) and then retired as a lieutenant general (May 1960).

Tupolev, Andrei Nikolaevich (1888–1972) Russian aircraft designer. Tupolev studied aeronautics at the Moscow Technical High School under Nikolai Zhukovski. Arrested for anti-tsarist activity (1911), he was released and worked at the Dax aircraft factory in Moscow. Following the 1917 Bolshevik Revolution he was rewarded for his pre-war revolutionary activities by being made chairman of the Special Committee for Heavy Aviation. After persuading Bolshevik leader Vladimir Lenin to create the Central Aerodynamics and Hydrodynamics Research Institute in Moscow, he was its director (1918–35). This Institute produced all leading Russian aviation designers. He benefited greatly from construction at the secret German Junkers aircraft facility in Moscow, built to circumvent a prohibition on military aviation imposed on Germany by the 1919 Treaty of Versailles.

Tupolev's ANT-2 monoplane was Russia's first all-metal airplane. His TB-3 (ANT-6) was operational in 1930 but went out of production in 1936. His SB-2 (ANT-40) all-metal, twin-engine bomber was successfully tested in the 1936–39 Spanish Civil War.

Arrested in the Great Purges (1938) along with many other aircraft designers, Tupolev was charged with passing technical secrets abroad. He and the other designers continued their work in prison. He designed both the Tu-7 strategic bomber and the Tu-2 twin-engine ground support dive bomber. Freed in late 1941, he participated in the design of such aircraft as the Tu-14 jet bomber, the Tu-95 turboprop bomber and the Tu-104, Tu-124, and Tu-134 transport aircraft.

Turner, Richmond Kelly (1885–1961) U.S. admiral. Turner graduated from Annapolis (1908) and was commissioned (1910). He attended the Naval Ordnance School (1915–16) and was a gunnery officer during World War I. He then served as an ordnance design officer at the Washington Navy Yard. He became a naval aviator (1927) and commanded the Asiatic Fleet air squadron. His next assignments included heading the Plans Division of the Bureau of Ordnance, advisor to the 1932 Geneva disarmament Conference, attendance at the Naval War College and head of its Strategic Section (1936–38), and director of the War Plans Division of the Navy Department (1940–42). He was promoted rear admiral (January 1941).

Turner took command of amphibious forces in the South Pacific (July 1942) and oversaw the landings on Guadalcanal (August). Though exonerated, he had command during the Battle of Savo Island (August), the worst defeat in U.S. naval history. He then directed the naval offensive in the Solomons and was promoted to command Fifth Amphibious Force (1943–45), which grew to 495 ships. As such he was responsible for the planning and execution of landings on Makin, Tarawa, Kwajalein, Eniwetok, Saipan, Guam, Tinian, Iwo Jima, and Okinawa.

He was promoted vice admiral (February 1944) and then admiral (May 1945) and had charge of planning Operation OLYMPIC, the projected invasion of Japan. Following the war he served as naval representative to the United Nations Military Committee until his retirement in July 1947.

Twining, Nathan Farragut (1897–1982) U.S. air force general. Twining joined the National Guard and saw service on the Mexican border before entering West Point (1917). He completed its shortened wartime course (November 1918) and was commissioned in the infantry. He served in the occupation of Germany (1918–19), then graduated from the Infantry School, Fort Benning (1920). He attended Flying School at Brooks Field (1923–24) and transferred to the Army Air Service (1926). After service as an instructor, he was with tactical air units in Hawaii and Texas. Promoted captain (1935), he graduated from Air Corps Tactical School (1936) and the Command and General Staff School, Fort Leavenworth (1937). Promoted to major (1940), he was then in the office of the Chief of the Air Corps (1940–41).

Most of Twining's World War II service was in strategic bombing. Promoted brigadier general, he was CofS of Army Air Forces in the South Pacific (August 1942), then commander of Thirteenth Air Force on New Caledonia (January 1943). Promoted major general (February), he provided air support for operations in the South Pacific (1942–43). He then commanded Fifteenth Air Force in Italy (1944–45), supporting operations in Italy but also striking targets in Germany, Austria, and the Balkans, including the Romanian oil fields. He also provided cover for the invasion of southern France (August 1944). Promoted temporary lieutenant general (June 1945), he commanded Twentieth Air Force (August), carrying out the final bombing of Japan, including the two atomic bombs in August.

After the war, Twining headed the Army Matériel Command at Wright Field (1945–47), then the Alaskan Command (1947–50). He became deputy CofS of the air force (May 1950). Promoted full general and appointed air force vice CofS (October), he became CofS (1953–57), then chairman of the Joint Chiefs of Staff (1957–60) before retiring (September 1960).

Tyrwhitt, Sir Reginald Yorke (1870–1951) British admiral. Tyrwhitt entered the navy (1883) and rose to commander of destroyer flotillas in the First Fleet (1913), a position he held until 1918. During World War I his two destroyer flotillas of 35–40 destroyers and 3–7 light cruisers formed a powerful group, known from its base as the "Harwick Force". His responsibilities included patrolling the southern portion of the North Sea and assisting the Grand Fleet in its sweeps. His force sank a German minelayer in the Thames estuary (5 August 1914), the first naval action in the North Sea; it also played a major role in the action at the Dogger Bank (January 1915). It also covered naval seaplane raids on Zeppelin sheds at Cuxhaven.

Tyrwhitt was a natural leader and one of the outstanding British fighting admirals of the war. He continually argued for more offensive action. His Harwich Force lost two cruisers and fourteen destroyers, and he and his men earned the reputation of having spent more time at sea and having engaged in more actions than any other naval force of the war. Created a baronet (1919), he commanded 3rd Light Cruiser Squadron in the Mediterranean (1921–22). Promoted vice admiral (1925), he was CinC, China Station (1927–29). Promoted admiral (1929), he commanded at the Nore (1930–33). In 1934 he became principal naval aide-de-camp to the king.

U

Udet, Ernst (1896–1941) German air force general. Udet entered the army in 1914 and later became a pilot and rose to command 11th Fighter Squadron in Manfred von Richthofen's elite 1st Fighter Group. At the end of the war, with sixty-two victories, he was the second leading German ace. After the war Udet worked as a stunt pilot and in the film industry, which took him around the world. He joined the Luftwaffe as a colonel (1935). His close friend General Hermann Göring placed him in increasingly more responsible positions, ultimately making him director general of equipment and head of the Office of Air Armament (February 1939) as a major general.

Udet had charge of setting parameters for aircraft and then selecting for production those types that met these requirements. Impressed with dive bombers, he championed them and medium bombers and fighters at the expense of heavy bombers. While he was a brilliant pilot, he was utterly lacking in administrative and organizational skills, and he impeded development of the Luftwaffe.

In 1941 General Erhard Milch, Udet's friend, blamed him for Luftwaffe matériel shortcomings in the 1940 Battle of Britain. This and attacks by Göring, along with fears that he would be soon removed from his post, led him to commit suicide. The German press reported it as an accident.

Ueda, Kenkichi (1875–1962) Japanese general. Ueda graduated from the Military Academy (1898) and Army Staff College (1908). He served as a staff officer in the Siberian Expeditonary Army (1918–19), then was promoted colonel (1919) and commanded a regiment (1923–24). Promoted major general (1924), he commanded a cavalry brigade (1924–25). As a lieutenant general (1928), he commanded the China Garrison Army (1920–30). He then commanded 9th Division (1930–32) in fighting in Shanghai in reaction to the Japanese takeover of Manchuria (1932). He lost a leg in a bomb blast in May.

Appointed vice chief of the General Staff (1933–34), Ueda then commanded the Korea Army (1934–35). Promoted general (1935), he commanded the Kwantung Army in Manchuria (1935–39) and supported militant policies toward the Russians in Siberia that brought fighting at Nomonhan (May–August 1939) and his dismissal and retirement in 1939.

Uehara, Yūsaku (1856–1933) Japanese field marshal. Commissioned in the engineers on graduation from the Military Academy (1879), Uehara studied in France (1881–85). He fought in the 1894–95 Sino-Japanese War but not in major actions. Promoted major general (1900), he fought in the 1904–05 Russo-Japanese War as CofS to General Michitsura Nozu during the siege of Port Arthur (June 1894–January 1895). While army minister (1912), he resigned his post, leading to the fall of the government and the precedent of army/navy veto power over governments.

Uehara was then inspector general of training (1915). As army CofS (1915–24) he defied the government's desire to leave Siberia (1919–22). Promoted field marshal (1925), he was a military councillor and helped block technical innovation over spiritual training. His positions led the way for the Imperial War faction in the military during the 1930s.

Ugaki, Matome (1890–1945) Japanese admiral. A graduate of the Naval Academy (1920), Ugaki was promoted lieutenant commander upon graduating from the Naval Staff College (1924). He was then resident officer in Germany (1928–30). Promoted captain, he was an instructor at the Naval Staff College (1932–35). He was then a staff officer with the Combined Fleet (1935–36) and commanded a cruiser, and then a battleship (1936–38).

Promoted rear admiral (1938), Ugaki was CofS to Combined Fleet commander Admiral Isoroku Yamamoto (1941–43). Promoted vice admiral, he commanded Admiral Takeo Kurita's Battleship Division in the Battle of Leyte Gulf (October 1944). He fought in battles in the Sibuyan Sea (24 October) and off Samar (24 October). He then commanded Fifth Air Fleet on the Japanese home island of Kyushu, then all naval aircraft there (June 1945). When he learned of the emperor's plan to surrender, he stripped off his insignia of rank and led a final *kamikaze* raid against U.S. ships, but his planes disappeared without trace (15 August).

Umberto, Prince of Naples and of Piedmont (1904–83) Marshal of Italy. Crown Prince Umberto, only son of King Victor Emmanuel III, was educated at the Royal Military Academy at Turin and rose rapidly in the military to the post of Inspector General of Infantry. On Italy's entry into World War II (10 June 1940), he commanded the Army of the Alps along the French frontier. Although it greatly outnumbered the French defenders, this force performed abysmally in its invasion of southeastern France.

Advanced by Benito Mussolini to marshal of Italy (October 1942), Umberto changed sides and was lieutenant general of the realm following Mussolini's overthrow (25 July 1943). He became regent after the Allies captured Rome and his father was obliged to step down (June 1944). When his father formally abdicated, he succeeded to the throne briefly as Umberto II (May–June 1946). Following a close vote against the monarchy in a national plebiscite (North Italy voted for a republic, while the South heavily favored keeping the crown), Umberto (known as the May King) went into exile in Portugal as count of Sarre.

Umezu, Yoshijirō (1882–1949) Japanese general. Umezu graduated from the Military Academy (1903) and the Army Staff College (1911). He fought in the 1904–05 Russo-Japanese War. Promoted captain (1912), he was resident officer in Germany (1913–14) and Denmark (1914–17). Promoted major (1918), he was military attaché in Switzerland (1919–21). He then served on the General Staff and in the Army Ministry (1921–24). Promoted colonel (1924), he commanded a regiment (1924–26) before returning to the General Staff (1926–28).

Promoted major general (1930), Umezu commanded the China Garrison Army (1934) and concluded the Ho-Umezu Agreement that favored Japan in north China (June 1935). Promoted lieutenant general (August), he became vice minister of war after the February 1936 Insurrection (1936–39). He then commanded the Kwantung Army in Manchuria and was ambassador plenipotentiary to Manchukuo

(1939– 42) and was promoted general (August 1939).

Umezu became CofS of the army when Hideki Tōjō was ousted from both that post and as prime minister (July 1944). An opponent of surrender, he grudgingly accepted Emperor Hirohito's decision and was among the delegation signing the formal surrender terms aboard the battleship *Missouri* (2 September 1945). Tried and convicted of war crimes, he died of cancer a year into his life sentence.

Upham, Charles Hazlett (1908–94) New Zealand officer. Upham is noteworthy as having won the Victoria Cross twice, both times during World War II. The first occasion came on Crete (May 1941) while he was a second lieutenant in 20th Battalion, 2nd New Zealand Expeditionary Force. Twice wounded, he nonetheless carried a comrade to safety when his unit was forced to withdraw and, some days later, killed twenty-two Germans at Sphakia, fighting off an attack.

Captain Upham won the bar to his Victoria Cross at Ruweisat Ridge in the Western Desert, North Africa (July 1942). Twice wounded, he refused evacuation to remain with his men. He then led his company in an attack in which he personally knocked out a German tank and several artillery pieces with hand grenades. His arm broken by machine gun fire, he continued to press the attack until he collapsed from lack of blood.

Urquhart, Robert Elliott (1901–88) British general. Educated at St. Paul's school, Urquhart was commissioned in the Highland Light Infantry (1920). During World War II, he fought in North Africa with the 51st Highland Division. He then commanded 231st Brigade in the invasions of Sicily (July 1943) and Italy (September). Promoted major general (1943), he took command of the 1st Airborne (the "Red Devils") Division, his first assignment with airborne troops. He led the division

into Arnhem in The Netherlands during Operation MARKET-GARDEN (September 1944), the attempt to secure access to north Germany across the Rhine and win the war that year. The operation failed for a variety of reasons beyond his control, and he was eventually able to withdraw only about a quarter of his 10,000-man force. He then commanded the Territorial Army and landed in Norway at the end of the war (May 1945) with British and Norwegian airborne troops.

After the war Urquhart commanded British troops in Austria and was CinC in Malaya (1950–52) during the height of the insurgency there. He retired from the military in 1957.

Ushijima, Mitsuru (1887–1945) Japanese general. Ushijima graduated from the Military Academy (1908) and Army Staff College (1918). He served on the staff of the Siberian Expeditionary Army (1918–19), then was an instructor at the Infantry School (1920–24). Promoted major (1924) and colonel (1930), he directed the Toyama Military School (1932). He commanded a regiment (1936–37) and was promoted major general (1937), then commanded an infantry brigade (1937–39), taking part in the siezure of Nanking (Nanjing). Promoted lieutenant general, he commanded 11th Infantry Division (1939–41).

During World War II Ushijima led his division in fighting in Burma (1942). He then commanded the Military Academy (1943–43). As commander of Thirty-Second Army on Okinawa (1943), he oversaw the construction of powerful inland defenses there and then commanded all land forces on the island against the U.S. Tenth Army invasion (April–June 1945), committing ritual suicide at the end of the battle.

Ustinov, Dimitry Fedorovich (1908–84) Soviet marshal and armaments minister. Ustinov graduated from vocational school (1927) and from the Institute of Military

Mechanical Engineering (1934). He worked as a design engineer and became director of a plant producing armaments for Soviet forces in the 1939–40 Russo-Finnish War. His efficient management attracted the attention of Joseph Stalin, who made him commissar (minister) of armaments just after the German invasion of the Soviet Union (22 June 1941). As armaments minister, he dramatically increased production of tanks and other military matériel. Commissioned colonel general of military engineers (1944), he continued as minister of armaments well after the war, until 1957.

An enthusiastic supporter of the space program, Ustinov was key factor in the successful launching of the first man into space, Yuri Gagarin (1961). Appointed minister of defense, he was that same year (1976) promoted marshal of the Soviet Union. He was responsible for the deployment of troops to Afghanistan (1979) and remained minister of defense until his death in 1984.

V

Van Deventer, Sir Louis Jacob (1874–1922)
Boer and South African cavalry officer.
"Japie" Van Deventer led mounted rifle-
men against the British in the 1899–1902
Anglo-Boer War. At the beginning of
World War I, as a colonel he led a South
African brigade against the Germans in
Southwest Africa. Adept at fast-paced
movements, he was promoted brigadier
general (1915) and he and his brigade were
transferred to fight against German East
Africa. In the course of this campaign, he
was promoted major general and com-
manded a division. Knighted (early 1917),
he took control of the British East African
Expeditionary Force, pursuing remnants of
German Major General Paul von Lettow-
Vorbeck's forces until the end of the war.
He retired in 1919.

Van Fleet, James Alward (1892–1992)
U.S. general. Commissioned in the infantry on graduation from West Point (1915),
Van Fleet then served on the Mexican
border. During World War I he went to
France with the AEF (July 1918) and saw
combat in command of a machine gun
battalion in the Meuse–Argonne offensive
(September–November).

After the war, Van Fleet was a Reserve
Officer Training Corps instructor and
studied and taught at the Infantry School.
Promoted colonel (February 1941) and
took command of the 8th Infantry Regiment, 4th Infantry Division. He distin-

guished himself in the capture of
Cherbourg (June 1944). Promoted brigadier general (July) and major general
(November), he commanded 90th Division, leading it in the siege of Metz and
the Ardennes counter-offensive. He commanded III Corps of First Army in the
breakout from the Remagen bridgehead
and in the subsequent campaign in central
Germany.

Promoted lieutenant general, he headed
the military advisory group in Greece
(1948), where he helped train the Greek
army to fight against the Communists in
the civil war. He then commanded Second
Army. During the 1950–53 Korean War
he took command of Eighth Army in
Korea (April 1951). His troops defeated
the Chinese spring offensive and then
launched a counterattack.

An effective and resourceful commander, Van Fleet nonetheless protested
against restrictions placed on the conduct
of the war in Korea. He left Korea
(February 1953) and retired two months
later as a full general.

Vandegrift, Alexander Archer (1887–1973)
U.S. Marine Corps general. Vandegrift
attended the University of Virginia
(1906–08) before enlisting in the Marines
(1908). Commissioned (1909), he spent
most of the next fifteen years on assignments in the Carribbean. He was then in
staff assignments at Quantico, Virginia

(1923–26). He served in China (1927–28) before returning to the United States, where he helped draft the training manual that laid out Marine amphibious doctrine used in World War II. He was again in China (1935–37), then returned to Washington as secretary and assistant to Marine Corps commandant General Thomas Holcomb (1937–41) and was promoted brigadier general (1940).

Assigned to the 1st Marine Division (November 1941), Vandegrift took command of it (March 1942), leading it in the first U.S. offensive of the war on Tulagi and Guadalcanal in the Pacific. In fierce fighting, the division managed to hold Henderson Field against Japanese attacks and Vandegrift was awarded the Medal of Honor. Promoted lieutenant general (July 1943), he headed I Corps during landings at Bougainville (November).

Vandegrift returned to the U.S. to become Marine Corps commandant (November 1944). He became the first Marine officer to become full general while on active service (March 1945). As commandant, he oversaw the rapid expansion of the Corps and its demobilization after the war, when he also fought hard to preserve the Corps as a distinct combat arm. He retired in December 1947.

Vandenburg, Hoyt Sanford (1899–1954) U.S. Air Force general. Vandenburg graduated from West Point (1923) and was assigned to the air service. An outstanding pilot, in 1927 he was a flight instructor at the Air Corps Primary Flying School, March Field, California. He held a variety of command and instructor positions, and he graduated from the Air Corps Tactical School (1936), the Command and General Staff School (1936), and the Army War College (1939). He was then assigned to the plans division of Air Corps Headquarters in Washington. Following U.S. entry into World War II he was promoted colonel.

Appointed CofS of Twelfth Air Force (August 1942), Vandenburg helped plan air aspects of the Allied invasion of North Africa. Promoted brigadier general (December 1942), he became CofS of the Northwest Africa Strategic Air Force but returned to Washington (August 1943) as deputy chief of the Air Staff. Promoted major general (March 1944), he joined General Dwight Eisenhower's staff to help plan the Allied invasion of France. He then headed Ninth Air Force, the world's largest tactical air armada. His exemplary performance won him promotion to lieutenant general (March 1945).

After the end of the war in Europe, Vandenburg became assistant CofS for operations for Army Air Forces. He then became chief of the intelligence division of the General Staff (January 1946), and headed the Central Intelligence Group, forerunner of the CIA (June). He was then vice CofS of the newly independent Air Force (September 1947). Promoted general, he succeeded General Carl Spaatz as Air Force CofS (July 1948) and oversaw U.S. Air Force participation in the 1948–49 Berlin Airlift and the 1950–53 Korean War. He retired in June 1953.

Vasilevsky, Aleksandr Mikhailovich (1895–1977) Marshal of the Soviet Union. Vasilevsky attended seminary before becoming an army officer. He joined the Red Army (1919) as a captain and was deputy commander of a rifle regiment during the 1918–20 Civil War. After commanding a rifle regiment, he was chief of the combat training department (1931–34). Following graduation from the General Staff Academy (1937), he was chief of the operations training section of the General Staff (1937–39). Allowed to join the Communist party (1938), he was then deputy chief of operations (1939–40) before heading the operations directorate (late June 1940). Encouraged in this by Joseph Stalin, he spent a third of his time visiting the front, more than any Stavka representative save Georgi Zhukov.

Vasilevsky succeeded General Boris Shaposhnikov as chief of the General Staff

(June 1942) and was promoted marshal of the Soviet Union (February 1943). A master of operational planning, he coordinated the 1st Baltic and 3rd Belorussian Fronts while Zhukov did the same for the 1st and 2nd Belorussian Fronts to the south.

On the death of Ivan Chernyakovsky, Vasilevsky took over as commander of his 3rd Belorussian Front. He then directed military operations against the Japanese. Replacing General Alexi Antonov as chief of the General Staff (November 1948), he then became defense minister (March 1949) and was then first deputy minister of defense until his retirement (1953–December 1957).

Vatutin, Nikolai Fedorovich (1901–44) Soviet general. Too young for World War I, Vatutin joined the Red Army (1920) and fought in the 1918–20 Civil War. He joined the Communist party (1921) and graduated from the Poltava Infantry School (1922), the Frunze Military Academy (1929), and the General Staff Academy (1937). He then became CofS, first of the Kiev Military District (1937–39), then of the Ukrainian Front. After distinguished service on the General Staff, he was promoted lieutenant general.

Following the German invasion of the Soviet Union (22 June 1941), Vatutin became chief of staff first of the Northwestern Front, then of the Kalinin Front, before returning to the Northwestern Front (July 1941–May 1942). He then became deputy chief of the General Staff (May–July), then commander of the Voronezh Front (July). One of the top Russian field commanders of the war, he then took charge of the Southwestern Front at Stalingrad (October) and commanded Russian forces in the outer encirclement ring of the German Sixth Army there (February), fighting off attacks by the German Fourth Panzer Army.

Promoted general of the army (February), Vatutin led an advance in Ukraine and took over the Voronezh Front until it became the 1st Ukrainian Front (October 1943). He held off the German attack in the Battle of Kursk (July 1943) and then counterattacked to take Kharkov and Kiev (January 1944). He died of wounds sustained in a Ukrainian ambush in February 1944.

Vian, Sir Philip Louis (1894–1968) British admiral. Vian graduated from the Royal Naval College, Dartmouth (1911) and served on destroyers in World War I. Following a variety of assignments, when World War II began (September 1939) he commanded 4th Destroyer Flotilla, Rosyth.

Modest, yet one of Britain's most aggressive and effective commanders in the war, Vian undertook the raid on the *Altmark*, a German supply ship servicing the pocket battleship *Graf Spee*. This stroke (16 February 1940), carried out in Norwegian territorial waters in Jossing Fjord, freed 299 British prisoners of war. He also destroyed a German convoy off Norway (October) and played a key role in sinking the battleship *Bismarck*, his desroyers scoring several torpedo hits (night of 26–27 May 1941). Promoted rear admiral (July), he commanded Task Force K in the Norwegian Sea, attacking German Arctic facilities and evacuating civilians from Spitzbergen.

Vian commanded 15th Cruiser Squadron in the Mediterranean (September), protecting convoys bound for Malta. He fought the Battle of Sirte (March 1942) against a larger Italian force and got his convoy through, for which he was knighted. Commanding a carrier force, he supported landings at Sicily (July 1943), Salerno (September), and Normandy (6 June 1944). Transferred to the Pacific, he commanded the British Carrier Task Force off Okinawa (1945).

After the war, Vian was fifth sea lord in charge of naval aviation (1946). He then commanded the Home Fleet (1950–52). Promoted admiral of the fleet (1952), he retired that same year.

Vietinghoff genannt Scheel, Heinrich Gottfried von (1887–1952) German general. Commissioned in the Prussian Guards (1907), he was later a staff officer. He became first commander of the 5th Panzer Division (1938) and led it in the invasion of Poland (September). Promoted lieutenant general (June 1940), he led XLVI Panzer Corps in the invasions of Yugoslavia (April 1941) and the Soviet Union (June). He then led Ninth Army in the U.S.S.R. before commanding Fifteenth Army along the English Channel.

After the Allied conquest of Sicily, Vietinghoff took command of the new Tenth Army in Italy (August 1943). Promoted full general (September), he conducted a masterful withdrawal to the Gustav Line. Following the injury of Field Marshal Albert Kesselring (October 1944), he was acting commander of Army Group C (October–January 1945). On Kesselring's return, he temporarily commanded Army Group Kurland in Latvia (January–March) but was unsuccessful in evacuating the Latvian pocket. Returning to Italy, he succeeded Kesselring as supreme German commander there (March 1945), surrendering to the Allies on 2 May 1945.

Villa, Pancho (1878–1923) Mexican revolutionary general. A controversial figure, his followers considered him a modern-day Robin Hood who took from the rich to give to the poor. More dispassionate observers saw him as a bandit who raped and killed at will.

Following the overthrow of Mexican dictator General Victoriano Huerta, Villa became governor of Chihuahua state. He was one of three principal leaders who claimed power, along with Emiliano Zapata and General Venustiano Carranza, who had the strongest claim to be president. Following U.S. recognition of Carranza's government (1916), Villa saw himself losing out and sought to embroil his country with the United States. He caused the murder of seventeen American mining engineers in Mexico (January 1916) and then raided Columbus, New Mexico (March), setting fire to it and killing sixteen people.

U.S. President Woodrow Wilson then ordered 6,000 men under General John J. Pershing to pursue Villa some 300 miles into Mexico (April 1916). Villa escaped and the incursion almost brought war with the Carranza government. With war with Germany looming, Wilson pulled all American troops out of the country (February 1917) without taking Villa, who nonetheless did much indirectly to prepare the U.S. military for World War I. Villa was later murdered by his political enemies.

Vlasov, Andrei Andreyevich (1900–46) Soviet general. Vlasov joined the Red Army (1919) during the Russian Civil War, distinguishing himself in the fighting in South Russia. He survived Josef Stalin's late 1930s purges of the military, perhaps because he was military attaché to China.

Following the German invasion of the Soviet Union (June 1941), Vlasov commanded Thirty-Seventh Army at Kiev, eluding the German encirclement. He fought in the Battle of Moscow (December) and commanded the new Twentieth Shock Army that pushed the Germans back. As reward, he was promoted lieutenant general and made a Hero of the Soviet Union (January 1942). He was then charged with relieving besieged Leningrad. Permission from Stalin to withdraw came too late and most of his force was cut off and killed or captured. Vlasov chose to stay with his troops and was taken prisoner.

Vlasov's hatred of Stalin was evident, and certain elements within the German Army attempted to enlist him to raise an army to fight against Stalin's regime. He became head of the Russian Liberation Army, which was doomed from the start as Hitler refused to promise a Russian state after the war. Although hundreds of thousands of Russians served the German

Army as auxiliaries during the war, many simply to stay alive, there was no independent Russian force fighting in alliance with Germany. Captured in Czechoslovakia (May 1945), he was turned over to the Russians. Returned to the Soviet Union, he was tried on charges of treason, convicted, and executed.

Vô Nguyên Giáp (1912–) Vietnamese general. Giáp was expelled from high school, then worked as a journalist and joined the Communist party. Arrested by the French, he served two years in prison (1930–32), then finished his studies at the Lycée Albert Sarraut (1934) and graduated from the Hanoi University law school (1938).

During World War II Giap worked closely with Indo-China Communist party leader Ho Chi Minh to form the Viêt Minh, which he led in the long struggle against the Japanese and the French. He employed Mao Tse-tung's (Mao Zedong) theories of revolutionary war but added an appreciation of the difficulties a democracy would face in fighting a protracted war. In 1946 he was promoted full general and commander of the People's Army of the Democratic Republic of Vietnam (PAVN). He directed the PAVN against the French during the 1946–54 Indo-China War, building it from a small guerrilla force into a large conventional army and winning the Battle of Diên Biên Phu (March–May 1954) that brought the end of the war.

In the 1960s and 1970s Giap led PAVN forces against the southern Republic of Vietnam and the Americans, although he opposed the 1968 Têt Offensive and the 1972 Easter Offensive. Although still defense minister, he did not direct the 1975 victory. Elevated to deputy prime minister (1976), he opposed the Vietnamese invasion of Cambodia (1978) and had little role in the 1979 war with China. He retired as minister of defense in 1986 and then lost his other government posts (1991).

Voronov, Nikolai Nikolaevich (1899–1968) Marshal of the Soviet Union. Voronov joined the Red Army (1918) and Communist party (1919). A specialist in artillery, during the 1918–20 Civil War he rose to command a battery. He was taken prisoner during the 1920 war with Poland. He then held a variety of assignments that included both battalion and regimental commands. A graduate of the Frunze Military Academy (1930), he became director of the Leningrad Artillery Officers School (1934–36). He was a military advisor to the Republican side in the 1936–39 Spanish Civil War and commanded the artillery of a front during the 1939–40 Russo-Finnish War. A favorite of Joseph Stalin, he was then chief of artillery of the Soviet Army, deputy commander of the artillery directorate, and commander of national air defense forces, as well as assistant commissar of defense.

As commander of artillery (1943), Voronov played a key role in planning all major campaigns. In order to maximize artillery effectiveness, he insisted on concentrating it rather than seeing it scattered among smaller units. He introduced both artillery divisions and artillery brigades for assault divisions, and he pushed mechanization. He was first of three officers promoted during the war to marshal of artillery (1943).

After the war Voronov became a champion of missiles and as president of the Academy of Artillery Sciences (1950–53), he oversaw the development of strategic nuclear weapons. He then commanded the Artillery Academy until his retirement (1958).

Vörös, János (1891–1968) Hungarian general. Commissioned in the artillery in the Austro-Hungarian Army in 1913, Vörös fought in World War I. After the war, he served in the army of the short-lived Hungarian Soviet Republic in its effort to retake lands lost to Romania and Czechoslovakia. He then attended the Hungarian Military Academy (1920–21), and joined the General Staff and rose to head one of its departments (November 1936–November 1940). He then commanded 2nd Motor Car Brigade. Promoted major general (May 1941), he was then chief of the Hungarian General Staff (August 1941). Promoted lieutenant general (February 1943), he then served in other posts. He was again chief of the General Staff (November 1943), then commanded II Corps, and was promoted colonel general (May 1944).

An opportunist, Vörös opposed resisting Germany's military occupation of Hungary (March 1944). Under German pressure, he also deserted Admiral Miklós Horthy when the latter sought to withdraw from the war (October). He then sided with the Soviets and became minister of defense in the Soviet-backed provisional national government (December 1944–February 1946). A victim of tightened Soviet control, Vörös was accused of treason, tried and convicted, and imprisoned (March 1949–June 1956). He was released just before the 1956 Hungarian Revolution.

Voroshilov, Kliment Yefremovich (1881–1963) Marshal of the Soviet Union. Born in humble circumstances, as a young man Voroshilov led a strike and was imprisoned (1899). Released, he joined the Bolshevik party (1903). Following the November 1917 Bolshevik *coup d'etat*, he fought in the 1918–20 Civil War as a "proletarian war leader," seeking to offset his lack of military knowledge by near-suicidal frontal attacks. His notable success was in fighting for Tsaritsyn (Stalingrad) (1918). He also fought in the 1920 Russo-Polish War, but on Stalin's orders failed to protect General Mikhail Tukhachevsky's flank.

Thanks to Stalin, he became commissar of defense (1925–40) and played a key role in the great purge of the military (1937). As commander of forces against Finland in the 1939–40 Winter War, he, as with all Russian leaders, grossly underrated Finnish endurance and ability. He was demoted after the war to deputy chairman of the defense committee (May 1940).

Voroshilov was the oldest Soviet military figure of World War II. As commander of the Northwest Front during the German invasion (22 June 1941), he had little success and was unable to stop the German encirclement of Leningrad. Replaced by Georgi Zhukov, he served the remainder of the war in staff positions. He held a number of political posts after the war but lost them all under Nikita Khrushchev (1960).

W

Wachi, Takaji (1893–1978) Japanese general. Wachi graduated from the Military Academy (1914) and Army Staff College (1922). He concentrated on Chinese affairs. In the China Section of the Army General Staff (1924–27), he was then military attaché at Tsinan (Jinan), China (1928–29). Promoted major (1929), he was serving as a staff officer with the Kwantung Army in Manchuria (1931–32) at the time of the Japanese conquest (September 1931–February 1932). After service as military attaché at Canton (Guangzhou) (1932–34), he was with the China Garrison Army (1935–36).

Wachi commanded a regiment at Tientsin (Tianjin) (1936–38) and was promoted colonel (1937). He helped create the Marco Polo Bridge Incident (7 July 1937) that led to the 1937–45 Sino-Japanese War. He then was with the Special Service Agency in Taiwan and China (1938–39) and a staff officer with the China Expeditionary Army (1939–40). Promoted major general, (1940), he was CofS to Fourteenth Army in the Philippines (1942–43).

Promoted lieutenant general (1943), Wachi was CofS for Southern Area Army (1943–45). He then commanded 164th Division in China (August). Tried for war crimes after the war, he was convicted and imprisoned (1945–50).

Waesche, Russell Randolph (1886–1946) U.S. Coast Guard admiral. Weasche attended Purdue University for a year before graduating from the Revenue Cutter Service School of Instruction (Coast Guard Academy) in 1906. He then held a variety of sea assignments and had his first command afloat (1912). He served in Coast Guard headquarters (1915–19), then held commands afloat (1920–27). He was Coast Guard chief ordnance officer (1928–32), then plans officer with the Navy Department War Plans Division (1932), then aide to the Coast Guard commandant (1932–36).

President Franklin Roosevelt appointed Waesche commandant (June 1936) with the rank of rear admiral. As commandant he carried out a number of reforms including integrating the Lighthouse Service into the Coast Guard, establishing the Coast Guard Institute and Correspondence School, and increasing the number of officers. Reappointed to a second term as commandant (1940) and promoted vice admiral (March 1942), he headed the Coast Guard during World War II, the period of its greatest expansion (to 250,000 men and women). In addition to its normal functions, the Coast Guard participated in all major invasions, escorted convoys, took part in anti-submarine patrols, sank twelve U-boats, and rescued survivors of sunken merchant ships.

Reappointed to a third term as commandant (1944), Waesche was promoted admiral (April 1945), the first Coast

Guard officer to attain that rank. He retired from the service after the war in January 1946.

Wainwright, Jonathan Mayhew IV (1883–1953) U.S. general. Commissioned in the cavalry on graduation from West Point (1906), Wainwright served in the U.S. and the Philippines. In World War I he rose to temporary lieutenant colonel and assistant CofS of 82nd Division in France.

After the war Wainwright reverted to the rank of captain and held a variety of posts and graduated from the Command and General Staff School (1931). Promoted brigadier general, he took command of the 1st Cavalry Brigade (1938). Promoted major general, he was sent to the Philippines to command the Philippine Division under General Douglas MacArthur (1940). He then commanded the North Luzon Force. Following the Japanese landings (December 1941), he delayed their advance to allow U.S. and Filipino defenders time to withdraw to Bataan. When MacArthur was ordered to Australia (March 1942), he was promoted lieutenant general and took command of U.S. forces in the Philippines.

Forced to surrender Corregidor (May), Wainwright was held in a succession of POW camps. Treated harshly, he maintained his dignity. Freed by the Russians in Manchuria, he attended the Japanese surrender ceremony (2 September 1945). Awarded the Medal of Honor, he commanded Fourth Army in the U.S. before retiring (1947).

Waldersee, Count Alfred von (1832–1904) German field marshal. Waldersee joined the Prussian General Staff during the 1866 Austro-Prussian War. He was military attaché in Paris, then aide de camp to King William I of Prussia (1869). During the 1870–71 Franco-German War he was CofS to the military governor of Paris (1871). Appointed quartermaster general of the General Staff (1882), he argued for

a "preventive war" against Russia. A close friend of Kaiser Wilhelm II, he was appointed chief of the German General Staff (1888), but his opposition to Admiral Alfred Tirpitz's naval construction program alienated the Kaiser and led to his replacement by General Alfred von Schlieffen (February 1891). Promoted field marshal, he commanded German troops sent to China to relieve the foreign legations besieged there during the 1900–01 Boxer Rebellion. He arrived too late (September 1900) to participate in serious fighting but conducted a number of punitive expeditions around Peking (Beijing) (September 1900–May 1901) before returning to Germany.

Walker, Frank Robinson (1899–1976) U.S. admiral. Walker graduated from Annapolis (1922) and held various commands in the 1920s and 1930s. He commanded a destroyer at Pearl Harbor during the Japanese attack (7 December 1941). Appointed to command Destroyer Division 8 in the Southwest Pacific (early 1942), he helped screen the U.S. landings on Guadalcanal and Tulagi (August) and participated in the battle of Savo Island (8–9 August), when the Japanese sank three U.S. and one Australian cruisers with no losses of their own. He then commanded Destroyer Squadron 4 in the Solomons, taking part in the night battle of Vella Lavella when his six destroyers tried without success to prevent nine Japanese destroyers and twelve smaller ships from evacuating the garrison ashore (6–7 October 1943).

Walker next commanded the Roosevelt Base and Small Craft Training Center at San Pedro, California (1944). After the war he commanded a cruiser (1946), then served on the Ships' Organization Board and Navy Regulations Board (1947). He retired as a rear admiral (1952).

Walker, Frederick John (1896–1944) British naval officer. Walker entered the navy (1909) and held a variety of assignments through World War I. He specialized in anti-submarine warfare (ASW) and by 1921 was considered an expert. While serving in the Far East Fleet in the 1930s he criticized the navy's over-reliance on sonar, which caused him to be passed over for promotion to captain. Appointed commander of the ASW training school at Portland (1938), he developed the techniques used with success in World War II.

At the beginning of the war Walker was operations officer for Vice Admiral Sir Bertram Ramsay at Dover and oversaw procedures for protecting the BEF's move to France and its extraction during Operation DYNAMO, the Dunkerque Evacuation (May–June 1940). In 1941 he commanded a sloop and, as senior officer of 36th Escort Group protecting Convoy HG-76 (December), put into practice procedures that sank four German submarines, although at the cost of an escort carrier, a sloop, and two merchant ships. Most other convoys were, however, suffering greater losses with no submarines sunk.

Ultimately vindicated and promoted captain (July 1942), Walker received command of escort groups in the Western Approaches Command (October), training "hunter-killer" groups to seek out and destroy U-boats. His "creeping attack" technique, coupled with new forward-throwing ASW Squid and Hedgehog weapons, brought results. These efforts took their toll on his health, and he died of a cerebral thrombosis.

Walker, Walton Harris (1889–1950) U.S. general. Like his mentor General George Patton, Walker attended the Virginia Military Institute (1907–08) before graduating from West Point (1912). Commissioned in the infantry, he participated in the occupation of Vera Cruz (1914). During World War I he served with the 5th Infantry Division's 13th Machine Gun Battalion in France and participated in both the St. Mihiel (September 1918) and Meuse–Argonne (September–November)

offensives. As temporary lieutenant colonel, he served in occupation duty in Germany (1919) but reverted to captain on his return to the United States.

Walker graduated from the Field Artillery School (1920), the advanced course at Fort Benning (1923), the Command and General Staff School (1926), and the Army War College (1936). He served with the 15th Infantry regiment in Tientsin (Tianjin), China (1930–33), and he taught at the Infantry School (1920–22), the Coast Artillery School, and at West Point (1923–25). He also served in the War Plans Division of the Army General Staff (1937–40). Promoted lieutenant colonel (1935) and temporary colonel (1941), Walker commanded the 36th Infantry Regiment. Promoted brigadier general (July 1941), he then commanded the 3rd Armored Brigade.

Following U.S. entry into World War II (December 1941), Walker commanded the 3rd Armored Division (January 1942) and was promoted major general (February). He established the Desert Training Center to train units for service in North Africa (September). He then took command of IV Armored Corps, Camp Campbell, Kentucky (April 1943). Redesignated XX Corps, it was sent to Britain (February 1944) and committed to France (July) as part of General George S. Patton's Third Army. Known as the "Ghost Corps" for its speed, it spearheaded Patton's advance across Europe, reduced Metz (November 1944), and Linz, Austria (May 1945). Promoted lieutenant general (May), he then headed 8th Service Command, Dallas, Texas.

After briefly commanding Fifth Army, Chicago (June 1948), Walker went to Japan to command the four divisions of Eighth Army, the ground force element of General Douglas MacArthur's Far Eastern Command (FEC) (September). His weak divisions (at only two-thirds' strength and equipment) were committed to the defense of South Korea following the North Korean invasion (25 June 1950), and he became the primary United Nations Command (UNC) ground forces commander in the early part of the 1950–53 Korean War. Skillfully managing the United Nations Command (UNC) retreat, he held the "Pusan Perimeter" in a tenacious mobile defense. Had that line been breached, the UNC would have lost the war. He commanded Eighth Army in the invasion of North Korea and rallied it following Chinese intervention (October and November) but was killed in a jeep accident (23 December). He was posthumously promoted full general in January 1951.

Wallis, Sir Barnes Neville (1887–1979) British aeronautical engineer. Financial circumstances forced him to leave school at age seventeen. He was soon developing new techniques of aircraft construction and helping to design commercial dirigibles. After recovery from a nervous breakdown (1928), he worked for Vickers Aviation with aircraft designer R. K. Pierson to develop long-range aircraft utilizing duralumin construction and basketweave geodetic structure. This made possible large fixed-wing monoplanes, culminating in the single-engine Wellesley and the twin-engine, mid-wing Wellington bomber (nearly 12,000 of which were built through 1945). However, he continued to use fabric instead of metal covering in the best British heavy bomber of the war, the four-engine Lancaster bomber (1942).

Convinced that the war would be decided through the destruction of German industry, Wallis set out to invent a special bomb to destroy the great Möhne dam serving the Ruhr. He came up with the spherical skip-bomb, which was used with success by Wing Commander Guy Gibson's "dam busters" (night of 16–17 May 1943). Wallis also produced deep penetration bombs "Grand Slam" and "Tall Boy" for high-altitude attacks on V-sites and U-boat pens. He continued his inventions after the war, retiring from

Vickers only in 1971. He was knighted in 1968.

Walt, Lewis W. (1913–89) U.S. Marine Corps general. Commissioned in the Marines following graduation from the Colorado School of Mines (1936), Walt saw service in China (1937–38) and fought in the 1st Marine Raider Battalion in the Solomon Islands (1943). He also fought on Guadalcanal, Cape Gloucester, and Peleliu. During the 1950–53 Korean War he commanded the 1st Marine Regiment (1952–53).

Promoted brigadier general (1962), Walt took command of the 3rd Marine Division in Vietnam as a major general (1965) concurrently serving as commander of III Marine Amphibious Force (MAF). When III MAF was elevated to the first corps-level headquarters in Marine Corps history, he continued in command and was promoted lieutenant general (1966). He also served as senior advisor and coordinator to the Republic of Vietnam I Corps area. In contrast to General William Westmoreland's preference for large-unit operations, he insisted on a balance of small-unit patrols, large-unit operations, and pacification efforts around Marine Combined Action Platoons (CAP) that operated with South Vietnamese forces.

Walt returned to the U.S. as assistant commandant of the Marine Corps and was promoted full general (June 1969). He retired in February 1971.

Warlimont, Walter (1894–1976) German general. Warlimont was commissioned in the artillery on graduation from the Danzig Military Academy (1914). During World War I he saw action on both the Western and Italian Fronts, and by the end of the war he was a battery commander.

After the war Warlimont served in the Freikorps as a lieutenant. He joined the Reichswehr (1922) and was selected for staff training. He briefly studied English in Britain (1926) and that same year was appointed to the General Staff as a captain. He served in both the economics and foreign armies intelligence sections. He was in the United States studying military mobilization (1929–30), then was in Spain as a major and military representative to the Nationalists in the 1936–39 Civil War (September 1936–37). Promoted lieutenant colonel, he commanded a battalion, then was promoted colonel in command of a regiment.

Warlimont then headed the Home Defense Branch of the Oberkommando der Wehrmacht (Army High Command, OKW). He then became deputy chief of the OKW operations section under General Alfred Jodl (September 1939–September 1944). He attended Adolf Hitler's major command conferences and drafted most operations orders. Promoted brigadier general (August 1940) and major general (April 1942), he was then raised to lieutenant general (April 1944).

Although loyal to his chief, Warlimont was never, like Jodl, a slavish admirer of Hitler. He was, however, held in contempt by field commanders for his lack of command experience and insensitivity to their problems. Injured in the bomb attempt on Hitler's life (20 July 1944), he left his post but was not recalled on his recovery.

A witness at Nuremberg, Warlimont himself was later tried and sentenced to life in prison for war crimes and crimes against humanity. Freed (1957), he published an important book, *Inside Hitler's Headquarters, 1939–45.*

Watson-Watt, Sir Robert Alexander (1892–1973) British scientist. Watson-Watt obtain a bachelor of science degree from the University of St. Andrews (1912). He worked in meteorology but is best remembered for his work in radio direction finding, which came to be known as radar. He proved in a trial (1935) that aircraft could be located in flight by bouncing electromagnetic waves off them, and a primitive radar system,

known as Chain Home, was installed along the east coast of Britain (1938). Further work led to Chain Home Low, designed to detect aircraft flying below the altitudes for Chain Home.

Watson-Watt also shepherded development of AI (airborne interception), lightweight radar that could be installed in aircraft, ASV (air to surface vessel) that allowed aircraft to locate vessels on the surface of the water, equipment to control antiaircraft artillery, a means to distinguish between friendly and hostile aircraft, and radio-navigation for bombers.

Radar and these other developments were of immense value in the antisubmarine campaign and almost all aspects of World War II. These technological advantages were shared with the United States, and radar was the single most important item of reverse Lend Lease. For his contributions, Watson-Watt was knighted in 1942.

Wavell, Archibald Percival, 1st Earl (1883–1950) British field marshal. Educated at Winchester, he graduated from Sandhurst (1901). He established his military reputation during the 1899–1902 Boer War, then saw service in India and graduated from Staff College. In World War I he was an intelligence officer and then served in an infantry brigade and lost an eye. On recovery he held staff slots and then fought in Palestine.

An effective trainer and innovator, Wavell took command of British troops in Palestine (September 1937). He returned to Britain to head Southern Command (1938), then returned to the Middle East to head British forces there (1939–41).

Wavell's forces had considerable success against the Italians both in Ethiopia and North Africa, and against anti-Allied elements in Syria and Iraq (1940–1941). Reversals in North Africa followed with the arrival of General Erwin Rommel and his Afrika Korps and removal of divisions to fight in Greece. Following the failure of Operation BATTLEAXE to push the Germans from Egypt and relieve Tobruk, Prime Minister Winston Churchill replaced him with General Claude Auchinleck (July 1941) and gave him command of British troops in India. Following U.S. entry into the war, he commanded Allied forces in the Far East. After the loss of Burma he prepared India against an invasion and then mounted a counterattack in Burma, which was unsuccessful. Promoted field marshal (February 1943), he became viceroy of India, a post he handled well until his retirement (1947) and return to Britain.

Wedemeyer, Albert Coady (1897–1999) U.S. general. Commissioned in the infantry on graduation from West Point (1919), Wedemeyer, among other assignments, completed the Infantry School, served in the Philippines, and studied Chinese in Tientsin. He graduated from the Command and General Staff School and from the Kriegsakademie. He was promoted lieutenant colonel (September 1941) and colonel (February 1942). Assigned to the Plans and Operations Division, he was promoted brigadier general (July 1942). As a major general (September 1943), he was named deputy CofS to Supreme Allied Commander in East Asia Admiral Lord Louis Mountbatten. When General Joseph W. Stilwell was recalled (October 1944), Wedemeyer replaced him as commander of the China Theater and CofS to Generalissimo Chiang Kai-shek (Jiang Jieshi). He did much to restore good relations with China.

In May 1946 Wedemeyer was promoted lieutenant general and left China. He commanded Second Army (1946–47) and then was director of Plans and Operations of the General Staff (1947–48). Finally he commanded Sixth Army until he retired (July 1951). In 1954 he was promoted to general on the retired list.

Wei Li-huang (Wei Lihuang) (1897–1960) Nationalist Chinese general. Wei began his military career as a volunteer in the forces of Wu Chung-hsin. He rose steadily and joined the Nationalists or Kuomintang (KMT, Guomindang) (early 1920s). He commanded 3rd Division in First Army of the National Revolutionary Army (1927) and fought in the 1926–28 Northern Expedition to reunify China. As a general in Chiang Kai-shek's (Jiang Jieshi) "Bandit Extermination" campaigns to suppress the Communists (1930–34), his military successes earned him the nickname of "Hundred Victories Wei". During the 1937–45 Sino-Japanese War he commanded First War Area and was one of the most effective Chinese commanders. Sent to south China to command Y Force, he worked well with the Americans and supported General Joseph Stilwell's Burma offensive. He attacked in Yunnan (May 1944), took Tengehung (July-September), and linked up with other troops in Burma at Wanting (January 1945).

After the war, Wei was sent to command KMT forces in Manchuria (October 1947). Cut off from the rest of China by the Communist capture of Chinchow, he planned to retake it but was refused permission to do so by Chiang and was replaced (October 1948). He fled to Taiwan (1949) but then returned to the mainland (1955). He was a vice chairman of the National Defense Council (1959).

Weichs zur Glon, Maximilian Maria Joseph von (1881–1954) German field marshal. Weichs entered a Bavarian cavalry regiment (1900). He attended the Bavarian War Academy and held a variety of command and staff positions during and after World War I, remaining in the Reichswehr after the war. Promoted brigadier general (April 1933), he commanded 3rd Cavalry Division and oversaw its transformation into 1st Panzer Division. Promoted lieutenant general (October 1936), he took over XIII Corps and commanded it in the invasion of Poland (September 1939). He then received command of Second Army (October), which as part of Army Group A fought in the invasions of France and Benelux (May 1940) and of Yugoslavia (April 1941). He led Second Army in the invasion of the Soviet Union (June). On sick leave (November 1941–January 1942), he then commanded newly formed Army Group B (July) for the invasion of South Russia. There is controversy over his role in the German defeats along the Don and at Stalingrad.

Following these setbacks, Field Marshal Weichs (promoted February 1943) was reassigned to Belgrade as supreme commander of German forces in southeastern Europe before being relieved of that command (25 March 1945). Arrested at the end of the war, he was indicted on war crimes charges but released on account of poor health in 1948.

Wemyss, Rosslyn Erskine, Baron Wester Wemyss (1864–1933) British admiral. Wemyss entered the navy (1877). Appointed naval aide to King George V (1910), he was then promoted rear admiral (1910). At the beginning of World War I he commanded 12th Cruiser Squadron in the English Channel with orders to protect the transit of the BEF to France. He then had charge of the island of Lemnos and the naval station at Mudros. He might have succeeded Admiral Sackville Carden as commander of forces at the Dardanelles (March 1915), but he recommended Rear Admiral John De Robeck while he remained at Mudros. A year later, as acting vice admiral, Wemyss commanded the 1st Naval Squadron during De Robeck's absence.

Wemyss commanded the East Indies and Egypt Station (January 1916) and supplied the advance into Palestine (August). Appointed deputy sea lord (1917), he was charged with reorganizing the war staff. He then replaced Admiral John Jellicoe as first sea lord. He helped plan the raid on Zeebrugge and represented the

Allied navies during armistice negotiations, and Britain at the Paris Peace Conference. Offended by calls for his dismissal by Admiral David Beatty, he resigned (November 1919) and was promoted admiral of the fleet and raised to the peerage.

Westmoreland, William Childs (1914–) U.S. general. Westmoreland attended The Citadel for a year and graduated from West Point (1936). As a major (April 1942) he commanded an artillery battery in Tunisia and Sicily, distinguishing himself in the Battle of Kasserine Pass (February 1943). He fought in France and Germany with the 9th Infantry Division, then was promoted colonel and was its CofS (October 1944).

Westmoreland completed parachute training (1946) and was CofS of 82nd Airborne Division (1947–50). He then taught at the Command and General Staff School and the Army War College. During the 1950–53 Korean War he commanded the 187th Airborne Regimental Combat team in Korea (August 1952) and was promoted to brigadier general (November). Advanced to major general (1956), he commanded the 101st Airborne Division at Fort Campbell, Kentucky. He was superintendent of West Point (1960–63), and then was promoted lieutenant general (August 1963) and commanded the XVIII Airborne Corps at Fort Campbell.

Westmoreland went to Vietnam as deputy commander of the Military Assistance Command, Vietnam (MAC) and was then its commander (June 1964–June 1968). Promoted general (August 1964), he fought the war on his World War II experiences, seeking large decisive battles with Communist forces. He was little interested in pacification. His optimistic reports (end of 1967) on the war's progress contributed to disillusionment in the U.S. following the January 1968 Têt Offensive, which was however a Communist military failure. Appointed CofS of the army (July 1968), he retired in July 1972.

Westphal, Siegfried (1901–82) German general. Westphal entered the military as an officer candidate in the 12th Grenadier Regiment in 1918. When the war ended, he remained in the army and was commissioned as a lieutenant in a cavalry regiment (1922). He was assigned to the 13th Cavalry Regiment in 1938.

When World War II began Westphal was operations officer of the 58th Infantry Division. Promoted lieutenant colonel (1941), Westphal became operations officer of General Erwin Rommel's Panzergrupppe Afrika (November). He then became one of the youngest German generals as a brigadier general and CofS to Field Marshal Albert Kesselring, commander of Army Group C in Italy (January 1943).

Promoted major general (1942), Westphal became CofS to commander of German forces on the Western Front Field Marshal Gerd von Rundstedt (September 1943). Promoted lieutenant general, he played a key role in planning the Ardennes offensive (Battle of the Bulge) (December 1944–January 1945). He then returned as CofS to Kesselring (March 1945) until the end of the war.

Wever, Walther (1887–1936) German air force general. Wever joined the army (1905) and, as a captain (1915), was Quartermaster General of the Army General Erich Ludendorff's adjutant during World War I. He continued in the Reichswehr after the war and was promoted colonel (1933), when General Erhard Milch selected him to be chief of the Air Command Office (September 1933). He was, in effect, first CofS of the Luftwaffe, nominally headed by Hermann Göring. He was promoted brigadier general (1934) and major general (1936).

Milch encouraged Wever to learn to fly, and he worked hard to improve and strengthen the Luftwaffe. A superb ad-

ministrator, he got along well with both superiors and subordinates. He was interested in technological advances and was the chief Luftwaffe advocate of developing a fleet of strategic bombing to cripple an opponent's industrial base and shatter morale. Toward that end he pushed the development of a four-engine "Ural" or "America" strategic bomber. Thanks to his efforts, Germany developed the Dornier Do-19, Junkers Ju-89, and Folke Wolfe FW-200 Kurier.

Wever's death in a plane crash near Dresden (3 May 1936) was a major loss to the Luftwaffe and saw the end of the production plans for the four-engine bombers. Germany fought World War II, including the Battle of Britain, with essentially a tactical air force, which, one could argue, was the best use of limited resources.

Weyand, Frederick Carlton (1916–) U.S. general. Weyand graduated from the University of California at Berkeley (1939), receiving a commission through ROTC. Called to active duty (1940), he was assigned to the 6th Artillery Regiment. During World War II he was an intelligence officer in Burma. After the war he transferred to the infantry. During the 1950–53 Korean War he was a battalion commander in the 7th Infantry and then operations officer of the 3rd Infantry Division.

Weyand was on the staff of the Infantry School, Fort Benning (1952–53), then graduated from the Armed Forces Staff College, Norfolk, Virginia (1953). He was an assistant to the secretary of the army (1954–57), graduated from the Naval War College (1958), served in Berlin (1960), and was then chief legislative liaison officer for the army in Washington (1962–64).

Weyand then took command of the 25th Infantry Division stationed in Hawaii, taking it to Vietnam (1966). He became deputy commander of II Field forces in Vietnam (March 1967) and its commander (July 1967–August 1968), playing a key role in shifting resources to meet the Communist Têt Offensive (January 1968).

Weyand was then chief of the Office of Reserve Components of the Army (1968–69). He was then military advisor to the Vietnam War peace talks in Paris (1969–70) before returning to Vietnam (April 1970) as deputy commander of the Military Assistance Command, Vietnam (MACV). Promoted temporary full general (October 1970), he succeeded General Creighton Abrams as last U.S. commander in Vietnam (July 1972–March 1973).

Weyand was next commander-in-chief, U.S. Army Pacific. In late 1973 he became army vice CofS. He retired as a full general in October 1976.

Weygand, Maxime (1867–1965) French general. Weygand graduated from St. Cyr (1885). He distinguished himself as a cavalry instructor at Saumur and as a student at the Centre des Hautes Études Militaires. At the beginning of World War I, he was a lieutenant colonel of Hussars in Fourth Army. French Army commander General Joffre assigned him as CofS to General Foch, who had taken command of the newly formed Ninth Army on the Marne. Weygand spent the entire war working as Foch's deputy. He was the ideal CofS and faithfully served Foch, even after the latter was named Supreme Allied Commander (April 1918).

His close association with Foch did much to advance Weygand's post-war career. He was chief of the general staff (1930–31) and vice president of the Supreme War Council and inspector general of the army (1931–35). Brought back from retirement to command the Eastern Mediterranean Theater of Operations at Beirut (August 1939), he replaced General Maurice Gamelin as French supreme commander (19 May 1940). Although he promised another miracle on the Marne, he ultimately advised capitulation to the Germans (13 June). Briefly minister of

defense of the new Vichy government (June–September 1940), he was distrusted by Pierre Laval, who sent him to North Africa as governor general of Algeria and delegate general in French North Africa. Convinced that he was planning an uprising, the Germans pressured the Vichy government into recalling him (November 1941).

Retired by the Vichy government, Marshal Henri Pétain recalled him and sought his advice following the Allied invasion of North Africa (8 November 1942). Weygand urged resuming the war against the Germans. Arrested and subsequently imprisoned by the Germans (12 November), he was later arrested by the de Gaulle government (1945) as a member of the Vichy government. He was released the next year and rehabilitated (1948).

Wheeler, Earl Gilmore (1908–75) U.S. general. Wheeler enlisted in the National Guard (1922) and graduated from West Point (1932). Commissioned in the infantry, he served in China (1937–38). He taught at West Point and spent the first part of World War II training infantry in the United States, but he became CofS of the 63rd Infantry Division (1944).

A protégé of General Maxwell Taylor, Wheeler was promoted full general (1962). He became deputy commander of the U.S. European Command (March 1962) and then was named CofS of the army (December). He then succeeded Taylor as chairman of the Joint Chiefs of Staff (JCS) (June 1964). Alarmed by a drawdown in U.S. military strength elsewhere in the world as a consequence of the Vietnam War, he urged a limited call-up of reserves. He also opposed the Johnson administration policy of gradual escalation in Vietnam. Following the January 1968 Communist Tet Offensive, he urged the commander of U.S. forces in Vietnam, General William Westmoreland, to request additional troops, hoping to force mobilization of the reserves. It did not. The Nixon administration also ignored his advice, but he was continued as JCS chairman for an unprecedented six years until his retirement in July 1970.

White, Isaac Davis (1901–91) U.S. general. White graduated from Norwich University (1922) and was commissioned in the cavalry. Commander of the 2nd Armored Reconnaissance Battalion of 2nd Armored Division (1940–41), he was promoted full colonel (1942) and then led one of the division's tank regiments in Operation TORCH, the invasion of North Africa (8 November 1942) as part of Western Task Force. He commanded the division's Combat Command B and led it in fighting in Northwest Africa, Sicily, and then northern France. Promoted brigadier general during the fighting in Normandy (1944), White led Combat Command B in the German Ardennes Offensive (Battle of the Bulge) (December 1944–January 1945) and surrounded and destroyed much of the 2nd Panzer Division at Celles. He then took command of the 2nd Division from General Ernest Harmon and was promoted major general (March 1945).

After the end of the war in Europe, White commanded the Cavalry School at Fort Riley, Kansas. He commanded X Corps in the latter stages of the Korean War. He returned to the U.S. in 1953, was promoted lieutenant general, and took command of Fourth Army. He then commanded U.S. Army forces in the Far East and was promoted general. He retired in 1961.

White, Thomas Dresser (1901–65) U.S. Air Force general. Commissioned in the infantry on graduation from West Point (1920), White graduated from the Infantry School and served in Panama (1921–24). On completion of flight training at Brooke and Kelly Fields, Texas, he served in the 99th Observation Squadron (1925). He studied Chinese at Peking (Beijing), China (1927–31), then was in the Air Corps Headquarters (1931–34). He then

was assigned to Moscow (1934–35) and Athens (1935–37) as assistant military attaché. He graduated from the Air Corps Tactical School (1938) and the Command and General Staff School (1939). Promoted major (1939), he was in the Office of the Chief of the Air Corps (1939–40), then military attaché in Brazil (1940–42).

Promoted lieutenant colonel (1941) and colonel (1942), White was on the staff of the Third Air Force at Dill Field, Florida (March); promoted brigadier general, he became its CofS (November). Assistant CofS for intelligence, USAAF (1944), he was then deputy commander of Thirteenth Air Force (September 1944–June 1945) and took part in operations against New Guinea, Leyte, Luzon, and Borneo. Commander of Seventh Air Force, he transferred it from the Marianas to Okinawa (June) and conducted final air operations against Japan.

Promoted major general (January 1946), White was CofS of Pacific Air Command (1946–47), then commanded Fifth Air Force in Japan (1947–48). He served in various assignments at Air Force Headquarters (1948–51). Promoted lieutenant general, he was deputy chief of staff of the Air Force (July 1951). Promoted general, he was vice CofS of the Air Force (1952–53), then CofS (1957–61), managing the early U.S. strategic missile program.

Wilhelm, Crown Prince (1882–1951) German general and last crown prince of the Hohenzollen dynasty. Commissioned in the army on his tenth birthday, Wilhelm began active service in 1900. Following the assassination of Archduke Franz Ferdinand (28 June 1914) and the outbreak of World War I, he took command of Fifth Army and led it in the Battle of the Frontiers, driving back French attacks in the Ardennes. He then took command of Central Army Group (1915) and had charge of it during the French offensives in Champagne. He oversaw the German offensive against Verdun (February–

December 1916). In the course of that long battle, he urged an end to the offensive and broke with his own CofS, General Schmidt von Knobelsdorf, and Army CofS General Erich Falkenhayn on this issue. Most of the German offensives at the end of the war took place in his sector of the front.

At the end of the war, Wilhelm accompanied his father Kaiser Wilhelm II into Dutch exile. He returned to Germany (1923). For a time he supported Hitler, but he refused to do so openly without the support of his father, which was not forthcoming.

Wilhelm II, Emperor of Germany (1859–1941) German emperor, 1888–1918. Wishing to plot his own course on his accession, Wilhelm II forced the resignation of Chancellor Otto von Bismarck and pursued his own aggressive foreign policy. His "Weltpolitik" and decision to build a powerful battle fleet led to the dismantling of Bismarck's complex alliance system, alienated Britain, and forced Germany into a close relationship with Austria-Hungary, its only ally. Wilhelm made only belated efforts to prevent World War I. Once the war had begun, he maintained a frequent presence at headquarters but left strategic decisions to the CofS of the army. His retreat to the background was particularly apparent after Generals Paul von Hindenburg and Erich Ludendorff took over (1916). At the end of the war Wilhelm II abdicated, but only after the decision was announced for him. He remained in exile in the Netherlands until his death.

Wilkinson, Theodore Stark (1888–1946) U.S. admiral. A graduate of Annapolis (1909), Wilkinson commanded the landing party that captured the customs house at Vera Cruz (1914), for which he was awarded the Medal of Honor. During World War I he served with the Bureau of Ordnance.

Promoted captain (1937), Wilkinson

was then a rear admiral and director of the Office of Naval Intelligence (1941). He then commanded a battleship division (1942–43), and then became deputy commander of the South Pacific Force. He took command of III Amphibious Force (July 1943) and became a proponent of "leap-frogging" to bypass Japanese island strongholds. He then directed assaults on Bougainville, Ulithi, Leyte, and Luzon.

After the war, Wilkinson's force transported Eighth Army to Japan. A month before his accidental death, he was named to a committee of the Joint Chiefs of Staff.

Wilson, Henry Braid (1861–1954) U.S. admiral. Wilson graduated from Annapolis (1881) and was commissioned (1883). Promoted lieutenant (1897), he proved an able commander and effective administrator. He headed the Bureau of Navigation's enlisted personnel section (1904–08), then was its assistant chief (1910–11). Promoted captain (1911), he took command of a battleship (1916).

Promoted rear admiral on U.S. entry into World War I (April 1917), Wilson commanded the Atlantic Patrol Force, which escorted ships carrying troops and supplies to Europe, Promoted temporary vice admiral (1918), he commanded all U.S. naval forces on the French coast, then all U.S. naval forces in France.

After the war Wilson was superintendent of Annapolis (1921–25), transforming it from a training school into a university authorized to award a bachelor of science degree. He then retired (1925).

Wilson, Sir Henry Hughes (1864–1922) British general. Wilson entered the army through the militia (1882). He served in Burma and participated in the 1899–1902 Boer War. Promoted brigadier general and given command of the Staff College at Camberley (1906), he advocated close ties with the French. He became director of military operations at the War Office (1910), where he drew up plans for the deployment of a British Expeditionary Force to France.

Promoted major general (1913), Wilson opposed Minister for War Lord Kitchener's policy of an independent stance for the BEF in France and accompanied that force to France. Promoted lieutenant general (early 1915), he became chief liaison officer with French Army headquarters. He then commanded IV Corps on the Western Front (December).

Wilson had a sucession of other assignments until Prime Minister Lloyd George appointed him the British representative to the Allied Supreme War Council (November 1917). Appointed chief of the Imperial General Staff (February 1918), he served as chief British military advisor at the Paris Peace Conference but found himself increasingly at odds with Lloyd George's policies. He retired from the army (February 1922), then served in Parliament where he opposed Irish independence. He was shot dead by IRA terrorists.

Wilson, Henry Maitland, 1st Baron (1881–1964) British field marshal. Educated at Eton and Sandhurst, "Jumbo" Wilson first saw action at the end of the 1899–1902 Anglo-Boer War. He fought in World War I, and at the start of World War II he was sent to Egypt as commander there and helped plan the British counterattack (December 1940) against the Italian invasion. General Archibald Wavell appointed him commander of the four-division BEF in Greece (March 1941) and he conducted a skillful withdrawal before superior German forces (April), keeping casualties to a minimum and bringing off 43,000 of the 57,000-man force. Wavell then gave him command of a two-division force to Iraq to reverse a pro-German coup there (May). He commanded the British invasion of Vichy-controlled Syria and the Lebanon (June–July).

Wilson then commanded the Persia–Iraq Theater and Ninth Army (1942)

before succeeding General Harold Alexander as CinC of the Middle East (January 1943). He replaced Eisenhower as CinC of the Mediterranean Theater (January 1944) and thus had overall authority for Allied operations in Italy. After the death of General Sir John Dill (November), he went to Washington as head of the British Joint Staff Mission there, and in this capacity he attended the final wartime conferences at Yalta and Potsdam. Made a baron (1946), he retired from the army (1947) and wrote his memoirs.

Wilson, James Harrison (1837–1925) U.S. general. Commissioned in the topographical engineers on graduation from West Point (1860), Wilson fought in the 1861–65 U.S. Civil War. He rose to brigadier general of volunteers (October 1863) and chief of the War Department's Cavalry Bureau (January 1864). He commanded 3rd Division in General Philip Sheridan's III Cavalry Corps in fighting in Virginia. Breveted major general of volunteers and appointed chief of cavalry for General William T. Sherman (October 1864), he fought in Georgia and Tennessee and played a major role in destroying General John B. Hood's army at Nashville (December). He then led a brilliant raid through Alabama and Georgia (March–April 1865).

After the war he left volunteer service and was appointed lieutenant colonel in the regular army (1866) but resigned from the army to enter the railroad business (1870). At the beginning of the 1898 Spanish–American War he volunteered for duty and was appointed major general of volunteers and given command of VI Corps. When this was not formed, he took command of 1st Division, I Corps, under General Nelson Miles for the invasion of Puerto Rico (July). He then served on occupation duty in Cuba. Reduced after the war to brigadier general of volunteers (April 1899), he was second in command to General Adna R. Chaffee in the Peking (Beijing) Relief Expedition (June–August 1900). Promoted brigadier general of regulars by special act of Congress (February 1901), he retired (March). He was promoted major general on the retired list in 1915.

Wingate, Orde Charles (1903–44) British general. Educated at Woolwich, Wingate was commissioned in the artillery (1923). He served in the Sudan (1928–33) and led Jewish irregulars in Palestine against Arab guerrillas (1936–39). His passionate conversion to Zionism led to his recall to Britain.

Sent to the Sudan during World War II (1940), Lieutenant Colonel Wingate led a highly successful series of raids by Ethiopian guerrillas against the Italians (1941) but was demoted to major for interfering in local politics. In 1942 General Archibald Wavell called him to India to organize deep penetration raids into Japanese-held Burma. Promoted brigadier general, his 77th Brigade, known as the Chindits, carried out a successful operation into Burma (February–June 1943). He launched a second operation (February 1944) but was killed the next month in a plane crash. A controversial commander, he attracted both devotion and dislike.

Witzleben, Erwin von (1991–1944) German field marshal. Witzleben joined the army (1901) and served on the Western Front during World War I. When Hitler came to power, he was appointed commander of the Berlin Military Area (1933). He was then promoted brigadier general (February 1934) and major general (December 1934).

In 1935 Witzleben assumed command of III Corps and was promoted lieutenant general (October 1936). As early as 1934 he opposed Hitler; these feelings crystallized in 1938 because of Hitler's purge of senior generals and the crisis over Czechoslovakia. He drew up plans to arrest Hitler but failed to act on them following the Munich agreement. His feelings were

not widely known, and he commanded Army Group C in the Polish campaign (September 1939). He was promoted full general (November) and commanded with distinction First Army in the Battle of France (May–June 1940). Raised to field marshal (July 1940) along with seven other generals, he then commanded Army Group D in France (October 1940). He was then CinC Army West (May 1941).

Witzleben's attitude toward Hitler became known and he was retired (March 1942). He was active in the 20 July 1944 bomb attempt on Hitler's life and was to have assumed command of the army had it succeeded. He dallied in carrying out the actual coup attempt in Berlin. Later arrested, he was tried and executed by strangling with piano wire on 8 August 1944.

Wöhler, Otto (1894–1987) German general. Wöhler joined the army as an officer candidate (1913) and saw front line service in World War I. After the war he continued in the Reichswehr, serving as a staff officer. Following the *Anschluss* with Austria, he was a staff officer for the new Fifth Army Group headquarters in Vienna, which became an army command under Colonel General Wilhelm List (1939).

After the start of World War II, Colonel Wöhler was CofS of XVII Corps (December 1939), then CofS of Eleventh Army under General Erich von Manstein, and CofS to Field Marshal Günther von Kluge's Army Group Center (April 1942). Given command of a corps in the northern Soviet Union (April 1943), he then commanded a group of divisions in the Ukraine (August) that became Eighth Army. Lieutenant General Wöhler also received supervisory authority over Romanian Fourth Army and Hungarian First Army (1944).

Appointed commander of Army Group South (December 1944), Wöhler tried to hold on to Hungary but was forced to withdraw into Austria, whereupon he was removed from command (7 April). Tried by U.S. authorities after the war on war crimes charges, he was sentenced to eight years in prison.

Wolff, Karl (1900–84) German SS general. Wolff joined the army and fought in World War I as an officer. He left the army after the war and became a businessman. He joined the Nazi party and the *Shutz Staffel* (SS), becoming personal adjutant to SS leader Heinrich Himmler (1933). Promoted *SS-Gruppenführer* (major general, January 1937), he was Himmler's CofS. Promoted *SS-Obergruppenführer* (full general, January 1942), he was the third most powerful figure in the SS after Himmler and Reinhard Heydrich. Until 1943 he was Himmler's liaison with Adolf Hitler's headquarters.

Promoted military governor and SS chief in northern Italy (September 1943), Wolff helped establish Benito Mussolini's Salo Republic. Realizing that Germany had lost the war, he opened secret negotiations with Allen Dulles of the U.S. Office of Strategic Services (OSS) in Switzerland (March 1945), the surrender taking effect on 2 May 1945.

Wolff was not tried at the International War Crimes Tribunal at Nuremberg but testified as a prosecution witness. Arrested by the German government (1962), he was tried and sentenced (1964) to fifteen years in prison for war crimes but was released (1971) because of poor health.

Woyrsch, Remus von (1847–1920) German field marshal. Woyrsch entered the Prussian Army (1860) and fought in the 1866 Austro-Prussian and 1870–71 Franco-German Wars. He then joined the General Staff and was promoted colonel (1896). Promoted brigadier general (1897), he commanded a brigade. Promoted major general (1901), he commanded 12th Division, then commanded VI Corps at Breslau (1903–04). Promoted

lieutenant general (1905), he retired in 1911 at age sixty-four.

Recalled to active duty with the start of World War I (August 1914), Woyrsch commanded his native Silesian Landwehr Corps in support of the Austro-Hungarian Army against the Russians at Krasnik (September). Following the Russian defeat of the Austro-Hungarians there (9 September), his corps covered their retreat. Although it lost 8,000 men, it saved the Austro-Hungarian First Army from certain annihilation.

The capable Woyrsch then returned to German command and led Army Section Woyrsch (October 1914–December 1917) against the Russians, assisting in victory at Thorn, for which he was promoted full general. His forces took advantage of the breakthrough by General August Mackensen's Eleventh Army at Gorlice–Tarnów (May 1915) to defeat the Russians at Sienno (June) and cross both the Vistula and Bug rivers. He then commanded Army Group Woyrsch in south Poland (August 1916) until it was disbanded (December 1917) after collapse of the Russian army. Then over seventy years old, he requested retirement and was promoted field marshal. After the war he commanded the southern wing of German border guards.

Wrangel, Pyotr Nikolaevich (1878–1928) Russian general. Graduating from technical school with a mining degree (1901), Wrangel entered the army but resigned to accept an engineering post in Siberia (1904). He rejoined the army during the 1904–05 Russo-Japanese War and fought with distinction in a Cossack regiment. He attended the General Staff Academy and on the outbreak of World War I led a cavalry squadron in East Prussia (August–September 1914) and a Cossack regiment in Galicia (1916). As a major general, he commanded 7th Cavalry Division in the Kerensky Offensive (July 1917). Following the failure of General Lavr Kornilov's coup attempt (September), he resigned and settled at Yalta.

After the Bolshevik *coup d'état* (November 1917) Wrangel joined the counter-revolutionary forces of General Anton Denikin's Volunteer Army (August 1916) and, as a lieutenant general, commanded a division. When Denikin took command of the Armed Forces of South Russia (AFSR), Wrangel commanded the Volunteer Army (spring 1919) and directed the capture of Tsaritsyn (later Stalingrad (June). After the failure of Denikin's drive on Moscow, he attempted to reorganize around Kharkov. He resigned at Denikin's request (February 1920) but returned after Denikin's departure to command the AFSR in the Crimea (April). Thanks in large part to the Red Army's distraction in Poland, he won a series of victories; but reversals followed, and he then carried out an evacuation of 146,000 soldiers and civilians at Sevastopol (November) and went into exile.

Wu P'ei-fu (Wu Peifu) (1873–1939) Chinese warlord. Wu joined Yüan Shih-k'ai's (Yuan Shikai) Peiyang Army as a private and later attended the Peiyang Academy and became an officer. After the October 1911 Revolution he became a protégé of 3rd Division commander General Ts'ao K'un (Cao Kun) and remained loyal to him. Later he commanded the division himself (1916), defending against Premier Tuan Ch'i-ju's (Duan Qirui) campaign against the Hunan warlords (1918). He defeated Tuan's Northwest Army and broke the Peiyang warlord clique (1921). He defeated the attempt of the governor of Fengtien, Chang Tso-lin (Zhang Zuolin), to control north China in the First Chihli–Fengtien War (1922).

A capable and determined soldier and incorruptible, Wu controlled much of central China. Defeated by Chang and his allies Feng Yü-hsiang (Feng Yuxiang) and Yen Hsi-shan (Yan Xishan) in the Second 1924 Chihli–Fengtien War, he counterattacked and drove Feng into alliance with the Nationalists or Kuomintang (KMT, Guomindang) in the south. With Wu's best troops tied down in the north, the KMT began the 1926–28 Northern Expedition. Wu hurried south but was defeated at Ting-ssu-ch'ao (October 1926) and forced into retirement.

Y

Yaeger, Charles Edward (1923–) U.S. Air Force general. Yaeger enlisted in the army out of high school (1941) and joined the Air Corps. Commissioned a reserve flight officer (March 1943) he was assigned to 357th Fighter Group in England (November). He flew sixty-four missions over Europe, and was credited with shooting down thirteen German aircraft, including an Me-262 jet fighter, in his P-51 Mustang. Shot down once himself, he was rescued by the French underground.

After the war, Yaeger became a test pilot. Volunteering for the X-1 rocket aircraft project (1947), he then flew the X-1 through the sound barrier, achieving Mach 1.1 speed in the world's first supersonic flight (14 October 1947). He set another speed record of 1,650 mph while flying the X-1A (1953).

As a colonel, Yaeger commanded the Aerospace Research Pilot School, Edwards Air Force Base, California. He retired from the Air Force as a brigadier general in 1975.

Yahara, Hiromichi (1902–81) Japanese army officer. A military attaché in the United States (1933–35), Yahara returned to Japan and taught at the Army War College (1938–40). He was then on the staff of Imperial General Headquarters and deputy military attaché in Thailand.

As senior staff officer of Thirty-Second Army under General Mitsura Ushijima,

Yahara drew up the defensive plans for Okinawa. He strongly insisted on adopting the example of Tadamichi Kuribayashi's defence-in-depth strategy in Iwō Jima. During the time Yahara had control of Thirty-Second Army operations, the Japanese garrison inflicted the heaviest casualties on the American forces (April–early May 1945).

Yahara lost influence after the failure of the early May offensive, initiated by his superior, CofS of Thirty-Second Army General Isamu Chō, which Yahara had adamantly resisted.

Yahara surrendered to American forces after the Okinawa campaign, the only surviving high-ranking officer of Thirty-Second Army Headquarters. In 1973 he wrote a detailed memoir of the Okinawa campaign.

Yamada, Otozō (1881–1965) Japanese general. Yamada graduated from the Military Academy (1903) and Army Staff College (1912). Commissioned in the cavalry, he was an instructor at the Cavalry School (1914–22), then commanded a cavalry regiment (1922–26) and was promoted colonel (1925). He was then CofS of the Korea Army (1926–27). He commanded a cavalry brigade (1931–32), was chief of the Transportation and Communication Division of the Army General Staff (1933–34), then headed the Military Academy (1935–37).

Commander of 12th Division in Manchuria (1937–38), he commanded Central China Expeditionary Army (1938–39) in the 1937–45 Sino-Japanese War. Next inspector general for Military Education (1939–41), he was promoted general (1940). Given command of the Kwantung Army in Manchuria (1944), he had the almost impossible task of halting the Soviet invasion (August 1945). He was then imprisoned by the Soviets as a war criminal (1945–56).

Yamagata, Aritomo (1838–1922) Japanese general. Yamagata served with distinction in the 1866 Four Borders War and 1868 Boshin (Restoration) War. He then studied Western military systems in Europe (1869–70) and became assistant vice minister of military affairs (1870) and then vice minister (1871). He was the major influence behind the introduction of conscription (1872). He was army minister (1873–78). As a lieutenant general, he commanded government forces in the 1877 Satsuma Rebellion.

Known as the father of the modern Japanese Army, Yamagata founded the Army General Staff and became the first CofS (1878–1882, 1884–85). He then served as home minister (1883–90) save for three months in travel to Europe (1888–89). He was next prime minister (1890), then justice minister (1892–93). During the 1894–95 Sino-Japanese War, he commanded First Army in Korea until he fell ill (December 1894). On his recovery, he became minister of the army. Promoted field marshal (1898), he was again prime minister (1898–1900).

Yamagata was responsible for the unfortunate political change requiring ministers of the armed forces to be selected from active duty admirals and generals (1900). This helped free the military from civilian control and gave it a veto over governmental decisions. Again chief of staff on the outbreak of the 1904–05 Russo-Japanese War, he held that post until he retired (1906), but he continued to influence policy as a member of the Privy Council (1905–22) and was made a prince in 1907.

Yamaguchi, Tamon (1892–1942) Japanese admiral. Yamaguchi graduated from the Naval Academy (1912). He attended Princeton University (1921–23), then graduated from the Naval Staff College (1924). He was a member of the Naval General Staff (1927). Promoted commander (1928), he was a member of the Japanese delegation to the London Naval Conference (1929–30). Promoted captain (1932), he was a naval attaché in Washington (1934–37). Promoted rear admiral (1938), he was then CofS in Fifth Fleet (1929–40) before taking charge (1940) of 2nd Carrier Division (*Hiryū* and *Soryū*), which he commanded in the attack on Pearl Harbor (7 December 1941) and in the Indian Ocean (April 1942). After *Hiryū* was fatally hit by U.S. aircraft in the Battle of Midway (June 1942), he lashed himself to the bridge and went down with his ship. He was posthumously promoted vice admiral.

Yamamoto, Gonnohyōe (Gonbei) (1852–1933) Japanese admiral. As a boy he fought in the 1863 Kagoshima and 1868 Boshin (Restoration) Wars. He then attended preparatory school in Tokyo and the Japanese Naval Academy (1870–74). He also trained with the German Navy (1877–78). He developed a new gunnery manual for the navy, commanded a cruiser, and then became director of the navy minister's Secretariat (1891). In this latter post he rid the navy of many ineffective officers, created a navy general staff similar to that of the army (1903), and favored an aggressive posture during the 1894–95 Sino-Japanese War. Promoted rear admiral (1895), he was then vice admiral and navy minister (1898). In the latter post he pushed large naval spending bills through the parliament, making the navy the backbone of the national defense. He supported the alliance with Britain (1902) and was raised to baron the same year. Promoted admiral (1904), he retired in 1906. Made a count (1907), he also served as prime minister (1913–14).

Yamamoto, Isoroku (1884–1943) Japanese admiral. Yamamoto graduated from the Etajima Naval Academy (1904). He fought in the 1904–05 Russo-Japanese War and was wounded in the Battle of Tsushima (27 May 1905). Promoted lieutenant commander (1916), he graduated from the Naval Staff College (1916) and spent two years in the U.S. studying English at Harvard University (1919–21). Promoted captain, he became deputy commander of the Kasumiga Ura Naval Air Station (1924–25). He learned to fly and became an advocate of naval air power. He was then naval attaché in Washington (1926–27) and held a succession of command and staff positions before promotion to rear admiral (1929) and command of the 1st Carrier Division (1933–34). Promoted vice admiral (1934), he was navy vice minister (1936), where he criticized escalation of the war in China and alliance with the Axis powers. He also opposed confrontation with the United States because of its economic might.

Appointed commander of First Fleet (1938) and CinC of the Combined Fleet (August 1941), Yamamoto held the latter post until his death. He planned the preemptive strike against the U.S. Pacific Fleet at Pearl Harbor (December 1941), hoping to gain an early advantage and purchase time, but also thinking this might cause the United States to give in to Japanese demands. In response to the Battle of the Coral Sea (May 1942), he planned an overly complicated trap for the Pacific Fleet and its carriers. The resultant Battle of Midway (June 1942) brought destruction of a major portion of his own carrier force. His operations were compromised in part by U.S. ability to read Japanese codes, which also brought his death when U.S. fighters intercepted

and shot down his plane, a severe blow to Japanese morale.

Yamanashi, Hanzvō (1864–1944) Japanese general. A graduate of the Military Academy (1886) and the Staff College (1892), Yamanashi was a platoon leader in the 1894–95 Sino-Japanese War and a staff officer in Second Army during the major battles in Manchuria during the 1904–05 Russo-Japanese War. Promoted major general (1911), he then was CofS of 18th Independent Division in the World War I siege and capture of the German port of Tsingtao (Qingdao) in China (August–November 1914). Promoted lieutenant general (1916) he became army war vice minister (1918). Promoted full general (1921), he was then army minister (1921–23). Later he served as governor of Korea (1927–29), his tenure marked by scandal.

Yamashita, Gentaro (1863–1931) Japanese admiral. A graduate of the Naval Academy, Yamashita was commissioned an ensign (1886). He served as a staff officer at the Yokosuka naval base during the 1894–95 Sino-Japanese War. He supervised ship construction for Japan in the United Kingdom (1896–99) and then was an executive officer aboard cruisers (1899–1900). He commanded marines at Tientsin (Tianjin) during the 1900–1901 Boxer Rebellion. Promoted captain (1903), he helped plan operations during the 1904–05 Russo-Japanese War. He then commanded a cruiser (1906).

While holding staff posts (1906–09), Yamahita was promoted rear admiral (1908). Promoted vice admiral (1913), he was then vice chief of the Navy General Staff (1914–15). He then commanded First Fleet (1917–19) and was promoted full admiral (1918) and served concurrently as commander of the Combined Fleet (September–October 1918; June–October 1919). He was then chief of the Navy General Staff (December 1920–April 1925). After several years in largely honorific posts, he retired and was made a baron in 1928.

Yamashita, Tomoyuki (1888–1946) Japanese general. A graduate of the Military Academy (1906) and Staff College (1916), Yamashita was trained as an infantry officer. Following service on the General Staff (1918), he was resident officer in Germany (1919–21). Promoted major (1922) and lieutenant colonel (1923), he was concurrently military attaché to Austria and Hungary (1927–29). Promoted colonel (1929), he commanded a regiment (1930–32) and then served in the Army Ministry (1932–36). He commanded a brigade in Korea (1936–37) and was promoted lieutenant general (1937). He was then CofS of the North China Area Army (1937–39) and commanded 4th Division (1939–40). He was inspector general of Army Aviation and traveled in Germany and Italy (1940–41).

Yamashita commanded Twenty-Fifth Army (November 1941) in the invasion of Malaya (8 December). Although outnumbered by British General Arthur Percival's forces (c.62,000 to c.89,000), his speedy advance and Japanese command of the air, coupled with ineffective British leadership, brought the surrender of Singapore (15 February 1942).

Largely because Premier Hideki Tōjō saw him as a rival, "The Tiger of Malaya" then commanded First Army in northern Manchuria (July 1942). Following Tōjō's fall from power (July 1944), Yamashita took command of Fourteenth Army defending the Philippines (October), only a week before the U.S. invasion. Plagued by divided command – he had little authority over naval and air assets – he was unable to prevent the fall of Leyte (December). Following U.S. landings on Luzon (January 1945), he gave defense of Manila to Rear Admiral Sanji Iwabuchi, who ignored his orders to withdraw and staged a suicidal defense.

Yamashita then withdrew into the northern mountains and, despite lack of supplies, held out until the end of the war (15 August). Charged with war crimes (15 September) for atrocities committed by Iwabuchi's Naval Defense Force, he claimed both ignorance of the crimes and inability to control his subordinate. In a controversial decision, the U.S. military court rejected this position, which became known as the "Yamashita defense." Found guilty, Yamashita was executed.

Yamaya, Tanin (1866–1940) Japanese admiral. A graduate of the Naval Academy (1886), Yamaya was on special duty in France (1891). As a navigator on a transport, he observed the Battle of the Yalu (17 September 1894) in the 1894–95 Sino-Japanese War. He attended the Naval Staff College (1896–97), then was an instructor there (1897–98). Promoted commander (1899), he was captain of a cruiser in the Battle of the Yellow Sea (10 August 1904) during the 1904–05 Russo-Japanese War. Promoted captain, he commanded a cruiser in the decisive Battle of Tsushima (27 May 1905). He is said to have instigated the crossing-the-T tactic used by Admiral Heihachirō Tōgō in that battle.

After the war Yamaya held various staff and line positions and was promoted rear admiral (1909). President of the Naval War College (1909–11, 1913), at the beginning of World War I he commanded the 1st southern squadron that searched for German ships in the South Pacific (October–December 1914). Vice chief of the Navy General Staff (1915–18), he was promoted admiral (1919). He then commanded the Combined Fleet (1919–20) before being placed on the inactive list (1922).

Yanagawa, Heisuke (1879–1945) Japanese general. Commissioned in the cavalry on graduation from the Military Academy (1901), Yanagawa served in Manchuria during the 1904–05 Russo-Japanese War. He graduated from the Army Staff College (1912) and returned there as instructor (1915–18). Military advisor to the Chinese government at the Peking (Beijing) Army Staff College (1918–20), he then served another assignment at the Japanese Staff College (1920). He was then detailed to the Army General Staff assigned to the League of Nations (1920–23). Promoted colonel (1923), he commanded a regiment (1923–25). He was then chief of the Maneuver Section of the Army General Staff (1925–27). Promoted major general (1927), he commanded first a cavalry brigade (1927–29) and then the Cavalry School (1929–30). Inspector general of cavalry (1930–31), he was promoted lieutenant general (1931). He then served as army vice minister (1932–34) and commanded 1st Division (1934–35). He then commanded the Taiwan Army (1935–36) and served on the Army General Staff (1936).

Placed on the reserve list (1936), Yanagawa was recalled to duty to command Tenth Army in China (1937–38) and was directly responsible, with General Yasuhiko Asaka, for atrocities committed by Japanese troops in Nanking (Nanjing) (December 1937). He then commanded Japanese forces at Hangchow (Hanzhou) (late 1939) but retired for a final time soon afterward.

Yang Hu-ch'eng (Yang Hucheng) (d. 1949) Chinese warlord. Yang's birth date and origins are unknown. A popular warlord, he came to control most of Shensi province (1926). Following defeat of the rebellion led by Feng Yü-hsiang (Feng Yuxiang) and Yen Hsi-shan (Yan Xishan) (1930), he subordinated himself to the Nationalists or Kuomintang (KMT, Guomindang) and commanded his own troops in the KMT Northwest Army. Following the 1934–35 Long March when the Communists (CCP) reached Yenan, KMT leader Chiang Kai-shek (Jiang Jieshi) ordered Yang (then known as "Old Yang") to join Chang Hsüehliang's (Zhang Xueliang) Northeast (Manchurian) Army and destroy the Commu-

nist base. Both men were impressed by CCP fighting prowess and supported the CCP position that all Chinese political factions should unite against the Japanese, whereupon Chiang flew to Sian (Xi'an) (December 1936).

When Chiang refused their demand that he form a united front with the CCP against the Japanese, they arrested him. When Chiang reversed his position, they released him and all flew to Nanking (Nanjing), whereupon Chiang had both Yang and Chang imprisoned. Yang was still in prison thirteen years later and was executed on Chiang's orders on the approach of Red Army forces to Nanking (Nanjing) (October 1949).

Yanushkevich, Nikolai Nikolaevich (1868–1918) Russian general. Yanushkevich graduated from the Mikhailovsky Artillery School (1888) and the General Staff Academy (1896). During most of the next decade he was in the Ministry of War. He became an instructor at the General Staff Academy (1910) and its commander three years later.

Largely because of political influence, early in 1914 Yanushkevich was promoted general of infantry and made CofS of the Russian army. An early advocate of forceful action in the summer 1914 European crisis, he superseded Tsar Nicholas' authority and ordered the general mobilization of the army (30 July).

During World War I, Yanushkevich's inadequacies as CofS to new supreme commander Duke Nikolai Nikolaevich were soon apparent. He also sought to deport Jews. His decision for a scorched earth policy during the Russian retreat from Poland (May 1915) caused serious problems, as the displaced inhabitants clogged the retreat routes, and helped alienate many from the government. Relieved as CofS (August 1915), he was relegated to duty in the Caucasus where he retired after the March 1917 Revolution.

Yashiro, Rokurō (1860–1930) Japanese admiral. Yashiro graduated from the Naval Academy (1881). Following a variety of staff and sea assignments, he fought in the 1894–95 Sino-Japanese War aboard a cruiser in the battle of the Yalu (17 September 1894). Naval attaché in St. Petersburg (1895–96), he was promoted lieutenant commander (1896) and commander (1897). He served on the Navy General Staff (1899–1900), graduated from the Naval Staff College, and was promoted captain (1901). He commanded a cruiser in the 1904–05 Russo-Japanese War and fought in battles off Inchon (February 1904), the Yellow Sea (August), and Tsushima (27 May 1905).

Yashiro was then naval attaché in Berlin (1905–07). Promoted rear admiral (1907), he held a succession of commands (1908–13). Appointed navy minister (April 1914), he removed Admiral Gonnohyōe Yamamoto and ended the period of Satsuma navy chiefs. His bluntness led to his forced resignation (April 1915). He then commanded Second Fleet (1915–17) and was made a baron (1916). Commander of Sasebo Navy Base (1917–18), he was promoted admiral (1918). He went on the reserve list in 1919.

Yeh Chien-ying (Ye Jianying) (1897–1986) People's Republic of China marshal. Yeh graduated from the Yunnan Military Academy (1919). He studied in France (1919–21), then was an instructor at Whampoa Military Academy. He joined the Communist party (CCP) and became a close associate of Communist leader Chou En-lai (Zhou Enlai) (1924). He commanded a division and then was CofS of First Army in the early part of the 1926–28 Northern Expedition to reunify China (July 1926–June 1927). But when Nationalist or Kuomintang (KMT, Guomindang) leader Chiang Kai-shek (Jiang Jieshi) sought to purge the Communists, Yeh rallied to the CCP side and took part in the unsuccessful August 1927 Nanchang and December 1927 Canton uprisings. He

then studied military tactics at Sun Yat-sen University in Moscow (1929–31).

Returning to China, Yeh helped lead military resistance to KMT "Bandit Extermination" campaigns, in which Chiang sought to liquidate the Communists (1930–34). He participated in the 1934–35 Long March to Yenan, supported Mao Tse-tung (Mao Zedong), and then assisted Chou En-lai in negotiations with Chang Hsüeh-liang (Zhang Xueliang) and Yang Hu-ch'eng (Yang Hucheng) for the release of Chiang Kai-shek at Sian (X'ian) (December 1936). During the 1936–45 Sino-Japanese War, he was CofS of Eighth Route Army (1937–40), then military liaison with the KMT government in Chungking (Chongqing) (1940–45). When the 1946–49 Civil War began, he resumed his position as CofS of CCP forces (No 1945) and helped plan the military campaigns. Following the Communist victory he held many important posts, including mayor of Peking (Beijing) and commander of forces in north China (1949–55). Named one of ten marshals (September 1955), he became minister of defense (1971) and tried through moderate policies to restore order after the chaos of the 1966–69 Cultural Revolution.

Yeh T'ing (Ye Ting) (1897–1946) Communist Chinese general. Graduating in the first class from Whampoa Military Academy, Yeh rose rapidly in rank in the Nationalist or Kuomintang (KMT, Guomindang) army and commanded 1st Division in the first part of the 1926–28 Northern Expedition to reunify China (July 1926–June 1927). A highly effective general, he remained loyal to the leftist faction when KMT leader Chiang Kaishek (Jiang Jieshi) sought to expel the Communists (CCP) and leftists from the party. He played a major role in the abortive August 1927 Nanchang and December 1927 Canton Uprisings and fled to Hong Kong. He remained in hiding until the united front against the Japanese (1936) when he was commissioned by

Chiang to gather scattered Communist elements in South China into the New Fourth Army. After he built this into a force of 45,000 men, Chiang ordered him north. Yeh remained south of the Yangtse (Yangzi) River with the headquarters and some 9,000 men, whereupon Chiang destroyed the southern group and imprisoned him. Released to join the CCP, he was killed when his plane crashed en route to Yenan.

Yen Hsi-shan (Yan Xishan) (1883–1960) Chinese warlord. A graduate of the Taiyuan Military Academy, Yen entered the Taiyuan New Model Army of the Ch'ing (Qing) empire (1904). During study at the Japanese Military Academy (1908–10), he made contact with Chinese nationalists. A regimental commander in the Taiyuan garrison, he supported the October 1911 Revolution and joined General Yüan Shih-k'ai's (Yuan Shikai) faction (1912). Appointed military governor of Shansi, he later deserted Yüan (1915) to support the faction of Premier Tuan Ch'i-jui (Duan Qirui) and received the civil governorship of Shansi. On Tuan's fall (1918), he alternated support for Wu P'ei-fu (Wu Peifu) and Feng Yü-hsiang (Feng Yuxiang). As a marshal, he joined Chang Tso-lin (Zhang Zuolin) (the Old Marshal) to drive Wu from north-central China (1925). He transferred his allegiance to the Nationalists or Kuomintang (KMT, Guomindang) during the 1926–28 Northern Expedition and commaned the KMT Third Army Group (September 1927–June 1928).

Rewarded with KMT government posts, Yen instead supported Feng Yü-hsiang and Wang Ching-wei's (Wang Jingwei) abortive revolt (1930). Exiled, within six months he again controlled Shansi (1931), which he governed effectively until the Japanese invasion (1937). Resisting their attacks (1937–38), he played off the KMT, Communists (CCP), and Japanese to preserve his autonomy. After World War II he employed an entire Japanese Army to keep the CCP out of Taiyuan (1945–49). When it fell (April 1949), he retired.

Yeremenko, Andrei Ivanovich (1892–1970) Soviet marshal. Drafted into the army (1913), Yeremenko fought in World War I. He joined the Red Army and Communist party (1918) and fought as a cavalry officer in the 1918–20 Civil War, ending it as deputy commander of a regiment. He then commanded a regiment and attended military schools, including the Military Political Academy and the Frunze Military Academy (1935). He commanded a cavalry division (1935–38), and then VI Cossack Cavalry Corps, which he led in the Soviet invasion of eastern Poland (September 1939).

Yeremenko took command of a mechanized corps (June 1940) and was promoted lieutenant general. He commanded First Red Banner Far Eastern Army at the time of the German invasion (22 June 1941), but was recalled and replaced General Dimitri Pavlov as Western Front commander, helping to restore a degree of stability. An outstanding tactician, he understood the importance of air power and the need to mass armor. He next commanded the new Bryansk Front (August), where he was seriously wounded (13 October). After his recovery, he was promoted colonel general and took command of Fourth Shock Army in the defense of Moscow. Again seriously wounded (February 1942), he commanded Southeast Front at Stalingrad (August). He took command of Southern Front (January 1943), pushing the Germans out of the Caucasus. Transferred to command the Kalinin Front (April), he was promoted general of the army (August). He commanded 1st Baltic Front (October–November) for the advance on Smolensk. He then led the Independent (Black Sea) Maritime Front in the eastern Crimea, then headed 4th Ukranian Front (March–July 1945).

After the war Yeremenko commanded

various military districts. He was then inspector general of the Ministry of Defense (1958–70) until his death.

Yi Hyŏng-Kŭn (1920–) Republic of Korea general. Yi graduated from the Japanese Military Academy (1942) and by the end of World War II was a captain in the Japanese Army. He returned to Korea after the war and attended the Military English Language School run by the U.S. military. His high marks there led to his receiving serial number 1 of all Republic of Korea Army (ROKA) officers.

Yi was the first commander of 8th Division (June 1949). Two weeks before the North Korean invasion of South Korea (25 June 1950), he was reassigned to command 2nd Division at Taejon and immediately clashed with ROKA CofS Ch'ae Pyong-dok over the employment of his division. Shortly after the start of the war, Ch'ae threatened him with a pistol and then removed him from command. After the incompetent Ch'ae was himself removed, Yi returned to field command. He took charge of III Corps (October 1950) and I Corps (January 1952). After the war he was promoted to full general (February 1954) and became the first chairman of the ROK Armed Forces Joint Chiefs of Staff and then (June 1956) CofS of the ROKA.

Yokoyama, Shizuo (1890–1961) Japanese army general. Yokoyama graduated from the Military Academy (1912) and the Army Staff College (1925). Promoted major (1928) he was assigned as a staff officer to Korea Army Headquarters (1929). Promoted lieutenant colonel (1932), he then held staff positions (1933–35). He then served as commander of the Kwantung (Guangdong) Army's Railway Zone (1935–37). He commanded a regiment (1938) and was promoted major general (1939).

Yokoyama held other railway commands (1939–42) and was promoted lieutenant general (1941). He then commanded 8th

Division (1942–44) and Shimbu Group defending southern Luzon Island in the Philippines (1944) before commanding Forty-First Army in the defense of Manila (January–March 1945). Tried and convicted on war crimes charges for actions committed by his troops during the defense of Manila, he was imprisoned for five years (1948–53).

Yonai, Mitsumasa (1880–1948) Japanese admiral. A career naval officer, Yonai graduated from the Naval Academy (1901) and the Naval Staff College (1914). Promoted commander (1916), he was a resident officer in Russia (1914–17), then was on the Naval General Staff (1919), before becoming resident officer in Berlin (1920–22). He held ship commands and commanded several bases. Promoted vice admiral (1930), he commanded the Combined Fleet (1936–37). He was navy minister (1937–39) and worked with Vice Minister of the Navy Admiral Isoroku Yamamoto to block the army's attempt to ally with Hitler's Germany. Briefly premier (June–July 1940), he was again navy minister until General Hideki Tōjō became premier (October 1941).

Yonai worked to build up the strength of the navy for war. In retirement, he advocated a negotiated settlement when it was clear that Japan was losing the war. He refused the opportunity to become premier when Tōjō was ousted from that post (July 1944), but he did agree to return as navy minister to first General Kuniaki Koiso and then to Kamtaro Suzuki. After Suzuki resigned (April 1945), he continued on as a member of the Supreme Council for the Direction of the War, helping to convince its other members that defeat was inevitable.

York, Alvin C. (1887–1964) U.S. soldier. York grew up in poverty and became a superb marksman while hunting for food as a boy. In 1911 he experienced a religious conversion and became a pacifist.

When the United States entered World War I (April 1917), he applied for conscientious objector status, which was denied. Drafted, he made clear during training his objection to war. His battalion commander, Major George E. Buxton, who was also a Bible scholar, convinced him that men of high moral convictions could fight. York arrived in France with the 328th Regiment of the 82nd Infantry Division and saw action in the Argonne Forest, leading seventeen men against a German strong point (8 October 1918).

The Americans took some prisoners, including a major, before coming under fire. With six men dead and the rest guarding the prisoners, York went on alone and personally shot down seventeen German gunners. When the remainder realized he was alone, seven rushed him, but he shot them all with a pistol. The major then promised to get the remainder to surrender and the Americans returned with 132 prisoners. For this deed, York was promoted sergeant and awarded the Medal of Honor and Croix de Guerre, among many other decorations.

The modest York, epitome of the "citizen-soldier," was one of the most famous Americans of the war and returned home to a New York City parade and a farm given by his home state of Tennessee. Eschewing commercial advantage, he did allow a film to be made of his life but used the money from *Sergeant York* (1941) to fund a vocational training center and Bible college.

Yoshida, Zengo (1885–?) Japanese admiral. Yoshida graduated from the Naval Academy (1904) and advanced in rank and responsibility to command the battleships *Kongō* and *Matsu*. Appointed commander of the Combined Fleet (December 1937), he followed Isoroku Yamamoto as vice minister of the navy (July 1939). He became minister of the navy (August 1939). He opposed army expansionist policies but was unable to resist them. In poor health, he resigned (September 1940) to protest Japan's signature on the Tripartite Pact. Promoted full admiral, he then became CinC of Japanese Fleets in China and then (1944) CinC Yokosuka Naval Station. During the last months of the war he was a member of the Supreme War Council.

Yüan Shih-k'ai (Yuan Shikai) (*c.*1859–1916) Chinese general and political figure. Yüan joined the army and commanded a brigade in Korea where he helped prevent a Japanese coup. Made ambassador to Korea, he attempted to maintain Chinese influence during a period of increasing Japanese pressure (1882–94). Driven from Korea in the defeat of Chinese forces in the 1894–95 Sino-Japanese War, he was given the task of creating a modern, western-style army for China. This Peiyang Army was completely loyal to him.

Yüan supported Empress T'zu-hsi (Ci Xi) in an 1898 attempted coup but, as governor of Shantung (Shandong) Province, refused to aid the 1900–01 Boxer Rebellion. As viceroy (1901–07), his power alarmed many at the imperial court and he was relieved of most of his posts (1907). Forced to retire altogether (1909), he retained *de facto* control of the army.

During the October 1911 Revolution, Yüan was appointed head of the army and navy and then prime minister (November). Unprincipled, he rebuffed pleas that he negotiate for the Empress and instead agreed to secure her abdication (February 1912) if he were made president rather than Sun Yat-sen (Sun Zhangshan), to which Sun agreed (April).

Yüan hoped to secure order and maintain China's territorial integrity but also attempted to set up his own dynasty. He crushed a revolt by Sun and others (1913) and proclaimed himself president for life (1914) and then emperor (1915). Deserted by his allies, he died before he could establish his regime and without naming a successor. China then again fell apart.

Yudenich, Nikolai Nikolaevich (1862–1933) Russian general. Yudenich graduated from the Aleksandrovsky Military College (1881) and General Staff Academy (1887), and served in a variety of staff assignments. During the 1904–05 Russo-Japanese War he distinguished himself commanding an infantry regiment, then a brigade. Promoted major general (1905), he became deputy CofS of the Caucasus Army (1907), then its CofS (1912).

While many of the best Russian units in the Caucasus were being sent to other fronts, the Third Turkish Army invaded. Yudenich resisted suggestions of Caucasus Army commander General Myshlaevsky that he withdraw. Promoted lieutenant general (January 1915), he took command of the Caucasus Army. He defeated another Turkish advance (1915) and then mounted a series of spoiling attacks that captured Erzurum, Trebizond, and Erzincan (1916).

Yudenich replaced Grand Duke Nikolai Nikolaevich as supreme civil and military commander of the Caucasus Front (March 1917). Soon recalled, he remained in Petrograd until the Bolshevik Revolution (November) forced him into hiding. Following Russia's withdrawal from the war, he joined the counter-revolutionary White movement and fought in the 1918–20 Civil War. His small force reached the outskirts of Petrograd (October 1919) before being forced to retreat into Estonia. He then went into exile in France in 1920.

Yuhi, Mitsue (1860–1940) Japanese general. A graduate of the Military Academy (1882) and Army Staff College (1891), Yuhi was a staff officer during the 1894–95 Sino-Japanese War and 1900–01 Boxer Rebellion. Promoted colonel, he was on Second Army Staff during the 1904–05 Russo-Japanese War. Promoted major general (1907), he was chief of the Operations Section, Army General Staff. Promoted lieutenant general, he commanded the Staff College (1914). He then commanded in succession 15th and Guards Divisions before becoming chief of staff of the Siberian Expeditionary Army (1918). Promoted full general (1919), he commanded the Tsingtao (Qingdao) Guard Army (1919–22) before his retirement (1923).

Z

Zapata, Emiliano (1877?–1919) Mexican revolutionary general. A small landowner in the state of Morelos, Zapata was a champion of land distribution in favor of the Indians. He had been imprisoned by the government of President Porfirio Diaz and had served in the army.

At the start of the 1911–14 Mexican Revolution, Zapata led the revolution in Morelos, supporting presidential aspirant Francisco Madero. He opposed the dictatorship established by General Victoriano Huerta, which he believed would not institute the desired land reforms. He cooperated briefly at different times with two other rivals for power: General Venustiano Carranza and another revolutionary general, Pancho Villa. Although he continued to hold Morelos and parts of neighboring states, he was killed at the orders of Carranza's ally General Pablo Gonzalez.

Zeitzler, Kurt (1895–1963) German general. Zeitzler joined the army just before World War I and commanded a regiment during it. He remained in the Reichswehr after the conflict, completing staff training. He was a lieutenant colonel in the Army High Command (OKW) in 1937. He helped plan the movement into Czechoslovakia (March 1939) and was chief of staff of XXII Corps in the invasion of Poland (September 1939) and of Army Group Kleist (later first Panzer Army) in

the Battle for France and Benelux (May–June 1940).

A competent staff officer, Zeitzler was then CofS of First Panzer Army in Russia (September 1941). He was then sent to France as CofS of Army Group D (April 1941). Promoted major general (September 1942), he replaced General Franz Halder as CofS of the army. His aggressive nature (his nickname was *Kugelblitz*, "Thunderball") seemed to fit Adolf Hitler's plans, but after Sixth Army was trapped at Stalingrad he pleaded with Hitler to allow its withdrawal. Following the collapse of Operation CITADEL, the Battle of Kursk (July 1943), which he had largely planned, he fell out with Hitler and was allowed to resign for reasons of ill health (June 1944). Imprisoned after the war, he was released in 1947.

Zhekov, Nikola Todorov (1864–1949) Bulgarian general. Zhekov graduated from the military academy and fought in the 1885 war with Serbia. He studied in Italy and returned to command a regiment, then a division. In the 1912–13 Balkan Wars he was CofS of Second Army. As war minister (August–October 1915), he readied the army as Bulgaria prepared to join the war in alliance with Germany and Austria. He then assumed direct command of the army (October).

As an element of Army Group Mackensen, Bulgaria's First Army helped the

Germans shatter Serbia's defenses in 1915. Bulgarian troops took the Aegean port of Kavalla as part of a successful offensive (August–September 1916). In the fall of 1916 he was pressed to detach troops to Field Marshal August von Mackensen for an offensive against Romania.

In addition to the friction with his German allies, Zhekov found himself caught up in a movement to oust Premier Rudoslavov. In 1917, aware of the severe conflicts between Zhekov and the government over army supply problems, an opposition group attempted to enlist his aid, but he reported the plot. He finally joined the anti-Rudoslavov movement, which ousted the premier (June 1918).

With Bulgaria losing the war and the army close to mutiny, Zhekov went into exile in Germany. Returning to Bulgaria in order to defend his reputation (1923), he was sentenced to a lengthy prison term but was released (1926) and returned to Germany.

Zhilinsky, Yakov Grigorevich (1853–1919) Russian general. Zhilinsky was commissioned in the Russian Army after graduation from the Nikolaevsky Cavalry School (1876). He held a variety of staff positions, before being promoted major general (1900). He then served on the staff of army commander General Aleksei Kuropatkin.

Selected as CofS of the Russian Army (1911), Zhilinsky visited France (1912), where he became an admirer of General Ferdinand Foch. He then commanded the Warsaw Military District (1913). With the outbreak of World War I he campaigned to be army CinC but received command of the Northern Front instead.

Zhilinsky believed that the key to Russian victory lay in defeating Germany first instead of Austria-Hungary. As commander of the Northern Front it was his task to coordinate the movement of the First and Second Armies against Germany. In this he failed. When the Germans did

attack, Zhilinsky was unaware of the danger. Appointed as Russian military representative to the French High Command (1915), Zhilinsky was also a failure as a diplomat. He returned to Russia and retired following the March 1917 Revolution.

Zhukov, Gregori Konstantinovich (1896–1974) Soviet marshal. Conscripted into the army (1915), Zhukov was a cavalry NCO during World War I and was twice awarded the St. George Cross for bravery. Following the November 1917 Bolshevik coup d'etat, he joined the Red Army (1918) and commanded a cavalry squadron in the 1918–20 Civil War. He attended cavalry schools (1920 and 1925) and then was in Germany to study at the underground Kriegsakademie. Returning to the Soviet Union, he studied at the Frunze Military Academy (1925–31). He survived Joseph Stalin's purge of the army through administrative error.

Sent to the Far East as commander of the Soviet First Army Group in Manchuria (1939), Zhukov defeated the Japanese Sixth Army near the Khalka River at Nomonhan (July–August 1939). He was then deputy commander (1939) and commander of the Kiev Military District (1940).

Following the German invasion of the Soviet Union (June 1941), he participated in the unsuccessful defense of Smolensk (August). Stalin was generalissimo of Soviet forces, but Zhukov was his chief deputy. Known as "Stalin's Fireman," he was the outstanding Russian general of the war and was called upon in every major battle on the Soviet Western Front. He organized the defense first of Leningrad (September–October) and then Moscow (1941–42), directing the counteroffensive there. As commander of the 1st Belorussia Front he directed the Battle of Stalingrad (1942–43), Kursk (July 1943), the great offensive in Belorussia (summer 1944), and the capture of Berlin (1945).

He was Soviet representative at the formal German surrender (8 May 1945).

Following the war Zhukov was the Soviet representative on the Allied Control Commission for Germany (May 1945–March 1946). Second only to Stalin in prestige in the Soviet Union, on his return Stalin immediately relegated him to a series of minor commands. Following Stalin's death (March 1953), Zhukov became deputy defense minister. In the secessionist struggle he supported Nikita Khrushchev and was made defense minister (February 1955). Removed from this post (1957), he then retired.

Zumwalt, Elmo Russell, Jr. (1920–2000) U.S. admiral. Zumwalt graduated from Annapolis in 1942. His World War II service included combat off Guadalcanal and the Philippines. He served on a battleship during the 1950–53 Korean War. He graduated from the Naval War College (1953) and in 1959 commanded the navy's first ship designed for guided missiles.

Zumwalt attended the National War College (1961–62) and became associated with Paul H. Nitze, a foreign policy advisor in the Kennedy administration. He became an aide to Nitze, then assistant secretary of defense (1962–63), and assistant to Nitze when he was secretary of the Navy (1963). Promoted rear admiral (1965), he was the youngest officer ever to gain that rank. He then headed the new Division of Systems Analysis (1966–68). He had opposed introduction of U.S. ground troops in Vietnam, but in September 1968 was promoted vice admiral and given command of naval forces there, a flotilla of more than 1,000 patrol boats in the Mekong Delta of South Vietnam, the so-called "Brown Water Navy."

Named chief of naval operations (CNO) (July 1970) Zumwalt was the youngest man ever to hold that position. As CNO, he carried out policies designed to end racial discrimination, improve conditions and morale in the fleet, and allow women to serve on ships. In all he issued more than 121 "Z-Grams" to change long-standing policies. He retired in July 1974.